TRAMP

Also by Joyce Milton

TRAMP

THE LIFE OF
CHARLIE CHAPLIN

JOYCE MILTON

HarperCollins*Publishers*

King of Comedy, by Mack Sennett and Cameron Shipp, is quoted by arrangement with the William Morris Agency.

Interviews from the Oral History Collection on the Performing Arts, De Golyer Institute for American Studies, Southern Methodist University, are quoted with the permission of Dr. Ronald L. Davis.

HarperCollins books may be purchased for educational, business, or sales promotional use. For information please write: Special Markets Department, HarperCollins Publishers, Inc., 10 East 53rd Street, New York, NY 10022.

FIRST EDITION

Designed by C. Linda Dingler

ISBN 0-06-017052-2

96 97 98 99 00 ❖/RRD 10 9 8 7 6 5 4 3 2 1

CONTENTS

Photographs follow page 342.

TRAMP

1

"They Were Nothing . . . *Nothing* . . . NOTHING!"

Born during the reign of Queen Victoria, Charles Spencer Chaplin now seems peculiarly modern. He became the first international movie star, celebrated around the world for his portrayal of the Little Fellow, a universal victim. But his sense of his own identity was as uncertain as the lineage of his character. For much of his life he claimed that he had been born in a hotel in Fontainebleau, France, and that his older half-brother, Sydney, had been born in South Africa. He often told friends that he was far from sure that his mother's husband, Charles Chaplin Sr., was his biological father. At times he thought his real father might have been Jewish or even African American. He was undoubtedly at least one-quarter Romany, or Gypsy, a heritage he sometimes denied and at other times took pride in. He was unsure, or pretended to be, of his mother's maiden name.

Chaplin rose from the marginal classes of the South London slums, a stratum of society among whom family history was not a source of pride but a catalog of humiliations and tragedies, to be glossed over with invention when they couldn't actually be forgotten. As he himself put it, "To gauge the morals of our family by commonplace standards would be as erroneous as putting a thermometer in boiling water."[1] As long as the facts remained mere bubbles, evaporating from the seething cauldron of the past, moral judgments were irrelevant.

In his sixties, when he was working on his autobiography, Chaplin decided that the time had come to set the record straight. He paid a visit to the central registry office of vital statistics in London, but his search for a birth certificate was unsuccessful. "I went to Somerset House, you know, on the Thames," he told a much younger acquaintance, "and *there is no Charles Chaplin.*"

Nor did he find any records of his mother's family: "They were nothing . . . *nothing* . . . NOTHING!"[2]

Thanks to Chaplin's dedicated admirers in Britain, many—though by no means all—of the mysteries surrounding his early life have been resolved. His mother was born Hannah Harriet Pedlingham Hill on August 6, 1865, the daughter of a shoemaker, and grew up in Walworth, a working-class district of South London. Hannah's mother, one Mary Ann Hill, had married her first husband, a sign painter named Henry Hodges, when she was about fifteen. They had one son, also called Henry. The elder Henry Hodges died in a fall from a horse-drawn omnibus, leaving Mary Ann a widow at thirty-four. In 1861 she married Charles Hill, and the couple had two daughters, Hannah and Kate. Mary Ann and young Henry worked side by side with Charles Hill as he plied his trade, but they never prospered. Hill suffered from rheumatism and very likely he drank. He seems never to have had his own shop, and the family moved every year or two, occupying a series of cheap rented flats.

Chaplin described his maternal grandfather as a "good old Irish Mick" with a shock of snow-white hair, who hailed from County Cork. He had been told that Grandfather Hill was somehow involved in the assassination of Lord Frederick Cavendish, but this is unlikely since Cavendish, the nephew of Prime Minister William Ewart Gladstone, was not murdered until 1882, long after Charles Hill took up residence in London. Whether or not he had revolutionary sentiments, Hill does seem to have been a combative sort. He quarreled with both his daughters and eventually turned his wife out of his house, allegedly because he caught her in bed with another man.

Hannah Hill was eighteen when she escaped from this grim environment. She later told her children that she eloped with the son of an English lord and married him in South Africa, where she lived on a plantation, waited on by legions of servants, and gave birth to her first son, called Sidney John. In fact her lover's name was Sydney Hawkes or something similar, and another version of the family story identifies him as a Jewish bookmaker. Jewish or not, Hawkes was hardly the son of a lord, although there is some reason to suspect that he may have been the black-sheep heir of a well-to-do family. Hannah often spoke of a legacy that was supposed to come to her son after Hawkes's death.

Hannah and Sydney Hawkes were never married, and by the time she gave birth on March 16, 1885, the relationship had ended. Sidney John (hereafter known as Sydney, the spelling he used later in life) was born at the home of Joseph Hodges, who was the uncle of Hannah's half-brother Henry. It is possible that Hannah had then already met Charles Chaplin, a twenty-two-year-old singer, whom she would marry on June 22, when her baby was just fourteen weeks old.

As far as anyone knows, Hannah Hill's story of her elopement to South Africa was a fantasy. But maybe not. The Chaplin family *had* South African connections: Three of Charles Chaplin's siblings eventually emigrated there, and one brother, Albert, became a prosperous farmer with business holdings near Durban. It is just possible that Hannah *did* run off to South Africa with Sydney Hawkes. She may even have met Charles Chaplin there and returned with him to England, where Hawkes was unlikely to pursue her or make any claim on his child.

More likely, however, Hannah and Charles met in London, drawn together by their shared ambition to become stars of the music hall stage. Variety—or vaudeville as it was usually called in America—was one of the few routes to success open to an ambitious young person from the lower classes, and the South London neighborhood where they had both grown up was the nerve center of the business, a venue of large theaters and booking agencies as well as pubs and eateries frequented by music hall entertainers. Charles and Hannah may have started out entertaining on street corners or working in "the halls" in some minor capacity. Within two years of Sydney's birth, each launched a career as a soloist.

Hannah Chaplin was not a great beauty, but she had striking violet eyes and a pert nose, and her mouth turned upward slightly at the corners, giving her a saucy expression. It is unlikely that she had much formal schooling, but she was a quick study. According to her second son, Charlie, she spoke four languages fluently. She knew many historical anecdotes, drawn more from popular plays than from books, and would retain to the end of her life an encyclopedic memory for the songs she heard performed in the music halls. Under the stage name Lily Harley she was billed as a "serio comedienne" who sang, danced, and did impersonations. Her repertoire included one song that she sang while costumed in a judge's robes and wig:

I am a lady judge,
and a good judge, too. . . .
I mean to teach the lawyers
a thing or two,
And show them just exactly
what the girls can do.[3]

While Hannah Hill Chaplin had pulled herself up from nothing, her husband came from a family of modestly prosperous pub keepers. Contrary to the myth perpetuated by outdated reference books like *Who's Who in American Jewry*, which traced the Chaplin family's origins to a Central European immigrant named Thonstein, Charles senior was not Jewish but the descendant of a long line of English yeoman farmers.[4] His ancestors hailed from the village of Great Finborough in Suffolk, where the surname Chaplin can be found in parish records as early as 1609.

The early Chaplins were farmers, sturdy and long-lived. Caleb Chaplin, the earliest identifiable direct ancestor of Charles, was born in 1670. His grandson, George, lived until 1819. George was illiterate but left a will signed with his mark, instructing his heirs to keep the expense of his funeral "moderate as may be." To his widow and son Meschach he left "All the life and ded Stock on my Farm together with all the growing crops thereon likewise." Six other children were to share the sum of eighty pounds, while the son of a child who had predeceased George received an inheritance of five pounds "good and lawful Money of Grate Britain."[5]

George's son Shadrach continued a family tradition by naming *his* three sons Shadrach, Meshach, and Abednego. Of this generation Abednego became an ironmonger and grew prosperous, while the younger Shadrach moved to the city of Ipswich and ran through a series of occupations—master brewer, pork butcher, hotel manager, coffeehouse proprietor, and shoemaker. His son, Spencer Chaplin, got married at the age of twenty to a sixteen-year-old Gypsy girl named Ellen Elizabeth Smith.

Ellen was one of the southern Smiths, a well-established Romanichal (English Gypsy) family whose members still visit caravan sites in the British Isles. She bore her husband five sons and two daughters. By the time the fourth child, Charles, was born in 1863, the family had moved to London, where Spencer became a pubkeeper and eventually the owner-manager of the Devonport Arms in Paddington. Ellen died at the age of thirty-five, and ten-year-old Charles, the future music hall singer, was brought up mainly by his father and older siblings. Spencer never remarried but, it seems, enjoyed a reputation as a ladies' man. His grandson, our Charlie Chaplin, would recall quite proudly that even when Spencer was "an old man with white hair . . . the family couldn't trust him alone with a woman."[6] Actually Spencer was only in his sixties when he died, so his distinction along these lines was not so great as Charlie thought.

Spencer's interest in women aside, the Chaplins were a hard-working and prosperous lot. Charles's eldest brother, Spencer William Chaplin, expanded the family's interests to South London, becoming the landlord of the Queen's Head pub on Broad Street, between the Albert Embankment and Lambeth Walk. While brother Albert established himself in Durban and became rich, fathering nine children, Charles took advantage of a pleasing light baritone voice and an affable personality to launch his career in the music halls as a "descriptive vocalist"—a specialist in musical monologues.

The Chaplins can hardly have approved of Hannah Hill, who had given birth to an out-of-wedlock child by another man less than four months before she married into their family. Hannah's mother, Mary Ann, was another cause for embarrassment. After being repudiated by her husband, Mary Ann was reduced to peddling old clothes on the street to support herself. Poverty, cheap gin, and perhaps mental illness all took their toll, and she became increasingly unkempt and eccentric as the years went by.

Charlie Chaplin believed that Mary Ann Hill, his maternal grandmother, was either a Gypsy or half-Gypsy. Judging from a garbled paragraph in his autobiography, in which he gives her maiden name as Smith, it would seem that he was confusing Mary Ann Hill with his paternal grandmother, Ellen Smith Chaplin. On other occasions, however, it is clear that he was basing his belief on childhood memories of his maternal relatives. His mother's people, he recalled in 1964, were in the "rag and bone business—junk collectors," and his aunt "used to be able to call better than all others, 'Come and buy my violets.' . . . This means almost certainly that she was a gypsy. They were the ones selling violets."[7]

All this is rather vague, and certainly Gypsies had no monopoly on either violet selling or the junk trade in turn-of-the-century London. Quite possibly Chaplin chose to believe that his maternal relatives had Gypsy blood because this put a romantic gloss on their otherwise humble and rather disorderly lives. On the other hand, it may be that there were Gypsies among Chaplin's maternal relatives and he was not telling all he knew. Romany culture is insular, and there is a strong bias, well grounded in centuries of persecution, against revealing oneself to the *gadje* (non-Gypsies). A number of Chaplin's associates who met his mother when she was in her late fifties accepted her as a Gypsy. Charlie himself, who never mastered a foreign language as an adult, was said to have been familiar with the dialect of Romany spoken in the British Isles, and he was fluent in the half-Romany patois spoken by Gypsies, street musicians, and circus and carnival performers. Harry Crocker, a close associate who at one time intended to write Chaplin's biography, often questioned him about his grandparents and concluded that he was being deliberately evasive. Charlie, he wrote, "had a secretive and suspicious side to his delightful character."[8]

To complicate matters, when Chaplin did talk about his mother's side of the family he often seemed to be referring to the Hodgeses, who were not blood relatives. Of Mary Ann Hill's biological parents nothing is known except that on her marriage certificate she described her father as a "mercantile clerk." It was Joseph Hodges, the brother of Mary Ann's first husband, who was a "general dealer" or trader in secondhand goods. This catchall phrase was often used in official documents to describe Romany (Gypsy) heads of families;

in fact, Ellen Smith's father was also a "general dealer." The Hodgeses appear to have functioned as a surrogate family, taking in Mary Ann and her two daughters when they were estranged from Charles Hill. Even though he was acquainted with his grandfather Hill, Charlie always listed his mother's maiden name as Hannah Hodges on his immigration documents.

Romany ancestry, on one side of the family or on both, was not a matter of pride in late Victorian London, and one can well understand why Chaplin, in his autobiography, would refer to his Gypsy forebears as "the skeleton in our family closet." Sedentary Gypsies, especially women who intermarried or led irregular sexual lives, were at the very bottom of the social scale, despised by traditional Romanies as well as society as a whole. The latter's attitude can be judged from an ostensibly sympathetic discussion that appeared in the *London Illustrated News* in 1879, when Hannah Hill was fourteen. The anonymous author reported that between four and five thousand semisedentary Gypsies were living in tents or wagons within the London city limits: "They take their meals and do their washing squatting on the ground like tailors and Zulus. Lying, begging, thieving, cheating, and every other abomination that low cunning craft backed by idleness can devise, they practice." In addition, he reports, an unknown number of urbanized Gypsies "have arrived at what they consider the highest state of civilized life [but] reside in houses, which in ninety-nine cases out of a hundred are in the lowest and most degraded part of the towns, among the offscouring of all nations."

Although the writer advocated education and, presumably, assimilation, he reserved his deepest scorn for younger generations of Romanies, many of whom had intermarried with non-Gypsies. Such families, he said, continued to resist cooperation with the census and frequently failed to enroll their children in school:

Considerable difficulty is experienced sometimes in finding them out, as the women often go by two names. . . . In many instances they live like pigs and die like dogs. The real old-fashioned gipsy has become lewd, and demoralised—if such a thing could be—by allowing his sons and daughters to mix up with the scamps, vagabonds, "rodneys" and jail-birds who now and then settle among them as they are camping on the ditch banks. The consequence is our lanes are being infested with a lot of dirty, ignorant gipsies, who, with their tribes of squalid children, have been encouraged by servant girls supplying their wants with eggs, bacon, milk and potatoes. . . . Children born under such circumstances, unless taken hold of by the state, will turn to be a class of most dangerous characters.[9]

The article went on to propose a national registration system that would assign a number to every Gypsy dwelling as well as a requirement that every Gypsy family carry a "book" recording each child's school attendance. The goal of encouraging literacy among Romany children was laudable, but one can also see why the intended beneficiaries of such schemes would be suspicious of government and less than eager to have their children "taken hold of."

By the time Charles Spencer Chaplin was born, on April 16, 1889, his father was already a well-known entertainer, popular enough to receive top billing in the provincial music halls. There were more than two hundred such theaters in Great Britain, and Charles was often away on tour. During the week his son was born he happened to be appearing in Hull, in the north of England, at Professor Leotard Bosco's Empire Palace of Varieties.

We can't be sure where Hannah was. Charlie was told that he was born in East Lane in the Walworth district, the same street where his grandfather Hill had worked at the shoemaking trade. Although the birth of Sydney John, who was illegitimate, had been properly registered, followed by his baptism into the Church of England, his half-brother Charlie came into the world unrecorded and unblessed. There was, however, a brief announcement of his arrival in a trade paper, the *Era*.[10]

It may be that Hannah and Charles's marriage was already in turmoil. Easygoing and popular with his peers, Charles had a weakness for alcohol and, when drunk, a violent temper. Nor was Hannah the type to sit at home and suffer in silence. She had her own circle of friends from the halls and enjoyed dressing up and going out in carriages to after-show suppers.

The year 1890 found Hannah living in a fashionable flat on West Square and Charles senior traveling to the United States, where he played an engagement at the Union Square Theater in New York City. Charles had recently introduced his first hit song, a number called "Eh! Boys!" written by George Le Brunn and John P. Harrington. No doubt the lyrics' nudging, winking evocation of the nagging missus at home sums up all too well the history of his married life with Hannah:

> When you're wed, and come home late-ish,
> Rather too late—boozy, too,
> Wifey dear says, "Oh, you have come!"
> And then turns her back on you. . . .
>
> We all of us know what that means,
> Eh, boys? Eh, Boys?
> When first she starts to drat you,
> And then throws something at you,
> We all of us know what that means—
> It's her playful little way.[11]

By the time Charlie was two years old, Hannah had embarked on an affair with Leo Dryden, another rising variety star, who specialized in sentimental evocations of Great Britain's far-flung empire. A good-looking man with blond hair and pleasant features, Dryden was enjoying the first flush of success, having recently introduced a ballad called "The Miner's Dream of Home." Hannah and Leo Dryden lived together for a year or so, and in August 1892 she bore him a son. Dryden's legal name was George Wheeler, and the baby was called George Dryden Wheeler Jr. By some accounts there was a second son, Guy Wheeler, of whom little is known. Once again the relationship quickly went sour, and during the spring of 1893 Leo Dryden departed, taking his son (or sons) with him.

Hannah was still under thirty, a vivacious woman with two children to support. Very likely Leo Dryden was not the only man in her life after she and Charles separated. Charlie would write in his autobiography that he saw the elder Charles Chaplin only three times before he was eight years old, twice on the stage and once when their paths crossed by accident on the street. However, in interviews given when he was a young man, he spoke of memories of a man he called his "father." Two such anecdotes appear in *Charlie Chaplin's Own Story*, a hastily produced "as told to" book that appeared in 1916. Here he relates: "When I was two or three years old my mother began to be proud of my acting. After she and my father came back from their work in the London music halls they used to have little parties of friends for supper, and father would come in and pull me out of bed to stand on the table and recite for them." He goes on to describe his father as "a large, dark, handsome man . . . his rough, prickly cheek hurt me."[12] This vaguely remembered "father" was certainly not the ginger-haired Leo Dryden, hardly a dark man. He may have been Charles Chaplin, but perhaps not.

Charlie Chaplin's Own Story also tells how his "father" was responsible for his stage debut. Alone once again, Hannah had attempted to revive her lagging stage career. One day, when Charlie was about five years old, "mother came in, staggering. I thought she was drunk." That night she was unable to perform and "father" decided that Charlie should go on in her place. The next thing he knew, a girl in tights and shiny spangles was smearing greasepaint on his cheeks, and "father" was shoving him on stage with the instruction "Go out and sing 'Jack Jones.'"

"Jack Jones" was a popular music hall song about a costermonger, or pushcart peddler, who has come into some money and begun to take on airs:

Jack Jones, you'd know 'im if you saw 'im,
round about the marketplyce . . .
I've no fault to find with Jack at all,
Not when 'e's as 'e used to be.
But since 'e's had the bullion left him
'E has altered for the worst. . . .

Charlie sang with gusto and was rewarded with a shower of coins.

Delighted, he interrupted his song and began scurrying around the stage to pick up the money. Momentarily remembering his audience, he promised them, "Wait till I get it all, and I'll sing a lot!" This earned him a big laugh, followed by another volley of coins. By the time the song was finished he had collected almost three pounds in tips. The next day, Charlie recalled, there was a quarrel. His "father" wanted him to go on stage again, but his mother protested, "He's too little yet!"[13]

During the 1920s Chaplin told this story to his friend Harry Crocker, recounting that the incident took place in a music hall at Aldershot, where the audience included a large number of soldiers. By the time he came to write his autobiography, however, Hannah's mysterious ailment, which made her stagger as if drunk, had become a case of laryngitis, and "father" was gone from the story, replaced by an anonymous stage manager who pushed little Charlie before the footlights. In the earlier versions of the anecdote Hannah is incapacitated, perhaps by alcohol, but still tries to protect her son from exploitation. In the later version it is Charlie who played the protector's role, taking Hannah's place on stage and winning over a hostile, jeering audience.

Somehow the earlier story is more believable. What motive could the stage manager have had for shoving a very young child onto the stage before an audience of rowdy soldiers? Why not simply move ahead to the next act on the program? Hannah's husband or lover, reluctant to lose the fee she would have earned from the engagement, would have been far more likely to insist that her little boy go on in her place.

Up to the time of Hannah's illness, she and her sons had lived well, if not always peacefully. She earned a good income on the stage and no doubt was supported by Leo Dryden and perhaps by other men. Charlie remembered his mother's favorite possessions from these years—stylish clothes, an enameled music box, and, of all things, a life-size portrait of Nell Gwyn. He had his own tiny chair, acquired from "the Gypsies."

Although Charles Chaplin Sr. was more prosperous than his wife, he seems to have done little or nothing for her and his son and stepson. Perhaps he even wondered if Charlie was his own child. Charles senior was a stocky man with brown eyes, a short upper lip, and a distinctively shaped jaw; Charlie was small and sickly, with curly black hair and deep blue eyes.

Many years later Charlie confided his own doubts on the subject to an assistant, Eddie Sutherland. "Apparently the mother had strayed from the path with several men—at least, she had romances with quite a number of men," Sutherland recalled. "And Chaplin told me, 'I don't know, actually, who my father was. There's some doubt about it.' He wasn't saying this against his mother; he said, 'This is what has been quoted to me.'"[14]

Hannah, on her part, dramatized her situation by identifying with the fallen women of history. She entertained Charlie by pretending to be Nell Gwyn, the barmaid mistress of Charles II, pleading with him for their son, "Give this child a name, Sir!" and threatening to fling the baby down a staircase if he refused. She also spoke of the Empress Josephine, another woman loved and then mistreated by a powerful man. She told young Charlie that his father resembled Napoleon—which he did, slightly.

Around the time of her humiliation at Aldershot, Hannah's health had begun to fail. She lost her voice to a throat ailment, probably psychosomatic, and suffered debilitating migraine headaches. Her behavior, always somewhat impulsive and unpredictable, became more so. Unable to earn a living on the stage or attract a good provider, she tried to support herself and the boys by doing needlework at home. Furniture, bric-a-brac, and her elegant clothes were sold off to pay the mounting bills.

In her troubles Hannah turned to religion for comfort, attending mass at Christ Church on Westminster Bridge Road. Now, instead of playing Nell Gwyn she began acting out Bible stories—the woman taken in adultery, Pontius Pilate washing his hands, and Christ gazing down from the cross at Mary, saying, "Woman, behold thy son." At times she spoke simply but persuasively of Jesus as a real person whose compassion was comforting because he, too, had suffered the world's scorn. Charlie was touched by the luminous sincerity of his mother's faith but less favorably impressed by the charity of her religious friends. The ladies of Christ Church tried to help Hannah by giving her piecework. She crocheted lace cuffs and handkerchiefs to order, but the needlework was time consuming and the pay scarcely enough to keep food on the table.

Before long Hannah drifted away from the Church of England and began attending the evangelical revival meetings that were a feature of South London life at the time. The evangelical meetings were closely allied with the temperance movement. Preachers urged abstinence from strong drink, often adding a populist twist to their message: Alcohol served the interests of the upper classes by keeping working people demoralized and quiescent, so swearing off liquor was the best way to undermine the class system. Well aware of the competition from the music halls, the revivalists put on a good show. By 1904 they would even begin to screen moving pictures during meetings.

At Spurgeon's Tabernacle, one of the largest permanently housed missions, Charlie saw an evangelist slide down a banister to demonstrate the swift descent into hell that awaited all who departed from the path to salvation. Another preacher, "a terrible man named MacDonald," solicited testimonials from the newly saved. Hannah's friends pressed Charlie to go forward and testify, a prospect he found terrifying. At last he screwed up his courage, but when he was face to face with the congregation he couldn't bring himself to shout "Hallelujah" with the required degree of fervor. His performance as a penitent sinner was "a flop."[15]

One evening, Charlie would recall, a well-meaning preacher offered to walk Hannah and the boys home after a meeting. As they neared the street where the family's dingy room was located, Hannah became frantic. She and the boys did not have proper beds; they were sleeping on a mound of blankets on the floor, and she didn't want the preacher to see their disreputable way of life. A block or so from the flat, Hannah protested vigorously that she and the children were quite all right and needed no escort the rest of the way. The preacher, guessing her motives, muttered, "I understand," and walked away. Perhaps there was nothing more he could do at that moment—Hannah was already receiving relief packages and handouts—but Charlie was furious at the inadequacy of the response.

There are hints that Hannah was often improvident, even after she turned to religion. At one point in his autobiography Charlie mentions offhandedly that his mother had won five shillings at the races, and so could afford to buy the boys some clothes. At other times her behavior was simply odd. For whatever reasons, Hannah had held on to her old theatrical costumes long after her other valuable possessions had been sold off or pawned, and when the boys had nothing to wear she busied herself cutting down some of these outfits for them. Syd inherited a fancy dress coat, which his buddies teasingly called "the coat of many colors." For Charlie she remodeled a frayed velvet jacket with leg-of-mutton sleeves slashed with deep gores lined in red. He wore the jacket with short pants and a pair of Hannah's old red tights, far too large for him and identifiable from their material and finishing as women's undergarments. When he appeared in this outfit, boys in the street ran after him, shouting, "Sir Francis Drake!" Charlie seems never to have questioned the necessity of this humiliation. There was, however, an active market in secondhand clothes in London, as Hannah had reason to know. Surely her costumes, of good material and elaborately constructed, could have been sold or bartered for more suitable children's clothing.

But even if she had been the best of managers, Hannah could scarcely have provided a decent living for herself and two children on her income from sewing. An 1863 study of the lowest-paid workers in Britain put female needleworkers at the bottom of the wage scale. Nor had matters improved by the turn of the century. While the living standard of most workers in England was rising, laborers in such traditional occupations had been left behind. William Booth, the founder of the Salvation Army, talked about the "submerged tenth," the lowest 10 percent of the laboring class who lived in a shadow country he called Darkest England. Tailors and seamstresses, along with charwomen, figured largely in Booth's heartwrenching tales of this forgotten class. The most Hannah was able to earn from piecework, assembling ladies' blouses at home, was six shillings ninepence a week. A 1901 survey conducted in the city of York, where costs were if anything lower than in London, concluded that workers earning less than eighteen shillings a week were living on a semistarvation budget, able to afford little more than potatoes, bread, tea, and margarine.[16]

It gradually became apparent that the underlying cause of Hannah's deteriorating health was mental illness, most likely a form of manic-depressive (bipolar) disorder. She was hospitalized for the first time in June 1895. Sydney was placed in Norwood, a public boarding school for indigent children, where he remained through the summer. Charlie was taken in by the Hodgeses. After a month in the hospital Hannah was discharged, but from this time on her mental state was precarious.

The situation was hard on both boys, but especially on Charlie. His half-brother, he would recall in 1915, was "a wide awake, lively, vigorous young person; I was always delicate and sickly." The sturdy Syd was a good-looking boy with a typical peaches-and-cream English complexion. He had been able to attend school regularly for several years while Hannah was still well off, and by 1895 he was working as a newsboy and taking classes at night, activities that kept him away from home most of the time. Charlie, by contrast, was almost always alone with his mother. "I had no life at all separate from her," he would remember. "My dreams were of making her happy and buying her beautiful things and taking her to a place in the country where she could rest and do nothing but play with me."[17]

As her situation worsened, Hannah began trying to force Charles senior to make regular payments of ten shillings a week in child support. Despite his heavy drinking, the elder Chaplin's singing career was flourishing. His most popular numbers included a song called "The Girl Was Young and Beautiful" as well as "Oui! Tray Bong!" the saga of a pair of Cockneys who conquer Paris with their masculine charms and fractured French:

To each little French dove,
Standing drinks and making love,
We fairly smashed the ladies
With our Oui! Tray Bong!

George Carney, a comedian who shared a bill with the elder Charles Chaplin on various occasions, remembered "Oui, Tray Bong!" as an immense success, earning Chaplin a record six encores at Seabright's London music hall. Chaplin's voice and mannerisms were so well known to audiences that a Scottish ventriloquist named Prince Bendon incorporated an impersonation of him into his own act. Chaplin, finding himself on the same bill with Bendon, decided to play a joke on the audience by hiding behind Bendon's chair and singing the part of the dummy. It was agreed that he would pop up at the end of the act and take his bow, but Charles had grown stout and out of shape and looked so uncomfortable that Bendon couldn't keep a straight face and had all he could do to get through one song.[18]

Charlie would recall that his father earned seventy-five pounds a week—and his mother, at the height of her brief career, had commanded twenty-five pounds. Seventy-five pounds weekly was a very ample income, and when Syd was admitted to Norwood, Charles Chaplin's failure to support his family came to the attention of the parish relief committee. Charles was not happy to be told that not only Charlie but Syd, who now called himself Syd Chaplin, were still legally his responsibility. Apparently he did come up with some of the money he owed, and Hannah, finding herself with cash in hand, promptly spent much of the windfall on a holiday, taking the boys to the resort town of Southend-on-Sea.

Within weeks Charlie was back living with the Hodgeses while Hannah attempted to revive her stage career. They enrolled him in school for the first time in his life, but he attended classes for only a few weeks, soon rejoining his mother. On February 8, 1896, billed as Lily Chaplin, "serio and dancer," Hannah made her last known professional appearance in a performance sponsored by the Hatcham Liberal Club.[19] By the following June, she was once again so ill that she had to be admitted to a public infirmary. This time the Hodgeses did not come to Charlie's rescue, and he and Syd were packed off to the workhouse.

"English people have a great horror of the poorhouse; but I don't remember it as a very dreadful place," Chaplin said in 1915. But then, he scarcely remembered it all. "The strongest recollection I have of this period of my life is of creeping off by myself. . . . And pretending I was a very rich and grand person." He never day-dreamed about starring in the music halls; instead he imagined himself going into law or politics and becoming a member of Parliament with a fortune of a million pounds.[20]

After a few days in the workhouse, Charlie and Syd were taken in a horse-drawn bakery wagon to the Hanwell Schools for Orphans and Destitute Children, twenty miles outside London—also known, for reasons impenetrable to the American mind, as the Cuckoo Schools. Like Norwood, Hanwell was a boarding school administered under the English Poor Laws. At first Charlie was excited and happy, thinking that he and his brother were embarking on a wonderful adventure. His spirits fell when he realized that they were to be separated. After a medical examination and a few days of quarantine, Syd was assigned to the upper division of the boys' school while Charlie was placed in the "infant" division. There, much to his horror, he discovered that the senior students from the girls' school were called upon to scrub the littlest boys at their weekly bath. Being vigorously soaped down by a fourteen-year-old girl was a mortifying experience.

The children admitted to Hanwell were rarely the shoeless street urchins who could still be found around London sleeping in doorways and under bridges. Rather they were sons and daughters of the striving poor. The essayist Thomas Burke, who spent four years in Poor Law schools, joked that getting into one of them was as difficult as gaining admission to Oxford. The local relief boards required a written application, a vaccination certificate, and character references. Successful applicants usually had the help of a relief board volunteer or social worker who helped move the process along.

At the time the Chaplin boys entered system, these public orphanages were well managed. The clothing issued to the children may have been drab, but it was warm and well made. The boys and girls received regular medical and dental checkups, thus enjoying better health care than the average working-class youngster. There were even periodic shoe inspections to discover footwear that needed repair or replacement. Meals were plain but filling, consisting of porridge for breakfast; meat, potatoes, and suet pudding at noon; and bread with cocoa at six in the evening. The students were taken to church on Sundays and got outdoor exercise during regular group walks outside the school walls. Classroom instruction encompassed academic and vocational subjects, and the quality of the teaching was generally superior to anything poor children were likely to encounter in neighborhood grammar schools.

"They couldn't do enough for us," wrote Burke, summing up the program as the "sentimental Christian's idea of heaven."

All this benevolence, however, was dispensed in highly regulated doses. A wake-up bell signaled the rising hour of 7:00 A.M. and sent the boys scurrying to the lavatories, where they washed up at a long row of basins. Another bell announced that it was time to march to the refectory, a huge vaulted room, where the children sat at long tables while student monitors collected plates of food from the kitchen staff and passed them around. Here, too, there were bells: one for the singing of grace, another for the moment to sit down and commence eating, and, exactly twenty minutes later, a third commanding the children to set aside their knives and forks and rise for the postmeal benediction.

Discipline was strict. E. H. Farley, a student at the Cuckoo Schools at the time of Queen Victoria's Jubilee in 1887, recalled:

It was just like being in the Army and the Head Officer, Mr. Hindrum, showed no mercy if ever a boy was rude to a nurse or officer. One instance I can recall was when a boy was hitting me, and I was too nervous to retaliate. We were seen—and made to box it out in the gymnasium. I finished up with giving the other boy a damn good hiding and the officer said to the other boy: "You won't hit Farley again in a hurry." [21]

On the whole Farley thought he was lucky to have attended his Poor Law alma mater. More surprisingly, so did Tom Burke, who had been a sensitive, dreamy boy, hopeless at games and the compulsory military drills: "Unhappy as I had been there, the unhappiness was of my own creating; and in retrospect I see it as others see Winchester, or Rugby, or Westminster. . . . It had its own tradition, and its own slang, and it had much to give that was good." [22]

Syd Chaplin, big for his age and eager to please, also fared very well at Hanwell and was soon chosen for a special cadet program on the training ship *Exmouth*. The lessons in seamanship he learned there qualified him for a job as a steward on a passenger steamer when he was only sixteen. But for Charlie, who was not only excruciatingly shy but hypersensitive to rejection, Hanwell was the scene of one humiliation after another. The bracing hikes outside the grounds were made torture by his embarrassment at being seen by the locals who, he felt sure, were staring at the children in scorn and mouthing the words "booby hatch," a slang term sometimes applied to workhouses and orphanages as well as lunatic asylums. One of a group of students who contracted ringworm that year, Charlie fell into "paroxysms of weeping" when the barber shaved his head. Placed in the quarantine ward, he was so deeply shamed that he refused to look out the window lest the boys in the play yard below see him and feel the same "loathing" for him that he had once felt for the ward's inmates. [23]

No doubt Hanwell was a difficult environment for a boy who was too small to defend himself effectively in the boxing ring, as young Farley had, and easily gulled by older children. Shortly before the Chaplin boys arrived at Hanwell, a boy and girl from one of the older classes had been discovered in a compromising situation, an event so uncommon that it was the talk of the school for many weeks. The girl was moved to a single room in a part of the building that happened to be accessible to some of the younger children, and Charlie was soon reported for peeking through the keyhole at her. As he recalled the incident, his motives were innocent. Some other boys had stuffed a button into the keyhole, or said they had, and then challenged him to pry it out. He was seen, and his name was added to the list for Punishment Day, a weekly ritual.

Punishments consisted of one to three whacks with a birch cane, administered by Mr. Hindrum, a retired army captain and the same headmaster who had made such an impression on E. H. Farley a decade earlier. The night before his caning, Charlie was too terrified to sleep. "Be a man," Syd advised, but to eight-year-old Charlie's eyes the basement gymnasium where the ritual took place was as ghastly as any medieval torture chamber. One by one the boys bent over a vaulting horse, their britches pulled down around their ankles. Hindrum then approached, his cane securely wrapped to his hand with twine, and administered the strokes.

Awful as it was, Punishment Day had its compensations. Surviving the ordeal gave a boy a certain status, and afterward, proud of their courage, they retired to the lavatory to compare welts. A far worse ordeal for Charlie occurred at Christmastime, after Syd was already on the *Exmouth*. During the boys' weekly physical the doctor was in the habit of rolling back their eyelids, on the theory that he could tell by the color of their eyeballs whether or not they were constipated. That week the doctor thought he detected the telltale hue in Charlie's eyes and prescribed a dose of "Black Jack," a powerful laxative. During the night Charlie soiled his bed. The next day happened to be Christmas Eve, and at suppertime the students stood in line in the refectory for their Christmas treats, an orange and a small packet of hard candy. As Charlie's turn to receive his gifts approached, one of the more unsympathetic masters clapped a hand on his shoulder and pulled him out of line,

announcing in a booming voice for all to hear, "This boy misbe-
haved." In a dormitory school there were no secrets. Everyone knew
the nature of the misbehavior. Even the sympathy of the other boys,
who gave him sections of their oranges and pieces of candy, could
not erase his shame.

Despite all this, Charlie must have gained something from
Hanwell. The eighteen months he spent there were the longest
period of continuous schooling he would ever have. He learned to
write his name, read a little, and perhaps more. Many years later he
would recall that the first time he ever heard of Socrates was at
Hanwell, where a bust of the Greek philosopher was displayed in a
hallway. Unlike Thomas Burke, however, Charlie did not allow his
feelings about the orphanage to soften with the passing years. For
him Hanwell would always be summed up as a place where "they
tried to break your spirit."

In his autobiography Chaplin recalls that the one bright spot in
his eighteen-month "incarceration," as he called it, was a visit from
his mother, who had left the workhouse and was once again living on
her own: "Her presence was like a bouquet of flowers; she looked so
fresh and lovely that I felt ashamed of my unkempt appearance."
But Chaplin had earlier told Harry Crocker a far different story:
Hannah had been transformed by mental illness and her stay in the
poorhouse. No longer a smart, pretty woman, she had become a
prematurely aged drudge, and for some reason she showed up at the
school carrying an empty oilcan. He was humiliated and shouted at
her, "Why do you come at all?"[24]

Charlie and Syd were discharged into their mother's custody in
January 1898. Six months later the family was destitute again and
once more forced to seek refuge in the workhouse. This time the
boys were promptly packed off to Norwood, but not for long. The
prospect of another lengthy separation was simply too much for
Hannah. After two weeks she declared her intention to leave the
workhouse and the boys were returned to her. Syd, who always
seemed to have some way of scraping together a little change, had
ninepence in his pocket, enough for a bag of black cherries and two
cups of tea, which the three of them shared while enjoying the afternoon sunshine in Kennington Park. But Hannah had no plan and
nowhere for them to spend the night, so at the end of the day she

and the boys presented themselves once more at the workhouse gates. The staff was furious since the whole family had to go through the admissions process a second time—their paperwork redone and their clothes fumigated.

The boys were proud of their mother's gesture of defiance, and perhaps rightly. She had given them a pleasant family memory, the last they would have for a long time to come. By September Hannah was once again too ill to carry on, and this time there was no doubt about the nature of her problem. She was committed to Cane Hill, a public mental hospital.

The local parish board, meanwhile, was still pursuing Charles senior. The relief committee can't have seen many cases involving fathers who so clearly had the means to live up to their responsibilities, and the Chaplin case must have been a source of considerable frustration. Before the boys were sent to Hanwell there had been a hearing that ended with Charles and Hannah trading insults, each accusing the other of being unfit. Charles brought up Syd's illegitimacy and Hannah's subsequent adultery. She pointed out that Charles, still her legal husband, was living with another woman and therefore could not provide her sons with a decent environment.[25] Hannah's commitment to Cane Hill simplified the board's work in a way, since her objections to giving Charles senior custody of the boys could now be ignored. Charles didn't want the children, but he was forced to take them anyway.

At this time Charles senior was living with a woman Charlie would come to know as Louise in a two-room floor-through apartment at 287 Kennington Road, a good neighborhood. Drinking more heavily than ever, he hadn't introduced a hit song in several years. Louise had problems enough of her own, and she was none too pleased to discover that the relief board had stuck her with responsibility for her common-law husband's two sons—or rather, one stepson and another whose parentage was uncertain. Charlie and Syd were equally unhappy with the arrangement, especially when they discovered that Charlie had a four-year-old half-brother whose existence had never been mentioned to them before. Syd, now thirteen, stayed away from the flat from early morning until he was ready to fall into bed, and once, when Louise screamed at him, he threatened to stab her with a button-hook. Charlie tried to cope by transforming himself into a little mouse in the corner.

In the early evenings Charlie watched in fascination as his father downed his pretheater meal of six raw eggs in a glass of port. When sober, which can't have been often considering that the eggs were his only nonalcoholic sustenance of the day, Charles senior showed some affection for the boys. Once he wrapped a towel around his head and chased Charlie around the table, clucking and crowing, "I'm King Turkey Rhubarb!" He told funny stories about his life on tour, and it was probably here that Charlie heard of Professor Leotard Bosco, at whose theater in Hull Charles had been playing the night Charlie was born. Professor Bosco, or at least his name, would remain alive in Charlie's imagination for many years, a symbol of the pathetic grandiosity that flourished in the seedier outposts of show business.

On weekends, however, Charles senior often failed to come home from the theater. Then Louise would start drinking too, progressing from morose self-pity to fantasies of revenge. When thoroughly drunk she would take out her rage on the boys by locking them out of the house.

This dreadful living arrangement lasted about two months until Hannah, discharged from Cane Hill, showed up to collect her sons. She and the boys then settled into another rented room, this one on Methley Street, near Kennington Cross, next to a pickle factory and a slaughterhouse. Charlie would remember his time at Methley Street as a relatively calm interval, when he was enrolled in school and managed to win a certain acceptance among his classmates. In fact, though, this time in school lasted only a few weeks.

Well groomed and fed during his time at Hanwell, Charlie had deteriorated into a neglected-looking boy in ragged clothes, whose matted hair hung down to his shoulders. He worked hard to ingratiate himself with other children by entertaining them with snatches of songs, dance steps, and stories he had learned from his mother. Otherwise he dealt with trouble by running away from it. Underneath his calm, almost passive exterior, he was a bundle of anxieties, plagued by phobias that would remain with him throughout his life. He was disgusted by the smell of warm milk, and by extension disliked touching milk bottles. In later years Chaplin explained that the pungent odor of unrefrigerated milk reminded him of sex, though why a child would have made this association is unclear. More strangely still, he had a phobia about stocking caps, especially the tasseled kind, and found it impossible to stand in the street speaking to a boy who happened to be wearing one.

His most extreme phobia was a fear of rubber. Although he found it impossible to say how or when most of his irrational aversions began, he associated this one with a visit to a rubber factory owned by one of his Chaplin granduncles, perhaps during the period when he was living with his father and Louise. Why the factory upset him, apart from the unpleasant smell and the noise, is unknown. He also thought his feelings had something to do with the cheap rubber balls sold as children's toys by street vendors. When new, these balls were dusted with white powder, which he considered filthy and repulsive. His sense that rubber was "dirty" remained so strong that even as an adult he would refuse to work with stage props made of rubber.

Charles senior's concern for his son may have been awakened during the time the boys spent living under his roof. Or perhaps he was simply looking for a way to evade paying more child support. At any rate he talked Hannah into letting Charlie audition for a troupe of child clog dancers being organized by a music hall acquaintance of his named William Jackson. Clog dancing was the craze at the time, and poor boys practiced on the sidewalk, spreading a handful of sand underfoot to accentuate the sounds produced by the rhythmic steps. The question, "What's your break?" was a challenge for a newcomer to prove himself by showing off his best moves. Charlie, for all his shyness, had become an excellent dancer, though it would take six weeks of intensive practice for him to learn the distinctive Lancashire style practiced by the Jackson troupe.

The Eight Lancashire Lads, as Jackson called the group, played in first-class theaters, including the Oxford and Tivoli music halls in London and the Empire theaters in Scotland and the north of England, on the same programs with some of the top acts of the day. Jackson's promotional gimmick was wholesomeness. The "lads" wore no stage makeup and were neatly turned out in knickerbockers and red shoes. Four of the eight dancers were Jackson's own children, one a girl whose hair had been cut short to disguise her sex.

Jackson's publicity was not entirely misleading. He and his wife were devout Catholics who made sure that all the children attended mass every Sunday. Charlie, the only Protestant in the group, was given the option of staying in his room but usually chose to go along to church. The Jacksons were also conscientious about enrolling the children in school wherever the "lads" happened to be performing. Since the troupe sometimes spent a month or even two in one town, it is possible that the children actually learned a little.

Despite their youth, the non-Jackson "lads," like chorus dancers anywhere, were a competitive group, each dreaming of going off on his own as a solo act. Charlie had admired a performer called Bransby Williams, a music hall actor who made a specialty of portraying characters from Dickens, and he worked up an impersonation of Williams doing Uriah Heep, Fagin, and so on. One night, while they were appearing at a theater in Middlesex he was given a chance to try out his act, but the audience was not amused, and his bid for a solo turn ended with one performance.

Even more than the actors, comedians, and singers he saw while on tour, Charlie was impressed by the clowns. During the summer the Lancashire Lads were booked at Transfield's Circus in Yorkshire, where he watched a clown named Rabbit perform an act called "The Road to Ruin." Standing on the back of a galloping horse, Rabbit mimed drinking and card playing, then tore off his fine clothes revealing the rags underneath. The act ended with him taking a mock-suicidal tumble off the fast-moving horse.[26]

In December 1900 the Lads returned to London, where they played cats and dogs in *Cinderella*, a grand holiday pageant produced at the Hippodrome arena. A spectacle with a huge cast and an array of dazzling special effects, *Cinderella* included an aquatic act, for which the floor of the arena was transformed into an artificial lake. The great French clown Marceline appeared as a fisherman angling for mermaids, with glittering "diamond" jewelry as his bait. Charlie had spent his childhood watching his mother do impressions of everyone from street vendors to the great Napoleon, but seeing Marceline at work opened up a new awareness of the possibilities of mime. Marceline was an "Auguste," a relatively extroverted clown personality rooted in the nineteenth-century European circus, and he would have worn the traditional costume of frayed evening wear and a battered-looking top hat. Here, perhaps, was the germ of an idea that Charlie would later use in developing his own comic persona. In fact, around this time, he and another boy in the troupe discussed creating a double act called "The Millionaire Tramps."

William Jackson was "essentially a good man," Charlie would say later, but at the time he and his mother suspected Jackson of exploiting the members of the group. Charlie's wages, sent directly to Hannah, were a half crown a week. This was the equivalent of two and a half shillings, a pittance by any standard. When Hannah complained, Jackson pleaded that the costs of traveling with eight children were ruinous. No doubt the Lancashire Lads were commanding much smaller fees than other acts higher on the bill, so perhaps Jackson was doing the best he could. But when the Lads opened in *Cinderella,* Charlie was able return home every weekend, and Hannah began fussing over his health and making demands that got on Jackson's nerves.

Perhaps she had good reason to worry. Charlie was skinny and tired looking, and one day while the Lads were playing on the bank of the Thames a worrisome incident occurred. The boys were pitching stones, and Charlie suddenly slipped and fell into the river. He would have drowned, he recalled, except that he was rescued by a "big black woolly dog belonging to a policeman." [27]

The *Cinderella* pageant continued its run through the Christmas holidays and into 1901, but soon after the New Year, Charlie was sent home by Mr. Jackson, who had tired of Hannah's fussing. No sooner was he back with his mother than he developed asthma. When an attack came on he fought for breath, and Hannah would drape a blanket over his head and try to get him to inhale the aroma of a bouquet of herbs. The attacks, which may have been triggered by stress, eventually tapered off.

Syd had left school and was working full time, and Hannah was soon able to move into better quarters, an apartment on Chester Street over a hairdresser's shop. Without expecting much to come of it, Charlie registered for work at the Blackmore Agency, which served clients in the legitimate theater. In the meantime, as Syd was departing for Cape Town, South Africa, on his first run as a steamship steward, Charlie inherited his former job as a surgeon's assistant. His duties included scrubbing down the surgery and accompanying the doctor on house calls, carrying his medical bag and assisting him with procedures. The work was too demanding and far too bloody for the overimaginative Charlie, but his employer, Dr. Kinsey-Taylor, took a liking to him and he offered to add him to his household staff as a page boy. The Kinsey-Taylors lived in a large, well-furnished house with a staff of twelve, and Charlie was issued a uniform and told that his main duty would be to ride on the back of the family's carriage. He was quite taken with his own glory and fantasized about making a career in service, perhaps becoming a butler one day. These daydreams were cut short, however, when he was let go for playing in the kitchen yard while he was supposed to be stacking scrap lumber.

For a time, according to Harry Crocker, Charlie also worked as a page to a certain Capt. A. T. Anderson, an officer in the British army in India who was home on leave and suffering from a bad back. The captain enjoyed Charlie's stories about his music hall experiences and became so fond of him that he bought him new clothes and took him to the zoo. Charlie, in turn, "worshipped" Anderson, who treated him more like a son than an employee. Eager for a role model, he began to think of emulating his employer by joining the army. All too soon, however, Anderson's leave was up. Charlie, devastated, "cried like a baby."

Meanwhile, during Charlie's stint with the Eight Lancashire Lads, alcoholism had caught up with Charles Chaplin senior. Chaplin's theatrical friends organized a charity benefit for him, and by a twist of fate Charlie found himself dancing to raise money for his dilatory father's support. One day some months after this concert, passing the Three Stags pub on Kennington Road, Charlie caught a glimpse of his father seated at a table and was shocked by his appearance. The once handsome Charles was in the final stages of cirrhosis of the liver, complicated by kidney disease. His face was puffy, his body swollen almost beyond recognition. In late April, Hannah received word that her husband had been admitted to the hospital. Forgetting their many battles over child support, she rushed to the infirmary to see him. Just thirty-seven years old, Charles senior died on May 9. Charlie, who was home alone that afternoon, was certain that he saw a blaze of white light hovering over the fireplace grate at the very moment his father passed out of this world.

A less welcome apparition was the Reverend O'Neill, a preacher friend of Hannah's, who showed up to pay a condolence call. O'Neill could not resist drawing a moral from Charles senior's early demise: "As ye sow, so shall ye reap." Syd, who was away at sea and must have been told of O'Neill's heartless comment later, said of it, "That just finishes religion for me." Charlie, who was still a believer or at least in awe of the church's authority, thought Syd's reaction highly sacrilegious.

Charles senior had died destitute and estranged from his common-law wife, Louise. The former music hall star was assigned a pauper's grave, but his younger brother Albert, who happened to be visiting from South Africa, did come forward to pay for a proper funeral. Afterward, Charlie recalled, Albert and his family went off to have lunch without bothering to invite Hannah and her son to join them.

As was customary, Charlie pinned a black muslin mourning band to his sleeve, and the sympathetic glances he received from passersby soon gave him an idea. He purchased some cut flowers and began making the rounds of the pubs, peddling them to customers. He earned fifteen shillings in a single day, about seven times his weekly salary with the Lancashire Lads. Using the deliberately ambiguous Cockney euphemism for "job," he proudly told his mother, "I've found a graft of my own." But Hannah objected that peddling flowers was no better than begging and put a stop to it.

Steady work continued to elude Charlie. The pattern established during his stint as a page with the Kinsey-Taylors was destined to repeat itself over and over. Charlie's small size and sweet personality prompted employers to take a chance on him, but their generous impulse was rarely rewarded. He became a clerk in a shop selling lamp oil and sundries, but his habit of taking home a candle or two every night led to an early dismissal. For a time he worked as a barber's assistant, lathering up customers for their shaves. He learned enough to be able to cut his own hair, using an arrangement of three mirrors rigged to allow him to see the back of his head, but once again his work habits were unsatisfactory and he was soon let go. He talked his way into a job as a printer's assistant with a stationery sup-

ply company, claiming prior experience even though he knew so little about the trade that when his boss called "Strike it"—the signal
to start the press—he thought he was being told to take a break. The
pay was good, but after two months the strenuous, high-pressure
work became too much for him.

At one point Charlie was hired as a glassblower's assistant, the
wrong job for a boy who could not tolerate heavy lifting and stress.
The wages were low—roughly the equivalent of $1.80 a week—the
glass factory was an inferno, and Charlie found the labor expected of
him "terrifying." He had been at work just a few minutes when he
was overcome by the heat, and the foreman sent him out into the
factory yard to recover. There a group of glassblowers on a smoking
break began to chide him for being soft. He readily agreed that he
was used to easier work and proved it by showing off a few dance
steps. The show was so entertaining that the men overstayed their
break and Charlie was in trouble for the second time that morning.

"I'll give you one more chance to get some work done," the
foreman grumbled. He pointed to some trays filled with finished
bottles and ordered Charlie to stack them in the loading area. The
trays were heavy, and Charlie, dizzy from the heat, reached out to
steady himself, burning his hand on a white-hot furnace support. He
left the factory on a stretcher, invalided off the job before lunch.[28]

Employment as a newsboy seemed better suited to Charlie's
abilities. Syd had previously worked for the Willing Co., owners of a
chain of newsstands, and his good record on the job may account for
Mr. Willing's confidence in Charlie, who was given the responsible
task of operating a newsstand near the entrance to the Clapham
Common tube station. One of the delightful perks of the job was a
cap emblazoned with the logo WILLING, entitling the wearer to
travel free on public transportation. Another was a small, primitive
vending machine on the counter, which dispensed a piece of choco-
late candy in exchange for a halfpenny coin. Charlie tinkered with
the machine until it gave up its sweets for free and attached a small
box to the outside with a sign advising DEPOSIT HA'PENNY HERE. The
scheme worked perfectly until his boss opened the machine and
totaled up the take. Charlie was unemployed again after just three
weeks.

With hindsight, no one could blame a boy whose mother often

didn't get enough to eat for succumbing to temptation and snitching a few ha'pennies. The striking feature of this incident is that Charlie didn't realize that the owner would be reconciling his income with the depleted stock, and when he was caught he thought it rather mean-spirited for such a substantial businessman to be counting halfpennies. His resentment of tradesmen persisted, even though he himself thought about money almost all the time, his head so filled with "capitalist" schemes that he couldn't concentrate on the jobs he actually managed to get.

The first installment of Syd's pay, turned over to his mother before he shipped out, was soon used up, and Charlie and Hannah were living with a chronic shortfall in their budget. They had moved from Chester Street to a top-floor room at 3 Pownall Terrace, a dilapidated building where the rent was five shillings tenpence a week and the landlady, a friend of Hannah's, not too particular about seeing the money on time. Once again reduced to the diet of the poorest classes, they lived on mashed potatoes and greens or bread-and-drippings, the latter a dish Charlie thought quite tasty. Once a week Hannah made a stew from fourpenny ends, miscellaneous scraps of meat the butcher shops sold by weight. If money was especially tight, she would make do with threepenny ends, which were the same, only slightly rancid.

Poverty is a curse but not necessarily a humiliation. Hannah, however, had come up from nothing and earned good money as a singer when she was still very young. That many of her old friends, not to mention her husband and her former lover Leo Dryden, continued to live well while she and her sons were destitute, must have been a constant preoccupation. After he became famous Charlie received a letter from a woman who had been a childhood friend of his at Pownall Terrace, recalling the good times they had playing dress-up and how Charlie would amuse her family by putting on a dress and pretending to be a lady. It would seem he had not been quite as solitary and friendless as he remembered. Still, he felt set apart from the children of the neighborhood, measuring his situation against what might have been.

"I was well aware of the social stigma of our poverty," he wrote of this period of his life. "Even the poorest of children sat down to a home-cooked Sunday dinner. A roast at home meant respectability, a ritual that distinguished one poor class from another. Those who could not sit down to Sunday dinner at home were of the mendicant class, and we were that. Mother would send me to the nearest coffee shop to buy a sixpenny dinner (meat and two vegetables). The shame of it—especially on Sunday!"[29] In fact many working-class Londoners did not have ovens during the first decade of the century, hence the continued popularity of boiled puddings. Undoubtedly he was reflecting the shame felt by his mother, whose middle-class aspirations and values were invariably abandoned during her manic episodes.

Hannah, it seems, was not completely estranged from her family and former friends. When healthy, she was a generous woman who reached out to help others even though she had little to share. Her father, Charles Hill, lived with her and the boys for a time when he was down on his luck and too ill to work, and she even visited Charles senior's child by his common-law wife, Louise, who had died, leaving the boy an orphan. In turn, Hannah's sister, Kate Hill Mowbray, who was fairly well off, seems to have tried to help her and Charlie. "Her occasional visits usually ended abruptly and with acrimony at something Mother had said or done," Charlie would recall. [30]

Sooner or later Hannah's unstable personality led to quarrels that drove away everyone who tried to come to her aid. One old friend from the music halls, a "Junoesque" former dancer who had become the mistress of a retired colonel, ran into Hannah during the time after Charlie had left the Lancashire Lads and invited them to move into her fashionable house on Lansdowne Square, which she shared with four servants and a younger boyfriend who disappeared whenever the colonel paid a visit. At this stage of his life Charlie was subject to devastating crushes on other boys, and his affections soon settled on the son of the family next door. He and Hannah were putting up a good front, and the boy accepted him as an equal. But Hannah and her benefactress soon had a falling-out, for reasons never explained, and Charlie found himself back in his frayed poor boy's clothes, picking up odd jobs on the street. One day, in this condition, he ran into the boy from Lansdowne Square: "He looked at me. I grew self-conscious. Quickly I said, 'Oh, I'm in my working clothes, you know. I'm studying carpentry.' He looked at my outfit—with disbelief. I never saw him again."[31]

Another well-meaning friend, a certain Mrs. Taylor, who knew Hannah from her attendance at the mission tabernacles, tried to help her and Charlie escape their dreary quarters at 3 Pownall Terrace by renting them a room on the second floor of her house for a very modest sum. This arrangement ended abruptly when Hannah got into a screaming fight with Mrs. Taylor's daughter, shouting at her, "Who do you think you are, Lady Shit?"

"That's nice language coming from a Christian," the younger woman retorted.

"It's in the Bible, my dear: Deuteronomy, twenty-eighth chapter, fifty-seventh verse, only there's another word for it," Hannah said huffily. "However, shit will suit you."[32]

For what it's worth, Deuteronomy 28:57–58 says nothing about excrement, but the chapter in which it is found is a litany of ritual curses on those who disobey God's laws, including madness, boils, abandonment, war, and hunger so extreme that the accursed will be forced to consume the "issue" of their own bodies. Hannah's constant Bible reading had led her into some dark corners indeed.

Evicted by the Taylors, Hannah and her son returned to Pownall Terrace. Hannah was headed for another breakdown, and Charlie began staying away from home as much as possible, hanging around the stables behind Kennington Road, where a semiderelict who slept in a loft taught him to make toy boats out of discarded wooden shoeboxes and scraps of string and tinsel. Charlie took pleasure in fashioning the little boats, and the work turned out to be surprisingly lucrative. His materials cost almost nothing, and after selling a few boats he would invest in a bag of candy and divide it into smaller lots wrapped in newspaper, which he peddled as well. But when he tried working on the boats in the close quarters of their room, Hannah complained that the fumes from the glue gave her headaches.

As Hannah's behavior became more and more erratic, Charlie began sleeping overnight in the loft. In her worst moments Hannah sometimes threw crockery or went up to people on the street and punched them for no reason. No doubt Charlie took his share of blows as well, and he must also have rescued his mother from the consequences of many public outbursts. Years later, when he was the world-famous Charlie Chaplin, he returned to Pownall Terrace, where the landlady remembered him and invited him to share a pot of tea. As he left the premises the dingy street, not much changed from his youth, brought back a vivid memory: "I saw myself, a scared, undersized, skinny kid, leading my mother by the hand, dragging her through the fog and the smells and the cold toward our miserable home, while other kids yelled and jeered at her."[33]

One day when he was not around, Hannah began knocking on her neighbors' doors, telling the children that she had a birthday present for them and then handing them lumps of coal. (Can it be a coincidence that the word for money in the Romany dialect spoken in England also meant, literally, "coal"?) This time the sympathetic landlady could not protect her. The neighbors insisted on calling in a doctor, and Hannah was readmitted to Cane Hill. The doctor who examined her on May 9, 1903, noted in his report that the patient "says the floor is the River Jordan and she cannot cross it." He also described her as "at times violent and destructive."[34]

After his mother was taken away Charlie examined the cupboards and found that there was no food at all. Later a doctor at Cane Hill told him that Hannah's condition was caused in part by malnutrition, so guilt over his failure to provide for her in his brother's absence was piled on top of sorrow and shame.

Syd was due back from his latest sea voyage, and the landlady let Charlie keep his room on credit while he waited. Afraid of being sent back to Hanwell or Norwood, he stayed out of sight during the day, earning a few pennies by chopping wood around the stables. When Syd did return, he decided to resign from the steamship company in order to make a home for his brother. It was no great sacrifice. Syd had been playing the cornet in the ship's band and entertaining passengers with jokes and impersonations. His heart was set on making a career in the music halls.

2

. . . A Romance of Cockayne

While trying to launch himself as a comedian, Syd found work as a barkeep. Just when the chances of either brother getting anywhere in show business seemed dim, Charlie unexpectedly received a note summoning him to the Blackmore Agency. Mr. Blackmore himself interviewed him and sent him on to the offices of the distinguished theatrical producer Charles Frohman, who offered him not one job but two: A featured role in H. A. Saintsbury's new play, *Jim, A Romance of Cockayne*, to be followed by the part of Billy the page boy with Saintsbury's touring company of William Gillette's *Sherlock Holmes*.

Charlie had no idea how to account for this sudden stroke of luck. One suspects that someone at the agency may have been familiar with the tragic history of Charles Chaplin senior and wanted to do something to help his son. But Charlie also had all the qualifications for a successful child actor. He was small for his age, with a large head, good features, and a winsome expression. At fourteen he could still easily be mistaken for a ten-year-old. He was a trained dancer, he moved well, and his Cockney accent was the real thing. Moreover, he had experience with a touring company, and with Hannah once again a patient at Cane Hill, Saintsbury could be spared having to deal with an overprotective stage mother. One qualification Charlie did not have was the ability to read well. Luckily Saintsbury did not expect him to audition at once; he gave him a copy of the play to study at home, where Syd coached him in his lines.

The title of Saintsbury's new play evoked the mythical land of Cockaigne, where the streets are paved with pastry and the houses made of barley sugar. The association between the legendary kingdom of idleness and Cockney London was far from the only whimsical touch in this comedy/melodrama, in which an aristocrat suffering from amnesia finds himself living in an attic room in the slums. The plot was hackneyed, but Charlie's role as a streetwise newsboy gave him some good lines, which he delivered with the pinched vowels and dropped aitches of a genuine Cockney, much to the delight of the audience.

Jim closed after two weeks, but later that same month, on July 27, Saintsbury opened his production of *Sherlock Holmes,* with Charlie once again playing a sprightly Cockney lad. William Gillette's *Sherlock Holmes* was authorized by Arthur Conan Doyle, whose own attempt to bring Holmes to the stage had been rejected by producer Charles Frohman as insufficiently dramatic. Frohman had persuaded Conan Doyle to turn the project over to the American actor-director Gillette, who borrowed from two of Holmes's best-known adventures, "A Scandal in Bohemia" and *A Study in Scarlet,* to create an original mystery-drama billed as "a hitherto unpublished episode in the career of the great detective, and showing his connection with The Strange Case of Miss (Alice) Faulkner." Following its premiere in New York in November 1899, *Sherlock Holmes* became a repertory staple. Gillette himself often played the title role, making his last appearance as Holmes in 1932 at the age of seventy-eight. The play had already been a hit in London during the 1901–2 season and had toured the provincial theaters, but the tall, austere H. A. Saintsbury was such a satisfactory incarnation of the sage of Baker Street that his revival was guaranteed a long, profitable run.

The role of Billy was an excellent showcase for a young actor, and Saintsbury doted on Charlie, giving him extra coaching. He taught him not to move his head too much and to wait for a laugh instead of rushing through his lines. Ironically, considering his experience as a dancer, Charlie was comfortable with his dialogue but nervous about the stage business, which required him to manage a tray, teapot, and other props.

Charlie quickly became an audience favorite. Offstage he was a

loner who became more withdrawn during the course of the tour.
Tom Green, a stagehand, and his wife, Edith, the wardrobe mistress, were assigned to keep on eye on the youngest cast member,
but Charlie did not enjoy their company and he felt that the other
players, though friendly, were not really comfortable about having a
teenager hanging around. He was so shy that he would cross the
street rather than face the ordeal of saying hello to the leading lady,
whom he worshipped from afar. Although he was earning two
pounds ten shillings a week, three times what he had made in the
print shop, he spent most of his free time looking for ways to aug-
ment his income. He bought a cheap camera and took photos in
working-class neighborhoods, developing the film in his room and
then selling the prints to the subjects for a few pennies each.

Mrs. Green recalled another of Charlie's moneymaking ven-
tures:

One day, when the company was staying at the Market Hotel, in
Blackburn, Charlie noticed that the hotel sitting room was filled with
farmers, in town because it was market day. He walked into the midst of
the country folks, and began singing songs in what was then a pronounced Cockney accent. And he finished his bit of entertainments by
going into a clog dance—and he was a real clog dancer too. His audience
laughed until the tears streamed down their faces, but their amusement
was somewhat lessened when Charlie circulated among them with his hat
in his hand. He intended that his audience should pay for the impromptu
show—and they did.

Charlie wasn't mean, but he never threw away money unnecessarily. I
recall how he used to check every item on the bills rendered him by landladies when we were on the road, and how he used to knock off items for
service he hadn't been given. If he had been out to tea one day during the
week, he would deduct a proportionate amount from the bill.[1]

Despite this scrutiny of their accounts, the landladies at the
rooming houses and small hotels where the company lodged usually
took a liking to Charlie, who was not too shy, it seems, to charm
them. On baking day he could usually be found in the kitchen, sam-
pling tea cakes as they emerged hot from the oven.

Concern for Charlie may have prompted Saintsbury's decision

to hire eighteen-year-old Syd to fill the featured role of Count von Stalberg, an elderly aristocrat, when it fell vacant in December. A month later the brothers were joined on tour by Hannah, who had been released from Cane Hill. The reunion was not a great success. Always an independent sort, Syd was highly interested in the opposite sex, and having his mother along on tour was inconvenient. Worse, Hannah was nervous and strangely subdued. Very likely she did not trust herself and was afraid of a lapse into odd behavior that would embarrass her sons. After a few weeks she returned to London, where she was able to move back into her former rooms on Chester Street.

Saintsbury's road company broke up during the summer of 1904, and Syd went to sea again as a steward. Charlie was announced for the leading role of "Ned Nimble, the newsboy . . . who works his way from gutter to palace," in an American play called *Rags to Riches*. The production sank from sight before its official London opening, but Charlie wasn't unemployed for long. The indestructible *Sherlock Holmes* was now being played by not one but three provincial road companies, and he was able to pick up his role of Billy in one of them. As a result he was away from London when Hannah had yet another breakdown. This time the doctor who examined her at the Lambeth Infirmary described her as "very strange in manner and quite incoherent. She dances sings and cries by turn. She is indecent in conduct & conversation at times and again at times praying and saying she has been born again." Committed to Cane Hill once more, Hannah still had periods when she was completely lucid and fretted about how she looked without her false teeth, which had been left behind or damaged when she took ill. These intervals of self-awareness were a mixed blessing for her and for her sons. It seemed cruel to keep her locked up in a public hospital when she still had her pride, and could even joke about being temporarily "on the shelf," yet her attempts to live independently always ended in disaster. Charlie found his trips to Cane Hill a strain and began to avoid them whenever he could.[2]

The tour of *Sherlock Holmes* was becoming a little seedy, as the rights to it had been sold to a second-rank producer and many of the key roles taken over by unknowns. But once again Charlie's theatri-

cal career was blessed by fate. The great William Gillette was opening in London at the Duke of York's Theatre in a play called *Clarice*,
and he hoped to warm up the audience with a curtain-raiser, a brief
theater piece entitled *The Painful Predicament of Sherlock Holmes*.
Originally written for a benefit performance at New York's
Metropolitan Opera House as a showcase for Ethel Barrymore, the
sketch re-creates Holmes's interview with a very talkative lady who
comes to him as a client and is gradually revealed to be quite mad.
Ironically Charlie's part—once again as the page boy, Billy—called
for him to recognize the lady's condition and summon the police to
take the madwoman away.

Despite the addition of the curtain-raiser to the program, *Clarice*
soon failed, and Gillette decided to fill out his engagement with yet
another revival of *Sherlock Holmes*. An old hand at the role of Billy
by now, Charlie found himself playing opposite the celebrated
Gillette in a first-rank theater, where the royal box was often occupied by such distinguished guests as the king of Greece, who interrupted the performance by remonstrating loudly with his son for giving away the plot, screeching, "Don't tell me! Don't *tell* me!" The
engagement with Gillette ended with a Royal Gala Performance in
November 1905, and Charlie returned to a road-company *Holmes*
until March of the following year. Then he was let go.

One month shy of his seventeenth birthday, Charles Spencer
Chaplin had reached that difficult stage in the life of the child actor
when he was, as he put it, "neither fish nor fowl for any form of theatrical work."[3] He had grown too tall for juvenile roles like Billy but
was not quite old enough for adult parts. In Charlie's case it seems
that the end of his legitimate stage career was helped along by a
tantrum. As he told it, Dion Boucicault, son of the celebrated actor
and one of the leading impresarios of the London theater, had recommended him for a role on tour with a new production starring
actress Madge Kendal. Charlie appeared for an interview, but Mrs.
Kendal kept him waiting, then offhandedly told him to return the
next day as she was too busy to talk to him. Charlie took offense and
walked out. One wonders if there was not more to this incident.
Charlie was a Cockney youth, very touchy about his class background, and Mrs. Kendal a grande dame of the theater. Whatever
the cause of the misunderstanding, the repercussions must have

been serious. Charlie gave up looking for stage roles and within a month he joined Syd, who was playing in a music hall comedy sketch called *Repairs*, about a group of innocently befuddled workingmen who deconstruct everything they touch.

When the summer came Charlie moved on to a leading role in an act called Casey's Court Circus. The company, all boys Charlie's age or younger, played a group of "street arabs" putting on an impromptu show on a vacant lot. Charlie's star turns included his impersonation of Dr. Walford Bodie, a stage hypnotist who claimed to cure the sick through "bloodless surgery." Charlie had seen Bodie in person but, amazingly, he had never witnessed the act he was called on to burlesque. Instead of resorting to the usual hypnotist's mumbo-jumbo, he decided to try for a realistic, understated character study. On opening night his noble intentions were undone by his silk top hat, which he had stuffed with paper so that it would fit his smallish head. In the middle of his act the paper fell out, and when he donned the hat it slid down over his eyes and came to rest on the bridge of his nose. The audience broke up, and Charlie learned the valuable lesson that there was nothing so humorous as the sudden collapse of a man's dignity.

"I had stumbled on the secret of being funny—unexpectedly," he told an interviewer a few years later:

An idea going in one direction meets another idea *suddenly*, Ha! Ha! You shriek. It works every time. I walk on the stage, serious dignified, solemn, pause before an easy chair, spread my coat-tails with an elegant gesture—and sit on the cat. Nothing funny about it, really, especially if you consider the feelings of the cat. But you laugh. You laugh because it is unexpected. Those little nervous shocks make you laugh.[4]

Casey's Court Circus was a very successful act, and Charlie had star billing. But compared to appearing at the Duke of York's Theatre with Gillette onstage and the king of Greece in the royal box, it didn't amount to much, and he left the company without regrets in the summer of 1907. For a while nothing he tried worked out. He wrote a sketch called *Twelve Good Men*, about a jury full of misfits for whom the term "deliberation" was an oxymoron, but his chief financial backer withdrew his support while the act was in rehearsal. Too softhearted to give his cast the bad news, Charlie kept holding run-throughs until Syd intervened, saying, "This is crazy," and insisted that he tell the eleven other players that there would be no opening night.

Next he tried a "Jewish comedian" act, using material commissioned from a gag writer as well as excerpts from an old American joke book. His first and last performance was at a theater on Mile End Road, near the heart of London's largest Jewish neighborhood, where the audience drove him from the stage, pelting him with orange peels. Their reaction was the first hint he'd had that his material might be considered anti-Semitic, and the fiasco cured him of any desire to work as a stand-up comic.

In two short years the fortunes of the Chaplin brothers had reversed. Charlie, after a brilliant start as a child actor, had no prospects and was living in a very modest boardinghouse, his keep subsidized by Syd, whose career in comedy had surged ahead when he was hired by Fred Karno, the leading producer of music hall comedy sketches. Born Fred Westcott, Karno had started life as a glazier's assistant, drumming up business by breaking windows along his boss's route. He trained as a circus acrobat, branched out into comedy, and within a few years he had become a producer with between six and ten troupes on tour, all run out of his headquarters, the "Fun Factory" in London's Camberwell district, which housed his offices, a rehearsal studio, and a prop warehouse.

There was a tradition of pantomime in the music halls, going back to the days when shows were staged as free entertainment for saloon patrons. In order to prevent drinking establishments from competing unfairly with theaters, English law forbade the performers in these saloon shows to speak on stage. By Karno's day the music halls had outgrown their origins, but comedy-sketch artists continued to rely on mime, using dialogue chiefly to set up the situation and end the act, and Karno quickly established his knack for developing foolproof material. Acts like *Jail Birds* and *Early Birds*, set in a flophouse, drew humor from the grimmer aspects of slum life. There was nothing shabby, however, about Karno's productions. He hired the best comic talent, trained them well, and showcased them in elaborate, inventive sets. And he excelled above all in generating publicity. The cast of *Jail Birds*, arriving in town for an engagement, would descend from the train dressed in striped convicts' uniforms, only to be herded into a paddy wagon and paraded through the streets to the theater. On other occasions the actors would arrive at the theater in a horse-drawn hearse, or following behind a cage containing a live circus lion that was mauling a realistic-looking dummy that had been smeared with meat.

By all accounts Fred Karno was a horrible little man. If he decided that an actor was below par, he would torment the poor fellow by standing in the wings and interrupting his performance with loud raspberries. He beat his wife, and once responded to her accusation that he was having an affair by mailing her a packet of photographs of himself and his mistress in pornographic poses. One actress recalled that her employment interview with Karno began with his ordering her to strip to the waist. She failed to comply quickly enough to suit him, and he taunted her, saying, "I won't *bite* them!" When he next demanded to feel her legs to see if they were firm, she stormed out of his office in indignation.

This interviewing technique may explain why Karno's troupes produced few outstanding female players. Yet Karno's male stars often looked up to him as a great teacher and mentor. "Fred went to infinite pains to train newcomers to his shows," says his biographer, J. P. Gallagher, "to teach them the slow delivery of lines, to slop about the stage, always to be 'wistful'—that was the secret of the great appeal of 'Karno's Komics,' they tugged at the heart-strings at the same time that they created belly-laughs. The audience was brought to *sympathise* with the poor comic."[5]

No doubt young players also looked up to Karno because he rarely missed a chance to thumb his nose at the class system. He kept a houseboat on the Thames, ablaze with multicolored lights, which was considered an eyesore and a public nuisance, and on the death of the Duke of Cambridge he purchased the ducal coaches at auction as transport for his players.

By early 1909 Syd had become one of Karno's chief writers, and he persuaded "the Guv'nor" to give Charlie a tryout in a sketch called *The Football Match*. Charlie was not quite twenty and struck Karno as too shy and physically unimposing to hold his own on stage, but he got the biggest laughs night after night. Cast in a supporting role as the villain, he would upstage the leads by painting his nose cherry red, tripping over his own cane, and even dropping his pants on stage. Karno knew ambition when he saw it, and by the end of his first year with the organization, Charlie was playing the lead role in *Mumming Birds*, Fred Karno's trademark act.

Karno had created *Mumming Birds* in 1904, when his theatrical lodge, the Grand Order of Water Rats, was asked to stage a gala charity performance in honor of the shah of Iran's visit to London. Karno's inspiration was to burlesque some of the worst acts in the business, a task that the lodge members undertook with gusto. *Entertaining the Shah*, as the sketch was originally known, was soon adapted for a commercial run under the title *Mumming Birds* and became the most popular and enduring act in the history of vaudeville. In one form or another it played for forty years in theaters all over the world.

The sets for Karno's production employed a false proscenium, with false box seats on either side. The "patrons" who occupied these boxes were Karno players and the real stars of the show. In the box at stage left were two actors who portrayed a doting uncle and his bratty nephew, who uses a peashooter to torment the hapless "dud" acts. The box on the right was occupied by a character in evening dress and top hat called the "Inebriate Swell." *Mumming Birds* begins with the Swell making a great commotion as he is escorted to his seat. Settling into his box, he opens a bottle of champagne, tries unsuccessfully to light his cigar on an electric bulb, and then, offered a light by an actor in another box, leans forward to reach it and falls head over heels onto the stage.

Karno's script for *Mumming Birds* was only a few pages long. Typically there were a dozen acts, each worse than the last, beginning with a male comic vocalist and a "Saucy Soubrette," who directed her naughty song to the Swell. Then came:

3. Lady Vocalist Comedy. Song "Come Birdie, Come and Live with Me." (Interruptions from Boy and Drunk.)
4. Chord on for Actor's Entrance. Recites "The Trail of the Yukon." (Boy and Drunk interfere again.)

5. Sustained chord for Quartette. Comedy Bus. to be explained.
    (Drunk gets out of Box and gets them off.)

And so on through act number twelve, invariably "Marconi Ali,
the Terrible Turk," a wrestler who offers to take on volunteers from
the audience. The Swell takes up the challenge, is ushered backstage for a quick change into tights and trunks, and returns to the
stage to flip Ali onto his back and win the bout. At the end of the
act, the Swell speaks his first and only line of dialogue:

Announcer: And what would you like now, sir?
Drunk: Bring on the girls!

The pantomime business that made the act funny was traditional, passed down from one cast to the next and modified to suit
their talents. Charlie approached the role of the Swell with the conviction, no doubt learned from hard experience, that there is nothing innately funny about drunkenness. Humor arises only from a
drunk's struggle to pretend that he is sober. He portrayed the Swell
as a man fighting a gallant but losing battle to hang on to his dignity.
However it was played, the Swell's role was physically punishing.
The prop list for the show included—in addition to oranges,
bananas and a whole pie for the horrible boy to fling at one of the
bad acts—a small mattress used to line the floor of the drunk's box.
But there was nothing to cushion the Swell when he fell *out* of the
box, which he did several times a night.

Now that they were both on Karno's payroll Charlie and Syd were
able to afford a comfortable flat in London, where their circle of
friends included Jimmy Hargreaves, who played in the halls as
"Magnini the Wizard Violinist," and Lester Garner, a member of
an act known as "The Ten Loonies." The young men would wander the streets all night, then stop for breakfast at a shop in Drury
Lane to gorge themselves on fried fish. Syd, who was fascinated
by machines, bought one of the first motorcycles sold in England.
Charlie begged to be allowed to ride it around the block and was
so exhilarated by the sensation of speed that he kept going for
fifty miles, stopping only when he had burned out the engine.

Luckily for him, Syd could never stay angry with his little brother for long.

On tour Karno's Komics were expected to cover traveling expenses out of their salaries. Like many in the company, Charlie had sidelines that enabled him pick up extra cash to defray these out-of-pocket costs. For a while he sold a metal polish made from nitric acid. Objects cleaned with this concoction had a tendency to turn black after a few days, but by then the troupe had moved on to a different town, so the sellers heard few complaints. Charlie later joked that he only sold the product in Scotland, where the theater-goers were so hard to please that they deserved to be cheated. Scottish theater managers often had to resort to giving away premiums to draw patrons, and the story among Karno players was that one man, attending on a day when the free gift was a clock, interrupted the show to inquire, "Hae it got a guarantee with it?"

By 1909 Charlie had grown into a slender, ascetic-looking young man whose deep blue eyes and long eyelashes were his most striking features. Considering that he had spent much of his childhood on tour, he was remarkably immature, still subject to devastating crushes. Over the years he had transferred his interests from other boys to women, but the objects of his adoration were invariably unapproachable, like the beautiful Marie Doro, who had played opposite William Gillette in the short-lived *Clarice*. During the summer of his first year with Karno, however, he began a flirtation with Hetty Kelly, a fifteen-year-old dancer with a troupe called Bert Coutts's Yankee Doodle Girls. Desperate to impress Hetty as a man of the world, he reserved a table at the Trocadero, one of the most expensive eating spots in London. Hetty was not prepared to find herself dining out in such a grand setting, and she was put off and even a little alarmed by Charlie's effusive insistence that she was to be his "nemesis." Nevertheless Hetty allowed him to call for her the next morning at seven to walk her to rehearsal. Charlie, who rarely went to bed before 2:00 A.M. anyway, was too excited to sleep, and in his overwrought state he became fixated on the notion that destiny had forged a "mystic" connection between him and Hetty.

After four days of sacrificing his sleep to escort Hetty to rehearsals, he belatedly noticed that she had some reservations about their union of souls. There was a quarrel, and Hetty spoke the dreaded words, "I like you—but . . . "[6] Stung, Charlie told her they had better not see each other again. He was devastated when Hetty agreed that this would be for the best.

As Chaplin himself later acknowledged, his feelings for Hetty had little to do with sex and perhaps even less to do with her personality. Hetty, he explained, had awakened him to "beauty." One might speculate that what he really meant was that she had awakened him to female beauty—the first female, at least the first who was at all approachable, to arouse his romantic interest.

A few weeks after his flirtation with Hetty ended, Charlie's troupe was booked in Paris at the Folies-Bergère. In addition to playing the Swell in *Mumming Birds*, Charlie was now doing a solo turn as a morose drunk who flamboyantly threatens suicide. At the end of the act he fired a revolver at his temple and tumbled over a balcony, landing in a sitting position on a couch underneath it, no worse for wear. During his free hours, he found Paris almost as intoxicating as the charms of Hetty Kelly. He spent his days walking the streets and sitting in sidewalk cafés, and every night after the show he would go out in evening dress in search of adventure. With the rest of the male cast members, he visited the brothels and drank absinthe. One night he negotiated for the services of a high-priced prostitute, only to flee from their cab in horror when the young woman glanced at her watch and explained that her exorbitant fee was only *"pour le moment"* and she had another engagement booked for later in the evening.

Charlie had arrived in Paris expecting to see Hetty, whose company had also been booked at the Folies. Showing up at the theater the night before Karno's Komics were scheduled to open, he went backstage and found a twelve-year-old ballerina who spoke English. The young dancer, Maybelle Fournier, informed him that the Yankee Doodle Girls had already left Paris and were on their way to play an engagement in Russia. Their conversation was observed by Maybelle's mother, who assumed that Charlie was making a pass at her daughter and angrily warned him away. After he explained that he only wanted news of Miss Kelly, she apologized and invited him to tea in the suite she shared with Maybelle and another daughter, fifteen-year-old Dolores. Charlie began dropping in on the family regularly. As he recalled, during the course of the next few weeks both Mrs. Fournier, who was thirty-nine and still handsome, and Dolores, whom he considered wild and coarse-looking, tried to seduce him.

Chaplin's unflattering memories of Dolores, however, may have had something to do with an article that later appeared in the British press, in which Dolores reminisced about his infatuation with twelve-year-old Maybelle. In private conversations, however, he confirmed the essence of Dolores's story: "I had a most violent crush on a girl only ten or twelve. I have always been in love with young girls, not in an amorous way. . . . It was funny: not in a sex way—I just loved to caress and fondle her—not passionately—just to have her in my arms."[7]

Charlie never saw Maybelle Fournier again. He did run into Hetty Kelly in England a year or so later, and was disappointed to notice that she had developed breasts, which he did not find attractive. He felt relieved that she had broken off their romance.

In 1910 Charlie was offered the lead in a new Karno sketch, *Jimmy the Fearless, or, the Boy 'Ero*, about a Cockney lad addicted to "penny dreadful" novels who dreams of himself as the hero in a fantastic series of adventures—fighting Indians in the American West, rescuing a damsel who has been left tied to the railroad tracks in the path of an oncoming train, winning the hand of a princess. Jimmy was a big part, and Charlie amazed everyone by turning it down. The sketch was new and untried, and perhaps he worried that Jimmy would invite comparison with his Billy in *Sherlock Holmes*. His refusal of the role created an opportunity for another young Karnoite, Arthur Stanley Jefferson, the son of a Glasgow theater manager. Jefferson—better remembered as Stan Laurel, the stage name he adopted a few years later—opened in the sketch, but when Charlie saw that the act was a hit he changed his mind and decided that he wanted to play Jimmy after all. Laurel accepted the situation philosophically. In September, Stan and Charlie were both asked to join Karno's American touring company, and they agreed to become roommates for the duration of the tour.

Accompanied by Alf Reeves, the tour manager, the company sailed for the New World on a freighter still redolent of its former cargo of beef on the hoof. When not actually seasick, they passed their time making up seasickness jokes. Laurel sized up young Chaplin as an unpredictable mixture of extreme shyness and self-dramatization. He later told his biographer, John McCabe, that as the ship approached land, Charlie raced to the rail and exclaimed, "America, I am coming to conquer you! Every man, woman, and child shall have my name upon their lips—Charles Spencer Chaplin!" Undercutting the drama of the moment, the land in question happened to be Canadian.

After a stop in Quebec, the players headed for Jersey City, New Jersey, for a weeklong tuneup before their New York City opening. Arriving in town the company repaired to a saloon, where Charlie addressed the bartender, "Well, old Top, I fancy I should like a mug of mulled ale and a toasted biscuit." Assuming that he was being mocked, the barkeep grabbed an oak "bung starter," a stick used to tap kegs of beer, and approached threateningly, growling, "You're in Jersey City now, young feller, not Piccadilly." Charlie panicked, and Alf Reeves had to intervene to pacify the bartender and assure him that no insult had been intended.[8]

Charlie's first impression of New York City was more favorable but still a little daunting. The buildings were tall and impersonal, and the people talked very fast and were in such a hurry that they even ate and drank standing up. Nor was Charlie the only member of the company to find American customs hard to get used to. On their first night in the city, Stan Laurel put his only pair of shoes outside his hotel room door to be shined. The next morning they were gone and the hotel clerk, instead of commiserating, lectured him on his foolishness.

The twenty-member company was a very young group. Alf Reeves, at thirty-four, was almost a father figure. Another player, tall, lanky Albert Austin, could make up to play a septuagenarian, but he was only four years older than Charlie. Stan Laurel was a few years younger, having dropped out of boarding school to go "on the halls" at sixteen. Unfortunately, although Karno's Komics had enjoyed great success in the States in the past, the new company was saddled with unpromising material, a sketch called *The Wow-Wows*, in which Charlie was cast as Archie Binks, an upper-class twit who is tricked into going through the initiation rites of a nonexistent secret society. Presumably Karno thought that Americans would enjoy seeing an English snob get his comeuppance, but the sketch was filled with topical jokes that were not very funny to begin with and lost on New Yorkers. Unlike *Mumming Birds*, which was basically a mime show, the humor of the *Wow-Wows* depended on dialogue, so the player's accents also became a problem. Reviewing the opening night at New York's Colonial Theater, *Variety's* East Coast reviewer observed, "A Karno company that talks seemed to hit the Colonial audiences as a bit queer."[9]

Determined to wring laughs out of the weak script, Chaplin had improvised makeup that accentuated Archie Binks's spotty complexion and unhealthy pallor. *Variety* disapproved of this "twenty-minutes-from-a-cemetery" look but observed that Charles Chaplin was "the sort of comedian American audiences seem to like, though unaccustomed to."

During the remainder of the tour, the company tinkered with their material, improvising a sketch called *A Night in an English Club*, which used *The Wow-Wows'* set but incorporated the amateur acts concept of *Mumming Birds*. At some point they simply gave in and began doing *Mumming Birds* in its entirety, billing the show under its American title, *A Night in an English Music Hall*.

Offstage the company amused itself by playing practical jokes on one another. One night Charlie spotted one of the actresses, an ingenue on her first tour, chatting with a local man in their hotel lobby. He approached and spoke confidentially, but quite loud enough for the man to hear: "Well my dear, when you finally shake *it*, tell the hall girl to give you the key to our room. I'm off to the pawnshop around the corner to get your wedding ring out of soak." The young woman took the joke in stride; however, the general feeling in the company was that Charlie did not quite fit in.

"People through the years have talked about how eccentric he became," Stan Laurel later told John McCabe. "He was a very eccentric person *then*. He was very moody and often very shabby in appearance. Then suddenly he would astonish us all by getting dressed to kill. It seemed that every once in a while he would get an urge to look very smart. At these times he would wear a derby hat (an expensive one), gloves, smart suit, two-toned side button shoes, and carry a cane."[10]

In San Franciso, Charlie bought another odd piece of clothing, a second-hand coat with a nipped-in waist, which he wore until someone told him he looked like a ringmaster. At every stop he haunted the used-book-stores. He carried around a Latin grammar, which he didn't find time to open for more than a year, as well as books on philosophy and economics. For a while he tried to teach himself ancient Greek but gave it up when he discovered yoga and went on a weeklong water-only fast that was supposed to cleanse his system. Moreover, he had brought his violin with him on tour and sometimes practiced three or four hours at a stretch. Stan Laurel reflected that the scratching at least served a purpose, covering up the sizzling sound made when they fried bacon over the gas jet, in defiance of hotel rules.

Chaplin's own memories of the American tour as recorded in his autobiography center on the friendly dice games run by the proprietors of midwestern drugstores, where patrons could gamble for free merchandise, and the plentiful whorehouses. He notes that Butte, Montana, had the prettiest prostitutes in the country while Chicago had the bawdiest and most vulgar, including an international brothel known as the House of All Nations. (One is always a little suspicious of the motives of those who find it necessary to boast of youthful exploits in brothels, and surely it is no accident that the state of Montana and the city of Chicago happened to be the homes of two prominent latter-day critics of Chaplin's morals.) Nevertheless it was true that in the American Midwest he was introduced to certain indulgences that had escaped his notice even in Paris. In St. Paul, Minnesota, he had an intense weeklong affair with the wife of a man who played in an act called the Four Fords. This woman happened to be a cocaine addict, and she assumed from Charlie's high-strung manner that he was also a user. For a few days he snorted coke and smoked reefers, but didn't care for the way they made him feel and soon gave them up.

Even the occasional drinking binges of his teenage years were now very rare events. It was a joke within the company that Charlie could nurse the same glass of port all evening long. Since the social lives of the male members of the company centered on drinking, the fact that Charlie was earning more than any of them and spending a good deal less of his salary in bars probably contributed to his reputation for being unsociable and a little stingy. Because of the long distances between engagements and the relatively high cost of living in the States, traveling expenses were running much higher than any of them had expected, and some of the players were having difficulty making ends meet. Charlie, meanwhile, had managed to save two thousand dollars, which he kept in a purse sewn to the back of his undershirt.

Chaplin's attitude toward his career at this stage of his life was ambivalent. Comedy was the family business and the only thing he had ever been really good at. The variety stage had taught him self-discipline and brought him a great deal of admiring attention. On the other hand experiences like his one-night stand as a "Jewish comic" had convinced him that he did not have a natural rapport with audiences. He wasn't the kind of comedian who rescues bad material by stepping out of character to charm the paying public with ad libs. At times he was bitter about his lack of education and wished he could have been a professional man, a classical musician or a composer. And like many poor boys, both he and Syd fantasized about making their fortune quickly so that they could retire young and enjoy the leisure they never had as children. Traveling across the United States, Charlie saw that it was a country where fortunes were waiting to be made, and no doubt there were better ways of making them than playing two or three shows a night on the Sullivan and Considine circuit.

He was far from the only performer thinking along these lines. For a time he became friendly with an acrobat named Ralph Lohse, who told him that land was only $2.50 an acre in Oklahoma. Lohse suggested that Charlie put up his savings and together they could start a hog farm. Charlie was interested enough to purchase a book called *Scientific Hog Breeding*. whose description of the process of castrating nonbreeding males cured him of any thought of becoming a farmer. Even less promising was the suggestion of another performer who claimed that there was a shortage of cheese in China; Charlie was prepared to invest $1,000 but, fortunately, thought better of it. Another idea, which he discussed with Alf Reeves, was to buy a camera and make motion pictures. This seemed no more practical than exporting cheese to China, since neither of them knew the first thing about how moving pictures were made and sold.

When the company returned home in June 1912, Charlie was

immediately struck by how class-bound his homeland was in comparison to the States. While he was visiting Fred Karno's houseboat on Tagg's Island, a punter came by in a rowboat and began mocking its *nouveau riche* tackiness, calling "Oh, look at my lovely boat, everyone!" It was fine for royalty to revel in display and ceremony, Charlie thought, but to the upper classes the pretty colored lights on Karno's houseboat would always be seen as an affront.

During his absence, Syd had married, which rather put a crimp in the fantasy that they would retire early and travel around the world together. Syd and his new wife, Minnie, had also given up the apartment that he and Charlie once shared and sold off some of the furniture, leaving Charlie without a home and feeling somewhat betrayed. He was more than ready to return to the United States, where the Karno troupe had been booked once again on the Sullivan and Considine circuit. This time the company traveled on a passenger ship, the *Oceanic*, which took them directly to New York, arriving on October 10.[11]

During his first American visit, Charlie had been competing against the public's memories of actors like Billy Reeves and his own brother Syd, who had preceded him in the role of the Swell. This time he was a returning star and confident enough to act like one. In New York he treated himself to a seat at the opera. The evening's bill of fare was *Tannhäuser*, and though he had only a vague notion of the story he was deeply moved by Elisabeth's song of redemption. Wagner would remain his favorite composer, his concept of musical drama inspiring Charlie to think about new ways of combining music and pantomime.

When the company reached Seattle, the demand for tickets was so great that the theater manager demanded that the troupe play an unheard-of five shows a night. Charlie refused and took the responsibility off the shoulders of Alf and the other players by confronting the manager personally. In Vancouver, where Karno's Komics shared a bill with a group of minstrel comedians called the Guy Brothers ("their comedy is the kind that everybody enjoys," said the local reviewer), *A Night at an English Music Hall* was reported to be "doing a phenomenal business and the house is packed at every performance." In Los Angeles the *Examiner* declared Charles Chaplin "the equal of Billy Reeves."[12]

Inevitably his success was noticed by American producers. In May, while the company was playing at the Nixon Theater in Philadelphia, he had been asked to come to New York for an interview with Charles Baumann and Adam Kessel, a pair of New York businessmen who were the chief backers of the Keystone Film Company. It hadn't occurred to Charlie that moving pictures paid better than vaudeville, but he asked around and was told that Fred Mace, the comedian he was being asked to replace, had been getting $400 a week—an enormous sum, especially for a job that involved no traveling or expenses. Charlie asked for half that and was offered $150 a week, with a raise in two months if his work was satisfactory. Excited as he was, he was in no hurry to start his career in the "flickers." Having lost good comedians to higher American salaries in the past, Fred Karno had made him promise that he wouldn't desert the tour. He kept his word, putting off Keystone until November, when Karno's commitment to the Sullivan and Considine circuit ended.

Charlie's departure did not bode well for the rest of the company, and in fact once their headliner was gone, bookings fell off and the American tour was abandoned. Before long Stan Laurel (still billed as Stanley Jefferson) would be trying to make it on his own in vaudeville as a Charlie Chaplin imitator with an act called the Keystone Trio.

Resentment over being abandoned may have been partly behind the nasty prank that company member Arthur Dandoe planned for Charlie's last night with the company, after a performance in Kansas City. Dandoe, who had never liked Charlie, found some lumps of greasepaint that looked very like feces and placed them in a gift-wrapped box with a card that read, "Some shit for a shit." That night, however, Dandoe saw Charlie standing in the wings, his eyes filled with tears, and when he also treated the entire company to drinks and handed out going-away presents, Dandoe was too ashamed to carry out his prank.

As for Charlie, he had no intention of remaining long in moving pictures. He figured that if he lasted five years he could save enough money to be set for life.

3

A Film Johnnie

In 1915 Chaplin told reporter Gene Morgan of the *Chicago Herald* an amusing story about his debut on film: At the time he signed with Kessel and Baumann, he was unfamiliar with the Keystone product. Under the impression that he was going to be acting in dramatic roles, he entrained for Los Angeles with "glorious visions haunting my lower berth dreams." He saw himself playing Hamlet, or perhaps "the ideal Romeo of the photo Shakespearean. You can imagine my feeling when I was told that the first character I would play would be a man with a limp and a backache trying to carry a scuttle of coal on his head while climbing a greasy stepladder."[1]

This story was not meant to be taken literally. When he agreed to go to Los Angeles, Chaplin knew very well that Keystone made slapstick comedies. He had even seen a few of them and was none too impressed, though he thought the girls were nice and admired the work of one in particular, the vivacious Mabel Normand. Hamlet and Romeo were not in his immediate future, but he did intend to be taken seriously as an actor.

Chaplin knew that comic acting of great subtlety was possible in motion pictures because he had seen it done by the great Max Linder, whose films he became aware of when he was still playing with Casey's Court Circus. Linder, who began making films with the Pathé company in France in 1905, was a master of the slow buildup. His character was an impeccably turned-out petit bourgeois whose ingratiating smile remained firmly in place even as circumstances deteriorated around him.

One of Linder's peculiarities was a fixation with shoes—he once made a picture in which his shoes came alive and fell in love with a pair of lady's shoes. Chaplin so admired Linder that during the Karno tour he had acquired a pair of shoes similar to the ones Linder wore in his films, two-tone high-top shoes in pearl gray and black. He continued to wear the same style until the early 1930s, long after high-topped shoes for men went out of fashion.

It was no accident that the American film industry had yet to produce a Max Linder. During the first decade of their existence, American motion pictures were dominated by a battle over control of the rights to the new technology. The problem was temporarily resolved by the creation of the Motion Picture Trust, made up of seven domestic and two foreign companies, which owned the relevant patents, but this arrangement began to break down almost immediately, as "outlaw" producers entered the business, taking advantage of the burgeoning demand. Many fans spent four to five hours a week at the "flickers," and some theater managers changed their programs every day or even twice a day. As a result, by 1913 the industry was made up largely of underfinanced companies churning out product as fast as possible.

To hold down costs producers did everything in their power to keep actors from developing a following, starting with omitting cast credits from their prints. The Biograph Company even answered mail from fans inquiring about specific players with the statement, "All Biograph players are named John Doe or Jane Doe." Chaplin was lucky to be entering the business just as this policy of keeping actors anonymous was on the point of collapse. Competition was giving actors bargaining power, and fan magazines like *Moving Picture World* and *Motion Picture Magazine* were springing up, feeding the public's interest in film actors as personalities. Meanwhile the success of multireel foreign films like *Queen Elizabeth*, starring Sarah Bernhardt, was changing the minds of established stage actors who previously considered film work beneath their dignity. However, Chaplin's new boss, Mack Sennett, was by no means resigned to the arrival of the star system. Like Fred Karno, he called his studio the "Fun Factory," and ran it according to the principles of mass production. Like so many of the great names in American comedy, Sennett was a Canadian. Born Mack Sinott, he got his start in vaudeville playing the rear end of a horse, and after a brief and uninspired career on the stage he joined the Biograph film company in 1908, appearing in many one-reelers directed by D. W. Griffith. Sennett's destiny as an actor was determined by his plain, broad face: He was inevitably cast as either a loutish peasant or an Irish cop, and by all appearances his career was going nowhere. "If there was one person in the studio that would never be heard from—well, we figured that person would be Mack Sennett," recalled Griffith's then wife, Linda Arvidson. Not only was Sennett lacking in physical appeal, most of his fellow actors regarded him as a chronic complainer. Mack, Arvidson said, "grouched" his way through his work. "He never approved whole-heartedly of anything we did, nor how we did it, nor who did it. There was something wrong about all of us—even Mary Pickford. . . . But beneath all this discontent was the feeling that he wasn't being given a fair chance; which, along with a smoldering ambition, was the reason for the grouch." [2]

Sennett liked to present himself to the world as a rough-hewn primitive, an image he cultivated throughout his life. (Belatedly honored at Cannes with a retrospective of his work, he got a huge laugh by addressing his remarks to "Ladies and gentlemen, and you people of France.") But while acting with Biograph he devoured books in his room every night, plowing through comic novels, short stories, and plays; by day he attached himself to Griffith like a lamprey, plying him with questions and watching everything he did. He was soon put in charge of Biograph's number two film unit, directing a string of successful comedies, and in 1912 he persuaded Kessel and Baumann, owners of the New York Motion Picture Company, to set him up in his own studio. Promising "A Comedy Reel Every Monday," Keystone began operations that September, and a few months later, Sennett moved his headquarters from East Fourteenth Street in New York City to Edendale, California.

Like Chaplin, Sennett the actor was an admirer of Max Linder, and during his acting days he had tried to emulate him, creating a comedy character he called "the French dude." Recalled Arvidson: "Mr. Sennett evolved a French type that for an Irishman wasn't so bad." When it came to directing and producing, however, Sennett evolved a comedy style of his own that was the opposite of Linder's. For Sennett the all-important characteristic of moving pictures was that they moved—and the more motion, or *com*motion, the better. He used quick cuts—up to ninety-five separate shots in a one-reel comedy that ran about sixteen minutes on the screen. To some degree Sennett's reliance on constant movement and extreme physical types was based on an already old-fashioned notion that subtle action wouldn't "register" in the minds of the audience. Mostly it came from his anarchic vision of a world in which men and women were just overgrown children, ready to start brawling and throwing bricks at one another at the slightest provocation, and the police were no better than playground monitors, comic in their futile attempts to impose order on a disorderly world.

Sennett and Chaplin got off to an awkward start. The night before he was to report to the Keystone studio, Chaplin decided to take in the show at the Empress Theater, where he had played during his previous visits to Los Angeles. Sennett and Mabel Normand happened to be in the audience, and after being introduced to Charlie by the theater manager, Sennett invited him to join them for dinner. Sennett proved to be a tough-looking man whose rumpled suit was stained with tobacco juice. Normand, his girlfriend as well as Keystone's greatest comedy asset, was just nineteen, a former artist's model from New York with Betty Boop eyes and a disconcerting vocabulary. Sennett and Normand were friendly enough, but obviously surprised to discover that the new male comedian, who appeared middle-aged in makeup, was a very young-looking twenty-four.

In the months since Chaplin had first been approached about coming to Keystone, the company had acquired a talented baby-faced comedian, Roscoe "Fatty" Arbuckle. What it needed more than ever was a mature actor who could replace not only the departed Fred Mace but the very popular Ford Sterling, who was about to leave the company, having been refused a raise on his $250-a-week salary. Sterling played Chief Teheezal, the leader of the Keystone Kops, but was perhaps better known for his comic villain, a character he called the Dutchman, identified by his false goatee, exaggerated eyebrows, and larcenous heart. According to Harold Lloyd, who played juvenile roles in some of Sterling's films, the Dutchman was perpetually embroiled in intrigues involving stolen pearls: "It was a rubber plot, and they'd stretch it in different directions, but somehow somebody always stole the pearls."[3]

"I can make up to any age," Charlie assured Sennett. Nevertheless the idea had been planted in his mind that he was expected to imitate Sterling, whom he thought of as "an old man in his forties" who worked in an outdated style. Actually Sterling was thirty-two, and it is difficult to believe that Sennett, just two years older himself, had a problem with youthful actors. However, it was typical of Sennett to sign an actor only to find some flaw in him as soon as he showed up on the lot. Disappointment and doubt were Sennett's constant companions: He just couldn't help himself. No sooner had he hired Fatty Arbuckle than he decided that Arbuckle's fair complexion and blond hair wouldn't show up on film. Sennett was talked out of this particular misconception by Mabel Normand, who took a liking to "Big Otto," as she called Arbuckle. Other talented players like Harold Lloyd never did work their way back into Sennett's favor.

The next morning Charlie found a cab and gave the driver the address of the Keystone studio on Allessandro Street in Edendale. The address turned out to be "way out in the suburbs," in a neighborhood of derelict farms, warehouses, and workshops. The driver got lost trying to find the place, and when Charlie reached the studio more than two hours late, Sennett was nowhere to be found. Suddenly a group of actors still in makeup poured through the gate, headed for a sandwich shop across the street. Almost pathologically shy about meeting new people and already worried by the previous evening's conversation, Charlie lost his nerve and ordered the cabbie to take him back to his hotel. There he remained for two days until Sennett called to find out what had happened to him. He made a lame excuse and, reassured that Sennett would be waiting to show him around, finally found the courage to get through the studio gates.[4]

Chaplin's first day on the Keystone lot was a revelation. Except for a row of offices with a spanking-new facade, the studio was still recognizable as the abandoned farm it had recently been. The main dressing room was a converted barn, surrounded by an assortment of ramshackle outbuildings. Filming took place on a vast wooden platform, hung with muslin sheeting to diffuse the sun's rays. While actors labored through a scene on one corner of the platform, workmen a few feet away were hammering together a set. Until that moment Charlie had assumed that motion pictures were essentially stage plays performed in front of a camera. It hadn't occurred to him that the scenes were chopped up and filmed out of order, or that he would have to work outdoors with so many distractions.

Still more daunting was the first question he was asked by a Keystone director: "Can you do a funny sprawl off a stepladder without breaking your bones?"

An hour later he found himself dressed in a pair of grimy trousers borrowed from a two-hundred-pound prop man, his hair "rumpled up like a Zulu's." The cameras rolled, and he managed to negotiate the greasy ladder without injuring himself.[5]

The name of the film in which this scene appeared, assuming it was used at all, has long been forgotten. However, it was Charlie's introduction to Sennett's methods. Actors were expected to fill in by playing bit parts when needed and even to pitch in and help build sets. This was a little disconcerting to Chaplin, and no doubt he was even less flattered to discover that his ability to take a fall was the aspect of his work in *A Night in an English Music Hall* that had most impressed Sennett. But, as Sennett recalled many years later, that had been the case: "In his act Charlie revealed most of the trade skills of the music-hall people. He could fall, trip, stumble, somersault, slap, and make faces. These were stock-in-trade items which we could use."[6]

If Chaplin was underwhelmed by the setup at Keystone, no one was overly impressed by him either. Comedienne Minta Durfee, Fatty Arbuckle's wife, thought Chaplin "an odd duck. . . . He just walked around staring at everyone." And Mabel Normand, whose opinion counted for a great deal, had taken an active dislike to "the Englisher."[7] As a result Chaplin played his first featured role in a slapdash one-reeler called *Making a Living*. The director, Henry Lehrman, had been given permission to film inside the print shop of the *Los Angeles Times*, and he cast himself as a young man

applying for a job as a reporter. Charlie was his nemesis, a
"sharper," or con man, who steals the affections of Lehrman's girlfriend and does his best to steal his job. Demonstrating that the
popular view of reporters hasn't changed over the decades, the film
included a sequence in which Lehrman reaches the scene of an
accident and interviews the victim—still pinned underneath his
overturned car.

Chaplin played the "sharper" role in what he called his
"Desperate Desmond" costume and makeup—a wasp-waisted frock
coat and drooping mustache. He didn't yet know how to relate to
the camera, and in the early scenes he stands around like an awkward teenager in a home video, thumbing his nose at the lens. He
adapted quickly, however, and managed to get in some good bits of
business: Interviewing for a job at the newspaper, Charlie uses the
boss's knee as a convenient armrest, and when a fight breaks out,
instead of throwing a punch he launches his whole body at his oppo-
nent, grabs him around the neck, and hangs on for dear life.

When it came time to view the finished film, Charlie was
appalled by his own awkwardness. "I was stiff. I took all the surprise
out of the scenes by anticipating the next motion. When I walked
against a tree, I showed that I knew I would hit it long before I
did."[8] He also blamed Lehrman for sabotaging his performance out
of jealousy by cutting some of his best work—and he may have been
right. Lehrman, whose approach to directing later earned him the
nickname "Suicide," was not a well-liked man, and Fatty Arbuckle
had already refused to work with him for the same reasons. Still,
Making a Living was hardly a disaster. In his first movie role
Chaplin managed to project a quality that critic Walter Kerr would
describe, many years in retrospect, as a "serene belligerence in
times of self-need." Nevertheless Keystone had invested heavily, by
its standards, in advertising the debut of "the famous English pan-
tomimist" (whose name they did not deign to reveal) and Sennett
saw nothing in Chaplin's work to reassure him that this lost-looking
young man would live up to his publicity. When he wasn't working,
Chaplin dressed shabbily and mooned about in the dressing room,
and once the camera started to roll, he was easily distracted and
touchy about taking direction. Sennett gave him an ultimatum:
Improve or else.[9]

One morning in early 1914, brooding over his situation in the dressing room he shared with Fatty Arbuckle, Charlie was seized by an inspiration. Keystone comic Chester Conklin would recall that moment vividly:

It was a rainy day. We tried to start a picture called *Mabel's Strange Predicament* and got soaked. The muslin drapes we had strung over the hotel entrance scene were dripping like dishrags. Then it came down in so many bucketsfull to the square inch that the Old Man [Sennett] couldn't even find sand for us to shovel or carpentry work for us to mash our thumbs with.

Some of us hid out in "Fatty" Arbuckle's dressing room and started a game of pinochle. Sterling and Arbuckle and I were cursing each other over the score and hoping the rain wouldn't let up so's we wouldn't have to go back to work being funny. The rule was that if the rain didn't stop by one o'clock, we could go home.

It was Chaplin's dressing room, too, so eventually he drifted in. All the boys were competitive and glad of any chance to cut each other's throats, but we had begun to feel sorry for the Limey.

He had told me a day or so before that he was going to quit motion pictures as soon as he could. "I'm going to get out of this business. It's too much for me. I'll never catch on. It's too fast. I can't tell what I'm doing, or what anybody wants me to do," Charlie said. "At any rate, I figure the cinema is little more than a fad. It's canned drama. What audiences really want to see is flesh and blood on the stage. I'm not sure any real actor should get caught posing for the flickahs."

I told him to stick it out. I told him he was going to be something very big in motion pictures. I lied like hell. I didn't think any such thing.[10]

Invited to join the pinochle game, Chaplin declined: He never wagered money. Instead he paced the room, deep in thought. Arbuckle's trousers were hanging over the back of a chair, drying out. Chaplin studied them. Would Arbuckle mind if he tried them on? "No, I don't mind," said Big Otto. Charlie tried on the trousers, did a few flip-flops, and got a laugh from the pinochle players. Inspired, he donned a coat belonging to Charlie Avery, a Keystone player and sometime director who was even slimmer than himself. The coat barely buttoned across his chest and the coattails jutted out in back. A derby belonging to Arbuckle's father-in-law completed the ensemble.

Next Chaplin ran off to the makeup room and returned with a piece of crepe hair. Cutting himself a mustache, he held it under his nose experimentally and trimmed the sides until he had fashioned a toothbrush-shaped rectangle, small enough to wiggle when he made a face. He fixed the mustache in place with spirit gum. Then he began strutting around the dressing room, doing a funny, splay-footed walk.

Continues Conklin:

He found a thin bamboo cane somewhere and began to do tricks with it. We'd never seen anything like it. The cane seemed to come alive in his hand. It gestured. He tipped his hat with it. His starched cuff came loose, slid down the cane, and shot back to his wrist.

I don't know whose brogans he got hold of, Ford Sterling's, I think. They were over-size. The rain slackened then and Charlie jogged over to the hotel lobby set and made like a drunk. He got his foot caught in the cuspidor. His cane betrayed him and tripped him up. The mustache wiggled like a rabbit's nose. A crowd gathered.

We helped him out. A couple of people pretended to be a honeymoon couple going to bed. Charlie blundered in, tittered, tipped his hat—from the rear—and spun around and made an exit hopping around a corner on one foot.

Want to know something? Chaplin is left-handed. Most people don't know that. As he took that exit he made it look as if the door smacked him full in the face. We were watching his right hand, of course. Everyone does that unconsciously. He caught the door with his left and fooled us.

Mabel and Ford and Hank and Avery and Arbuckle and Minta Durfee were laughing at Charlie. We didn't notice the Old Man had come down from the tower and was standing in the rear. All of a sudden we heard him. "Chaplin, you do exactly as you are doing now in your next picture. Remember to do it in that get-up. Otherwise, dear old England is beckoning." [11]

Many years later Chaplin would recall the thrill he felt when he looked at the group that had gathered to watch his antics and saw Ford Sterling in the second row, peering over the shoulder of the person in front of him for a better view and laughing along with the rest.

The character born that day on the rain-sodden hotel set would come to be known as the Little Fellow, or simply the Tramp. Contrary to Conklin's impression, he was probably not the invention of a moment. Chaplin later told his son Charles junior that he once wore oversize shoes and trousers and a too-small derby while filling in for an absent comedian at a music hall where he was doing janitorial work. Elsewhere he said that the Tramp's walk was inspired by Rummy Binks, a poor sod who once held customers' horses outside the Chaplin family pub in Lambeth.[12] The one-footed running turns, and no doubt other bits of Tramp business, were part of the Karno company's stylistic repertoire.

Chaplin himself said that the defining characteristic of the Tramp was "shabby gentility." The character personified the eternal loser, struggling to keep up appearances and preserve a modicum of human dignity. The Tramp's silhouette—the baggy trousers seat and pinched shoulders—made him instantly recognizable, even from the rear, and lent him a childlike appeal. At this early stage of his existence, however, he was basically an antisocial character who worked at various occupations—sometimes drunk, often lewd, and always disorderly.

In *Mabel's Strange Predicament* the Tramp character appears as a drunk making a nuisance of himself in a hotel lobby, his eyes so riveted to the backsides of passing women that he literally slides out of his chair. Meanwhile Mabel, in her pajamas, has accidentally locked herself out of her room. Charlie wanders upstairs, and his leering attentions so unnerve her that she flees into the room across the hall—occupied by Chester Conklin—and hides under the bed.

Mabel and her young man (Harry McCoy) were supposedly honeymooners, but the chopped-up story makes their relationship so ambiguous that Chaplin scholar Harry Geduld has speculated that Mabel was meant to be seen as a prostitute.[13] At any rate the idea of a woman in pajamas, even those as unrevealing as Mabel's, which appear to be worn over several layers of clothing, was still considered naughty. Meanwhile Charlie's character, tippling from a pint bottle while he ogles the ladies, is obnoxious by the standards of any era.

Keystone comedies were frequently denounced for their crudeness. In today's supposedly more liberated times they probably couldn't be made at all. Interestingly, when director Richard Attenborough re-created the Tramp's film debut for his biographical film *Chaplin*, he found it necessary to present a heavily bowdlerized version of Mabel's "predicament." Instead of wandering a hotel corridor in her pajamas, Mabel is seen as a bride, posing with her entire wedding party in the hotel lobby. And Charlie, played by Robert Downey Jr., is no longer a leering drunk but a harmless madcap. The scene recreates the silent film era as many prefer to remember it, bathed in sepia-toned nostalgia. In the process it makes Chaplin's lecherous antics politically correct—and insipid.

Not only were men perpetually on the prowl in the early Keystones, women were only slightly encumbered by a veneer of restraint—portrayed, at times, as hypocrisy. If lust usually went unconsummated it was only because a brawl inevitably broke out before matters could proceed to their expected conclusion. The Keystone version of romance was typified by comedies like *The Fatal Mallet*, released in April 1914, in which Charlie and Mack Sennett, rivals for the attentions of Mabel Normand, engage in a spitting contest and pelt each other with bricks and then join forces against a third suitor, Mack Swain, braining him with a ridiculously oversize mallet. The Fatal Mallet was already an old vaudeville gag by 1914, made famous by Weber and Fields, and versions of it survive today, in the Big Red Hammer wielded by performers on the television comedy show *The Newz*, for example. The Mallet would reappear in other Chaplin films over the years, along with custard-pie-throwing, which was Fatty Arbuckle's specialty, but the gesture that became the Tramp's trademark was the swift kick in the rear, delivered with grace and well-timed malice.

Although Sennett and the company were delighted with his work in *Mabel's Strange Predicament*, Chaplin had not gotten off to a good start at the Fun Factory. "Movies"—a term still more often applied to the people who made motion pictures than to the pictures themselves—were considered a disreputable element, and they tended to stick together. The "gang" at Edendale was like a big family—often quarrelsome and competitive but a family nonetheless. (And to a degree they *were* a family: Fatty Arbuckle, within six months of joining the company, had managed to get his wife, Minta Durfee; his nephew, Al St. John; and even his dog on the payroll.) Charlie, however, did not fit in. Though he had played the Folies in Paris and big theaters in the United States and England, he dressed shabbily and lived in a rundown hotel in downtown Los Angeles, and as soon as his face became familiar to the public, he made an arrangement with the owner of a nearby restaurant, which let him dine free on the theory that he would draw in other customers. George B. Stout, Sennett's business manager, also noticed that Chaplin's paychecks were not being cashed. When he inquired he learned that Chaplin was in the habit of carrying the checks around in his pants pocket, cashing them only when he needed the money.[14]

Despite his reputation for being close with a dollar, Charlie did purchase an automobile, which he drove with remarkable ineptitude. Once, while passing through the studio gates, he realized he was too close to a pillar, and rather than correct the problem by steering, he instinctively let go of the wheel and tried to shove off from the offending post, as one might do when docking a boat. Luckily he was moving so slowly that his arm wasn't seriously hurt. Another day, approaching an intersection where a policeman was directing traffic, he panicked and stepped on the accelerator instead of the brake. The policeman avoided being run over and fined Charlie seventy-five dollars—a hefty penalty at the time.

At Edendale as on the variety circuit, a leading man was expected to drink with the cast and crew, and to spread his money around by buying rounds of drinks for others. Charlie had no use for this custom—and little wonder, since it had been his father's downfall. He was also, it seems, notoriously reluctant to take his turn picking up the tab for lunch. One day a member of the crew suggested that everyone at the table write his name on a slip of paper and place it in a hat; the person whose name was drawn would pay for everyone. The others at the table were all in on the ruse and wrote down "Chaplin." It is not recorded whether he realized that he had been conned, or understood why.

Soon, however, he managed to turn the tables. One of the "heavies" in the company had made the toilet stall in the bathroom of the men's dressing room into his private office, repairing there for long stretches of time to read the paper. As a prank, some of the men rigged the toilet seat to give an electric shock. Although the contraption wasn't meant for Charlie, he showed up in the dressing room at an opportune moment, and the temptation to try it out on him was too much to resist. He entered the bathroom, and the conspirators outside closed the circuit and waited for a reaction. Inside the men's room there was . . . silence. When Charlie did not emerge after some minutes, the pranksters ventured inside and found him sprawled on the floor of the toilet stall. He maintained the illusion of death long enough to prove that he had a sense of humor after all.

Jealousy also had something to do with Chaplin's cold reception on the Keystone lot. Fatty Arbuckle had recently costarred with Mabel Normand in a two-reeler—a full half hour of comedy—called *In the Clutches of the Gang*, and he was poised to replace Sterling as Keystone's biggest star when Chaplin arrived. Chester Conklin— whose repertoire of characters included an innocent rube called Fishface as well as Walrus, the sort of opportunistic villain who steals candy from babies—was also ambitious. Doubtless it was no accident that the first Fun Factory regular to befriend Chaplin was Ford Sterling, who was about to form his own company, Fred Balshofer's Sterling Comedies, and had no reason to fear Chaplin's success.

Sterling invited Charlie out for a drink at the Alexandria Hotel bar and introduced him to Elmer Ellsworth, a heavy-set man who wore his skin like a suit that was a size too big. A former newspaper reporter, Ellsworth was perhaps the original disaffected Hollywood screenwriter. Though he was making a good living turning out scenarios and gags, mainly for Universal Pictures, he considered the work beneath his dignity. Sterling introduced Ellsworth as "an expert on everything," which was pretty much how he saw himself. He was a socialist, with a fund of stories about the glory days of the IWW (Industrial Workers of the World, also known as the Wobblies), and he soon began inviting Charlie to his house for home-cooked meals and introduced him to his socialist friends.

Charlie had already encountered radical and agnostic ideas through books he picked up at stalls during his travels with the Karno company, and he may also have been influenced by the ser-

mons of the tabernacle preachers, some of whom emphasized class
pride and the solidarity of the working poor. For a young man who
had often felt humiliated because of his class, socialism had obvious
appeal. Not that Ellsworth and his friends ever did much to promote their beliefs beyond sitting around in coffee shops talking.
Charlie, however, found the talk more interesting than the endless
pinochle games at the Fun Factory.

In the short run Ellsworth teased Chaplin about being Sterling's
replacement, asking him belligerently, "Well, are you funny?" No
doubt his digs helped to plant the idea in Chaplin's mind that he
would have to combat Sterling's influence at the studio in order to
make his mark: "I wondered what Sennett expected of me," he
wrote much later. "He had seen my work and must have known that
I was not suitable to play Ford's type of comedy: my style was just
the opposite."[15] Chaplin concluded that the writers at Keystone were
unconsciously tailoring their material for Sterling and that everyone
was imitating him to some extent, even Fatty Arbuckle. Perhaps he
was right, though it would seem that a good deal of what he thought
of as the Ford Sterling style was actually the Sennett style. As
Chaplin himself acknowledged in a 1924 article, Sennett and his
directors were far from being unself-conscious about their work.
They argued constantly about the theory of comedy, and debated
whether audiences would laugh at this or that sequence. In variety,
where performers faced two or three audiences a day, no one had to
ask what the public wanted. At Edendale, Chaplin thought, the talk
about the public too often became an excuse for refusing to take
chances with new ideas. "The businessman, the banker, the artist, or
whoever he is who puts up the money wants to be assured," Chaplin
wrote. ". . . And therefore, we all argue about what 'they' want. . . .
The public does not stand at the box office and say: 'We want a
drama after this pattern. . . .' Quite frankly, I do not believe the public knows what it wants."[16]

Chaplin argued with Henry Lehrman that it wasn't necessary to
end every picture with a chase. Nor was it necessary to cut short a
good scene in order fit some abstract concept of pacing. From the
director's point of view, Chaplin's preference for longer cuts no

doubt appeared to be just an attempt to get more screen time for himself, and certainly when Charlie got his way he managed to take over the films he appeared in.

Though his arguments eventually prevailed, there was little Chaplin could do about the pace of the work. Sennett was now aiming to turn out at least two comedies a week, and to eke out the quota his directors alternated story films, shot mainly at the studio, with improvised comedy shorts filmed on location, typically in a single day. In his first ten months with Keystone, Fatty Arbuckle had completed 41 comedies, and Mabel Normand, still in her teens, had already appeared in 129 movies by April 1914. No one except Chaplin seems to have regarded this as a killing schedule, but then he was a perfectionist, who irritated the crew by asking for reshoots, a practice considered a waste of film.

During a hiatus in the production of *Mabel's Strange Predicament*, Henry Lehrman took two cameramen and Chaplin, dressed in his Tramp costume, to a soapbox derby at the amusement park in Venice Beach. Chaplin pretended to be a camera hog, wandering out onto the racecourse in the path of the competitors, peering into the camera lens, and generally interfering with the efforts of Lehrman and his number one cameraman, Frank Williamson, to document the race. The shooting of *Kid Auto Races at Venice* took less than an hour, and the finished film, barely six minutes long, was released on a split reel with a documentary short, *Olives and Their Oil*. By happenstance it reached the theaters on February 7, 1914, before *Mabel's Strange Predicament*, thus becoming the public's first glimpse of the Tramp.[17]

Another strategy for turning a quick one-reeler was to take a crew to nearby Westlake Park and improvise a "masher" story. The idea of using a park bench as an impromptu movie set was almost as old as the movie camera itself, but Sennett elevated the park picture to a genre in its own right. Inevitably the action involved a pesky character who flirts with unescorted ladies, annoys courting couples, and liberates the occasional umbrella, pocket watch, or purse. Chaplin did his first park film, *Between Showers*, in February. In a variation on the theme he and Ford Sterling played "rival mashers," with Charlie getting the better of Ford in a dispute over a stolen umbrella.

Still another Keystone quickie was *Tango Tangles*, for which Sennett took his cast—including Chaplin, Arbuckle, and Sterling—to a commercial dance hall, or "tango parlor," where they pretended to be rivals for the love of the same girl (Minta Durfee). The most interesting thing about the film, in retrospect, is the reaction of the other patrons, who go along with the gag willingly but appear none too impressed by the presence of a movie crew in their midst. Chaplin appeared in the film in his own clothes, without makeup, doing a comic tango.

The tango parlor was not a totally foreign environment for Charlie, who around this time won a trophy in a dance contest with Keystone ingenue Peggy Pearce.[18] Pearce, however, lived with her parents and was too conventional—meaning, too marriage-minded—for his taste. Otherwise his efforts to meet girls were largely ineffectual. Mack Sennett would recall watching Chaplin chatting up a young lady at a party and being encouraged by her body language and breathy squeals until he belatedly realized that he had accidentally backed her against a hot radiator. Fortunately for his public, Chaplin had the wit to transform his social gaffes into material, and he would use the incident in his 1916 comedy, *The Adventurer*.

Henry Lehrman had annoyed Sennett by trying to date Mabel Normand, and as Ford Sterling's departure neared he decided to leave with him. Chaplin was not sorry to find himself assigned to another director, George Nichols, a man in his sixties. Unlike Lehrman's pictures, which too often seemed to start in the middle, Nichols's films had a comprehensible plot line as well as elements of originality and wit, and the four films Chaplin made with Nichols undoubtedly did a great deal to establish his popularity.[19]

The most interesting of the Nichols pictures was *A Film Johnnie* (as in "stage-door Johnnie"). Charlie is a nickelodeon patron who develops a crush on the "Keystone girl," a reference to the unbilled ingenue known to the public only as the "Biograph girl." Tracking his beloved to the Edendale studio he wanders onto the lot unchallenged, where he appropriates a prop pistol and idly picks his teeth with it. Mistaking a staged abduction scene for the real thing, he rushes to defend Minta Durfee's honor, firing the pistol and causing a panic on the set. Not content with making fun of the naïveté of movie fans, Nichols added an interesting twist to the story. Mack Sennett, hearing the sirens of fire engines on the street, orders a cast and crew to race to the scene of the fire and improvise a story with the burning building as a backdrop. This was by no means a fantasy—Keystone crews literally did chase fire engines—and Nichols leaves the audience to wonder who is more deluded, the fan who mistakes movie hijinks for reality, or the actors who see a human tragedy only as background for yet another one-reeler. The film ends with a gag that would become an audience favorite— doused by the fireman's hose, Charlie twists his ear and a jet of water squirts out of his mouth.

The Nichols films gave Chaplin a chance to be mischievous, melodramatic, and even romantic—at any rate more than a mere drunk and an ambulatory id. Still, he regarded Nichols as just another hack, who cut off every suggestion he made, screaming, "We have no time! No time!" Of course Nichols was right. The pro- duction schedules, over which he had no control, didn't allow for second thoughts. The rest of the cast sided with the director, who complained to Sennett that Chaplin was a "son of a bitch" and impossible to work with.[20]

At a loss what to do with his difficult star, Sennett next handed him over to Mabel Normand, who had decided that Chaplin had tal- ent after all and was prepared to work with him. Normand had begun directing late in 1913, with *Mabel's Stormy Love Affair*, and was now embarking on a two-reeler, *Mabel at the Wheel*, a parody of the action serial *The Perils of Pauline*, whose first episode had just been released. Normand played the girlfriend of Harry McCoy, a dashing race-car driver. Charlie, back in his Desperate Desmond costume and makeup, was a gambler who has money riding on another driver and orders his henchman to kidnap McCoy and hold him captive until after the race. When Mabel thwarts his plot, driving McCoy's car for him, Charlie tries to cause a pile-up by wetting down the racetrack with a hose.

Charlie, as usual, had a notion to flesh out his part with some clever business. He would step on the hose, peer into the nozzle wondering what the matter was, then absentmindedly remove his foot. Mabel vetoed the suggestion. She was the star of the picture, and the race was her big moment. The sequence, moreover, was already complicated, with shots of cars doing 180-degree spins on the Venice speedway. "Do what you're told," she snapped.

"I will not do what I'm told. I don't think you're competent to tell me what to do," Charlie replied. And with that, he sat down on a curb and refused to finish the scene. Normand's biographer, Betty Fussell, says of his account of this incident, "Chaplin's sexual bias has obscured one of Mabel's brightest achievements."[21]

No doubt it is true that Chaplin would not have defied a male director so openly in front of the crew, but the fact was that he didn't think *any*one was competent to direct him. In any case conflict over *Mabel at the Wheel* was inevitable for reasons that had nothing to do with the director's sex. Just when audiences were coming to look forward to seeing him as the Little Fellow, he had been cast once again as a Ford Sterling villain, with a frock coat and drooping mustache.

His argument with Mabel Normand almost marked the end of Chaplin's career in moving pictures. Sennett, he recalled, was ready to fire him on the spot, but he had just received a letter from Kessel and Baumann in New York, informing him that Chaplin's pictures were outgrossing all other Keystone productions. Chaplin told Sennett that he wanted to direct his next picture himself, and if it was no good he would cover the cost of the production with fifteen hundred dollars of his own money. In the meantime he agreed to finish *Mabel at the Wheel*.

A few days after the race-car picture was completed, Chaplin was informed at 9:00 A.M. that the studio needed a one-reeler by 3:00 P.M. the same day. He quickly rounded up a few actors who happened to be free and took his cast to Westlake Park to shoot a "masher" picture. "Then I thought of my story," he would recall. "A beginning came to me, and we rarely had more than a beginning in those days": The Tramp is standing on a bridge, ready to jump, when a pretty girl passes by.[22]

This may have been the premise that Chaplin used to motivate his performance, but no such scene appears in the finished film. Instead *Twenty Minutes of Love* begins with Charlie mocking a courting couple by extravagantly hugging and kissing a tree trunk.

He then sits down on the park bench beside the couple and tries to feel the woman's thigh while she is busy kissing her boyfriend. But the boyfriend has switched places with his sweetheart, and Charlie ends up stroking his leg instead. Later he steals a watch from a pickpocket and makes the mistake of trying to sell it back to its original owner, who calls the police. Charlie escapes by biting the policeman and kicking him in the stomach. The plot, in short, was not significantly different from a typical park masher film like *Between Showers*. What Chaplin had added to the formula was a realistically motivated performance—and the motivation was spite. The desire to revenge himself on the more fortunate turns the Tramp's thoughts away from self-destruction and gives him a reason for living.

The Tramp's next outing was a happier one. Mabel Normand did not hold a grudge, and she and Chaplin collaborated on a two-reeler called *Caught in a Cabaret*. Charlie is a waiter at a café with a rough clientele, who wins Mabel's affection by pretending to be a VIP—"Baron Doobugle, Prime Minister of Greenland." When Mabel and her friends drop into his café for a lark, Charlie is in danger of being exposed as an impostor, but he does some fast thinking, assuring her, "I'm slumming, too." *Caught in a Cabaret* showed a relatively romantic, even chivalrous side to the Tramp's character, and for the first time a trade-paper reviewer for *Moving Picture World* not only singled out his performance for praise but spelled his name right.

Twenty Minutes of Love had been an experiment, and it may be that Chaplin's work was supervised by Sennett or another of the studio's directors. The success of *Caught in a Cabaret*, however, meant that his ambition to direct more substantial films could no longer be denied. After campaigning so relentlessly that he'd alienated much of the company, Chaplin finally had a chance to prove himself, and he immediately felt "a slight attack of panic." Now that he had the freedom to invent his own story, what he came up with was a conflation of scenes from pictures he'd already made. *Caught in the Rain*, his first major directing assignment, starts with Charlie flirting with a married woman in the park, then moves to the same hotel set used in *Mabel's Strange Predicament*, where he reprises his obnoxious-drunk act.

When it came time to screen the finished picture, Sennett's

directors gathered expecting to see Chaplin fail, and prepared to enjoy the sight. Sennett recalled sitting in his rocking chair in the dark, hearing his staff "suck in lungfuls of air, getting ready to let loose jeers and catcalls. Instead they applauded from the first scene."[23] Almost nothing in the film was new, but Chaplin had done it better. The physical comedy was brilliant, and when he scrambled up the stairs in the hotel lobby, his arms and legs flailed away so fast that the steps seemed to melt under him.

Caught in the Rain was the thirteenth comedy Chaplin had appeared in since joining Keystone less than five months earlier. By the end of 1914 he would play featured roles in twenty-two more, most of which he also directed. Some of the twenty-two were forgettable, like *The Face on the Barroom Floor*, a parody of the melodramatic poem by Hugh d'Arcy, or *Those Love Pangs*, which revisited the park-bench territory of *Between Showers*, with Chester Conklin replacing Ford Sterling as the "rival masher."

Another, *His Musical Career*, about a pair of piano movers (Chaplin and Mack Swain) who make a delivery to the wrong address, is interesting mainly in comparison to Laurel and Hardy's famous 1932 remake of the same story, *The Music Box*. Chaplin's film is a parable of injustice: Mr. Rich buys a piano on a whim, while another customer, a starving musician, is in danger of having his instrument repossessed. Laurel and Hardy would strip away everything but the central joke—the Sisyphean task of hauling the piano up a flight of stairs.

Other comedies from this period are memorable mainly for their performances. In *The Rounders* Chaplin and Fatty Arbuckle teamed up to play a pair of drunks, Mr. Full and Mr. Fuller, whose night of revelry ends with the two of them sleeping it off peacefully, even as the rowboat in which they are lying fills with water and sinks. In *The Masquerader* Chaplin anticipates Dustin Hoffman's dual role in *Tootsie*—fired by his director, Charlie takes revenge by returning to the studio disguised as the eerily seductive actress Señorita Chapelina.

The Masquerader was actually Chaplin's second drag role. The first, *A Busy Day*—whose title reflects the amount and quality of the time that went into making it—was filmed during a parade honoring the opening of the new San Pedro harbor facility. Chaplin wore a borrowed dress, but this time he made no attempt at a convincing female impersonation; his heavy shoes and long underwear are clearly visible under his skirt. His character is a nightmare wife who blows her nose into her dress and physically abuses her husband, the mountainous Mack Swain. After catching Mack flirting with a pretty young thing, she works herself into such a fury that she attacks him and any male who gets in her way with full frontal kicks to the groin. Keystone comedies were often issued under different titles, and some of the titles later applied to *A Busy Day*—including *A Militant Suffragette* and the French *La Jalousie de Charlot*— reflect the distributors' inadequate efforts to provide some motivation for the wife's rage. In fact she appears to be insane, at times pausing to enjoy the parade or to break into a little dance before resuming her rampage. One can only wonder if Chaplin was recalling—and, one hopes, exaggerating—the demons that at times took possession of his mother.

Of course moviegoers did not take Keystone comedy violence literally, any more than later generations of filmgoers would be upset by the Marx Brothers' tormenting of Margaret Dumont, the rough-housing of the Three Stooges, or Wile E. Coyote's efforts to dismember the Road Runner. But the combination of slapstick sensibility and Chaplin's intense, realistically motivated acting could be volatile. In *Laughing Gas* Charlie is a porter in a dentist's office who takes over in the absence of his boss. Trying to revive a patient who has been given an overdose of gas, he applies reverse logic and bops the unconscious man on the head with a very large mallet. Later, he uses a pair of tongs to tweak the nose of an attractive female patient. The routine has a riveting manic energy, though as Harry Geduld notes, the underlying theme is "a dentist exploiting his opportunities for lechery and sadism."[24]

As Chaplin's comedies became more popular, reviewers began to complain about the sadistic twist he gave so much of his humor. *The Property Man*, a backstage comedy in which Charlie takes out his frustrations on an elderly assistant, prompted *Moving Picture World* to comment: "There is some brutality in this picture and we can't help feeling that this is reprehensible."[25] Chaplin took such comments to heart; however, there was no overnight way to make the Tramp sympathetic. The character's transformation from nuisance/provocateur to soulful victim first became dramatically clear in *The New Janitor*, which begins with Charlie, in the title role, climbing the stairs of a downtown office building while more favored employees ride the elevator. Even when he heroically captures a robber, the police, arriving on the scene, try to arrest him instead of the better-dressed crook. Filming a scene in which the janitor, unjustly fired, pleads for his job, Chaplin noticed that an older actress on the set was in tears. Nothing could have thrilled him more. He had made the Tramp touching as well as funny.

Chaplin was now responsible for the scenarios for his own pictures. In some cases the story lines of his comedies were directly inspired by familiar music hall and vaudeville sketches—the mad dentist, for example, was a comedy staple. But Keystone directors were already turning to other motion pictures for inspiration on occasion. Although Chaplin had attended the "flickers" during his youth in England, he never had much to say about his memories of them, apart from his preference for Max Linder.

Still, it's worth noting that one of the best-known early British films was *The Tramp and the Baby Bottle*, in which a depraved and hungry-looking vagrant tries to steal a milk bottle from the pram of a middle-class baby.[26] Chaplin made a comedy with Mabel Normand called *His Trysting Place,* in which the action is reversed—Charlie the Tramp eats his fill at a lunch counter and then—rather grudgingly—brings a milk bottle home as a "treat" for his baby. Was *His Trysting Place* a cryptic comment on the class bias of the earlier film? There is no way to be sure, though considering that milk bottles were among Chaplin's least favorite objects, the choice of "treat" was a strange one in any case. The more one looks at Chaplin comedies, the more one suspects that they are filled with allusions, intended less for the audience than to motivate his performance.

Chaplin's most successful Keystone comedy, the two-reeler *Dough and Dynamite*, was a joint effort with Chester Conklin. As Sennett recalled it, Charlie and Chester were racking their brains for an idea when they happened to get off the trolley at the same stop and found themselves standing in front of a bakery with a BOY

WANTED sign displayed in its front window. Simultaneously, they turned to each other and cried, "There's our story!"

While the sign in a bakery window may have been the inspiration for putting Charlie and Chester together in a bakery, it also happened that Ford Sterling, now the star of his own production company and still considered by some to be Chaplin's chief competition, had recently made a picture called *Love and Dynamite.* Somewhat to the disappointment of Chaplin's later admirers on the Left, Charlie cast himself in his picture as a hardworking scab, keeping the bakery going while the striking workers scheme to blow up their former place of employment with a stick of dynamite hidden in a loaf of bread—the "FATAL LOAF" (as a title card informed the audience). Chaplin knew he had a winner in *Dough and Dynamite,* and in the absence of Sennett, who was on Catalina Island working on a picture with Mabel Normand, he authorized the construction of a new and—by Keystone standards—rather elaborate set. He and Conklin decided to expand the picture into a two-reeler only after they realized that they had gone a thousand dollars over budget. Sennett grumbled, as usual, but the expense paid off as *Dough and Dynamite* more than earned back the investment.

During the latter half of his one-year contract with Keystone, Chaplin had begun to discover, as he put it, that "success makes one endearing."[27] The extras and crew members who once snickered at him and made him the butt of their practical jokes now greeted him like a pal, and he joined the Fun Factory "gang" in their weekly expedition to the fights, held at Doyle's on Sante Fe Avenue in Vernon. Doyle's saloon featured an extra-long bar, said to accommodate four hundred patrons, and a prominently placed sign warning: IF YOUR KIDS NEED SHOES, DON'T BUY BOOZE. While the saloon was for men only, women were admitted to the boxing arena in the back through a separate entrance, and Mabel Normand was among the company's most avid fight fans. The boxers were technically amateurs, getting $7.50 per appearance, win or lose. However, they were also awarded medals, which could be redeemed under the table for cash. It was a rough crowd, and in addition to battling their opponents, the fighters had to contend with bottles, chairs, and other objects thrown by disgruntled spectators as well as crooked referees, who were known to trip the less favored fighter or even hold his arms or the waistband of his trunks to give his opponent a stationary target.

Several of the fighters were taken up by the crowd from Edendale, especially Al McNeil, who eventually went to work for Sennett as an editor. On one occasion Fatty Arbuckle and Chaplin agreed to act as seconds in a bout between McNeil and a fighter named Frankie Dolan. Betting was heavy, and, unknown to the seconds, the fight was fixed. Dolan was supposed to win, but in the first round he walked into McNeil's right hand and crashed to the canvas. The audience went crazy, and both the fighters and seconds had to flee the arena. Arbuckle made good use of this experience in a film called *The Knockout*, casting Charlie as a rubber-legged referee who takes more punishment than the fighters.

In those relatively carefree days of moviemaking there were no lines to learn and no early makeup calls, and shooting was often finished by early afternoon. But, while few at the Fun Factory approached their work with as much nervous intensity as Chaplin, taking pratfalls and doing chase scenes day after day was physically punishing, and the pressure to come up with new material was constant. Mack Sennett got through the day on neat Scotch and raw onion sandwiches, and the gentle Roscoe Arbuckle, only twenty-seven, had turned to whiskey to "cure" his insomnia. Almost everyone drank at least a little, and before long a member of the carpentry crew at the studio would begin selling a magic white powder, obtained cheaply in Mexico, that made it possible to work hard all day and still party at night. This was probably after Chaplin's time, though perhaps not; a Keystone publicity release of the era gives *Jim, a Romance of Cocaine* as one of Chaplin's credits.

For the most part, however, these were innocent times. Although they had started off badly, Charlie's closest friend during his last months at Keystone was probably Mabel Normand. Mabel looked fragile but was a fearless athlete who did all her own stunts and was determined to prove that she could keep up with men in every respect, including their practical jokes. Charlie often found himself playing straight man to Mabel's pranks. Strolling down a busy street, she would pretend to throw a fit while he earnestly explained to passersby, "My wife is a homicidal maniac. I'm taking her to the hospital right now." But Mabel also had a serious side. She was another secret reader (Hollywood at this time seems to have been filled with people who felt obliged to hide their interest in books), and she and Charlie talked about literature and studied French together. One night, after they had appeared together at a charity function in San Francisco, he gathered his courage and made a pass at her; Mabel politely but firmly told him that they weren't each other's types.[28]

By midsummer Sennett was engrossed in his plans to produce a feature-length film. D. W. Griffith was at work on an epic about the Reconstruction era, eventually released as *Birth of a Nation*, and Sennett saw no reason why comedies shouldn't become longer and more ambitious as well. Kessel and Baumann, however, were not enthusiastic. Why go into debt to finance a six-reel movie when they had orders for as many comedy shorts as they could make? Sennett sold the money men on the project by promising to sign Marie Dressler, a major stage and vaudeville star.

A large, remarkably plain woman, comedienne Marie Dressler was known for her signature greeting, "Hiya all my gals and all my pals!" In her latest Broadway play, *Tillie's Nightmare*, she had introduced the hit song "Heaven Will Protect the Working Girl." In reality it was Dressler who protected the working girl; she was pro-union and a few years later she would risk her career to back a strike of Broadway chorus girls. Dressler was already fifty-five years old in 1914. Ahead of her lay blacklisting on account of her union activities, and the discovery that her husband was a bigamist, engaged in embezzling her savings. Washed up at sixty, she would survive to have a second career in talking pictures, win the Oscar for Best Actress in 1932, and become Hollywood's top box-office draw. When she died in 1934 she left $35,000 to her maid and to her sister, a solid gold toilet seat. [29]

Sennett was a great admirer of Dressler, a fellow Canadian. When he was an assistant boilermaker, hoping to get into show business, he had gone to see her on the strength of a letter of recommendation from one of his customers, a lawyer named Calvin

Coolidge. Dressler had advised him to give up singing and go into comedy. Unfortunately, while Sennett remembered all this vividly, Dressler did not. Her husband (the embezzler) was a hard bargainer, and Dressler was eventually signed at $2,500 a week, more than ten times the salary of Fatty Arbuckle, the highest-paid actor on the lot. Chaplin's contract would be up for renewal at the end of the year, and Dressler's deal was an eye-opener.

Craig Hutchinson, Keystone's chief story editor and the writer of *A Film Johnnie*, collaborated with Sennett on a scenario loosely based on *Tillie's Nightmare*. Dressler was to play a farmer's daughter who flirts with a passing stranger, capturing his attention in the approved Keystone manner by hurling a brick at his head. The stranger eventually marries Tillie, in the belief that she has inherited a fortune from a rich uncle. The scenario of *Tillie's Punctured Romance* called for an enormous cast by Keystone standards and would include a chase scene to end all chase scenes—or so it was thought—culminating with Dressler and a car loaded with Keystone Kops tumbling off the end of the Santa Monica pier. Kessel and Baumann, meanwhile, were insisting that Sennett continue to deliver his usual quota of one- and two-reelers, so the actors in this epic were working on other movies in their off hours.

No one could convince Marie Dressler that film acting called for a more restrained style than playing before a live audience. She gesticulated wildly and mugged for the camera. Had she been able to, she would have climbed right through the lens and given each and every movie patron a hearty slap on the back. She also broke Fatty Arbuckle's heart by insisting that he be banned from the cast. It was nothing personal, but Dressler meant to be the biggest thing in the picture, and Fatty's size and broad acting style would distract attention from her. Instead she tapped Charlie Chaplin for her leading man. For the most part they got along well, though there were a few rough moments.

One day, Sennett recalled, Miss Dressler took him aside before filming began and asked him, "You know Chaplin's neck?"

Mack said he did.

Dressler then explained that she didn't necessarily mind that the neck in question had been enclosed in the same celluloid shirt collar for sixteen days running. But "I'm a mite squeamish about that same piece of decaying banana on the same collar for the past sixteen days. As a matter of fact, Mr. Mack Sennett, if the banana is not removed, I shall enact you the goddammedest vomiting scene in the annals of the drammer."[30]

It may have been after this incident that Sennett introduced Chaplin to the Los Angeles Athletic Club, persuading him to take a room there. He also found him a valet to deal with his wardrobe.

Charlie was pleased with his work in *Tillie*. Writing to Syd on August 9, around the time the filming was completed, he boasted: "I have hog [*sic*] the whole picture. It is the best thing I ever did." He also reported having $6,700 in savings in banks in New York and London, and could not resist mentioning that he was about to go "automobiling" with friends and then "to the beach to dine."[31]

If he really thought that he had hogged the picture, he was kidding himself. Chaplin, during the course of his career, would play opposite beautiful women, adorable children, and dogs, but never was he upstaged as he had been by Marie Dressler. For all her over-acting, her presence was riveting. Still, even though Chaplin was definitely the second banana, so to speak, his comic tango with Dressler—not to mention prominent billing as her costar—brought him to the attention of a whole new audience. *Tillie* was not released until November, a month after *Dough and Dynamite*, and the two pictures together made it clear that Chaplin was not just this year's new face but a phenomenon.

On November 9, a week before *Tillie* opened, Syd and his wife Minnie arrived in Los Angeles. Syd was still a bigger name than his brother in England, and Sennett had been happy to sign him. Approaching his thirtieth birthday, Syd already had a receding hair-line, a slight paunch, and none of Charlie's nervy intensity. His favorite comic character was Gussle, a shambling hapless soul in baggy pants and a porkpie hat. To all appearances he was the nor-mal, easygoing Chaplin brother, and Sennett had high hopes that he would become just as popular.

But appearances did not tell the whole story. Although he was a brilliant comic when he cared to be, Syd had a way of sabotaging his own efforts. He drove Keystone director Charlie Avery nearly mad with his habit of slipping obscene gestures into his performance, often so subtly that they weren't noticed until the sets had been struck and the footage was being edited. No one, it seemed, could make Syd understand that such foolery cost a great deal of money and could get the company into serious trouble if one of his little jokes made it into the theaters. It almost seemed that Syd, after a childhood filled with hard work and adult-size worries, was determined to make up for lost time.

Charlie hoped that Syd would do a few pictures for Keystone on a week-to-week basis and they could then go into business together, forming their own production company. To his disappointment, Syd had opted for a one-year contract instead. This left Charlie's own plans in limbo. He had asked Sennett for a raise to $1,000 a week. Sennett was prepared to pay, even though he wasn't making that much himself, but Kessel and Baumann insisted that no mere actor was worth that much money. Charlie, who recalled that Miss Dressler *had* been worth it, continued to hold out.

Sennett now offered a three-year deal, escalating from $500 a week the first year to $1,500 in the final year of the contract. Charlie suggested starting with $1,500 decreasing to $500. Sennett thought he was joking, but Charlie had a point. Who could say what he'd be worth in three years? The very fact that the $1,500 salary was being discussed suggested that it was a reasonable salary at the time. By holding out for so much money Chaplin was taking an enormous risk. The desire of producers to snatch away Keystone's hot new star was balanced by their reluctance to set a precedent that would jack up salaries throughout the industry. But Chaplin had been approached by other producers, including promoter Marcus Loew, and he had confidence that the gamble would pay off.

In November Charlie took a crew to Tom Ince's ranch to film *His Prehistoric Past*, a caveman comedy in which he appeared in his trademark derby, oversize shoes, and a moth-eaten loincloth. The props for the picture included a basket of snakes, and Charlie entertained the cast by pretending to be a snake charmer and demonstrating that it was actually possible to juggle serpents.

Meanwhile the Chicago-based Essanay Film Manufacturing Company had come through with an offer of $1,250 a week, plus a $10,000 bonus. Charlie had met one of the company's owners,

Gilbert M. Anderson, and was favorably impressed. Anderson was an actor himself, a good-looking man with startlingly white teeth, dancing eyes, and a quizzical sense of humor, very unlike the conventional business types who always made him a little uneasy. Anderson assured Charlie that Essanay wouldn't think of trying to force him into a mold, as Keystone had. He approved a clause in his contract guaranteeing that all films he made for Essanay would be designated as "Chaplin Brand" pictures, and released only with his approval of the final product. It was almost too good to be true.

4

Work

Chaplin didn't know it, but in signing with Essanay he had put himself in the middle of a quarrel between business partners.

George K. Spoor, the S in Essanay (S and A) was an inventor and businessman whose interest in a projector called the Magniscope had made him a player in the "patent war" of the previous decade. Technology remained Spoor's passion. He was experimenting with color film processes, and by the 1920s he would be promoting a version of 3-D. For him motion pictures would always be "product," necessary but relatively uninteresting compared to the hardware side of the industry.

In 1907 Spoor had joined forces with Gilbert M. Anderson, who hoped to parlay his appearance in *The Great Train Robbery* into a career as a cowboy star. With Spoor's backing he took a company to Golden, Colorado, and began cranking out two-reel westerns, starring himself as "Broncho Billy." In time Anderson moved to an abandoned ranch in Niles, California, about sixty miles from San Francisco, but the Broncho Billy pictures remained much the same. Anderson made no claims to be an artist or even a good actor, but he took genuine delight in the magic of the cinema. It tickled him that he, born Max Aronson, had become the best known cowboy in America, even though he wasn't especially adept at riding. "I was good enough to be thrown and break my back," he recalled many years later. "I was fairly good." He also exulted at being an expert shot "in pictures." In one of his Westerns he and the bad guy exchanged taunts by writing with bullets on a barn wall. "He took out his gun and started to shoot, and he spelled out 'Keep away from my gal.' And then I spelled out 'Keep away from me.' I put my bullet in every one of his bullet holes until it came to 'my gal' and I rubbed that out and put in 'me.'"[1]

By 1914 Anderson was concerned that Essanay was falling behind the times. The Argyle Street studio in Chicago produced the popular "Sweedie" comedies, featuring the gravel-voiced Wallace Beery in drag as a not terribly bright Swedish maid, but it was mainly known for "sophisticated" dramas. The Essanay version of glamour was epitomized by its reigning male star, Francis X. Bushman, who wore an amethyst pinkie ring and drove a custom-made lavender automobile. Bushman's wife and numerous children were carefully kept out of sight, in accordance with the prevailing belief that audiences wouldn't accept a married romantic lead.

Anderson thought he could do better, and he also happened to have a wife and children in Chicago whom he claimed to love dearly though he hadn't seen much of them in recent years. He had signed Chaplin on the advice of Essanay producer Jesse Robbins, but he was planning to move back home and supervise the production of Chaplin's comedies himself. "I was going back to work with Charlie on the pictures there," he recalled. "I was bored with westerns. In fact, I get bored with everything except girls."

Chaplin joined Anderson in San Francisco in mid-December, and they boarded the train for Chicago, accompanied by a group of actors from Niles who were to form the nucleus of a repertory comedy company. Ex-musician Bud Jamison was a "heavy," a role he would later play in a number of Three Stooges comedies. Sharp-faced Leo White was a stock comedy villain, frequently cast as a wily Frenchman. Ben Turpin, formerly a handyman at the Niles studio, was just a funny-looking guy with a cross-eyed squint. Buster Keaton once said that the biggest laugh Ben Turpin ever got was when he entered on the line, "Here he comes, a man's man." Turpin, said Keaton, "didn't *do* anything." And he didn't need to.[2]

Awaiting Chaplin in Chicago were a serious of unpleasant surprises. To begin with, Jesse Robbins had decided that he would be billed as Charlie Chaplin, not Charles. Although, in fact, everyone called him Charlie, Chaplin considered the nickname demeaning and was furious that the decision had been made without consulting him. The Essanay publicity department was also touting him to the press as "the greatest comedian in the world," a claim that almost begged contradiction. Meanwhile, he had yet to see the five-thousand-dollar check representing the half of his bonus that was due on signing. George Spoor, who happened to be the company's chief financial officer, complained that he had never heard of Chaplin and hadn't approved his salary. Spoor was in New York on business, or so Chaplin was told, and it was far from clear that he would honor the contract.

Chaplin also received a chilly welcome from the other Essanay contract players, who looked him up and down and wondered why "this hamfat"—a slapstick comedian and a shabby dresser at that—was worth more than seventy thousand dollars a year. Moreover, despite the clause in his contract giving him control over his own pictures, it was clear that no one who worked at Argyle Street had much autonomy. While Sennett pushed through pictures quickly, the social atmosphere at Keystone was that of a slightly disreputable summer camp. Essanay really was run like a factory. Scenarios were produced by a writing department, supervised by a young ex–newspaper reporter named Louella Parsons, and directors were expected to follow the story lines as written. Lunch breaks were sacrosanct, and quitting time came promptly at 6:00 P.M., when cast and crew dispersed to their homes throughout metropolitan Chicago. After-hours socializing was almost unknown. Presiding over this cold but efficient operation was the studio manager, a man named Bouché, for whom schedules and time sheets were almost sacred documents.

Chaplin also found himself besieged by requests for interviews, a new experience for him. In 1915 New York was still the center of the movie industry; even the fledgling fan magazines had their headquarters there, and few members of the entertainment press ventured west to California. This was the first opportunity for the press to size up the popular new star of *Tillie's Punctured Romance* and *Dough and Dynamite*. May Tinee of the *Buffalo Courier*, one of the first to seek Chaplin out, was told by a frustrated studio employee that he was "scared to death" of reporters. "I have my hands full" to get him to agree to talk to the press at all, the man added. Tinee persisted and tracked down Chaplin in the screening room, where he was seated at a child-size desk watching a print of a recent Essanay production, *When Love and Honor Called.* Cornered, he explained that he was uncomfortable about the big buildup the publicity office was giving him. He would much rather be thought a "comer" than an overpriced star. "When a man's been boosted to the skies, they're apt to sit back in their seats and say, 'I don't see anything so wonderful about that chap. Nothing to make a fuss about. He's over-rated.' But if a man's not made, they take pride and joy in discovering him."[3]

For all his nervousness, once Chaplin started talking he couldn't stop. To Tinee and other reporters, he told stories about his childhood, his experiences at Keystone, and his future ambitions, including what he self-deprecatingly called "the usual desire of a comedian to play tragic roles." He improved a little on his past, substituting a private boarding school for Hanwell, for example, and his claim that he signed with Kessel and Baumann in the expectation of playing Shakespeare was obviously an absurd distortion of the facts, but overall he impressed the reporters as engaging, unaffected, and eager to please. Gene Morgan of the *Chicago Tribune* became so friendly with Chaplin that he volunteered to lead him on a tour of second-hand clothing stores in search of a pair of dilapidated size fourteens to replace Ford Sterling's castoffs, which he had left behind in Edendale. The search proved more challenging than expected, causing Morgan to reflect that Chicago might be known as "the city of big shoulders" but it certainly wasn't the city of big feet.[4]

Rather than use a script from the story department, Chaplin decided to improvise a backstage comedy about a stagehand who suddenly finds himself promoted to leading man when the film company's "unpunctual star" fails to appear. A scene in which Charlie appears for a job interview recalled his Keystone debut in *Making a Living,* but the story line was probably based on the experience of Ben Turpin, the former Niles handyman.

On the first day of filming a crowd of skeptical Essanay employees gathered on the set to watch the Limey comic at work. Before cameras began to roll, Chaplin launched into an energetic clog dance, reeling off a succession of tricky steps while crooning, "Got to limber up. A little pep, everybody. A little pep. Come on boys, shoot your set. I'm ready."

"He did [all this] so seriously that everybody wondered if he was out of his mind," noted *Motion Picture Magazine*'s Charles McGuirk, but with his warm-up finished, Chaplin quickly established his authority as a director, issuing a series of rapid-fire instructions, mixed with a running monologue of "musings and comments on the world of today."

"When any actor went thru a piece of 'business' that appealed to Charlie," McGuirk observed, "he was quick to step out, pat him on the back and tell him, 'You're a bear. Good stuff. You're goin' along right, old top. Keep it up—keep it up.' It took a little while, but Chaplin finally injected enough enthusiasm into his people to make them work hours without thought of time. The proof of it came at the noon hour. Nobody knew it was twelve o'clock."[5]

As Chaplin worked, McGuirk noticed Francis X. Bushman among the spectators, looking "a little bit peeved." Surely Bushman had noticed that the "unpunctual star," as played by the hefty Bud Jamison, appeared to be a caricature of himself. Bushman, who considered himself a serious exponent of what Marie Dressler called "the drammer," failed to appreciate the joke.

Jesse Robbins had told Chaplin that he could have any actress under contract as his leading lady, and his choice fell on a cool, slightly haughty fifteen-year-old bit player named Gloria May Swanson. It is tempting to think that Chaplin recognized some special quality in the future star. Most likely, however, he picked Swanson out of a desire to please Leona Anderson, his hostess during his stay in Chicago. Swanson's Aunt Inga had been the nanny of the Andersons' daughter, and Mrs. Anderson was eager to help out Inga's family.

Swanson was more confused than flattered by Chaplin's attention:

He picked me and spent one whole morning trying to get me to work up routines with him. These all involved kicking each other in the pants, running into things, and falling over each other. He kept laughing and making his eyes twinkle and talking in a light, gentle voice and encouraging me to let myself go and be silly. He reminded me of a pixie from some other world altogether, and for the life of me I couldn't get the feel of his frisky little skits.[6]

After several hours of feeling like "a cow trying to dance with a toy poodle," Swanson told Chaplin that she simply couldn't see what was supposed to be so funny about these antics. Chaplin demoted her to a walk-on and cast the lovely Charlotte Mineau as the female star fancied by Charlie the stagehand. Although he was polite, Swanson sensed that he was hurt and a little angry.

George Spoor eventually signed Chaplin's bonus check, but only after he learned that the Chicago film exchange had received sixty-five orders for Chaplin's first Essanay comedy before the picture was even officially announced. By this time Broncho Billy had already had his fill of the studio manager, Bouché—"a smart aleck"—and perhaps also of domesticity. Anderson had decided to head back to California, and Chaplin soon followed, bringing his little company with him. Essanay's PR department announced that Chaplin simply couldn't get used to the cold weather in Chicago, but this was an excuse. As Anderson put it, Charlie "didn't like to be regimented."

Chaplin had already passed through Niles on his way to Chicago, and he knew that the facilities there were primitive. Still, he was shocked when he arrived at the ranch and saw his new living quarters. The crew occupied a series of bungalows that had been constructed mainly to serve as a backdrop for street scenes. The rooms were tiny and little expense had been wasted on luxuries like plumbing. Anderson had a bungalow to himself, furnished with an iron bedstead, a packing crate that served as a nightstand, and a rickety table and chair. His only ashtray appeared not to have been emptied in years. The toilet had not worked in some time either, and could only be flushed by pouring a bucket of water down it, a task Anderson didn't always make time for. Chaplin could hardly believe that Anderson, who was worth more than a million dollars, would voluntarily live in such squalor—and, actually, he didn't. Anderson would knock off a Broncho Billy two-reeler in a day or two, then spend the rest of the week in San Francisco, where he kept a suite at the St. Francis Hotel.

The other individual bungalow, which would have been Chaplin's, was now occupied by Wallace Beery, who had recently fled to Niles with his "Sweedie" crew to avoid an outraged Chicago mother who was trying to have him arrested for dating her teenage daughter. Chaplin was assigned to share another cabin with several other men, including Bud Jamison and Roland H. Totheroh.

A former minor league ball player, "Rollie" Totheroh had been hired by Anderson because he needed a ringer for the studio baseball team. When Totheroh couldn't learn to ride well enough to make the grade as a cowboy, he switched to the technical crew, eventually becoming Anderson's head cameraman. Totheroh and the rest of the Niles regulars had seen Chaplin's movies but were confused about his nationality. "We all thought he was a little Frenchman," he would recall. While Chaplin made no effort to hide his displeasure at the shabby quarters, Totheroh looked him over and decided that he had no cause to feel out of place. The influence of the valet Chaplin employed for a time while with Keystone was no longer in evidence, and his luggage consisted of a single valise containing a spare shirt, a few dingy changes of underwear, and a frayed toothbrush.

"Jesus, he hasn't got much in his bag, has he?" one of the men blurted out.[7]

At the first opportunity Chaplin took the train to San Francisco and returned with a violin, which he'd had strung backward so that he could play it left-handed. He practiced up to three hours a day, often making up little tunes of his own, and his bunkmates were relieved when he decided to move to Niles's only hotel. The rooms were almost as seedy as the bungalow, but at least Chaplin had privacy.

At Niles as at Edendale, Chaplin quickly earned a reputation for being close with a dollar. He was in possession of "some of the oldest money in California," Bud Jamison would recall. "One of the boys had to show him how to write a check." Jamison was wrong in thinking that Chaplin didn't have a bank account, however; he already had at least three, as well as some Canadian railroad stock.[8]

Chaplin may not have been in the habit of spending money on her personal needs, but he was used to a more modern approach to filmmaking than that practiced at Niles. To his amazement the lab had no facilities for developing. No one ever screened dailies, and Anderson edited his films by slicing up the negative—an irreversible process—without making a work print or even screening the footage he had shot. At some point it must have dawned on Chaplin that there was more to this situation than Anderson's personal eccentricity. George Spoor did not approve of Anderson's plans to get more involved in production, and he was trying to force him out by keeping a tight rein on his expenses. Spoor also hoped to drive down the value of the Niles property so that when Anderson decided to sell, Spoor could buy his shares at a more favorable price. Signing Chaplin had been a brilliant countermove on Anderson's part since he was now allied with a star who was destined to become Essanay's greatest financial asset.

Though the facilities at Niles were unpromising, Chaplin at least had the beginning of a decent company. Besides Jamison, Leo White, and the middle-aged Charles Insley, the Chaplin comedy team now included young Billy Armstrong, another Karno veteran who was attuned to Chaplin's pantomime style. There remained, however, the problem of a leading lady. Anderson took Chaplin on an expedition to interview chorus girls at San Francisco vaudeville theaters, but Chaplin saw no one who had the fresh quality he wanted. He had a romantic notion of discovering an unknown, a girl with no acting experience whom he could mold into his ideal partner. As Totheroh so cyncially put it, Chaplin preferred to work with actresses "who didn't know their ass from their elbow."

Chaplin later gave a rather fanciful account of how he found the comedy partner he was looking for. Carl Strauss, a handsome cowboy actor from the Broncho Billy unit, had seen a lovely young woman at Tate's Café on Hill Street in San Francisco. He didn't know her name, but with the help of the café's proprietor she was tracked down and persuaded to come to an interview at the St. Francis Hotel. The young lady's name was Edna Purviance (rhymes with reliance), and she proved to be a miner's daughter, born in 1894 in Paradise Valley near Lovelock, Nevada. Edna's parents had divorced, her mother remarried, and at seventeen she came to San Francisco to do secretarial work. Becoming an actress had never entered her mind.

Edna told a somewhat different story. Charlie had placed an advertisement in the San Francisco papers announcing an open audition, and hundreds of women showed up at Niles on the appointed day, ranging from experienced actresses to schoolgirls. Edna had no intention of auditioning, she would insist. She had come out to the ranch to visit a friend and enjoy a day's outing in the country, and while she was familiar with Charlie's pictures she didn't recognize him when he appeared without his costume and makeup:

While we were watching a little man with dark curly hair, who had been walking among the girls, looked over at me, and pointing in my direction, called out: "That's the type I want!" I was scared at first, and when the young man who was with him came over to me, I asked him who the little man was, "Why, that's Charles Chaplin our comedy star," he answered. "He wants to see you about the position."[9]

Totheroh's memory confirmed that Edna was at the ranch because she was dating an employee, not handsome Carl Strauss, but handyman Fritz Wintermeyer. His memory also backs up Chaplin's recollection that he wasn't completely sure of Edna until she turned up at a "beer and sandwiches" party given by a crew member. Charlie had been boasting that he could hypnotize anyone he wanted. Edna bet him he couldn't and challenged him to put her into a trance. Charlie went into his act, meanwhile whispering in Edna's ear, "Go along with me!" She did, and sank to the floor in a very realistic faint.

When Charlie asked Edna to costar with him in his first production at Niles, her reaction was, "Why not? I'll try anything once."

"Before I began to be a picture artist," she said a year later,

I had thought of myself as gifted with a little more than ordinary intelligence. After the first day in front of the camera, I came to the conclusion that I was the biggest boob on earth. Charlie was very patient with me, and after my first picture, in which I think I was terrible—*A Night Out*, you know—I began to get used to the work, and although I have had occasional relapses, as Charlie calls them, I am at least "camera wise" by now.[10]

Edna wasn't, and never would be, one of those people who naturally come alive in front of a camera. Outtakes from the Chaplin archives show a giggling, fun-loving Edna, more animated than she would ever be when consciously trying to act. Still, she did have qualities that made her an ideal foil for Chaplin. Five-foot-four, with a lush figure and masses of blond hair, her regular features were made more interesting by a slightly short upper lip. In looks and style, she was somethng like a prototype Diane Keaton; no matter how crazy the shenanigans going on around her she never lost her dignity. She also projected warmth, a quality that Chaplin could reflect and react to but never generate from within himself.

Edna, it seems, was still recovering from an unhappy love affair at the time she joined the company. Charlie had seen something in her that no one else had, and she responded by falling in love with him almost instantly. Within a few weeks they were a couple, apparently a very well-matched one. Charlie was moody; Edna had almost endless reserves of patience. She sent him before the camera with the motherly admonition "Go on. Be cute."

Edna's debut film, A Night Out, was about a pair of drunks on the town, with Ben Turpin as second lead not quite living up to the standard set by Fatty Arbuckle in The Rounders. The picture took longer than expected to complete, in part because Chaplin had ordered the construction of a new set. When the shooting was finally finished, Chaplin went off to San Francisco for a few days' rest and relaxation. He returned earlier than expected and found that "Billy" Anderson had decided to hurry things along by cutting the film for him. Anderson's approach to editing was crude. He measured film like dry goods—the distance between the tip of his nose and his outstretched thumb equaled a close-up, and since he was working directly on the negative, what he had done couldn't be undone. Charlie was furious. He refused to start another picture until the lab had a film developer. The machine took two weeks to arrive, and then was missing a part.

According to Anderson, while they were waiting for the lab to be set up, he and Charlie amused themselves by swapping assignments. Charlie directed one of his films and he, in turn, took over the directing chores for Charlie's next comedy, a boxing story called The Champion. Recalled Anderson, "[Charlie] was a little skinny prizefighter and I had him put a horseshoe in his glove. He could hardly lift it, and then he swung at the fellow and hit himself with the horseshoe and down he went."

Anderson wasn't credited as the director of The Champion, which would prove to be one of the more popular pictures Chaplin made with Essanay. Perhaps he exaggerated his contribution, but he does appear in the small role of an excited fan at ringside. Chaplin, meanwhile, played a bit part in Anderson's picture *His Regeneration.*

The Champion was not ready for release until March 11, and the home office was becoming very unhappy about Chaplin's work habits, which by 1915 standards were leisurely. He liked to improvise his story with the cameras rolling, and often reshot scenes that didn't satisfy him, which was considered an unconscionable waste of film. After *The Champion* Chaplin caught up a bit, quickly finishing two more pictures—*In the Park*, yet another variation on the familiar Keystone theme of "rival mashers," and *The Jitney Elopement*, a car-chase picture but without that manic driver Mabel Normand. But he hadn't signed with Essanay just to keep on producing Keystone knock-offs. For his next comedy he was determined to try something very different.

In *The Tramp*, for the first time, Charlie's character was literally a hobo, earning his keep by doing casual chores for a family of farmers. After he is injured fending off a gang of burglars, he is misled by the solicitous attentions of the farmer's beautiful daughter (Edna) into thinking that she is in love with him. Then her sweetheart shows up, and reality sets in. "I thort your kindness was love but it aint cause I seen him good bye," he says in a crudely scrawled farewell note. *The Tramp* concludes with a shot that would become Chaplin's signature—heartbroken but undefeated, the Tramp shrugs his shoulders and shuffles off down the road.

Chaplin knew he was taking "an awful chance," but he thought the public would be willing to accept this gentler, more romantic side of the Little Fellow's character. The home office in Chicago was less sure. "Down in the projection room at Essanay," wrote Charles McGuirk, "the men who passed on the picture felt a chill across their backs as the tramp discarded his humor and became pathetic. That chill was fear."[11]

The Tramp did well at the box office, but Essanay was still obsessed with getting out more product. Charlie was no longer just a popular new comedian—he was becoming the object of a national craze, unfortunately dubbed "Chaplinitis" by the pundits. On March 26 *Variety* reported that when *In the Park* played in theaters, audiences applauded Charlie's first appearance on the screen. Two weeks later the *New Jersey Mail* observed that "in many cases,

Chaplin films are renting for bigger prices than feature films twice their length." Unfortunately for Essanay, many of these rental fees were being earned by Keystone, which had more Chaplin comedies in circulation than they did.

It is never easy to explain what goes into the making of a craze, but Chaplin's instantly recognizable costume and makeup made his image easy to exploit. A Chicago craftsman, Cyrus LeRoy Baldridge, had begun manufacturing Charlie statuettes, which he sold through mail-order catalogs. Newsstands, gift shops, and street vendors were soon peddling an array of other Charlie souvenirs—spoons, lapel pins, balloons, "squirt rings," ashtrays, and postcards. The Hampton Company in New York City had its own version of the Charlie statuette, designed by one G. Grandelis, and in May 1915 it won a five-thousand-dollar judgment against a rival manufacturer for copying its design.[12]

Vaudeville was also doing its part. The first professional Chaplin imitator may have been his former roommate, Stan Laurel, who had joined with a married couple, Wren and Edgar Hurley, to form the Keystone Trio. Laurel did Chaplin, while Wren and Edgar played Mabel Normand and Chester Conklin. Connors of the vaudeville team of Connors and Duveen also did a Chaplin imitation. A less benign impersonator was former Karno star Billy Ritchie, who claimed that Chaplin had stolen his act. It may have been true, as Ritchie claimed, that he had once worn a costume similar to Chaplin's. For that matter many of Charlie's best-known walks and tricks were taken from the Karno tradition. Very little is new in the world of comedy, and young comics are especially likely to imitate their elders. Ritchie would later make a series of slavishly imitative comedies that proved he was no match for Charlie.[13]

Vaudeville houses still showed motion pictures in 1915, and many were promoting the Chaplin vogue by sponsoring amateur Charlie look-alike contests. Among the early winners was Bob Hope, who took first prize in a Chaplin contest in Cleveland. Charlie himself was not so lucky. When he entered a contest run by a theater in San Francisco, he failed even to make the finals. "I am tempted to give lessons in the Chaplin walk," he told a reporter, "out of pity as well as in the desire to see the thing done correctly."[14]

As "Chaplinitis" swept the country, the clamor for new Chaplin pictures became so great that on April 4, the General Film Company, which distributed Essanay releases, issued a statement denying that Chaplin was dead. One doubts that such a rumor was actually circulating, but denial gave the company an excuse to reassure anxious theater managers that more Chaplin comedies were in the pipeline.[15] Unfortunately, it wasn't true.

On April 8, following a quarrel with the head office, Chaplin suddenly decamped to Los Angeles, taking his company with him. They improvised a short comedy called *By the Sea* on the beach at Santa Monica, but this proved to be the last new Chaplin comedy that Essanay would see for two months.

Ironically, Chaplin and George Spoor were anxious for the same reason: Everyone seemed to be making money from the Chaplin boom but them. Flo Ziegfeld wanted to pay Charlie eighteen hundred dollars to appear live in his latest Broadway revue. When Essanay vetoed the deal, arguing that it had exclusive rights to Chaplin's services, Ziegfeld himself traveled to Chicago to present his case, to no avail. In the end the production number went on without Chaplin. Chorus girls in "Charlie" mustaches danced to the song "Oh, Those Charlie Chaplin Feet!"

Frustrated at working under primitive conditions at Niles while his films were minting money for the company, Chaplin was demanding his own studio. As Jesse Robbins hurried to California to negotiate, Chaplin moved his cast into the old Bradbury mansion at 147 North Hill Street and began filming a story based on an old music hall premise—the destruction wreaked by a team of incompetent paperhangers.

Work begins with a shot of the master paperhanger seated in a two-wheeled cart piled high and wide with ladders, scaffolding, and the other tools of his trade. Between the stanchions, pulling the oversize load is—our Charlie. So focused is he on the task at hand that he fails to notice that he has narrowly missed being run over by a streetcar, not once but three times. Laboring to pull the cart up a steep hill (actually the camera has been tilted sideways), he is literally lifted off his feet, his legs pumping in midair.

Chaplin's English biographer, David Robinson, has observed that *Work*'s opening sequence, filled with "horror-comedy images of slavery," looks ahead to the Soviet avant-garde films of the 1920s. Roger Manvell called it "almost surrealist" in impact, anticipating Beckett's *Waiting for Godot*.[16] *Work* implies that the condition of labor for hire is inherently degrading. Charlie's boss treats him like a beast of burden, and once they are inside the house, he uses him as a human sawhorse to hold up one end of his scaffold. And Charlie, in turn, is anything but willing. On the job his thoughts keep drifting to sex, also the main preoccupation of the family that inhabits the mansion—the wife is hoping to get her husband out of the house before her lover (Leo White) shows up; the husband is chasing the pretty maid (Edna); and the maid prefers to flirt with Charlie. While the rich and the poor play, the middle-class capitalist, the paper-hanger, is not only an exploiter but a fool. *Work* may well have owed something to Chaplin's exposure to socialist ideas, but the protest was also highly personal. He had hitched himself to the rickety cart of the Essanay Film Manufacturing Company, hauling its do-noth-ing partner, George Spoor, up the steep slope of profitability.

Chaplin's attitude toward work was a puzzlement to his col-leagues in the film industry. If he had been lazy, he could easily have knocked off a park-masher comedy every week, leaving himself plenty of time to enjoy the high life in San Francisco or Los Angeles. Instead he spent long hours on the set and lived modestly. On his return to Los Angeles, he had set himself up once more in the modest Stowell Hotel. Edna had her own room in the nearby Engstrom Hotel, and although they dined together almost every evening, they never spent the night together, whether by choice or for fear of causing a scandal. What Chaplin really objected to was not work per se, but working for others. He wanted the freedom to make his kind of movies according to his own schedule. This was the attitude of an artist who cared a great deal about quality, but Chaplin often didn't talk like an artist. Harry Carr, a *Los Angeles Times* reporter who interviewed Chaplin extensively after his return to LA from Niles, observed that it was an "open secret" that he did not intend to remain in the movie business for long. "I want to make all the money I can. Then in a few years, I am going to quit," Chaplin told Carr.[17]

Despite his success Chaplin still had mixed feelings about acitng. One of the more irksome side effects of "Chaplinitis" was the appearance of popular songs like the "The Chaplin Strut," "The Chaplin Waddle," and "Oh, Those Charlie Chaplin Feet!" He wrote songs himself, and dreamed of being recognized as a composer, not just a knockabout comic. One of his few public appearances in Los Angeles after his return to the city was a concert at the Shrine Civic Auditorium on July 29, where he was invited to conduct the orchestra in a performance of one of his own compositions.

In the meantime Syd, who was living with Minnie in modest quarters not far from Charlie's hotel, had taken over the task of sifting through the business proposals that came pouring in, while Edna shielded Charlie from social distractions. "If you only knew the hundreds of inconsequential things people want to see him about, sometimes you wouldn't think badly of him—or of me—for turning them down," she told sometime Essanay player Fred Goodwins.

"Of you?" Goodwins wondered aloud.

"Yes," Edna acknowledged. "You see, he feels so badly about having to do it that sometimes he has to get poor me to answer phone messages and act as a right-hand diplomat."[18]

By early June, Jesse Robbins and Syd had agreed to renegotiate Charlie's contract. Essanay rented the former Majestic Studio on Fairview Avenue as his new base of operations. Robbins would remain in Los Angeles as studio manager and the company's on-site representative, while Billy Anderson limited his well-meaning interference to a visit every two weeks or so. In return, according to George Spoor, Chaplin made a verbal agreement to complete ten more pictures for Essanay before his contract ran out on January 1, 1916. For each of the ten, starting with *Work*, he was to receive a $10,000 bonus—the same per-picture bonus that Mary Pickford, the only star receiving a higher salary than he, was said to be getting from Jesse Lasky.[19]

The outdoor stage at the Majestic happened to be protected on three sides by a high embankment, and Robbins, in an effort to protect Chaplin from distractions that were taking a toll on his nerves and concentration, hired security guards and barred unauthorized visitors from the studio. Still, the combined efforts of Robbins, Syd, and Edna could not always keep Chaplin's mind on making movies. One New York promoter got his attention with an offer of $25,000 for a two-week engagement at the New York Hippodrome, promising that he would have to be on stage only fifteen minutes every evening. In a 3:00 A.M. phone call to Anderson, Chaplin pleaded with him for permission to accept, promising that he would come up with an idea for a picture while he was on the train, and shoot it using New York locations. Anderson refused to sanction the engagement but approved an additional $25,000 bonus to placate his jumpy star.[20]

Meanwhile, even as Chaplin's popularity at the box office soared, reviewers continued to find fault. When *Work* was released on June 21, *Variety*'s influential critic, Sime Silverman, called it "the usual Chaplin work of late, mussy, messy and dirty." He continued:

Chaplin has found the public will stand for his picture comedy of the worst kind, and he is giving them the worst kind . . . the Censor Board [a creature of the distributors] was passing matter in the Chaplin films that could not possibly get by in other pictures. Never anything dirtier was placed upon the screen than Chaplin's "The Tramp," and while this may have been objected to by the censors, it merely taught Chaplin what to avoid and how far to go.[21]

While Silverman's objections to *Work* are understandable, it is difficult to imagine, today, how he could have considered *The Tramp* a "dirty" picture. Apparently, the very appearance of a protagonist who wore grimy clothes (and used an old tin can as a finger bowl) was an affront to genteel taste.

A Woman, the first comedy Chaplin made at his new studio, stirred up even more of a fuss. Cross-dressing roles were a standard part of the vaudeville and movie comic repertoire. Unlike Wallace Beery's "Sweedie" and Roscoe Arbuckle's "Miss Fatty," however, Chaplin in drag looked fetching, even seductive. Four days after *A Woman* opened, the *Chicago Tribune* ran excerpts from letters it had received objecting to his latest effort, including one from a man who called it "as coarse a film as I have ever seen."[22] Swedish censors later banned the film in its entirety. Once again, the aspects of *A Woman* that were considered objectionable in 1915 are not necessarily obvious today. The censors, it seems, were not so much troubled by Charlie's flirting with other men as by his leering attentions to a dressmaker's dummy.

The other major complaint about Chaplin's comedies was more understandable. "Chaplin needs a scenario writer, and if he doesn't Essanay does," wrote Silverman in his review of *A Woman*. "Too much money could not be paid the man who could fit Charlie Chaplin in his present brand of comedy as he should be fitted." This was by no means the last time a movie critic would complain about the difficulty of finding suitable material for a comic actor, but it was true that Chaplin's improvised stories often began strongly only to go nowhere. Chaplin took such criticisms seriously, but rather than rely on scenario writers for his next three pictures, he recycled old material. *The Bank* was a near remake of *The New Janitor*. *A Night at the Show* was built around Fred Karno's *A Night in an English Music Hall*, with Chaplin playing both the drunken Swell and a rambunctious working-class fan in the balcony. *Shanghaied*, the most original of the three, was shot on board a rented fishing boat, the *Vaquero*, and ended with a motorboat chase reminiscent of the finale of *Tillie's Punctured Romance*.

If the stories were familiar, the style of these Essanay comedies was a far cry from the frenetic, hard-sell approach of the Keystones. Chaplin now took more time to set up and develop his gags, and the editing was leisurely, resulting in a more intimate, relaxed brand of comedy reminiscent of what Max Linder had been doing in France for some years.

But in spite of his revised agreement with Spoor and Anderson, Chaplin was soon as dissatisfied as ever. During the Los Angeles run of *Birth of a Nation*, Chaplin had seen the Griffith epic at least once a week, and like Sennett a year earlier, he was determined to try his hand at making a feature-length film. The immodest title he had in mind was *Life*, and the story line may have been meant as a skeptical commentary on Billy Anderson's *His Regeneration*, about the reformation of a burglar. In Chaplin's version the do-good preacher who approaches the Little Fellow on his release from prison is actually a con man, who distracts his prey with the consolations of the Good Book in order to steal his watch. After failing at a menial job as a dishwasher and all-around cleaning man in the kitchen of a wealthy family, and being turned out of a flophouse for lack of a few pennies to pay for a bed, Charlie joins forces with a former confederate in crime to commit a burglary. While ineptly stripping the main floor of valuables, he and his partner are surprised by Edna, who has been upstairs nursing her invalid mother. She tells the burglars to take what they like but begs them not to go upstairs and frighten her ailing parent. Charlie recognizes Edna as the maid in the house where he formerly worked and is so touched by her courage and sweetness that he reforms on the spot.

Chaplin's desire to make a feature-length film was certainly understandable. Features were the coming thing, and their popularity was having an impact throughout the industry. Longer movies meant bigger budgets and, in turn, audiences large enough to pay premium rentals. Small, low-overhead nickelodeons were being replaced by well-appointed movie houses, and film distribution companies were altering their rental policies, setting their fees according to a sliding scale depending on the size of the house. Chaplin undoubtedly hoped that Essanay would accept *Life* in lieu of three or more two-reelers. So far, however, General Films, Essanay's distributor, had not instituted the sliding fee scale, and George Spoor insisted that he couldn't release a comedy feature profitably.

With the dispute over *Life* still unsettled, Chaplin began *Burlesque on Carmen*, a parody of Cecil B. De Mille's silent film version of the Bizet opera. (De Mille's project was not quite as pointless as it sounds. His star, diva Geraldine Farrar, was as celebrated for her acting skills as for her voice, and when the film played in the larger theaters a professional orchestra provided suitable musical accompaniment.) In Chaplin's freewheeling interpretation of the story, his character, Don José, became "Darn Hosery," and Lillas Pastia was transformed into Lilias Pasta.

By December of 1915 George Spoor had finally been able to resolve some of his long-standing business problems. He negotiated the buyout of Anderson's share of the company and, along with other producers from the old Edison Trust, set up a new distribution company, Vitagraph-Lubin-Selig-Essanay, or VLSE. Spoor now felt that he had a good chance of re-signing Chaplin for another year and came out to Los Angeles to discuss a contract renewal, opening with an offer of $350,000.

Chaplin, however, was already being courted by other producers, especially the Mutual Film Corporation. Through a business deal with Kessel and Baumann, Mutual had acquired prints of Chaplin's Keystone comedies, which proved to be a bonanza for the company. The prints, however, were fast wearing out, and Mack Sennett, who had recently formed his own company with Hollywood's leading directors of dramatic films, Tom Ince and D. W. Griffith, was not about to provide Mutual with replacements. According to film historian Terry Ramsaye, who was working in the publicity department of the company's New York headquarters at the time, Mutual began pursuing Chaplin as early as the spring of 1915, hiring a freelance press agent named Casey Cairns to disguise himself as a cowboy actor and get a job as an extra with the Broncho Billy crew in order to get close to Chaplin. After Chaplin's move to Los Angeles, the competition for his services heated up, as other production companies joined in the pursuit: "The business of stalking Chaplin honeycombed the cafes and hotels of the [West] coast with intrigue. Niles and Los Angeles were full of spies and special agents on to the Chaplin situation. The Mutual had relays of watchers, negotiators and emissaries. . . . Chaplin was extremely aware of the situation."[23]

Unfortunately for Chaplin, both Mutual and Essanay—and presumably the other companies pursuing him as well—wanted to sign him to make two-reelers. Even though *Tillie's Punctured Romance* had proved that full-length comedies could make money, two-reelers were still much in demand as program openers. Chaplin comedies in particular were so popular that a producer could force an exhibitor to rent an entire line of films in order to get them, a practice known as block booking.

Escape from the shackles of slapstick two-reelers was possible if Chaplin chose to become an independent producer. Billy Anderson, flush with cash from the buyout of his shares by George Spoor, was eager to go into business with him. In fact, as far as he knew, they had a deal. Meanwhile Syd Chaplin, whom Anderson found "pretty hard to take," had gone ahead to New York to talk business with John Freuler, the president of Mutual, who was offering a compensation package totaling $670,000 for a one-year commitment. Syd quickly agreed on the details of a contract. Charlie had only to take his insurance physical and sign the papers.

As soon as he finished shooting *Burlesque on Carmen*, Chaplin boarded the train for New York. It was the first time he had ventured East since the country was swept by "Chaplinitis," and he was completely unprepared for the reception that awaited him. Telegraph operators, probably alerted by Mutual's head office, had passed the word of his travel plans to stations along the train's route, and huge crowds turned out at every stop. In Amarillo, Texas, he was hustled from his compartment in midshave, his face still decorated with puffs of lather, and found himself face to face with the entire town, which had gathered to watch him eat a sandwich and drink a Coca-Cola with the mayor. In Kansas City cheering fans lined the tracks. In New York City the police were afraid that his arrival at Grand Central Station would cause a riot, and they persuaded him to leave the train at 125th Street in Harlem. Syd met him there in a limousine and escorted him to midtown Manhattan, where he registered at the Plaza Hotel as Charles Spencer.

Chaplin reacted to all this adulation by becoming starkly conscious of his own loneliness. Slipping out of his hotel he walked up Fifth Avenue to the address where Hetty Kelly was living with her sister, who had married the American millionaire Frank Gould, but he could not bring himself to ring the bell. He stopped at a Child's restaurant for pancakes, one of his favorite breakfasts, but the waitress recognized him, and he had to flee before he finished his meal.

Chaplin was far from sure he wanted to sign with Mutual, but Syd outlined a plan that would ultimately lead to financial independence. He and Chaplin would incorporate as equal partners in a film production company. The incorporation would cut Charlie's tax burden, enabling him to save more of the $670,000 he received from Mutual. True, he would have to devote another year to producing short subjects, but in the long run he would be free from having to rely on Billy Anderson or any other outside partner.

While considering Syd's plan, Charlie insisted on reviewing personally all the competing offers he had received. There followed a series of steak dinners at fashionable midtown restaurants, during which prosperous businessmen in custom-tailored suits plied him with brandy and assured him that they had his best interests at heart. Anderson, who had come east from Los Angeles on the same train, was among the wooers, but he could not match Mutual's salary package. George Spoor either couldn't or wouldn't. Spoor took the position that he was still owed four two-reelers under the agreement he and Chaplin made the previous June. But their agreement had never been committed to paper, and Chaplin, or someone advising him, obviously didn't think the promise was enforceable. In the end Chaplin decided to go with Mutual after all. Terry Ramsaye speculated that Charlie was impressed by the white-haired, well-spoken John Freuler, who looked "more like a millionaire than anyone else in the film trade."

More likely he had decided to place his trust in Syd.

5

The Vagabond

Chaplin's signing with the Mutual Film Company, on February 26, 1916, was a major news event. Not only would he be earning more than the president of the United States, as editorial writers gleefully pointed out, his salary for 1916 would equal 94 percent of the payroll of the entire U.S. Senate. With the possible exception of steel magnate Charles Schwab, he would be making the highest salary of any individual in the country.

A Mutual film crew was on hand to record the signing of the historic contract, and Charlie tried to work off his jitters by pretending to direct the crew's efforts. "What is the action in this scene?" he asked no one in particular.[1]

After the cameras stopped rolling, the Chaplin brothers' New York attorney, Nathan Burkan, shocked Terry Ramsaye by auctioning off his fountain pen for thirty-five dollars. Ramsaye was even more taken aback when the newly wealthy Charlie, leaving the office with the check for the first installment of his salary in hand, turned to him and said, "Well, I've got this much if they never give me another cent. Guess I'll go and buy a whole dozen neckties."[2]

Chaplin's only major New York public appearance, a benefit concert at the New York Hippodrome six days earlier, had not gone well. Among the charities sponsoring the event was a British actors' fund, and in addition to the usual society figures and business tycoons the concert drew a large number of Britons connected with show business and the arts. In addition to John Philip Sousa marches, conducted by the composer himself, the program featured the "futurist" pianist Leo Orenstein, playing a "Cubist" composition called "The Wild Man's Advance," and cornet soloist Herbert L. Clarke.

A critic from the *New York World* went backstage to see Chaplin before the performance and found him shaking with stage fright. "It's several years since I've been on the stage, and I don't know how to act," he confessed.

"Be funny," the critic advised.

"I don't want to be funny," Chaplin protested.[3]

And, indeed, when Chaplin was introduced, he strode on stage in evening dress, sans makeup, to conduct the orchestra in his own compositions, including a march called "The Peace Patrol." The audience reaction was tepid, and Charlie, sensing their disappointment, hastily did a few steps of his shuffling, splay-footed walk and twirled an imaginary cane. He left the stage more shaken than before.

It may be that Chaplin's appearance as a conductor was so unexpected that the audience was simply confused. But there was another explanation for the cool reception. Great Britain had been at war with the Central Powers for a year and a half, and had more than 2.5 million men in uniform. Some 28,000 had died evacuating Gallipoli, and just a week before the concert, the Battle of Verdun had begun with the Germans lobbing shells loaded with phosgene gas at the Allied lines. Proneutrality sentiment was still strong across the United States, but not among New York business circles, and certainly not among British expatriates. That the best-known Englishman in the States had chosen this moment to present a tune called the "Peace Patrol March" could only have come as an unpleasant surprise.

A second public appearance, on March 6, was even more unpleasant from Chaplin's point of view. The ratification of the Thirteenth Amendment to the Constitution in 1913 had introduced the first federal income tax, and the U.S. Treasury Department had asked him to inaugurate the opening of a new branch office of the Internal Revenue Service in midtown Manhattan. Charlie dutifully posed for photographers, smiling as an official showed him how to fill out a tax form.

In fact he had been none too happy to discover that the two-year-old income-tax law applied to resident aliens like himself. Moreover, while the average wage earner paid no tax at all, and the levy for most upper-income people was only 1 percent, he would be among a small number of the very wealthy assessed at 6 percent. This was a calamity Syd had already taken steps to avert by incorporating with him as the Charles Chaplin Film Company. By splitting the profits they took out of the company, the brothers hoped to avoid the 6 percent bracket. Fortunately the IRS agents appeared not to be paying attention when Charlie indiscreetly mentioned to reporters that he was paying Syd a $75,000 commission for his services in negotiating with Mutual. If Syd had really been really getting half the income from the contract, a commission would have been superfluous.

For the moment, however, the income tax and the war were distant concerns. Chaplin's contract had touched off a debate, still going on today, about just how much entertainers are worth. Many, perhaps the majority, found it inspiring that a young man could arrive in America with empty pockets and make a fortune before his twenty-seventh birthday. Others wondered what it said about our society that a man who was famous for impersonating drunks and park mashers should earn a thousand times more than a typical public school teacher. Already an outraged citizen of New Orleans had written to his local paper to demand that Chaplin, "the acme of vulgarity," be deported. Few were prepared to go quite that far, but the king of slapstick, along with the sexy "vamp" Theda Bara, were invariably cited as horrible examples of what was wrong with American culture. The *Minneapolis Tribune*, for example, reported that ministers and teachers blamed Chaplin for leading "low grade persons" to become addicted to motion pictures.[4]

No one was more eager to see his image upgraded than Chaplin himself. A few months earlier, in an interview with J. B. Hirsch of *Motion Picture Magazine*, he had announced the arrival of a "new Charlie Chaplin," practicing a better-mannered style of comedy. "It is because of my music-hall training and experiences that I am by force of habit inclined to work into my acting little threads of vulgarisms," he told Hirsch. "This Elizabethan style of humor, this crude form of slapstick comedy that I employed in my work was due entirely to my environment and I am now trying to steer clear from this sort of humor."⁵ No doubt many readers suspected Hirsch of putting words in his subject's mouth, but Chaplin really did talk this way. By offhandedly linking the music hall tradition to Elizabethan drama while defining himself as a victim of his "environment," he showed an almost uncanny sense of how to appeal to people who considered themselves progressive.

Other attempts to define the "new" Chaplin were less successful. Soon after signing his contract, he informed Terry Ramsaye that he no longer wished to be known as Charlie Chaplin: "Charlie is a jitney-house name. I've outgrown it just as the pictures have outgrown their former character."⁶ Ramsaye dutifully wrote to newspaper editors and reviewers across the country informing them of Chaplin's desire to be referred to, in the future, as *Mr.* Charles Chaplin. Recipients of the letters had a good laugh, then forgot all about them. No matter how he was billed, Chaplin would remain "Charlie" to his fans.

Chaplin's desire to be taken seriously got a huge boost in May 1916, when *Harper's Weekly* published an article by Mrs. Minnie Maddern Fiske, the reigning "First Lady of the American Stage," hailing him as a "genius" in the art of pantomime. "Chaplin is vulgar," conceded Mrs. Fiske, but "there is vulgarity in the comedies of Aristophanes, and those of Plautus and Terence and the Elizabethans, not excluding Shakespeare. Rabelais is vulgar. Fielding and Smollett and Swift are vulgar."⁷

The lively, opinionated Mrs. Fiske had fallen into the habit of visiting nickelodeons to ease her boredom on tour, and she had singled out Chaplin as comedian of special merit when he was just starting out with Keystone. Her praise was totally sincere. Nevertheless, a whiff of the ghostwriter hangs over the *Harper's Weekly* article. Deeply in debt and hoping to raise money for a new production, Minnie Fiske had agreed to publish a book, *Mrs. Fiske Speaks*, which was being written for her by a young critic named Alexander Woollcott, an early and enthusiastic Chaplin fan. Woollcott, one suspects, was the one to invoke Plautus, Aristophanes, and all the rest.

It takes nothing away from Chaplin to point out that for Alexander Woollcott and his generation any cultural phenomenon that upset the likes of Protestant ministers from Minnesota and schoolteachers from the Deep South was worth championing. Urbanized, sophisticated, and sympathetic to modernist trends, they were opposed to the distinction between high and low culture, and even more opposed to any suggestion that art should uphold bourgeois values. It was more than a little ironic that the representative of popular culture who captured the fancy of Woollcott and his contemporaries was Chaplin—the most cerebral of the slapstick comedians, and surely the only one who could talk glibly about his roots in Elizabethan tradition.

Even while he courted the approval of the intellectuals, Chaplin at times found being a "genius" something of a burden. Touched and flattered by Mrs. Fiske's tribute to his work, he tried to read a play by Aristophanes and found that he couldn't get through it.

By the middle of March, the "new" Chaplin was back in Los Angeles and ready to begin settling into the former Climax Studio on Lillian Way in Hollywood, now renamed the Lone Star Studio. Lone Star was better equipped than the Majestic, and Chaplin was given a few weeks grace to assemble a comedy company that suited his needs. Leo White, Charlotte Mineau, and a few others had joined him from Essanay. Replacing Bud Jamison was a new "heavy," the mountainous Eric Campbell, a former Gilbert and Sullivan specialist with the D'Oyly Carte light opera company. Young Billy Armstrong was also gone, succeeded by another Karno graduate, Albert Austin, who had been part of the company that Chaplin toured with in A Night in an English Music Hall. Tall, thin, and curly-haired, Austin could appear boyishly earnest, dim-witted, or a bit of both.

Perhaps the most important addition to Chaplin's staff was Rollie Totheroh. Chaplin had taken a liking to Billy Anderson's head cameraman, and on learning that Totheroh was in Los Angeles and unemployed he took him on as an assistant. When his head cameraman, William Foster, left for a job with Universal just three pictures into the Mutual contract, Totheroh was promoted, beginning one of the longest and most productive collaborations in motion picture history.

✲ ✲ ✲

As Totheroh explained in an interview shortly before his death in 1967, the director's job in those days was to manage the actors. Decisions about camera angles, lighting, and exposures were largely left up to the cameraman. Moreover, since the cameras were hand-cranked, the operator was also able to control the speed at which the film was shot. Totheroh soon learned, however, that the chief requirements for a Chaplin cameraman were patience and vigilance. As he recalled:

> He'd rehearse everybody, and even in the silents we had dialogue. It came to a little woman's part, and he'd go out there and he'd play it. He'd change his voice and he'd be in the character that he wanted the little old woman to play. . . . He rehearsed it so many darn different ways with them that when he came in there, it'd be all changed around with what he put down. You had to be on the alert for him.
>
> I never got away from that camera, looking through that lens. And all those rehearsals, I sat right there, watching every move he made. Then if he came along and something spontaneous hit him, you had to be ready there to take it and get it.[8]

Delighted to be liberated from Essanay, Chaplin started his new contract brimming with energy and good intentions. In New York he was already on the lookout for new gag ideas, and Terry Ramsaye had been fascinated by the way Syd followed him through the streets, notebook in hand, ready to jot down his comments. When Charlie happened to pass a window dresser setting up a display in a department store window he briskly instructed his brother, "Here's business, Syd—get it in the book, put it down." Whether aided by Syd's notes or not, Chaplin had a way of drawing on these passing observations years, even decades, later. The window dresser would make his appearance in *City Lights*, released in 1931.

Other aspects of the New York scene would be put to more immediate use. One day, while walking on Sixth Avenue at Thirty-third Street, Chaplin saw a man on the escalator leading to the elevated train station lose his balance and skid down the moving staircase. The pedestrian's bad luck was his inspiration. As soon as he had moved into the new studio, Chaplin ordered the construction of an elaborate department store set featuring a working escalator for his first Mutual comedy, *The Floorwalker*.

The American department store, as envisioned by Chaplin, could be said to illustrate the maxim Capitalism Is Theft. Everyone is stealing; the customers merely shoplift while the manager and the floorwalker (played by Lloyd Bacon) are embezzling in a big way. The Tramp, no longer the troublemaker he was in his Keystone and Essanay days, is now a relative innocent; he merely cops a free shave from some supplies on display at the gentlemen's toiletries counter. Still, as Buster Keaton put it, Charlie's character remained "a bum with a bum's philosophy . . . he would steal if he got the chance. My little fellow was a workingman and honest."[9]

Chaplin was probably influenced even at this early date by the socialist ideas of friends like Elmer Ellsworth, though his outlook owed even more to an ingrained Cockney cynicism. For the most part, however, the early Mutuals were light on social commentary and heavy on physical comedy and byplay with inanimate objects. "Chaplin did not care a whoop about the floorwalker as a type," Terry Ramsaye concluded, somewhat overstating the case. "What he sought were the wonderful possibilities of an escalator as a vehicle upon which to have a lot of the most amusing troubles."[10]

In his second Mutual film, *The Fireman*, Charlie served coffee from the gleaming boiler of the fire engine, shinnied *up* the pole in the firehouse, and talked into the wrong end of a telephone. In *One A.M.*, reprising his role as the "Inebriate Swell," he had his innings with an animal-skin rug, a revolving table, a pair of carpeted staircases, and a Murphy bed. *The Pawnshop* gave him an opportunity to roll out pastry by running it through the hand wringer of a washing machine, perform major surgery on an alarm clock, and balance precariously atop a teetering stepladder.

A fan magazine features writer who visited Lone Star during the making of *The Pawnshop* was struck by the lighthearted atmosphere on the set. On the first day of shooting Chaplin appeared late, about ten o'clock, carrying a jumble of notes, and playfully called the cast and crew to order: "Attention! Ladies and Gentlemen! We are about to open the pawn shop." In between set-ups, he candidly explained that the film drew on his memories of his experiences as a none-too-willing temporary clerk—"the seamy side of my life," he sighed. "It reminds me of the good old days."

Minutes later, his pensive mood forgotten, Chaplin was on the floor demonstrating for the cast how to imitate a can of condensed milk.[11]

The Pawnshop marked the debut of a new member of the company who was destined to have a long and close relationship with Chaplin. Henry Bergman was a former operatic tenor who had sung at Covent Garden and various European houses. He appeared at the Metropolitan Opera House in New York in 1906 and then moved to Broadway, joining the cast of the Ziegfeld Follies. On hearing that it was possible to earn five dollars a day in motion pictures, he made the switch, establishing himself as a comic "heavy."

Bergman was an American, born in San Francisco, but he had spent most of his life abroad, attending schools in Germany where his father was an officer in the U.S. consular service. His natural milieu was the coffeehouse, exchanging gossip over *Kaffee mit Schlag*, and on arriving in Hollywood in 1914 he was dismayed to find himself in a town where there wasn't a single restaurant or café that stayed open late in the evening, much less a decent bookstore. For a time Bergman held court on the steps of his apartment building. A little later he purchased a Hupmobile sedan, whose backseat was soon crammed full of show business trade papers, literary monthlies from back East, and assorted hard-to-find books. Bergman was a well-known local character, and when Chaplin heard that he was unhappy working at the L-Ko studio under Henry Lehrman, his old nemesis from Keystone, he invited him to join Lone Star.[12]

It was in *Behind the Screen*, Chaplin's seventh film for Mutual, that Bergman showed his mettle. The backstage comedy had become much more self-conscious since the days of *A Film Johnnie* and *The Masquerader*, and the props for *Behind the Screen* included six hundred berry pies—preferred to custard because they showed up better in black and white—as well as a trap door. Bergman happened to be standing half-on, half-off the trap door when a technician misunderstood a cue and it suddenly fell open. Even as he narrowly avoided breaking his leg, he had the presence of mind to shout to the cameraman, "Keep on grinding! I'm all right!"[13]

The acme of physical humor was reached in Chaplin's next picture, *The Rink*, a movie version of *Skating*, a sketch Syd had developed during his stint with Karno. For extras Lone Star hired every professional roller skater in the Los Angeles area, which in those days was not a great many. Chaplin hadn't skated in years, but within a week he was outperforming the pros. The rest of the company were somewhat less sure of themselves. Edna skated tentatively, her face a mask of anticipated disaster. Eric Campbell, who had never been on roller skates before, was immobile, too frightened to move his feet. To get him out onto the rink, crew member Dave Allen stood out of camera range and prodded him with a long stick. So many pokes were required that Campbell's backside became black and blue, and Allen finally attached a crosspiece to the end of the stick so that his pokes wouldn't be quite so painful.

"When you pushed him into the scene, he had no idea what was coming," Chaplin later reminisced with Allen. "I had it all figured out. As I was skating backwards on one foot—the other raised gracefully in mid-air—I planned to kick him right in the stomach just as you pushed him into the scene. It worked. The unsuspecting Eric got my skate right in the abdomen."[14]

Such was the lot of the comic heavy.

Amazingly, when Chaplin told Terry Ramsaye that he had no plans beyond buying a dozen neckties, he had meant what he said. In 1915, when he was already very well compensated, his total expenses had been somewhat less than five hundred dollars, and during the first six months after signing with Mutual he continued to live in the same modest style. He and Edna socialized with other members of the company—and occasionally with Mabel Normand and a few old friends from "the bunch" at Keystone—at favorite haunts like Doyle's in Vernon or Barney Oldfield's, a saloon owned by the famous racing driver.

Rollie Totheroh recalled that Chaplin would often signal his readiness to call it quits for the day by asking, "How's the light, Rollie?"

"It's better down at Barney's," Totheroh would reply, the signal for everyone to adjourn to Barney Oldfield's for a light beer or two—light beer, or lager, being the favorite drink of the crew.

Although Charlie was now receiving invitations to go out in Los Angeles society, Edna had few social ambitions, and at first he was painfully aware of his own lack of polish. Attending his first formal dinner party, he worried that he would embarrass himself. He arrived armed with a list of topics for socially acceptable small talk, only to be confounded when the ultrarespectable matron seated next to him inquired casually, "Tell me, Mr. Chaplin, do you believe in the immortality of the soul?"

But the principle that success makes one endearing applied even in the higher reaches of society. *The Count*, Chaplin's fifth Mutual comedy, provides an amusing illustration of this phenomenon. The guests at Miss Moneybags's party, having mistaken Charlie for the aristocratic Count Broko, are prepared to forgive him anything. His shabby clothes are assumed to be a clever costume. His appalling table manners—he scratches his head with his fork and buries his face in a slice of watermelon—draw disapproving looks but no more. His rubber-legged partnering of Miss Moneybags (Edna) is greeted with applause.

Chaplin, however, was not prepared to play the gauche outsider indefinitely. Stars of the New York and London stage were migrating to Los Angeles to try their luck in the movies. Chaplin was drawn to these newcomers and more or less consciously used them as mentors in a program of self-improvement. One of his new friends was Julian Eltinge, a female impersonator whose one-man shows had won him a large following in New York. The three films he made with Famous Players–Lasky were not successful; his act depended largely on verbal wit and a keen eye for social hypocrisy, all lost on the silent screen. He remained in LA long enough, however, to persuade Charlie to give up his rooms at the Stowell Hotel and return to the LA Athletic Club. Chaplin began working out in the club's gym for an hour almost every evening and, if his Mutual publicity can be believed, he also received daily visits from a chiropodist and a barber.[15]

Around this time Chaplin also acquired another valet, Tom Harrington, who had been a "dresser" for the English comic Bert Clark. Harrington, who would remain with Chaplin for more than a decade, was a great reader, and introduced him to the works of

Lafcadio Hearn and Frank Harris. An exceptionally thrifty man who rarely paid retail for anything, Harrington took control of Chaplin's daily expenses as well as his clothes. Chaplin continued to wear off-the-rack suits, but he had begun to dress up more often and slick down his wiry hair.

At the urging of Syd, who worried that he would get into a serious accident, Charlie also acquired a new car, a magnificent twelve-cylinder Locomobile, and a full-time driver, Toraichi Kono. Born in Hiroshima in 1883, Kono was the rebellious son of a well-to-do family and a descendant of samurai warriors. His parents had sent him to live with relatives in the state of Washington when he was still a teenager. On returning home after finishing his schooling, he found that he could no longer adapt to traditional ways, and in 1906, he returned to the United States, settling in California. Kono longed for a life of adventure; he dreamed of somehow learning to fly and became a chauffeur only reluctantly, because the steady income would give his family security.

Undoubtedly Charlie's most important mentor during this period was Constance Collier, a leading lady of the British stage during his youth. Collier had made a lucrative sideline of coaching Hollywood's newly minted stars in acting, speech, and deportment. There is no suggestion that Charlie was ever a paying client, but Collier took a more-than-casual interest in cleaning up his accent and broadening his social horizons. One of the first people she sent him to see was Sir Herbert Beerbohm Tree, who was to be her costar in a silent film version of *Macbeth*.

As Chaplin told it, he was so intimidated at the thought of meeting the great English actor that when he found himself outside Tree's hotel suite he failed to notice that the door was ajar and knocked a bit too forcefully. The door flew open and he literally fell into the room, where the august Sir Herbert was in the process of demonstrating to his director how he wanted the witches in *Macbeth* to skip daintily through their scene. Sir Herbert continued his mincing performance, acknowledging his visitor's unorthodox arrival without missing a step: "This way, Chaplin, *this* way."[16]

Minutes later Sir Herbert announced that he had to make a phone call and departed, asking Chaplin to please look after his "little girl." Chaplin was relieved, thinking that baby-sitting would be less of a strain than trying to impress the veteran actor. His confidence vanished when the "little" girl proved to be eighteen-year-old Iris Tree, nearly six feet tall, formidably endowed, and already the author of a book of poetry. Chaplin overcame his awe and later took Miss Tree and her friend, Mrs. William K. Vanderbilt, to a fish restaurant in Santa Monica, where a policeman tried to arrest Mrs. Vanderbilt for smoking in public. (At the time men were permitted to smoke in Santa Monica but women were not.) Unimpressed by Mrs. Vanderbilt's name, the policeman dropped the charges when he recognized Charlie.

Chaplin seems to have spent a great deal of time with the older generation and very little with his peers. He resisted Connie Collier's efforts to introduce him to Douglas Fairbanks on the grounds that he disliked "bright young men" types. When they did meet, at a dinner party given by Collier in March 1917, the two men hit it off at once. Fairbanks was a born optimist, Charlie a worrier, but they were both romantics at heart and developed a firm if very competitive friendship.

Mary Pickford, Charlie's only serious rival as a box-office draw, was married to actor Owen Moore but already conducting a very discreet affair with Fairbanks. She met Charlie separately, on a rainy evening during the winter of 1916–17, at a "movie ball" in Long Beach, and was struck by his dramatic appearance—"very young and aesthetic, all eyes, with a great big black cloche [ascot] necktie." Her reaction is interesting since in those days nearly *everyone* in Hollywood was young. Pickford herself was only twenty-three and had been supporting her entire family as well as her hard-drinking husband since she was seventeen.

Charlie's romance with Edna Purviance was already on its way to becoming a casualty of his success. Edna believed, no doubt with good reason, that he had been unfaithful to her, and she was hurt when he failed to write her during his stay in New York. Doubtless another source of friction was Edna's lack of interest in making herself over to keep up with Charlie's new image. A Mutual press release that went out under Terry Ramsaye's name in the summer of 1916, doubtless with Chaplin's approval, is evidence of a clumsy attempt to upgrade Edna socially. Edna is quoted as saying:

Six years ago this fall I went East to Vassar. I was chosen to play the leading parts in several Shakespearean tragedies, presented by the dramatic society, of which I was a member. We gave "As You Like It" *a la* Ben Greet [the English actor Sir Ben Greet was the leading producer of Shakespeare in the United States from 1902 to 1914], two years ago this June, on the campus. No, I wasn't "Rosalind": I had to be content with "Celia's" role that time—class politics.

Then, after graduation, I returned to San Francisco, and went into charity and settlement work. I was asked to be the heroine in a playlet given under the auspices of a charity organization with which I was connected. . . . The evening of the performance, while I was bowing after the second curtain call, a very dear friend of my father's and mine came to me and asked to present a "Mr. Chaplin" who wished to congratulate me on my success with the part I had taken.[17]

As You Like It does not happen to be one of Shakespeare's tragedies, but never mind. Edna Purviance had never been near Vassar either; nor had she done settlement work or appeared in a "playlet" in San Francisco. Edna responded to this effort to make her into a college girl by giving a rare interview to former Essanay actor Fred Goodwins, in which she made a point of describing herself as "thoroughly Western" and spoke with pride of her mastery of Pitman shorthand. She also confided that she had refused to change her name, even though Charlie kept urging her to do so: "I hate assumed names, and as mine is so distinctive I want to keep it."[18]

Even if Edna had had a taste for social climbing, which she did not, she would hardly have been in a position to indulge it. Mutual's heavy investment in Chaplin left no room for other stars. They had budgeted ten thousand dollars per two-reeler, a sum that had to cover the entire payroll, exclusive of Chaplin's salary. Thus, Edna was earning two hundred dollars a week while Chaplin made ten thousand. It hadn't occurred to him to use his bargaining power to win a better salary for his leading lady, an omission that says a great deal about their relationship.

❖   ❖   ❖

Even while Chaplin was gradually learning to live like a rich man, one of the more unfortunate by-products of "Chaplinitis" was the growing curiosity about his past. With his wiry hair and sharp features he did not look like a typical Englishman. As early as April 1916 Ivan Gaddis reported in *Motion Picture Magazine* that there was "much speculation" over his origins and nationality.[19]

As Chaplin explained late in life, when he first got into the movies, "the first producer who looked after me [Charles Baumann?] naturally took me for a Jew. I did not disillusion him. Born in the poorest class in England, with no past, nor castles, nor ancestors to defend, I was not a man to encumber myself with prejudice. If they wanted me Jewish, they would have me Jewish."[20]

One can imagine several reasons why Chaplin would not have been eager to get into a discussion about his family background. His childhood poverty, his junk-dealer relatives, and his mother's reputation as a woman who'd had several lovers were all embarrassments. Hannah was also mentally ill, and insanity was then considered to be a hereditary "taint," which could morally disqualify its carriers from marriage and parenthood.

It is also worth noting that Gypsies have a taboo against revealing themselves to non-Gypsies. Even today many assimilated Romanies in the United States do not acknowledge their heritage, either because this is traditionally just not done or because they fear that their neighbors will shun them as con artists and thieves. The late Yul Brynner was a Romany movie star who sometimes claimed to be Mongolian. A leading man still active today used to talk about his Gypsy roots but no longer does.

While there is no proof that Chaplin was aware of any Gypsy forebears at this stage of his life, during his year with Essanay he told interviewers that his mother was half Irish and half Spanish. Spain was popularly thought of as the land of the Gypsies, so this may have been a roundabout acknowledgment. Certainly the possibility that Chaplin was aware of some Romany blood on his mother's side and had been advised by Syd to keep it secret would explain some of his more puzzling behavior, including his preoccupation with the thought that every dollar he made in pictures would be his last. With hindsight, of course, one may wonder if his public would have cared, but social attitudes were very different in 1916, and Chaplin was a nervous, anxiety-ridden man.

Already, shortly after he signed with Mutual, a correspondent for the *New York Telegraph* had sought out Hannah Chaplin's sister, Kate Mowbray, in London. Mrs. Mowbray obligingly talked about Charlie's early talent for the violin, volunteering that he had inherited his mother's musical ability and was like her in everything but appearance. "Outwardly he is the image of his father," Mowbray declared. (In fact, most people were struck by the *lack* of resemblance between Charlie and Charles Chaplin senior.) The talkative Mowbray, just forty-one years old, was suffering from terminal cancer. She died before some enterprising interviewer had a chance to pry loose the secrets of Hannah's unhappy life.[21]

Chaplin, meanwhile, was stuck with the fanciful stories he had spun for the press. Aside from making Hannah half Spanish, he had told several interviewers and, indeed, close associates that he had been born in a hotel in Fontainebleau, France, where his parents happened to be performing. Strangely, and much to the confusion of his friends as well as reporters, Chaplin was highly suggestible and often seemed to believe his own inventions. Perhaps, since he was far from sure that Charles Chaplin Sr. was his natural father, he had some excuse for giving his imagination free rein.

In the early twenties, confessing his doubts about his paternity to his assistant, Eddie Sutherland, he said: "You see, I think I might have Jewish blood. I notice my characteristics are very Semitic, my gestures are, my thinking is certainly along money lines."[22]

Given this level of reasoning, Chaplin's belief that Syd, the money man of the family, was half Jewish must be regarded as questionable. One suspects that Charlie, having misled certain producers, covered his embarrassment by making his half-brother the designated Jew of the family.[23]

As his fame spread, Chaplin became less certain of his parentage rather than more so. Total strangers approached or wrote to him claiming to have information about his family history—information he was tempted to believe since almost anything was preferable to being the son of a drunkard who'd done his best to avoid supporting him. Some years later, perhaps exaggerating for dramatic effect, Chaplin joked that he'd heard from 671 English Chaplins who swore they were related to him, as well as nine women who claimed to be his mother. The existence of English Jews surnamed Chaplin undoubtedly compounded the confusion.

By far the most exotic story about his parentage was told to him by a sleeping-car porter who approached him on a train during one of his first cross-country trips. The porter claimed to be related to Charlie via John Gwynne Chaplin, a Pennsylvania-born artist of mixed African-American and white ancestry. John G. Chaplin had been a painter of considerable talent, specializing in biblical, mythological, and historical subjects in a conventional, somewhat academic mode. Though light-skinned, even white in appearance, in the United States he was labeled a "race artist"; and around 1850 he moved to Europe, where for a time he had a studio in Düsseldorf, Germany. He later returned to the United States and settled in the vicinity of Youngstown, Ohio. John Chaplin had three daughters and a son; all of them were fair skinned and at least one of the daughters had blue eyes.

According to family tradition, John Chaplin's son, also a painter, returned to Europe during the 1880s. He became involved in a common-law relationship with an Englishwoman, had a child with her, and brought his new family back to Ohio when the child was still an infant. The visit was a disaster—not because of the racial factor, insists one present-day family connection—but because the Ohio Chaplins, a very proper and religious family, knew that the couple were not legally married and were appalled by the woman's coarse, ill-mannered behavior. The couple returned to England, where the relationship soon dissolved. The American Chaplins had no idea what became of the woman and her infant son, but when the English comic Charlie Chaplin began appearing in the movies they believed, quite sincerely, that he was that child.

It would have been an extraordinary coincidence if Hannah Hill Chaplin had met a man who bore the same name as her husband, had a child by him, and even traveled to the United States. Although, as it happens, Charles senior was in the United States in 1891, there is no evidence that Hannah ever left England. Nevertheless Chaplin heard out the porter's story, and was suggestible enough to think, at least for a time, that it might be true.[24]

The implications of the tale were twofold. On the one hand, even a suspicion of "Negro" blood would very likely have ended Charlie's American career. On the other, the story gave him the option of imagining that his biological father was not a hard-drinking music hall singer but a man of talent, culture, and education—persecuted in his own country for reasons beyond his control. This version of his ancestry allowed Charlie to forgive his mother and to believe that he was the product of a romantic love affair, thwarted by social injustice and the hypocrisy of the system.

Chaplin's fascination with this version of his family history did not last, though he seems to have been in sporadic contact with John Chaplin's descendants over the years. Meanwhile, it gave him the basis for his fantasy autobiography, which was incorporated into a number of his more ambitious films, starting with *The Vagabond*, his third Mutual two-reeler—a film so different in tone and subject matter from its predecessors that it seemed to have come out of nowhere.

The Vagabond gives us Edna Purviance in the role of a young woman kidnapped in infancy from her wealthy parents and brought up by a Gypsy chieftain and his wife to slave as their all-purpose "drudge." The Gypsy as child snatcher was one of the earliest motion picture villains, used by the British director Cecil Hepworth in *Rescued by Rover* and by D. W. Griffith in his first directing assignment for Biograph, *The Adventures of Dolly*, released in July 1908. At first glance *The Vagabond* serves up the expected stereotypes. The Gypsy chieftain, played by Eric Campbell, chases a cowering Edna around the yard outside his caravan, threatening her with his bullwhip while his wife (Leo White in a scraggly fright wig) looks ready to catch a ride on the next broomstick out of town. Charlie enters the film as a soulful itinerant musician who plays left-handed violin (as did Chaplin—and, for that matter, some Romany musicians—in real life). Is he also meant to be a Gypsy? Perhaps. Meeting Edna, he serenades her with "Hungarian Goulash," the comedic idea of Gypsy music.

Smitten with Edna, Charlie rescues her from the chieftain's blows and they escape together by stealing his horse-drawn wagon. Edna is dewy eyed with gratitude, and Charlie dares to believe that his dream of love is coming true. After a chaste night under the stars, he plans a romantic picnic. But when Edna goes off to fetch water, she happens upon an artist who has set up his easel in a nearby meadow. He asks Edna to pose for him. She innocently agrees, then invites him back to the wagon to share the meal that Charlie has so lovingly prepared just for her.

Some time later the painter enters his portrait of Edna as *The Eternal Shamrock* in an exhibition. There it is seen by her still-grieving mother, who recognizes her long-lost daughter from a characteristic birthmark, which the artist has obligingly rendered. The mother prevails on the artist to show her where Edna can be found. Together they return to the caravan site in a limousine and whisk Edna off to reclaim her rightful place in society.

Chaplin originally planned to end *The Vagabond* with a comic suicide: In despair at losing Edna, Charlie throws himself into the river. He is rescued by the hatchet-faced Phyllis Allen, but one look at her homely face tells him that gratitude would be a fate worse than death, and he plunges back into the river.[25]

This would hardly have been a more downbeat ending than that of *The Rounders*, which concludes with a pair of stupefied drunks, Charlie and Fatty Arbuckle, laid out in a rapidly sinking rowboat. Still, Chaplin decided that it wouldn't do and substituted a more cheerful resolution. As Edna is driven away from the campsite with her mother and the handsome artist, she looks back through the rear window at the heartbroken Charlie, and in a flash she experiences "the awakening of real love." Ordering the car to turn back, she does not get out to rejoin Charlie, as might be expected in a traditional tale of romantic love, but insists that he join her.

It is difficult to imagine how the scruffy Charlie could fit into Edna's new existence. But then, *The Vagabond* is a fairy tale. Moreover, throughout the story, the Little Fellow behaves not like a man in love but an impetuous child. When the artist appears to spoil his picnic, Charlie drops an egg on his foot and shoos a fly in his direction, like a little boy in a snit, jealous because his mother is paying attention to another male.

In July 1916, the same month *The Vagabond* was released, Syd and Charlie learned that the Bobbs-Merrill publishing company was about to publish a book entitled *Charlie Chaplin's Own Story,* by Rose Wilder Lane, a features writer for the *San Francisco Bulletin* who had interviewed Charlie at the Niles ranch during the early months of his Essanay contract.

Mrs. Lane had transformed her notes into a first-person story, filled with fictionalized dialogue in a fractured Cockney dialect that owed more to Edinburgh than to Lambeth. Among the numerous errors in her manuscript were phonetically spelled names and a few unrecognizable ones, perhaps deliberately changed to avoid libel suits. Nevertheless, it was not Mrs. Lane's errors that upset Syd Chaplin but the things she got right, or nearly right. Apparently Lane had caught Charlie at a moment when he was in the mood to dwell on the miseries of his early life, including the sleazier side of the music halls. She memorably summed up the Casey's Court Circus company as "fifteen ragged, hungry-looking, sallow-faced boys desperately being funny under the direction of a fat greasy-looking manager who smelt strongly of ale." William Jackson came off even worse, as a cruel exploiter of children. The manuscript also contained numerous references to young Charlie's memories of his "father"—a "dark" man who may or may not have been Charles senior—as well as a vague but suggestive reference to Hannah's first breakdown.

Chaplin could be quite bitter about his experiences as a child performer, and these distortions undoubtedly owed more to his flair for self-dramatization than to Mrs. Lane's imagination. Her version of Charlie's life had already appeared as a syndicated newspaper feature without objection from Chaplin, but Bobbs-Merrill's plans to bring it out in book form, advertised as an "as-told-to" autobiography, went too far. Syd appealed to Nathan Burkan, and a few sharp letters from Burkan to the publishers resulted in the book's being withdrawn.[26]

The suppression of *Charlie Chaplin's Own Story* was just one of many campaigns undertaken by Nathan Burkan on Chaplin's behalf. To begin with, on April 9, 1916, three weeks before Chaplin's first Mutual comedy appeared in the movie houses, Essanay had opened *Burlesque on Carmen* at the Broadway Theater in New York City.

Essanay had discarded Chaplin's cut of the film in favor of an expanded four-reel version that made liberal use of Chaplin's "n.g.s"—"no goods," or outtakes—as well as new scenes directed by Leo White, starring Ben Turpin as the comic smuggler Don Remendado.

To compound the insult, George Spoor gave an interview to the *New York Morning Telegraph* in which he took issue with Chaplin's claim that he edited his own pictures. Spoor insisted that Jesse Robbins had edited all Chaplin's Essanay comedies with the exception of *Burlesque on Carmen*, which was Chaplin's "first attempt at cutting" and such a mess that Essanay felt compelled to recut it.[27]

What had really happened was obvious to everyone in the business. Now that he was distributing films through a new company, VLSE, Spoor could release a four-reeler profitably, and padding *Carmen* to four reels was a way to recoup the money he had lost because of Chaplin's low output. Reviewers certainly didn't buy Spoor's argument that the longer version of the film improved on Chaplin's efforts. The *Brooklyn Eagle* headlined its review A MONOTONY OF CHAPLIN, which previously would have been considered an oxymoron. The paying public was less discriminating, however, and *Burlesque on Carmen* broke box-office records in New York and Chicago.

Chaplin's contract with Essanay had been a scant two and half pages long. Still, it clearly spelled out his right of approval over any film he appeared in, and Nathan Burkan asked a federal judge in New York to grant an injunction against *Burlesque on Carmen*. Essanay promptly countersued, arguing that Chaplin had voided his contract when he failed to deliver four of the ten pictures he promised the company in June 1915.

Court papers from these lawsuits offer a glimpse of the acrimony that prevailed during Chaplin's year with Essanay. His insistence on taking full writing and directing credit obviously rankled. Although the claim that Chaplin never edited his own pictures went too far, his claim to have been writer, director, and star of all his pictures was contrary to Essanay's usual practice, and the cause of much bad feeling. In an affidavit Spoor credited Essanay staff writer Anthony J. Kelly with proposing the idea for *Burlesque on Carmen* and writing the scenario.[28]

Oddly enough, the best evidence to support Spoor's assertion comes from Chaplin's autobiography. Describing a visit to the Metropolitan Opera during the time he was negotiating with Mutual, Chaplin tells how his host, diva Geraldine Farrar's agent, Morris Gest, having confused the matinee and evening programs, mistakenly insisted that the opera they were watching was *Carmen*. Chaplin had his doubts, he recalled, but let himself be persuaded, and during an intermission, when he and Gest went backstage to meet one of the performers, the great Enrico Caruso, he embarrassed himself by saying that he was looking forward to hearing the toreador music.

"That's *Carmen*," snapped Caruso. "This is *Rigoletto*."

Doubtless Chaplin and Gest were not the first operagoers to sit through a first act without having a clue as to what they were seeing. But the author of *Burlesque on Carmen* was obviously quite familiar with Bizet's opera as well as the Prosper Mérimée novel on which it was based. If Chaplin had truly written this script just weeks earlier, could he have confused *Carmen* and *Rigoletto*? Chaplin's endearing, self-deprecatory anecdotes were often inadvertently revealing. This habit of "telling on himself" did not fit well with his appetite for litigation and would cause him a great deal of trouble over the years.

In any event Essanay contended that the real cause of Chaplin's unhappiness with the Chicago head office was its refusal to release *Life*, his story of the house burglar's reformation. Essanay executives thought the picture too long and unfocused and wanted it cut on artistic grounds. When the same executives became enthusiastic about the *Carmen* parody—which had not been Chaplin's idea in the first place—and asked him to expand it to feature length, he lost his temper and refused. According to court papers, Chaplin knew when he left California in December 1915 that Leo White was shooting additional footage—an assertion confirmed by the fact that White had since joined the Lone Star company.

On April 22 a federal court in New York denied the Chaplin brothers' request for an injunction. Encouraged by the decision, Essanay released the shortened version of *Life*—retitled *Police*—on May 25. Worse, the court awarded Essanay $125,000 in damages for each of the four films Chaplin owed it at the time of his departure.

On June 10 a federal appeals court refused to overturn the judgment, and Chaplin suddenly found himself owing George Spoor half a million dollars. This was an enormous judgment in 1916 and threatened to eat up most of the earnings from his Mutual contract. On June 11 the *Los Angeles Examiner* reported that Charlie and Syd had quarreled violently—a story the studio "vigorously" denied. Meanwhile Nathan Burkan promised to appeal the award all the way to the Supreme Court.

The dispute with Essanay promised to affect Chaplin's income in other respects too. Movie piracy did not exactly begin with Chaplin, but it certainly fed and grew strong on his success, and now Essanay was standing by, doing nothing to protect Chaplin's interests against imitators and black marketeers.

When Mack Sennett became a producer, just a few years earlier, the motion picture was considered a disposable product. Once the original prints wore out physically, usually after ninety days, the company had no further interest in them. Keystone did not even bother to register its films for copyright. In fact, the law as it then stood recognized a common-law copyright for unpublished plays, and it was far from clear that copyright registration was desirable.

For Keystone investor Charles Baumann, the age of innocence ended on August 16, 1915, when he stopped by the office of an establishment that called itself the Chaplin Film Company on West Forty-fifth Street in Manhattan. Baumann had received a tip that the company, which had no connection with Charlie or Syd, was renting out "dupes"—unauthorized duplicate prints—of *Dough and Dynamite*. He discovered to his horror that the office was well stocked with prints of the most popular Chaplin comedies. Keystone took the company to court and got it shut down.[29]

Essanay, by contrast, did nothing when travesties of *The Champion*, one of its more popular movies, began appearing in theaters. Two enterprising Bronx natives, Jules Potash and Isadore Peskov, had obtained a copy of the film, masked out the background, and overprinted it with footage from Herbert Brenon's undersea fantasy, *Daughter of the Gods*. The result, billed as *Charlie Chaplin in a Son of the Gods*, was a crude pastiche in which the Tramp visits King Neptune's court and cavorts with a bevy of mermaids. The picture's financial backer, George Maienthau, boldly booked this mess into the Crystal Palace on Fourteenth Street in New York City, a movie house that showed Chaplin comedies almost continuously and was a mecca for his dedicated fans. Another Potash and Peskov epic, *Charlie in the Harem*, soon followed. The advertising poster for this number featured Charlie surrounded by harem girls who were, by 1915 standards, half naked.

Since Chaplin did not own the copyright to *The Champion*, it was far from clear that he could do anything to stop the piracy. Nathan Burkan, however, raised the novel argument that Chaplin had ownership rights to the character he played on the screen, independent of the copyright to any particular movie. The judge who heard the Maienthau case agreed at first, then revised his decision to cover only the advertising material and lobby posters. Maienthau could distribute the pastiche films—he just couldn't advertise them as Charlie Chaplin comedies.

This limited decision actually encouraged other pirates. The brothers Joseph and Jacob Seiden had already gone into business in Chicago with a "Chaplin" pastiche called *The Fall of the Rummy-Nuffs*—a pun on *The Fall of the Romanovs*. Seeing a loophole in the law, they included a Chaplin imitator in their next effort, the aptly named *The Dishonor System*, and billed him as Charlie Chaplinski. Unforunately for the Seidens, theater owners had a way of dropping the final "ski" from their marquees. Burkan took them to court and won.

But even as Burkan piled up legal precedents in Chaplin's favor, fake Charlie comedies kept turning up. As late as October 1917 *Charlie in the Trenches*, another Potash and Peskov epic, was shown at the Crystal Palace. A month later, *The Fall of the Rummy Nuffs*, already under federal injunction, was distributed to theaters in Chicago followed by *The Mirth of a Nation: A Chaplin Review*. And a few months later a raid on a warehouse in Tennessee turned up multiple copies of all the most notorious fakes as well as a few new ones—*Charlie's Nightmare* and *Charlie's Picnic*.

No doubt the Chaplins and Burkan were doing the industry a service by energetically pursuing the likes of Potash, Peskov, and the Seidens. Still, the argument that Charlie owned the Tramp character provoked mixed feelings. If stealing material was a crime, then few comics could be considered innocent, including Chaplin; and the Tramp was so popular that almost everyone was imitating him to a certain extent. By 1917 the Russian-born Billy West, supported by Mack Swain lookalike Oliver "Babe" Hardy, was turning out comedy shorts that bore an uncanny resemblance to Chaplin Keystones. Other imitators ranged from Billy Ritchie, who claimed Charlie had stolen the Tramp from him, to Harold Lloyd, whose Lonesome Luke character was obviously derivative.

Chaplin pursued only a few of the most blatant imitators, though it's far from clear that performers like Charles Amador, who at times billed himself as "Charlie Aplin," were crossing the line between parody and theft. On the whole Chaplin's reputation for litigiousness probably won him more enemies than friends. Meanwhile, in his own mind—and to some degree in fact—he was the beleaguered victim of people who were trying to cash in on his work. One suspects that Chaplin occasionally tried to take revenge on his imitators by stealing from them. A barbershop scene in Billy West's *His Day Out* (1917) appears to have been an inspiration for his 1919 film *Sunnyside*.

The Court of Appeals ruling in favor of George Spoor was far from being Chaplin's only problem during the summer of 1916. A group of English theater operators had announced a boycott of Chaplin, placing signs in their lobbies proclaiming: NO CHARLIE CHAPLIN FILMS HERE.[30] The boycott was inspired by the revelation that his contract contained a clause prohibiting him from leaving the United States. Britain had begun drafting men into the armed forces, and Mutual obviously wanted to protect its investment.

According to Terry Ramsaye, the flap was instigated by a rival distributing company. "An uproar was raised, intended to hold Chaplin up as a slacker and seeking to cast shame on him and the Mutual Film Corporation because he was not offered up as cannon fodder."[31] No doubt this was true, although families who had shipped their sons and husbands off to be slaughtered in the trenches might be forgiven for wondering about Chaplin's motives in agreeing to the clause. Did he plan to blame Mutual for his decision not to return home and submit to the draft? Hundreds of letters from England containing white feathers, the symbol of cowardice, began arriving at the Lone Star studio.

Certainly Chaplin needed no encouragement to stay as far as possible from the war. As he later told Milton Gross, a friend, his instant reaction on reading newspaper accounts of the slaughter was, "Not for me! Not for me! Not for me! I'd have gone to jail rather than have gone into it! I'd have gnawed off my fist rather than get into that sort of thing."[32]

Chaplin's aversion to death and dismemberment hardly required political justification, but he was absorbing one nonetheless from his friend and part-time secretary, Rob Wagner. A stocky, barrel-chested man, Robert Leicester Wagner liked to present himself as an ordinary working stiff who more or less blundered into a talent for art and writing. In a 1918 letter to socialist novelist and lecturer Upton Sinclair, Wagner explained that he had formerly worked on a Ford assembly line and that his "last job was handing out leaflets." In fact Wagner had studied engineering at the University of Michigan, and after graduating with the class of 1895, he became a newspaper artist in New York. During the Spanish-American War he saw one day's combat at San Juan Hill, enough to convert him to pacifism. In 1901 he went to London with his best friend, the writer Rupert Hughes, became an illustrator for the *Encyclopædia Britannica*, and was converted to socialism.

After a few years abroad Wagner returned to his hometown of Detroit. Married to his high school sweetheart and with two sons to support, he did work for a time at a Ford tractor plant. In 1906, however, his wife died in childbirth and he brought his sons to Los Angeles, where the arrival of the first "movies" soon created opportunities for freelance journalists. He sold his first article to the *Saturday Evening Post* in 1910 and could justly claim to be the first reporter on the West Coast to cover the film industry.[33]

Wagner also worked for a time as a writer on the Keystone comedies but lost his job because Mack Sennett didn't buy his argument that he got his best ideas while napping for two hours during the afternoon. Wagner wasn't lazy; it was just that he was perpetually juggling two or three jobs, including coaching high school wrestling, serving as a part-time organizer for the Socialist Party, writing political articles, and publishing his own socialist newsletter.

Wagner became friendly with Charlie sometime in 1915, perhaps because they both patronized Harlow's Cafe on Third and Spring Streets in downtown LA, and by the following year he was working for him part-time, helping him with his correspondence. Just as Constance Collier improved Charlie's diction and manners, so Wagner became his political mentor. He gave Chaplin a copy of Upton Sinclair's *The Jungle*, an exposé of the meat-packing industry, a book that made a deep impression on Chaplin.

As an antiwar socialist, Wagner saw the Great War as the death throes of the old imperialist powers. His sympathies, insofar as he had any, lay with Germany, where a well-organized Social-Democratic Party had appeared to be on its way to taking power before the war. He was most enthusiastic, however, about the rise of revolutionary sentiment in Russia.

Wagner talked like a radical, but he usually took care to keep his politics and his income-producing activities separate. Charlie, however, lacked this self-protective instinct. As early as December 1916, Mabel Condon, a writer for *Picture Play Magazine*, asked him, "Suppose you were going to take a long vacation—then what?"

"Russia," was his unexpected reply. "The thought of it fascinates me."[34]

Strike-ridden Russia was not a popular vacation destination in 1916, and Chaplin's answer may have raised a few eyebrows among those who had wondered about the message of the "Peace Patrol March." However, his lack of interest in putting on a British uniform did not hurt him with his American fans. The European war was unpopular, and his position was widely interpreted as a sign that his allegiance was now to the United States.

Even in Britain feelings were mixed. Charlie Chaplin comedies were being shown in army camps and were praised for their value in keeping up morale. However, when a fad for Charlie Chaplin mustaches began to spread among enlisted men, the symbolism was worrisome enough to cause some commanders to ban them. On the home front Charlie's reputation as a slacker became part of wartime folklore, incorporated in children's jump-rope rhymes and at least one popular song, sung to the tune "Red Wing":

Oh, the moon shines bright on Charlie Chaplin,
His boots are crackin'
For want of blackin'
And his little baggy trousers they need mendin'
Before we send him
To the Dardanelles.

Some years later Chaplin told his friend Alistair Cooke that the first time he heard the song he suffered an attack of paranoia. "I went home and read about the Dardanelles after that, and for a time I was certain they were out to get me." (It isn't clear who "they" were—presumably the British.)[35]

Mutual had so far been an understanding employer even though it was obvious that Chaplin would never fulfill his obligation to produce twelve two-reelers by the following February. Since Chaplin's ten thousand dollars a week was predicated on this output, his slow pace of work was a matter of some concern. Nonetheless Mutual, earning handsome profits from Chaplin's films, was prepared to be flexible.

By late October, however, Charlie's increasingly erratic work habits had begun to worry his producers. One day, while cutting *Behind the Screen*, he had an idea for a comedy set in a slum neighborhood. Excitedly he summoned set designer Danny Hall and described a street scene reminiscent of the Methley Street neighborhood, where he and Hannah had lived in a barren room around the corner from a slaughterhouse. The set was even more elaborate than the one he had ordered for *The Floorwalker*, but Chaplin insisted that he needed it immediately. In fact, it had to be ready the next day.

Rising to the challenge, Hall had rounded up some two hundred day laborers who worked around the clock to get the job done—if not literally overnight, certainly in record time. When the set was ready Chaplin appeared at the studio, pronounced it "great!" and then didn't mention it again. He had decided to make *The Rink* instead, and spent the next three weeks rehearsing his cast on roller skates.

The cost of this "big and very pretentious" street scene, as Terry

Ramsaye called it, came to ten thousand dollars, much of which went for overtime. Mutual's head office in New York naturally wondered when they would see it in a movie, and they besieged Henry Caulfield, Lone Star's studio manager, with telegrams asking for progress reports. He cabled back: "Rain. No light. Set waiting."

"If the rain reports from Los Angeles were correct, submarines could dock in Hollywood," Terry Ramsaye groused.[36] Actually Los Angeles *was* slogging through a period of unusually heavy rain, making it impossible to use the outdoor shooting stage, but this was only part of the problem. In making *The Rink* Chaplin shot some thirty thousand feet of film, only a little over seventeen hundred of which he would eventually use. He then went to work on the street scene set, but for the first time since the previous May, Mutual missed a release date and was forced to issue an apology to exhibitors.

In the event *Easy Street* was only a week late, and well worth the wait. A satire on the evangelical missions Chaplin remembered from his youth, it begins with Charlie, who has just stolen a mission poor box, experiencing a religious conversion. Setting out to right the wrongs of his little corner of the London slums, he feeds hungry children, joins the police force, and does battle with a bully twice his size (Eric Campbell). *Easy Street* was Chaplin's most caustic film so far. The neighborhood poor, down to the smallest urchin, are an unappealing lot. The beautiful missionary (Edna) inhabits a mental la-la land, and a bomb-wielding anarchist (Henry Bergman) is similarly irrelevant. Even God, working his will through Charlie, is not up to the task of reforming this moral cul-de-sac. However, when Charlie accidentally sits on a drug addict's hypodermic, the cocaine cocktail works miracles.

After wrapping up *Easy Street*, Chaplin began *The Cure*, a satire on health spas. He started, as usual, with no definite plot in mind, preferring to "write" his story with the camera—improvising take after take until the action felt right to him. Originally he planned to play a bellhop at the spa, then a white-jacketed attendant. He didn't settle on the role of a foppish drunk, arriving at the spa for a "water cure," until take eighty-four. The change required jettisoning everything he had shot so far, including an intricately choreographed scene in which Charlie did a turn directing wheelchair traffic in the hotel lobby.

Outtakes from *The Cure* make up a segment of Kevin Brownlow and David Gill's fascinating documentary, *Unknown Chaplin*. From one point of view they are a study in artistic perfectionism; from another, evidence of a director who just can't make up his mind. Chaplin took four months to complete *The Cure*. Since many fans of slapstick comedy consider it to be one of Chaplin's best films, and a classic of the genre, it would be difficult to say with hindsight that this was too long a time. From Mutual's point of view, however, it *was* too long.

At any rate there was more to Chaplin's inability to finish films on time than artistic perfectionism. His moodiness and irritability were beginning to take a toll on the other studio employees. Carlyle T. Robinson, who joined Lone Star as a publicity agent during this period, soon discovered that Chaplin was a man of many whims. On a given day it was hard to know whether to address him familiarly as Charlie or keep out of his way altogether. The staff competed to stay in his good graces. The most successful at this game was Henry Bergman, whose tendency to play the yes-man made him unpopular with Chaplin's other aides. Chaplin soon rewarded Bergman's loyalty by setting him up in the restaurant business. "Henry's" grew from its origins as a coffee shop to become one of the most popular lunch spots in Hollywood.

Embarking on his eleventh film, Chaplin planned a romance set on the Left Bank in Paris, another variant on the premise of the innocent girl who falls in love with a painter. Shooting the opening café scene took more than a week, with Edna condemned to eat plate after plate of beans while Chaplin twice replaced the actor cast as the waiter. Then he abruptly decided to change to a story in which Charlie and Edna are immigrants who meet on shipboard en route to America. The café scene was still used, but it was moved to the end of the film.

On orders from Chaplin, Danny Hall rented a tramp steamer registered out of San Pedro harbor at thirteen hundred dollars a day. For ten days Chaplin didn't get around to using the boat at all. On the eleventh everyone went aboard, and the steamer was pulled out of the harbor by a team of tugboats. When they were finally at sea, Chaplin turned to Hall and said, "We'll start with the fish."

"What fish?" wondered Hall.

"You know. The fish gag."

Chaplin had planned a gag in which he is seen from behind, hanging over the rail apparently in the throes of seasickness. Suddenly he turns around, triumphant, with a freshly caught fish on the end of his line. Unfortunately he had neglected to mention his idea to the crew. Hall ordered an assistant to take a launch and row back to San Pedro for a supply of mackerel. Meanwhile the rest of the crew improvised lines and started fishing.[37]

Once again the results justified the confusion. *The Immigrant* was another gem, romantic and wistful, in sharp contrast to *The Cure*, which stressed the sadistic side of slapstick humor. The café scene in particular is an epic in miniature, recording Charlie's attempts to hold on to a coin that is not only his last hope for a good meal but for retaining a shred of dignity in the eyes of the woman he loves. The meanderings of the coin—found, lost, found again by a hobo, dropped and deftly recovered by Charlie just in time to pay his check, and finally tested by the waiter and pronounced counterfeit—chart the ups and downs of a poor man's hopes.

In making this intimately scaled romance, a little more than twenty-four minutes long, Chaplin shot some ninety thousand feet of film—worth "about thirty dollars a reel to the buyer and nothing at all to Mr. Chaplin," as Terry Ramsaye put it. This was approximately the same amount of film stock used by D. W. Griffith in making *Birth of a Nation*, released in twelve reels.

While Mutual seethed over Chaplin's mushrooming budgets and lateness, Syd worried about the depiction of Charlie and Edna's arrival in the United States. As the immigrants' ship passes the Statue of Liberty, a pair of unctuous customs officials burst onto the deck and herd them behind a rope. Charlie, poked and prodded like a piece of livestock, is sent off into the New World with a kick in the behind from the representative of the U.S. government.

As it happened, Syd had been negotiating to get a visa for Hannah Chaplin, and just six months earlier, the Bureau of Immigration (later the Immigration and Naturalization Service) had obligingly bent the rules against admitting mentally incompetent persons and granted her a special one-year permit. Unfortunately, because of the wartime disruption of transatlantic travel and red tape in London Hannah was unable to use the permit. Syd expected to ask for a renewal later on, which made Charlie's unflattering depiction of the treatment of immigrants somewhat ill timed. Over Syd's objections, however, the scene stayed in the picture, with no repercussions from either the officials or the American public, which was not in the habit of waxing sentimental over bureaucrats.

But Chaplin soon had a far more serious clash with the government and public opinion. By the spring of 1917 U-boat attacks on American shipping, followed by the revelation that Germany had proposed an anti-American alliance to Mexico, had prompted Woodrow Wilson, recently elected on a peace platform, to ask Congress for a declaration of war. Many Americans still had qualms about entering a bloody conflict whose causes they did not understand, but these doubts only increased the pressure on prominent individuals to demonstrate their patriotism by supporting the president's decision.

The country's entry into war put Charlie in a double bind, subject to the draft in both Britain and the United States. On April 6, the day the war resolution passed the House of Representatives, the Friars Club, a New York–based theatrical lodge, became one of the first fraternal organizations to voice its support, urging draft-age members to volunteer. According to *Variety*: "The general tenor of the talk of those who are actors was to the effect that the men on this side of the world would show up the "slackers" of the other countries and immediately enlist."[38]

Meanwhile Britain, which had previously made no attempt to extend the draft to subjects living in the United States, opened a recruitment mission in New York City. So far at least, the mission was not issuing official draft notices. Rather, its strategy was to target stars of vaudeville, the stage, and the movies, pressuring them to set an example by joining up. Those who failed to cooperate, reported *Variety*, were being "marked for special mention in the [newspaper] pages at home." The mission, *Variety* went on, was swamped with inquiries, but mostly from men who were looking for a "soft snap" in a noncombat unit.[39]

The notion that theater people, normally one of the least military-minded segments of the population, should lead the march to the recruiting offices was something new. No doubt it was unrealistic and even unfair, but for better or worse it was a product of the same trends that made it possible for a music hall comic like Charlie Chaplin to become a national idol, and one of the highest-paid men in the country.

On June 5, 1917, Lone Star issued a statement saying that Chaplin had registered for the U.S. draft in Los Angeles and failed the physical. At five feet four inches tall and 129 pounds, he had been ruled undersize. The circumstances of this visit to the recruiting office were never made clear, however, and the report was greeted with well-deserved derision. Chaplin had claimed to be five six in the past and, on paper at least, he would soon regain the two inches he had lost when he stepped inside the induction center. Moreover, while five four was officially the lower height limit, the *average* height of World War I draftees was five seven, and the *average* weight was 141 pounds. No doubt there were valid reasons why a conscientious physician could have declared Chaplin unfit for service, including nervous instability and a history of asthma, but the explanation that he was too small to wear an American uniform smacked of evasion. Julian Johnson of *Photoplay* would soon take sarcastic note of the rumor that Chaplin "has hurled himself ineffectually, again and again, upon the bayonets of the medical examiners."[40]

In retrospect one can only agree with Chaplin's biographer and staunch admirer Theodore Huff, who wrote: "Had [Chaplin] done military service an Allied army would have gained an indifferent soldier but lost a valuable morale booster."[41] If anything this understates the case. A man who was too nervous to drive did not belong on the front lines with a rifle in his hands. However, by 1917—as opposed to earlier in the war—this was hardly the issue. Editorials in the *Toledo Blade*, the *New York Telegraph*, and other papers were already citing Chaplin as an example of a public figure whose importance in building morale made him too valuable to waste in combat. Moreover, Chaplin's friend Doug Fairbanks, who wanted to serve even though he was three years too old for the draft, had been refused induction. Fairbanks received a personal rebuff from Secretary of the Treasury William G. McAdoo, who informed him that it was his patriotic duty to remain stateside, selling Liberty Bonds.

The real issue, at least in Hollywood, where Chaplin's antiwar views were not unknown, was whether he planned to support the war effort. Since the United States had entered the war, Chaplin had been telling acquaintances around town that rather than serve in uniform he was thinking of throwing over his career and departing with his savings for South America. In an extraordinary article headlined CHAPLIN IN WRONG, *Variety* reported that he had refused a demand from the British War Office (no doubt via the recruitment mission) that he return to England. He was also in trouble with American authorities because he had reportedly failed to file an income tax statement for 1917. More recently, *Variety* continued, Chaplin had been heard to say that he was "indifferent to appearing before the cameras in the future" and boasted of transferring his savings into gold certificates in case he decided to emigrate. In response the Secret Service was investigating and had obtained permission to examine his safe deposit boxes.[42]

While Hollywood digested the revelations, Chaplin literally took to the hills. On location in Las Flores Canyon in the Santa Monica Mountains, he was filming *The Escaped Prisoner*, eventually released as *The Adventurer*, in which he played an escaped convict who passes himself off as a millionaire yachtsman.

Reporter James Hilbert, who sought Chaplin out in the mountains in mid-July, found him wandering the canyon in his striped prisoner costume, disconsolate over his inability to find decent English breakfast tea and gulping down quantities of the nearest facsimile, which he brewed himself, using "three handfuls per cup." Hilbert ascribed Chaplin's jumpiness to the date, which happened to be Friday the thirteenth. Chaplin insisted he was not superstitious, but he was certainly having difficulty concentrating. When he happened to glimpse a good-size rattlesnake sunning itself on the road, he was so unnerved that he canceled shooting for the rest of the day.[43]

The plot of *The Adventurer* was almost an allegory of Chaplin's situation. The recent passage of the Espionage Act had transformed other antiwar socialists into lawbreakers, subjecting them to arrest and (in the case of aliens) deportation. Meanwhile Chaplin was hiding out among the rich, protected by influential friends. Syd had gone off to New York to consult with Mutual executives and Nathan

Burkan, while Rob Wagner had joined the studio payroll and was doing his best to stanch the bad publicity arising from the draft story. The most helpful of all was Doug Fairbanks, who happened to be a personal friend of Treasury Secretary McAdoo and his much younger wife—who was also President Wilson's daughter. Fairbanks had agreed to become a high-profile Liberty Bond salesman, and doubtless he was instrumental in persuading Charlie to bend his principles and join in the effort. By the end of the summer Chaplin had purchased a large quantity of war bonds. He continued to steer clear of parades and other overtly military events, but he and Edna appeared at war-related charity functions.

The British embassy in Washington, pointing to Chaplin's considerable investment in war bonds, even issued a statement denying that he was a "slacker." And in early 1918 Chaplin wrote to a British correspondent, saying:

I only wish I could join the English army and fight for my mother country. But I have received so many letters from soldiers at the front, as well as civilians, asking me to continue making pictures that I have come to the conclusion that my work lies here in Los Angeles. At the same time, if any country thinks it needs me in the trenches more than the soldiers need my pictures, I am ready to go.[44]

6

"Camouflage"

One steaming hot evening in July 1917, Charlie was in his room at the Los Angeles Athletic Club, dressed in nothing but a towel and playing music from *Tales of Hoffmann* on his violin, when Syd burst in to announce that he had just negotiated a contract with the First National Film Corporation worth $1,250,000.

"I suppose that's wonderful," Charlie said languidly—a response that he acknowledges in his autobiography involved the "tinge of a pose."[1]

In fact, if Chaplin had not been avidly following the progress of Syd's negotiations, he was the only one in Hollywood who wasn't. Despite frustration over Chaplin's disregard for schedules and budgets, Mutual was eager to re-sign him. The sale of the UK rights to Chaplin's comedies alone had recouped the cost of his salary. Mutual was even prepared to pay off George Spoor, relieving Chaplin of having to worry about the half-million-dollar judgment hanging over his head.

Jesse Lasky and the newly formed First National Film Corporation were also involved in the bidding war for Chaplin's services. Formed just three months earlier by Los Angeles businessman T. L. Talley to service independent theater owners, who were rapidly losing ground to chains owned by Loew's and Paramount, First National badly needed credibility, and it broke with tradition by offering a deal that would make Chaplin an independent contractor. In addition to a signing bonus of $75,000, he would receive

$125,000 for each of eight two-reelers, to be completed within eighteen months. Chaplin would finance his own pictures out of these payments and split the profits from distribution on a fifty-fifty basis. He would retain the copyrights to his own work, and after five years the worldwide distribution rights would revert to him. In the short run the money First National was offering was somewhat less than he would have gotten from Mutual, and he would also be left owing George Spoor $500,000 if his appeal failed in the courts. But the tax advantages were substantial. Best of all, he would no longer have to answer to carping executives from New York, and over the years—assuming a continuing demand for his pictures, a big if in those days—he stood to profit handsomely.

Announcing the deal to the press, Talley hailed it as a triumph of "quality over quantity." First National had no intention of pushing Chaplin to churn out a picture every three weeks, he said. The company was prepared to wait two or three times that long in order to get pictures that were "perfect."

There was only one small hitch. First National, like Mutual, wanted two-reel comedies, and Chaplin had no desire to make more two-reelers for any amount of money. Syd, who knew this, tried to get an escalator clause written into the contract that would raise Chaplin's compensation if he delivered a movie three or more reels long. But the most he could wrest from Talley was a symbolic $15,000-per-reel bonus.

No doubt it seemed very unfair to Chaplin that despite all his achievements, businessmen who had never been before a camera in their lives were still trying to tell him what kind of movies to make. Nevertheless, the economic reality was that First National needed a steady supply of short films to keep exhibitors happy. Chaplin therefore signed his new contract with his fingers crossed, hoping that the company could be induced to change its position.

The first order of business was to build himself a studio. Chaplin purchased an orange grove on the south side of Sunset Boulevard, between La Brea and Fairmont Avenues, for $34,000, and while waiting for the land to be cleared, he and Edna sailed for Hawaii on the *Matsonia*, accompanied by Rob Wagner. The idea, Wagner later wrote, was for Charlie and Edna to travel incognito and stay in Honolulu about three and a half weeks. Instead they were recognized "in about three and a half minutes," and rumors flew that they were planning to be married. Chaplin was tracked down on Waikiki Beach by a reporter for *Motion Picture Magazine*, and when asked for his sentiments on the wedded state he commented enigmatically: "Don't be a heap of dust in a windy corner."[2]

In fact he and Edna had broken up earlier in the year, and while they had reconciled for the Hawaiian trip, their affair was essentially over. Chaplin often talked of wanting to marry someday and have a family, just as he talked about retiring from the movies. For the present, however, marriage was the last thing he wanted, and Edna's total devotion no doubt became a burden at times. "I was uncertain of her and for that matter uncertain of myself," he recalled many years later.[3]

Personal insecurities aside, one can easily see why Chaplin felt no temptation to marry. No longer a backwater village, Hollywood was rapidly becoming a mecca for glamorous stage personalities, and Charlie Chaplin—young, single, rich and enormously popular— was in great demand socially and having a wonderful time. At a Fourth of July gala thrown by Blanche Ring Winninger, who introduced the song "In the Good Old Summertime," the revelers, in addition to Charlie and Edna, included Julian Eltinge; diva Geraldine Farrar; Jesse Lasky; Sam Goldwyn; actor Wallace Reid; D. W. Griffith and his wife, Linda Arvidson; and Winninger's good-looking brother-in-law, actor Tommy Meighan. Arvidson, perhaps the earliest chronicler of inane Hollywood conversation, was standing on the terrace taking in the commanding view of the lights of Los Angeles when she heard a fellow guest remark: "This reminds one of a diamond bar pin." A little later Charlie wandered out on to the lawn, where he improvised a version of Mendelssohn's "Spring Song," while Morris Gest did an interpretive dance with a borrowed lady's scarf.[4]

At such times Edna was all but forgotten, and when she felt she had been neglected long enough she would sometimes stage a fainting scene and allow herself to be helped to a couch in a quiet corner, where Charlie rushed to her side. There came an evening in early 1917 when Edna fainted at the home of Fanny Ward, an actress described by screenwriter Francis Marion as filmdom's "first exponent of the plastic surgeon's art," but instead of asking for

Charlie, she allowed herself to be consoled by Tommy Meighan.[5] Too proud to admit that he minded—and perhaps unconsciously he didn't—Chaplin greeted Edna curtly the next morning at the studio, informing her that she and Tommy had his blessing. Edna's flirtation with Meighan did not last long. Undoubtedly it was a ploy to nudge Charlie into declaring his intentions. But Chaplin was phenomenally sensitive to rejection and, one suspects, more than a little relieved to be off the hook. Only years later would he realize that his blessing to pursue other men was the last thing Edna wanted.[6]

His relations with Edna strained, Chaplin found little relaxation in Hawaii. He hated the beach, and his first encounter with the game of golf was not promising. He was all too happy to get back to Hollywood in mid-October, and now that he was about to be a studio owner, he was eager to prove he could be a socially responsible businessman. Mindful of the complaints of Sennett's neighbors in Edendale, he issued a statement reassuring residents in the vicinity of La Brea Avenue that his new facility would have "no factory appearance in any way." The studio's open stage and working areas were to be camouflaged behind a row of mock-Tudor bungalows housing offices and his dressing room. A large frame house known as the "mansion," which had been the home of the orange grove's owner, was left standing. Chaplin also ordered the construction of a tennis court and a swimming pool for his employees, though—as he conceded to reporter Walter Vogdes of the *New York Tribune*—"Probably, they'd rather have a saloon."

Syd and Rollie Totheroh had set up a time-lapse camera to document the construction in Charlie's absence. On his return they all continued shooting a lighthearted in-house documentary, *How to Make Movies*. They shot footage of Tom Harrington ceremoniously removing Charlie's battered Tramp's shoes from their place of honor in the studio vault, and of actors from the company, ranging in size from the six-foot-four Eric Campbell to the diminutive Loyal Underwood, about four ten, frolicking in the pool. In the years to come Chaplin would add to the record by filming many distinguished visitors, from the resolutely wooden Winston Churchill to Lord and Lady Mountbatten, who were such enthusiastic amateur actors that they improvised a minidrama about murder and mayhem on the lawn of an English country house.

Adding to the family feeling at the studio, Alf Reeves, the former manager of Karno's American touring company, had arrived in California and would soon take over the job of studio manager. Meticulous and always impeccably groomed, Reeves was a cheerful man given to signing his correspondence with tag lines like "Yours for light wines and beers." He could hold his own with Charlie, and at times the offices rang with their arguments:

"You're a bloody slut!"

"Well, you're a bigger bloody slut!"

None of this was serious, however. Reeves and his wife, Amy, were delighted to be released from the grind of the music hall circuit and resettled in a neat Santa Monica bungalow, and their loyalty to Charlie was unshakable.

All in all it was happy period in Chaplin's life. Still, he remained a man of quicksilver moods. When Walter Vogdes met him for the first time in December at Rob Wagner's house, Chaplin impressed him as charming and gregarious. Having recently seen a popular mystery play, *The Thirteenth Chair*, he had figured out "whodunit" during the first act, and he made up for revealing the ending by reenacting all the key scenes, with hilarious asides. A few days later, at the studio, Vogdes found Charlie moping in his dressing room. "What I need, you know," confessed a melancholy Charlie, "is someone to keep me from feeling pathetic about myself. Someone to say, 'Here, you poor little devil, what business have you feeling sorry for yourself, you poor, lonely child with no one to love you and only about $5,000,000 between you and starvation.'"[7]

Two months later, in an overly euphoric frame of mind, Charlie decided to entertain a group of photographers by climbing the scaffolding over the outdoor shooting stage. Forty feet above the ground he demonstrated the Tramp's splay-footed walk and showed off his flexibility by doing high kicks until he lost his balance and very nearly fell. Syd wrote the New York office of First National that he had been so frightened that "my heart almost quit work."

Although First National was doubtless looking for a big laugh-getter, pathos predominated in *A Dog's Life,* the first film shot at the new studio. As Chaplin recalled it, this was not necessarily a conscious decision. At a certain point the Little Fellow had begun to take on a life of his own: "Sentiment was beginning to percolate through the character. This became a problem because he was bound by the limits of slapstick."[8] The more sympathetic—and pathetic—the Little Fellow became, the harder it was to think up appropriate story lines.

Filmed on the *Easy Street* set, which had been reconstructed at the new studio, *A Dog's Life* featured Charlie as a homeless man, first seen sleeping in a vacant lot, who finds a wallet dropped by a pair of thieves.

Its best joke, borrowed from a routine Syd had done in one of his Gussle comedies at Keystone, involved Charlie's attempt to smuggle his pet dog into a seedy dive called the Green Dragon by stuffing the animal into his baggy pants. The dog's wagging tail, protruding through a hole in the seat of the trousers, gives away his secret.

A number of Charlie's friends and employees played extras in the Green Dragon café scene. Rob Wagner was a patron who makes a pass at Edna; Syd's wife, Minnie, was one of the dancing patrons; Alf Reeves appeared drinking at the bar. The role of the bartender was taken by Granville Redmond, a deaf-mute painter friend of Charlie's who had set up his easel in the studio prop room. Directing so many amateurs, not to mention a canine costar, presented difficulties, and *A Dog's Life* fell a little behind in its ten-week production schedule. Chaplin worked around the clock to get the film edited and ready to ship so that he could leave for the East Coast to kick off the Third Liberty Bond drive with Doug Fairbanks and Mary Pickford.

As part of a public relations effort organized by Rob Wagner, Chaplin had already donated ten thousand boxes of candy for soldiers' parcels and autographed three thousand photos for a Red Cross auction. Still, he was worried that the public had not forgotten the flap over his draft physical. At the drive's kick-off rally in Washington, he was so keyed up that he slid off the stage, pulling Marie Dressler with him. They landed in the lap of Assistant Secretary of the Navy Franklin Delano Roosevelt. In New York City on April 8, a noontime rally on Wall Street drew a crowd in excess of twenty thousand. Speaking through a megaphone, Chaplin started off a bit awkwardly. "Now listen," he shouted. "I have never made a speech before in my life, but I believe I can make one now. You people out there—I want you to forget all about percentages in this third Liberty Loan. Human life is at stake and no one ought to worry about the rate of interest the bonds are going to bring. . . . This very minute the Germans occupy a position of advantage, and we have got to get the dollars. It ought to go over so that we can drive that old devil, the Kaiser, out of France."[9] His words could scarcely be heard over the din of the crowd. Doug Fairbanks obligingly hoisted him onto his shoulders so that everyone could at least have a good look.

After New York the stars split up. Chaplin, escorted by Rob Wagner, had been asked to make a whistle-stop tour of the southern states. In New Orleans local politicians refused to appear on the same platform with a mere slapstick comedian, but an estimated forty thousand people turned out to see Chaplin, and they bought bonds. Everywhere the public was so avid to get close to him that Rob Wagner admitted to feeling a bit resentful over being physically shoved aside by autograph seekers and reporters. "But what was I? I was ten thousand persons fewer than a stewed prune. . . . Simply litter in the path of greatness." At last he met an attractive young woman who told him that she had read his work in the *Saturday Evening Post* and wanted to talk to him. He was flattered, but the first question she asked was, "Tell me, Mr. Wagner, what is Charlie Chaplin really like?"

After completing half of his three-week itinerary, Chaplin began canceling appearances, and he eventually cut the tour short and returned to New York. Rob Wagner attributed the cancellations to "exhaustion." Some newspaper accounts described the problem as stage fright.

Nevertheless, at the tour's final event, an outdoor rally in City Hall Park, Chaplin seemed much more at ease. "It means nothing to say you've bought a $100,000 bond at 4½ per cent . . ." he began, only to be interrupted by laughter and a heckler who shouted, "If you've got the $100,000!" Soon, however, he hit his stride, offering to kiss the first girl who bought a bond. "I'll go further and kiss the first married woman who buys a $100 bond," he added to general applause and encouragement. "I'll *marry* the first girl who takes a $1,000 bond. Isn't that fair?"[10]

Chaplin's personal views hadn't changed—he still loathed the "ogre of militarism" and believed that war put people in a frame of mind to accept authoritarian rule. One can only wonder if his lack of faith in what he was doing had something to do with the cancellation of almost half the tour, in cities where his nonappearance was unlikely to attract national publicity. Nonethless he had sold millions in war bonds and purchased some $350,000 worth himself. Public opinion and Secretary McAdoo were more than satisfied.

On the return trip to LA Chaplin decided to make a movie about the war. His working titles were usually revealing, and this film was provisionally called "Camouflage"—a term that also applied to his Liberty Bond activities, which had effectively disguised his antiwar, antinationalist convictions. Originally he planned to begin the story with the Little Fellow as a henpecked husband for whom a summons from the draft board is almost a welcome relief. There followed the Little Fellow's draft board physical, about which there is (literally) something shady—the scene was photographed through a smoked glass door so that only the silhouettes of Charlie and the punnily named Dr. Francis Maud are visible. Dr. Maud probes Charlie's insides with a soup ladle, a screwdriver and other unsuitable instruments.

Eventually Chaplin decided to drop this section of the film along with a concluding segment in which Charlie, who has captured the kaiser, is feted as a hero. He had enough material for a five-reel opus but was not prepared to face the inevitable battle with First National. *Shoulder Arms,* as the comedy was eventually called, was finished as a three-reeler, concentrating on the Little Fellow's exploits on the battlefield, where he was a reluctant hero—when the order comes to go over the top he politely steps aside, motioning the rest of his platoon to go ahead of him with an "after you" gesture that seems perfectly sensible under the circumstances.

One episode in the film called for the bunker where Charlie and three members of his platoon are sleeping to be flooded by heavy rains. Charlie and another private (played by Syd) have been assigned to the lower bunks. They do their best to get some sleep even as the waters rise around them.

The flood scene was being filmed in the studio swimming pool, and one morning the crew arrived to find that a frog had made itself at home on the set. Rollie Totheroh got a shot of the frog perched on Syd's foot, but Charlie wanted more—the frog must swim out to Syd's foot and hop onto it. While a crew member launched the amphibian off-camera, Charlie shouted instructions at the animal through his megaphone: "Not that way! To the right, I say, to the right!"

The frog kept getting it wrong, and eventually a crew member pointed out that the poor thing was exhausted and needed to "take five."

"We can't be here all day catering to the whims of a frog," Charlie snapped. The frog was given its release, and in the final cut of the film it is seen only briefly.

Shoulder Arms ended with Charlie delivering a swift kick to the kaiser's behind, followed by the title: "Peace on earth, good will to all." In a coda he wakes up in his cot, still in basic training; his adventures were just a dream.

The film was irreverent but in its way closer to the truth of the soldier's experience than many dramatic pictures—it acknowledged that heroes aren't made by brass bands and fine words but by force of circumstance. But trench warfare had hardly been a laughing matter, and when *Shoulder Arms* was finally finished, after four months' work, Chaplin had qualms about releasing it. D. W. Griffith advised him that it would be better to wait until peacetime, and when he mentioned the subject of the film to Cecil B. De Mille, he was warned that making fun of the war could be "dangerous." Doug Fairbanks disagreed. At a private screening he laughed uproariously and assured Charlie that the picture would be an enormous success.[11]

He was right. *Shoulder Arms* became Chaplin's biggest hit yet. It set the tone for an entire genre of battlefield comedy, and some of the scenes, with their undertones of dark humor and antiheroic point of view, probably also influenced serious war pictures as well. But the picture was not, as Chaplin remembered it, "a great favorite with soldiers during the war." It was not released until October 20, 1918, three weeks before the Armistice. A year or even six months earlier, *Shoulder Arms* very likely would have been controversial, and perhaps even unreleasable. Ironically, since Chaplin had little sense of public opinion and rarely thought about his audience until he had finished a project, he seemed to have a genius for timing.

      ❋   ❋   ❋

In mid-August Chaplin took a few days' break from filming *Shoulder Arms* to make a five-minute promotional film for the war bond drive. Four brief skits illustrated the different kinds of bonds that hold society together—friendship, love, marriage, and, of course, Liberty Bonds. In the love segment Charlie, seated next to Edna on a park bench, is shot through the heart by an impish girl cupid. In the marriage tableau Edna appears in a traditional white wedding gown. Finally the kaiser (Syd) is dispatched by Charlie, who wields an enormous version of the Fatal Mallet. Edna looks so radiant in her wedding dress, and Charlie so blissfully resigned to his fate as Cupid's captive, that one is tempted to imagine that they were once again a loving couple.

But it wasn't so. Shortly after the end of the Liberty Bond tour, Charlie had become involved with another woman, or rather a girl. Owen Moore, Mary Pickford's estranged husband, shared a beach house in Santa Monica with his brother-in-law, Jack Pickford, actor Elliot Dexter, and Eddie Sutherland, a social acquaintance of Chaplin's who later became an assistant director at his studio. Chaplin had been invited to a party at the beach house, and since Kono happened to be unavailable, Sutherland had offered to pick him up at his club in Owen Moore's car. In the backseat was another nondriving guest, actress Mildred Harris. "They had never met before," Sutherland would recall. "And boy, they got together like glue in two minutes and a quarter. We had this party and I remember Charlie devoting a lot of attention to Mildred, who was then about sixteen or seventeen and very beautiful. He did an imitation of somebody imitating him doing the Charlie Chaplin waltz."[12]

"He was wonderful," Mildred herself remembered. "He was so fatherly in this way—he acted to me as if I had been a mere child—but I was only seventeen. He kept saying, 'Wow, how young you are!'"[13]

Time and Hollywood biographies have dealt harshly with Mildred Harris. Chaplin, in his memoirs, has little to say about her except that she was "no mental heavyweight." And, he adds, "the only possible interest she had for me was sex." In the Richard Attenborough movie *Chaplin*, Mildred appears as a zombielike creature, presumably thrust into Charlie's path by her ambitious mother. Charles Higham's recent life of Louis B. Mayer calls her "ruthless" as well as "self-indulgent."

In reality Mildred was an immature, rather spoiled but well-meaning girl. Born in Wyoming in November 1901, she was sixteen, not seventeen as she claimed, when she and Chaplin met. Her parents had separated when she was very young, and her mother worked as the supervisor of the wardrobe department at Triangle Films. Mildred appeared in her first movie when she was eight, and during her early teens she was signed by Lois Weber, an able director chiefly known for socially conscious "message" films. Mildred, however, appeared mainly in domestic dramas, invariably cast in undemanding roles as the star's younger sister or loving daughter. Unfortunately she had reached that stage, common in the lives of child actors, when inflated ambition clashed with her desire to catch up on the fun she had missed while she was growing up. Her china-doll looks seemed to assure her of a brilliant future in the movies and got her a lot of attention from men, which she naively mistook for genuine affection. She had already survived a crush on Doug Fairbanks and was infatuated with Elliot Dexter at the time she met Charlie.

After the party Mildred called Charlie at the Athletic Club. He found her prattle "fatuous" but let himself be drawn in, teasing her about being unfaithful to Dexter. He did not think about her again until Kono, who had picked him up at Moore's house when the party broke up, called Mildred "the most beautiful girl in the world." Kono's comment "appealed to my vanity," Chaplin would recall.[14]

Whatever sparked his interest, Chaplin gave every indication of being madly in love. The Cadillac Hotel, where Mildred lived with her mother, was deluged with bouquets of roses, and after Mrs. Harris expressed the opinion that Mildred was too young for a serious relationship, he began sitting in his car outside Mildred's studio in the afternoons, waiting to see her when she left work.

Mildred had played a bit part in the Babylonian orgy scene in *Intolerance* and become quite friendly with Lillian and Dorothy Gish. She was often on D. W. Griffith's set, and for a time he promoted the romance. When he rounded up a party for dinner and dancing at the Ship, a popular Santa Monica nightspot, he made sure Mildred and Charlie were invited. Griffith was attracted to much younger women himself, and he thought Mildred would be the cure for Charlie's loneliness.

"Mildred, why don't you marry Charlie?" he asked her one evening.

According to Mildred, she hadn't taken the possibility of marriage seriously until Griffith planted the idea in her mind. Afterward she thought of little else. She told Charlie that she had always assumed she would remain single until she was twenty-three or -four. "When do you think you'll marry?" she wondered aloud.

"Never," he replied.[15]

Even so, by late June the couple's friends were confidently expecting an early wedding, and it was reported in the trade papers that Chaplin had been to see Lois Weber to discuss buying out Mildred's contract.

Having conquered, however, Chaplin soon began to grow bored. During the late summer he was preoccupied with finishing *Shoulder Arms* and saw Mildred less often. On the eve of the picture's release, however, came Mildred's frantic announcement that she was pregnant. Chaplin didn't want to marry her but could see no alternative, so Tom Harrington arranged for a quiet ceremony. On October 23 Chaplin reported to the studio as usual, leaving just in time for the private ceremony. *Shoulder Arms* had opened only three days earlier, and Chaplin was worried that news of his marriage to a sixteen-year-old would hurt him at the box office. The local papers agreed to suppress all mention of the wedding— "at the urgent request of Mr. Chaplin," as they later explained.[16]

The next day at the studio Chaplin announced to his cast and crew that he was about to depart for a weeklong honeymoon cruise around Catalina on a yacht borrowed from Thomas Ince. Edna, who was as surprised by the wedding as everyone else, wrote him a sweet note of congratulations, closing with the wish that he would "catch lots of fishes."[17]

If not lots of fishes, Chaplin did hook a big one—a 175-pound sailfish, so feisty that it yanked him off his feet. Mildred grabbed his legs and screamed for help from a crew member, who arrived just in time to save them both from being swept overboard. Chaplin was an avid deep-sea fisherman, but Mildred was not the outdoor type, and a week on the water watching her husband fish was not her idea of a wedding trip. Chaplin had talked about visiting England as soon as the war ended, and Mildred had envisioned herself returning with him, basking in the glow of being the girl who snared one of the world's most eligible bachelors. Now she was beginning to realize that Charlie had no such intentions. "I don't know whether I've had a honeymoon or not," she would soon confide to a reporter.

On her return to Los Angeles, there was more disillusionment in store. Chaplin had rented 200 De Mille Drive, a comfortable but modest home in chic Laughlin Park. But the lease was only for six months, and he showed no signs of wanting to take his new wife out in society. Indeed on November 4, four days after the wedding trip, he departed for the Phelps Ranch, where he was to begin location shots for his next film.

Sunnyside was meant to be a takeoff on the sentimental rural comedies made popular by actor Charles Ray. At times in this film, music hall turnabout humor shaded into surrealism. As the overworked handyman of a small country inn, the Little Fellow cooks breakfast by having a hen lay an egg directly into the frying pan and milking a cow in the kitchen. A herd of cows stampedes into a church only to emerge as fearsome-looking longhorns. There are dreams within dreams, including one in which Charlie dances with a quartet of nymphs in homage to Vaslav Nijinsky's performance in the ballet *L'Après-midi d'un Faune*.

In a sense Nijinsky may have been an inspiration for the film. The great dancer, who happened to be a manic depressive, had visited the Lone Star studio during the filming of *The Cure* and spent three whole days watching Chaplin work, unnerving him by his failure to do so much as crack a smile. Later, Chaplin attended a performance of the Ballets Russes de Monte Carlo and was mesmerized by Nijinsky's "godlike" dancing, which suggested to him the mysterious depths of primal emotions beneath the superficial innocence of rural life.

Chaplin hoped to suggest these mysterious forces in *Sunnyside*, and to a degree he succeeded. Admired by intellectuals, the dark comedy laid a foundation for a Chaplin vogue among French *cinéastes*. For the most part, though, his fans were bewildered. The cast played their roles with an air of disengagement that at times makes them appear not mysterious but mildly retarded. Edna, as the country girl whom Charlie almost loses to city slicker Albert Austin, looks seriously depressed, and some reviewers objected to a scene in which Charlie rids himself of her pesky younger brother, a village-idiot type, by tying a blindfold over his eyes and sending him out to play in traffic.

Recalling *Shoulder Arms*, *Sunnyside* ended with Charlie throwing himself in front of the car that is carrying Edna and her new lover away from the village—followed by a coda in which he wakes up from his dream suicide, dispatches the city slicker, and regains Edna's love. The happy ending seems perfunctory, and one can only wonder if it was Chaplin's attempt to undo, through wish fulfillment, the moment when he declined to compete for Edna's affections. Moreover, there are so many dreams in *Sunnyside* that one is tempted to suspect that Charlie's suicide was "real" and the coda his dying fantasy.

Part of the problem with *Sunnyside* was that in making a work of art about depression it doesn't necessarily help to *be* depressed. On his return from location work at the Phelps ranch, Charlie and Mildred had gotten into a volcanic argument. Mildred wanted to bill herself professionally as Mildred Harris Chaplin, which Charlie regarded as a mediocre actress's attempt to trade on his name. During the course of the quarrel, it seems, Mildred confessed that she was not actually pregnant. Charlie was devastated, and Mildred soon checked into Good Samaritan Hospital, where she remained for three weeks. The announcement that she would be unable to continue work on her current picture because of a "nervous breakdown" finally prompted the newspapers to break their silence about the marriage.

In early December Mildred was well enough to attend a San Diego air show with Charlie, Doug Fairbanks, Mary Pickford, and a group of employees from the Chaplin studio. She and Charlie spent Christmas together at De Mille Drive, but by New Year's Day they were quarreling again, and Mildred reentered Good Samaritan. Now her doctor determined that she was indeed pregnant, and he was so worried about her ability to carry the baby to term that he ordered her to take several weeks of complete rest at the Mt. Lowe sanitarium north of the city. Charlie declined to accompany her, so

Mildred went off to the mountains with her mother. When they returned to Los Angeles several weeks later, Mrs. Harris moved into the spare bedroom at De Mille Drive. Chaplin's friends commiserated that he was the victim of a conniving wife and interfering mother-in-law. As far as Mildred was concerned, however, she had been abandoned. Charlie rarely came home, and when he did he typically refused to talk to her and snapped at her when she said anything to him. As she put it: "Charlie married me and then he forgot all about me."[18]

Mildred had grown up believing that life was a fairy tale and she was the princess. Nothing in her experience prepared her to understand why Charlie had pursued her ardently only to turn cold. Somehow it must be her fault, and she tried to win back his love by playing the model wife, diligently mending his underwear. Since Charlie was spending his nights at the Athletic Club, she deluged the studio with calls, begging for a chance to talk things over. Now it was her turn to wait in her car outside his studio, hoping to catch him as he left for the day.

In the midst of this marital disaster, Chaplin's honeymoon with First National had also come to an end. The fantastic success of *Shoulder Arms* had prompted him to approach the company's new president, J. D. Williams, about rewriting his contract to allow him to make feature-length films. To his amazement Williams refused even to discuss the subject. Almost a year and a half had passed since Chaplin signed with the company in June 1917, and so far he had delivered only two films—not the eight he had promised. *Sunnyside*, his third film, would not be ready for release until June 1919.

First National, moreover, had been drawn into Chaplin's still-simmering dispute with George Spoor, whose judgment—now grown to $650,000—was upheld by the U.S. Supreme Court in April 1918. Within days of the decision Spoor obtained a warrant for U.S. marshals to search First National's headquarters on East Forty-first Street in New York City and attach any property of Chaplin's they could locate. The search was embarrassing for the company's executives and ultimately unsuccessful. The marshals found a check for $140,500, but it was made out to Sydney as treasurer of the Charles Chaplin Film Corporation. To collect on his judgment, Spoor needed to locate Charlie's personal assets, which had so far proved impossible.

In a huff Chaplin told Williams that if necessary he could quickly churn out six more short comedies, but the company would bear the responsibility for discouraging him from raising the artistic standard of his work: "Your indifference shows your lack of psychology and foresight," he said. Williams replied that if that was true, so be it.[19]

Syd, meanwhile, had been hearing gossip that the major production companies were secretly discussing a consolidation that would enable them to drive down actors' salaries. Syd talked the rumors over with Mary Pickford and Doug Fairbanks, who were nearly at the end of their respective contracts with First National and Paramount. Neither company had so far shown any interest in discussing renewal terms, and they too feared that the producers were plotting against them. A convention of exhibitors was meeting in Los Angeles, and Chaplin, Pickford, and Fairbanks hired a female private investigator who used her charms—sparingly, it seems—to win the confidence of a libidinous film executive. She reported that a megamerger of all the major production companies was indeed in the works.

The facts were that Jesse Lasky of Paramount had indeed been trying to tempt First National into a merger, but First National's directors had rejected the deal. It was true, however, that there was a trend in the industry toward consolidation, and the highest-paid stars had reason to be worried about their futures. The merger rumors prompted the Chaplin brothers, along with Mary and Doug, to talk seriously about an idea that had been percolating in their minds since the Liberty Bond tour, when Bill McAdoo had suggested to them that they band together to form their own company. On January 14 Syd held a meeting at his house, and by the end of the day the participants had come up with a business plan for a new corporation, which they called United Artists. D. W. Griffith and cowboy star Bill Hart were recruited as partners, and Bill McAdoo agreed to serve as general counsel. Hiram Abrams, an able executive with ties to McAdoo, and Pickford's lawyer Dennis "Cap" O'Brien, were instrumental in working out the partnership arrangement. Abrams would become the company's first general manager, O'Brien a board member.

For some time the stars had been unhappy about the practice of block booking, under which theater owners who wanted to show the movies of Charlie Chaplin or Mary Pickford were forced to order an entire slate of films from the same company. With hindsight block booking could be defended as a way of introducing order into a boom-or-bust industry, creating a market for films that were not necessarily commercial blockbusters. As far as the stars (and most theater owners) were concerned, however, it was an unfair trade practice. Chaplin, Pickford, and Fairbanks saw their very popular movies being used as engines to pull a whole train of mediocre films, to the detriment of their profits.

United Artists was intended to eliminate this problem. Its partners would function as independent producers, financing their own productions. The company would then act as a distributor, placing the partners' pictures with exhibitors in the United States and abroad. The partners agreed to capitalize the company by purchasing preferred stock, and in return they would pay a fraction of the usual distribution fee. The problems with this approach would not become evident until some time later.

The attitude of the industry toward United Artists was that "the lunatics have taken over the asylum." Bill Hart dropped out almost immediately, having pried a better offer out of his producers. Griffith was notorious for his inability to control costs; Chaplin for being slow. Doug Fairbanks, never a businessman, treated the planning meetings as a lark, made enjoyable by the need to keep them secret from the producers. He delighted in making up code words, referring to cabbages instead of shares of stock, and so on. A reporter for *Moving Picture World* caught up with Fairbanks at his studio soon after the first public announcement of United Artists' existence and found him "sizzling around like a bottle of old-fashioned soda pop. 'Happiest man in the country,' he said. 'We are doing what we have all wanted to do for years.'"[20]

Chaplin's attitude toward the new company was less efferves-
cent. He recalls in his autobiography feeling resentful of Mary
Pickford, who had taken it upon herself to involve O'Brien and
Abrams in drawing up the business plan. At the organization meeting, moreover, he was "saddened" by Mary's mercenary attitude,
which showed itself in a sudden eruption of talk about contract language, capitalization, and stock assignments. When Mary uttered
the phrase: "Gentlemen, it behoves us [sic]," he said, he could not
help collapsing into a fit of giggles.

Chaplin's memory fails him on this subject, since Mary Pickford
did not even attend the meeting in question. Home in bed with the
flu, she was represented by her mother, Charlotte. Chaplin was fortunate to have Syd to handle the nuts and bolts of his finances,
allowing him the luxury of being as scornful of mere "merchants" as
any class-conscious British aristocrat. In the long run this pose of
detachment worked to his advantage, since he could always claim to
be interested only in the creative side of the business, dismissing
contract clauses as mere details, unworthy of his attention. In fact
Chaplin originated the tactic, later to become so common in
Hollywood, of agreeing to anything, on the theory that he could
always renegotiate later—when his opponents were worn down and
ready to make sacrifices to protect their investment.

Amazingly Chaplin's individual partnership agreement with
United Artists, signed on February 5, 1919, called for him to produce nine short films of two or three reels each. He could not begin
to deliver on this quota until he had worked out his contract with
First National, which he promised to do as soon as possible but "in
no event later than September 1920."[21] Why Chaplin would commit
to making nine more short films, when he was already chafing over
the six owed to First National, is a mystery. Presumably he told his
partners what they wanted to hear.

In the meantime nothing much was happening at his studio,
which was dark so often during the first three months of 1919 that
the rumor spread that Chaplin was planning to quit the business and
retire to England. On March 28 *Variety* reported that Chaplin had
been complaining to his friends that he was broke. Although this
could hardly have been true, Chaplin had to be worried about
George Spoor's efforts to attach his assets. He had no real incentive

to complete any more films as long as there was the possibility that Spoor would find a way to place a lien on the profits.

Chaplin was not completely idle, however. On March 4 he and Rob Wagner went to hear a "Hands Off Russia" lecture by the charismatic Max Eastman. Lanky and boyishly handsome—"the Byron of the Left," his biographer William O'Neill called him— Eastman had been the editor of *The Masses*, a magazine founded on the principle that a revolutionary agenda was compatible with the best in avant-garde art and literature. For a few years the formula had worked brilliantly. The heyday of *The Masses* coincided with the flowering of Greenwich Village bohemia, a time when it was quite possible for serious people to believe that there was no contradiction between Marxism, unfettered self-expression, and fun. But World War I had divided American socialists, and *The Masses'* antiwar stance drove the magazine out of business. Eastman was twice indicted for conspiracy to obstruct the draft, though he spoke so eloquently in his own defense that both juries acquitted him.

For Eastman the Bolshevik Revolution was a thrilling event. "What makes us rub our eyes at Russia is the way all our theories are proving true. Nothing else could give us this feeling of crazy surprise. One by one the facts fall exactly as they were predicted by Marx and Engels and the philosophers of syndicalism." Of course he had never actually visited the new Promised Land, but his friend Lincoln Steffens had and assured him that the rule of the "mob" was proving to be a miraculous success.[22]

Eastman's "Hands Off Russia" lecture tour had once again exposed him to the threat of jail, or worse. He was threatened at gunpoint in several towns, and in Cleveland he hid in a closet from vigilantes who talked of lynching him. In Los Angeles police cordoned off the auditorium, and Chaplin, along with other attendees, was forced to run a gauntlet of armed officers to get inside the hall. Nevertheless quite a few celebrities took the risk. "Cecil B. De Mille was rather nasty to me. . . . He is a screaming patriot,—also an ugly fat fool," Eastman wrote after the lecture. D. W. Griffith, however, had congratulated bim, saying, "I take my hat off to you. You're a braver man than I am."

Chaplin had been expecting a rigid ideologue, and was pleasantly surprised and intrigued by Eastman's youth, looks, and informal speaking style. Backstage he shook his hand, telling him, "You have what I consider the essence of all art, even of mine, if I may call myself an artist—restraint." Eastman refused to take credit on that score, joking: "Did you see those policemen?"

That evening Rob Wagner, Eastman, and Chaplin had dinner together, and the next day Eastman visited the studio, where he and Charlie swam in the pool and posed for the inevitable "home movie," picking lemons off a tree and pretending to enjoy eating them like oranges.

Eastman, as always, was trying to raise money, on this occasion for his new magazine *The Liberator*. Uncomfortable about asking Chaplin for a donation, Eastman left the task to Isaiah McBride, a veteran organizer who was accompanying him on tour. Charlie listened to McBride's appeal, expressed enthusiasm for the cause, and wrote a check for twenty-five dollars. The puny sum amazed Eastman, who was already under no illusion that he had made a serious political convert. "Nobody 'knew Charlie well,'" he later wrote,

who did not know how deep down he was an actor. . . . The day after he so praised my radical speech in Los Angeles I heard him express a glowing belief in slavery as an immortal institution, backing it up with arguments and illustrating it with a pantomime that left his hearers breathless if not convinced. . . . I sensed very early, through watching with keen attention these wholly unintegrated flights of his mind, that he could not be relied upon to be, or to continue to be, anything in particular, and I never expected him to be. If he was irresponsible toward me, instead of nursing the injury, I cured it by being irresponsible to him.[23]

In spite of his reservations, Eastman was impressed by Chaplin's intensity. He was a great listener, and when he turned his attention on Eastman and began to ply him with questions, the experience was both flattering and exhausting. Charlie, Eastman thought, was "high-strung and aesthetic, with an instantaneous distaste for anything false-faced or cheap, and no hesitation about extruding it from his attention or abruptly leaving it."[24]

By the end of Eastman's four days in Los Angeles it was clear to him and Charlie that they had much in common. For one, both men were often mistakenly identified in the press as Jewish. Born in 1883, Eastman was actually the son of two ordained Congregational ministers. His father had been an invalid or, some suspected, a malingerer. His mother, the vivacious Annis Eastman, was a popular evangelist, promoting a progressive social agenda including woman's suffrage and family planning. At the age of fifty-nine Annis entered psychoanalysis, lost her faith, and resigned her ministry, dying not long after. Max himself suffered from psychosomatic back pains as a young man, as well as a tormenting sexual drive and fears of impotence. He, too, tried analysis and was told that his problems stemmed from an incestuous attachment to his mother—though, one might note, his symptoms sound suspiciously similar to the troubles that plagued his father. Eastman dismissed the analyst's diagnosis, though he often brought it up in conversation. Charlie, he would note, also took pride in denying that he suffered from a "mother complex."

A pupil of John Dewey, Eastman believed that he had largely overcome his demons by embracing laughter, love, and literature. He often lectured on the topic "The Sense of Humor," and was in the process of transforming his theories on the subject into a book. As for love, he belonged to a generation of young intellectuals who saw free love as the path to self-knowledge. Recently separated from his first wife, Eastman had begun a passionate affair with the chestnut-haired actress Florence Deshon. Deshon had attracted unusual attention for her roles in two dramas, both filmed in New York, and the readers of one movie magazine had voted her the most beautiful woman in the movies. At the premiere of her second film, the now-forgotten *Jaffrey,* released in 1917, Deshon attracted another kind of notice by refusing to stand for the national anthem. The daughter of a Welsh trade union organizer and a Czech-Hungarian mother, she considered herself an internationalist who owed allegiance to no flag. Since that time Deshon had received inquiries from producers, and the Coca-Cola company had expressed interest in using her in a national advertising campaign, but all of these offers evaporated mysteriously after a few weeks. Eastman suspected that Deshon was being blacklisted, partly because of what happened at the *Jaffrey* premiere but mainly for her association with him.

Eastman desperately wanted Deshon to get back into film work. A movie contract would release her from the dreary round of roles in second tier productions in Boston and Philadelphia and restore her spirits. Not incidentally it would give Eastman, who was amazingly starstruck for a radical, an excuse to spend more time in Hollywood. Very likely he discussed all this with Chaplin, but if he didn't the situation was certainly known to Rob and Florence Wagner, at whose house he was staying in LA.

After a few days Eastman reluctantly departed for New York via San Francisco, while Chaplin put the finishing touches on *Sunnyside* and resumed his war of attrition with his wife. Louis B. Mayer, a newcomer to Hollywood, had succeeded in luring Lois Weber away from Universal, and now he was using Weber as bait to sign Mildred. Mayer thought enough of Mildred's future to propose a six-picture contract at fifty thousand dollars per picture, under terms that would make her a coproducer, her films to be released through First National as "Chaplin-Mayer Productions."

The deal was irresistible to Mildred. Just as surely Chaplin loathed everything about the proposal. Justifiably, in this instance, he regarded the "Chaplin-Mayer" logo as a shameless bid to cash in on the prestige of his name. He was also deeply suspicious of an arrangement that would forge a link between Mildred and First National. When he and Mildred divorced, as inevitably they would, his wife and the company might discover that they had common interests.

Less rationally, Chaplin suspected Mayer of wanting to sleep with his wife, who was having a difficult pregnancy and hardly in the mood for a romantic encounter. Chaplin was so insanely jealous that one evening when Mayer came by to discuss the proposed contract over dinner with Mildred, he hid in the sun parlor expecting to catch Mayer in the act of seduction. Mayer guessed that he had walked into a setup and left as quickly as possible.

Far from contemplating an affair, Mildred still loved Charlie. If only she could stop crying so much and be more cheerful, she told herself, perhaps he would care for her again. In her desperation she turned to a quasi-religious sect that preached the gospel of "positivity." No matter how bad their problems, devotees were advised to banish all negative thoughts and approach life with a smile. For

Charlie this was the final proof that Mildred was irredeemably stupid.

Mildred went into labor on the evening of July 6, and the following morning at 6:00 A.M. she gave birth to a son. Charlie did not show up at the hospital, and the baby's birth certificate, based on information provided by the mother, gave his place of birth as France, and the infant's name as "Charles Spencer Chaplin, Jr."—a name he objected to when he heard it. The baby survived only two days. Kono was told that the infant was born with "its stomach upside down"—a condition that caused peristaltic action to work in reverse. The death certificate gives the cause as "rudimentary development of the large intestine."

The appearance of a child eight months and fifteen days after the wedding makes it necessary at least to reconsider Chaplin's explanation that Mildred's claim to be pregnant when they married was a "false alarm." Is it possible that Mildred was indeed pregnant in October, even if awfully quick to get Charlie to the altar? At any rate she may well have been pregnant in November, when she and Charlie quarreled. During her three weeks' stay at Good Samaritan she was probably treated with drugs to calm her shattered nerves, and drug intake early in pregnancy is one of numerous possible causes of the type of birth defect the baby suffered from.

Chaplin had not wanted the baby, but still he grieved for it. "That's the only thing I can remember about Charlie," Mildred said many years later, "that he cried when the baby died."[25] Within twenty-four hours, however, the bereaved parents were at odds again. The funeral director Mildred chose was a member of her church, and Charlie objected that the man had fixed an artificial smile on the infant's face. He avoided the wake out of dislike for Mildred's religious friends, and later, she complained, dickered with the mortician over the price of the funeral. He also refused to accept her choice of a name. On the death certificate the infant was identified as Norman Spencer Chaplin.

Awkwardly enough, within two weeks of little Norman's death, Chaplin was hard at work on a new picture, *The Kid*, and had put out a casting call for babies. However cold it may seem to others, for a creative person even tragedies can be grist for the mill, and there was undoubtedly some connection between Chaplin's own dismal experience of fatherhood and his decision to make a film in which the Tramp adopts an abandoned baby and becomes a tender, devoted caretaker. Nevertheless the immediate inspiration for *The Kid* was more cheerful. In the dining room of the Alexandria Hotel, Chaplin had been introduced to Jackie Coogan Jr., four years old and already a seasoned vaudevillian, whose act he had earlier caught at the Orpheum Theater.

Oddly enough, in retrospect, many people considered Chaplin's movies children's entertainment, and he was constantly being approached by parents who wanted him to meet their photogenic offspring. In fact children had seldom been seen in Chaplin's comedies, and when they did appear, as in *Easy Street*, his attitude toward them was hardly sentimental. But Chaplin must have seen something of his younger self in Coogan—who had the look of a ragamuffin and could dance the shimmy, tell jokes, and reel off words like *prestidigitator*. When Chaplin's aide Chuck Riesner happened to mention that Fatty Arbuckle had signed Coogan, meaning Jackie Coogan senior, Chaplin suddenly realized that he would never forgive himself if he missed a chance to sign the son.

As for the story line of *The Kid*, it is worth noting that it was a twist on the popular early British film *Rescued by Rover*, the story of a baby kidnapped by a Gypsy. In Chaplin's version of the story, the Tramp is a doting father and it is bourgeois society, in the form of child protection workers, who try to kidnap the infant away from him.

Of course *The Kid* was also another brief on behalf of the unwed mother, and by extension a defense of Hannah Chaplin. The story begins with an aspiring singer (Edna Purviance), who has been loved and abandoned by—naturally—a handsome young painter. After giving birth to her illegitimate child, she leaves the hospital, destitute and alone. HER ONLY SIN WAS MOTHERHOOD, a title proclaims. Lest anyone miss the point, there is a quick cut from Edna with the blanket-swaddled infant in her arms to an image of Christ carrying his cross up Calvary. The mother, sinless, has taken on the burden of man's sin in the form of her illegitimate child.

Unable to care for the baby, Edna leaves it inside an expensive automobile, in the hope that the wealthy owners will take pity and adopt it. Instead, through a series of mishaps, the basket containing the baby ends up on the slum doorstep of the Tramp. When we next see the pair it is several years later, and Charlie and the kid are a team. Charlie earns his living as a glazier. The kid—like the young Fred Karno—drums up business by breaking windows. Their hardscrabble but happy life is threatened by the police and social workers, who snatch the kid away.

The most memorable aspect of *The Kid* would be the remarkable performance of Jackie Coogan, especially in the scene where he sobs inconsolably as the welfare authorities prepare to cart him away. (Improbably, Jackie has been dumped into the open bed of a truck—perhaps a reminder of Charlie's arrival at the Hanwell orphanage in a baker's van.) Coogan's triumph owed a great deal to Chaplin, who showed remarkable patience in directing child actors, and was not too proud to listen to their suggestions on occasion. Nine year-old Raymond Lee, who played a bully who picks on the smaller Jackie, recalled Chaplin guiding the two of them through more than fifty takes of a brief fight scene: "Boys, this is a very simple scene. Very simple. Two boys fighting. All boys fight. Must be a million boys fighting all over the world this very minute. It's born in you—like tonsils. But boys, you aren't fighting. You're dancing with each other."

And again: "There is hunger in this scene. A boyish hunger makes Raymond steal Jackie's toy. And Jackie fights for his hunger . . . It's not an ordinary hunger. It's been going on for thousands of years but it still isn't an ordinary fight. I've been so hungry I could eat a shoe!"[26]

Chaplin talked to Coogan as if he were an adult, explaining that the motivation of the scene was to create sympathy for his character and urging him to think of himself as David confronting Goliath. This helpful suggestion was undone by Jackie's mother, Lillian, who was present on the set and volunteered with some embarrassment that her boy was unfamiliar with the source of the tale. Eventually, little Raymond Lee spoke up, offering his opinion that the scene had been choreographed badly. "Jackie and I are little boys, but you want us to fight like you fight."

"Very well," said Chaplin, admitting defeat. "Mr. Raymond, you direct the scene. I won't even sit in my chair while we shoot it."

The boys then put their heads together, agreed on their moves, and got the action right on the first take. When the scene was in the can, Chaplin shook Lee's hand, and the boy felt that at that moment he had "come of age" as an actor. What made *The Kid* work, Lee thought, was insistence that every moment of every performance be emotionally true. "Chaplin, the director, had no favorites. What amazed me was how Chaplin judged himself. A wall of mirrors in front of him couldn't be more critical."[27]

The Kid was an enormous risk for Chaplin, who borrowed half a million dollars from the Bank of Italy to finance the five-reeler, even though First National had made it clear it didn't really want a feature-length film and was under no obligation to pay more than $170,000 for it. For that matter, the relatively tepid audience response to *A Dog's Life* was grounds for wondering if anyone would want to see the Tramp in such a pathos-laden story. In short, there was no reason to make *The Kid* except that Chaplin felt like making it. He worked on the project sporadically over the course of a year, in no rush to finish and face the inevitable fight with First National's head office and the judgment of his fans. In the meantime his personal life was becoming even more of a melodrama than the tale he was laboring to bring to the screen.

1

"The Black Panther"

On July 9, while Charlie and Mildred's infant son lay dying at Good Samaritan Hospital, Florence Deshon boarded a train for Los Angeles, where she was about to begin a long-term contract at Sam Goldwyn's new studio in Culver City. Deshon was traveling with her mother, Caroline, and to while away time on the long journey she was trying to read Robert Burton's *The Anatomy of Melancholy*, a seventeenth-century treatise on the varieties of melancholy, which Burton called "an inbred malady in every one of us." Long sections of the book were in Latin and Greek, but, she reported to her lover, Max Eastman, she found the work interesting, "at least those parts of it that are in English."

After so many disappointments Deshon had been quite surprised to hear from Goldwyn, who offered her a generous salary of four hundred dollars a week. On arriving in California she was even more pleased to discover that Goldwyn was taking a personal interest in her career. Actresses were still expected to supply their own costumes, and Deshon's contract called for her have at least four suitable dresses, but Goldwyn took her aside and gave her a thousand dollars for wardrobe expenses. Her dressing room, actually a detached bungalow, was another pleasant surprise; it was being redecorated to her specifications with "sun yellow" walls, cheerful print curtains, and white wicker furniture.

Considering that Florence hadn't made a picture in two years, had no agent, and was about to become just another contract player in nonstarring roles, she was being paid a great deal of attention. Goldwyn, whose pictures were being distributed through United Artists at the time, happened to be a good friend of Chaplin and often did him favors. Almost certainly he had signed Deshon at Chaplin's suggestion, and very likely the generous thousand-dollar wardrobe allowance came from Chaplin's pocket. Chaplin may have balked when it came to making a large contribution to *The Liberator*, but he liked to help out friends and often preferred to do so quietly without drawing attention to himself. In arranging a contract for Florence Deshon, he was coming to the aid of a noble and beautiful woman who had suffered for her allegiance to socialism. Her presence in LA also guaranteed that Max Eastman would be returning to California for a lengthy visit, giving Chaplin an opporutnity to get to know him better.

Although Chaplin didn't know it, his good deed was a mixed blessing for Florence. Her hopes were raised high by Goldwyn's personal interest in her, only to be crushed when she was cast in supporting roles that offered few opportunities to show off her looks or her talent. She felt vaguely that her colleagues at Culver City resented her, and had no idea why.

Nor did she feel she belonged in Hollywood. Deshon's extraordinary complexion and graceful figure had made her an actress, but her intellectual interests condemned her to being a lonely one, out of place even in relatively bookish theatrical circles. She wrote poems in her spare time, and judging by the few surviving examples she had the potential to become a published poet of some distinction. She read Li Po in translation as well as her favorite author, John Milton. ("He reminds me of you," she wrote Eastman, "I don't mean his struggle between passion and puritism. I think you have been more victorious in that than he was, but he cared so much for perfection. And then too he cared so much for the truth.") She could dissect a Van Wyck Brooks essay on Mark Twain with clinical precision, and had no hesitation about dismissing Brooks and others as overrated. ("Frank Harris was always an unstable quantity in my mind," she told Eastman.)

Although film acting provided her with a steady income, Florence missed the the bohemian intellectual life of the Village. Politically the climate was hostile. Los Angeles was in the midst of a wave of strikes, and soon after she started work at Culver City, the studio employees were summoned to a forty-five minute lecture warning them against having anything to do with representatives of the IWW. She was also having problems with her mother, who was so intimidated by being in a strange city that she insisted on coming to the studio with Florence every day.

Then, too, there was the considerable distraction of Eastman's letters. Max wrote long, effusive epistles every two or three days and expected equally lengthy replies. His correspondence was always challenging and occasionally erotic, inviting her to reimagine moments of passion when "my hot muscle plunged up through you to the inmost thrusting nerve, and we were lost, lost, lost in the madness of each other's life."[1] Max complained that their separation was making him physically ill and actually consulted nerve specialists who, much to his annoyance, could find nothing wrong with him. And yet, when Deshon replied that she was not happy in LA and thinking of returning to New York, he urged her to stay on—and to save up enough money for a car, so that they could enjoy California when he came for a visit.

Eastman had asked Elmer Ellsworth and Rob and Florence Wagner to take an interest in Deshon. Chaplin was busy at his studio during July and August and didn't meet her until the beginning of September, when he showed up at a dinner party at the Wagners'. A few days later, Hiram Abrams, the chief executive of United Artists, appeared at Culver City and made a point of asking to meet her. This time Deshon realized that Chaplin must be responsible, and she gave him a thank-you gift, a photograph of Max taken by her friend Margarethe Mathers, an associate of Edward Weston. A few weeks later Max arrived for his promised visit, and it seemed natural to invite Charlie and Margarethe, a lanky ash blond, to make up a foursome for dinner.

From then on the quartet was inseparable. After dining together they would return to the house on South Oxford Drive that Chaplin had rented after the lease on the Laughlin Park "cottage" ran out. Chaplin's personal interest in Margarethe Mathers was perfunctory at best. The glue that held the foursome together was intellectual camaraderie, so highly competitive and absorbing that Chaplin's work at the studio became an afterthought.

The layout of the Oxford Drive house happened to be ideally suited to parlor theatrics. The dining room, which served as the stage, was set off from the living room by an arch resembling a proscenium, and its twin staircases were perfect for exits and entrances. At first the foursome played charades, ransacking the upstairs bedrooms for costumes and props. Later they invented their own "drama game," in which each couple was required to improvise an entire one-act play based on a title drawn at random.

Charlie invited other friends to join in the fun, but the level of acting ability and general knowledge, not to mention the ferocity of the competition, was sufficient to intimidate even the bravest souls. To loosen up the tongue-tied, Charlie and Max invented an exercise in which each of the guests was asked to think of a suitable topic for a speech and write it down on a slip of paper. On a second slip of paper they were to write the description of a character. The slips were placed in two hats. Each guest had to choose a slip from each hat and then deliver a one-minute extemporaneous speech in the persona of the chosen character. Improvised costumes were permitted, but the speech was to be done straight, without joking around.

For Chaplin this was a meat-and-potatoes exercise. One night he would be Carrie Nation lecturing on "Some Doubts as to the Origin of the Species," the next a "toothless war veteran" expounding on "The Benefits of Birth Control." Another of his assignments was to play a minister delivering a sermon on "David and Goliath," an exercise that found its way into his acting advice to Jackie Coogan. His casual guests, however, were often so overcome by stage fright that they were unable to squeeze out a single sentence. "After they have suffered through one of those lonely minutes," wrote Eastman, "they are ready for anything that is done in company."[2]

While Chaplin and the others partied, Mildred remained upstairs in her room with the door shut. "Charlie invited his socialist friends to my home, but I refused to receive them," she later told a reporter. Max, Florence, and Margarethe failed to notice that they were being snubbed. When he thought about it at all, Max assumed that Mildred simply wasn't up to their caliber intellectually and preferred not to take part. No one, it seems, bothered to wonder if she might be resentful of a group of strangers who spent every evening playing dress-up with her curtains and tablecloths. Long after midnight Max and Florence headed for Pasadena, where Max had rented an apartment in a neighborhood beyond the notice of industry gossip, while Charlie departed to spend the night at the Athletic Club.

By day Chaplin was working fitfully on a short film orginally called *Charlie's Picnic*, which he had begun as a sop to First National. An enthusiastic driver, Florence had purchased a Ford for herself and Max to use during his visit. The car, not to mention the dealer, a certain Mr. Clark, were the source of endless complications, and Charlie was inspired to rename his comedy *The Ford Story*, adding a sequence in which the Little Fellow is stuck in traffic while taking his wife and children on a Sunday outing. Deshon was borrowed from Goldwyn to drive her own car in the traffic jam—though her role as an impatient motorist was cut from the finished film.

Distracted by Eastman's visit and his desire to return to *The Kid*, the project close to his heart, Chaplin became so frustrated that he cut the traffic scenes to a minimum, rented an excursion boat, the *Ace*, out of San Pedro harbor, and finished the shooting in a single day. Edna Purviance, recently returned from a leave of absence, replaced the four-hundred-pound male actor whom Charlie had cast to play his wife in drag. Jackie Coogan was one of the children. The theme of the harassed family man, suffering through a day of leisure with the wife and kids, was reduced to a series of crude seasickness jokes, indifferently performed.

Retitled *A Day's Pleasure,* the picture opened on December 15, 1919. "Everybody is very disappointed in it," wrote Deshon. "I mean everybody. The ones who care about him (Charlie). The audiences seem to like it well enough."[3]

Two days before the premiere of *A Day's Pleasure*, Max Eastman had departed for New York, having raised enough money from Chaplin and other West Coast friends to put out another issue of *The Liberator*. "Give my love to Charlie, and try to keep my memory green—or at least not too red—among the child millionaires of Hollywood," he wrote Florence soon after his return home.[4]

Max's parting words to Charlie had been to ask him to look after Florence for him—a request that was to have fateful consequences. Deshon herself was immediately suspicious, wondering if Max wasn't hoping, perhaps unconsciously, that she and Charlie would have an affair. Though he claimed to miss her desperately, Max did not want her back in New York and Florence wondered why. As a believer in free love, she would not have dreamed of demanding fidelity from Max, but she did want some assurance that she would always come first in his life, and Max replied to her hints about commitment and permanence with evasions. In fact he was already deeply involved with Lisa Duncan, an Isadora Duncan dancer, who had moved into the Croton, New York, cottage Max once shared with Florence, repainting the living room in Chinese red. (Lisa was not related to Isadora—like the other "Isadorables," she had taken her teacher's name as a gesture of respect.)

Though he was not aware of any such motive at the time, Max would later realize that he probably had set up a situation in which it was inevitable that Florence and Charlie would fall in love. Though he loved Florence, he was not ready to dedicate himself to any one woman. Florence, moreover, was subject to unpredicatble mood swings and at times had a violent temper, which he called "the black panther" side of her personality. Considering Max's manipulative behavior, however, Florence's anger seems hardly surprising. When they were together, she earned the money and did all the chores so his mind would be free for thinking deep thoughts; when they were apart, he had affairs. Nevertheless Max found her moods irrational and wearying, and no doubt it was true that she suffered from a form of depression.

There were good reasons for Chaplin to be attacted to Florence. Back in 1916 he had told a reporter for the *New York World* that he was looking for an intellectual woman. Most men prefer to "look down" on women, he explained, "but I haven't got the brains to feel that way."[5] The cure for the contempt he felt for his ditsy wife was to find a woman of intellect, and Florence, whose mind was as clear and sharp as a diamond, certainly offered a stimulating contrast to Mildred Harris. And if Max Eastman could be believed, she was a passionate lover—Eastman credited her with being the first bed partner to free him of his sexual inhibitions. Unfortunately Florence's unpredictable moods were part of the attraction. Chaplin might be insecure about his masculine appeal, especially in competition with the charismatic Max Eastman, but he had grown up catering to his emotionally volatile mother, and he was comfortable in the role of caregiver.

On Christmas Eve Charlie invited Florence to dine alone with him at his club, presenting her with a gift that was considered, at the time, personal but not too intimate—a set of monogrammed, hand-embroidered handkerchiefs. Before two weeks had passed, he was reorganizing her personal life. The unhappy Caroline was persuaded to return to New York, and Chaplin's assistant Chuck Riesner found Florence a better apartment, a charming bungalow on DeLongpre Avenue, not far from the studio. He had already seen to it that the Ford, never satisfactory, was replaced by a Buick convertible, which Tom Harrington obtained at a steep discount.

Chaplin also tried to help Florence work out her problems at the studio. Goldwyn's studio manager, Cliff Robertson, had taken a dislike to Florence and offered her only minor ingenue roles. Robertson complained that she was hard to cast because of her strong resemblance to the studio's reigning star, Pauline Frederick, but Florence thought his motives were probably political. It was the winter of the Red Scare and the Palmer raids. Federal agents were rounding up scores of left-wing aliens for deportation, the public's mood was conservative, and Robertson may well have been reluctant to promote the career of a woman closely associated with a notorious radical agitator.

Doubtless at Charlie's instigation, UA executive Hiram Abrams once again appeared at the Culver City studio and made a point of inviting Florence to dinner. She went, much to the horror of an actress friend who told her, "A kike will never do anything for a girl for nothing." But the only thing Abrams wanted was to give Florence career advice. "Every girl should have a publicist," he counseled. Before she could act on this tip, Florence was suddenly offered a featured role opposite the romantic leading man Reginald Pole.

Even so, Florence was ready to leave California at the slightest sign of encouragement from Max. "Darling, I understand why all these movie people are so restless and discontented," she wrote him. "There is absolutely no purpose or beauty in their lives." In motion pictures, she complained, there was no such thing as artistry, only "material": "All this talk about a new art being born is untrue, it's simply a new business. It's [sic] name gives it away. Moving pictures, that's all they are and the only art is that of photography."[6] Max's response was to urge her to stick it out a while longer.

Reginald Pole, meanwhile, had developed a crush on Florence, and one night he broke into her bedroom and woke her from a sound sleep to declare his passion. More amused than alarmed, she described the incident in a letter to Max, who was wildly jealous. Strangely, it did not occur to him to wonder about her growing friendship with Charlie, even though she was now living close to his studio and obviously spent much of her time there. On January 22nd Florence saw an unfinished print of *The Kid*. The picture was "wonderful, wonderful. I cried and laughed," she wrote. The cast and crew were all working in high spirits, well aware that the picture was going to be very special . . . if, indeed, it was ever finished at all. Charlie, she added, "is very bad about his work and takes scenes over and over again not because he is striving for perfection, but because something in him can't go forward."[7]

She was also present on February 12 when Charlie's idol, the great Max Linder, paid a visit. Linder, Florence noted with amazement, was a tiny man, a good deal smaller than Charlie but handsome and impeccably groomed: "Charlie was quite jealous of him for a few minutes. Then he went into his dressing room. He pulled off his cap and roughed up his hair and you know how he always looks charming that way. So he caught a fleeting glimpse of himself in the glass and all was well in the world again."[8] Linder's first stint in American movies, as Essanay's replacement for Chaplin, had not been a success. His new production venture was to be better favored. He tooled around town in a yellow limousine and made a spoof of *The Three Musketeers*, with advice and help from Doug Fairbanks.

But Linder, who had been injured in World War I, was not a well man, and seeing him merely deepened the malaise and inertia that had beset Charlie ever since his marriage The state of his career would soon be summed up in an open "Letter to a Genius," published in the April 1920 issue of *Photoplay*: "*Sunnyside* was anything but sunny. *A Day's Pleasure* was certainly not a pleasure. . . . Since you have been out of sorts the world has gone lame and happiness has moved away. Come back, Charlie!"

In an era when even ambitious films were made economically and shot in a matter of weeks, not months, Charlie's working habits had always been considered eccentric. But his progress, or lack of it, on *The Kid* was the talk of Hollywood and a serious concern even to longtime employees accustomed to his moody ways. When inspired, Chaplin shot prodigious amounts of film—up to four thousand feet in a single day. Unfortunately, since he had yet to settle on a story line, many takes, and even whole incidents, could never be used. At other times he would seize on any excuse to cancel filming. The studio was dark for an entire week at Christmastime, ostensibly to give Jackie Coogan a vacation. In mid-February, Charlie seemed to lose interest in the movie entirely, and work ground to a halt.[9]

This time the distraction was Florence. Soon after Christmas she and Charlie had begun sleeping together. He was desperately in love and talked about wanting to marry her. But he had reached the point, familiar to all who suffer from depression, where he felt trapped in a mental maze. He could not marry Florence until he divorced Mildred. But if he divorced Mildred, his profits from *The Kid* would doubtless go into the settlement. The prospect was so dismaying that he could not bring himself to wrap up the picture.

Elmer Ellsworth, meanwhile, had negotiated a buyout of Florence's contract with Goldwyn, so she was not working either. Chaplin wasted days shopping for a yacht, and talked constantly of his fantasy of leaving Hollywood to sail around the world with Max Eastman, Florence, and Ellsworth. The inclusion of Max in this fantasy was curious, and could hardly have pleased Florence, who was growing impatient. "Charlie speaks of going away," she wrote "but it depends on this picture and at the rate he is working, he will never finish it. I know I am naughty, but I have become tired of Charlie's marital troubles. He stays in that frightful situation at his home, and his powerlessness to move wears me out."[10]

Hollywood was buzzing with rumors of the affair, but since Mildred, so far, didn't seem to know about it, Florence and Charlie could not appear together in public. The violinist Jascha Heifetz was in town, and Florence longed to meet him, but Charlie went alone to the reception for fear of encouraging gossip. Through letters, however, she initiated a friendship with novelist Theodore Dreiser, and perhaps it was via this connection that news of her relationship with Charlie filtered back to Max in New York. A bit belatedly he began to worry that the pairing off of two such emotionally volatile individuals could only lead to disaster. He warned Florence in a letter that he was "frightened of Charlie in two ways"—for his own sake and for hers.

Even so, when Max learned that Florence had been offered a contract by director Maurice Tourneur at $350 a week, he was emboldened to confess his affair with Lisa Duncan. Reminding Florence that he had been separated from his wife for just twenty-five days when they met and fell in love, he argued that as a man who "loved liberty" above all else, he was entitled to a chance to enjoy a little of it.

"Shall I tell you what I felt when I read your letter," she replied. "I was sad for you, then I was angry. . . . I felt like one who had walked and trotted a long way. Now I can rest."[11] And, she added, she had made up her mind to find that rest by marrying Charlie.

While waiting for Charlie to get a divorce, Florence was determined to concentrate on her career. She had become friendly with Mabel Normand and was "very excited" about writing a screenplay for her. Meanwhile, with the Maurice Tourneur movie finished, she immediately had another good offer from Bill Russell, a Fox director, and was about to go on location in San Francisco.

Mildred Harris, however, was far from resigned to ending her marriage. Somehow she had persuaded herself that if it hadn't been for little Norman's death, she and Charlie might have worked things out. During the Christmas holidays the Los Angeles papers had carried the story of a woman who was abandoned by her common-law husband at the hospital shortly after going into labor. Mildred visited the woman, befriended her, and offered to adopt the baby. The arrangement collapsed because Charlie refused to sign the adoption papers, but Mildred was now determined to become a mother, and a few weeks later she learned of a destitute single woman who had given birth to triplets and wanted to place them in a good home. This time Mildred told the newspapers about her plan, and Charlie was forced to admit to a reporter that he was standing in the way of Mildred's desire to adopt.

No doubt it was true that Mildred wanted the children for all the wrong reasons. However, it seemed hypocritical of Chaplin, even while filming the story of the Little Fellow's love for an abandoned waif, to oppose his own wife's desire to care for needy children. For that matter it was hard to say what he *did* want for Mildred. His attorneys were also in court trying to void her agreement with Louis B. Mayer on the grounds that she was a minor who needed his consent to enter into a contract.

Divorce was still uncommon and professionally risky for a movie star, especially one about to release a picture like *The Kid*. It was also, as his friends Doug and Mary had recently learned, very expensive. The previous November, Fairbanks had given his wife, Beth, a half-million-dollar settlement in exchange for an amiable end to their marriage. More recently Mary Pickford had agreed to pay Owen Moore, a notorious drunkard, one hundred thousand dollars for her freedom. What Chaplin really wanted was to keep Mildred in limbo—unable to work, adopt, or date other men—until she filed for divorce from him, if possible to marry another man. Then he would appear to be the injured party, and the easily intimidated Mildred would be too grateful for her freedom to ask for a settlement.

The loyal Kono had already been deputized to keep an eye on 674 South Oxford Drive in the hope of catching Mildred in a compromising situation, and one evening he summoned Chaplin with the news that she was entertaining a young man. Chaplin hurried to the scene, and he and Kono peered into the living room window, but Mildred and her guest, fully dressed, were decorously sipping tea. Seconds later Chaplin found himself being hauled backward through the shrubbery by a burly private detective. Mildred's "assignation" had been a setup. The young man was the brother of her friend, actress Anita Stewart, and the detective had been hired to catch Chaplin in the act of spying. Kono offered the private eye a bribe to turn on his employer, but he indignantly refused, saying,

"That skunk of an actor hasn't got enough money to make me double-cross her."[12]

Chaplin took Kono's loyalty for granted, and it did not seem to occur to him that the chauffeur deeply resented being drawn into his extramarital adventures. Kono and his wife were living temporarily in the "mansion" on the studio grounds, and Chaplin had taken to meeting Florence—and perhaps, on occasion, other women—there. Mrs. Kono was expected to serve Chaplin and his date supper in front of the fireplace and then discreetly disappear upstairs—a task Kono considered an insult to his wife's honor. Kono put up with the humiliation because Chaplin had promised him that he and his wife were named in his will as heirs to one-third of his estate. Older than his boss, Kono had few expectations of ever enjoying the money himself, but he believed that by holdiing on to his job he was guaranteeing future financial security for his wife and their children.

Her adoption plans frustrated, Mildred finally hired an attorney, and on March 19 she announced that if she filed for divorce she planned to name a co-respondent. "There is another woman back of all this. It is a woman he used to go with before he knew me," she told reporters, apparently in the belief that her rival was Edna, not Florence. In the next breath she insisted that what she really wanted was her husband back: "I still love Charlie to death."

Meanwhile Mildred continued to practice positivity by surrounding herself with all the luxury money could buy. When Louis Mayer decided to bring his wife and daughters to California, Mildred was dispatched to greet them at the train station. Mayer's daughter Irene, a schoolgirl at the time, was dazzled to find herself seated next to the honey-blond movie star, dressed in white from head to toe, in the richly upholstered passenger compartment of a brand-new Marmon tonneau limousine, perfectly appointed down to a crystal bud vase holding a single rose.

Mildred's idea of luxury was what Marie Antoinette might have aspired to if she could have had Flo Ziegfeld as her decorator. The actress and sometime features writer Marjorie Daw, a childhood friend of Mildred's, waxed lyrical over her bedroom—"a symphony of lavender and ivory" with a canopied four-poster bed and a profusion of vases filled with calla lilies, Mildred's favorite flower.[13]

Now that Mildred had escalated the conflict, Chaplin struck back by offering to show reporters canceled checks representing the fifty thousand dollars Mildred had spent over the past two years. She countered with a statement that made it clear that she did not think this an exorbitant outlay for the wife of one of the richest men in the United States. Following this exchange Chaplin fled to Catalina, where he spent the week fishing on a friend's boat. By April 8, however, he was back in LA, dining with a group from the studio at the Alexandria Hotel. Louis B. Mayer happened to be in the hotel dining room as well, and after an insulting note signed by Mayer was delivered to Chaplin's table, he confronted him in the lobby and challenged him to step outside. Mayer glared, saying nothing. "Take off your glasses, then," Chaplin demanded. When Mayer did, he socked him, and Mayer struck back. Neither man landed a solid blow, but Chaplin slipped and hit his head on a chair.

According to Chaplin biographer David Robinson, the note that set off the fight may have been forged as a practical joke by Jack Pickford, Mary's brother, who was a member of Chaplin's party that evening. Certainly everyone but Chaplin thought his jealousy of Mayer ludicrous.

By now Chaplin was taking steps to hide his assets, and he handed over $300,000 in cash to Elmer Ellsworth to hold for the duration of the crisis. Ellsworth was not only Chaplin's employee but his oldest friend in Hollywood, but $300,000 was an enormous sum in 1920, and no sooner had Chaplin given Ellsworth the money than he began to worry whether he'd ever see it again. In his anxiety he snapped at Ellsworth on the set and avoided him socially. Florence, who didn't know about the money, was perplexed by this shabby treatment of the unassuming older man. Since Charlie hated to be around physically unattractive people, she suspected that he was displeased by Elmer's new false teeth, which fit him badly.

Ellsworth found his own way to protest. Months later, when the time came to return the money, he remembered that Chaplin, in a burst of enthusiasm over a scene he directed, had promised him a $10,000 bonus. Chaplin frequently made such promises only to forget them when his mood changed. This time Ellsworth decided to award himself the bonus, returning just $290,000. Chaplin was so furious yhat he fired Ellsworth and didn't speak to him for two years.[14]

Summer came, and Mildred continued give interviews, offering reporters glimpses of her husband's miserly ways. "I don't think he had a decent pair of socks when we were married, and his shirts and underthings and pajamas were frightful, all full of holes and tears," she said. "Mother looked after that and when she had fixed him up he was delighted."[15] Chaplin, whatever his faults, had no taste for this sort of public sniping. However, this did not stop his partisans from spreading the story that Mildred and Lillian Gish were having a lesbian affair.

At the studio Chaplin had spent the better part of May and June adding a new twist to the story of *The Kid*—a dream sequence in which the Tramp falls asleep and wakes in a sort of Cockney heaven, populated by streetwise angels wearing homemade-looking wings. While the heavenly gatekeeper dozes, a devil sneaks into the neighborhood and whispers into the ear of a young female "angel," who tempts Charlie with sly wink and a glimpse of her stocking-clad leg. Her jealous boyfriend then pulls a gun and shoots him.

As a number of critics noted at the time, the dream sequence was out of place in *The Kid*, raising issues about the Tramp's character that had nothing to do with the story. One can only wonder if it was inspired by Chaplin's guilty conscience over sleeping with his friend's lover. With *The Kid* approaching completion, the day when he would have to go to New York to negotiate with First National executives was drawing near—and no doubt he dreaded confronting Max, who now knew that he and Florence were planning to marry.

Florence, meanwhile, had not been well. Illness had forced her to cancel her commitment to Fox and return early from San Francisco, and she was bedridden for almost a month. She was also beginning to wonder whether Charlie intended to get a divorce at all. By the beginning of July he had begun saying that rather than pay Mildred a lot of money, he would find a way to "make it up with her."[16]

The shooting of *The Kid* was over at last, though Chaplin next faced the daunting task of editing nearly half a million feet of film. On August 3, however, Mildred's attorneys unexpectedly filed divorce papers. Realizing Chaplin's worst fears, they had joined forces with First National in asking the California courts to seize the negative of his movie as collateral against a future settlement. To make matters worse, George Spoor had petitioned a federal court judge to grant him a lien on the picture as well.

Chaplin was warned of the impending seizure the night before the California judge issued his order. In the middle of the night he called Rollie Totheroh and asked him and his assistant, Jack Wilson, to pack the negative in coffee cans. Chaplin and Tom Harrington met Totheroh and Wilson at the train station, and they all decamped to Salt Lake City, where they began cutting the negative in a hotel room.

Chased by process servers, Chaplin's party later made its way east and hid out in a rented barn in New Jersey while completing the editing. When Chaplin showed up in New York offering to screen the finished picture for First National's executives they were furious. But *The Kid* was clearly destined to be a tremendous hit, and faced with a choice between a profitable movie and a ruinous lawsuit, they were prepared to bargain. The executives offered to count the film as the equivalent of three two-reelers. Including bonuses this would bring Chaplin an advance of something over $400,000. He, however, had spent more than that to make the picture, and demanded $1,500,000 as well as 70 percent of the profits after his advance was earned back.[17] Grumbling all the while, the executives met his price.

First National's deal with Charlie left Mildred in the cold. By now she had indeed begun dating another man and did not want to risk a scandal. Rather than charge adultery, she petitioned for divorce on grounds of "mental cruelty," complaining that Charlie had neglected her and refused to speak to her for long periods of time. By way of an example, her divorce petition mentioned his habit of going for long solitary walks while brooding over the next day's shooting, even when it happened to be raining—"the harder it rained the longer he walked and the harder he thought." The editorial writers at the *New York Times*, who rarely commented on the personal problems of movie stars, took this complaint at face value, expressing amazement that a wife could be so selfish that she "objected that her husband was devoted to thought."[18]

Wiser than Mildred in the ways of public relations, Chaplin avoided interviews while making sure that his influential New York writer friends were well apprised of his side of the story. Borrowing a dress and hat from his sister-in-law, Minnie, who along with Syd was sharing his suite at the Ritz, he sashayed through the crush of reporters in the lobby and cabbed uptown to pay a call on Frank Harris, for whom he rehashed his recent phone conversations with Mildred, mimicking her voice with occasional asides of his own: "I am entitled to a settlement. (Eh?) I am too ill, physically and mentally, to work at present, and this notoriety and exposition of my personal affairs is very disagreeable to me. (Really? You needn't engage in it, Madam, unless you want to.)"

Mildred, he told Harris, would agree to the first figure he proposed only to ring back minutes later, whining, "Oh, I'm sorry, but my lawyer won't let me take fifty thousand; he says it is ridiculous. Won't you give me a hundred thousand, and I can satisfy him? Please, I'm so nervous and ill." He took revenge by offering half a million, then dialing back fifteen minutes later to say that *his* lawyer had vetoed the plan: "He says a year's earnings for a week's marriage is too much."

Charlie related this story, Harris later wrote, with "a smile on his lips and a little sub-acid contempt for human, and especially for feminine, nature."[19]

In the end Mildred did get her hundred thousand, though after eight months of wrangling a substantial percentage went to pay her attorneys' fees. Meanwhile she had given up positivity in favor of whiskey, and within a year she was bankrupt, her looks frayed. Mildred eventually remarried and had a healthy son. She appeared in many films, and as late as 1931 was billed along with Clark Gable and Barbara Stanwyck in *Night Nurse*. But the stardom that seemed so sure in 1918 never materialized, and she was eventually reduced to acting as a foil for the Three Stooges. An alcoholic, she died of pneumonia at the age of forty-three.

Chaplin could hardly be blamed for Mildred Harris's unhappy life—certainly, as biographer John McCabe noted, "alcoholism is not a disease imposed on one by others"[20]—on the other hand, he didn't do her any good, either.

8

"A Total Stranger to Life"

Florence Deshon had joined Charlie in Utah and traveled east with
him as far as Chicago. There Charlie had a mysterious business
meeting, probably in order to work out a settlement with George
Spoor, who had to be pacified before *The Kid* could be sold.
Florence was feeling extremely ill, and she decided to go ahead to
New York, where Max Eastman met her train and was shocked to
find that she was running a high fever and almost too weak to walk.
He immediately took her to the office of gynecologist Herman
Lorber, who discovered that she was carrying a three-month-old
fetus that had died in the womb. Without treatment she would have
been dead from blood poisoning within a few days. Had it lived, the
the baby would have been Charlie's.

Writing of the incident in later years, Eastman would refer to the
death of the fetus as a "tragic accident." However, Lorber's bitter
comments about incompetent California doctors suggest that the
cause of Florence's condition may have been a bungled abortion.
Florence had already had one abortion during the first year of her
affair with Max, and considering that Charlie had been suggesting
he might not divorce Mildred after all, she had reason to try to end
her pregnancy.

      ✿   ✿   ✿

After emergency surgery Florence recovered quickly, nursed by Max at the cottage in Croton. (Lisa Duncan had moved out, leaving Max the Chinese red living room to remember her by.) Max found it difficult to comprehend how any man—even one as self-absorbed as Charlie—could have allowed a woman so ill to travel alone from Chicago to New York. Presumably he was so focused on rescuing *The Kid* from being tied up in litigation that he was too distracted to notice Florence's deteriorating physical condition.

At first Max's attentions were platonic, but after several weeks with no word from Charlie, they resumed their sexual relationship. Then Charlie did show up in New York with the finished print of *The Kid*. Florence visited him at the Ritz, found him contrite and deeply hurt that she had lost faith in his good intentions, and began sleeping with him, too.

Thus for a time she was commuting between her two lovers. As Eastman saw it, he and Charlie owed it to Florence to give her a chance to make up her mind between them; indeed, they were feeling rather noble about their broad-mindedness: "We both had a sense of humor and of the varieties of human experience, and we both admired her extravagantly. There was something royal in her nature that gave her the right to have things as she pleased."[1]

In truth Max was probably secretly hoping that Florence would choose Charlie. Though he loved her in his way, he and Florence couldn't seem to live together without getting involved in titanic quarrels that wore both of them out. Charlie's position was more complicated. Max had no doubt where his friend's heart lay: "Florence was the only girl he had ever loved with total respect and admiration," he later wrote.[2] The problem was that Charlie suspected that Florence would never love him with the same passionate intensity she felt for Max. This might have been true in any case, but Charlie's diffident behavior made it certain. Instead of trying to compete with Max, he summed up the situation by telling Florence that he was "satisfied to have sneaked in where a better man belonged."

Florence, one suspects, was unsure of both men and waiting for one or the other to deliver an ultimatum. In an obvious attempt to spark a confrontation, she persuaded Charlie to accompany her to

Croton, but while walking up the path to Max's cottage his courage failed him. He left her there and hurried back to New York alone.

Shortly afterward, on October 2, Florence dined with Max at the Nikko Inn, a Japanese restaurant at the junction of the Croton and Hudson Rivers. During dinner she confessed that she was consumed by a rage against him that was "absolutely insane." She had made up her mind that she could never marry any man but Charlie, but "I would have a child by you before I married him." On this unsatisfactory—and to Max, thoroughly bewildering—note, she left for Los Angeles, where she was soon to begin shooting another picture for Fox, *The Twins of Suffering Creek*. Charlie was still negotiating with First National and Mildred's attorneys and was unable to follow her for the time being.[3]

Once back in Los Angeles, Florence was able to think things through more calmly. Her feelings for Max were as unresolved as ever, but she saw that she could never marry Charlie. Her attraction to him was based on the fantasy that he would take care of her—"I know I childishly longed for a mother, that was all."[4]

With hindsight it would seem that Chaplin had almost willed Florence to reject him. Had he been more willing to assert himself, she would have respected him more. Had he made a timely settlement with Mildred, he and Florence could have been married months earlier, and—assuming that Florence did something to end her pregnancy—that whole tragic experience need never have taken place. In any case it seems that Charlie hadn't known Florence was pregnant at the time, and still wasn't sure exactly what had gone wrong. Having already fathered one child with a fatal birth defect, he drew the lesson that he was incapable of fathering a healthy baby.

As it was, the sorry situation cast a shadow over his greatest career triumph. First National had caved in to all his demands, and *The Kid* opened in New York on January 5, 1920, to raves from the critics and a huge box office. Since 1916 Chaplin had been a favorite of the New York style setters, but in a slightly condescending way. Slapstick comedy represented the vitality of pop culture, therefore progressive critics thought they should like it. With the release of *The Kid*, however, Chaplin began to be accepted as a serious filmmaker and a prophet of modernism. Looking at the movie today, it is hard to see why. *The Kid* is a lovely piece of filmmaking, but an unabashed tearjerker, almost Victorian in its sensibility. And even at the time intellectuals who adored *The Kid* found their passion hard to justify. Hart Crane, a still-unheralded poet who was just beginning his mature work, saw the picture at a neighborhood theater in his hometown of Cleveland and was enthralled. When his friend, critic Gorham Munson, complained that it was far too sentimental, Crane responded that, yes, the sentiment was excessive, but its deliberate excess had to be seen as a protest against the "mechanized, deracinated" quality of modern life. *The Kid*, he summed up, was the cinematic equivalent of "the futile gesture of the poet in the USA today."[5] Crane loved *The Kid* so much that he wrote a poem about it, "Chaplinesque." At the time he knew of no one who would publish it, but he mailed off a copy to Chaplin at his studio.

Although Crane framed his reaction to *The Kid* in terms of his situation as a struggling poet, he was also a homosexual, like many of Chaplin's most devoted admirers. Charlie's appeal to gay men was established almost from the beginning. The Tramp was never a conventionally masculine figure, and several early Chaplin comedies contain relatively explicit references to homosexuality. In *Behind the Screen* Eric Campbell catches Charlie smooching with Edna, who is disguised as a man, and comes to the wrong conclusion. Confronted by a bully, as in *Pay Day*, Charlie often responds by flirting with him.

No doubt it was tempting to guess that Chaplin was dropping hints about his own sexual orientation, and in her 1940 biography, *Charlie Chaplin, King of Tragedy*, Gerith von Ulm refers to widespread speculation on this subject, relaying Toraichi Kono's opinion that Charlie was "essentially normal." Coming from the chauffeur/valet who knew Chaplin's most intimate habits, this comment strikes one as equivocal, but one can only observe that if Chaplin had physical relationships with men he conducted them with a discretion that he could not manage to bring to bear on other areas of his life. What matters is that while Chaplin the man was often uncomfortable with the contradictions of his personality, Chaplin the artist understood instinctively that androgyny was in tune wth the modern temperament.

And *The Kid* went a step farther. In this film Chaplin did not simply portray a dispossessed and sexually indeterminate character, he made him heroic. The appeal of the film was not just to poets or homosexuals, but to anyone who felt marginalized by society. The Tramp, a social outcast, was a better father to the kid than his biological father, a better mother than his real mother, more responsible and caring than the community and the state. He demonstrated the moral superiority of the lonely, alienated individual.

Another reason for Chaplin's growing reputation among intellectuals was quite simply that he courted them, imitated them, and made every effort to talk like them. The critic Benjamin de Casseres, who saw Chaplin frequently during the latter's stay in New York, was not at all impressed by his wistful desire to play Hamlet, recalling that vaudeville comedian Eddie Foy had once confided to him a dream of playing Lear to Marie Dressler's Cordelia. What did amaze him was the quality (and, more so, the quantity) of Chaplin's talk, his ability to go on for hours in the mode of an "ultra-advanced thinker." De Casseres tried to record Chaplin's stream-of-consciousness monologues as accurately as he could, emphasizing that his transcripts were just brief excerpts from hours of similarly one-sided conversation:

My clowning, as the world calls it—and I dislike the word clown, for I am not a clown—may have esoteric meanings. I prefer to think of myself as a mimetic satirist, for I have aimed in all my comedies at burlesquing, satirizing the human race—or, at least, those human beings whose very existence is an unconscious satire on this world. The human race I prefer to think of as the underworld of the gods. When the gods go slumming they visit the earth. You see, my respect for the human race is not 100 per cent.

My antics on the screen to you are no doubt ridiculous. Well, the antics of men—even in their most serious and what they choose to call their sublimest occupations—are just as ridiculous to the gods or beings who live in the higher dimensions.

In a word, the whole of humanity seen from the angles of the cosmic imagination are Charlie Chaplins.

In my antics, my clothes, my horseplay, my illogical movements and comic pathos I show mankind itself as it must look to spectators Higher Up. If there be any who are looking at this Charivari on earth. . . .

Although not a pessimist or a misanthrope, there are days when contact with any human being makes me physically ill. I am oppressed at such times and in such periods by what was known among the Romantics as world-weariness, I feel a total stranger to life.

Here de Casseres ventured to interject a comment: "In the wrong flat?" he suggested.

"On the wrong star," replied Chaplin. And he continued:

I once had a day vision. I saw at my feet in a huddled heap all the trappings and paraphernalia of my screen clothes—that dreadful suit of clothes!—my mustache, the battered derby, the little cans, the broken shovel, the dirty collar and shirt. I felt as though my body had fallen from me and that I was leaving behind an eternal seeming for a vast reality.

That day I had resolved never to get into those clothes again—to retire to some Italian lake with my beloved violin, my Shelley and my Keats, and live under an assumed name a life purely imaginative and intellectual, but the instinct to be other than I really am, which is universal, is so strong in me, and I went in for just one more picture—the last; like the drunkard's eternal last drink and Patti's eternal farewell."[6]

One's first thought on reading this is that Chaplin was putting his interviewer on. Surely the talk of retiring to a villa "with my Shelley and my Keats" was a bit of a pose. But when he talked of the Tramp as an addiction, like drink, he was quite serious. Work kept him going; it was a reminder of who he had been before he was overcome by fame.

Unfortunately, Chaplin's tendency to swing between periods of mild depression and hyperexcitability—probably established years earlier—was becoming more pronounced. The Tramp was the depressed half of the equation, a man of good intentions but fated to perceive the world around him as shabby and gray. Charles Spencer Chaplin was the manic persona, addicted to the pursuit of women, money, and petty legal squabbles.

Chaplin was well aware of his divided self, and would make use of it in his next First National comedy, *The Idle Class*, which he began on his return to California. The story called for him to play dual roles as a rich drunkard and his hobo look-alike. Edna, who had toyed with the idea of going over to Goldwyn's studio but decided against it, was cast as the rich man's "neglected wife."

In Chaplin's personal life the manic side of his personality was definitely in the ascendancy. Consoling himself about Florence's rejection, he had begun an affair with first likely candidate to present herself—May Collins, an aspiring actress who had been hired in New York by Syd to handle his correspondence. Collins followed him to Los Angeles, and it soon became apparent that she was more than a secretary. On April 12 the studio confirmed a report that she and Chaplin were engaged to be married.

Florence, who remained on close and perhaps even intimate terms with Charlie, considered May a good influence on him and felt no resentment of her. Max Eastman, who arrived for a visit a few weeks later, also approved, describing May as "plump, round, rosy, bright-eyed, unscheming, full of happy laughter. She was fun. . . . the kind of girl who made you think she came from home. She had plenty of sophistication, but wore it as part of her nature, not an acquired adornment." May, he added, was not at all the sort of woman the public would expect Charlie Chaplin to be interested in.[7]

Unfortunately Chaplin had acquired this sensible fiancée almost absentmindedly while on the rebound from Florence, and their relationship was complicated by the repercussions of earlier entanglements.

Soon it was reported that actress Claire Windsor had been kidnapped while horseback riding in the Hollywood hills. A deceptively fragile-looking blonde, Windsor (born Olga Cronk) was the mother of a two-year-old son whose father's name she declined to reveal. Charlie had been close to Windsor for a time, and after being approached by her agent, he publicly offered a thousand-dollar reward and joined the search party. A few days later a young couple picnicking in the canyons discovered Windsor lying under a tree, looking dazed and claiming amnesia. Chaplin's aide, Carlyle Robinson, suspected a hoax and questioned Windsor until she admitted that the disappearance had been a stunt, cooked up by her agent.[8]

This, at least, was the story as told to Carl Robinson, but there was more to it. Chaplin had abruptly ended an affair with Windsor sometime earlier, and the kidnapping appears to have been staged in a deliberate attempt to embarrass him. Exactly why Windsor felt ill used is unclear, but Florence and Max were sympathetic, as they probably wouldn't have been if the only point of the hoax was publicity. They took Windsor out to dinner and spent the evening with her. Charlie said nothing directly, but May, in a "nervous-cross" mood, passed the word that he was deeply offended.

Now that he was divorced Chaplin had moved into a much grander house, a Moorish-style mansion on Beechwood Drive. May was under the impression that they were soon to be married, but in early June Charlie suddenly decided that he could scarcely stand to be in the same room with her. Rather than tell May that his feelings had changed, he began to avoid her. Since she was still working as his secretary and had an office at the studio, this wasn't easy. Charlie stopped coming in to work, sending word that he was suffering from a bad case of influenza, which May knew to be a lie. Bewildered and hurt, she began dropping in to see Florence, whom she knew Charlie still visited. She had no idea what had caused the chill and went on a crash diet, thinking that her weight might be the problem.

"Poor boy," Deshon wrote of Charlie. "He can't stand May and it is very hard to get her to realize it. She comes over here all the time."[9] In fact May hadn't done anything to offend, possibly apart from being so well adjusted and loyal that Charlie had grown bored with her. The chief reason for the change was that Max's visit had not gone well, and Florence and Charlie were now drifting back together.

This time there was no discussion of marriage, and Charlie's attitude was guarded. His pride had been wounded when Florence began sleeping with Max again in New York, and, Max observed, Charlie was not one to let himself be hurt by the same woman twice. Despite this, he resumed his role as Florence's lover and guardian angel. He took over the payments on the Buick, and Tom Harrington had the car repaired, with a new convertible top and tires. (The alternative, buying her a new car, seems never to have occurred to Chaplin, who did not spend freely on himself either.)

Unfortunately it was not so easy to solve Florence's professional problems. After Charlie's engagement to May was announced, the stream of lucrative film offers Florence had been getting suddenly dried up—a sure indication that she had been getting work mainly because she was thought to be in line as the next Mrs. Charlie Chaplin. Though she must have already suspected this, the truth was painful. Reduced to doing regional theater in Santa Barbara and at the Pasadena Playhouse, she began to talk of switching careers. She was working hard on several articles, including a piece for *Vanity Fair* on the Hollywood scene. She called it "The Dictatorship of Mediocrity," a title she expected she would have to change before submitting it. An earnest exposé of mediocrity in the movie business was doubtless the last thing the style-chasing, celebrity-fancying *Vanity Fair* was looking for, and it is no wonder that Florence's writing career was doomed to frustration.

In New York, Max Eastman had recently spent a day at a publicity event in Bayside, Queens, sponsored by the Astoria Studios, where a considerable number of feature films were still being made. In an awkward attempt to entertain Florence and provide some material for her *Vanity Fair* article, he wrote her a long and uncharacteristically catty account of the event. Norma Talmadge's looks were disappointing, he reported, as she had a "cast" in one eye. But she, at least, had a sense of humor. He was "bored to death" by her better-looking sister Constance. Anita Loos was a "terrible-voiced" woman who suffered from the illusion that she was an intellectual. Max's nastiest comments were reserved for Mae Marsh, a "nice little freckled mick" whom he described as the kind of girl respectable families would work hard to keep as a maid. Marsh had recently given birth, groused Max, "and she is so crazy about her baby that you know there is no use talking about any other subject. I hate to see people in that condition."[10]

Florence failed to see the humor in this description. She replied to Max's effusive letter with a curt note: "Your neurotic selfishness has wiped any memory of you from my mind. It is though [sic] I had never known you." He never did figure out what he had written to provoke this reaction.

Florence was now deeply depressed, and the "black panther" side of her personality more often taking control. She was furious with Max for being too in love with "liberty" to enter into a committed relationship, disgusted with Hollywood, and probably also angry with Charlie, who certainly hadn't mourned their breakup very long before taking up with May Collins. Complicating the situation, May refused to fade gracefully out of the picture and hung around town for several months, insisting that Charlie owed her an explanation for his behavior. In addition Hannah Chaplin had recently arrived from England, escorted by Tom Harrington, who made a quick round trip to London to handle the sailing arrangements.

In his autobiography Chaplin expresses annoyance at the U.S. immigration authorities who put Harrington through "a lot of red tape" after the unpredictable Hannah addressed an official on Ellis Island as Jesus Christ. He implies that the Bureau of Immigration had put obstacles in the way of his desire to be reunited with his mother. On the contrary, Hannah Chaplin's immigration file reveals that Syd Chaplin's requests for a visa for his mother had been expedited at the highest level. Hannah was admitted to the United States for a "special course of treatment," a polite fiction to evade the rule against admitting mentally ill persons. Her original visa, issued in January 1917, was promptly renewed on request in April 1919 and again in early 1921.[11] Once the war ended there was nothing in the way of bringing Hannah to California but Charlie's resistance to the idea. In 1919, for example, he had pleaded with Syd that he couldn't handle his mother's arrival while he was so unhappy about the situation with Mildred.

When Hannah Chaplin did reach the States, Sydney settled her in a Santa Monica cottage with a couple to keep house for her and a full-time nurse-companion. The years had transformed Hannah into a ruddy-faced, solid-looking matron who used henna on her silver hair. Max Eastman, who went with Charlie to visit her soon after her arrival, found Hannah "perfectly bewitching." She knew all the old music hall songs and with the slightest encouragement could sing them in tune without benefit of an accompaniment. "She was a little crazy," Eastman added, "but was aware of it and able to manage it some of the time."[12]

Sydney, Minnie, and even Alf and Amy Reeves took an active interest in Hannah's welfare; Charlie was paying her bills but didn't visit often. He loved his mother but could not quite forgive her for failing him when he was a child. And despite his attack on the double standard and the stigma of illegitimacy in *The Kid*, one feels that on some level he still thought she had been promiscuous and blamed her for it. When Charlie did make an effort to spend time with Hannah, their visits were as hard on her as on him. Brought to the studio to watch Charlie at work, she became distressed seeing her son in ragged clothes and makeup that made him look sickly and pale. She knew that he was in the movie business but had trouble keeping the distinction between him and his character fixed in her mind. There was a tension between her and her younger son that did not seem to extend to Sydney. Hannah had vested all her hopes and ambitions in Charlie—her childhood nickname for him had been "The King"—but now that he had succeeded beyond all expectations she was unable, or unwilling, to recognize the fact.

Since before he married Mildred Harris, Chaplin had been talking about making a trip back to England. Now the frustrations of dealing with Florence, May, and his mother made the time ripe for escape. Florence was talking about moving back East soon anyway, and in mid-August Chaplin shut down the studio, abandoning a half-finished comedy that would have featured him and Mack Swain as a pair of *nouveau riche* plumbers.

Stopping for a few days in New York, Chaplin played host at a luncheon party at the fashionable Elysée Cafe. He now had two sets of friends in New York—the Greenwich Village bohemians and the uptowners, who included Frank Crowninshield, the editor of *Vanity Fair*, the critic Heywood Broun, publisher Condé Nast, and assorted theatrical types. With some trepidation he decided that the time had come to mix the two circles. He needn't have worried; the "Red" Max Eastman was a great success with the uptown crowd, charming everyone. Eastman in turn threw a party for Charlie in the Village, where the most interesting guest was a Bulgarian refugee, a former secretary of the IWW, who was out on bail after serving two years of a twenty-year sentence.

The political climate had softened considerably since the "Red Scare" period, and Chaplin now felt confident enough to talk about politics in public. In an interview with a representative of the movie magazine *Shadowland*, he said, "Wealth has allowed me to think. I used to be afraid to have ideas," and went on to speak earnestly of his admiration for Lenin "because he trims his sails and modifies his ideas to meet the changes of each day." And he added: "Whenever I mention my ideas on Russia to newspaper men, they ask me to compare Lenine [sic] to someone in American history. This desire to compare everything and anyone to something or someone else is one of the platitudes of mass thinking."[13]

As a result of these comments, Chaplin would be pursued in New York and in Europe by reporters asking him to confirm his pro-Bolshevik sentiments. Perhaps this accounted for the cloud of paranoia that had descended on his entourage. On the day that Chaplin, Carl Robinson, and Tom Harrington boarded the liner *Olympic* for the voyage to England, a news service reporter happened to approach Chuck Riesner on the pier and was startled when Riesner began berating him for a mildly negative review of *The Idle Class*, circulated by his syndicate. Riesner was so upset that Chaplin had to step in and smooth things over with the reporter, telling him that Riesner "always has a chip on his shoulders [sic] where I am concerned. He rather mothers me in his rough way. We talk about everybody's ingratitude for what he and I have done for people."[14] Presumably he was speaking ironically.

Several news organizations had put reporters on board the *Olympic*, and their bulletins, filed by radio, built up excitement in England about the Cockney comedian's homecoming. When the *Olympic* reached Southampton, thousands were waiting on the pier, and a reception ceremony complete with speeches by the Lord Mayor and band music had been prepared. Orchestra leaders everywhere had dusted off their arrangements of the old tune "Charlie Is My Darling," and the newspapers predicted: HOMECOMING OF COMEDIAN TO RIVAL ARMISTICE DAY. In the event, the crowds were not quite as large as those that had turned out to greet Douglas Fairbanks and Mary Pickford a few months earlier. Chaplin managed to be at once panicked by their size and slightly peeved that they were not larger.

In Los Angeles earlier in the year Chaplin had confided to Max Eastman that he was thinking a great deal about Hetty Kelly, the teenage Bert Coutts dancer he had adored during his Karno days. Hetty was married to the son of a British MP and had written him a friendly letter in 1918, but it was only more recently, following his failed marriage and his ill-fated love for Florence Deshon, that her memory had become almost a "fetish." His hopes for a reunion soared when her brother, Arthur Kelly, now an executive with a film company, turned up among the welcoming party in Southampton. On the train to London they shared a compartment, and Chaplin mentioned that he was thinking of dropping in on Hetty. It was an awkward moment. Kelly stammered out the news that Hetty was dead, a casualty of the great influenza epidemic of 1918. Chaplin felt as if he had been "robbed of an experience." As he later wrote, he thought that Hetty would be his "audience": "My success I had looked upon as a bouquet of flowers to be addressed to someone, and now that address was unknown."[15]

At the London Ritz a second tumultuous reception awaited. Thousands of fans filled the street in front of the hotel. Someone had given Chaplin a bouquet of roses, and he impetuously tossed them to the crowd. The police immediately sent a representative, begging him not to repeat the gesture for fear of causing a riot. In his room Chaplin found a mountain of mail—invitations, letters from former members of the Karno and Casey's Court troupes, and requests for financial help from total strangers. There was also a solicitation from a man who had noticed his prematurely graying hair and claimed to be the only person in the kingdom able to restore its natural color.

Aside from meeting Hetty, Chaplin had hoped to accomplish two things in England—to make a sentimental pilgrimage to the locales of his youthful struggles and, as he candidly put it, "cash in on this celebrity business" by meeting the sort of people who once would have disdained him. On both counts he was disappointed. He could not really enjoy his visits to places he had known as a child—the past was still too vivid. On the social front he found himself meeting mainly "Hollywood" people and their British equivalents. A dinner invitation from the Prince of Wales turned out to be a hoax. A banquet in his honor at the Garrick Club, attended by J. M. Barrie and Gerald du Maurier, proved to be slightly awkward. Chaplin had been quoted in the press as saying he was homesick for treacle pudding, so this working-class dish was on the menu at the Garrick, as it was nearly everywhere else he went.

Even his invitation to dine with H. G. Wells and his common-law wife, Rebecca West, did not quite live up to expectations. The author of *An Outline of History* was a hero of Chaplin's, and when he received a fan letter from Wells during the filming of *The Idle Class* he carried it around in his pocket and proudly showed it off to Max Eastman. He didn't quite know how to reply, however, and put off the task so long that he was finally embarrassed to answer at all. Wells did not hold this against him, but on the day of the dinner Chaplin found himself dragooned into attending a screening of a movie based on one of Wells's stories. He hated the movie, refrained from saying so, and then became annoyed when Wells remarked, "There is no such thing as a bad film."

In Paris the crowds were larger than in England. Doug Fairbanks and Mary Pickford were already ensconced at the Hotel Crillon. Also in the city were two good friends of Max Eastman, the novelist Waldo Frank and attorney Dudley Field Malone, who volunteered to show him the city and introduce him to the literary figures who gathered at the Brasserie Lipp. Little remembered today except as the author of many *New Yorker* profiles, Frank was considered an important writer, the leader of a generation of Americans who were overcoming the provincialism of the past. Frank loathed bourgeois hypocrisy and the "puritanism" that drove Americans to launch moral crusades like Prohibition, and at this point in his life he still believed that communism might show the way to a world of individual freedom and unfettered self-expression.[16]

One day Frank showed up at Chaplin's hotel with Jacques Coupeau, an innovative theatrical director and editor of the *Nouvelle Revue Française*. The two men announced that they were going to take Chaplin to the Cirque d'Hiver to meet the Fratellini brothers, a famous pair of clowns. Chaplin had admired circus clowns and indeed borrowed from some of them, but he had mixed feelings about being called a clown himself. One suspects that he was less interested in the Fratellinis than in the discovery that intellectuals like Frank and Coupeau were connoisseurs of clowning and considered it a great art form.[17]

What Frank remembered about the outing was Chaplin's reaction when the audience recognized him and surged around their party at the end of the show, nearly tearing their clothes off. As the three of them made their escape, he heard Chaplin muttering under his breath, "It means nothing. Nothing."[18]

After Paris, Berlin was another letdown. Chaplin's pictures were largely unknown, and he had trouble getting a hotel room at the overbooked Adlon. At a fashionable restaurant he was seated in an obscure table near the kitchen until, by chance, he was recognized by Paramount executive Al Kaufman. Kaufman was in town to negotiate a Hollywood contract for Pola Negri, whose films *Passion* (also called *Madame Dubarry*) and *Gypsy Blood*, based on the opera *Carmen*, had been hits in America. The minxlike Pola greeted Chaplin as, "Jazz boy, Sharlie," the only English words she knew. During the next few days they were seen and photographed everywhere, usually with Pola's much taller lover glowering in the background.

Aside from Kaufman, the only other familiar face Chaplin saw in Berlin was "George," the IWW stalwart he had met at Max Eastman's village party. George had skipped bail and was now, he proudly explained, the European purchasing agent for the Bolshevik government.

By the time he returned to Paris, Chaplin's mood had improved. Dudley Malone and Iris Tree took him on a late night tour of Montmartre, where he encountered a beautiful White Russian singer called Skaya in a dive known as Le Rat Mort and took the opportunity to question her on the subject that seemed to be very much on his mind.

"Are you a Bolshevik?" he asked her.

"No, they are wicked. Bolshevik man, he's very bad. Bolshevik good idea for the mind, but bad for practice."

Chaplin then asked Skaya if she had given the Bolsheviks a "fair opportunity."

"Plenty," she said. Her mother was one.[19]

Chaplin decided that Skaya, whose full name was Moussia Sodskaya, could become a great film artist. He talked of doing a movie with her, but nothing came of the idea. For the moment, at least, Skaya was a stateless person, marooned in France without a passport.

Returning to England, Chaplin spent a weekend at H. G. Wells's country house; this time everyone avoided the subject of the movies, and the visit was a success. (In later years, Chaplin bragged that he had seduced Rebecca West during the course of the weekend.) Then it was back to Paris. On his first visit he had been approached by Anne Morgan, the daughter of J. P. Morgan, for permission to hold the French premiere of *The Kid* (*Le Gosse*) at the Trocadero theater as a benefit for the war-devastated villages of France. Chaplin did not really want to attend—one gets the impression that the French *cinéastes* who idolized him as *Charlot* made him a little nervous—but Miss Morgan had assured him that "you will be decorated" and mentioned the possibility of his getting the Legion of Honor. Arriving in town on the day of the premiere, Chaplin was rushed to a gala dinner attended by members of the French cabinet, boxer Georges Carpentier, publishing magnate Henri Letellier, and Princess Xenia of Greece and assorted other crowned heads. At the theater, after lengthy speeches and a lengthier show—*The Kid* having been augmented by a documentary on the plight of the war-damaged countryside—Chaplin was at last presented with a rosette of the Order of Public Instruction.

The cartoonist Cami, one of the organizers of the event, was incensed. "Chaplin did not know the value of the decoration and accepted it with eyes full of tears," he wrote. But the Order of Public Instruction was the sort of award given to retiring school principals and—considering that the evening had raised two hundred thousand francs—almost an insult. Madame Cecile Sorel, who was seated in the official box with Charlie and Cami, "could not suppress a cry of indignation and muttered under her breath, "He should have *la croix*, or nothing."[20]

Chaplin, quite sensibly, thought that receiving an award given to schoolteachers put him in good company. He could nevertheless be excused for feeling more than a little irritated with his hosts. Anne Morgan and others had raised expectations that he was about to receive the Legion of Honor, and now he had been humiliated in front of a select audience that showed up expecting him to get it. If he expressed disappointment, he would seem petty and ungrateful. If he didn't, everyone would assume he was too ignorant to know that he had been slighted.

Cami had sent drawings and letters to Chaplin in Los Angeles and received friendly replies—apparently in French, since he was startled to learn on meeting *Charlot* that they had no common language. They communicated through gestures, but at one point, Charlie had hugged Cami, telling him, "I feel as if you are my other self." With some justification Cami considered himself Chaplin's best friend in France, and the following evening, at a dinner party hosted by Georges Carpentier and Henri Letellier, he vowed to right the wrong done by his government. Over the next ten years, he would make obtaining the Legion of Honor for Chaplin a crusade, enlisting the support of influential writers like Louis Delluc, a founder of the French Ciné Club movement, who produced the first book-length critique of Chaplin's films.

Returning to New York, Chaplin extended his vacation for a few days. Max Eastman was soon to depart for an extended stay in the Soviet Union, and knowing he would be gone for years, he made an effort to introduce Chaplin to as many of his New York circle as possible. Charlie was especially impressed by the Jamaican poet Claude McKay, who, he thought, looked and often acted like an "African prince."

He also spent time with the writer Frank Harris, who took him to visit Sing Sing penitentiary, where he was dismayed by his brief glimpse of the electric chair but observed that the prisoners, in general, seemed to have "quite a bit of freedom" and more visitors than he would have dreamed possible. "Why are sinners always loved?" he mused. "Why do sinners make such wonderful lovers?"

None of Chaplin's intellectual friends would ever be as close to him as Eastman, who had a childlike (and occasionally childish) belief in the importance of "play." For one thing, Eastman knew that Chaplin rarely read a book all the way through, and yet did not mind his literary name-dropping. Indeed, he thought men of action were as important as thinkers, and was gratified that Charlie cared for books as much as he did.

With Eastman's departure imminent, Charlie did begin to grow closer to another charismatic character, Konrad Bercovici, a Romanian-born musician, composer, and writer of mixed Jewish and Gypsy descent. A gregarious man who sported a luxuriant mustache and outsize enthusiasms, Bercovici told colorful stories of his youthful experiences living among the people of the Rom. Chaplin had met Bercovici in 1915 when he was a reporter for the *New York*

World. Since that time he had published a book about the slums of New York and the failures of reform called *Crimes of Charity*, with a foreword by John Reed. Bercovici was interested in writing for the movies and would soon turn up in California with his wife, Naomi Librescu, a French-Romanian sculptor. Their younger daughter, Mirel, recalls that Chaplin visited the house often, invariably bearing gifts for her and her sister—"and good ones, too"—on one occasion a wooden monkey that climbed a stick. The toys were fascinating, though Chaplin would embarrass the girls by asking, "Don't you love me more than you love your daddy?"[21]

On the train back to California, Chaplin dictated the story of his European trip to journalist Monta Bell, who would soon join his staff as an assistant director. A magazine had offered $25,000 for the serial rights, a sum that would repay his expenses, and perhaps because he and Bell were working quickly, the narrative was unusually candid. Chaplin acknowledged that during a visit with his cousin Aubrey Chaplin he showed off his radical political opinions, largely for the pleasure of shocking him. ("I find myself deliberately posing, and just for him. I want to be different, and I want him to know that I am a different person.") Perhaps the most interesting revelation was his confession that he found passing through immigration control a frightening experience: "I am terrified of American officials." Why this should be, he never said.[22]

Despite his public praise for Lenin, Chaplin had not received an invitation to visit the Bolshevik "worker's paradise." His films were unknown in Russia, and it had not yet occurred to the leaders of the international Communist movement that a mere slapstick comedian might be worth cultivating. On his return to Los Angeles, however, he was to meet a sculptor who not only knew Lenin but had persuaded him to model for her. Clare Sheridan was a well-connected bohemian and a cousin of Winston Churchill. Chaplin had read her book *From Mayfair to Moscow* before he left for Europe and commented to Sam Goldwyn that she was the one woman in the world he wanted to meet. Sheridan was in San Antonio, Texas, in the final stages of a lecture tour, when she received a telegram from Metro-Goldwyn-Mayer president Abraham "Sam" Lehr offering to pay her expenses if she would come out to Los Angeles immediately. Expecting to be offered a writing assignment, Sheridan canceled her remaining lecture dates and hurried to Los Angeles, only to discover that she had been summoned as a sort of surprise homecoming gift for Charlie Chaplin.

Sheridan was outraged by Lehr's deception but decided that if she could persuade Chaplin to sit for her the publicity might generate other commissions. So far Sheridan had found that Americans were easy to scandalize—asked by a reporter if it was true that married women in England took lovers, she quipped, "As many as they can get," a mildly titillating witticism that rated tabloid headlines and outraged editorials during what must have been a slow week in the newsrooms. Unfortunately this kind of attention had not helped her to line up wealthy patrons.

The Lehrs' intimate dinner party was held just hours after Chaplin's arrival in LA. Sheridan set out to impress Charlie and found herself impressed in return. "It has been a wonderful evening," she wrote in her diary that night, "I seem to have been talking heart to heart with one who understands, who is full of deep thought and deep feeling. He is full of ideals and has a passion for what is beautiful"[23]

Though a child of privilege, Clare Sheridan knew about rejection. Her mother had been one of the glamorous Jerome sisters, American heiresses much admired in British society. Clare had been groomed to make a brilliant match, and when she turned out to be a plain, outspoken, bookish young woman, her mother could not forgive her. Charlie won her heart by listening sympathetically to her complaints about her unhappy childhood, though they paled in comparison with his own bitter memories. "I loved my mother almost more when she went out of her mind," he told Sheridan. "She had been so poor and so hungry—I believe it was starving herself that affected her brain."

A widow, Sheridan was traveling with her eight-year-old son, known as Dickie, and on the afternoon following Lehr's dinner Chaplin invited them for a tour of the studio and a special screening of *The Kid,* providing an improvised accompaniment on a harmonium. During the scene in which Jackie Coogan is carted off to the orphanage, Dickie began to sob, much to Chaplin's distress. This part of the film was intended to provoke tears, he explained, but he wasn't used to seeing its effect on a child.

The next day Sheridan brought her clay and modeling tools to Beechwood Drive, where Charlie sat for her, "with his wild hair standing on end, his orange dressing gown dazzling against the white walls of his Moorish house." He was a difficult model since he couldn't keep still, turning the sittings into nonstop performances that alternated between philosophical discussions and clowning for Dickie's amusement.

When the portrait head was finished, Charlie proposed a camping trip. The arrangements for this expedition illustrate how far he had come from the simple life. In addition to Kono he brought along his Japanese cook, and the party traveled in three cars, with five individual tents and a complete portable kitchen. Their weeklong idyll of camping, hiking, and swimming ended abruptly when a group of children who had been visiting their campsite on the beach mentioned its location to adults, who tipped off the press. Pursued by photographers, Charlie, Clare, and Dickie fled back to Beverly Hills. At the studio, meanwhile, a reporter cornered Carl Robinson to ask him if Mr. Chaplin and Miss Sheridan were engaged. "Why, she's old enough to be his mother!" Robinson sputtered.

Sheridan, who was all of four years older than Chaplin, was understandably offended. It was probably true, however, that Chaplin's feelings for her had less do to with romance, or even with sex, than with his longing for a ready-made family. Chaplin had spent at least as much time trying to impress Dickie as he had his mother, and there was something needy and even slightly inappropriate about his focusing so much attention on a little boy he would never see again.

Sheridan soon returned to New York, where she was taken aside by Bernard Baruch, a family friend, who gravely advised her that the status of mistress might be acceptable in Europe, but in the States it just wouldn't do: She must either marry Mr. Chaplin or publicly disavow him. "But there is no question of marriage and I refuse to break off a link with the most beautiful soul . . . the most alive, fascinating person I have ever met," Sheridan protested. Nevertheless both she and Charlie viewed the time they spent together as an episode without a future. Sheridan opened a studio in New York, and Dickie was dispatched with his nanny to England, where his uncle noted disapprovingly that the boy went around in a cap that had been worn by Jackie Coogan, a gift from Chaplin, ate with his fingers, and seemed "babyish" and "prone to excitement."[24]

Chaplin's associations with Clare Sheridan and Max Eastman, and his published comments on the Bolshevik revolution, meant little or nothing to most of his fans. Within the small world of left-wing politics, however, the discovery that the most famous man in the movies—and perhaps in the world—was a sympathizer was electrifying news. As early as 1919 Hart Crane's friend Gorham Munson had heard third-hand reports of Chaplin's sympathies, and he wrote the studio asking for a donation to his new radical magazine, the *Modernist,* and was thrilled to receive a ten-dollar contribution. The amount was secondary to the satisfaction of having Charlie Chaplin as a sponsor.[25]

Others who knew Chaplin better questioned just how deep his commitment went. Max Eastman, good friend that he was, complained that when the *Liberator* needed three thousand dollars in an emergency Charlie came through with only one thousand. The extra two thousand, Eastman noted, would have meant nothing at all to Charlie and everything to the magazine's hard-pressed staff and readers. One rather sympathizes with Chaplin on this score. Financial "emergencies" were a constant in the lives of Eastman and his circle, and Chaplin had before him the example of Kate Crane Gartz, the widow of a Pasadena plumbing supplies magnate, whose generosity to socialist causes often led to her being taken advantage of. At one point, when Eastman and Florence Deshon hoped to go to Europe together, they even planned to talk Mrs. Gartz into to sponsoring their trip as a sort of "scholarship."

Although it was sometimes reported that Chaplin was a member of the Socialist Party, his only active political involvement was with the Severance Club, a loosely organized group that met more or less regularly for dinner and discussion. Apart from Chaplin, the best-known film industry regular was William de Mille, the playwright brother of Cecil B. De Mille, though Doug Fairbanks occasionally attended meetings. Rob Wagner was one of the organizers and

Upton Sinclair an occasional speaker. Socialist in its leanings but nonideological, the Severance Club had three main areas of interest: censorship, union organizing, and the promotion of left-wing films.

Anticensorship activities were the special interest of Rob Wagner, and Chaplin probably indirectly subsidized an informal survey of state and local censorship actions that Wagner had begun compiling in 1918. But when it came to supporting political messages in films, Chaplin was leery. Chaplin had discussed the relationship of politics to art with Clare Sheridan, who had warned him against letting his films become vehicles for propaganda. Sheridan's advice must have made an impression, because Charlie followed it for a long time, disappointing left-wing friends who hoped that he would speak out on social issues or finance their own pet projects. Upton Sinclair, for one, was continually promoting films, including, in 1921, a remake of *The Jungle* (prints of the original film had been damaged or lost) and a screen version of his novel *The Millennium*, perhaps with Doug Fairbanks in a starring role.

Since Chaplin's own films were comedies, and silent ones at that, the opportunities for explicit political statements were few. No doubt this was just as well for his friends, since Chaplin's perspective was far from orthodox. As he told an aide, Jim Tully, a few years later, the socialists wanted men to live by the product of their own labor, whereas *he* didn't think they should have to work at all. And he wasn't kidding. Chaplin's jaundiced view of the workingman's life was summed up in his sixth First National film, *Pay Day*, which he began filming in November 1921, shortly after Clare Sheridan left town. In *Pay Day* the Little Fellow is a construction worker caught between a scary-looking boss (Mack Swain) and an even scarier wife (Phyllis Allen), who is to the rolling pin what General Patton would be to the tank corps. Late arriving at work, Charlie tries to pacify his boss by bringing him a lily and batting his eyelashes—it's a case of the aesthete trying vainly to charm a man who cares about nothing but schedules and profits. Just as Chaplin felt pressured by First National to keep up his quota of two-reelers, so here the Little Fellow is caught in a work speed-up—high on a scaffold he frantically tries to lay bricks as the boss tosses them to him from the ground. The boss keeps picking up the pace, and Charlie is forced to become a contortionist, catching flying bricks between his legs, in the crook of his knee, even balancing one on the upturned sole of his shoe.

Pay Day was a funny film and had its share of admirers, among them Max Eastman, but Chaplin himself thought little of it. Unfortunately, he shared the general prejudice that comedy is less important than tragedy, and it was certainly true that *The Kid* had won him a great deal of flattering attention from the sort of people who dismissed his two-reelers as beneath their notice.

For his next project Chaplin had envisioned a role that would get him out of the Tramp's baggy pants and derby hat. He would play an escaped convict who dresses up in clothes stolen from a minister, only to be mistaken for the young preacher sent to rescue the western cow town of Heaven's Hinges from its wicked ways. Chaplin's idea was to have the minister follow the example of the tabernacle evangelists he had heard in his youth by putting on a show that would compete with the town dance hall, substituting ragtime for hymns and dice games for the passing of the collection plates.[26]

Work on *The Pilgrim* got under way in April 1922, not a good time to be making a movie that poked fun at organized religion. In September of the previous year, while Chaplin was in England, Fatty Arbuckle had been arrested for the rape and murder of Henry Lehrman's girlfriend, Virginia Rappé. In time, his accuser exposed as a liar, Arbuckle was acquitted by a jury, but by then he had already been tried and convicted in the newspapers. In a pattern that would be repeated often in Hollywood over the years, the industry initially rallied to Arbuckle's support, then caved in when confronted with the full force of public opinion. Arbuckle was no rapist but not quite an innocent. He had hosted a drunken party in his hotel room—during Prohibition. More important, to delve into the real cause of Rappé's death—almost certainly a ruptured bladder caused by an incompetent abortionist—would have meant even more negative publicity.

No sooner had Hollywood begun to recover from the Arbuckle scandal than on February 2, 1922, William Desmond Taylor, a leading director, was found shot to death in his home. Edna Purviance, a neighbor of Taylor's, was among the first on the scene, and someone, perhaps Edna or one of the servants, summoned a representative of Taylor's studio, Paramount, who removed certain personal effects before the police arrived, including a packet of letters written by Mabel Normand. Suspicion in the Taylor killing touched Edna only briefly—she was too unassuming to make good newspaper copy—but came to rest on her friend Normand, the last person known to have seen him alive.

Mabel Normand's behavior had grown erratic over the years. Some blamed her cocaine habit; others thought she had never been the same since she suffered a concussion when she jumped off the Santa Monica pier after discovering Mack Sennett "rehearsing" in a state of semiundress with actress Mae Bush the night before he and Mabel were supposed to be married. Even though Normand's chauffeur confirmed that Taylor was still alive when she left his house, many in Hollywood continued to think she might have done it. According to Sidney D. Kirkpatrick, whose investigation of the Taylor murder is reported in his book *A Cast of Killers*, Paramount encouraged the press stories about Normand to distract attention from the unmentionable subtext of the killing—this time, not abortion but homosexuality. Taylor's chauffeur had been arrested for soliciting in a public park, perhaps on behalf of his boss, and was scheduled for a court hearing the day after the murder.[27]

Chaplin may well have had his own theories about what happened to William Desmond Taylor. He and Taylor had both lived at the LA Athletic Club, and they had many friends in common, including playwright Edward Knoblock, who had played social mentor to Chaplin during his recent stay in England and had been Taylor's housemate when he came to Los Angeles to write a screenplay for Doug Fairbanks. Certainly the rapid demolition of Arbuckle and Normand's reputations was sobering to witness and fueled his disdain for the hypocrisy of the industry.

Taylor's murder remained unsolved—no doubt in part because the studios did not want to see it solved. Meanwhile, fearing that the next Hollywood scandal would cripple their business and inspire a rash of state and even federal censorship laws, the producers formed a trade association, the Motion Picture Producers and Distributors of America (MPPDA), inviting Will Hays, a former U.S. postmaster general and elder of the Presbyterian church, to become its head. Hays proved to be less a censor than a public relations man who did his best to reassure politicians and the public that the industry was policing itself; the restrictive production code was not to be instituted for another decade. On the other hand Hays quickly affirmed the banishment of Fatty Arbuckle and approved the use of morality clauses in the standard actor's contract.

Chaplin was the only studio owner, indeed the only major star, to boycott the "Welcome, Will Hays" celebration held in Hollywood that March. Nevertheless he toned down the satire in *The Pilgrim*, replacing the scenes of dancing and gambling in church with a comic sermon on the subject of David and Goliath.

The Pilgrim's conclusion expressed Chaplin's growing ambivalence about the United States and bourgeois respectability in general: A sympathetic sheriff escorts Charlie, the escaped convict, to the border and pointedly suggests that he wander into Mexican territory to pick some flowers. Helped along by a kick in the backside, Charlie takes the hint only to be scared back to U.S. soil by a gang of gun-wielding *banditos*. The final shot shows him waddling away from the camera, one foot in each country, unable to decide between the land of anarchy and that of puritanism.

Around this time Chaplin's name accidentally found its way into the files of the Justice Department's Bureau of Investigation (later, the FBI) as the result of a surveillance of radical activity in San Francisco. A Communist organizer named Plotkin had visited Los Angeles in 1922 to raise money for striking railroad workers and, according to an anonymous source, approached Chaplin armed with letters of recommendation from Konrad Bercovici and Kate Crane Gartz (neither of whom were Communists, then or later). By the summer of 1922 the BI had developed an informant inside the Severance Club who reported that Chaplin held a fund-raiser at his studio for William Z. Foster, the leader of the 1919 strike against the steel industry who had recently gone over to the Communist Party.

At the reception Chaplin told Foster, "We are against any kind of censorship, and particularly against Presbyterian censorship." Laughing, he led Foster to the men's toilet and pointed out a pennant emblazoned with the words WELCOME WILL HAYS that was tacked to the door.[28]

The bureau helpfully forwarded this report to Hays himself,

who wrote back that he thought "the party mentioned [Chaplin] is really a little odd in his mental processes, to say the least." [29]

In December the same informant told the bureau that Chaplin had donated one thousand dollars to the Communist Party. A few weeks later two of Chaplin's Essanay comedies, A Night at the Show and Work, were screened at Sverdlovsk University—the first time any of his pictures had been seen in the Soviet Union. Nikolai Ledbedev, in an enthusiastic review in Pravda, reported that "Chaplin is an old member of the Socialist Party of America. According to the latest information he has joined the American communists." Ledbedev's review ends with the jocular prediction that once the Soviet Union acquires its own "laugh factory" the Presidium "will have to consider the request made by a group of Communist Movie Workers: 'for a swift transfer, as a point of party discipline, of Comrade Chaplin from America to the RSFSR. . . .' However, even without this he has long been keen about us."[30]

There was much talk in 1922 of the Communists joining forces with other leftists to develop a united prolabor political movement, and it is quite possible that what Chaplin joined was the so-called Worker's Party, a short-lived organization secretly controlled by Communist activists but billed as an above-ground "mass" party. Max Eastman became a Worker's Party member shortly before his departure for Europe, a decision that would have been a powerful recommendation to Chaplin.[31] At any rate the party was not well organized in the United States outside of a few strongholds of labor, and by 1923 Chaplin's personal links to radicalism were weakening. Eastman was abroad, and Rob Wagner, after losing his teaching job at Hollywood's Manual Arts High School on account of his links to Upton Sinclair, had become relatively inactive in socialist affairs. Several years would pass before the Soviets attempted to take advantage of Chaplin's sympathies.

9

A Woman of Paris

In February 1922, just days after William Desmond Taylor was murdered, there was tragic news from New York. Florence Deshon had committed suicide by turning on the gas jets in her apartment at 120 West Eleventh Street in Greenwich Village.

Florence had returned to the city several months earlier, determined to resume her career on the New York stage. She and Max Eastman were friendly though no longer intimate, but after several of her visits to Croton ended in angry scenes, he asked her not to return. On February 2, when Max ran into Florence by chance on a midtown street corner, he passed by with a brief greeting, dreading another difficult encounter. Later that afternoon, feeling guilty about his coldness, he stopped into Scribner's bookstore and purchased a copy of *The Sense of Humor,* the book he had been writing during his first visit to California. He planned to deliver it personally that afternoon, but fell asleep instead and awoke just in time to make a theater date.

During intermission a man approached and told him that Florence Deshon had been found unconscious in her apartment. Max rushed to St. Vincent's hospital, where a doctor informed him he and Florence had "friendly blood" and allowed him to give a transfusion in an effort to save her life. Nevertheless she died that night. She was twenty-nine years old and had just entered psychotherapy.

Deshon's death was the talk of New York intellectual circles.

The *New York Times,* delicately describing her as a "friend of Charley [*sic*] Chaplin and of Max Eastman," mentioned rumors that the actress was despondent over the latter's plans to go abroad for an extended stay in the Soviet Union. Eastman denied this, saying, "Miss Deshon was a dear friend of mine, and I am sure her death was accidental."[1]

In fact he knew it was suicide, and though he didn't know why Florence had done it, he took some comfort in the assurance of her close friend Marie Howe that the "the cause of Florence's mental despair was her sense of failure in her work—it wasn't you." Florence, Howe went on, had been deeply ambitious, though she rarely showed this side of herself to others, and when she failed in the movies her pride had been grievously wounded. "The Goldwyn contract fed her ego with flattery and false hopes. The day she signed that contract was the beginning of the end." Another friend, Marie Thomas, wrote: "She loved Freedom more than any woman I ever knew—to me she was the very symbol of Freedom—and now she is Free—from all the shackles of Society and convention."[2]

Chaplin never spoke of Florence's death. He does not mention her in his autobiography, and years later, when Eastman tried to bring up the subject he dismissed it, saying only, "Florence was a noble girl." Eastman, who often brooded over the tragedy, noted that he had never heard Chaplin express a sense of regret or responsibility about anything; indeed he doubted that Chaplin had a conscience in the usual sense of the word—"there seemed to be some almost weird disconnection between his earnest judgments and his acts of will. . . . He not only never acquired in childhood the habit of self-discipline, but he never apparently even caught on to the idea. It just didn't occur to him that he might stand up against a strong flow of feeling, or even move against it for a time."[3]

Perhaps so, though the evidence that Florence remained very much on his mind is to be found in his semiautobiographical 1952 film *Limelight,* which opens with a scene that recreates the circumstances of Florence's suicide—in the film, however, Chaplin's character arrives in time, smells gas, and rescues the despondent heroine from the brink of death. *Limelight* would reflect Chaplin's image of himself as a man of limited masculine appeal but great empathy, who earns a young ballerina's love by restoring her belief in her own talent, then gives her up in favor of a "better" man. In reality, if Marie Howe was correct, Chaplin's attempts to help Florence had been counterproductive, raising expectations that were never fulfilled and undermining her self-confidence. One doubts that Chaplin ever came close to seeing matters in this light.

Seven months into 1922 Chaplin finally completed *The Pilgrim*. Worn down by four years of acrimony, First National agreed to accept the four-reel film in lieu of two shorter comedies, thus bringing his contract to a close. At thirty-three Chaplin had already made seventy-one films; over the next forty years he would complete only ten more.

Although United Artists assumed that Chaplin would go on making comedies, his status as a partner gave him complete freedom to do anything he wished, and he was looking forward to trying a straight dramatic film, one that could serve as a vehicle for Edna Purviance, who at twenty-eight had grown too "matronly" to serve as his comic foil. Edna had always had a problem keeping her weight down, and over the years she had turned to alcohol (and very probably cocaine) as a substitute for food. Needless to say, drinking didn't help her looks, and when she lost Charlie's love, she had lost what little confidence she had in her abilities as an actress. Edna, in short, was another of Chaplin's failed projects, and his decision to cast her in a major dramatic role at this point in her career represented the triumph of loyalty over artistic judgment. He toyed with the idea of doing an adaptation of *The Trojan Women*, or perhaps an original story about the Empress Josephine. The problem with the latter idea was that the more he read, the more he realized that while he admired Napoleon—a "flamboyant genius"—he found Josephine boring.[4]

Chaplin's affinity for dangerous women was already well known in Hollywood—the Claire Windsor episode was a case in point — and around this time director Marshall Neilan introduced him to Peggy Hopkins Joyce, who had achieved tabloid notoriety by marrying and divorcing five wealthy men in quick succession. Peggy Joyce was already the subject of a famous vaudeville joke about a soapbox orator who, in painting a glorious vision of the future, promises his audience: "Comes the revolution you'll all eat strawberries and cream. . . . You'll have chicken every Sunday. . . . Why, comes the revolution, you'll all sleep with Peggy Hopkins Joyce." At this a voice in the crowd pipes up, protesting, "But I don't *want* to sleep with Peggy Hopkins Joyce." The orator fixes the troublemaker with a cold stare: "Comes the revolution," he tells him, "you'll sleep with Peggy Hopkins Joyce whether you want to or not."[5] And that was more or less how it went between Peggy Joyce and Chaplin.

Joyce had come to Hollywood to play a role in a movie and troll for husband number six. Charlie quickly saw through her veneer of sophistication, and soon she was regaling him with anecdotes of her marital and nonmarital adventures. On one of her several wedding nights, she said, she refused to let her husband into the bedroom until he wrote her a check for half a million dollars and slipped it under the door. She later hit the same husband over the head with a champagne bottle, and "he seemed to like it."[6]

In spite of it all, Joyce insisted, she was a nice Midwestern girl who "just wanted to have babies." She had discovered this for herself in France when she embarked on an affair with Henri Letellier, the same Paris publisher who had been a sponsor of the French charity premiere of *The Kid*. She went to bed with Letellier on the assumption that the affair would lead to a marriage proposal, only to learn to her horror that in his world there were two mutually exclusive categories of women—mistresses and wives. When she began hinting broadly about her unfulfilled maternal instincts, Letellier had responded by buying her a large, expensive doll.

Sixteen days after they met, Charlie and Peggy were invited by Tom Ince to spend the day aboard his yacht. Peggy, who had figured out by this time that Charlie was not likely husband material, got drunk and a little rowdy, and began flirting outrageously with Ince. Suddenly it occurred to Charlie that he was about to get the champagne bottle treatment himself, and he "gently" threatened to throw her overboard unless she behaved.[7]

This was the end of a relationship that Chaplin would characterize as brief but highly educational. His next romantic adventure would take a more serious turn. It began in September when he agreed to conduct the orchestra at an Actor's Fund benefit at the Hollywood Bowl. A number of other stars were to appear during the

evening costumed as characters from Shakespeare. On the night of
the event, newspaper photographers gathered at the entrance to the
staging area, busily snapping pictures of each celebrity as he or she
arrived, and soon Chaplin found his car stuck in a traffic jam of the
chauffeur-driven limousines that were already a feature of such
Hollywood events. Suddenly Chaplin's Locomobile was bumped by
the vehicle behind it. He got out to exchange apologies with the
occupant of the other car and found himself face to face with a
"much bejeweled and very nude" brunette dressed as Cleopatra. It
was Pola Negri, recently arrived in America, and under contract at
Paramount.[8]

The following night Pola awoke at three A.M. to the sound of a
ten-piece Hawaiian band, sent by Charlie to serenade her.
(Doubtless this was the same band, house musicians from the
Vernon Country Club, that Douglas Fairbanks had hired when be
was courting Mary Pickford.) Flowers and an expensive diamond-
and-onyx bracelet soon followed.

Thus began an affair that Chaplin described as "exotic" and Pola
Negri would eventually look back on as high camp. While it lasted,
however, it was no laughing matter to either of them. The essence of
mittel-European café society sophistication, Pola Negri dressed
provocatively in black, spoke limited English apart from swear words,
and lied often and confusingly about her age and antecedents. Fan
magazine stories circulated at the time of her arrival in the United
States claimed she was a Hungarian Gypsy, though in fact she had
been born Apolonia Chalupec, the daughter of a middle-class family
of Polish Jews. She was insecure and hyperemotional—but also a
serious artist, who had worked with Ernst Lubitsch and the great
theatrical director Max Reinhardt. A major star in Europe, Pola had
signed with Paramount's Famous Players–Lasky division, which
brought her to the United States with much fanfare and no idea at all
of how to use her talents effectively. In her first American film she
was ludicrously miscast as an Englishwoman. Meanwhile the studio's
publicity department seemed intent on turning her into a cartoon.
She went along with a manufactured feud between herself and
Gloria Swanson, but became frightened when the studio floated a
story that she had criticized the decor of Mary Pickford's former
dressing room, which she had inherited. Pickford—Hollywood's

social arbiter as well as "America's Sweetheart"—was not especially noted for her sense of humor.

Pola remembered Charlie from Berlin and very likely contrived the meeting at the Hollywood Bowl in the hope that he could help her smooth things over with Pickford. To her surprise she soon decided that he was the most sympathetic man she had ever known. Charlie made up for his lack of macho appeal by being an excellent listener. He wanted to know everything about her past and dealt patiently with her anxieties over the progress of her career. Even his long silences, which had so unnerved Mildred Harris, were appreciated by Pola as a thoughtful gift from one busy, self-preoccupied adult to another. She found it very restful to have a companion capable of sharing the beauty of the sunset without a lot of distracting chatter.

Pola understood, as some of Charlie's longtime friends did not, how deeply he longed to escape from the image of the Tramp and be taken seriously as an actor and director. Her heart ached for him when the guests at one of Doug and Mary's parties laughed at his talk of wanting to make a film about Napoleon. And while Charlie already had a reputation for pursuing young girls, Pola sensed that what he really wanted was someone to mother him: "He was at his best when he created situations to which he could react with the confusion and bashful awkwardness of the young."[9]

Chaplin had recently purchased a sixty-six-acre parcel of land down the hill from Pickfair, Doug and Mary's hilltop showplace in newly fashionable Beverly Hills, and at Syd's urging he was planning to build a house commensurate with his income. Pola began suggesting improvements in the architect's plans, and was seduced by the idea of moving into Charlie's new house as his bride. Together they would rival Doug and Mary for honors as the screen's reigning couple.

Unfortunately she felt no physical attraction to him whatsoever—a drawback in the relationship that she was prepared to overlook. Why Charlie was prepared to overlook it is a more difficult question. According to Pola's account, three months into their relationship, with the newspapers already speculating about an engagement, they were not yet on intimate terms.

Displays of temperament compensated for the lack of sexual

electricity. When Pola tried to get Charlie's attention at a party by pretending to faint (the same ploy tried by Edna), he stretched out beside her in a swoon worthy of Camille. She in turn had discovered his habit of memorizing a list of ten new vocabulary words before a party so that he could use them in conversation. Secretly she learned the same words and used them as ostentatiously as possible, before he had the chance.

Politics, too, provided the subject matter for many an argument. Pola's father, a moderate constitutional democrat, had been imprisoned for attempting to introduce liberal reforms in Poland, and she herself had lived through the Spartacist riots in Berlin. Charlie, she complained, brushed off her attempts to explain the differences between Communists and Social Democrats by telling her, "One reason why you're only intelligent and not an intellectual is that all intellectuals are radicals, and you're not."

On Christmas Eve, Charlie arrived at Pola's house late for dinner, bringing with him a five-carat diamond, which, he said, he hadn't had time to have set. She glanced at it and tossed it carelessly into her jewel case. They were now officially engaged, and when she was invited to dine alone with Charlie at his house on Beechwood Drive on New Year's Eve, Pola knew that sex could no longer be postponed. After dinner Charlie sat down at the piano to play a love song, one of his own compositions, then switched to the violin. Pola had never seen a left-handed violinist before, and she spoiled the mood by remarking on how bizarre he looked. Charlie, nervous to begin with, was overcome with self-consciousness. "He started moving towards me, moving in a gait that was a parody of seductiveness," she would recall, his passion expressed in "an uproarious dumbshow of rolling eyes and waving hands."[10]

Unlikely as it may seem, the relationship was consummated that evening and Pola actually began to look forward to the wedding. Charlie's new house on Cove Way was going up—complete with a two-story-high vestibule, to be used as a screening room, a pipe organ, and, of course, a private swimming pool and tennis court. Pola's vision of herself and Charlie becoming the next Doug and Mary came ever more clearly into focus. However, as she belatedly realized, she had overlooked one small detail: Doug and Mary "were polite to each other as they were to everyone else."[11]

Although there had been plenty of conflict before, it was only after their New Year's Eve rendezvous that the serious fights began. Now that they were engaged, Charlie began trying to manage Pola's career. He also accused her of having an affair with her latest leading man, Charles de la Roche: "You never have time for me," he berated her. "This young Frog's the reason why."

Charlie, on his part, told friends that he was getting tired of the late-night hysterical phone calls from Pola's maid, who would screech: "Queek, queek, Mr. Chaplin, queek. You must come over. Miss Negri is terrible." He consulted a Polish acquaintance, Richard Ordinsky, and was told that his only defense was to be as temperamental as she. "Attitudinize," Ordinsky told him—surely superfluous advice.[12]

In March the newspapers quoted Chaplin as saying that he was too poor to be married—exactly the complaint he had made when his marriage to Mildred Harris went sour. Pola summoned reporters and announced that *she* was too poor to marry Charlie, and the engagement was off: "I end—just like that! I am very extreme."[13] POLA NEGRI JILTS CHAPLIN proclaimed the *Los Angeles Herald Examiner* on March 22. This, however, was not quite the end. Chaplin showed up on Pola's doorstep, pleading for a second chance in front of a delegation of startled reporters. She relented, and the engagement was on again.

At some point during one of their nastier quarrels, Pola said something hurtful and noticed that "a strange joyous expression of suffering passed over Charlie's face." Suddenly it dawned on her that he craved rejection and knew exactly how to provoke her until he got it. Once she understood this, the game no longer had any appeal. Still, she allowed herself the final cut. This time she signaled the end of the engagement by appearing at a Hollywood night spot on the arm of Charlie's good friend, tennis star Bill Tilden. Since Tilden was gay, Pola may intentionally have been sending Hollywood a message.

By the time she came to write her memoirs, Pola Negri was able to look back on this melodrama with a degree of perspective, even humor. Chaplin, characteristically, could not. In his conversations with friends, and even in his autobiography, Chaplin would invariably portray himself as a passive, even unwilling pawn of the women in his life. Just as Mildred had snared him by pretending to be pregnant, so "Miss Pola" made a play for him and suddenly, "I found myself in the role of Casanova."[14]

There could be no doubt, however, that Chaplin was often the pursuer. Even while he was engaged to Pola, he had other liaisons, and during this period he confided to Sam Goldwyn that his first date with actress Signe Holmquist ended at her apartment with her holding a revolver to his head and demanding that he vow eternal fidelity to her. He was frightened, but not unpleasantly so. "What a hot one she was!" he said.[15]

One woman who was definitely the pursuer was Marina Varga, an obsessed fan, said to be the daughter of a Mexican general, with a husband in Vera Cruz. Varga, whom Chaplin had never met before, managed to sneak into his house, where she was discovered by Kono in bed in the master bedroom, dressed in Chaplin's pajamas. Charlie happened to be dining that evening with Pola and Dr. Cecil Reynolds, the neuropsychologist who treated his mother. He insisted that they all go upstairs to talk to Varga, and refused to press charges. The next day his generosity was rewarded when Varga was found lying in his driveway, semicomatose. She claimed to have taken poison and was rushed to the hospital, where Chaplin paid her bills, and she promptly gave a press conference proclaiming him the greatest artist in the world. His entanglement with this disturbed young woman would probably not have ended there had Pola not put a stop to it.

And yet, while Chaplin had a low opinion of women in particular, he continued to idolize womanhood in general. During the period when he was trying to disentangle himself from Pola Negri, he was beginning to shoot *A Woman of Paris,* another variant on his favorite theme of a young woman from a repressive home who falls in love with a naive painter. Marie St. Clair (Edna), a girl from the French provinces, is about to elope to Paris with her sweetheart when the young man's father suffers a heart attack. Marie, believing that she has been abandoned at the railroad station, takes the train alone. When next seen she has become the mistress of Pierre Revel, a smooth, amoral sophisticate much like Henri Letellier. Later the worldly Pierre discovers that the young artist has reentered Marie's life, but he is more amused than jealous. He, after all, is about to enter into a marriage of convenience with a woman of his own class. Unfortunately the artist is not so philosophical. Armed with a gun he follows Marie and Pierre to a fashionable restaurant, where, overcome by despair, he commits suicide in the lobby.

The film's working title, *Public Opinion*, tells us what Chaplin thought was to blame for this tragedy. Quite deliberately the screenplay gives no hint of the experiences that transformed Marie from an innocent country girl into a rich man's kept woman. Chaplin's point is that only accidents of "fate," not character, separate the good girl from the fallen woman. "The world is not composed of heroes and villains," one of the film's opening titles informs us, "but of men and women with all the passions God has given them. The ignorant condemn but the wise pity." Maybe so, though the suggestion that the specifics of Marie's story are too well known to be worth recounting amounts to conceding that they are not very interesting.

Just as Chaplin's efforts to write a film about Josephine were sidetracked by his fascination with Napoleon, so in filming the story of Marie St. Clair he became mesmerized by the amoral Pierre Revel. Pierre is supposedly a hollow man, incapable of love, but he emerges on film as a male fantasy figure. He lives an enviable life, savoring all the pleasures Paris has to offer apparently without having to work for a living, and enjoys sexual freedom without guilt or responsibility, jealousy or fear of rejection.

If the real-life model for Pierre Revel had not been a Parisian, Chaplin would have had to make him one. In 1923 American audiences expected adulterers to suffer for their sins, but an occasional exception might be made for a Frenchman. Chaplin hired Harry d'Abbadie d'Arrast, a Basque actor who had lived in France, as a consultant on the Parisian backgrounds. Even so the film's depiction of decadent high life at times suggests Kansas City rather than Montmartre. Louise Brooks, who saw the film at the time of its release, sniffed that the women's clothes were five years out of date, and when Pierre Revel dines in an elegant restaurant he orders "champagne and truffle soup"—a Hollywood prop man's notion of haute cuisine. When the movie opened in Paris, Chaplin's French fans were, as usual, forgiving. One critic would note, generously, that Chaplin was using Paris "to suggest the whole world," and therefore should not be held to account for inaccuracies.

Chaplin might have played Pierre himself—the role, in many ways, was suited to him—but perhaps he realized that this was asking too much of moviegoers used to seeing him as the Tramp. Instead he cast the Pittsburgh-born Adolphe Menjou. In an era when leading men were still expected to supply their own costumes, Menjou's extensive wardrobe made him much in demand for parts that called for European sophistication and first-rate tailoring. Tipped off by Monta Bell that Chaplin was looking for an Henri Letellier type, Menjou campaigned for the part by appearing regularly at Chaplin's favorite luncheon spots, Musso & Frank's and Armstrong's, sporting a different outfit each day—first a dinner jacket, then white flannels, and then well-cut tweeds.

Once he had Chaplin's interest, Menjou demanded five hundred dollars a week, twice Edna Purviance's salary. What's more, he insisted on being paid even when Chaplin wasn't ready to shoot his scenes on schedule, as was the custom everywhere else. Alf Reeves was aghast: "But you haven't worked!"

"That isn't my fault," said Menjou.

Much to Reeves's amazement, Menjou got his check. Pierre Revel would not have asked for any less.

Menjou would recall making *A Woman of Paris* as a thoroughly enjoyable experience. He admired Chaplin's perfectionism and credited him with correcting his tendency to overact. At the slightest sign of overplaying, Chaplin would remind him of the intimate relationship between the screen actor and the audience, warning: "Remember, they're peeking at you."[16]

Menjou was also delighted by the La Brea Avenue studio, a world unto itself, "as full of junk and eccentric characters as a country store." Timekeepers, accountants, and efficiency experts, ubiquitous figures at other studios, with the power to "ruin the product," were unknown. Chaplin's employees tended to have whimsical titles that had little or nothing to do with their duties. Monta Bell, for example, was a "literary advisor." Others received stipends and did no work at all, or received no salaries but used the premises for their own projects. Granville Redmond, the deaf-mute painter who had appeared in *A Dog's Life*, was ostensibly working on a portrait of Edna Purviance as Marie that would be used in the movie. Redmond labored many days over the painting, which became progressively more abstract until by the time the it was needed as a prop, Edna was unrecognizable. In the end one of the set crew made a crayon copy of an old fan magazine photograph. The job took a little over an hour, and the shot was quickly completed, but Redmond painted on.

Another frequent presence at the studio was Konrad Bercovici, who occupied a vacant office where he was writing a book of "Gypsy tales," later published under the title *Murdo*, with a florid dedication to Chaplin. By this time Chaplin had become so close to Bercovici and his family that he chose the name of Bercovici's elder daughter, long known as "Girlie" because her parents had never been able to agree on what she should be called. When "Girlie" decided that she wanted a real name, everyone sat around the table throwing out possibilities. Chaplin's suggestion—Rada—was the one she liked best, and so he became her godfather.

In 1925 Chaplin used Bercovici to announce to the world his Gypsy ancestry via an "authorized" interview published in *Collier's* magazine.

Chaplin is quoted in the article as saying that he had only just learned from his mother the "thrilling" news that he had a Gypsy grandparent. This is almost certainly a lie—Max Eastman, for one, seems to have heard about Chaplin's Gypsy forebears as early as 1921 and Charlie had for years described his mother as "half-Spanish." Bercovici expressed his own doubts, saying, "As Charlie looked dreamily up at the ceiling and closed the subject by suddenly beginning to talk about something else, it occurred to me that he, too, knew more than he was telling me."

Bercovici went on to cite Chaplin's work habits as an example of a Romany approach to life:

He is unable to work unless he feels like it. Although there are hundreds of people in the studio waiting for him, hundreds of people who are being paid huge [*sic*] salaries for waiting time, Charlie cannot be induced to work when he does not feel like it. And the time he loses! Sometimes, when everything is ready and the cameramen are waiting to "shoot"

Charlie will suddenly begin to play his violin or dance and sing. Who else would do that but a Gypsy?[17]

Although one suspects that plenty of people would work this way, given the opportunity, a case could be made for Bercovici's observation. Chaplin's frequently stated opinion that he did not believe people should have to work was not an endorsement of laziness but a protest against the necessity of working for other people, according to their schedules and rules. Though Charlie's dislike of regimentation could be ascribed to artistic temperament, his attitudes on this score also bear some relation to the Romany view of work as described, for example, by Jean-Pierre Liégeois: "Labor is an independent activity. The nobility of association is contrasted to the dependence of wage-labour. . . . Even in the face of great obstacles, Gypsies continue to try to work in the Gypsy way."[18] Chaplin not only planned his career to insure his independence from outside producers, he went to great lengths to create the illusion that his studio was not a typical movie factory but a collection of people who happened to enjoy spending time together.

For that matter one could argue that a number of Chaplin's strongly held attitudes—his suspicion of nationalism and government officials, his sense of being an outsider, even his aversion to birth control, reflect traditional Romany culture. With Chaplin, however, one could never be sure of the line between fact and his overactive imagination. Mirel Bercovici came to believe that Chaplin had "misled" her father, inventing a Gypsy heritage out of a desire to romanticize "certain deficiencies" in his own background. She continued to insist on this in 1995, even though she acknowledged hearing in childhood that Chaplin spoke the Romany dialect used in England. Told that there was independent confirmation that Chaplin did have at least one Gypsy grandmother, she dismissed this as immaterial, saying, "We're talking about tea-drinking Gypsies here."[19]

This comment gives some indication of why Chaplin came to regret the *Collier's* article. Not only do Roma from Central Europe regard English Gypsies as not quite authentic, but the motives of any mixed-blood or assimilated individual who publicly identifies himself as a Gypsy are likely to be questioned. Konrad Bercovici himself faced such criticisms. In spite of his lonely campaign to draw attention to the persecution of Gypsies in his native Romania and Germany, many Roma dismissed him as a fraud. "Coming out" as a Gypsy did not win Chaplin acceptance among other Gypsies. Nor did it do him any good with mainstream critics who tended to regard Gypsies as semimythical creatures.

In addition to Granville Redmond and Konrad Bercovici, another colorful figure who became a regular at the studio at this time was Jim Tully, the "Hobo Author." A pug-nosed, disheveled Irishman, barely five feet tall, Tully had spent part of his youth in orphan asylums, graduating to riding the rails and sleeping in hobo camps while supporting himself as an itinerant laborer. He described his experiences in a book called *Beggars of Life*, which received enthusiastic reviews and led to his being lionized by some critics as that longed-for literary phenomenon, the authentic "working stiff" genius. A sudden success on the party circuit, Tully found himself invited to dinner by Hollywood's more socially conscious writers and directors, even though he still had no regular income and couldn't afford a decent suit of clothes.

Chaplin met Tully at one such party, hosted by Paul Bern, the brilliant director who later committed suicide following a brief marriage to Jean Harlow. Noticing Tully sneaking glances at the other guests, hoping for a clue as to which fork to use first, he whispered, "Don't look at me, Jim. I pick the wrong one every time." Later he sent Tully an autographed picture of himself addressed to "Dear fellow comrade," and at Bern's suggestion, offered to put him on his studio payroll at $50 a week.

Tully no doubt reminded Chaplin of a younger version of himself—one might say a more authentic version, since Tully had actually been a tramp and known acute poverty well into his adult years. Chaplin was eager to hear about Tully's life history, spent a lot of time with him, and for a while made him the "fair-haired boy" at the studio, as Rob Wagner would put it, valuing his advice over that of veteran aides like Chuck Riesner and Henry Bergman.

Tully soon learned that Chaplin brooded about the possibility of losing his sanity and blamed Hollywood for his frequent bouts of depression. One day Tully wondered aloud what the world would be like if everyone were a genius—what if every waiter and bootblack were born with the brains of a Thomas Hardy or an Anatole France? Chaplin considered the question and remarked that on the whole, the world would be a better place: "But—a lot of people would have to die in Hollywood first."

Tully joined the studio just as Chaplin was in the process of trying to come up with an ending for *A Woman of Paris*. He was confronted by the question, What becomes of Marie St. Clair after Jean, her artist lover, kills himself? Some of the possible answers were either too gloomy or too morally unacceptable for a commercial movie, even a daring one. Convention required that Marie repent her wicked ways, even though this was totally at odds with the picture's claim to be a "drama of fate" as opposed to personal responsibility and free will.

Eddie Sutherland, an assistant director on the picture, would recall that Chaplin's original solution was "a dilly": "One day he came in all steamed up. He'd dreamed this up during the night—the whole thing was going to end up on a leper's island. Edna Purviance (as Marie) had seen the light and she was going to nurse little lepers." Sutherland had learned from experience that it was mistake to tell his boss straight out that he'd had a bad idea, since Chaplin overreacted to criticism. Instead he prevaricated, saying, "Well let's investigate if it has possibilities."

After a few days the leper colony was transformed into a sunny cottage in the country, where Marie and her dead lover's mother, united by grief, are found caring for a brood of smiling, healthy-looking orphans. "Time is a great healer," explains one of the film's closing titles, "and time teaches us that the road to happiness is in the service of others."

Tully was invited to a screening and, less circumspect than Sutherland, he pronounced the ending "hackneyed. . . . A woman like that would never be contented to spend the rest of her life with the cows and the chickens," he observed. "There's no reason why she should go to the country—she's no more spiritual than an ox—as you portray her."

Chaplin waved aside the objection. "Maybe she stayed only an hour or so in the country after the picture ended."

Chaplin knew that showing Marie's repentance struck a false note. He was, however, a businessman who had invested almost half a million dollars of his own money in an off-beat move. A second ending was shot for the European market, in which Marie, only briefly troubled by Jean's death, soon returns to Pierre. A program note Chaplin prepared for the New York premiere had the ring of an apology: "The story is intimate, simple, human, presenting a problem as old as the ages—showing it with as much truth as I am allowed to put into it—giving a treatment as near to realism as I have been able to devise."

This didn't satisfy Tully, who later called the final scenes of *A Woman of Paris* "one of the saddest tributes that talent ever paid to commercialism."[20] This was the sentiment of a disillusioned man who was beginning to discover that his "comrade," Chaplin, was after all a commercial filmmaker, not to mention a star whose established entourage resented being shunted aside in favor of a newcomer. As he grew more aware of the intrigues within Chaplin's "brain trust," most of them directed at ousting him from his favored position, Tully also became cynical about Chaplin himself. "Charlie is always bored by the stupidity in Hollywood and at the same time is relentless in his pursuit of it," he observed.[21]

In spite of having to compromise on the ending of *A Woman of Paris*, Chaplin had great hopes for the movie. It was not only his first venture into straight drama, but the first picture he had directed without appearing in it himself. He and Edna traveled to New York for the East Coast premiere on October 1, 1923, at which the film was introduced by a live dramatic prologue, written and staged for the occasion by Eddie Sutherland. The audience's warm reception was followed by enthusiastic reviews.

The critics singled out Chaplin's directorial efforts for special—and quite justified—praise. He had drawn a remarkable performance from Adolphe Menjou, one which would keep Menjou happily employed in movies for many years to come. He had also displayed a flair for economical, allusive storytelling and irony, which led some critics to compare him to de Maupassant. During a conversation among Marie and her friends, for example, Chaplin had the camera focus on Marie's masseuse, whose eyes register an eloquent commentary on their superficial prattle. Chaplin's display of versatility was so impressive that the reviewers went more than a little overboard, ignoring the doubtful premise and Edna Purviance's uninspired performance. (Edna did have one great moment, however, in a scene in which Marie's friends show her a newspaper announcement of Pierre's forthcoming marriage. This was very close to the way Edna herself had learned of Charlie's marriage to Mildred Harris, and the look in her eyes says it all.)

A few evenings after the premiere, still incandescent over his triumph, Chaplin knocked on the door of Waldo Frank's apartment on Irving Place. Though he announced that he was just stopping by for a few minutes, four hours later he was still talking, and when Frank happened to mention that he knew Hart Crane, who was living in a furnished room nearby, they trooped around the corner and roused Crane out of a sound sleep. Still groggy, Crane found himself and Frank trailing Charlie Chaplin through the streets of New York while a pack of street urchins surged around them, alternately begging for Charlie's autograph and shouting off-color suggestions about the purpose of his late-night expedition.

Back in Frank's apartment, Chaplin regaled Frank and Crane with another six hours of nonstop talk. Chaplin described his marathon battles with Pola Negri and, Crane reported in a letter to his mother, spoke candidly "about his life, his hopes and spiritual desires which were very fine and interesting. He has been through so much, is very lonely (says Hollywood hasn't a dozen people he enjoys talking to, or who understand his work) and yet is radiant and healthy, wistful and gay and young."[22]

Still buoyed up by this visit and his glowing reviews, Chaplin returned to Los Angeles in the company of Eddie Sutherland and Arthur Kelly, Hetty's brother, whom he had brought to the United States to work in the executive offices of United Artists. At a station somewhere around Albuquerque, Sutherland would recall, Chaplin's spirits suddenly plummeted, and for no apparent reason he began to complain bitterly about the smoke in the air.

"This is a railroad station," Sutherland pointed out.

Back on board the train, Chaplin launched into a long diatribe against capitalism. This was something new to Sutherland, who was not one of Charlie's politically oriented friends. "He kept talking about Bolshevism, or whatever it was called in those days. He was expounding this to me, how this was a bright, wonderful, new possibility in life."

"Now I know you have three million dollars in the bank," Sutherland said after a time. "How does this give-away-the-money affect you?"

"Oh, Eddie, don't be silly," Chaplin answered. "It doesn't affect artists!"[23]

Chaplin's rising anxiety level was soon justified by the disappointing box office reception of *A Woman of Paris*. Perhaps, and this was certainly Chaplin's conclusion, the picture's failure was the fault of the audience. Americans expected movies to be populated by heroes and villains and were rather bewildered by the film's detached, ironic point of view. On the other hand, it may be that the unsophisticated public was right. There was something false, and even unconsciously hostile, in Chaplin's portrayal of Marie St. Clair. While claiming to be cool and objective, the script actually gave all the advantages to Pierre Revel, making him far more attractive than such men are likely to be in reality.

Any remaining hope that *A Woman of Paris* might lead to future dramatic roles for Edna Purviance was shattered on January 1, 1924, when a man named Al Kelly summoned the LA police to an apartment on North Vermont Avenue. The police found millionaire oil broker Courtland S. Dines lying on a sofa in the living room, bleeding profusely from a gunshot wound to the abdomen. Edna Purviance and Mabel Normand were in the kitchen, hysterically insisting that they had no idea how Dines came to be shot.

Courtland Dines was a popular amateur golfer and society gadabout, recently divorced by his second wife on grounds of "inebriety." Newspaper reports in the wake of the shooting described Edna as his fiancée, though the Dines family soon issued a statement denying this. Kelly, also known as Horace Greer or Joe Greer, was Mabel Normand's chauffeur—though not the same one who had given her an alibi in the William Taylor murder. Kelly gave a statement to the police taking the blame for shooting Dines. As he told it, Miss Normand had gone to Dines's apartment earlier in the evening to deliver a New Year's present to Edna. Kelly was supposed to pick Normand up at 8:00 P.M. He arrived on time and after waiting in the car for an hour, he decided to go inside and ask when he would be needed. Entering the apartment, he noticed that "Miss Normand was in no condition to remain any longer," but when he insisted on taking her home, Dines grabbed a bottle and lurched toward them threateningly. Kelly shot him in self-defense.

The problem with Kelly's story was that the pistol used in the shooting was identified by Mabel Normand's maid as one that Normand normally kept in a drawer in her night table. At a January 2 press conference, Mabel Normand greeted reporters dressed in black velvet and reclining on a chaise longue. She admitted that the pistol was hers, but could give no adequate explanation of how Kelly came to be carrying it on the night of the shooting.

During Kelly's trial for assault, which opened on January 18, the picture became murkier still. Dines, who fortunately suffered no permanent injury, testified that he blacked out before the incident began and had no idea who shot him. Edna Purviance pleaded "faulty memory." Normand, who was more creative, said that when Kelly entered the apartment Edna had her corsets unlaced. She had pushed Edna into the bedroom to help her lace herself up, and that was how she happened to miss the excitement.

The only helpful testimony came from the arresting officer, who recalled that as they were driving to the jail, Kelly told him: "I shot Dines because he kept Mabel all hopped up."[24]

The trial ended with Judge J. Walker Hanby observing that "there appears to be a conspiracy on the part of the witnesses to keep from the court many things that the court should know about this case." Hanby threatened to have Purviance, Normand, and Dines prosecuted for obstruction of justice, but no charges were ever filed. One explanation for the conspiracy of silence was that drugs were somehow involved, and none of the principals wanted to provoke Kelly into mentioning this in his sworn testimony. Another is that Dines had become obstreperous and violent after a long holiday binge, and Edna called on Mabel, who arrived with her pistol just in case. Kelly, said by some accounts to be in love with his employer, may have volunteered to take the blame.

By the time Kelly's trial ended, the Ohio Board of Film Censorship had already banned the showing of films starring

Normand and Purviance. The state of Kansas and the cities of Boston and Detroit were considering similar bans. Normand's career was effectively finished. Chaplin, to his credit, stood by Edna. His studio issued a statement saying that she was still on the payroll and would remain his leading lady. In fact she never appeared opposite him again, though a few years later he attempted to revive her career by financing a Josef von Sternberg film called *Woman of the Sea,* with Edna in the leading role. The film was unreleasable, and Edna, still receiving her salary as an unofficial "pension," settled into obscurity. She spent some time in Hawaii, where she became the victim of a jewel thief, and was mentioned in connection with a messy San Francisco society divorce, but for the most part remained out of the news, plagued by a life-threatening heart condition and stomach ulcers before she turned forty.

One can't help reflecting that the plot of *A Woman of Paris* pales beside the true-life saga of Edna Purviance, a "Woman of Hollywood." For that matter Chaplin was surrounded during this period by women like Florence Deshon, Pola Negri, and even Peggy Hopkins Joyce, who were by no means innocents, much less passive pawns of fate and the double standard, but certainly a lot more interesting than the two-dimensional Marie St. Clair.

Thanks to a relatively successful box office run in Europe, *A Woman of Paris* eventually turned a profit, earning $634,000 on an outlay of $351,853. Chaplin could certainly have continued making unconventional, modestly commercial movies, but in the long run he would have been forced to accept outside financing and resign himself to turning out films on schedule and economically—in short, giving up his hard-won freedom to work as and when he liked. The alternative was to revive the Tramp.

10

The Gold Rush

The beginning of 1924 found Chaplin filled with enthusiasm for his latest project, a comedy on an epic scale set during the Klondike gold rush of 1898. The idea, he would recall, came to him at Pickfair, where he happened to see a stereopticon slide showing a line of prospectors struggling up the steep face of the Chilkoot Pass, on their way to seek their fortune in the gold-fields. Viewing this striking and justly famous image may have brought home the visual possibilities of the subject, but Chaplin surely had heard a great deal about the Klondike from other sources.

Many of the "stampeders" who descended on the Klondike in 1898 hoping to strike it rich eventually found their way to the next promised land, Southern California, where they became successful businessmen. Among the gold rush veterans who thrived in Los Angeles were Wilson Mizener, founder of the Brown Derby restaurant; theater chain owner Alexander Pantages, and Chaplin's good friend Sid Grauman, whose father had operated a tent show in Dawson City during the long, hungry winter following the arrival of the stampeders, when gold nuggets were plentiful and food of any description extremely scarce.

The Grauman family later operated vaudeville theaters in San Francisco and Los Angeles, where Chaplin played while touring with the Karno company. Charlie and Sid Grauman were already good friends by 1922, when Sid opened his Egyptian Theater, a fantasy picture palace whose "King Tut" theme extended to the ushers, who were dressed in "Egyptian" togas and sandals.

An inveterate practical joker, Grauman once phoned Charlie from his bachelor apartment in the Alexandria Hotel, telling him that he was in terrible trouble and needed help as soon as possible. Charlie arrived to find an inert female form lying in the blood-soaked bed. Grauman said he could see no way to save himself except by getting rid of the body, and he desperately needed Charlie's help. Horrified, Charlie refused. When he began to insist on calling the police, Grauman revealed that the corpse was a dummy, artfully smeared with ketchup.[1]

Grauman, it seems, had once circulated a script about the Klondike written by an old prospector friend, and it is possible that Chaplin preferred not to acknowledge him as a source lest the author of the script get suspicious and try to claim that his ideas had been stolen. Nevertheless Grauman remained in the background as an unofficial adviser, and a number of studio regulars assumed that the film was inspired by his anecdotes.

Wherever it came from, sending the Little Fellow into the Klondike was a once-in-a-lifetime idea. Gold fever was a great leveler, uniting men and women from all stations in life, and a universal metaphor for the hopes, dreams, greed, and folly that make up the human condition. From a practical standpoint, moving the Little Fellow out of his urban setting into the great outdoors opened up new possibilities for dramatic situations and funny business.

By January 1924 Chaplin had a tentative title, *Lucky Strike*—later simplified to *The Gold Rush*. If he also had a plot in mind, he didn't share the secret with his aides. "As per the Chaplin formula of moviemaking," recalled Eddie Manson, who was writing publicity for the studio at the time, "it was just an idea; a title, something, anything, to hang a story on, a story that as yet had no outline. About the only thing we knew for sure, it was going to be about the frozen North and for that background of a plot, we had to have snow."[2] Even so, Danny Hall and his crew went to work, recreating the Arctic on the studio's back lot. The set would take months to complete, eventually using 239,577 feet of lumber, 200 tons of plaster, 22,750 feet of chicken wire and 22,000 feet of burlap. One hundred barrels of flour and 285 tons of salt served as "snow."

Chaplin's first order of business was to find a new leading lady. Although he could have had his pick of experienced actresses, he was still taken with the idea of discovering a fresh face, a newcomer he could mold. A tersely worded advertisement in a local newspaper drew hundreds of applicants, ranging from the hopeless to the merely inept.

On February 3 Lillita McMurray showed up in the studio reception area with her high school friend Merna Kennedy, a petite redhead who had already toured as part of a brother-sister dance act on the Pantages circuit. Lillita and her mother, Mrs. Lillian Spicer, were neighbors of Chaplin's assistant Chuck Riesner, and they had worked as extras for Chaplin in the past. During the making of *The Kid*, Chaplin had chosen Lillita, then twelve, to play the part of the Angel of Temptation in the dream sequence. As a Cockney angel, the girlfriend of the bully (Chuck Riesner), she had tempted the Little Fellow with a flirtatious wink. Although Lillita's role in *The Kid* was small, Chaplin had promoted her heavily, inviting her to pose with Jackie Coogan for publicity shots. According to Lillita, he had also flirted with her on the set—telling her, "I've been peeking at you"—and, later on, tried to coax her into sneaking out of her house to attend a birthday party he was giving for May Collins, his then girlfriend. Lillita's mother found out about the birthday party invitation and made it clear that her daughter would not be going anywhere unchaperoned. When Mrs. Spicer and her daughter finished their roles as maids in *The Idle Class*, their contracts were not renewed.

Now three months shy of her sixteenth birthday, Lillita had grown into an attractive, big-boned girl, mature for her age. Eddie Sutherland noticed her in the waiting area near the studio's front gate and told his boss, "Say, Charlie, we've tested everybody in North America. I just saw Lillita McMurray out there and she looks wonderful."[3]

Chaplin summoned her inside and asked her, "What have you been doing with yourself?"

"I've been in school," she answered.

The next thing his aides knew, Lillita had been given a screen test. Rollie Totheroh wondered aloud if Lillita's broad face and full cheeks, though very attractive in person, might be hard to photograph.

Jim Tully thought the fifteen-year-old had "less acting ability than any girl who appeared," but this is hard to believe, given her brief but charming moment in *The Kid*. The real objection to hiring Lillita McMurray had less to do with her personal qualifications than with Chaplin's motives for hiring her. "I'm going to marry that girl!" he had exclaimed on seeing Lillita's screen test. This upset Syd, who warned: "If you do, the headlines will say: CHAPLIN ROBS THE CRADLE."

"I'll keep it out of the papers," Charlie assured him.[4]

Tully foresaw disaster and seethed with indignation as Harry d'Arrast and Henry Bergman—"stooges," the irate Tully called them—assured the boss that Lillita was "marvelous." The decision was made, and Tully, along with Eddie Manson, orchestrated the publicity campaign that accompanied the signing of the contract. Lillita was rechristened Lita Grey, and on March 3 the studio announced: "The picture plum of 1924 has been plucked by one of California's native daughters, picked by Charlie Chaplin to be his leading lady in his premier comedy for United Artists." The publicity release noted that Lita was descended through her maternal grandmother from one of California's old Spanish land-grant families. Less accurately, it described her as nineteen years old and a business school graduate. Her salary was to be a minimal seventy-five dollars a week.

Chaplin, meanwhile, had made a quick trip to the Sierras to scout locations. He settled on Summit, California, just below the Donner Pass. Summit was a way station for the crews of the "pusher" engines used to get trains over the steepest part of the pass, and there wasn't much to the town apart from a small hotel, precariously shored up on the side of a gully, recently used as location headquarters for a Western directed by John Ford. The lobby was furnished with homemade chairs and tables in painted pine, and large sawdust-filled spittoons. There were only two bathrooms, and the fixtures from one of them had been thrown out of the window into the gully, perhaps by disgusted members of Ford's crew.

Weeks of preparation would be necessary before shooting could begin. While carpenters hurriedly renovated a suite in the hotel for Chaplin, Eddie Sutherland went on to Sacramento to recruit extras for the Chilkoot Pass scene, and Chaplin went back to the studio, where he began shooting a sequence in which Charlie and another prospector, Big Jim McKay (Mack Swain), are driven by a snowstorm to take refuge in the cabin of the villainous Black Larsen. Snowbound, without provisions, Charlie nibbles on a candle, which, in his delirium, he has mistaken for a stalk of celery. Thanksgiving Day arrives and he is reduced to cooking up one of his oversize shoes, which he prepares and serves with the pride and concentration of a master chef, testing it for doneness, basting with pan juices, and dexterously separating the top from the sole.

Mack Swain had only to look on in alarm, a reaction that became more heartfelt by the day. The shoes used in the scene were made by a Los Angeles confectioner out of licorice with rock candy "nails" holding the sole and uppers together. Swain happened to loathe licorice, and by the end of the third day of shooting he had consumed so much of it that his digestive system was in a state of extreme rebellion.

Chaplin needed no reminder of what it was like to be so hungry that he fantasized about food, but some pamphlets on the Donner party that Eddie Manson had picked up in Truckee, the nearest town to Summit, inspired him to take the cabin scenes in a more surrealist direction. Instead of having Mack Swain's character conjure up a vision of a juicy roast turkey, as he originally planned, Chaplin had him hallucinate that the Little Fellow himself had been transformed into a man-size chicken.

One of the studio painters, a man named Pete, was chosen to play the chicken. Pete, recalled Eddie Sutherland, got into the chicken suit constructed in the studio shop and "walked on [the set] and looked like a painter in a chicken skin." Charlie was none too eager to don the hot, uncomfortable costume, but when he did "he was a chicken. Now, I'm sure that Chaplin never consciously studied or even looked at a chicken, consciously, but he knew just what a chicken did and how it moved its wings and its feet and everything else."[5]

Sutherland had recently returned from Sacramento, where some hard bargaining had been required to talk the state authorities into approving Chaplin's plan to take hundreds of hobos—or "bindle stiffs," as they were called in those days—into the High Sierras to play prospectors crossing the Chilkoot Pass. Worried that the hobos would get drunk and harass local homesteaders or freeze to death in the snow, the state insisted that none of the men be paid until they were safely back in Sacramento. The hobos, however, were far from enthusiastic about signing up without seeing cash up front. Ninety percent of the men "wouldn't even look at you," Sutherland recalled; 10 percent stared as if they "hated your soul," but "the other ten per cent [*sic*] were willing to listen," provided Sutherland established his trustworthiness by drinking with them, a daunting proposition since the only alcoholic beverage available was Sterno strained through a sock and diluted with water.

Eventually Sutherland rounded up more than five hundred men, who were transported to Summit in Union Pacific boxcars. The cars were parked on railroad sidings that were roofed over to prevent them from being buried under drifting snow. Although the hobos were supposed to sleep inside the boxcars, many of them were unable to tolerate being packed together and spread out their blanket rolls outside. Few of them were complaining, however. Sutherland had arranged for the railroad to provide food service from its regular dining cars, which were well stocked with roast beef, hams, vegetables, and crusty breads and pies, all served buffet-style.

With the help of the Truckee ski club, meanwhile, a technical crew from the studio had transformed a trail through a narrow defile on the slopes of Mount Lincoln into a reasonable facsimile of the Chilkoot Pass. Nearby, carpenters constructed a set for the mining camp, where Charlie, the "lone prospector," would meet and fall in love with a dance hall girl, to be played by Lita. By the time the set was complete and the extras ready to work, it was already early April, and a spell of unseasonably warm weather was melting the snow out from under their feet, turning the trail into a slough of mud. As it happens these were precisely the conditions faced by the great majority of the "stampeders" of 1898, who crossed the pass during the summer, when mudslides were far more of a problem than snow. Chaplin and his assistants either didn't know this or didn't care. Hollywood reality, such as it was, called for snow.

With the preparations at Summit almost complete, Chaplin and his party left Los Angeles in a private railroad car. In addition to Harry d'Arrast, Henry Bergman, Jim Tully, and Chuck Riesner, the group included Lita Grey and her mother, as well as Sid Grauman. In high spirits, Chaplin organized a mock revival meeting, calling on the members of the party to come forward one by one to "testify."

Luckily a fresh snowfall covered the chewed-up portions of the trail just before Chaplin's party arrived in Summit, and Eddie Sutherland scheduled the filming of the Chilkoot Pass crossing for the very next day. To make the file of "stampeders" look as large as possible, all available personnel, including Lita Grey, the leading lady, joined the march. The altitude at the base camp was more than 9,500 feet, and the trail rose another 1,000 feet to the spot where Rollie Totheroh had placed his camera. The climb was hard, cold work, even for the young and fit, and the glare reflecting off the snow was blinding.

Chaplin, Jim Tully would recall, appeared in his Tramp costume and was driven to the base camp in a horsedrawn sleigh, cheered lustily by the hobos who shouted, "Hey Charlie, boy! Hurrah for Charlie! He's our kind!" After directing the action for a while, he turned over his megaphone to Eddie Sutherland and joined the long file of men struggling with their heavy packs up the steep trail. "As he stepped along with the army of vagabonds," observed Tully,

his face slowly and miraculously took on a sadder and sadder expression, until, as he near[ed] the camera, you saw a broken explorer in a lonely moment, worn and heartsick, and trudging onward to a very uncertain destiny. He was able to interpret perfectly his companions' sufferings on his mobile face. I stood near a cameraman who had photographed the comedian for seven years. He sighed as he looked at Chaplin's face and turned the camera. Here, indeed, was the man Chaplin great.[6]

Strangely this remarkable moment is not seen in the finished film. Although Chaplin and his cast were on the trail, none of them are clearly identifiable in the crowd shots. There is something almost willfully uncinematic about this, as if D. W. Griffith had filmed the blizzard scenes in Way Down East using Lillian Gish as an anonymous extra.

Perhaps Chaplin would have used his cast more effectively if it hadn't been for a flu epidemic that struck down most of the actors and kept him in bed for four days. He, at least, had his private suite.

Accommodations for the rest of the party, about fifty in number, were none too comfortable. The nearest showers were in Truckee, twelve miles away by train, and while most of the bindle stiffs were well behaved, a few of them had taken to lurking outside the hotel at night, peering through the windows at the crew's nightly poker game. Some of Chaplin's assistants began to worry that if the work weren't wrapped up quickly, the hobos, desperate for drink, might stage a mutiny.

In such close quarters few could fail to observe that Lita Grey had begun visiting Chaplin's suite. Eddie Manson claimed that Mrs. Spicer dressed her daughter in a fetching pink kimono and instructed her to knock on Chaplin's door to ask if she had a call the next morning. Lita recalled that, on the contrary, she was fully dressed and had been summoned by Henry Bergman, who told her that Mr. Chaplin wanted to see her. Still ill with the flu, Charlie was wearing red silk pajamas. He showed her a book about Napoleon and Josephine, then pushed her down on the bed and began rubbing against her and kissing her, stopping only when he realized that she was completely inexperienced.

To varying degrees, the other men were amused or scandalized. Eddie Sutherland saw nothing really wrong with the situation. Mack Swain, a conservative family man who had a heart condition and was already suffering from the high altitude, was the most distressed. Jim Tully tried to point out to Chaplin that mixing casting and seduction was exploitive as well as potentially dangerous. Didn't he see that no teenage girl could conceivably be interested in him if he didn't have the power to make her a star? Chaplin sorrowfully agreed. "If I were a clerk, she would not want me. . . . Would you blame her? All the words of Byron in a clerk!"[7]

For the most part, the aides blamed Mrs. Spicer for putting temptation in the path of a vulnerable man. She, however, was being very effectively distracted by Sid Grauman, who rarely left her side and gave every appearance of being besotted with love. Sometime after the cast's return to Los Angeles, Grauman dropped out of the picture, but Chaplin, who boasted to Lita that he was a "planful" man, began dating Thelma Morgan Converse, the beautiful twin sister of Gloria Morgan Vanderbilt. With Thelma as chaperone, Chaplin took Lita to Musso & Frank's restaurant, the opening of

Douglas Fairbanks's latest picture, dinner parties at Sam Goldwyn's house, and swimming at the Santa Monica Beach Club. When they were alone he told her that she had become such an obsession with him that his work had begun to suffer. Believing that she and Charlie shared a true love that the world could never understand, she promised to keep their deepening physical relationship secret from her mother.

Chaplin knew that society disapproved of his passion for young girls but rationalized to Lita that he had nothing in common with nasty old men who merely wanted to despoil innocence. "I'm not like that—God, I *know* I'm not," he protested. He was an artist, who simply appreciated the perfect beauty of the first bloom of woman-hood. Even when she came to write her life story many years later, Lita Grey would agree that there was a "purity" in Charlie's passion, and that he couldn't be compared to, say, Errol Flynn, a compulsive seducer of teenagers.[8]

Certainly it was true that Chaplin was no Errol Flynn. But even his own staff recognized that his pursuit of Lita was more than just the natural attraction of a mature man for a young woman. "He always used to be very worried about his sexual ability," said Rollie Totheroh. "He'd want to be the teacher. He didn't want anybody who had any experience of anything whatever."[9]

Distracted by his pursuit of Lita, whom he saw mostly during the day, Chaplin got little done until midsummer, when he finally resumed shooting on the back lot. In the sweltering heat Mack Swain, dressed in a heavy parka, chased Charlie through drifts of salt and flour until the exertion became too much for him. "I love this part. I love Charlie. I love you," he told Eddie Sutherland. "But if I do this, it'll kill me."

Chaplin happened to be in a bad mood that day, and abruptly told Swain that he couldn't work with an actor who was in no condi-tion to do action scenes. No sooner had Mack left the studio, how-ever, than he had second thoughts. Their association went back to 1914, and reshooting all of Big Jim's scenes would be a major expense. When he called the Swain house to tell him that he wanted him back, Mack exclaimed, "You're too late!" He had just come from the barbershop, and the grizzled beard he had grown for the part was but a memory. Rather than try to cover Swain's bare chin with a false beard, Chaplin decided to abandon shooting until the real thing grew back.[10]

Chaplin's dilatory work habits were already a point of contention between him and Mary Pickford, the only one of the United Artists partners who took an interest in the day-to-day fortunes of the company. By the end of 1924, Pickford would have released eleven movies through UA, Doug Fairbanks seven, and D. W. Griffith, working out of his studio in Mamaroneck, New York, nine. In the summer of 1923, looking forward impatiently to Chaplin's first contribution to the company, Pickford wrote her attorney, Cap O'Brien: "Charlie is thoroughly frightened and realizes he has to get down to business if he hopes to keep in public favor and he needs the money, so I am looking forward to getting a picture from him very soon now."[11] The picture she got was *A Woman of Paris*, a financial disappointment.

Pickford was also upset that Chaplin had used the foreign rights to *The Kid* to strike a better deal with First National. When Griffith followed suit by giving another company the overseas distribution to *Way Down East*, Pickford, "very much incensed," complained to O'Brien:

If Mr. Griffith and Charlie are going to equivocate about giving us their pictures for foreign release and when they do get pictures like Way Down East and The Kid, sell them to the highest bidder and leave us with their mediocre output such as The Idle Class and Dream Street, then Douglas and I should insist that they should be shown no favors but they should pay 40 percent instead of 30 percent (as a distribution fee).[12]

Griffith, Pickford pointed out, had voted at a recent board meeting to expand UA's foreign operations, an expansion that was being paid for with the profits from her *Pollyanna* and Douglas's *The Mark of Zorro*. But when she asked Charlie to sign a letter to Griffith, remonstrating with him, he refused, telling her that he didn't feel that Griffith—or he himself for that matter—was obligated to United Artists "in any way."

By the fall of 1923 Pickford and the UA management had

another worry. Chaplin, in New York for the premiere of *A Woman of Paris*, was entertaining a group of UA executives in his suite at the Ritz-Carlton, when Nathan Burkan delivered a message that William Randolph Hearst was upstairs in the penthouse and wanted to talk to him. Burkan assured Cap O'Brien and Hiram Abrams that the meeting would be purely social, but the UA executives didn't believe it, and O'Brien speculated that Hearst was about to make separate production deals with Griffith and Chaplin and "practically get our own company without paying for it."[13]

Hearst was planning to move his production company, Cosmopolitan Pictures, to the West Coast, and in his ceaseless search for a director who could make a star of his mistress, Marion Davies, he probably was making an effort to strike a deal with Chaplin. Nothing came of the discussion, but Chaplin became friendly with Hearst, who spent millions almost absentmindedly, without anxiety or guilt. Like many others in Hollywood, he had blamed the Hearst newspapers for destroying Fatty Arbuckle, and he was amazed to learn that Hearst himself was scarcely aware of the case. For better or worse, his power was wielded by hired hands while he remained aloof.

By the summer of 1924 Cosmopolitan had become a subsidiary of MGM. For the moment there was no suitable space for the company's productions at MGM's facility in Culver City, so Hearst arranged for Marion Davies's next picture, *Zander the Great*, to be shot at the United Artists (Doug and Mary's) studio. When trouble developed on the set, he called from New York to ask Charlie to help him out.

The *Zander* script called for Marion to do a scene inside a lion's cage, but the animal borrowed from a local zoo had arrived in a feisty mood and when it displayed a full set of teeth by snapping its jaws near Marion's head, she became too frightened to continue. The director ordered a thick sheet of plate glass erected between the lion's half of the cage and Marion's, but she was not reassured. "I think a lion can go right through glass," she later wrote. Chaplin, who had recently used a trained bear in *The Gold Rush*, happened to be friendly with an animal trainer named Charles Gay, the son of a Parisian jeweler, who had nineteen lions at his ranch in Del Monte, California. He rented one of them for *Zander*, and showed up on the set to coach Marion through the scene. The substitute lion displayed the manners of a pussycat, but Marion was paralyzed by fear.

Eventually, according to her account, Chaplin dressed up in her costume and a wig and did the shot for her. Vera Burnett, her aide, remembered that the role was played by the lion's female trainer. By no means the untalented bubblehead many in Hollywood took her for, Marion Davies was a talented comedienne, ambitious but also warmhearted, who wisecracked her way through life. Never convinced of her own talent, she organized elaborate practical jokes on the set and reeled off wicked imitations of Lillian Gish, Mary Pickford, and Al Jolson. Chaplin was drawn to her and began visiting her dressing room almost every day, at times hiding under a cot to avoid being seen by Hearst's spies, who were legion. In the evenings he and Marion went nightclubbing, accompanied by Hearst reporter Louella Parsons, former head of the story department at Essanay, and another journalist, the tall, good-looking Harry Crocker.

Years later Davies would insist that her relationship with Charlie was never serious. As she told Hearst reporter Adela Rogers St. Johns, "Nobody ever made passes at me except Chaplin and everyone knew he was harmless and anyway it was for laughs. Either men worshipped W.R., or they worked for him, or they were our guests and gentlemen, or they hated W.R.'s guts but were scared of him. My leading men—they went whoosh the instant the camera stopped grinding."[14] This, of course, was exactly her problem. Just twenty-eight, she was also the mistress of a married man thirty-four years her senior who had no intention of divorcing his Catholic wife and, so far, had failed to provide her with the financial security she felt she deserved. She was bored, often lonely, and far from resigned to spending the rest of her life with W.R., as she called him, but men who would risk the wrath of Hearst and his newspapers were few indeed. For Charlie, whose enthusiasm was close to being a full-blown manic high, the danger was no doubt part of the attraction.

By the beginning of November, Charlie and Marion's good times were beginning to attract notice, and brief items mentioning their visits to nightclubs appeared in the non-Hearst papers. Chaplin was still seeing Lita, who considered herself secretly

engaged, but in eight months he had yet to shoot more than inci-
dental footage of her. Chaplin shot his films in roughly chronological
order, a necessity since he often didn't know how the story would
end until he had acted it out, and the girl's first appearance had
been put off until relatively late in the story. One is tempted to think
that he was bored or having second thoughts, and perhaps even considering replacing Lita with Marion.

A few days after the items about him and Marion were published, Charlie entertained Lita and her increasingly suspicious
mother at a dinner party, also attended by Alf and Amy Reeves; his
physician, Dr. Cecil Reynolds; and Mrs. Reynolds. During the
evening Mrs. Spicer suddenly doubled over with an attack of severe
abdominal pain. Dr. Reynolds gave her a sedative and advised her
and Lita to spend the night in the guest room. Some hours later
Spicer awoke, wondered what had become of her daughter, and
made her way to Chaplin's bedroom, where she found him and Lita
in bed together.

Mrs. Spicer was indignant. No doubt she had been hoping that
Chaplin would develop a romantic interest in her daughter. Perhaps,
as Chaplin's friends suspected, she was even scheming to get herself a
rich son-in-law. But the discovery that Lita was already sleeping with
Chaplin, and keeping the secret from her, was shocking. According to
Lita's account, Chaplin calmed Mrs. Spicer's hysterics by telling her
that he loved Lita and had every intention of marrying her.

Chaplin would later deny that he ever propsed to Lita or told
her mother that he and Lita were engaged; however, he had made
similar glib promises to other women in the past, and his denials are
difficult to take seriously. Moreover, shortly after this confrontation,
he began making preparations to shoot the dance hall scene that
would introduce Lita's character in *The Gold Rush*—surely in order
to placate Mrs. Spicer. Meanwhile, Mrs. Spicer visited a gynecologist who diagnosed her condition as a blockage of the fallopian
tubes, fortunately operable. During the same visit, he examined Lita
and found her to be pregnant.

Lillian Spicer may have encouraged, or at least winked at,
Chaplin's pursuit of her daughter, but she had done so expecting
that it would lead to marriage. Instead, when she confronted him in
his office at the studio, he offered to pay a ten-thousand-dollar set-

tlement and have Kono arrange an abortion at the office of a doctor "in the Valley." Spicer, a Roman Catholic, refused even to consider this proposal. Chaplin then suggested finding a young man closer to Lita's age who would be willing to marry her in exchange for a twenty-thousand-dollar "dowry." Lita was present during this meeting, and, hearing her future being disposed of so cavalierly, she burst into tears and protested that she didn't want to marry anyone. Far from seeing that she was at least as much—and surely more—a victim of the situation as he was, Chaplin took her outburst as evidence that she had never loved him and was just leading him on.

"I was stunned and ready for suicide that day when [Lita] told me that she didn't love me and that we must marry," he said of this moment in a statement released by his studio several years later. "Lita's mother often suggested to me that I marry Lita, and I said I would love to if only we could have children. I thought I was incapable of fatherhood. Her mother deliberately and continuously put Lita in my path."[15]

Where fatherhood and contraception were concerned, it is difficult to imagine how Chaplin's mind worked. While the death of his son by Mildred Harris may have given him reason to doubt that he was capable of fathering a healthy child, surely that tragedy, combined with the unhappy aftermath of Florence Deshon's pregnancy, should have made him acutely aware of the importance of contraception. On the contrary Chaplin's aversion to rubber and rubber-like materials extended to condoms, which he considered repulsive. This phobia, however, does not quite explain his mode of self-denial. Surely he had wanted Lita to get pregnant, even if unconsciously, in order to prove himself and give himself a reason to marry her despite her youth.

No doubt it was also far from coincidental that the women Chaplin became romantically involved with were almost invariably fatherless. This time, however, Chaplin belatedly learned that his part-Mexican "waif," as he called her, had a maternal grandfather, William Curry, who owned several apartment buildings in Los Angeles, as well a a paternal uncle, Edwin McMurray, who was a prominent San Francisco attorney. The family summoned Chaplin to a conference, and when he continued to rule out marriage as unthinkable, Edwin McMurray pointed out that under California law, sexual intercourse with a fifteen-year-old was statutory rape, punishable by up to fifty years in jail.

Chaplin caved in under pressure, but he intended to keep the marriage secret as long as possible, the better to finesse future questions about Lita's age and pregnancy. Chuck Riesner and Eddie Manson were dispatched to Guaymas, Mexico, in the state of Sonora, to arrange for a quiet wedding ceremony. Riesner discovered that the normal procedure called for marriage licenses to be cleared through a central registry in Mexico City, a process that would give numerous bureaucrats and telegraph operators an opportunity to leak the story to the newspapers.

An accommodating clerk suggested that the law could also be satisfied by posting the banns—displaying an announcement of the couple's intentions for two weeks in a public place. Riesner had a notice placed on a town bulletin board, but while the ink on the notice was still wet he rubbed his thumb through it, smudging Chaplin and Grey's names.

The waiting period suited Chaplin, who faced a critical series of United Artists board meetings during the forthcoming week. Desperate over the company's mounting debts, and unsure of when they would see Charlie's new comedy, Mary Pickford and Doug Fairbanks wanted to invite an outside producer, Joseph Schenck, to join UA as a partner and chief executive. Schenck was an able producer and controlled the contracts of two major box office draws— his wife, actress Norma Talmadge, and the romantic heartthrob Rudolph Valentino (and of *his* wife, designer Natacha Rambova). Chaplin had no practical alternative to propose, but he planned to use his vote as a lever to force the company to renegotiate his contract.

The week would also be a busy one for Nathan Burkan. On Monday, November 17, Burkan's law firm filed papers in the state of Delaware, incorporating the Charles Chaplin Film Corporation as a successor to his New York–based production company. The laws of Delaware would make it very difficult for his future in-laws to get information about the corporation's income and assets.

✿   ✿   ✿

Meanwhile, on Saturday, November 15, William Randolph Hearst's 220-foot yacht, *Oneida*, departed from San Pedro, California, on a weekend cruise. Among the guests were Marion Davies, her sisters Ethel and Reine, her niece Pepi, British author and screenwriter Elinor Glyn, actresses Aileen Pringle and Seena Owen, Hearst's aide and secretary Joe Willicombe, and Dr. Daniel Carson Goodman, Cosmopolitan's studio manager. The *Oneida* sailed for San Diego, where the next morning the director Tom Ince joined the party. Ince was in the final stages of negotiating a production deal with Hearst's International Film Corporation.

At dinner on Sunday night the guests celebrated Ince's forty-third birthday. Early the next morning a water taxi was summoned to the vessel, and Tom Ince went ashore, accompanied by Dr. Goodman. According to a statement Goodman later gave the San Diego district attorney, he and Ince boarded a train for Los Angeles, but when Ince fell ill they got off the train at Del Mar and checked into a nearby hotel. Goodman called a doctor, A. T. Parker, who arrived with his nurse. He also phoned Nell Ince, Tom's wife, who immediately headed for Del Mar in her chauffeur-driven car, accompanied by her teenage son. Goodman departed before Nell Ince arrived.

Late on Tuesday, Tom Ince died at home. His personal physician, Dr. Ida Glasgow, signed the death certificate, giving heart failure as the cause of death. To the surprise of Ince's hundreds of friends, employees, and admirers, his body was immediately cremated and the memorial service, held the following Friday, was private. Nell Ince soon departed on an extended tour of Europe.

Although Ince was known to suffer from stomach ulcers and angina, gossip that there was something suspicious about his death began to circulate almost immediately, fueled by a statement issued by the Hearst organization saying that Ince had fallen ill while visiting Hearst's "upstate ranch" in the company of his wife and two sons. The story perplexed colleagues, who knew very well that Ince had been on Hearst's yacht.

Why the lie? One obvious possibility is that Ince had come aboard the *Oneida* with a woman, reportedly actress Margaret Livingston, and the story was a clumsy attempt to spare his family embarrassment. This might also explain why Ince tried to get back to Los Angeles on his own, instead of summoning his car or asking to be taken to a local hospital.

Similarly, Daniel Carson Goodman's role gave cause for suspicion. A licensed but nonpracticing physician, Goodman was married to actress Alma Rubens, a notorious heroin addict who was being carried by Hearst's studio despite the threat of scandal. In his statement to the district attorney, who conducted only a perfunctory investigation, Goodman seemed confused as to whether Ince suffered a heart attack or just indigestion. Also briefly questioned by a representative of the San Diego DA was nurse Jesse Howard, who attended Ince at the hotel. Howard attributed the director's condition to "bad liquor"—a common problem during the heyday of bathtub gin but hardly likely to trouble Hearst's guests.

What, if anything, did all this have to do with Charlie Chaplin? Although Chaplin would deny, at times none too convincingly, that he was even present on the *Oneida* that weekend, few believed him. One witness to the contrary was Vera Burnett, who later told Davies's biographer, Fred Lawrence Guiles, that she remembered Chaplin and Louella Parsons picking up Marion at the studio on their way to San Pedro. Hearst biographer W. A. Swanberg, who dismissed gossip about Ince's death as ridiculous, also lists Chaplin among the guests. At the time the most damaging alleged witness was none other than the normally discreet Toraichi Kono. Supposedly on the dock in San Diego waiting to pick up Chaplin, who was scheduled to meet with UA executives later that day, Kono was present when Ince was brought ashore, and he saw something that upset him. Kono confided in his wife, and the story spread among the network of Japanese domestic workers in Beverly Hills.

By the time the gossip reached the ears of actress Eleanor Boardman, the future wife of directors King Vidor and Harry d'Arrast, it was being said that Kono had seen Ince bleeding from a bullet wound to the head.[16]

That William Randolph Hearst shot Tom Ince became part of Hollywood legend. It was often alleged, though never proved, that Hearst made a private settlement to Ince's estate, paying off the mortgages on the Château Elysée apartment building in Hollywood and another rental property. Fred Guiles, who discussed Ince's death with many of Marion Davies's surviving friends in preparing his 1972 biography, found that there were two schools of thought. One faction dismissed the Ince shooting as a fantasy; the other claimed that Hearst had found Marion and Ince together in the yacht's galley late at night. Ince was looking for something to calm his upset stomach, but Hearst, mistaking him for Chaplin in the poor light, assumed he had walked in on an assignation and shot him.

A variation on this story, impossible to attribute to any particular eyewitness yet all too plausible, is that there was some sort of struggle over a gun belowdecks, and the bullet passed through a plywood partition into Ince's cabin, wounding him. Certainly if Chaplin was on the yacht, the party can hardly have been uneventful. That weekend he was, by his own account, "almost suicidal" over his forthcoming shotgun marriage. An excitable man at the best of times, Chaplin owned a .38, and it was not unknown for him to brandish the gun melodramatically, threatening to shoot himself. In the confined quarters of a yacht, such carryings-on could all too easily lead to a struggle and the accidental discharge of the weapon. Despite what Kono was supposed to have seen, Tom Ince was ambulatory when he left the *Oneida*. Whatever happened on board cannot have done his ulcers any good, but if he was indeed shot, no one expected the wound to be fatal.

Suspicion about the circumstances that led to Ince's death could be easily dismissed were it not for the inconsistent statements made about the incident in later years. Everyone involved seemed determined to exaggerate the amount of time between the yacht party and Ince's death. Marion Davies, whose denials were often highly revealing, said of the Ince rumors: "So if he'd been shot, how long can one keep a bullet in his system?" As Fred Guiles noted, the answer to this question is: Any amount of time.[17]

In 1968 veteran reporter and Hearst loyalist Adela Rogers St. Johns set out to squelch the misconceptions about Tom Ince's death once and for all in her memoir, *The Honeycomb*. For some reason St. Johns chose to rebut at length the possibility that Ince was poisoned—which had never been rumored. "I can see Mr. Hearst shooting an enemy—maybe even in cold blood," she wrote. "Everybody can shoot somebody some time for something. But poison a guest at his own table in a birthday toast—NO."[18] Some defense.

St. Johns went on to reprint a letter from Nell Ince, expressing indignation over the many false stories told about her husband and extolling Hearst: "such kindliness—and such a splendid dancer." Nell then gave her own account of what happened after Dr. Goodman summoned her:

From the moment we met in Del Mar I was never separated from him for a minute. Tom had been treated by a specialist MD for chest pains which were diagnosed as angina. When my son Bill became a doctor, in his medical studies and experience and in many talks with physicians, he giving all the symptoms he saw in his teens, Bill says it all fits what we know today as a thrombosis, and the end came at home a week later. He had been improving steadily, the doctors and nurses were pleased—the end was unexpected as with thrombosis it generally is.[19]

This is an extraordinary statement. After enduring slanders for four decades, the indignant widow decides to set the record straight but gets her husband's date of death wrong by a week.

Nell Ince's letter concludes with a somewhat suspect description of her husband's cremation. Four people went to the crematorium with her husband's body, she says—Ince's attorney; his studio manager Reece Houck; Dr. Day of the Day and Strother mortuary; "AND [her capitals] the Chief of Homicide of Los Angeles. . . . They made the necessary legal examination before the cremation." In fact, if an individual dies of a preexisting condition, no post mortem is necessary. Witnesses to a cremation are present only to identify the remains and have no reason to examine the corpse. Why the LA chief of homicide would have been at the crematorium is a mystery, especially since Nell Ince also insists that she was unaware of any suspected foul play until after her husband's funeral.

The investigation by the San Diego DA did not begin until a month later.[20]

Chaplin's comments on Ince's death in his autobiography are equally bizarre. After denying that he was on the *Oneida*, he goes on to say that he, Hearst, and Davies visited Ince's bedside together a week after he fell ill. Ince seemed to be improving, Chaplin says, but died two weeks later.

Why would Chaplin, Hearst, and Davies have paid a joint call on

Ince unless they had all been together on the yacht? On the other hand, why would Chaplin invent such a story? At any rate Ince survived not three weeks but less than forty-eight hours. That Friday Chaplin was a pallbearer at Ince's funeral. On Saturday he completed the renegotiation of his United Artists contract and on Sunday he departed for Guaymas, accompanied by Nathan Burkan. He had good reason to recall the chronology of this tumultuous and unhappy week.

Toraichi Kono, widely thought to know the truth about the *Oneida* incident, was later the chief source for Gerith von Ulm's gossipy but generally accurate biography of Chaplin. Published while Hearst and Davies were still alive, the book makes no claim that Ince was shot, but it does say that Chaplin's decision to marry Lita Grey devastated a certain film star, since "retired from the screen." This star was surely Marion Davies, though von Ulm, who had reason to fear a libel suit, chose to identify her by the pseudonym "Maisie." After Chaplin's marriage to Lita, the affair continued, kept alive by "Maisie," who wrote naive and highly indiscreet love letters, using Kono as an intermediary. The envelope of one such letter, Kono recalled, bore the imprint of her lipstick-smeared mouth—the lover's code for "sealed with a kiss."[21]

Lita had already been dispatched to Guaymas, accompanied by her mother, grandmother, and Kono, as well as an entire film crew, supposedly planning to film location shots for *The Gold Rush*. The large party was put up in the town's only hotel, which was even seedier than the inn at Summit. The rickety beds had a tendency to collapse in the middle of the night, and the rooms had only half-length doors, affording no real privacy. A few suspicious reporters had followed the party to Guaymas, and when Chaplin and Burkan arrived they waited until after dark to leave the train. Chaplin slipped out of the window on the opposite side from the station platform. This method of egress was hard on the portly, unathletic Burkan, who was hoisted to the ground by several of his aides.

There followed a postmidnight dash for the nearby town of Empalme in three broken-down Fords, the best cars Riesner had been able to round up. The roads were primitive, and one of the Fords narrowly avoided striking a mountain lion. A local magistrate was rousted from his bed at three A.M. to perform the wedding ceremony, and the party immediately returned to Guaymas. The next day Chaplin went fishing while the women stayed out of sight, guarded by Kono. Boarding the train back to California, Chaplin was heard to announce to his companions, "Well, boys, it's better than the penitentiary, but it won't last long."

According to Lita, while she and Charlie were standing on the rear platform of their Pullman car, she ventured the observation, "Everything's going to be all right," and he began to mock her, saying, "If you can't cope with your misery, just mumble 'Everything's going to be all right' three times and the clouds will disappear for all us children." He then suggested that the best way out for all of them would be for her to jump from the moving train.[22]

Amazingly, considering this beginning, Lita would later insist that her life with Chaplin was not always unbearable. At times he was bitingly sarcastic, as times cold and distant, but when in control of his moods, he could also be considerate. Chaplin always became sentimental at Chistmastime, and in a mellow mood, he allowed Lita to invite her mother and various relatives for a house party. The gossip columns, no doubt reflecting the attitude of Chaplin's aides, made snide references to a "Mexican invasion" of Cove Way. Mrs. Spicer, meanwhile, settled down in the guest bedroom and never left.

Like Mildred Harris before her, Lita suspected that Charlie did not find her mother's presence entirely inconvenient. At times he seemed to get along with his mother-in-law better than he did with her, and now that she and Charlie were married, her mother often took his side in arguments.

When New Year's came they were invited to Marion Davies's fancy-dress ball at the Ambassador Hotel, and Charlie decided they should go as Napoleon and Josephine. He ordered the custom-made costumes himself, supervising every detail of the design. During the course of the evening Lita was cornered by a very drunk John Barrymore, who broke the news to her about Marion's interest in Charlie and gallantly offered her a chance to get even. She declined.

Pregnant and miserable, Lita slept away her days for several months, and then developed insomnia and could scarcely sleep at all. Kono, making no secret of his disapproval, doled out her allowance and delivered messages from Chaplin, who sometimes failed to come home nights, sleeping at the studio. Kono continually emphasized Chaplin's need for quiet and regularity, telling Lita: "Mr. Chaplin does not like change." Syd Chaplin, who was more sympathetic, told her that Charlie was afraid that he was going insane, like his mother before him, and worried that he had some inherited defect that would cause their child to be born deformed.

Despite his miserable situation at home, Chaplin had pulled himself together and was doing some of the best work of his career. The studio announced that Lita Grey had retired from acting, and Chaplin tested a number of possible replacements, including Jean Alice Peters, the future Carole Lombard. But Peters was just seventeen, and Chaplin could not risk the publicity that would accompany signing another underage "discovery." At a private screening of Josef von Sternberg's low-budget *The Salvation Hunters,* Chaplin was impressed by the work of Georgia Hale. Hale idolized Chaplin, and to her delight, Doug Fairbanks, who had recently signed her for his forthcoming *Don Q, Son of Zorro,* agreed to release her from her contract.[23]

A former Miss Chicago, Georgia Hale was an interesting combination of glamour and Midwestern straightness. She was well cast as the fiery-tempered but good-hearted bar singer, and the shooting of the complicated dance hall scenes moved along briskly.

Later in the story Georgia and the other dance hall girls stop by the tiny cabin where the lone prospector is keeping an eye on things for a friendly miner. The girls are in a teasing mood, and Georgia impulsively accepts his invitation to return with her friends for dinner on New Year's Eve. Chaplin was supposed to register his elation with a little dance of joy. With the cameras rolling, he seized the pillows off his bed and hugged them until they split open, releasing a blizzard of feathers. The tearing of the pillows came as a surprise to the crew on the set, who gasped in admiration. The weightless down feathers were the perfect metaphor for the Little Fellow's exuberance.

During this period Chaplin also shot his famous Dance of the Rolls. The routine was a variation on an old music hall turn attributed to the British comic, G. H. Chirgwin, who made a pair of clay pipes "dance" on a tin tray.²⁴ Spearing two dinner rolls with forks, Chaplin turns them into a pair of dancing feet. The plump "feet," spindly fork-handle "legs," and Chaplin's face hovering above them combine to create the illusion of a young girl dancing—coy, grace- ful, and in some indefinable way, weirdly seductive.

In the climactic segment of *The Gold Rush,* the prospector and Big Jim McKay return to Black Larsen's cabin in the hopes of locat- ing his lost gold strike. While they sleep, a fierce storm comes up, and the cabin is blown down the mountain and left teetering precar- iously on the edge of a crevasse. Charlie is up first the next morning, notices the cabin seems to be rocking a little, and blames it on his having had too much to drink the night before. Then Big Jim wakes and begins to move around. The rocking becomes more alarming. Charlie starts outside to investigate and finds—an abyss.

When it came time to film the exterior shots of the cabin, air- plane engines were brought onto the back lot to blow up a storm of mica and corn flakes. Their roar was so ear-splitting that Eddie Manson had to stand by with a starter's pistol, firing in the air to sig- nal the beginning and end of each shot. The "cabin," actually only a facade, was mounted on a track so that it could be moved up and down the slope. To maintain the proper perspective (or rather the lack of it) Totheroh's camera was also mounted on a track, its move- ments coordinated with the cabin's. Later, in the cutting room, Chaplin would splice these shots with footage of a scale model. The illusion, though primitive by today's standards, was surprisingly effective. The cabin facade is so obviously a fake that one is tempted to mistake it for a miniature—until, suddenly, the door swings open and Charlie comes sliding out, his legs pumping furiously as he strives to avoid falling into the void below.

According to Jim Tully, Chaplin had originally planned an "ironi- cal" ending to the prospector's story. Fortunately this impulse passed. Like Chaplin himself the Little Fellow strikes it rich in the goldfields. When last seen he and Big Jim are millionaires. To please a newspaper reporter who is writing his story, Charlie agrees to pose in his old rags on the deck of the steamer that is carrying him and his partner back to civilization. Georgia, who happens to be on the same ship, mistakes him for a stowaway and tries to help him. When she realizes he is now rich, romance blossoms instantly. Chaplin surely knew that this conclusion would disappoint his left-wing admirers. In a lighthearted rebuff to this segment of his audience, the final title card of the film is the photographer's complaint that Charlie and Georgia have ruined his carefully arranged pose by exchanging a kiss—"Oh, you've spoilt the picture!"

Many years later Georgia Hale told Chaplin biographer David Robinson that when Charlie kissed her she knew for the first time that her romantic feelings for him were reciprocated. On the way back from the filming, which had taken place on board an actual commercial passenger steamer bound for San Diego, the cast and crew stopped at a nightclub, where the band recognized Chaplin and broke into his unofficial theme song, "Charley, My Boy." The dance floor cleared, and she and Charlie danced together.[25]

Georgia knew that Charlie was married—a serious obstacle for her, since she happened to be religious—but she may not have realized how close he was to becoming a father. Charles Chaplin Jr. was born on May 5, 1925, just three weeks after the scene on board the steamer was shot. During the final weeks of Lita's pregnancy, Harrison Carroll, an energetic reporter for the *Los Angeles Times*, had begun staking out Cove Way, hoping for an interview, and Chaplin had rented a house for Lita and her mother in the Whitley Heights section of Hollywood. Lita returned to Chaplin's house to give birth to Charles junior, and then she and her mother were immediately sent into hiding, first to a primitive cabin in the San Bernardino Mountains and later an apartment in Manhattan Beach, where they were looked after by Amy Reeves. Chaplin also bribed the obstetrician to change the date on his son's birth certificate from May 5 to June 28—a not-uncommon ruse in the days when a "six-month baby" was still considered scandalous. One suspects that Chaplin's fans would have happily forgiven him for fathering a child before the wedding, but with the opening of *The Gold Rush* just weeks away, he didn't want to risk it.

Lita was mortified and bitter over being hidden away, though at the time it didn't occur to her to protest. Busy wrapping up *The Gold Rush*, Charlie ignored his family until he learned that Lita had fallen ill with complications from a breast abscess. He then hastened to Lita's bedside, and when he held his son, he felt a rush of fatherly pride and decide to bring his wife and the boy back home.

Lita was still in hiding on June 26, and so was unable to attend the premiere of *The Gold Rush* at the Egyptian Theater. Sid Grauman, who felt a special connection to the picture, staged a spectacular live show for opening night. Trained seals cavorted on a mountain of ice, "Eskimo dancing girls" frolicked on ice skates, and one Lillian Powell performed a "balloon dance." *Variety*, which had often been critical of Chaplin in the past, was ecstatic about the movie: "It is the greatest and most elaborate comedy ever filmed and will stand for years to come as the biggest hit in its field, just as *The Birth of a Nation* still withstands its many competitors in the dramatic field."[26]

United Artists, delighted to have a Chaplin comedy at last, and a good one, pulled out all stops in its publicity campaign. Chaplin, however, insisted that he wanted to so some reediting, and the New York premiere was delayed until August 15. Fired up by *Variety's* review and the UA publicity department, the New York press awaited Chaplin's arrival in town as if it were the Second Coming. On July 13 Mack Swain was dispatched East to satisfy the clamor for interviews. When Swain failed to arrive as expected, the tabloids, hungry for a story, speculated about his mysterious "disappearance." Swain, who had stopped en route to visit relatives, finally showed up on July 22, telling reporters that Chaplin was already planning his "next laughfest," to be entitled *The Suicide Club*.[27]

The reporters were a little confused—none of them, it seems, had ever heard of the Robert Louis Stevenson story of the same name, but they were even more bewildered when Chaplin finally arrived in town, accompanied by Harry d'Arrast. The amiable if occasionally overserious Chaplin of earlier times had been replaced by a frenetic pleasure seeker. Canceling a full schedule of interviews on the grounds of exhaustion, Chaplin nevertheless began making the rounds of nightclubs and private parties, pursuing every woman in sight. One of them, the actress Blyth Daly, took offense at an unwanted kiss and bit him hard enough to draw blood. The incident would have gone unnoticed, except that Chaplin created a fuss, dancing around the room and shrieking about "blood poison."

Chaplin did manage to find time to pose for photographer Edward Steichen, who had been asked to do his portrait for *Vanity Fair*. Impeccably attired, and holding a dress cane and a Stetson,

Chaplin struck a pose that suggested he was about to break into a soft-shoe step. Steichen saw something darker in his subject's mood, and lit the photo from below, an angle that lent Chaplin's grin the suggestion of a goatish leer. His shadow, thrown onto a scrim behind him, bears an almost subliminal resemblance to a satyr.

Chaplin had been keyed up—or as he put it, enthused—throughout the filming of *The Gold Rush*. Another name for what he was going through would be hypomania, a mood disorder sometimes characterized by increased creativity and goal-directed behavior, but also insomnia, irritability, feelings of grandiosity, and risky behavior including sexual indiscretions. Although he had experienced periods of such behavior in the past, this one had gone on for a long time. He was worn out, but even though the picture was finished, he couldn't rest.

On the night of August 11, he suddenly sat up in bed and began to shout, "Quick! I'm dying! Call a lawyer!"

"Don't you mean a doctor?" asked Harry d'Arrast, rushing to his bedside.[28]

No, Charlie insisted. He needed a lawyer. He was dying and wanted to make a new will. D'Arrast called a doctor anyway. The next day d'Arrast announced that he taken ill, suffering from "shattered nerves, low blood pressure, and a high fever." Chaplin would recall years later that his main problem was that he kept weeping, about nothing in particular.

He managed to pull himself together to attend the opening of *The Gold Rush* at the Mark Strand Theater at midnight on August 15. Considering the picture's enormous success with the public, the initial response of the New York critics was somewhat tepid. The reservations of the Hearst newsapers' movie critic Dorothy Herzog were typical. Calling *The Gold Rush* "not the star's best offering," she complained that the plot "tried to cover too much territory" and "generous cutting would benefit the whole greatly."

Meanwhile, Dr. McKenzie, who had been called in to treat Chaplin, suggested that he needed a few days of rest away from the overstimulating environment of Manhattan, so d'Arrast arranged for a car, and he and Charlie, incognito, headed for Brighton Beach, where they checked into a modest beachfront hotel. D'Arrast left Charlie in his room while he went out to do some errands, and when he returned Charlie was frantic. As he sat gazing out the window, he said, he had seen a swimmer in trouble, but he was too far away to do anything but watch helplessly. At last a lifeguard spotted the struggling figure and swam to his rescue, but it was too late. An ambulance arrived and took the body away. No sooner had the ambulance departed than another swimmer screamed for help. Then another. These two men were pulled out of the water alive, but by this time Chaplin was hysterical, and he begged d'Arrast to take him back to the relative calm of midtown Manhattan.

Both Chaplin and Harry d'Arrast retold this story often. In the version of the tale heard by Harry Crocker a few years later, the victims had become not three but five heavy-set Jewish men. (How Chaplin knew they were Jewish is a mystery.) Three were rescued and two drowned. It was a good story, but not true. Lifeguard rescues, not to mention drownings, were reported daily in the newspapers in 1925. The only incident during Chaplin's New York stay that he could conceivably have witnessed was the rescue of one H. Kugal, who was pulled from the surf at Twenty-Ninth Street on Coney Island on August 18. No one drowned, except in Chaplin's overheated imagination.[29]

Although neither Lita nor Georgia Hale had come East for the premiere, Edna Purviance was passing through the city on her way to make a movie in France, and Chaplin introduced her to his latest flame, Ziegfeld Follies dancer Louise Brooks. Just eighteen, "Brooksie" wore chiffon gowns and had not quite perfected the elegant, boyish look that would later make her the object of an adoring cult. Onstage in the Follies, she paraded in six-inch heels to such tunes as "Syncopating Baby" and "Fine Feathers Make Fine Birds." Her costume for the latter number consisted of a slinky, backless gown and a peacock feather headdress almost as high as she was tall. She was also featured in two solo numbers, and in the show's finale she and Will Rogers stood together atop a fifteen-foot pyramid while he twirled a lasso.

Cheerfully cynical about show business glamour, Brooks read Aldous Huxley's *Crome Yellow* in her dressing room and appeared to enjoy encouraging speculation that she and her best friend, Ziegfeld vocalist Peggy Fears, were involved in a lesbian relationship. It almost certainly wasn't true, but Brooks, like Chaplin, was ahead of her time in perceiving that androgyny was chic.

Charlie met Brooks at a cocktail party given by Paramount producer Walter Wanger, and he soon abandoned the Ritz-Carlton and moved in with her at the Ambassador Hotel. The two of them were seen everywhere together, occupying box seats at the theater and drinking in the fashionable speakeasies, usually accompanied by Harry d'Arrast and Peggy Fears. In the early hours of the morning they made the rounds of the ethnic restaurants and watering holes of the Lower East Side, where Charlie was constantly seeking out Gypsy (or putatively Gypsy) musicians. Brooks later wrote fondly of Chaplin, describing him as a dapper man ("clean as a pearl") and a sensual, resourceful lover who had allowed neither fame nor his domestic problems to sour his zest for new experiences. "I never heard him say a snide thing about anyone. He lived totally without fear," she wrote. She also recalled, "He adored his mother's madness, and credited her with giving him his comic viewpoint."[30]

At the end of August, Harry d'Arrast sailed for Europe to do advance publicity for the London and Paris premieres of *The Gold Rush*. His place as Peggy Fears's escort was taken by A. C. Blumenthal, a financier with playboy aspirations. The two couples retired to Blumenthal's penthouse for a weekend-long party, catered by room service. Champagne flowed freely, and no one bothered to get dressed. Blumenthal played the piano, Peggy and Louise sang, and Charlie treated his companions to one dazzling impersonation after another—John Barrymore reciting *Hamlet* while picking his nose; Isadora Duncan, lost in a fog of self-expression, unfurling streamers from a roll of toilet paper; and so on.

Someone had told Charlie that he could protect himself from venereal disease by painting his private parts with iodine, and at one point he burst out of the bathroom naked, his iodine-red penis in full erection, and gleefully chased Louise and Peggy around the room.

The salaries earned by Follies girls were not quite commensurate with their glamorous images, and it was understood that wealthy men who dated them would express their appreciation with gifts of jewelry and furs. Blumenthal bought Peggy Fears a diamond ring and eventually married her. Chaplin told Brooks that he couldn't risk the bad publicity of having her seen around town wearing an expensive gift that everyone would know had come from him. Some weeks later, however, he sent her a generous check. She was not insulted.[31]

In 1925 there was still a distinction between public and private life, and men's dalliances with showgirls definitely belonged in the latter category. Not a word of Chaplin's affair with Brooks appeared in the newspapers, even though some reporters were shocked, considering that he had a teenage wife and infant son in LA. As long as he was in town, Harry d'Arrast had kept the press pacified, explaining Chaplin's absence from the Ritz-Carlton by saying that he had "gone to the country" for a rest and assuring them (falsely) that Charlie called his wife long-distance every night. But d'Arrast was no longer around to play nursemaid on September 24, when Chaplin finally held his often deferred luncheon meeting with the press at the Ritz-Carlton. As Dorothy Herzog put it, "After two months of freedom and breaking engagements, Charlie Chaplin violated precedent and actually kept a date." If the reporters expected an apology they were in for a surprise. Asked about his previous cancellations, Chaplin waved off the question, saying, "That's the beauty of having money and independence. I don't have to keep dates. I'm a rebel."

Asked if he missed his wife and baby son, he said he hadn't seen them in two months and was in no hurry to return to them. "In fact," wrote Herzog, "he rather amused us by declaring that he could easily love 12 women at the same time." Later, when a woman seated at another table brought her little girl over to meet him, Chaplin turned to the reporters and quipped, "That girl is almost as old as my wife."

Herzog's account of the luncheon leaves no doubt that the journalists were smiling in spite of themselves at Chaplin's refusal to mouth the expected platitudes. "He delights in shocking people," she wrote, "and nothing pleases him more than to be the cynosure of all eyes."[32]

But if sexual dalliances were considered off limits to the press, income tax returns were still a matter of public record. At the beginning of September, the day after the Treasury Department opened its files on the previous year's tax rolls, the *Daily Mirror*, in a story headlined NINE NOTED INCOME TAX PAYERS, informed its readers that Henry Ford had anted up $3,290,594 to the government and John D. Rockefeller Sr. only $128,420. Among Hollywood's elite, the highest tax was paid by Douglas Fairbanks, who turned over $132,190. Gloria Swanson had paid $87,075, Mary Pickford $34,075, and Buster Keaton $12,762. "The big surprise of screenland is Charlie Chaplin," the *Mirror* reported. His tax for 1924 had been only $345.81.[33] Chaplin (or rather his film company) had incurred losses during 1924 on *A Woman of Paris* and invested almost a million dollars in *The Gold Rush*. Still, the figures were startling.

In mid-October Chaplin was due back in Los Angeles for an important UA board meeting. Shortly before he was to leave New York, a special delivery letter arrived from Lita, informing him that she was pregnant for the second time. "Oh, no! She can't do this to me!" he wailed.

"Haven't you found out yet what causes it?" asked his distinctly unsympathetic aide Eddie Manson.

Manson had never seen a man look so beaten. Chaplin was "in a stupor, pitiable."[34]

11

The Circus

Charlie Chaplin had returned to Los Angeles. But how long would he stay? On October 15, the very day he arrived in town, Chaplin issued a statement saying that after making one more picture he planned to sell his home in Beverly Hills, rent out his studio, and move his operations to New York City. A month later a source close to Chaplin told reporters that Charlie would make his next picture in London and was talking about deserting the United States entirely. The press speculated that Chaplin's threats to leave Hollywood were motivated by his unhappy domestic situation. In fact his main concern at the moment was a bitter battle with Mary Pickford and Doug Fairbanks over the future of United Artists.

A business founded on antibusiness principles, United Artists had been in trouble almost from the beginning. Chaplin and his partners had assumed that their pictures would sell themselves. They soon learned, however, that like every other company in the field, UA needed a steady flow of product to justify its overhead and retain a first-class sales force. But UA, unlike traditional production companies, did not provide financing for the films it released, and very few independents could afford to do business on these terms. Failing to lure major talents like Harold Lloyd, UA had to make do with pictures from lesser producers. By 1924 even D. W. Griffith found it impossible to raise financing on his own and bolted to Paramount.

Under Joe Schenck UA's policy became more flexible, and he

was able to sign independent production deals with Sam Goldwyn, recently ousted from his own company by a stockholders' rebellion, as well as Gloria Swanson, who had financial backing from her lover, Joe Kennedy. Still, the company was fighting an uphill battle against the industry trend toward consolidation. Independent movie theaters were being gobbled up by theater chains, which in turn had business relationships with major studios. The recently formed Metro-Goldwyn-Mayer (MGM), for example, was owned by Loew's, which controlled a network of profitable theaters. Joe Schenck's brother, Nicholas, happened to be a vice president of Loew's, and while Chaplin was in New York, Schenck had negotiated an agreement for United Artists and MGM to distribute their films jointly.

Strictly speaking the deal was an amalgamation, not a merger. UA would continue to release movies under its own name; however, owners of UA and MGM stock would swap for shares in a new corporation. MGM was prepared to pay well for an association with UA's big-name stars. By Schenck's estimate the value of the UA partners' stock would increase by half a million dollars overnight.[1] Pickford and Fairbanks both had qualms about sacrificing the principle of independence, but considering UA's chronic debts they saw no alternative.

Chaplin had taken almost no active part in UA's business affairs over the years, and he certainly had offered no plan to resolve the company's long-standing problems. Nevertheless, shortly after his return to Los Angeles, he suddenly made up his mind to oppose Schenck's proposal.. According to Chaplin, his opposition was a matter of principle. MGM was a "trust" and represented the triumph of monopoly capitalism and the studio system, which was nothing more than an attempt to reduce the art of motion pictures to a form of mass production. Never one to mince words, Chaplin was quoted in *Variety* deriding MGM as "the three weak sisters" and calling the proposed amalgamation "a club for Metro-Goldwyn-Mayer to force exhibitors into line, using the 'block booking' as a means to foist its film 'junk' on the exhibiting market."[2]

Joe Schenck suspected that Chaplin's antimonopoly sentiments were being stoked by Sam Goldwyn. Having been ousted from the his own company—the "Goldwyn" of Metro-Goldwyn-Mayer—Sam deeply resented the MGM management, and he feared that his productions would not be treated fairly under the amalgamation. For once even Doug Fairbanks, who rarely let business interfere with friendship, was openly exasperated. Speaking to a reporter from *Variety*, Fairbanks called Chaplin a "kicker," explaining, "Charlie is kicking over the traces just as he did when United Artists organized. He is suspicious of the proposed combine which I am convinced is for the good of the whole industry."[3]

After two weeks of frustrating negotiations, Chaplin told Schenck that he couldn't give his final word on the deal until Nathan Burkan came out from New York to advise him. In the meantime he decided to get away from the pressure by taking a drive up the California coast to Del Monte, where he could work on ideas for his next picture.

By this time Chaplin had given up the idea of making a movie called *The Suicide Club* in favor of a circus picture, which would be made in Hollywood after all. Word of his decision filtered out, generating relief and excitement. To the industry a circus theme meant a children's picture, and the trade press speculated that Chaplin was planning a reunion with Jackie Coogan, whose career had been stalled by poor material. In fact he had something quite different in mind.

It is always tricky to trace an artistic idea to a single moment of inspiration. Chaplin had talked about making a picture about a clown for years, since 1920 at least, but his experience on the set of *Zander the Great* surely helped clarify his intentions. The scene in which Marion Davies found herself face to face with a lion had enormous possibilities. Imagine what the Tramp would have done in the same situation!

Also, while in New York Chaplin had read Maurice Willson Disher's book *Clowns and Pantomimes*, which mentioned him in flattering terms as an outstanding "mimetic satirist" and the heir to the great music hall comic Dan Leno. Disher's main theme was the familiar paradox that the funny men of the world are often driven by despair. Dan Leno, as Charlie well knew, had died insane. Marceline, the French clown he had admired in his childhood, was now a broken man. (In 1927 Marceline would commit suicide, and Chaplin paid for his funeral.)

Disher's book told the story of an even more tragic clown, the

Italian, Joseph Grimaldi, who performed in Drury Lane, London, during the eighteenth century. It was said that a London physician of the period advised a severely depressed patient, "Go and see Grimaldi. He will cheer you up."

"But I am Grimaldi," the patient replied.

According to Disher, Grimaldi's black moods were so well known to his contemporaries that they joked that the correct pronunciation of his name should be "grim-all-day." But then, wrote Disher, for a clown laughter is always just a means to an end. "Satisfy people's desire for the ridiculous and they will accept your idea of the sublime."[4]

Responding to Disher's advice, Chaplin envisioned *his* circus movie as a tragedy in which his character, the clown, dies in the center ring, even as the audience applauds wildly, mistaking his demise for part of the act. Or, perhaps, the clown would suddenly go blind, his helpless flailing mistaken for slapstick.

It was easier to envision such a conclusion than to figure out how to set up a plot that would justify it. How, for example, would he establish his character as a circus clown in the first place? For Charlie Chaplin to play an ordinary clown doing a routinely funny act was a recipe for boredom. His character's clowning must be *really* funny—it had to be the funniest thing ever done.

With only a vague story outline in mind, Chaplin ordered Danny Hall and his crew to begin constructing a circus set at the studio. Meanwhile he prepared to depart for Del Monte with Harry Crocker, whom he had just hired as an all-purpose assistant. A Yale graduate and the scion of one of San Francisco's leading families, Crocker had showed early promise as an actor and playwright and worked off and on as a newspaperman, but for several years he had devoted himself mainly to partying.

Crocker had no illusions about why he'd been hired. Chaplin was laying the groundwork for divorcing Lita and he needed a "constant companion," as Crocker put it, to keep him out of trouble. Crocker happened to be a good friend of Marion Davies, and was discreet enough to act as a go-between. It may be, however, that he was less a beard than a chaperone, whose function was to gently discourage Marion Davies's expectations of intimacy. Chaplin had suspected for some time that William Randolph Hearst had hired detectives to follow him. Very likely he was right, though Hearst was the sort of man who paid detectives to uncover a loved one's infidelity and then refused to look at the evidence they gathered. Too conventional to accept that Marion might be entitled to cheat on him, even as he cheated on his wife with her, Hearst preferred to accept a verdict of "not proven." In the meantime, he assured her loyalty by giving her the house of her own she had always wanted—a beachfront "cottage" in Santa Monica with 110 rooms and fifty-five baths.

Marion was prepared to live up to her half of the bargain, but in moments of loneliness she still turned to Charlie for emotional support. Her habit of writing sweet, semiliterate letters could easily lead to disaster if they fell into the wrong hands. Moreover Marion was drinking more heavily. Charlie couldn't afford to offend her lest she do something rash, like confessing the affair to W.R. in a moment of alcoholic candor.

Officially Harry Crocker was replacing Harry d'Arrast, who was about to become a director at Paramount. He joined the studio on October 29, and just twelve days later he and Chaplin departed for their working vacation in Del Monte. They traveled in the Locomobile, driven by Chaplin's chauffeur, Frank Kawa. Kono, who now devoted himself to his duties as Chaplin's valet and manager of the household, followed in his own car.

No sooner were they under way than Chaplin began to outline for Crocker's benefit a scheme to reform American capitalism: Once a company began earning one hundred thousand dollars or more in annual profits, it should be required to turn over 25 percent of everything it produced to the government, which would sell the goods to pay for social welfare projects. Of course, to ensure that the government could dispose of its share promptly, it would have to be able to sell at a lower price, say 2 percent below what the company charged. The beauty of the scheme, Chaplin concluded, was that it would make the government a partner in every business, with a say in determining policy and setting production goals.

Crocker, a banker's son, listened in amusement. "And you are just the man to inaugurate the experiment," he suggested sarcastically.

"I should say not!" Chaplin protested. "This scheme is not for me. I'm not a businessman; I'm an artist!"

Later Chaplin decided that they should stop overnight at a lodge in Pebble Beach, where he continued his monologue through dinner and well into the evening. He described an idea for a short story involving a giant and dwarf, then moved on to pantheistic philosophy, explaining to Crocker that there was just so much "soul matter" in the universe—transferred at death into another, newborn creature. Next he recited the better part of acts three and four of the Gillette play, *Sherlock Holmes*, acting out all the parts, and segued into a discussion of the Prometheus myth—which in turn reminded him of a story about a man who could snap his fingers and make the stars fall out of the sky.

At last Chaplin began to rhapsodize over the beauty of the scenery, but when the by-now-exhausted Crocker mumbled his agreement, he changed gears again, exclaiming, "Thank God for New York! It [meaning the beauty of nature] is all too much! It crushes a man!"

The next day Chaplin once again suggested stopping early, this time to spend the night at the Highlands Hotel south of Carmel. The weary Crocker had been listening steadily since they left Beverly Hills, but Chaplin, bristling with energy, insisted on hiking into town. As they walked by a number of picturesque, secluded beaches, he began to formulate a plan to buy one of them for a summer retreat. The location was so exceptional that the most accomplished people in the world would be happy to be his guests. "You could invite someone like H. G. Wells," he enthused.

A stray dog had followed them into Carmel, and Chaplin decided that the humane thing to do would be to see that the animal was well fed before it had to make its way home. They stopped at a restaurant, where he had a difficult time making the waitress understand that he wanted to order a nice dinner, not for himself or his friend but for the dog.

Back at the hotel that evening, Chaplin was still in no mood for sleep. His mind was like a mountain goat, making dazzling leaps from one narrow crag to the next. He suggested a walk through the woods, then challenged Crocker, asking him what he'd do if a madman suddenly appeared out of the darkness, gibbering, "I can't help it!"

"I know what *I'd* do," Chaplin said, answering his own question, "I'd jump behind you and grab your coat."

Then it was back to the beauty of the stars, which he compared to "young girls showing off. . . . Why has no artist painted the stars? What a camera shot from this angle!"[5]

The Del Monte trip lasted nine days in all. At one point, Chaplin talked for twenty-eight hours straight. Crocker understood that this was not normal behavior, but the content of Chaplin's talk was so dazzling that he was more impressed than worried.

Unfortunately, although Chaplin had resolved to his own satisfaction the mysteries of God and man, he had not come up with a solution to the problem of how his character comes to join the circus. According to Crocker, it was he who eventually suggested having the Tramp, pursued by the police, run into the circus tent, where the audience mistakes the Keystone Kops–style chase for part of the regular clown act.

On his return to LA Chaplin consulted with Nathan Burkan and then suggested to his partners that he would agree to the MGM amalgamation if the term of the agreement were shortened from fifteen years to five. The papers were redrawn, but Chaplin changed his mind again. Schenck, Fairbanks, and Pickford had the voting power to push the deal through over his objections, but out of friendship and a desire to avoid further dissension, they declined. Mary Pickford, however, would never forget that but for Charlie's stubbornness she could have earned millions from the success of MGM.

Chaplin next stunned his aides by deciding not to renew Georgia Hale's contract. Hale's work in The Gold Rush had been singled out for praise by the critics, and she was a cooperative actress who had never given him a day's trouble. One suspects that the decision was personal rather than professional. Although Georgia spoke with the accent of a Chicago gun moll, she was a religious woman, and in an interview given at the time of the release of the Gold Rush, she summarized her approach to her work by saying: "Out of hard work we learn that failure is due to our wrong thoughts."[6] Georgia may well have had qualms about conducting an affair with a married man, and Lita Chaplin, on her part, had begun to suspect that Georgia was in line to be the third Mrs. Chaplin.

Charlie had no desire to give his wife ammunition to use against him in divorce court, so Georgia departed for a contract with Paramount, and he placated Lita by signing her high school girlfriend, Merna Kennedy, who was living in Glendale and working as a dancer in vaudeville. Merna was a pretty redhead with no discernable talent as a dramatic actress, but she was athletic. Cast as an equestrienne, she learned to ride bareback well enough to perform her own stunts.

Try as he might, Chaplin had been unable to develop a story that would justify a dramatic death scene, and the plot of *The Circus* developed along more conventional lines: After his accidental debut as a clown, the Tramp finds himself competing with Rex, a handsome tightrope walker, for Merna's love. One night Rex is unable to go on, and the Tramp volunteers to perform in his place, secured in a safety harness, which gives him the courage to perform marvelous feats of balance and acrobatic skill. The act is a great success until the Tramp looks up and sees that his safety harness has come undone. His confidence vanishes—and so does his illusion of himself as a worthy suitor for the lovely Merna. *The Circus* had been transformed into a film about stage fright—or rather, performance anxiety in art and life—surely a more original and interesting theme than that of the suffering clown.

By December 3 Chaplin was hard at work at the studio, practicing his tightrope-walking skills under the watchful eye of Henry Bergman. Harry Crocker joined in the lessons and did well enough to be cast in the role of Rex. After just five weeks of instruction, Chaplin was ready to begin shooting.

The obvious way to film the tightrope scenes was to place the rope near the ground and use backdrops and camera angles to create the illusion that the action was taking place high in the air under the roof of the big tent. Chaplin, however, insisted on realism. Stagehands stretched the rope thirty-seven feet above the floor of the set, with a platform built up underneath it in case of a fall. Rollie Totheroh was also high off the ground, filming from atop a scaffold.

One idea for the scene had come to Chaplin in a dream. He saw himself up on the high wire with two monkeys on his back. (A Freudian pun if ever there was one—were the two monkeys Lita and Marion, or were they the two children he had begotten on a wife he now wanted to be rid of?) The dream image was promptly re-created in the studio, with three monkeys instead of two.

Monkeys and all, the tightrope shots were finished by February 8, 1926, very good time by Chaplin's standards. Unfortunately a technician in the studio's lab scratched the film, destroying three weeks' work. The scenes were reshot, but the energy level was never quite the same. The dye that Chaplin used to touch up his prematurely gray hair had begun to fade by the time the reshoot was completed, and in the final cut one can see that his hair is different from one moment to the next. Also, a close-up of Crocker's legs was substituted for one of Chaplin's. Overall the tightrope scene proved entertaining, but not quite the show-stopper it should have been.

The opening minutes of *The Circus*, on the other hand, rank with Chaplin's best work. The movie begins in the sideshow, where a pickpocket working the crowd temporarily stashes a stolen wallet in Charlie's pocket. So hungry that he has been reduced to stealing bites from a baby's hot dog, Charlie is surprised to find himself in possession of a well-stuffed billfold. He is prepared to cope with his good fortune, but the wallet's original owner spots him and a policeman gives chase. There follows a mad dash into a funhouse shaped like Noah's ark, through the hall of mirrors, and finally into the circus tent proper, where Charlie leaps onto a revolving turntable that is a prop for the clown act. The audience roars with delight, and the next thing he knows, the befuddled Charlie is being auditioned by the owner of the circus, who commands him to "do something funny."

Regardless of who first thought of having Charlie chased into the ring by the police, the beauty of the sequence comes from Chaplin's ability to turn a standard slapstick mixup into a minidrama that becomes almost an allegory of the human condition. Certainly the action neatly recapitulated his own biography—from a childhood that seesawed between extreme need and sudden windfalls to his pell-mell rise to fame via the funhouse (Karno's Fun Factory) and Sennett comedies (the cops and Charlie running on the turntable).

April was another productive month, with shooting divided between the studio and the Venice Beach amusement park, the site of the Noah's ark fun house seen in the film. After that bad luck returned to plague *The Circus*. There were delays caused by the widening of Sunset Boulevard, which required several studio buildings to be moved back from the original property line. Additional days were lost due to spells of unseasonable rain, extremely hot weather, and problems with the props, such as, on July 21, "waiting for snakes from Texas." Then, on September 22, a fire broke out in the studio, destroying the circus tent set and most of the props.[7]

In the long run, however, civic progress, inclement weather, herpetological delays, and even the fire were less of a problem than Chaplin's mercurial moods. When in a manic state, as he was during October and November, Chaplin often made rash personal and business decisions, but he was also "enthused," as he put it—full of energy and working at a high level of creativity. By the summer of 1926, however, his energy had flagged, and he was depressed and irritable. Story conferences, which tended to be drawn-out affairs even at the best of times, became agonizing ordeals.

These meetings of the "brain trust" were held in a mock-Tudor building called "the stable" that fronted on North Formosa Avenue. Originally built to house a saddle horse Chaplin purchased during the days when he went riding with Doug Fairbanks through the scrublands of present-day Beverly Hills, the stable had been remodeled into a bungalow whose living room was used for staff meetings and, occasionally, for informal parties. Though sparsely and cheaply furnished, the room contained two objects of great significance for Chaplin—the bronze portrait head of himself sculpted by Clare Sheridan, and a silver basket with artificial roses, a gift from Max Linder. As the summer dragged on into autumn, however, these artifacts failed to inspire, and Chaplin spent hours, even whole days, stretched out on the couch, racking his brain for ideas while his aides sat around, doing their best to be encouraging.

When Chaplin did begin shooting, he ordered even more retakes than usual. For the scene in which Charlie is trapped inside a lion's cage he filmed for three weeks, accumulating much more footage than could ever be used. After the fire, while waiting for the circus tent set to be rebuilt, he took the cast out onto Sunset Boulevard to film an entire sequence that was later discarded.

✧   ✧   ✧

During this period, though still living under the same roof as his wife, Chaplin resumed his bachelor routine. Every Tuesday, Harry Crocker recalled, he and Charlie attended the boxing matches, usually finishing off the evening at the Coconut Grove or some other popular nightspot. Most days Chaplin worked at the studio until 8:30 or so, then stopped at home, where he would take a hot bath, followed immediately by a cold one, and go out again, picking up Crocker for a late dinner. Often they wound up at the budget-priced Orpheum Cafeteria. Chaplin liked plain meat-and-potatoes fare and enjoyed watching the other customers, a relaxing change from being watched. Few expected to find Charlie Chaplin dining at a cafeteria, and the general public hardly knew him without his mustache anyway, so he was rarely recognized. But, Crocker noted, he often left a tip larger than the cost of the meal out of fear that some disgruntled busboy would complain to the gossip columnists, inspiring yet another story about his miserly habits.

Lita would remember Charlie's routine at this time as being less orderly. He took eight or ten baths a day, she writes, and sometimes went out in the middle of the night, his .38 in hand, to roam the property in search of prowlers. News of the death of a show business acquaintance, or even listening to somber classical music, could throw him into a deep funk for days. Although they now went out as a couple occasionally, Charlie rarely spoke to her when he was at home, and he took little interest in Charles junior.

Lita no longer had anything in common with her old school chums, and Merna kept turning down her suggestions that they get together, saying she was too busy preparing for her role as the bareback rider. Ironically, the one person she felt she could confide in was Marion Davies. Admitting to a "little fling" with Charlie, she insisted that was all in the past. At any rate, she was such a friendly, unaffected person that it was hard not to like her.

Reassured by Charlie's marriage, W. R. Hearst began inviting him and Lita to San Simeon, his "ranch" on the coast west of Paso Robles. The new 73,500-square-foot main house, Casa Grande, had just been completed. Charlie was impressed by the splendor, and also by how *un*impressed Marion was. She evaded W.R.'s rule against drinking during the day by sneaking sips from a silver flask, and chided him in front of guests for talking business during the cocktail hour.

For Charlie these excursions to Hearst's castle were an opportunity to mix with interesting Hollywood newcomers like screenwriter Donald Ogden Stewart, a former *Vanity Fair* writer and Yale graduate. Though not yet interested in politics, some years later Stewart would be converted to Marxism after reading John Strachey's *The Coming Struggle for Power*, a book that also influenced Charlie. Lita, meanwhile, lounged around the pool. Her pregnancy not yet apparent, she could take satisfaction in noticing that she looked better in a bathing suit than fellow guest Greta Garbo. Marion, no doubt with the best of intentions, commiserated that Charlie could not be anyone's idea of a "prize package" as a husband and advised her that if she wanted to stay married to her high-powered husband she would have to learn to take the good with the bad. "Mildred Harris was no saint, but she wasn't really a bad kid, and Charlie, God bless him, loused her up good," Marion rambled on. She also advised Lita that she had better be prepared to look out for her own interests—"Girls get old, sugar."[8]

On March 30, 1926, seventeen-year-old Lita gave birth to her second child, another boy. Sydney Earle Chaplin was five weeks premature, and thanks to Charlie's falsification of Charles junior's birthdate, the two boys were officially nine months and two days apart in age—a circumstance that gave rise to a certain skepticism about Chaplin's claim that he had been entrapped into a loveless marriage.

During the summer, as Charlie's depression worsened, he berated Lita almost daily, calling her a "Mexican tramp" and worse. But when she suggested that if things were that bad they'd better divorce, he was livid, telling her: "I'll divorce you when I'm good and ready, and strictly on my terms." He threatened that if she went to the newspapers, he'd put out a contract on her life. "I have contacts who can do the job quickly and quietly and not think twice about it." One such quarrel ended with him pulling a gun from his desk drawer and aiming at her while he ranted on. Lita recognized that the "lunatic side" of Charlie's character, as she put it, was a symptom of an illness that was beyond his control, but this did not make such confrontations any less harrowing.[9]

Like Pola Negri before her, Lita also came to see that in a bizarre way Charlie enjoyed these scenes, and enjoyed hating her.

When she lost her temper and screamed back at him, he was sexually aroused and quite ready to hop into bed.

Meanwhile Merna Kennedy finally agreed to meet Lita for lunch and promptly told her of Charlie's plans to have her play Empress Josephine to his Napoleon. Merna was sporting an expensive bracelet, a gift from Charlie, and when Lita accused Charlie of having an affair he not only admitted it but taunted her by reeling off the names of women he'd slept with since their wedding day— Marion included.

In early November, Lita escaped from an intolerable situation by taking a cruise to Hawaii with her mother. During the course of their vacation together, Lita poured out her heart to her mother, telling her about the episode with the gun, and Charlie's threats to have her killed. Mrs. Spicer was unsympathetic. She dismissed the gun-waving as a melodramatic gesture and urged Lita to try harder to be "nice" to him.

Soon after Lita's return to Cove Way, Todi, the trusted nanny who had been left in charge of the babies, confided that Chaplin had been talking to Kono and Frank, telling them that when Lita finally left him they were to do their best to prevent her from taking the children. No doubt Chaplin understood that if a wife moved out leaving her children behind, even temporarily, she could be accused of abandonment. Todi's warning frightened Lita so badly that she packed her bags at once, calling her grandfather Curry to get herself and the babies out of the house. Kono showed up as the houseboy was carrying Lita's suitcases downstairs and protested that Lita could take nothing from the house without Chaplin's permission. Mr. Curry was in no mood to hear this, and in the end Lita, the babies, and the suitcases all left with him.

The dark side of Chaplin's character was, of course, well known to his male friends and employees. When Harry Crocker went to work for Chaplin, Eddie Sutherland told him, "If you're smart, you'll write Chaplin down in your books as a son of a bitch." Harry d'Arrast was even more explicit, warning that Chaplin had a definite "sadistic streak. He'll try to try to lick you mentally. He can't help it."[10]

Nevertheless Chaplin's male associates were amazingly ready to accept his view of himself as the hapless victim of a manipulative teenager. Rob Wagner, for one, would recall an afternoon patio party he and his wife attended at Cove Way in the fall of 1926. Charlie was sitting by the pool talking with his guests, including Elinor Glyn, when Lita interrupted to coax him into joining her in the pool. Lita suggested a game. She would dive into one end of the pool, Charlie into the other, and they would meet in the middle of the pool for an underwater kiss. The guests watched this display of adolescent foolery with some embarrassment. "A few weeks later," Wagner wrote indignantly, "Charlie suddenly heard himself pronounced a marital monster."[11]

Wagner mentions that Merna Kennedy was among the guests at the pool party, which gave Lita an understandable motive for flirting with her husband in public. At any rate Wagner's reaction suggests that Chaplin was not getting much realistic advice on his situation from his friends. Whether or not it was true that Lita's relatives had been planning to get their hands on a chunk of his fortune from the beginning, Chaplin's behavior had given them plenty of motivation to try for it now. Summoned from San Francisco, Lita's uncle Edwin McMurray heard about Charlie's threat to file for divorce "when I'm good and ready" and recognized that these were the words of a husband who was hiding his financial assets.

The adage that disasters come in threes appeared to be coming true for Chaplin. In December, while waiting for Lita and her attorneys to file divorce papers, he learned that his former aide Jim Tully was about to publish a series of articles about him in the *Pictorial Review*. Tully had been present the day Lita was signed for *The Gold Rush* and made no secret of his disapproval. Damaging revelations were to be expected, and Nathan Burkan asked a federal judge in New York for an injunction.

Although the content of the articles was protected, Burkan claimed that the *Pictorial Review* had violated Chaplin's rights by using his name and image in advertising the series. His suit was mostly bluster, but, faced with a half-million-dollar action, the magazine's editors caved in and agreed to allow him to review Tully's manuscript.

Far more worrisome, Chaplin had learned through Sam Goldwyn and UA that he was being investigated for underpayment of his income taxes and a possible criminal charge of fraud. "Some auditor had fixed up the books," Rollie Totheroh would recall, "and the FBI said Charlie was going to have to go to the penitentiary. For a while he had some pull in Washington, but not this time."[12] Actually it was the IRS enforcement division that was conducting the investigation; otherwise, Totheroh had it right. The charges were potentially very serious, and Chaplin's friend Bill McAdoo was no longer secretary of the Treasury and in a position to protect him.

The trouble began when a Price Waterhouse accountant, brought in to do an independent audit of UA's books, questioned Chaplin's title to his preferred stock. The original agreement among UA's founders had provided that each of the partners would invest one hundred thousand dollars in the company, receiving a thousand shares of preferred stock valued at a hundred dollars each. Chaplin paid fifteen thousand dollars by personal check on March 21, 1919, and another fifteen thousand on July 29. The balance, according to UA's legal files, was not paid until some time "after Joe Schenck came in"—which would have been 1924 at the earliest. For some reason the Price Waterhouse auditor either overlooked this payment or questioned its propriety. His report listed the preferred stock as on loan to Chaplin, not owned outright. For the IRS this raised the question of who had been claiming it for tax purposes.[13]

So many years after the fact it is impossible to say exactly what the auditor's objections were. However, he was not the first to question Chaplin's financial dealings with United Artists; one UA treasurer had already resigned in protest rather than sign a check made out to Chaplin's company. By 1926 the office of treasurer was held by Arthur "Sonny" Kelly, the brother of the late Hetty Kelly. Chaplin had arranged for Kelly to be hired by United Artists, and it is certainly possible that Kelly was allowing Chaplin to use his transactions with UA to conceal assets from his wife's attorneys, and perhaps also from the IRS. If so, then Chaplin's motive for opposing the MGM amalgamation was not irrational after all.

Chaplin, for example, had made a loan to Sam Goldwyn of $150,000. In return for the cash, Goldwyn assigned Chaplin the profits from two pictures, *Stella Dallas* and *The Winning of Barbara*

Worth. The principal of the loan would come due in the second half of 1927, when repayment would be made in a roundabout manner. A memo from the files of Dennis "Cap" O'Brien, UA's legal counsel, observes: "Strictly speaking, Samuel Goldwyn is not paying the Charles Chaplin Film Corp. any moneys directly, as the United Artists corporation is acting as a third party in this instance."[14] In other words, Chaplin had given Goldwyn $150,000 (worth slightly more than ten times that sum in today's dollars), to be returned later, via United Artists, to his company. By this time, presumably, Lita Chaplin's attorneys would have completed their survey of his net worth.

The IRS subpoenaed Goldwyn's records and from there began to look at the Chaplin brothers' claim to be equal partners in the Charles Chaplin production company. In recent years Syd had been pursuing an independent film career, and it was increasingly obvious that his half-ownership was a tax dodge.

Syd moreover had a variety of other business interests that provided him with opportunities for creative bookkeeping. From about 1918 to 1920, he was in the garment business, manufacturing something called "Saucy Jane" dresses. An early aviation enthusiast, he invested in an air-taxi service in Florida and for a time controlled the airplane landing rights on Catalina Island. When the U.S. government sold off military surplus airplanes after World War I, Syd reportedly purchased more than four hundred of them, becoming for a time the largest owner of private aircraft in the United States. There was simply no way that any commercial air service at the time could have used forty planes, much less four hundred. Either Syd was a very great optimist or the purchase was part of a scheme to reduce his tax liability and move money around.

By December 1926, however, Treasury agents had succeeded in tracing a large payment from the Charles Chaplin Film Co. to Syd, proving that money from the company eventually found its way back to Charlie as undeclared personal income. Charlie knew he was in deep trouble, and a jail term for tax fraud was a very real possibility.

Paralyzed by fear and anxiety, he retreated to the old "mansion" on the north side of the studio lot, refusing to see anyone but Alf Reeves and a few of his closest associates. Formerly inhabited by the Konos, and later by Syd and Minnie Chaplin, the house had been empty for some time, and the dilapidated furniture was covered with dust and cobwebs. Reeves arranged for Charlie's meals to be delivered to the door, but the trays remained untouched. The stress had upset Charlie's stomach, and he was racked by bouts of vomiting and gas. Doubled over with pain, he refused to see a doctor.

Chaplin had been through nervous crises before, but this time he was in the grip of what would surely have been diagnosed as a major depressive episode. He could have taken steps to limit the scope of his troubles—consult with his attorneys, work out a temporary support arrangement with Lita—but he was paralyzed with indecision, and Alf Reeves was seriously worried that he would take his own life. To prevent a suicide attempt, Reeves assigned Eddie Manson to stay with Chaplin around the clock.

Hour after hour Manson sat in a dusty armchair, sipping scotch and staring out the window at the passing traffic on Sunset Boulevard while Chaplin paced the room, complaining that his enemies were out to get him and bemoaning his bad luck. "The punishment is greater than the crime," he wailed. "This shouldn't happen to me! I don't deserve this."

"Never once did he admit any guilt of his own doing," recalled Manson. "Fear gripped him like a vice. His greatest concern was monetary, his ruin at the box office, fame and fortune wiped out, a fallen star."[15]

Meanwhile news of Lita and Charlie's separation had leaked to the newspapers, and on December 10 Charlie released a statement through Eddie Manson saying that he "would be satisfied to take one of his sons and let his existing wife [sic] keep the other." Lita dismissed this proposal as "absurd."[16]

On January 9, 1927, Chaplin managed to get himself on board a train for New York. Ostensibly he was heading East to confer with Nathan Burkan about his suit against the *Pictorial Review* and Jim Tully. In reality he had been advised to get out of California because both Lita's attorneys and the LA Internal Revenue office were planning to subpoena him in an effort to gather information about his personal finances.

The following day, January 10, Lita Chaplin filed for divorce in

Los Angeles Superior Court. The divorce complaint said that during Lita's first pregnancy Charlie repeatedly called her a "gold digger" and a "blackmailer," telling her that "if she had not been selfish and had loved him, she would have 'gotten rid' of said baby—as many other women had done for him."

The petition also charged him with pulling a gun on his wife, threatening her life, changing the locks on his house while she was out of town, and insisting that she accompany him to the house of "a certain motion picture actress" against her will. Moreover:

> throughout the entire married life of said parties and at times too numerous for plaintiff to more particularly specify, defendant has solicited, urged and demanded that plaintiff submit to, perform and commit such acts and things for the gratification of defendant's said abnormal, unnatural, perverted and degenerate sexual desires, as to be too revolting, indecent and immoral to set forth in detail in this complaint.[17]

Specifically Chaplin had demanded that his wife perform "an act of perversion defined by Section 288a of the Penal Code of California," telling her, "all married people do those kind of things. You are my wife and you *have* to do what I want you to do. I can get a divorce from you for refusing to do this." Section 288 was the criminal sodomy law, which made oral sex, among other practices, illegal, even in marriage.

Rarely did a divorce petition go into such salacious detail. So many reporters and curious citizens lined up at the county clerk's desk waiting their chance to read the legal papers that security officers could no longer control the crowd and closed the office temporarily. It was too late, however, to prevent a private citizen from printing the entire fifty-two-page text of the document in pamphlet form. Within three days *The Complaint of Lita* was being hawked on every street corner in downtown Los Angeles.

Charlie's demands in the bedroom were actually far down on Lita's list of grievances, and publication of the intimate details of her sex life was as mortifying for her as it was for Charlie. Her uncle, however, had shrewdly guessed that whatever residents of Hollywood and Beverly Hills might think about the subject, there were plenty of local politicians across the country who would be scandalized. Indeed, within a matter of days censorship boards in Seattle, Washington, the state of Ohio. and the province of Ontario were already debating a ban on Chaplin films. Will Hays, the czar of the producers' association, declined to comment for the time being.

From the industry's point of view, meanwhile, the complaint's references to abortions were potentially far more explosive. Illegal abortions were fairly prevalent among upper-class women in general and no doubt far more common among motion picture actresses, who in those days turned out four or five pictures or more a year without interruption and rarely became mothers. This, however, was a subject that was never, ever publicly discussed. Not only did the petition charge that Chaplin had offered to pay Lita to have an abortion, it quoted him as bragging that a certain motion picture actress, unnamed, had undergone two abortions for his convenience. It was universally assumed that the actress in question was Edna Purviance, who was working in France and scheduled to be deposed there by representatives of Lita's attorneys.

Chaplin learned of the divorce filing while aboard the Twentieth-Century Limited, and when the train reached Cleveland, he emerged long enough to issue a statement asking for the public's support. "I realize that I am temporarily under a cloud, but those who know me and love me will not pay any attention to the charges as they will know they are untrue," he told reporters. He also promised to fight for custody of his sons. "I have two wonderful children," he said. "They are of different temperaments, one being very musical and the other more serious." Since Charles junior was just twenty-one months old and baby Sydney was nine months old, it isn't clear which was which.

Whatever good this interview may have accomplished was quickly undone by Chaplin's attorneys, who proposed to pay Lita Chaplin twenty-five dollars a week in temporary alimony and child support, an amount so insultingly inadequate that women's groups across the country were incensed. Judge Walter Guerin of the Los Angeles Superior Court promptly ordered Chaplin to pay four thousand dollars a month. Lita, however, could not collect because the IRS had staked its own claim to Chaplin's assets, filing seven liens against his property for back taxes from 1918 through 1925 (1920 excepted), for a total of $1,073,721.47. Chaplin had thirty days to post a bond. If he failed, the government could seize his property and sell it at auction.

Judge Guerin ordered the studio padlocked and appointed receivers to do an inventory. They reported that the premises appeared to have been stripped of valuable photographic equipment, and Alf Reeves could not be found to unlock the vault. In Hollywood rumors flew that the vault contained pornographic home movies of Lita and Charlie.

Whether it was meant that way or not, Chaplin's public demand for custody of one of his two sons had all the earmarks of emotional blackmail and certainly did nothing to convince the public that he was a loving father. Meanwhile, Lyndol Young, Edwin McMurray's Los Angeles associate, competed for honors in the Scrooge category by asking Judge Guerin to cut off Edna Purviance's thousand-dollars-a-month stipend. Young also threatened to name six women as co-respondents in the divorce action and to subpoena Mildred Harris to testify about Chaplin's fitness as a father.

Had Young followed through on this last threat, he would have been disappointed. Around this time Mildred Harris dropped by the studio where Rob Wagner was working as the director of Will Rogers's films and told Wagner that she hoped Charlie *would* get to keep one of the two babies. Remarried and a mother at last, Mildred still had a soft spot in her heart for Charlie.

On the assumption that Chaplin had secreted a substantial portion of his assets, McMurray and Lyndol Young had named ten codefendants in the divorce action: Alf Reeves, Toraichi Kono, the Charles Chaplin Film Corporation, the Charles Chaplin studio (which was separately incorporated), United Artists, the Bank of Italy (later the Bank of America), and four domestic banks. Also named were "Doe #1" and "Doe #2," reportedly Chaplin's LA attorney Loyd Wright and Sam Goldwyn. As it turns out, McMurray and Young did not cast their net widely enough. According to Mirel Bercovici, Chaplin had parked his money with her father. Unlike Elmer Ellsworth, who held cash for him during the divorce from Mildred Harris, Bercovici told no one and eventually returned every penny.

Meanwhile Chaplin's major tangible asset, the negatives of the completed portions of *The Circus*, were traveling east with him under the care of Eddie Manson and Rollie Totheroh. When their train reached New York, Arthur Kelly was at the station to meet them. "As far as this Lita Grey case goes, that doesn't mean a thing," Kelly assured Chaplin. "If we get out of this tax thing we're okay."

For the moment, however, Chaplin's chances of working out the "tax thing" did not look good. Nathan Burkan was attempting to raise a bond against the tax liens, and he had sent one of his partners to Washington to negotiate with the IRS. But neither the IRS nor Burkan's contacts in Congress were sympathetic. The IRS was willing to forgo prosecution, but only if Chaplin signed a consent decree acknowledging that he was guilty of a criminal misdemeanor. If he accepted the bargain, he could be deported.

Chaplin was in an agitated state when Rollie Totheroh helped him check into his suite at the Ritz-Carlton: "I left Charlie at his hotel and came back the next morning," Totheroh recalled. "Kono, his valet, told me that Charlie had tried to jump out the window."[18]

Chaplin's weight had dropped to 116 pounds, and his suicidal impulses made him difficult for Kono to manage. Dr. Gustav Tieck, a neuropsychiatrist, was called in, and he later told the press that Chaplin had suffered an uncontrollable nosebleed, losing a pint of blood. In spite of this alarming report, Nathan Burkan ruled out sending him to a hospital. A warrant for tax fraud might be issued any day, and he didn't want his client to be arrested in a psychiatric ward. Burkan took Chaplin to stay at his own apartment, promising him that he would use any legal weapon available to prevent the authorities from serving an arrest warrant. "I can keep you here for a year," he assured him.

Chaplin was telling friends who visited him that he was the victim of a "plot" engineered by his enemies. His paranoia was encouraged by Syd, who wrote from California giving his own theory that "some one must have a personal grudge against you." Syd claimed to have heard reports that Charlie's socialist politics were the cause of the trouble. He suggested the usual remedy, fleeing the United States for Europe.[19]

Just when he appeared to be a ruined man, Chaplin pulled himself back from the brink. Within a week he had recovered from his nervous breakdown and was passing the time by writing short stories, including one about a mythical race of winged people. Ignoring Burkan's warnings that he was not to leave the apartment, he donned a disguise and headed for the Bronx Zoo, where he was recognized immediately by a ticket taker. Fortunately the man was discreet, and for several hours Chaplin sat unnoticed in the zoo cafeteria with a hat pulled down over his eyes. Within two weeks he was well enough to attend a stag dinner, performing two of the "blue" routines he reserved for private gatherings.

Burkan, for his part, was continuing his negotiations with the IRS, which eventually dropped its demand for a plea, and on April 20 Chaplin agreed to pay one million dollars in back taxes and penalties. The money was promptly anted up, even though the receivers in Los Angeles had been able to locate only $913,372 in bank deposits and negotiatble securities and about a half million dollars' worth of property, a fraction of Chaplin's estimated wealth of sixteen million. On June 9 the padlocks were removed from the studio's gate and Chaplin returned to La Brea Avenue to resume production of *The Circus*.

As far as the divorce action was concerned, Chaplin's California attorneys, Loyd Wright and Gavin McNab, had offered a settlement in the vicinity of three hundred thousand dollars. McMurray, however, was holding out for a million. Wright and McNab set out to build a case that Lita was an unfit mother, but the strategy backfired when Chaplin's Japanese houseboy broke down during his deposition and admitted that he had been told he must support Mr. Chaplin's story or be fired. McMurray also learned through the deposition that Chaplin had tried to bug his wife's conversations with her mother with a primitive dictaphone machine that he used to record story ideas that occurred to him in the middle of the night.

Then a cook no longer in Chaplin's employ came forward, volunteering the more explosive information that on March 30, 1926, Chaplin had given him five dollars to leave his room in the servants' quarters so that he could use it for a tryst with Marion Davies. At the time Lita had been in her bedroom on the second floor, in labor with Sydney Earle.

The cook's information gave Lyndol Young the ammunition he needed to revive his threat of naming six co-respondents with whom

Chaplin allegedly had sexual relations after his marriage to Lita in November 1924. Although the list was never actually presented in court, it was said to include Merna Kennedy, Edna Purviance, Peggy Hopkins Joyce, Claire Windsor, and Pola Negri. Except for Merna Kennedy and, possibly, Edna Purviance, it is highly unlikely that Chaplin had been intimate with any of these women in 1925 or 1926, though he may well have told Lita otherwise in order to provoke her. On the other hand, there were women Lita and her attorneys didn't know about, including Louise Brooks.

At any rate the only name on Lyndol Young's list that mattered was that of Marion Davies. The whole world might know Marion Davies as the mistress of William Randolph Hearst, but he was well known to be fiercely protective of her public reputation and prepared to retaliate against anyone rash enough to question her virtue in public. Anticipating that Hearst would put pressure on Charlie to keep Marion's name out of divorce court, Lita went to see Marion and told her of Young's intentions.

The warning had the expected result. The next day Hearst showed up at the studio, furiously demanding to see Charlie, who was so frightened that he sprinted for the "mansion" and hid out in the attic. Hearst, however, meant to have it out if he had to wait all day, and he began pacing up and down the walkway in front of the dressing rooms. "His eyes were dynamite," said Rollie Totheroh.[20]

Some time later Marion Davies showed up and managed to get Hearst to calm down. Charlie was talked down from the attic, and the two men had a brief meeting alone.

Hearst's temper tantrum worked a miracle. As Lita Grey heard the story, Chaplin summoned Nathan Burkan from New York and asked him what he should do about Hearst's threats. Burkan said "settle" and took the next train back to New York. The trial that had promised to be the ugliest contested divorce in the annals of Hollywood began on August 22, 1927, and in one hour it was over. Lita Grey Chaplin received $625,000, and her sons were provided for with a $200,000 trust fund. The settlement was said to be the largest ever awarded in California, and perhaps anywhere in the United States; all things considered, however, it was in line with the trend set by other high-profile divorces of the period. Chaplin could have resigned himself to his million-dollar mistake months earlier and spared himself, his young wife, and his loyal public a great deal of unpleasantness. No one profited from all the wrangling except the lawyers.

"I left Hollywood to keep from being named in the Chaplin trial, and now they go and name nobody," joked Will Rogers on the radio. "Not a name was mentioned except for Charlie's bank."

The paradox that good art can come from people who live disorderly personal lives was never more true than in Chaplin's case. His most focused and, indeed, most humane movies—the later Mutual comedies, *The Kid*, and now *The Circus*—were all made during a period when he was not only troubled, but in a state that could only be described as borderline psychosis. Though it had its share of technical flaws, *The Circus* was a lovely movie, a deceptively simple blend of pathos and humor. Any Hollywood director could make the point that show business is full of fakery and hypocrisy—and quite a few have. Chaplin saw the circus as a mirror of life. We all play roles, and fate—the ultimate casting agent—may thrust us into parts for which we feel totally unsuited. At the end of *The Circus* the Little Fellow steps aside in favor of the tall, handsome Rex, and the circus pulls of out town, leaving nothing behind but a scrap of torn paper from the hoop through which Merna jumped at the climax of her act. Charlie picks up the torn paper, gazes at the star printed on it, and tosses it away, giving it a final kick with the heel of his shoe as he saunters off down the road.

Increasingly aware of the importance of music in complementing the images on the movie screen, Chaplin worked closely with the composer who had been hired to do the orchestral score for the picture. (In premium-priced theaters such scores would be performed by house musicians.) The Academy Awards had just been established, and *The Circus* made Chaplin one of the first winners, earning him a special (noncompetitive) Oscar for versatility in directing, writing, and acting.

No doubt there were fans who would never feel quite the same about Chaplin again, but this was hardly evident when *The Circus* opened officially in New York on January 6, 1928. The picture was a hit with the public, and Chaplin's admirers in the press were eager to forgive and forget the unpleasantness over the divorce. In a piece entitled "Picking on Charlie Chaplin," *The New Yorker* said: "If, in order to produce films that are a public necessity the world over, he finds it indispensable to get into a mess with every designing woman who meets him, a grateful government should grant him a special dispensation from alimony and the punishment for bigamy, with Flo Ziegfeld retained at public expense to round the ladies up."[21]

Chaplin's fervent admirer Alexander Woollcott was reading from the same script when he groused about the delays in bringing *The Circus* to the screen: "Thanks to the witless clumsiness of the machinery of our civilization, someone (a wife, I think it was, or something like that) was actually permitted to have the law on Chaplin as if he were a mere person and not such a bearer of healing laughter as the world had never known."[22]

There is something to be said for the argument that public opinion must make allowances for the excesses of creative people. Less understandable was the vitriol aimed at Lita Chaplin. The most extreme example was a broadside entitled "Hands Off Love: A Surrealist Manifesto," which appeared in the summer 1927 issue of *transition*, a prestigious English-language literary quarterly published in Paris. The signers of this document were among France's best-known artists and intellectuals—Louis Aragon, André Breton, Robert Desnoes, Max Ernst, Elliot Paul, Raymond Queneau, Man Ray, Georges Sadoul, and Yves Tanguy, among others.

"Hands Off Love" began by expressing amazement that in the United States there were still people who considered fellatio a perversion, calling the divorce complaint against Chaplin "typically characteristic of the average moral standard of 1927 America." Chaplin, the authors went on, was the personification of love. Indeed, he had asked Lita Grey to abort their child in the name of love (meaning his freedom to love others). Lita, on the other hand, was a representative of the decadent, bourgeois institution of marriage—"a domestic hitching machine" as well as "one of those bitches that in all countries constitute the good mothers, the good sisters, the good wives, those pests and parasites of all kinds of love and true emotions." On top of her other misdeeds she had even managed to "exact" a second baby from him: "Everything is criminal to this woman who believes or pretends to believe that the breeding of brats is her sole function in life, who will breed brats in return."

Chaplin, the authors went on, had already exposed the lie of the American dream in films like *The Immigrant*, which showed

the brutalities of the law's representatives, the cynical examination of the emigrants, the dirty hands fumbling the women on arrival in this land of prohibition, under the classic statue of Liberty lighting the world. What the lantern of this particular liberty projects through all his films is the threatening shadow of the cops who run down the poor, the cops popping up at every street corner, full of suspicion.

A man trapped in such a society might even be justified in holding a revolver to his wife's head and pulling the trigger. "For a man to become aware of such a possibility, i.e. insanity, murder, seems surely to indicate that he has been subjected to a treatment capable of driving him to insanity and murder."

In retrospect the most amusing aspect of this document is that the Surrealists, striving to be as outrageous as possible, managed to be more literal-minded than Chaplin's fans in the benighted American "provinces," who generally understood that the oral sodomy charge was a lawyer's ploy. They were also more naive than the Americans if they truly believed that babies came into the world because wives "exacted" them from unsuspecting husbands. One can't help thinking that Chaplin's fans, especially in Europe, looked at the androgynous image he presented on the screen, concluded he was highly unlikely to be a pursuer of women under any circumstances, and therefore were all too ready to think the worst—not only of the woman who "entrapped" him into marriage but of the society that encouraged such mismatches to occur.[23]

One good thing did come of *Chaplin* v. *Chaplin*—Vladimir Nabokov's 1955 novel, *Lolita*, generally considered one of the great novels of midcentury American literature. Nabokov had no desire to be thought of as a writer of "topical trash," as he put it, and certainly no desire to be sued by the story's real-life models, yet his book is peppered with clues that lead to the conclusion that the similarities between his Lolita and the real-life Lillita McMurray Grey Chaplin are no accident.

Like Chaplin, Lolita's seducer/victim Humbert Humbert wears a "toothbrush mustache," plays tennis, and suffers bouts of insanity. He is a man who, at least so he tells us, could conquer "at the snap of my fingers any adult female I chose." Just as Chaplin had his Hetty Kelly, Humbert had a youthful crush on a girl named Annabel, who died young. Lolita's mother is named Charlotte—the female equivalent of Chaplin's French nickname, *Charlot*—and late in the novel Lolita is found living in a town called Gray Star. Humbert, telling his story from his prison cell, looks up the biography of his victim, Clare Quilty, in a reference book called *Who's Who in the Limelight*—a title that evokes Chaplin's autobiographical film *Limelight*, released in 1952.

Nabokov's *Lolita* poses, but never answers, an interesting question: Did Humbert Humbert, "a foreigner and an anarchist," corrupt Lolita? Or was it the other way around—did Lolita's all-American "philistine vitality" corrupt him? One could ask a similar question about Chaplin: Was he an artistic genius corrupted by the bourgeois commercialism of Hollywood—the artist as victim? Or was he guilty of corrupting it?

12

City Lights

As far as the public was concerned, Chaplin's feud with Jim Tully
had been merely a footnote to the Lita Grey divorce. His friends felt
otherwise. Years after the *Pictorial Review* series appeared, Rob
Wagner was still indignant. Writing to "Uppie" Sinclair, Wagner
recalled a confrontation with Tully at the Hollywood Writer's Club,
an organization Wagner had helped to create:

> About three years ago I was lunching with him and Fred Palmer at the
> Writers and after burning up Charlie Chaplin in a most outrageous way Jim
> announced that he was preparing a series of articles that would "show up
> the s.o.b. as a fake and a cheap skate." As I happened to know that Jim was
> at that moment, and for a long time had been, on salary from Charlie I
> accused him of it, he replying, "Yes, but we writers are all prostitutes."
>
> He asked me not to tell Charlie, but I refused. When I did tell the
> poor kid he blushed crimson and then calmly observed: "Rob, I'm afraid
> Jim is a tramp at heart." He then went on to tell me how Paul Bern, or
> somebody, had asked him to give this poor tramp author a job as he was in
> desperate straights [sic]. This he did, although he had no particular use for
> him. His salary was $75 a week.
>
> Charlie, however, found Jim's overwhelming ego too terrifying and he
> began to sidestep him on the lot. This hurt Jim, but instead of leaving he
> stayed on, Charlie continuing his salary and giving him an office in which
> he wrote his novel, at the same time preparing his "exposure" articles.
>
> Sometime later I got a wire from Wheeler of *Liberty* [magazine]

telling me he had received a scorching article about Charlie from Jim and asking about Jim's credibility. I replied that the stuff was undoubtedly based upon a strong personal prejudice. He killed it.

Jim finally sold the stuff to *Pictorial Review* and when I read it I was surprised at this relatively temperate tone. But later on in NY I met the editor and he told me he had cut out the venom.

What do you think of a pup who would *poisonously* bite the hand that is feeding it? Ingrate is a mild word.[1]

Tully, of course, had his own version of these events. Still, Wagner's letter reveals the mixture of fealty and overprotectiveness that Chaplin evoked in his longtime friends and employees. Tully was guilty of taking Chaplin's money—though for a shorter period of time than Wagner himself—and of being generally an unattractive personality. Wagner, on the other hand, was a type familiar to every journalist and biographer—the longtime friend who insists that he alone is qualified to tell the Great Man's story—though of course, out of loyalty, he never will.

Wagner had in fact completed a fully authorized biography, which he sold to a publisher in 1925 for a hefty advance. Chaplin approved the manuscript and supplied a foreword, but when the book was ready for press, Wagner recalled, "Syd got squeamish; he didn't want the world to know the details of their poverty, their father's intemperance and mother's insanity. Charlie didn't care, but Syd made him self-conscious. Syd has always wanted to be a gentleman." Chaplin asked Wagner to withdraw the manuscript until after he retired from pictures—which, he promised, was only one or two movies away. Wagner returned the advance, money he had hoped to use to pay off debts incurred when a fire damaged his house. He was still holding the manuscript when he died in 1942.[2]

Harry Crocker's objections to Jim Tully were less understandable. Crocker blamed Tully for portraying Chaplin as nervous and troubled. Crocker had seen as much of his boss's "chameleon moods" as anyone. Even so he preferred to think of him as a happy person, one who had overcome early adversity to live a remarkably full and rewarding life. Chaplin, he insisted, had a humorous view of life— unlike, say, Buster Keaton, who in Crocker's opinion merely practiced comedy as a trade. Perhaps most important from Crocker's

point of view, Chaplin was also living proof that Hollywood had outgrown its raucous, money-grubbing origins and become a mecca for
bright, creative, glamorous people. Crocker had not one but two
manuscripts in his drawer—one of them titled, no doubt with unin-
tended irony, *Small Talk of Great People*, a collection of Hollywood
anecdotes and table talk in which Chaplin figured prominently.

Playing Boswell to Chaplin's Johnson, Crocker recorded Chaplin
discussing the craft of writing with Michael Arlen, author of the
1924 bestseller *The Green Hat*, over lunch at Montmartre (one of
the better restaurants in town—but chic only at lunchtime, Crocker
noted) and interrogating Carl Sandburg about how much of the
Lincoln material in *The Prairie Years* was the product of his original
research. "Ten per cent," Sandburg estimated.

Dining elsewhere with Waldo Frank and someone called the
Comte de Chasseloup Laubat, Chaplin lamented the decline of
American songwriting. The currently popular number, Rodgers and
Hart's "You Took Advantage of Me," he opined, was a sad come-
down from "vigorous, compact" dance music like the Charleston
and the Black Bottom: "Everything urged young America to strain
to become one hundred percent efficient, and the music was taut
and vibrant. But now their souls are devitalized with the effort. . . .
Dancing has become loose."

Waldo Frank, along with Chaplin and the rest of his circle, saw
America as a sink of parochialism. "Instead of prohibiting alcohol it
would be better to prohibit hypocrisy," Frank liked to say. When a
play about lesbianism, called *The Captive*, opened in Los Angeles
and was quickly banned, Chaplin snorted that it would make more
sense to ban depictions of Christ's crucifixion. "Why could not it be
said that such a spectacle urged the spectator towards sadism?"

But when it came to form as opposed to content, Chaplin was a
conservative. He dismissed Shakespeare in modern dress as "bunk"
and abstract painting as a hollow exercise. "Beauty alone is not
enough. That is where the modernist errs in art, in thinking that
paint spilt on the floor is art because it happens to be a lovely color.
If that were true, I could spit [*sic*] in the snow and the lovely crystals
which resulted would be art." The possibility that the modernist
painter might not be primarily, or even secondarily, interested in
"beauty" did not occur to him.

On another occasion, in conversation with Crocker and John Barrymore, Chaplin boasted—stretching the truth considerably—that he had once been a glassblower.

"What did you blow?" asked Barrymore.

"Chandeliers," Chaplin replied quickly.

More incongruously Crocker tells of Chaplin discussing the prophecies of Nostradamus and cases of multiple personalities with Upton Sinclair and, during a Beverly Hills party, expatiating at length on pantheism to a group consisting of William Randolph Hearst, newspaperman Irwin Cobb, Ethel Barrymore, and comedienne Beatrice Lillie. Confessing to being "a bit of a Buddhist," Chaplin defended reincarnation, saying: "I believe we are all part and parcel of the same substance. Today I may have an individual life, but when I die I return to the same substance. . . . Even the life of a louse is important."

"Especially to the louse," muttered Hearst, putting an end to the monologue.

Minutes after this conversation, Crocker noted, Chaplin borrowed a lady's scarf and did a devastating impression of the Spanish dancer Raquel Meller, complete with an outpouring of nonsense syllables that sounded very like Spanish to anyone unfamiliar with the language. In truth, Crocker added, the only Spanish words Chaplin knew were the names of cigars.

One suspects that Chaplin's opinions on Nostradamus and pantheism were interesting mainly because they came from such an unexpected source, but Crocker does convey a sense of his kinetic mind, constantly skimming the surface of esoteric subjects and translating them into comic material. Among the odd topics that intrigued Chaplin was the work of the trainers who supplied animal performers to the studios. Observing that the trainers were becoming ever more specialized, Chaplin claimed to have overheard a conversation on the corner of Sunset and Gower in Hollywood between a "cat man" (like his friend Charles Gay) and a specialist in worms and other exotic species:

"How's tricks?" asked the worm man.

"Fair," said the cat man. "Have Betty working at Universal and Tom doing a bit at MGM."

"I can remember when I was the only worm and fish man in

Hollywood," complained the exotica specialist. "Now there's half a dozen. But there's none of them have a worm like Longfellow. Paramount wants to sign him up for five years, but the price isn't right." Longfellow, he went on, had recently lost one job because the leading man was jealous of him and passed up another in a picture called *The Early Bird Catches the Worm* because he was insulted by the producer's insistence that he audition, and anyway, the script of that picture was heavy on "symbolic stuff." When last heard from the worm man was bragging about the versatility of his star cockroach—why, he could even do cricket roles with the help of "wooden attachments."[3]

Once Chaplin was divorced from Lita, Georgia Hale had reentered his life—a cheerful, undemanding companion whom he tended to take for granted. Crocker records a conversation about modern child rearing with Georgia, during which Chaplin told her: "The one reason why I married is because I wanted children. I wanted to have the sensation. I wanted to look at the little bundle of flesh and feel that it was part of me. And I was sadly disappointed. I didn't have that feeling at all." Of course, wanting children was hardly the reason for either of his marriages—a detail Georgia was too discreet to point out. But the most striking thing about this statement—and the saddest—is the description of fatherhood as a "sensation," tried out and found wanting.

The polished raconteur, dominating the conversation over French food at Montmartre and steaks at Musso & Frank's, may have been one side of Chaplin's persona, but as Crocker well knew, Chaplin was still haunted by the fear that his next breakdown would leave him permanently insane. No doubt one reason he avoided visiting his mother in Santa Monica was that he dreaded ending up unable to care for himself, as she was. Hannah's visa had been renewed twice—though Charlie resented having to post a five-hundred-dollar bond against her becoming a public charge—and for the most part she seemed happy. But Hannah's awareness of her surroundings could fade in and out from one minute to the next, and she sometimes behaved strangely in public or went on bizarre shopping sprees, once purchasing dozens of yards of brightly colored silk for which she had no use.

When Hannah fell ill with an infected gall bladder in August

1928, Charlie visited her daily and was holding her hand as she sank into a coma from which she never awoke. Erratic about so many things, he was normally conscientious about funerals. He rarely missed the last rites of a friend and often served as a pallbearer. Syd being in Europe, he took care of the funeral arrangements for his mother, but he refused to view her in her coffin. Perhaps he was thinking of the false smile the undertaker had given his son by Mildred Harris and wanted to spare himself a similarly disconcerting last memory.

Even before Hannah's death, her personal physician, Dr. Cecil Reynolds, had become Charlie's as well. Reynolds had been trained during the era when there was no separation between neurology and psychiatry, and his practice included performing delicate brain operations as well as doing Freudian-influenced therapy. A colorful character, born in Huntingdonshire, England, he sang Gilbert and Sullivan arias while operating, kept a collection of venomous snakes, believed in numerology, and held seances at his home at which the dead played his piano. Unfortunately Reynolds suffered from the very maladies he treated in others. He washed his hands compulsively, and when he dined in a restaurant he insisted on washing his silverware before he used it. In a mischievous mood, Chaplin once pressed his thumb into a pat of butter that had been delivered to their table, nearly throwing Reynolds into hysterics.

Even at the best of times, Chaplin's behavior occasionally crossed the fine line between eccentricity and madness. It was one thing to avoid unpleasant encounters, like facing May Collins to tell her their affair was over, but quite another to become filled with a dread of seeing casual acquaintances whose company he had formerly enjoyed. When Prince Paul Troubetskoy, whom Chaplin had liked in the past, dropped by the studio unexpectedly, Chaplin hid in a crawl space under the stage to avoid seeing him, remaining there so long that he fell asleep. Harry d'Arrast had also noted Chaplin's tendency to become paralyzed by the smallest emergency, as when d'Arrast's dog fell into the Cove Way swimming pool; instead of helping him climb out, Chaplin stood rooted to the spot and screamed for help.

Avid for insight into his problems, Chaplin plied Reynolds with questions about psychoanalytic theory. Supposedly he was in therapy with him, though it is doubtful that he got much treatment since Chaplin's fame and assiduous charm made it difficult to keep up even the pretense of a professional relationship. Instead Reynolds was bitten by the acting bug, played a few roles in amateur productions, and began to dream of giving up his successful practice to become the next John Barrymore. In a community theater production of *Hamlet*, the nearest he came to attaining his dream, Reynolds interpreted the melancholy Dane as a cyclothymic manic-depressive.[4] Cyclothymic individuals experience pronounced mood swings, which fall short of full-blown psychosis. During the "up" cycle, the cyclothymic feels confident and energized: The person's imagination works overtime; he or she is often restless and extremely talkative. Such a state of mind may lead to authentic insights and important creative artistic achievements, but also to a reckless overconfidence that can have disastrous repercussions in business and personal life. Inevitably the "up" cycle is followed by a downturn, and a lapse into depression.

Whether or not this description applies to Hamlet, it certainly applies to Chaplin, who was well aware of the seasonal nature of his moods. The celebrity astrologer Darios, on meeting Chaplin, told him to take special care during April and May. Chaplin was amazed, since those happened to be the months that were invariably most difficult for him. Darios may simply have been a good-enough observer of human nature to notice that spring is often a precarious time for sufferers from mood disorders in general.

Chaplin was invariably drawn to others who shared the same fears of losing control. Among his closest friends during this period, closer perhaps than Georgia Hale or Dr. Reynolds, was the illustrator and cartoonist Ralph Barton. A frequent contributor to *The New Yorker*, Barton was distinctive looking, with penetrating blue eyes and a face prematurely marked by deep vertical creases. He owned an antique Egyptian ring with the outline of a phallus incised on the seal and wore it above the knot on his neckties, a rather daring fashion statement for the time. He and Chaplin had met in New York, where Barton and his wife, the actress Carlotta Monterey, gave chic dinner parties for their artistic and theatrical friends, despite the limitations of their studio apartment. (It is said that they once staged a professional wrestling match as entertainment—a story suggesting that theirs was not a typical New York studio.)

The Bartons divorced in March 1926 after Carlotta became fed up with Ralph's compulsive philandering, and he came out to Hollywood to enjoy the sunshine while finishing a book of drawings. Like Chaplin, Barton had manic-depressive tendencies, and he brooded about the warring masculine and feminine sides of his nature. From today's perspective he was clearly bisexual, and one can't help wondering about the nature of his relationship with Chaplin. For a time they were so close that that they had the noted New York photographer Nickolas Muray do a double portrait of them in what he called a "Greek coin pose."[5]

Unfortunately, having a label for his condition did not offer Chaplin any reassurance. Some cyclothymics learn to manage their moods. Others deteriorate, experiencing hallucinations and incoherent thought patterns. Chaplin tried to keep on an even keel mentally by avoiding overexcitement. The bedroom of his Cove Way mansion was severe as a monk's cell, painted stark white and furnished with twin beds, a cheap dresser, and a battered Persian carpet that he refused to replace, even when it became so worn that the backing showed through. Chaplin spent many hours in this refuge, reading, mulling over his story ideas, and staring at his neighbors down the canyon through a powerful telescope.[6]

He also spent hours alone playing his pipe organ or relaxing in his living room, as cheerfully cluttered as his bedroom was austere, and furnished with his beloved Steinway grand and an eclectic mix of furniture, ranging from valuable antiques to pieces that might have come from the Salvation Army. Here he kept his special Oscar, as well as an array of souvenirs from his travels. A permanent feature of both living room and bedroom was a thick, unabridged Webster's dictionary: In fact there were five Webster's in the house, including one in the bathroom, resting in a custom-designed niche.

Chaplin felt anxious about running out of things, and he liked the house to be well stocked, buying everything in quantity, including his favorite cologne, Mitsouko. The Japanese cook, George, served solid, English-style meals—roast meat with baked potatoes and peas and a dessert pudding for dinner and English tea and crumpets at 4:00 P.M. Breakfast might consist of pancakes or eggs with a side of bacon, but sometimes there were kippers or even kidneys. Chaplin worried about keeping his dancer's figure, and went on stringent diets, consuming nothing but celery for days at a time, but he always returned to George's comforting meals.

This quiet, well-ordered bachelor existence was only half of the story, however. Throughout the twenties Chaplin continued to live a fairly extensive double life, often disappearing into the poorer neighborhoods of Los Angeles for hours, and sometimes for days. He would stroll aimlessly for miles, picking out likely characters and following them to study their walks and gestures. Unlike in the old days, however, he now often asked Kono to wait nearby in one of his less conspicuous cars, ready to whisk him away if he was recognized. Kono found his employer's habits mysterious in the extreme: "Mr. Chaplin is a strange man," he once told Rob Wagner. "When he go joy riding, he go by himself."[7]

According to Jim Tully, Chaplin also had a succession of working-class girlfriends, including one Tully knew only as "Hotsy Totsy." It delighted Chaplin that when he picked Hotsy Totsy up at her modest bungalow, her mother, who lived with her, had never bothered to come out of the kitchen to meet him. Chaplin's habit of approaching good-looking women on the street and offering, quite seriously, to arrange a screen test, worried Tully, who tried to tell him it would get him in trouble sooner or later, but he paid no attention.

In 1928, when Konrad Bercovici returned to Los Angles after several years of living in Paris, he was told by Tom Harrington, who now worked just part-time, that neither he nor Alf Reeves had seen Charlie for two days and had no idea where he was. Chaplin eventually showed up, explaining to Bercovici that he had been avoiding the studio because he was frightened of a strange old man who had been hanging around on the sidewalk outside the La Brea Avenue gate. Bercovici investigated and discovered that the man was a deluded but harmless soul who was searching for his lost son; someone had told him that Charlie Chaplin might be his missing offspring. Told this, Chaplin commented bitterly: "Father love? No father of mine has been looking for me so assiduously."

In the late afternoon Chaplin invited Bercovici to join him in visiting Doug Fairbanks's studio, where they found Doug and two stunt men practicing a scene that involved leaping back and forth between two nets made from knotted ropes. Chaplin insisted on trying the stunt, too. Light and acrobatic, he proved to be an even nimbler jumper than Fairbanks, who was in excellent shape and prided himself on his athletic prowess. Chaplin told Bercovici that coming off second best in the stunt would doubtless leave Fairbanks too distracted to work for the next two days, just as he had been distracted by the odd-looking man lurking on La Brea Avenue: "I have been the 'old man' for him tonight."[8]

Later Chaplin invited Bercovici to come along for one of his incognito forays downtown. Simply by shifting the angle of his cap and visibly shrinking inside his clothes, Chaplin so changed his appearance that he was able to walk the streets unrecognized. They stopped to listen to a socialist organizer harangue a small crowd, and Chaplin became so caught up in the rhetoric that he began to mutter loudly in agreement. "Gee, that's right, my boss bought two new cars inside a month. By God, with everything going up the way it does, something's got to be done." He spoke with such conviction that the refrain, "Something's got to be done," was taken up by the crowd around them. He and Bercovici then quietly slipped away.

The evening continued with Kono delivering them to a boxing match, where Chaplin identified so strongly with one of the fighters that he doubled over in pain when the man was knocked out. "He always picks the losers," a mutual friend commented.

Back on the street he quickly picked up two young women and invited them to join him and Bercovici at a nearby ice cream parlor. Chaplin kept up a nonstop line of patter, claiming to have been Rudolph Valentino's fencing coach. "The wop was all he was cracked up to be," he assured the young women. (In fact, Chaplin had been a pallbearer at Valentino's funeral.) He was especially taken with the more skeptical of the women, an Irish redhead who responded to every boast with a cutting remark. But when he pulled a thick roll of bills from his pocket to pay the check, she became suspicious and insisted to her friend that they leave at once.

The evening ended at a Russian émigré nightclub where Chaplin and Bercovici were the only customers for the floor show, entertained by White Russians dressed as Gypsies and Cossacks.

Bercovici found the ersatz "gypsy" tunes and fake folk dances unbearably depressing, but the café was a favorite haunt of Chaplin's. While the performers sang and danced for them alone, the conversation turned to the racial theories then taking hold among some segments in Europe, and Chaplin launched into a voluble defense of the "superman" concept. According to Bercovici:

Christianity had hurt the world by making the humble one and the unsuccessful one appear in a favorable light. It was all against nature, against the trend of history. . . . Doctors maintained the cripple and the weakling. They were against the interest and the welfare of the strong, the only ones who should be protected and encouraged.

Bercovici understood that Charlie was simply adopting a position for the love of argument. Still, he suspected that behind the attitudinizing was a profound ambivalence. On the one hand Chaplin identified with the poor, unwashed masses. On the other he felt a certain contempt for the audience that idolized him. During the course of the evening, Bercovici remembered, Charlie suddenly turned to him and snapped, "Don't you *ever* become a successful man."

"What about yourself?" Bercovici asked.

"I am sorry. But it was either that or die."[9]

Under the circumstances it is hardly surprising that work on "Production No. 4" for United Artists, soon to be known as *City Lights*, proceeded only by fits and starts. One theme Chaplin had in mind was a romance between the Tramp and a blind girl who sells flowers on the street. The idea evolved gradually, but for once Chaplin had a clear vision of the story's end before he started to film: The Tramp has stolen money so that the flower girl can have an operation to restore her sight. Thanks to him she can see for herself that he is not at all the rich, handsome benefactor she has imagined. His bold, romantic gesture gives her the gift of sight, even while it shatters her romantic illusions.

For some time he also considered giving the Tramp a sidekick who was even lower on the social scale, someone whose admiration and independence would force the Tramp to reveal another side of his character. Chaplin settled on a black newsboy, and tried for months to work the character into his story, planning out scenes involving their meeting in a café and, later, in a library. Eventually, the newsboy was dropped; he reverted to making the Tramp's companion a drunken millionaire. In 1921 Chaplin had brought the Inebriate Millionaire and the Tramp together in *The Idle Class*, playing both parts himself. This time the millionaire was envisioned as a role for Henry Clive, an Australian and Chaplin's newest assistant. The millionaire is a manic-depressive type, whose moods depend on his alcohol intake. In his manic phase he recognizes the Tramp as the Good Samaritan who saved him from suicide by drowning. When sober he forgets all about him.[10]

While Chaplin spent 1928 tinkering with the plot of *City Lights*, the rest of the industry was in turmoil. The arrival of talking pictures had been predicted for years, but everyone had assumed that sound technology would take decades to develop. In late 1925, however, Warner Bros. decided to begin production of a series of demonstration films using the new Vitaphone sound system. Even the Warners did not think the public was ready for dialogue pictures. Their idea was to record musical numbers, primarily for the benefit of small-town movie houses, which did not have their own orchestras.

Comedian Harold Lloyd recalled a dinner party at the home of cowboy star Fred Thompson, at which Thompson, leading man John Gilbert, and Chaplin argued about the future of sound: "Gilbert was the one that was championing the talking picture. . . . He was absolutely right, of course, but Charlie didn't want it. He had a lot of good points, too. People could go to the theater and use their own imagination. The silents had certain qualifications and attitudes that were good."[11]

The "good points" in favor of the silents were substantial. The movies had revived the art of pantomime, forcing film actors to develop a vocabulary of subtle gestures and expressions for communicating complex emotions. Writers had learned to tell their stories visually. The art of film music was still developing, but the best scores, performed by first-rate orchestras in showcase theaters, complemented the action on the screen to create a new and unique form of musical drama.

Moreover, left-wing critics hailed the silent film as the first truly international art form. For Chaplin this was not merely a matter of ideology. He was, uniquely, an international star, whose income from abroad rose steadily over the years until it exceeded what he earned from showing his pictures in the United States. Once the Tramp opened his mouth and spoke his first words in English—and with a slight British accent, at that!—he would lose his status as a universal character. In the immediate future, since subtitles had not yet been invented, this meant losing a large segment of his audience.

This was a great deal to give up in order to have talking pictures that were still, in many respects, technically inferior. The Vitaphone process required bulky cameras enclosed in soundproof booths, and it was impossible for cameramen to film at varying rates of speed. The early talkies tended to be full of static shots of actors standing around talking.

Nevertheless the release of *The Jazz Singer* in August 1927, the same month Chaplin reached a settlement in his second divorce, marked the turning point in favor of talking pictures. Against the advice of his producers, Al Jolson had insisted on ad-libbing introductions to his songs. *Photoplay*'s reviewer sniffed, "Al Jolson is no movie actor," and dismissed *The Jazz Singer* as "Al Jolson with Vitaphone noises."[12] But the public was galvanized. The response to Jolson's movie was so enthusiastic that when *The Circus* was previewed two months later, Chaplin felt compelled to defend the silent film. In an interview printed in the *Circus* press book, Chaplin speculated that the talkies would destroy the pleasure of moviegoing for children because "they can't follow the dialogue." And, he added, "Talking pictures are not motion pictures but a poor excuse for a genuine stage play."

By the time Chaplin was ready to begin shooting *City Lights* in December 1928, the debate had become academic. The public didn't care about the presumed artistry of the silent film; it voted at the box office in favor of sound. Moreover, once the studios began investing millions in the new technology and exhibitors made the decision to equip their theaters for talking pictures, they had a vested interest in promoting the superiority of the talkies. That October *Photoplay's* James Quirk, a staunch defender of the silents, was forced to concede defeat. Even though many of the talkies being rushed into release were junk, he wrote, "It's up to us to sit tight, cross our fingers, and let the scientists tinker."[13]

In the beginning of the sound era, it appeared that Charlie's half-brother would be one of the talkies' bright new stars. In 1925 Syd broke away from Charlie's orbit and scored a great success in a movie version of the theatrical warhorse *Charley's Aunt* and another comedy, *The Missing Link*. As enthusiastic about technology as Charlie was suspicious of it, Syd starred in one of the first Vitaphone demonstration films, *The Better 'Ole*. Just when Syd was winning recognition as a first-rate comedian in his own right, he suddenly departed for London, where he had signed a production deal with British International pictures to do a movie version of *Mumming Birds*. In England, Syd worried incessantly about Charlie's refusal to accept the triumph of the talkies, but when his brother made up his mind on an issue there was no changing it.[14]

As Chaplin told Rob Wagner, he had decided that "the Tramp must never be allowed to speak." The decision was certainly his to make, but there was no artistic reason why it had to be so. Syd wasn't the only Karno veteran to adapt to the sound era. Stan Laurel made an effortless transition, appearing with Oliver Hardy in the cleverly titled *Unaccustomed As We Are*. Buster Keaton, another great mime, had no hesitation about talking and even singing before the cameras. It was not sound technology but poor scripts and an unsuitable partner, Jimmy Durante, foisted on Keaton by MGM, that eventually did in his career.

The real reason for Chaplin's trepidation was that he had everything to lose and little or nothing to gain. For more than a decade he had been universally hailed as a genius. As he wrote many years later: "I was unique, and without false modesty, a master."[15] The moment the Tramp spoke his first line of dialogue, his reputation would be open to reassessment, and Chaplin had been in the business long enough to know that the very critics who pump up a star's reputation can take childish delight in puncturing it.

Fourteen years in the movie business had also given Chaplin a long respite from attacks of stage nerves, and his first encounters with a live microphone called up all his old fears. In March 1928, he joined other United Artists stars—Fairbanks, Pickford, Griffith, and Joe Schenck's wife, actress Norma Talmadge—in a live appearance on the Dodge Brothers' Hour, a popular radio show. The stars chatted about their latest films, and Chaplin tried to tell a few jokes. He was obviously ill at ease, and later, leaving the bungalow on the United Artists' lot where the show was recorded, he confessed to a reporter that he had suffered from a bad case of "mike fright."

Confirming his worst fears, the broadcast was poorly received. Movie theater owners around the country had delayed the start of their regularly scheduled films to play the broadcast over their sound systems. Audiences, no doubt tired of being subjected to such ill-conceived promotional events, greeted the broadcast with jeers and catcalls. The response to the event gave Chaplin even more reason to avoid microphones.[16]

While others bowed to necessity, Chaplin remained a holdout. In May 1929, when a reporter from *Motion Picture Magazine* asked him about his attitude toward the talkies, he said, "You can tell 'em I loathe them. . . . They are ruining the great beauty of silence." This prompted a rebuttal from Al Jolson, who said that anyone who spouted off as much as Chaplin had his nerve going on about the beauty of silence. If Chaplin loved silence so much, "let him lock himself in a room—become a nun's brother, or something."[17]

Jolson's suggestion that Chaplin's attitude was just "sour grapes" was too harsh. Chaplin was the world's greatest pantomime artist, and the discovery that the public regarded his art as disposable was a stunning blow. His inability to adapt was no doubt partly due to the same inability to move forward noticed some years earlier by Florence Deshon. At this stage of his career, unlike actors who were less financially secure, he also lacked the incentive to adapt.

"Charlie didn't want to make any more films" says Douglas Fairbanks Jr. "Neither did my father. He had done his best work and he had no interest in doing any more. But they were forced to, because they were obligated to UA for a few more films. Almost every afternoon Charlie would come over and they would sit in this elaborate dressing room my father had, and tell stories."

Visits to Fairbanks's dressing room on the UA studio lot invariably began with Charlie, Joe Schenck, and other regulars sitting around in the steam room, after which they retired to the dressing room proper to continue their conversation. Fairbanks kept his bar stocked with white wine and the makings of light cocktails for those who insisted on drinking, but he was a teetotaler and did not encourage it. The main attraction of these afternoon gatherings was all-male conversation, much of it supplied by Charlie, who had an endless fund of stories that, Doug junior recalls, were "mostly off color" and always hilarious. "My father and everyone would laugh until the tears ran down their cheeks and they fell off their chairs."[18]

Moreover, because of the economics of silent filmmaking, it didn't matter very much to Chaplin if it took him a year, or even two years, to finish a film. "It wasn't costing him much," reiterates Fairbanks. "It was mainly boredom."

If *City Lights* were made today, it would no doubt be picketed by advocates for the disabled. The story asks us to believe that a blind woman, capable of earning her living selling flowers on the street, can't tell the difference between an impeccably groomed millionaire and a smelly tramp. Chaplin had long ago scoured the Cockney from his everyday speech, and ironically, had the film been made with dialogue, his excellent diction and British accent would have made the premise more credible. On the other hand, dialogue would have spoiled the central metaphor: Just as the girl's blindness enables her to "see" the Tramp's noble spirit, so the silent film reveals things that the talkies do not.

When shooting finally began at the end of December, Chaplin was still far from sure of his story. He planned a number of scenes that were later dropped, including a dream sequence with a Hindu servant and a harem girl that vaguely evokes the more fantastic elements of Stevenson's Suicide Club stories. Another idea, reminiscent of Saintsbury's *Jim, a Romance of Cockayne*, was to have the Tramp living in a cheap rooming house, where the other inhabitants mistake him for a famous author who is living among them to research his next book.

As for the specifics of how the girl mistakes the Tramp for a millionaire, he intended to work them out in front of the camera, just as he had done in his Mutual days. Matters got off to a bad start, however. Chaplin had once again cast a nonactress as his leading lady. Virginia Cherrill was a lovely blond who bore a slight resemblance to Edna Purviance. She also happened to be quite nearsighted, and when Chaplin happened to spot her in the audience at a prizefight, he realized that her slightly unfocused gaze suggested blindness.

Unfortunately, as soon as they began to work together, Chaplin expressed frustration. Cherrill's timing was all wrong, he complained. She didn't know how to hold a flower properly, or to ask a simple question, "Flower, sir?" in a way that made her appear to be speaking naturally.

Cherrill had a different explanation for the lack of chemistry. "It really was true about Chaplin and young girls," she later told film historian Gerard Molyneaux. "Most of the girls that worked for him had been involved with him. I was too old. I was twenty and had been divorced."[19]

Not only was Cherrill divorced, but her ex-husband was Irving Adler, a prominent agent. She had excellent contacts in Hollywood, and she was neither in awe of Chaplin nor impressed by her minimal seventy-five-dollar-a-week salary. On one of her first days at the studio, she left to have lunch with friends at a nearby restaurant, not realizing that the cast was expected to remain on the premises all day. Later she angered Chaplin by requesting permission to leave early for a hairdresser's appointment. Chaplin complained bitterly that her attitude was unprofessional, but then, she *wasn't* a professional.

As for the hairdresser, it might have been wise for her to visit him more often. The studio didn't provide Cherrill with one, and she herself observed that one sequence, in which the Tramp visits the blind girl's home, took so many weeks to complete that her hair is noticeably longer in some takes than in others.

The difficulties Chaplin experienced in filming his first scenes with Cherrill were exacerbated by major distractions. For one thing Ralph Barton was on the set, documenting the production with a sixteen-millimeter camera. For another Chaplin was entertaining a visitor, the Czech writer Egon Erwin Kisch, who was brought to the studio by Upton Sinclair and stayed for eight days. Kisch had been a friend of Kafka, and he was a great storyteller whose elfin personality enabled him to get away with saying outrageous things. He liked to greet women with the salutation: "Hello my darling, hello my duck. Give me a hug, and I'll give you a kiss."[20] He also happened to be a high-ranking agent of the Comintern, the propaganda arm of the international Communist movement—a complex and manipulative man who had been deeply involved in pro-Communist intrigues since 1918.

Ostensibly Kisch had come to the United States in late 1928 to work on a book of essays about American life, and while in New York he was introduced to Upton Sinclair by a mutual friend, the German émigré screenwriter, Bertholt Viertel. The true purpose of his visit seems to have been to establish contacts in the American film industry and prepare the way for the Soviet director Sergei Eisenstein to work in Hollywood.

The Communist movement had failed to exploit Chaplin's expressions of support in 1921 and 1922, but it was now trying to make up for the oversight. A few years earlier, with young left-wing critics in Europe extolling film as the ultimate expression of the "collective soul" of the working class, the Comintern had decide to focus its propaganda efforts on workers in the film industry. It was the Comintern's bad luck that just as their plan was beginning to take shape, the talkies arrived. The Soviet film industry estimated that retooling and equipping theaters for sound would take five years at least, somewhat tarnishing its claim to be in the vanguard of cinematic art. And even at that, Sovkino, the Soviet film ministry, had no intention of paying Vitagraph and other patent holders in the West hard currency for licensing fees.

A plan to sidestep this last difficulty began to form when Doug Fairbanks and Mary Pickford made Moscow a stop on their 1926 European tour. Mary and Doug filmed a brief scene for a Soviet film called *A Kiss from Mary Pickford* and were introduced to Eisenstein, who happened to be a distant relative of Joe Schenck. After a screening of *The Battleship Potemkin*, Fairbanks praised the film effusively and suggested that that Eisenstein make a movie in the United States, adding, "How long does it take you to pack your bags?"

One suspects that the ebullient Fairbanks forgot this remark as soon as it passed his lips. However, the Soviet perspective on the meeting was quite different. Eisenstein's assistant, Grigory "Grisha"

Aleksandrov, was present during this discussion and recalled that it began with Joe Schenck, who was traveling with Pickford and Fairbanks, establishing that he was distantly related to Eisenstein on his mother's side. Aleksandrov, who spoke no English at the time, recalled that Schenck had "come to Moscow for the purpose of establishing business relations with Soviet cinema artists."[21]

Working in the United States was a dream of Eisenstein's, and Sovkino for its own reasons was eager to see him go. The Russians believed they had a firm invitation to produce motion pictures under the aegis of United Artists.

Meanwhile Chaplin's interest in politics had been a casualty of his troubled personal life. In December 1926 members of a delegation from the Moscow Art Theater were in Los Angeles and tried repeatedly to arrange a meeting with him at his studio. Unaware that Chaplin was busy having a nervous breakdown, the visitors were mystified and disappointed that their calls to the studio went unreturned. Amkino, the New York office of Sovkino, also made periodic attempts to obtain prints of Chaplin's films for release in the Soviet Union, but Chaplin, unlike other left-wing artists, expected to be paid in hard currency, raising doubts about his sympathies.

There is no record of what Kisch and Chaplin discussed in the spring of 1928. Probably, Kisch's main goal was to fire up his enthusiasm for the Communist cause. Since he was a subtle, persuasive man and Chaplin was all too easily swayed, he probably succeeded. Interestingly enough, during Kisch's stay in Los Angeles, Chaplin was mysteriously absent from the studio for more than a month— failing to show up on February 25 and not returning until April 1. Although he was said to be ill, suffering from ptomaine poisoning and then influenza, he very likely spent some of this time with Kisch.

As for Kisch's eight days on the set, he later published his observations in an article for the *Frankfurter Zeitung*, extolling the artistry of silent film.

Still searching for a way to show how the blind girl comes to believe that the Tramp is a millionaire, Chaplin had added a bit of business in which an elegantly dressed man steps out of his limousine just as the Tramp approaches the girl to buy a flower. The girl mistakenly thinks that the man who descended from the car is her customer.

After playing through the scene with the camera running, Chaplin asked Kisch and Upton Sinclair to describe what they had seen. Concentrating on the interaction between Charlie and the girl, neither of them had paid any attention to the man and his car.

"Didn't anyone go by?" Charlie probed.

"No, not so far as I know."

"Oh, the devil. The devil. Didn't you notice the auto again, the gentleman?"

"No, I noticed nothing."

Charlie buries his face in his hands with despair. His assistants are depressed, too, by what has happened. Why is it so terrible if a foreigner, passing through town, does not understand one of his gags?"

But it is much more than a gag. It is the fundamental idea of the film.

Over the following week Chaplin tried many variations of the scene, sometimes asking Kisch or his own assistants to act out the parts of the flower girl, the rich man, and rich man's chauffeur. Kisch also volunteered his own solutions:

How would it be if the girl, whom the public now recognizes as blind, should say to Charlie when he buys his second flower, "Give this to the chauffeur"? How would it be if Charlie were trying to help the gentleman into the automobile and the flower girl tried to hand the second flower through the window? But the window would be closed and it would not be the window but the open door of the automobile behind which Charlie would be standing.

"Wonderful, wonderful!" cries Charlie and tries it out. He goes back to his acting, but suddenly he leaps out of his shell and falls back again, saying, "It won't do. I couldn't act the part of a lackey immediately after I had been overwhelmed by the knowledge that the little girl was blind and that I was in love with her."

At last Chaplin came up with a solution, creating a few seconds of action that appear so inspired that it is difficult for a viewer of the completed film to imagine that they were the result of days of hard work and frustration. In the process of evading a policeman, the Tramp takes a detour through the empty backseat of the rich gentleman's car. The action is funny and surprising, so the audience can't miss it, and they understand immediately why the girl is confused.

Kisch was a keen observer, and his article goes far to explain why many who had worked in both media considered silent movies superior—their very limitations forced Chaplin to make every moment, every gesture, count. Published under the title "I Work with Chaplin," Kisch's article may also have conveyed a message to those who were aware of his role as highly placed agent of the Comintern.[22]

Later that same year Ivor Montagu, a young English film enthusiast and Communist activist, arrived in Los Angeles, expecting to set up a contract for Sergei Eisenstein to work as an independent director at the main UA studio. Montagu had apparently been led to believe that the groundwork for the contract was in place. Instead he was received with polite evasions. Fairbanks invited him to join his afternoon steam bath and cocktail parties but managed to avoid any situation in which the two of them would be left alone to talk business. Charlie simply failed to answer his calls and letters. At long last Montagu got through to Alf Reeves, who told him, "Mr. Chaplin has not forgotten. . . . Only at present he cannot think what to do."[23]

Since United Artists was not a traditional studio but a collection of independent producers, taking on Eisenstein would been difficult. Eventually Jesse Lasky, who had been approached separately in Paris, offered the Soviet director a contract with Paramount. He arrived in the United States in May 1930, accompanied by his assistant director, Grisha Aleksandrov, and cameraman Eduard Tisse, and set to work on his first project, a screenplay called *Sutter's Gold*, based on Blaise Cendrars' novel *L'Or*, about the California gold rush of 1849. Eisenstein's sojourn in America has been extensively chronicled, usually by writers who consider it a tragic example of the hostility of Hollywood to creative artists. Harry Geduld and Ronald Gottesman, whose book on the episode is scholarly and generally fair, call it "the old, familiar tale of the artist among the Philistines. Time and again the American film capital has lured original creative talent to its studios, and then destroyed it for refusing to conform to the box office."[24] But Eisenstein's misadventures also had elements of black comedy, and their moral is far from clear. Sovkino had not gone to the trouble and expense of sending Eisenstein and his crew to Los Angeles for the sake of his artistic development. His chief mission was to "study" American sound-film production methods— stealing as many trade secrets as possible in the process. For a while at least, Eisenstein and his crew went about their mission assiduously. During a tour of the Paramount lot, they even broke off chunks of soundproofing equipment, stuffing them into their pockets for later analysis by Soviet engineers.

Chaplin stayed clear of the Russian filmmakers and their British colleagues, the Montagus, until they were well settled at Paramount, then invited them for tea at Cove Way and told them they could use his swimming pool and tennis court any time. The Russian and British Communists were a bit stunned, at first, by their introduction to the Beverly Hills way of life. Eisenstein, who was just thirty-two but built like Winnie-the-Pooh, worried about losing his pants on the tennis court and violated the "tennis whites" dress code by appearing for a match wearing both a belt and fire-engine-red suspenders. Ivor Montagu's wife nearly succeeded in drowning herself in Chaplin's swimming pool.

One night Charlie took Sergei Mikhailovich to the amusement park in Venice Beach, where they took turns knocking down mechanical pigs in a shooting gallery. Rather than accept one of the plaster of paris statuettes of Felix the Cat that were being offered as prizes, Charlie kept a running total of his score, hoping to acquire enough points for an alarm clock.

Later he invited the entire group on a tuna-fishing expedition off Catalina. While Eisenstein, Montagu, and Georgia Hale sunbathed on deck, Chaplin talked about the scene in *Easy Street* in which he scattered food to a group of hungry children as if they were chickens.

"You see, I did this because I despise them. I don't like children," he explained.

While Eisenstein pondered this revelation from the director of *The Kid*, Chaplin went on: "I despise elephants. To have such strength and be so submissive."

"What animals do you like?"

"The wolf," said Chaplin.[25]

In a letter to the French critic Léon Moussinac, Eisenstein relayed his first impressions of Chaplin and the Hollywood scene:

Except for him, Sternberg and Lubitsch (this latter makes up for his faults by great personal charm) everyone is stupid or of mediocre interest. William De Mille is cretinous beyond belief. Vidor and Stroheim are not in Hollywood. I'll see them when they get back. Gloria Swanson is in Europe. I'll see the Feyders and Garbo Saturday. Harold Lloyd is in Florida.

To tell the truth we're so comfortably settled here that we don't even feel like seeing people except on official visits! We often go to Chaplin's house to play tennis. He's really nice. And extremely unhappy (personally).[26]

Eisenstein's *Sutter's Gold* script proved to be ahead of its time in interpreting the California dream as the folly of European white male imperialism. However, his grasp of American history and geography was shaky, and his script was filled with absurdities, including totem poles rising from the sands of the desert. If there had ever been any chance of this monumentally expensive, anticapitalist epic being made, Eisenstein squelched it by insisting that he would work only with an all-amateur cast.

Chaplin praised *Sutter's Gold* in his autobiography, but he showed no interest in producing it at the time. He also continued to spurn suggestions that he release his films for exhibition in the Soviet Union. "It is the principle of the thing," he told Montagu. "Pictures are worth something. They give Henry Ford valuta for tractors and my pictures must be worth as much as several tractors."[27]

Montagu was trying to arrange a deal under which Chaplin would receive furniture seized from the czar's palaces in exchange for the Soviet distribution rights to his films. Before the deal could be worked out, however, L. I. Monosson, the chairman of Amkino, came out to Los Angeles, vowing, "Once and for all, I will determine Chaplin's attitude to the Revolution." Montagu brought Monosson around the studio where Charlie lured the old Bolshevik into a discussion of ideology. Suddenly he appeared to take offense at something Monosson said, crying out, "That doesn't sound very

Communist to me. . . . Are you a Communist?" Monosson conceded that he was a "Soviet conservative." Charlie smiled. Having proved himself more ideologically correct than the Amkino bureaucrat, he indignantly refused to grant him the rights to his films.[28]

In November 1930 Representative Hamilton Fish began to raise questions about Eisenstein's mission in Hollywood. The Soviet director also became a favorite target of Maj. Frank Pease, an anti-Semitic right-winger who saw him as a prime example of the Jewish-Bolshevik conspiracy to take over Hollywood. Under pressure, Jesse Lasky terminated Eisenstein's six-month contract a few weeks before it was due to expire.

Eisenstein, however, did not want to go home. Inspired in part by Douglas Fairbanks's *The Mark of Zorro*, he had become fascinated by Mexico and hoped to make a film there about the Mexican revolution. Ivor Montagu, whose job it was to keep the great director from defecting, was distraught, and Chaplin took his side—although "principle" prevented Charlie Chaplin from making a gift of his own films to the Soviets, Eisenstein had a duty to return to Moscow and serve the cause of the workers' state. When Eisenstein ejected the Montagus from his rented house in Santa Monica, Chaplin took them in and even offered Ivor Montagu a job at the studio. He turned down the offer and returned to England.

Upton Sinclair stepped into the breach, raising money from private investors, including Kate Crane Gartz, to enable Eisenstein to go to Mexico, where he shot 234,000 feet of film, much of it on politically sensitive topics, and pursued pubescent boys with a lack of discretion that terrified Hunter Kimbrough, his production manager, who also happened to be Upton Sinclair's brother-in-law. Worried about his responsibility to his investors, Sinclair enlisted Rob Wagner to plead with Charlie to go down to Mexico and persuade Eisenstein to mend his ways. Chaplin refused, and Sinclair, who had run out of money and was being badgered by the Russians about his support for the director's unpatriotic behavior, terminated the project. Eisenstein's visa had expired, and he was forced to return to the Soviet Union. His unfinished film, which he intended to call *Que Viva Mexico!* remained behind.

Sinclair, in the hopes of recouping something for his investors, turned Eisenstein's footage over to director Sol Lesser, whose cut was released in 1933 as *Thunder Over Mexico*. In return for his efforts to help Eisenstein, Upton Sinclair found himself vilified by Communists and cinema buffs as a bourgeois capitalist, hypocrite, and protofascist, who had destroyed a masterpiece of revolutionary cinema out of greed. The mystique of the Soviet Union as the vanguard of socialism was still so great that even though Sinclair knew that the Communists were spreading scurrilous lies about him, he refrained from criticizing the Communist Party or Sovkino publicly. Like Chaplin, he was most exasperated with Eisenstein, writing: "He exploited me shamelessly mainly for the purpose of keeping from having to go back to Soviet Russia."

Chaplin, along with Rob Wagner and Doug Fairbanks, endorsed Sol Lesser's *Thunder Over Mexico*—further evidence that he was far from bound to the Communist line at this point. On the other hand, Chaplin's role in the affair reflects an unhealthy frame of mind. Like Rob Wagner, he was scornful of Paramount for not doing more for Eisenstein, even while he refused to risk his money and reputation by getting involved.

Wagner, who had recently launched a small literary magazine, *Script*—probably with Charlie's support—provided the all-purpose rationalization for hanging on to his radical illusions while protecting his own interests.

"I never felt stronger about things than I do now—but I gotta live under this ridiculous, but, thank heaven, rapidly cracking up system."[29]

Amazingly, as late as the early 1960s, Chaplin still refused to acknowledge the possibility that Eisenstein had good reason to be panicked at the prospect of returning home to function as an artist under Josef Stalin's regime. In fact he was punished for his rebellion, and not allowed to direct another film until 1938. Chaplin surely was aware of this but failed to mention it in his brief account of the affair. But then, in 1967, Ivor Montagu, still a close friend of Chaplin's, dismissed the persecution of Eisenstein by Stalin as cause for "cold war crocodile tears." Both men had no hesitation, however, about condemning Hollywood for failing to adapt to the Soviet director's whims.

Eisenstein, on his part, would sum up his feelings about Charlie Chaplin in an essay entitled "Charlie the Kid." Chaplin's art, he observes, grew out of a "comical-childish vision" of reality, one that followed naturally from his own personality. Whenever he thought of Chaplin, Eisenstein added, he remembered a photo caption he once saw in an English tabloid—"His Majesty, the Baby." The phrase said it all.[30]

The extreme unhappiness that made such an impression on Eisenstein continued to dog Chaplin throughout the making of *City Lights*, until the project became an ordeal for all concerned. One chilly morning, while filming the scene in which the drunken millionaire tries to drown himself, Henry Clive asked if his first plunge into the studio pool couldn't be delayed until the sun had warmed up the water. Clive had been working very hard and had picked up a nagging cough, but Chaplin lost his temper and fired him on the spot, replacing him with another actor, Harry Meyers.

A few months later Harry Crocker was suddenly informed that Charlie never wanted to see him again. He left the studio and his job without so much as a word of explanation from Chaplin.

For Virginia Cherrill the whole experience had become "painful. It seemed that the times you thought it was good, he'd hate it, and the other times when you felt flat and forced, he'd say it was great. If he enjoyed something, he'd do it forever until he was bored."[31]

Chaplin had been dissatisfied with her from the beginning, but for some reason soldiered on, ordering dozens upon dozens of takes. Then, nearly a year into the filming, he suddenly decided to replace her with Georgia Hale. Georgia desperately wanted the role and no doubt could have handled it, but for some reason, Carl Robinson opposed the change—perhaps he was just desperate to get the picture wrapped up. Robinson played on Chaplin's suspicions by insinuating that Georgia was using her personal relationship with him to further her career. Chaplin let himself be influenced by this, and began testing other actresses, including a sixteen-year-old named Violet Krauth (later known as Marion Marsh). He was prepared to sign her, but Alf Reeves was so alarmed by the prospect of another Lita Grey situation that he held up the typing of Krauth's contract until he could persuade Charlie to change his mind.[32]

Part of Chaplin's problem with Crocker and Cherrill may have been that they were both friendly with Marion Davies, who continued to pay unannounced visits to the set. Early in 1929 Chaplin had cast Marion's nephew, Charlie Lederer, in a small role as a messenger boy. As the months went by, however, Marion had become an irritant, and he no longer wanted to be bothered with her.

Marion got revenge in a small way by acting as Virginia Cherrill's confidante. When Cherrill was fired, Marion guessed that Charlie would be forced to take her back eventually. Realizing that Cherrill's contract, signed before her twenty-first birthday, was unenforceable, she advised her to hold out for a raise. Cherrill did and, interestingly enough, Chaplin seems to have found Cherrill more satisfactory at $150 a week than she had been at $75.

When *City Lights* was finally completed in October 1930, it was no longer commercially feasible to release a pure silent film. In many places the theater orchestra, combo, or piano player was a relic of the past. Chaplin may have balked at dialogue, but he relished the opportunity to compose a score for the separately recorded sound track. "I am writing every bit of it myself," he boasted to Rob Wagner, though in fact he did not read music and had considerable help from composer/arranger Arthur Johnson. Chaplin had nothing left to prove as an actor or director, and from this point on in his career, he would find more challenge in composing music and writing. As a composer he would write a few hit songs over the course of his life, and his ideas about using music in film were relatively sophisticated. Nevertheless, much of his music for *City Lights*—which includes a waltz, "hurrying music," and a brass fanfare whose title in the published score is given as "Proud and Pompus [*sic*]"—is rather pedestrian. Chaplin simply couldn't bring himself to apply the same rigorous standards of self-criticism to his work in this area as he brought to his acting, and while the results were not bad, exactly, an element of self-indulgence had begun to creep into his films that was destined to become more of a problem as the years went by.

Moreover, despite Douglas Fairbanks Jr.'s observation that silent film production was relatively cheap, the bills for *City Lights* were staggering. Chaplin, who made a point of not looking at the balance sheets until the last foot of film was in the can, must have been taken aback to learn that the movie had cost more than $1,568,000, a hefty sum for a silent picture shot in the studio without big-name stars. Wardrobe costs on the film were only $4,338, and the sets had required an outlay of only $36,325.

The budget breaker had been the schedule, which required keeping cast and crew on payroll for twenty-two months, including only 179 days on which the camera actually rolled.

Chaplin tried to assure his profits by demanding that United Artists give him 50 percent of the picture's gross, a better deal than any of his partners were getting. UA's sales force was already less than confident about the film's prospects, and in the end Chaplin decided to "roadshow" the film, underwriting the New York first run himself and setting a premium ticket price of $1.50.

The Los Angeles premiere of *City Lights* was set for January 30, 1931, and as the date approached, Chaplin was braced for disaster. The year 1931 would be a banner one for American movies. The Joan Crawford musical *Dance, Fools, Dance* was already a hit, soon to be followed by Greta Garbo in *Susan Lenox: Her Fall and Rise*, James Cagney in *The Public Enemy*, Bette Davis in *Bad Sister*, Adolphe Menjou in *The Front Page*, Boris Karloff's *Frankenstein*, and the Marx Brothers in *Monkey Business*. Audiences had come to expect entertainment that was ironic, realistic, wisecracking, hard-boiled—almost anything but sentimental, and the silent film was a relic of another era. When *City Lights* was screened in a sneak preview at the Tower Theater on January 19, the patrons appeared more confused than disapproving, and some walked out.

On the night of the premiere, an ashen-faced and weak-kneed Chaplin entered the theater accompanied by Georgia Hale and his special guests, Mr. and Mrs. Albert Einstein. One look at the audience should have reassured him. Once again Chaplin's slow production methods had worked in his favor. Now that the talkies had triumphed, the industry could afford to feel nostalgic, and the stars had turned out in force. Similarly, influential entertainment writers like the *New York Times*'s Mordaunt Hall had been running stories about the production since 1929, and one gets the sense that their reviews were written before they ever saw the picture. But the public was almost as enthusiastic. At the George M. Cohan Theater in New York, *City Lights* ran continuously from 9:00 A.M. until midnight, earning Chaplin a net profit of $288,074. The Paris run alone would cover the costs of the production.

In the opinion of many of Chaplin's most devoted admirers, *City Lights* remains his masterpiece—funnier than *The Circus*, but with more romance and character development than *The Gold Rush*. But the picture was not to everyone's taste. Reviewing the picture in *Script*, Rob Wagner observed that too many of the gags were recycled from earlier comedies, and he regretted that "Charlie's three years of puzzlement . . . has taken some of the edge off his spontaneity."[33]

Arguably, in *City Lights* the Little Fellow had crossed the line between pathos and self-pity. Even the famous final shot of Charlie's face—flooded with love, hope, and awful self-knowledge as he realizes that the blind girl can now see him for what he is—made some critics uneasy. The *Nation's* Alexander Bakshy commented that Chaplin almost seemed to be throwing himself on the mercy of the audience, pleading with them to continue to love him and accept him as a pantomime character. But the plea was futile. Chaplin had hoped that *City Lights* would prove that the silent film was still viable. On the contrary, its success was based on the audience's sense that they were watching the gallant swan song of a dying art form. *Variety* said as much, praising the picture but warning that Charlie Chaplin was "in danger of becoming an anachronism."[34]

13

"Disillusion of Love, Fame and Fortune"

The Charles Spencer Chaplin who went to Europe in 1921 was an opinionated but shy young man, homesick for his roots and avid for recognition. Ten years later, when he decided to celebrate the completion of *City Lights* by making a world tour, both he and the world were less innocent. "The disillusion of love, fame and fortune left me somewhat apathetic," he would write. "There seemed nothing to turn to outside of my work and that, after twenty years, was becoming irksome. I needed emotional stimulus."[1]

He was soon to find more of it than he could handle.

In New York to publicize *City Lights* before sailing for Europe, Chaplin looked up Ralph Barton. Barton's fourth marriage had ended, and he was far behind deadline on various projects. Panicky over his inability to work, he had begun to think obsessively about his ex-wife Carlotta. During their marriage she had provided a stable home and a fixed routine that kept him functioning. Now she was living in France with Eugene O'Neill, whose reputation continued to flourish with her support. Barton had already made a trip to France, where he tried in vain to persuade Lillian Gish to deliver a letter to Carlotta, begging her to see him.

Fifteen minutes before Charlie, Carlyle Robinson, and Kono were to leave for the docks, Charlie impulsively invited Barton to come to Europe with them. It was a terrible idea, but Robinson and Kono had no say in the matter. On shipboard Charlie and Ralph disappeared into Charlie's suite, where they spent the rest of voyage in a marathon conversation, and instead of calming his friend, Charlie himself became more irrational by the day.[2]

Disembarking in Southampton, where a private railroad car had been provided to whisk him to London, Chaplin was greeted by a crowd of reporters. "Is there any chance that you'll reconcile with Lita?" one shouted. Chaplin turned pale and hurried aboard the train. Later he told Robinson that he hated all journalists and intended never to speak to one again. "I didn't come here to be interviewed." But in fact he had. The trip was intended to be partly business, a promotional tour for *City Lights*.

On his first morning in London, Chaplin arose early, slipped out of his suite at the Hotel Carlton, and took a cab to Kennington where he stood on the street corner, overcome by emotion. It was the first of several pilgrimages to sites associated with his childhood—Lambeth, Brook Street, West Square, Westminster Bridge. In Kennington Park he suddenly saw an image of himself, aged about five, running from the playground toward a park bench where his mother was seated, and realizing that she was weeping.

A few days later, on February 20, he and Barton set out for Hanwell, a grim venue he had avoided in 1921. The school was still in the same fortresslike building, but, the headmaster explained, the military discipline had long ago been relaxed. Although the children appeared to be content and well cared for, Chaplin returned to the hotel in a state of agitation and took to his bed, weeping. An hour later he summoned Robinson and outlined a plan for a return visit to Hanwell, bringing gifts for the orphans—a movie projector, a saxophone for the school band, two hundred bags of candy, two hundred of the shiniest apples and most perfect oranges (not easy to find in London that winter), toys, and envelopes containing bright, uncirculated shillings.

Robinson scurried around assembling the gifts, but on the afternoon slated for the return visit, Chaplin took Ralph Barton off to have tea with Lady Astor, leaving Robinson and Kono to deliver the presents on his behalf. As their car approached the orphanage, Robinson's heart sank. The locals had decorated their cottages with Union Jacks and the Stars and Stripes, and crowds lined the road, waiting for a glimpse of Hanwell's most famous alumnus. Robinson stopped the car at a phone booth and called Charlie, pleading with him to change his mind. He refused but promised to reschedule his appearance for another day. This was small comfort to the orphans, who had turned out in their Sunday best. At one end of the hall a table had been laid out for Chaplin and his party to take refreshments. It stood forlorn and empty, reminding Robinson of the scene in *The Gold Rush* in which Georgia and the other dance hall girls accept Charlie's invitation to dinner and never show up. Chaplin never did find time for the Hanwell orphans, excusing himself on the grounds that his first visit had been so emotionally wrenching he couldn't face another.

Meanwhile Chaplin had become just about unstoppable on the subject of politics. Having read H. Douglas's *Social Credit*, which explained that all value is derived from labor, Chaplin had sold his stocks before the 1929 crash. Now he was working on a plan to end the depression. At a dinner at Chartwell, Winston Churchill's home at Westerham, he argued economics with John Maynard Keynes and reproved a guest who made a slighting remark about Gandhi, telling him, "The Gandhis and the Lenins do not start revolutions. They are forced up by the masses and usually voice the want of a people."

"You should run for parliament," Churchill quipped.

"I prefer to be a motion picture actor these days," Chaplin replied. "However, I believe we should go with evolution to avoid revolution."

During a visit with Labour prime minister Ramsay MacDonald at Chequers, his official residence in the country, he was less restrained, expounding at length on his ideas for resolving the world economic crisis:

Shrink the government.

Control prices, interest and profits.

Make England's colonies into "an economic unity."

Support world trade and abolition of the gold standard.

Shorten working hours and guarantee a "comfortable" income to all.

"Stand for private enterprise" provided it does not run counter to the "well-being of the majority."[3]

Of course, the politician who could accomplish all these contradictory goals simultaneously would not be a Labourite or a Tory but a wizard. Chaplin, however, was quite serious and a bit peeved that his prescriptions were not being taken seriously.

While strolling on the grounds of Chequers, he and the prime minister came upon a poor family having a picnic. MacDonald brusquely ordered the family to leave. Chaplin was shocked, he told friends, and decided on the spot that MacDonald had turned against the class he was pledged to serve. One suspects, however, that there were other reasons for his disenchantment. MacDonald and the Labour Party weren't especially interested in Chaplin's economic theories, but they did hope to persuade him to contribute to the gross national product by making one or more films in England. Although Chaplin had talked of moving his studio to London in the past, he was not about to make such a major commitment and resented being pressured. For all his talk about homesickness for England, he was atill bitter toward his homeland, blaming the entire nation and its preoccupation with class for the slights he had suffered in his youth.

Although their talks at Chequers were not a great success, MacDonald had made up his mind that bestowing a knighthood on a former child of the London slums would be good politics. Chaplin's name was placed on the honors list to be presented to King George V later that year, and MacDonald planned a dinner party to be held in the private dining room of the House of Commons, where Chaplin would be introduced to leading Labour MPs.

Chaplin dearly wanted the knighthood, but when it came to socializing with politicians he preferred the company of the Tory aristocrats he'd been meeting through Sir Philip Sassoon, whom he knew through Doug Fairbanks. The Tories were not in power at the time and didn't want anything from him, or if they did they were more subtle about asking for it. Chaplin was especially taken with Lady Astor, so much so that he accompanied her to a rally in support of her campaign for a seat in Parliament and sat next to her on the platform, much to the dismay of the Labourites.

Another distraction presented itself at the February 26 premiere of *City Lights*, in the form of a brunette dancer named Sari Maritza.

Instantly infatuated, Chaplin ignored the distinguished guests at the after-screening party—including Churchill and George Bernard Shaw—to tango the night away. Robinson, who'd made the mistake of inviting Maritza to the party as his own date, was frantic when he learned that Maritza, whose real name was Patricia Nathan, and her stunning blond friend Vivien Gaye, originally Sanya Bezencenet and later Mrs. Ernst Lubitsch, had a considerable reputation in London as ruthless fortune hunters. After the party, Sari was prepared to settle into Chaplin's suite at the Carlton. Robinson threatened to resign unless she left, but even though he won his point, Charlie continued to slip out of the hotel to meet Sari at various nightclubs.

By this time Ralph Barton's behavior had become so bizarre that Robinson was staying up most of the night to keep watch on him. Relentlessly if artificially enthusiastic at first, Barton had now grown morose. He had developed a phobia about time and went around the suite cutting the cords of all the electric clocks. At all hours he paced the halls of the hotel "like a caged animal," and one day Robinson surprised him staring intently at a revolver he held in his hand.

Finally, much to Robinson's relief, Barton announced that he wanted to go home. Perhaps he had learned that Carlotta and Eugene O'Neill were no longer in France, having left on February 25 for a vacation in the Canary Islands. Following their stay in the Canaries, the O'Neills were planning to return to the United States, and Barton, borrowing his return fare from Chaplin, also headed home.

On May 16, four days after Carlotta and her husband reached New York, Barton committed suicide in his Manhattan penthouse. He left a note expressing his undying love for Carlotta and attributing his despair to "manic depressive insanity."[4]

Meanwhile the political muddle Chaplin had gotten himself into became more complicated. On Tuesday, March 3, Chaplin was the guest of honor at a dinner for Tory notables, hosted by Lady Astor in the private dining room of the House of Commons. Astor had stolen a march on Prime Minister MacDonald, whose Labourite party in Chaplin's honor was scheduled for the following Monday. The insult was compounded when Chaplin decided to move his departure for Berlin up to Sunday, so that he wouldn't be able to attend MacDonald's dinner after all.

Carl Robinson was terrified that Charlie was getting ready to marry Sari Maritza—a mistake for which he, Robinson, would inevitably be blamed—and he thought it best that Chaplin get out of England even if it did mean standing up the prime minister. Unfortunately, neither he nor anyone else could persuade Charlie to call Ten Downing Street and make his excuses to MacDonald in person. Charlie promised to write a letter, but he never did, leaving a secretary hired from a temporary agency to break the news.

To make matters worse, Sari showed up on Sunday morning, glued herself to Charlie's side, and began telling him horror stories about the Channel crossing, predicting a winter storm and high winds. It took little persuading for Charlie to decide that a night with Sari would be more pleasant than a wintertime journey to Berlin. Robinson was frantic, envisioning the scandal if Charlie were still in London on the evening of MacDonald's dinner and it became known that he had failed to show up because he was closeted in his suite with Sari. Desperate, Robinson resorted to manufacturing a fake weather report, which he handed Charlie to convince him that his journey across the Channel would be uneventful.

On the strength of the weather report, Charlie allowed himself to be hustled off to the train. Unfortunately Sari's prediction proved correct. As soon as they boarded the ferry, the wind blew up, and Charlie retreated to his cabin, violently seasick. Kono had left his pigskin valise on the bed, and Charlie, who detested the smell of leather almost as much as he did rubber, began to see a plot on Kono's part to torture him.

Chaplin reached Berlin at 5:30 in the afternoon on Monday. Marlene Dietrich was on hand at the Friedrichstrasse train depot to greet him on behalf of the German film industry, and huge crowds, whistling and shouting "Hoch" and "Gold Rush Charlie!" filled the street in front of the posh Hotel Adlon. Chaplin, however, was not impressed with Berlin. Prince Henry of Prussia took him on a tour of the palace at Potsdam, whose baroque decor reminded Charlie of "the interior of an oyster bar or a concession at Coney Island." As for Berlin's famously decadent nightlife, in one café, "two effemi-nate youths danced together. This was the big noise of the evening, the something unspeakable we were privileged to see. Each time fresh customers would enter, the same youths would hurry to their feet again." Only a production of Ferenc Molnar's *Liliom* at the Workers' Theater restored his faith in the German avant garde.[5]

As the *New York Times* correspondent observed, Berliners welcomed Charlie Chaplin's visit as a respite from fractious street demonstrations and fighting between Nazis and Communists. But the respite did not last long.

On March 13 a spokesman for a Communist-led group claiming to represent unemployed workers in the German film industry called the Adlon, threatening to bring four thousand rioters to smash the hotel's windows unless Chaplin met with him. He agreed to receive a delegation of four of the group's leaders. The next morning a small Communist newspaper, *The Young Guard*, said that in a phone interview with its editor Chaplin had extended sympathetic greetings to the Communist youth of Germany.

Criticized for adding fuel to the volatile political situation, Chaplin issued a somewhat unconvincing denial, saying that he was only an artist who knew nothing about politics; however: "I believe in the five-day week and the six-hour day, and I am convinced that if it could be realized conditions would be improved." As for the delegation of unemployed film workers, he said, "I told them that conditions in the United States were perhaps worse than here. Los Angeles has perhaps 100,000 unemployed film folk."[6]

Hollywood was beginning to feel the impact of the depression, but it was hardly worse off than Berlin, where both the Communists and the Nazis were doing their best to bring down the government and destroy the social fabric. (Ironically, however, among those who were unemployed in Hollywood were former employees of the Charles Chaplin Studio, left to fend for themselves while Chaplin spread the good word about the thirty-hour week in Europe.)

As word spread of Chaplin's meeting with the pro-Communist workers' delegation, his suite at the Adlon was besieged by representatives of political factions. His presence in the city had become so disruptive that he was encouraged to leave without fanfare. A day ahead of schedule, he departed on a swing through Vienna, Budapest, and Venice. His temper was now so unpredictable that even the loyal Kono was threatening to resign, and he talked of little but his quest for attractive female companions. Unfortunately the ones he found were invariably married to influential men or otherwise disastrously inappropriate.

All this was a warm-up for Chaplin's arrival in Paris. Chaplin was to be awarded the Cross of the Legion of Honor by foreign minister Aristide Briand, capping a decade-long campaign by the artist Cami, who had mobilized the writers and artists of France on Chaplin's behalf. Cami had traveled to London at his own expense to apprise Charlot of the situation, but Chaplin's staff was preoccupied by the Barton-MacDonald-Maritza situation, and Cami was left cooling his heels in the hotel lobby.

At the Gare du Nord, Chaplin's train was met by a screaming crush of fans, held back by scores of policemen. Somehow the tiny, self-effacing Cami was thrust forward by the surging crowd, and he latched onto Chaplin and mouthed the words, "Bonjour, Paris," prompting Chaplin to greet the crowd in their own language. At almost the same moment, a reporter for a radio station stuck a microphone in front of Chaplin's face.

Chaplin had made up his mind that microphones were infernal tools of the sound technology that was killing pantomime. Although he had relented in Vienna and addressed a few words to the radio audience, this time he recoiled. Pushing away the microphone, he made a dash for his limousine, where he found the assiduous Cami waiting. Leaping to the conclusion that Cami was part of a plot to get him to talk on the air, Chaplin was furious with him and spent the ride to his hotel making faces at Carl Robinson over Cami's head, communicating his desire to get rid of him. Robinson was "stupefied" by this treatment of a gentle, sensitive man who had worked so hard on his idol's behalf. Still, in order to avoid a scene he agreed to bar Cami from the gala reception that awaited them at their suite in the Hotel Crillon.

Inconsolable and bewildered, Cami wrote an abject letter reminding Chaplin that he understood and supported his rejection of the talkies and begging him to explain why his feelings toward him had changed so suddenly. Chaplin did not bother to reply.

The following day Chaplin lunched with Briand and a company of assorted government ministers and aristocrats. The Legion of Honor, however, was not mentioned. Briand, it seems, had become nervous about reports of Chaplin's behavior in London and Berlin, and intimidated by political cartoons in the right-wing press, including an imaginary dialogue between himself and the slapstick comedian:

Chaplin: "All the world laughs at me."
Briand: "There are some who don't take me so seriously either."

Chaplin eventually did get his decoration, but it was awarded a week later without fuss or ceremony by Briand's secretary at a private reception in the foreign minister's office.

In England the newspapers were still raising a flap over Chaplin's insult to Ramsay MacDonald, and exhibitors were threatening to boycott *City Lights* because United Artists, in order to pay off Chaplin's special deal, was demanding 50 percent of the box office gross instead of the usual 30.

The French film critics, already upset over the slight to Cami, saw *City Lights* and were struck by certain parallels to a play called *Les Plus Beaux Yeux du Monde*, by Jean Sarment, a prolific playwright who happened to be a favorite of the influential *La Nouvelle Revue* and *Le Journal*. Sarment's play, written in 1922 but not produced in Paris until 1925, concerned two young men, the ambitious but dull Arthur and the romantic Napoleon, who leaves home to pursue his dream of becoming a famous writer. Years later, his clothes as tattered as his dreams, "Napo" returns home to find that Lucy, the girl he loved, has married Arthur, now a wealthy businessman. Lucy has also lost her eyesight in an accident, mercifully for Napo, since she cannot see how low he has fallen. As he puts it, "The most beautiful eyes in the world are those which do not see me."[7]

The Most Beautiful Eyes in World, to use the English title, was considered by many of Sarment's admirers to be his best play. There were plans for a Broadway production, which fell through, but his American agent hoped for a movie sale and had circulated a literal English translation in Hollywood. At least two studios made offers, but Sarment rejected them because he feared that they would not be faithful to the romantic spirit of his work.

The plots of Sarment's play and *City Lights* were in fact quite different. The resemblance lay mainly between Napo's closing line and the final moments of *City Lights*—which, of course, happened to be the most memorable things about the two works. Even if Chaplin had taken his inspiration from Sarment, it would be hard to say that he was guilty of plagiarism. As a memo emanating from United Artist's legal department observed, no one could have a monopoly on the subject of a sighted man's romance with a blind woman. Since Sarment was known to be reluctant to sell the rights to his work to anyone who planned a free adaptation, where did that leave Chaplin?

Still, Chaplin's insistence that he had never heard of Jean Sarment or his play evoked skepticism. And with hindsight, it is difficult to imagine that a play about a tramp named Napoleon could circulate in Hollywood without someone bringing it to Chaplin's attention. No doubt it is also significant that Chaplin originally planned to set *City Lights* in Paris, and, almost uniquely, he had envisioned the ending of the story early on in his work on the script.

Jean Sarment declined to sue, but UA was not so lucky with the agency that controlled the rights to "La Violetera," which Chaplin used as the *City Lights* theme song. When the strains of Padilla's haunting melody, made famous by chanteuse Raquel Meller, were heard in theaters over the credit "Music composed by Charles Chaplin," there were snorts of indignation and amusement. The Spanish film director Luis Buñuel would sum up the European reaction by joking that Charlot went to sleep and dreamed that he had written "La Violetera."

This time there was no question of plagiarism. United Artists had cleared the rights for "La Violetera" and other copyrighted material incorporated by Chaplin into his score. The problem was that the publishers, still used to the days when movie scores were played in theaters by live musicians, had given no thought to the question of screen credits. "La Violetera" was not only the best song in the score but very prominently featured. Chaplin's stinginess with screen credits had long been notorious, but it is difficult to imagine how he could have failed to see that in this instance he had left himself open to ridicule.

Almost nothing of the problems that sprang up everywhere Chaplin went was being reported in the States. Even the *New York Times* tended to bury such news in stories with headlines like CHUCKLES FOLLOW CHAPLIN IN FRANCE—COMEDIAN IS UNABLE TO

AVOID HUMOR, NO MATTER HOW SERIOUS HE IS.[8] In reality chuckles were few. Chaplin's knighthood was now out of the question—published reports said that Queen Mary herself had demanded that his name be struck from the honors list, on account of his failure to serve during World War I. The French critics were bitterly divided into pro- and anti-Chaplin camps, and Berliners were still debating whether he had endorsed Communist demonstrations or not. Carlyle Robinson was relieved when the formalities of launching *City Lights* were completed and he was able to deliver Charlie to the French Riviera, and into the hands of Syd and Minnie.

Syd's association with British International Studios had ended in July 1930 with a flurry of trouble including a contract dispute, a bankruptcy filing, and a tangled affair with a British actress, Molly Wright, who filed suit against him charging libel and slander. None of these troubles appeared to have left their mark on Syd, who had found his paradise on the Riviera and was quite content to be retired. He lived rather modestly in a suite of rooms at a Nice hotel but spent a good deal of his time at the casino, owned by the American tycoon Frank Jay Gould, who had once been married to Edith Kelly, sister of Arthur Kelly and the late Hetty.

Syd, it seems, enjoyed certain perks in exchange for functioning as a very discreet celebrity guest. At any rate Frank Gould invited Charlie to stay at one of his hotels, the Majestic, on the assumption that he was free to exploit the visit. Gould's press agent, Boris Evelinoff, issued bulletins to the newspapers on Chaplin's activities, and when he dined at another Gould hotel, the Mediterranean Palace, the management sold nearby tables to the highest bidders and charged other regular customers for seats on the terrace, where they could have a view of Chaplin and his party as they ate.

Chaplin was indignant when he realized what Gould was doing, though not quite indignant enough to leave. His attention had been captured by May Reeves, a willowy black-eyed beauty who had been hired to handle his correspondence. The glamorous and rather mysterious Miss Reeves, also known as Mitzi Muller, claimed to be a former beauty contest winner from Czechoslovakia, though other accounts say she was half English, or perhaps half French. Her occupation was as questionable as her background. Though Charlie didn't know it, she was an "intimate friend" of Syd Chaplin, and when Syd introduced May to Carl Robinson in the casino, Robinson's first thought was, "If she's a secretary, I'm a grand duke."[9] However, she was fluent in six languages and performed creditably for an entire morning until Charlie caught sight of her and fell instantly in love.

Charlie insisted on taking May everywhere, creating an awkward situation for Syd, who was jealous, and Minnie, who was irate over having to socialize with her husband's onetime girlfriend. The Goulds were also upset, as Charlie insisted on introducing a woman who was, as Robinson delicately put it, déclassé, to their stuffier guests. At last Mrs. Gould broke the stalemate by presenting Charlie with an exquisite pair of diamond-encrusted platinum cufflinks, announcing that they were his going-away present.

Chaplin took the hint and decamped to Algiers, but May followed on the next boat. Before long Charlie was scouting possible studio locations and Alf Reeves, in Hollywood, gave an interview announcing that Chaplin planned to make a picture in Algiers before returning to the United States.[10]

After a few weeks, however, Charlie and May tired of North Africa and took a boat back to Marseilles, where Carl Robinson was waiting for them. Syd didn't have the courage to tell Charlie about his own relationship with May, but Minnie feared that Charlie planned to marry the woman and insisted that the truth had better come out before he did. Syd delegated the unpleasant task to Carl, who for some reason agreed to take it on.

Charlie listened to Robinson's information in a state of horror and stupefaction. After a sleepless night he made his decision. Syd, as usual, was not to be blamed. Although Syd had steered Charlie wrong on several occasions, he was still his beloved big brother as well as the man who knew most about the disposition of his overseas bank accounts. Instead, his displeasure fell on the messenger, Robinson. After working for Charlie for fifteen years, Robinson found himself dispatched on an unnecessary errand to New York; the news that he had been fired reached him there. May was also forgiven for the moment, and she and Charlie, accompanied by Kono, soon moved on to the resort of Juan-les-Pins. In the car, May would recall, Charlie serenaded her with Marlene Dietrich's song from *The Blue Angel*, "Falling in Love Again."[11] But their relationship could never be the same. Charlie was excessively jealous, and the details Robinson confided preyed on his mind.

The news that the May Reeves spell had been broken had reached Hollywood by the summer. In late July, Alf Reeves sent Rob Wagner some of Chaplin's box seat tickets for the forthcoming Hollywood Bowl concert season, saying:

> You know a certain party is not in town. . . . He is still in that Sunny France, but not for good, as some of the press clippings say. We can make a good guess he will be back here by November, leaving Juan-les-Pins quite soon and possibly traveling via Japan and [the] Pacific Ocean to Beverly Hills. Reckon he will make his next picture in Hollywood—where *City Lights* came from.[12]

Reeves had the itinerary about right, but he was wrong about the timing. Charlie decided to spend an extra month in France, visiting Harry d'Arrast in Biarritz. A highlight of the visit was to be a brief trip across the Spanish border to attend a bullfight, but the day was ruined by his rage at Kono, who had forgotten to bring his passport, causing some delay at the border. Charlie retaliated later, d'Arrast told a friend, by cutting the fly buttons off Kono's trousers.[13]

Although it would seem that Carl Robinson had not done a very effective job in his role as a "suppress agent," as he put it, once he was gone Chaplin's press managed to get worse.

Chaplin had been invited by George Black, manager of the Palladium Theater, to appear at the annual Royal Variety show. The charity event was not a "command performance," but members of the royal family did attend, and an invitation to perform was considered an honor. Chaplin was in Algeria when the invitation arrived, and Carl Robinson declined for him on the grounds that he was proceeding with his trip around the world and would not be returning to England. Some days later, when Chaplin returned to France, he was asked about the reply to Black, and he commented that he had sent Black a donation of a thousand pounds, equal to his earnings during his last two years in England.

If the sarcastic implications of all this were not clear enough, he soon gave an interview to a reporter for the *Express* of London accusing his countrymen of being "hypocrites" and declaring: "They say I have a duty to England. I wonder just what that duty is? No one wanted me or cared for me in England seventeen years ago. I had to go to America for my chance, and I got it there. Only then did England take the slightest interest in me."

In the same interview he had a few sharp words for the French critics who had accused him of stealing the story of *City Lights*. He had plenty of ideas of his own, he said, and no need to borrow them from Europeans, especially Frenchmen. And he went on: "I have been all over Europe in the last few months. Patriotism is rampant everywhere, and the result is going to be another war. I hope they send the old men to the front next time, for it is the old men who are the real criminals in Europe today."

And, finally: "I am by way of being a student of history. I know that the jester always pays, for the king inevitably kicks him downstairs. The most famous Court clowns eventually are beheaded, but what happens to the monarch then? In nearly every case, kicking the jester has presaged the fall of the throne."[14]

It was not true, of course, that no one in England had paid attention to Chaplin during his years with Karno. As for his comments on "patriotism," they might have been better received had he used the word "nationalism"—Chaplin never did seem to grasp that there was a distinction. But to imply that the price of insulting Charlie Chaplin would be the "fall of the throne" was sheer megalomania. Chaplin, it seems, made these comments on the tennis court, not realizing that he was speaking to a reporter. Regardless of the circumstances, however, the interview was an awesome demonstration of one of Chaplin's most salient traits—his genius for rancor. He had a way of framing his insults in terms so venomous that their targets would find them unforgivable.

The *Express* interview outraged the English tabloid press and won him no friends among French intellectuals either, as can be judged from an article in the May 23 issue of the journal *Comoedia*, which took note of "this peculiar interview" in which "the great comedian almost sneered at the whole of Europe, and France in particular." Mr. Chaplin complained of being unappreciated, *Comoedia* went on, but he had not bothered to meet with any of the writers who had done so much to promote his reputation in France. Instead "he lunched with a minister who pinned a red ribbon on his coat. Mr. Charlot is a good fellow, but Mr. Chaplin is ill-mannered."[15]

Chaplin's statements played rather well in the United States. One editor noted that perhaps he was "simply getting even with Bernard Shaw [who] . . . has a nifty way of using every suitable occasion (which means every occasion) to slam the United States."[16] For such, Chaplin could do no wrong.

Chaplin had returned to England in September, where his cool reception became even chillier when the press learned that he was in the country to defend a lawsuit filed by May Shepherd, who had been his secretary during his stay at the Carlton earlier in the year.

Shepherd claimed that she had been underpaid by one hundred pounds (then worth $332) and was suing for payment. When Chaplin left England in March, Shepherd had submitted her bill to Maurice Silverstone, the managing director of the London office of United Artists, who objected that she was asking five times the going rate for secretarial help. Not only that, he complained to UA treasurer Arthur Kelly, but while working in Chaplin's suite she had run up a considerable room service bill—charging expensive meals and bottles of champagne.

The normal rate for secretaries "has nothing to do with it," Shepherd replied through her solicitor. The situation in the suite had been so chaotic that she was left by default to handle problems far beyond the duties of any secretary. For one thing it had fallen to her to inform Ten Downing Street that Mr. Chaplin was standing up the prime minister. She had ordered the champagne and food to pacify reporters disgruntled over Chaplin's failure to show up for interviews. By way of thanks Chaplin and his party had suddenly decamped from the hotel, dismissing her on one day's notice even though she had been promised that she would work for another week.

More to the point, Shepherd's representative told UA's solicitor, F. M. Guedalla, his client had other complaints, which she would make public if her claim was not settled promptly. The nature of the charges can be inferred from Guedalla's report that although Shepherd had no problems when she worked for Rudolph Valentino during his London visit, since on that occasion "Madame Valentino was constantly in the office," she'd had a similar experience with Douglas Fairbanks.

Both Arthur Kelly and Carl Robinson urged Silverstone to pay Shepherd and be done with it. Instead he chose to take the advice of Guedalla, who was viscerally offended at the thought of a secretary getting one hundred pounds for three weeks' work. "Personally, I should object to being blackmailed," he wrote in October. "She and her solicitor have approached Mr. Silverstone and Mr. Chaplin in a most offensive manner."[17]

Pumped up by Guedalla, Chaplin was "very strong" on fighting the suit. When the trial opened on December 1, he was not only present but insisted that he had a right to sit beside his barrister and make an opening statement—practices unknown in the English court system. As might have been predicted, Shepherd's account of the goings-on in Chaplin's suite won the sympathies of the judge and spectators. Nevertheless Chaplin insisted on testifying and took the stand in a feisty mood, only to collapse when the opposing barrister asked him about his knowledge of the incident involving Shepherd and Douglas Fairbanks. Chaplin immediately demanded a recess and instructed his advisers to pay Shepherd in full. He didn't mind about his own reputation, but he could never allow Douglas's name to be dragged through the mud.

The embarrassment of the Shepherd lawsuit was completely unnecessary. Chaplin's habit of making some kind of pass at practically every woman who crossed his path, including his secretaries, was not especially attractive, but one doubts that he was any worse on this score than Fairbanks or numerous other male stars of the era. A far more serious problem was that he saw himself as surrounded by people who were trying to take advantage of him. All too often there was someone on the scene—typically a lawyer—who was prepared to encourage his paranoia.

What Chaplin was also learning in Europe was that in certain rarefied social circles, episodes like the Shepherd suit and his "fall of the throne" comment were considered beneath notice. The Prince of Wales entertained him in England nevertheless, as did Ottoline

Morrell, the Bloomsbury hostess, who gave a luncheon to introduce him to Lytton Strachey, Aldous Huxley, and Augustus John. He was also summoned to an audience with Gandhi. Left alone on a settee to chat with the saintly Mahatma, Chaplin suddenly had a moment of clarity: How on earth do I get into these situations? he asked himself.[18] Nevertheless, within minutes he was debating the merits of the machine age and, for once, defending the necessity of industrialization.

By early 1932 Chaplin's mood had improved, and for almost six months his tour continued without incident. He spent two of them in Saint Moritz with Douglas Fairbanks, who was separated from Mary and preparing to marry Lady Sylvia Ashley. In March he sailed for the Far East, accompanied by Kono and Syd. In Bali, like so many other European and American artists, he fell in love with the intricate beauty of Balinese music and dance, so much so that he hired a cameraman to film performances and talked of doing a documentary on the subject.

Long fascinated by Japanese culture, Chaplin had even higher expectations for his visit there. He was disappointed to find Tokyo so Westernized, but made the rounds of museums and galleries in search of Hokusai and Utamuro prints.

Unfortunately Tokyo, like Berlin, was awash with political intrigue and on May 15, the day after Charlie and Syd arrived, nine terrorists, members of a militarist sect opposed to pacifism and internationalism, invaded the house of Premier Ki Tsuyoshi Inukai and shot him dead. Charlie had been scheduled to meet the premier that day, and Kono worried that he had been an intended target of the attack. Despite Kono's warnings Charlie made a point of dining with the premier's son at a restaurant, where he had his first taste of tempura and consumed thirty prawns.

On June 3 he sailed for home on the *Hikawu Maru*. The trouble in Japan had revived his conviction that he had the solution to the world's problems, and he spent the journey in his cabin, setting down on paper his plan for restoring economic prosperity. Arriving in Vancouver, he told reporters, "I am reputedly a comedian, but after seeing the financial conditions of the world, I have decided I am as much an economist as financiers are comedians"—which actually wasn't saying much. "Financiers," he continued, "will have to take less profit and they will have to get it on the basis of larger volume of business and smaller return."[19]

Kono was by now so jittery that he persuaded his employer to destroy his notes on his socialistic plan before he passed through U.S. Customs. As soon as Chaplin reached Seattle, however, he sent for a stenographer and began to dictate his ideas for publication in the *Post-Intelligencer*.[20]

In Los Angeles, meanwhile, the county assessor was compiling a list of the city's richest residents. By his reckoning Charlie Chaplin topped the roster of show business personalities, with $7,687,570 in taxable stocks and bonds as well as $285,600 in cash and cash equivalents. Douglas Fairbanks, who was second on the list, had only $639,000 in stocks and bonds. Considering that Chaplin bragged that he had liquidated most of his stocks before the crash and put his money into gold in Canadian banks, the assessor's estimate probably represented only a fraction of Chaplin's true net worth.

14

Modern Times

Chaplin returned from his world tour just in time for a meeting with the Internal Revenue Service. IRS auditors were going through the books of his production company, and once again he and Alf Reeves had no doubt that he was a victim of harassment. Certainly it was true that the IRS could be hard on celebrities, in the hope of making examples of them, but there were good reasons why the Charles Chaplin Film Corporation should have found itself the object of special attention. Chaplin had completed only two movies since 1925, and for the past year and a half his studio had been idle, yet everything he owned was in the company's name and therefore potentially deductible. Even the Cove Way house was company property. Neighbors recalled that much of the construction had been done by stage carpenters from Chaplin's studio. The workmen weren't used to building things to last, and the house took years to settle, occasionally emitting noises loud enough to alarm the servants, and shedding railings, facings, and woodwork in the process—problems so notorious that the locals had nicknamed the place Breakaway House.

The physical plant at La Brea Avenue studio, on the other hand, encouraged suspicions that it existed only as a tax dodge. The interiors of the mock-Tudor cottages hadn't been remodeled since they were built, and Chaplin's personal office was a filthy hovel with a scarred linoleum floor and soot-covered walls. The rest of the facility was hardly better. The film laboratory was a boarded-up relic.

The cameras, lights, and electrical equipment belonged to an earlier era of movie production.

Nor did the studio books make sense from a business standpoint. The auditors questioned, for example, why Edna Purviance, who hadn't been before a camera in several years, continued to receive a salary. Chaplin's generosity was admirable, but Purviance had never had a written contract with the studio, much less a pension plan. Under the circumstances they were justified in wondering whether her stipend was a legitimate business expense or conscience money paid to an ex-mistress.

Wrangling with the auditors kept Alf Reeves busy for months, but in the long run Chaplin's eccentric business practices worked in his favor. The IRS had started from the assumption that Chaplin's assets were undervalued but were forced to concede that the reverse was true.

Meanwhile the audit gave Chaplin an excuse to put off making a decision about his next project, if indeed there *was* to be a next project. During his year and a half abroad, Hollywood had been going through rapid changes. The major studios had borrowed heavily to finance the conversion to talking pictures, and the moguls of Chaplin's generation now had to answer to outside investors. Many of his contemporaries had retired rather than adjust to the new way of doing things. His friends Doug and Mary had split up. Even the compliant Georgia Hale was no longer at his side; unable to forgive him for failing to send her so much as a postcard during his year and a half abroad, she had told Charlie it would be better if they didn't see each other again. For a time, Chaplin seriously considered retirement.

Sam Goldwyn, one of the hardy survivors of the industry shakeout, was producing musicals at UA's corporate studio, and once again he took it upon himself to cheer Charlie up by finding him a new girlfriend. On the set of his latest production, *The Kid from Spain*, he introduced him to Paulette Goddard, an ambitious young actress who was one of the dancing "Goldwyn Girls."

"Mr. Chaplin," said Paulette "I've been married, I'm divorced. I want to meet and get on with the greatest actor in Hollywood, and that's you."

"Right away she showed her honesty," Chaplin reported to

friends in amazement. "She told me exactly what's what."[1]

Chaplin promptly took the starlet to dinner at the home of Alf and Amy Reeves, who were less favorably impressed by her candor. Any woman Chaplin showed an interest in was automatically suspected by the Reeveses and Henry Bergman of being a gold-digger, and in Goddard's case there were some grounds for their belief.

A gum-cracking peroxide blonde, known to old friends as "Sugar," Paulette Goddard had made her film debut in 1929 in the Laurel and Hardy short *Berth Marks*. She soon left town, however, and married Edgar James, the heir to a North Carolina lumber fortune. In 1931 she returned to Hollywood, richer by $100,000 thanks to a Reno divorce and driving a Duesenberg sedan worth $18,000 (this at a time when a new Model-A Ford could be purchased for $260).

Like Chaplin, Paulette had known hard times, and she was evasive about her past. She claimed to have been born Pauline Marian Levy on June 3, 1911, in Whitestone, Queens, New York, but the date is uncertain, and she may have been born as early as 1905. Her father, a Jewish salesman named Joseph Levy or Levee, and her Roman Catholic mother, Alta Hatch, were divorced when Paulette was very young, and she attended Catholic schools in Michigan, the state of New York, and Caldwell, New Jersey—"Mother traveled around a lot," she vaguely explained years later. Eventually Alta and Paulette returned to Long Island, where for a time they were so poor that they did field work, harvesting potatoes. After a time Alta married (or by some accounts, became the mistress of) a Great Neck businessman named J. L. Goddard, whose brother arranged an audition for Paulette with Flo Ziegfeld. She was cast in the 1925 edition of the Ziegfeld Follies, playing the featured role of Peaches. Her part consisted of sitting in a swing, wearing a large picture hat, and holding a lapdog. "I could tap, but I was never given a chance. Ziegfeld used to say I was a great sitter. I sat, and I walked. I didn't mind. I was only fourteen, and I was paying for my lessons at Ned Wayburn's [dancing school]."[2]

Adding to the uncertainty about Paulette's age, there were people in Hollywood who felt sure they recognized her as the same young woman who for a time had been a "roper" for a professional card sharp, working the first-class lounges of ocean liners on the

Southampton to New York route. Paulette would pretend to be a naive young thing, striking up conversations with men and encouraging them to make large wagers.

Douglas Fairbanks Jr., who costarred with Paulette in the 1938 United Artists film *The Young in Heart*, once asked her if the rumor about her past was true, and she laughingly admitted that it was. "But," she insisted, the card sharp had been "a very nice man. He was the prince of gamblers. The Robin Hood of gamblers. He stole from the rich, and he gave to me."[3]

Like many wealthy men, Chaplin instinctively feared that women were out to fleece him. By some mystifying reverse logic, Paulette Goddard's bank account, even though acquired in Reno, reassured him that she was not simply after his money. She was also amusing, a compulsive talker, a good tennis player, and an avid sailor. Within weeks of their meeting, Charlie bought a fifty-five-foot yacht, the *Panacea*, and he and Paulette began taking weekend cruises to Catalina. Before long she had moved into Cove Way—soon to become known as 1085 Summit Drive as the result of a reassignment of addresses in fast-developing Beverly Hills. Much to Kono's consternation, Paulette brought along her Scandinavian maid and her pet dog, Puddles.

Chaplin bought out Paulette's contract with the Hal Roach studio, arranged for her to take acting lessons with Connie Collier, and sent her to dance and exercise classes to rid her of her Ziegfeld-girl walk. He also insisted that she let her hair return to its natural brunette coloring. She complied with a sigh. "Life was easy as a blonde," she later said. "I didn't have to think. I didn't have to talk. . . . [As a brunette] I had to learn to live all over again."[4]

But this was only the beginning. Paulette had started reading "in a bumpy way" before she met Charlie, hoping to fill the gaps in her formal education. She now began her intellectual makeover in earnest, with the help of a female professor of English literature from the University of Southern California who set up a reading program of classics, starting with *Beowulf*. She read up on art history, haunted the galleries, and began purchasing paintings—a Modigliani, a Dufy, and a "tiny" Renoir—the beginning of a collection eventually valued at more than three million dollars. Later she audited classes in world history, French, and Spanish at USC and

UCLA. And for a time she also studied abnormal psychology—"I needed it," she said later.[5]

Whatever led her to get involved with Charlie, Paulette became fond of him and took up the considerable challenge of trying to make him happy.

Winning over Kono proved impossible, but Paulette was more successful with his friends, taking an exercise class with Connie Collier and talking politics with Upton Sinclair and his wife, Mary Craig. She also made an effort to create a semblance of family life with Charles junior and Sydney Earle. Charlie had seen his sons only sporadically since his divorce, but soon they were spending weekends at Summit Drive. Trim and athletic in her shorts and sailor shirts, the bubbly Paulette was more like a big sister than a stepmother to the boys. She planned picnics, skating parties, and trips to Arrowhead Lake, and she bought them amusingly extravagant presents including a motorized go-cart and a pair of Bedlington terrier puppies.

Encouraged by Paulette, Charlie gradually began to make efforts to act like a typical father, organizing Christmas celebrations and putting on a tweed jacket on Sunday afternoons to take her and the boys on family outings. Though he hadn't driven in several years, since he crashed a brand-new Rolls-Royce roadster into a pole on Sunset Boulevard three blocks from the studio, he purchased a Ford sedan and took to the canyon roads. His inability to keep the car on the right side of the center line made these expeditions exciting for the children. Paulette, an excellent driver herself, sat in the front seat, smiling bravely and making jokes about their close encounters with oncoming traffic.

Unfortunately these efforts got under way even as Chaplin was once again in court with the boys' mother. Lita Chaplin's huge divorce settlement had evaporated in a few years thanks to extravagance, poor money management, and the collapse of the stock market. She became a singer, touring on the Keith vaudeville circuit as an opening act for Jack Benny, then took the children to France for a time. Chaplin had not bothered to try to see his sons, who were living on the French Riviera during his stay in Monte Carlo, but his interest in them was reawakened when Lita returned to the United States in the summer of 1932 to announce that she had signed a

$65,000 contract for her and the boys to appear in a movie called *The Little Teacher.* Chaplin had bitter memories of his youthful experiences on the music hall stage, and he instructed his attorney Loyd Wright to file suit to save his sons from "exploitation." Public opinion sided with him on this issue, and, considering the unhappy histories of so many child actors it would be hard to say in retrospect that he was wrong. Still, one suspects that he was motivated less by his concern for the children, which so far had been nonexistent, than horror at the prospect of three actors named Chaplin appearing in a film over which he had no control.

No sooner was the issue resolved than Chapliin filed another action, challenging Lita's administration of the boys' trust fund. He demanded and got an accounting of every penny she spent, down to their $2.50 haircuts. Next he decided that young Charles and Syd were subject to too much female influence (their mother and grandmother) and insisted on enrolling them in boarding school, specifically the Black Foxe Military Institute in Hollywood. The boys lived at school during the week but came home on weekends. He quipped to friends that he was sending his sons to Black Foxe so that they could learn to hate the military. In fact, when it came to education his ideas were highly conservative. Despite his bad memories of the regime at Hanwell, Chaplin chose strict schools for his children.

Young Charles and Syd benefited from some of these lawsuits, especially since Lita was forced to set aside 25 percent of their income as savings. On the whole, however, the disputes were handled badly. Chaplin had no perspective on his second marriage. He loathed Lita so intensely that when she showed up with his sons at Hannah's funeral in 1928, his aides had hurried him away before he could catch sight of her. Four years later he still couldn't bring himself to discuss the boys' futures with her, deputizing the task to the abrasive Loyd Wright, who preferred court battles to reasoned negotiation.

Lita had begun drinking again, and in time she began to believe that Charlie was persecuting her, setting spies to watch her house and even poisoning the air she breathed. In 1936, in the throes of a nervous breakdown, she blurted out the unhappy history of her marriage and how Charlie hadn't wanted either of his children to be born—information that, to her credit, she had kept from the children up to that time. Sydney Earle, who resembled his uncle in some ways, was a chubby, happy-go-lucky youth and seemed to take the revelations in stride. Charles junior, on the other hand, brooded. He idolized his father but was mystified by his alternating moods of gentleness and volcanic temper.[6]

Speculation that Charlie and Paulette were about to marry began as early as the fall of 1932, after a photographer snapped them saying good-bye as she prepared to board a TAT flight for the first leg of a journey to New York. In reality Charlie was more determined to avoid marriage than ever. He explained to friends that a Gypsy fortune teller had predicted years earlier that he would have three unhappy marriages, followed by a fourth and happy one. So far the prophecy was proving accurate, and the prospect of a third marital disaster was simply too much to contemplate, hence he had made up his mind never to marry again. He told Paulette that not marrying would work to her advantage; by keeping the press guessing about their relationship, they would generate curiosity and valuable publicity for her.[7]

Maybe so, but Hollywood still frowned on the open flouting of middle-class morals, and the game depended on encouraging speculation that they were secretly married. In April 1934 it was reported that Charlie and Paulette had been wed on board the *Panacea* by the skipper, David Anderson, a former Keystone Kop. A few months later Paulette began wearing a wedding ring, and Syd senior, in London, told reporters he had reason to think his brother and Paulette were husband and wife. Anyone who believed that the skipper of a private yacht could perform a legal wedding ceremony in California waters was welcome to buy this story.

Meanwhile Paulette was being groomed for a role in a nonexistent movie. As long as the IRS audit continued, Chaplin was reluctant to invest in the upgrading of the studio. He had signed a contract with the *Woman's Home Companion* for a fifty-thousand-word account of his world tour, and rather to the distress of the editors, he insisted on doing the work himself without a ghostwriter—a task that consumed eight months.

Reading these articles it is easy to understand why Chaplin wanted to write them. As an author he could exercise the self-control that had been sorely lacking at the time. On paper the anxious, manic-depressive Charles Chaplin who had lived through the world tour vanished, replaced by a worldly, whimsical raconteur. But writing was both a rewarding and a frustrating experience. Chaplin had a wry sense of humor, and he certainly knew a lot of big words, but he lacked the formal education—and probably the attention span—necessary to translate these elements into polished, grammatical prose. His secretary, Catherine Hunter, did some of the editing, but the pieces still required major reworking by an editor at the magazine.

Nevertheless an old childhood dream had been reawakened. "At the tender age of nine, even before I was aware of such mystifying things as split infinitives and dangling participles," he wrote Rob Wagner:

I was afflicted with that unpardonable ailment known as *cacoethes scribendi* [the writing itch]. In those days my literary aspirations arose from a desire to compete with the authors of those penny weekly "bloods" I had read. It seemed such an easy way to make a living—the sort of thing one could do as homework—in between times, as it were.[8]

Wagner urged Chaplin to contribute to his literary magazine, *Script*, and in early 1934, Chaplin submitted not a short story but an *outline* for a story he wished he could write—a "Platonic dialogue" between a great physician and a student over the relative importance to civilization of scientists and poets. One is not surprised to find the verdict going to the poets: "Their dreams are beyond dreams—their desires beyond desires. The scientists are merely dabblers in speed—the makers of gilded beds upon which we never rest—the promoters of luxuries which we seldom enjoy." In later issues of *Script*, there followed a lyric poem, "Nocturne," and a tongue-in-cheek ghost story, "Experiment in the Dark." The poem was a respectable amateur effort and the story quite amusing, but Wagner did some heavy editing on both before they were published.[9]

On the movie front Chaplin toyed with several ideas, even thinking about returning to Indonesia and doing a documentary on Balinese dance. Most of his efforts, however, went into reviving that old chestnut, the Napoleon and Josephine film. During the summer of 1933, he granted a rare interview to the *Manchester Guardian*, and he was so pleased with the interviewer, an aspiring young playwright named Alistair Cooke, that he invited him to return to Hollywood the following summer to develop the Napoleon script. Cooke in turn found himself fascinated by Chaplin—he would later recall, vividly, Chaplin's tiny hands and feet and his delicate, graceful movements, which made even ordinary tasks like eating sausages or rowing a boat into acts of celebration. Working for Chaplin was pleasant and none too taxing. Cooke was invited to come fishing for swordfish on the *Panacea*, and when the fish failed to bite, Chaplin entertained him with wicked imitations of Jean Harlow as a bride and a speech by the Prince of Wales.[10]

Simultaneously Chaplin was working with another assistant, the former vaudevillian Carter de Haven, on a story to which he gave the working title *The Masses*. As both Max Eastman and Rob Wagner later pointed out, Chaplin had been talking for years about making a satire on "the factory system." Back in 1921, stopping in Detroit on his return from his first world tour, he had visited a Ford assembly plant. Viewing the assembly line from a catwalk high above the factory floor, he was deeply impressed—or rather depressed—by the mechanical, repetitive nature of the work.

Chaplin never said specifically what motivated him to go back to the factory idea after so many years—indeed, this would become the subject of much controversy later on—however, his early story notes show that he started with a vision of the Little Fellow causing chaos on an assembly line: The film would open with a shot of a factory chimney belching smoke, a fiery blast furnace, and then the foremen at the "Electrical Metal Corporation" starting up a huge dynamo to signal the beginning of the workday. In his office the boss interrupts his reading of the comics to address the workers over closed-circuit television, exhorting them: "SPEED UP. WE ARE WAY BEHIND." All comply except Charlie, who is bothered by a pesky bee.

These notes would provide the basis for perhaps the best-remembered sequence in any Chaplin film. Developing a plot around them proved to be far more challenging. For a time Chaplin considered a story line involving rebellious workers:

Shot in factory, men pull machine apart.
Men could conspire to destroy the machine.
They put me to work for the purpose, but I am innocent of their plan.
A drama of communism and everybody getting two cars.[11]

Whatever this cryptic reference to "a drama of communism" meant, the days were long gone when Chaplin could casually introduce the theme of industrial sabotage as a device to move the plot along. In 1934, moreover, most workers were worried about survival, not regimentation and boredom.

Outside the studio, meanwhile, Chaplin was under pressure to choose sides in the political phenomenon that was polarizing California—Upton Sinclair's campaign for governor as the standard bearer of an independent socialist movement known as End Poverty in California, or EPIC. Sinclair's fourteen-point program called for a state tax of 50 percent on all incomes over fifty thousand dollars a year and equally heavy levies on businesses, large farms, and inheritances. The taxes were intended to pay for the most generous social welfare benefits offered by any state in the Union, and—as Sinclair frankly acknowledged—to tax the rich into extinction. There can be no doubt that Sinclair's utopian program would have bankrupted California in short order, but the voters were desperate for change, and the promise of universal prosperity, 100 percent financed out of the pockets of the rich, was alluring. If this was socialism, who could be against it?

No interest group in the state felt more betrayed by the EPIC program than did the movie industry. Although few of Sinclair's film projects made it to the screen, the studios had been generous to him over the years.

Irving Thalberg of MGM had paid twenty thousand dollars for the rights to Sinclair's Prohibition novel, *The Wet Parade*, and an additional ten-thousand-dollar consulting fee on a never-produced script, also authorized by Thalberg, had enabled Sinclair to buy a home in Beverly Hills. Sinclair had then turned around and accepted twenty thousand from the eccentric producer William J. Fox to write a book that exposed alleged dirty dealings by Fox's competitors and advocated nationalizing the movie industry. Fox commissioned the book in the spirit of extortion, inviting his business adversaries to pay him off in exchange for his promise that it would never be published. Sinclair learned of the scheme and released the book anyway.

Aside from being out of patience with Sinclair personally, studio executives were galvanized into action by the prospect of having a governor who advocated confiscating their businesses. The opposition to Sinclair was led by Louis B. Mayer, while Irving Thalberg personally supervised the production of an anti-Sinclair newsreel.

But Sinclair's campaign also caused dissension on the left. While many individual Communists were excited about the EPIC program, the party hierarchy denounced Sinclair as an enemy. Their reasoning was tortured, but what it came down to was that the Communist Party could not tolerate the success of a leftist movement that was not under its control. Moreover President Roosevelt had established diplomatic relations with the Soviet Union, and the party feared that the Sinclair candidacy would lead to a backlash, to the detriment of Roosevelt's 1936 reelection campaign.

Rob Wagner—and very likely Chaplin as well—had early on heard and encouraged Sinclair's plans. Wagner, indeed, designed the "golden bee" logo of the EPIC movement. But once it appeared that Sinclair stood a good chance of becoming the official Democratic candidate, they refused to endorse him. In a telegram to Sinclair dated December 4, 1933, Chaplin explained that he had thought it over and decided it would be a "mistake" to get involved in politics: AS IN THE PAST MY PRINCIPLE IS TO MAINTAIN A NON-PARTISAN ATTITUDE.[12]

Wagner for his part declared that *Script* would remain officially neutral. "As an editor I've decided I'm in a stronger position if I don't join parties or organizations," he wrote Sinclair:

> I've never said in Script I'm a Socialist, with the result that I can slip over Socialism. I'll be able to boost your candidacy better that way.
>
> I can also understand Charlie's position. He is essentially an entertainer. If politics get hot and he is publicly lined up, he'd lose half his audience. As it is now, his Red stuff leaks out, helps the cause, and doesn't crab his profession.

You must understand that politics *is* your profession, and you mustn't be impatient of us who are for you and are helping in our own way, which really is the stronger way so long as we are not professional politicians. Will Rogers is another. If he took the brand, *he'd* lose half his audience and with it his influence. Hope you understand. You know I'd tear my shirt for you within my métier.[13]

Political cowardice is usually a believable excuse, but not this time.

In letters to friends and to Sinclair's wife, Mary Craig, Wagner gave a variety of reasons for his change of heart, from his fear that a Sinclair endorsement would drive *Script* into bankruptcy to doubts about Sinclair's fitness for the job. Writing to Arthur Browne, one of *Script's* more conservative subscribers, Wagner confessed: "I love Uppie as a great artist and a friend, but I did not want him to run for office and—just between us—*I do not wish for his election.*"[14] In a phone conversation with Sinclair himself, Wagner said bluntly that he considered him a great propagandist but "a bum executive," which was true.

However, there was a more immediate reason for Wagner's change of heart. He and his wife, Florence, had been moving closer to the Communist Party for some time, and the party's opposition to Sinclair had caught Wagner flat-footed. Wagner was an organizer of the California Authors' League, a group whose members ran the gamut from Jesse Lasky Jr., Anita Loos, and Groucho Marx to Charlie Chaplin, Donald Ogden Stewart, and Lincoln Steffens. The league's secretary, Frank Scully, happened to be an enthusiastic Sinclair supporter, and he had sent out a letter on official league stationery that gave the impression that all these members, and more, were campaigning for Sinclair. Scully also took it upon himself to sign the letter in the name of the league's executive committee, made up of Dorothy Parker, Jim Tully, Morrie Ryskind, Lewis Browne, and Wagner. The letter upset almost everyone, but especially Communists like Parker and Stewart, who assumed that Wagner had approved of the letter and was deliberately misrepresenting them.

During the summer of 1934 Sinclair planned a major fundraising rally at Grauman's Chinese Theater. The highlight of the evening was to be a performance of a one-act play he had written called *Depression Island*, about three sailors marooned on a desert island who live in harmony and comfort until they begin to gamble for coconuts, introducing the evils of private property and inequality. (It seemed not to have occurred to Sinclair that his play also demonstrated that the "profit motive" was an innate part of human nature and would triumph even when there was nothing of real value to fight over.) At any rate Sinclair was proud of his play and he decided that Chaplin must be present to introduce it. "Everyone said it was preposterous to imagine him consenting," Sinclair recalled.[15]

All other considerations aside, Chaplin had never paid a dollar in taxes if he could think of a way to avoid it. How could he possibly support a candidate who wanted to impose a 50 percent state tax on wealthy individuals like himself? And yet he did. To the surprise of everyone, including Sinclair himself, Chaplin paid for the rental of the theater and appeared on stage at the rally, where he forgot his nervousness and delivered a rousing political speech. Perhaps Chaplin was reacting to the new and highly restrictive censorship code, recently imposed on Hollywood productions by Will Hays, an anti-Sinclair activist. Perhaps he was simply swept along by the excitement of EPIC's moment in history. In any event, Sinclair would recall, Charlie had an "uproarious" time that evening.

Sinclair, after cruising to a surprisingly easy victory in the Democratic primary, now appeared to have a decent chance of winning the general election, and he soon began invoking Chaplin's name in his campaign speeches. Studio moguls like Louis B. Mayer, Joe Schenck, and Jack Warner had warned that they would move their operations to Florida if Sinclair won. He dismissed these threats as "the biggest piece of bunk in this entire election. They couldn't move out even if they wanted to. Their investment is too great. Besides think of what those Florida mosquitoes would do to some of our film sirens." If the movie barons did try to leave, Sinclair added, he would simply seize the studios and put the state of California into the movie business: "I'll ask Charlie Chaplin to run that part of the show."

This may have been Sinclair's idea of humor, but the studio owners weren't laughing, and the press seized on his comments.

Arthur Brisbane, the influential Hearst columnist, observed in his October 23 column that since Chaplin could only manage to finish one film every five years, his appointment would not bode well for the future of American movies.

These adverse reactions, while hardly surprising to others, prompted Chaplin to hop back onto his seat on the political fence. He didn't disavow Sinclair's candidacy, but privately he made it clear that he didn't want his name used in EPIC campaign literature in the future. This took some doing, as EPIC activists kept turning up at the studio seeking interviews, endorsements, and contributions. Sinclair couldn't always control his followers, though at Mary Craig's urging he wrote to Paulette, giving her advance notice of one such approach.

Brief as it was, Chaplin's involvement in the Sinclair campaign seemed to shake him out of the inertia that had beset him ever since his return from Japan. On August 19 he invited Alistair Cooke up to Summit Drive and they began amusing themselves by playing piano duets. In the middle of a slightly risqué cabaret song called *Titine*, Chaplin turned to Cooke and said, "By the way, the Napoleon thing. It's a beautiful idea—for somebody else." The project was scuttled, as of that moment.

Chaplin nevertheless promised that he would stand as best man at Cooke's wedding, which was just five days away. On the appointed day, however, he failed to show up. Cooke called Summit Drive and was told by Kono that he and Paulette had gone to Lake Arrowhead, where he was laying final plans for his next movie. Cooke heard nothing from his errant best man until Chaplin called him up, in high spirits, and without a word of explanation or apology suggested that Cooke and his bride join him and Paulette for an evening at the Coconut Grove nightclub.

At first all was well. Chaplin was cheerful and talkative, and Paulette almost pathetically excited by the prospect of a night on the town. Suddenly, however, Chaplin took exception to some falsetto notes sung by the evening's headliner, tenor Gene Austin, and launched into a denunciation of "eunuch" singers, jazz, nightclubs, and Hollywood decadence in general.

"What are we going to do, stay home and write *theses?*" protested the frustrated Paulette.

"One night a year is enough of that rubbish," Charlie snapped.

The uncomfortable evening ended at Summit Drive, where Chaplin called for a pitcher of water to toast the newlyweds' happiness. Although Cooke knew that Chaplin had given up drinking and disapproved of others who drank, he couldn't help finding the choice of beverage a bit severe.[16]

At the studio Chaplin had given orders to move ahead with his antimachine story. On September 18 *Variety* trumpeted, CHAPLIN THRU WITH HIT AND MISS SKED, HAS SCRIPT—EVEN LOCATION. Construction of sets for his long-awaited "Production No. 5" had begun the previous day and Chaplin's associates were predicting that the movie would be finished by the end of the year. "In the past, he has never worked on schedule, preferring to obey his moods," *Variety* noted, but the rising cost of labor and of projected location shots on the San Pedro docks made a leisurely pace out of the question.

But *Variety* spoke too soon when it predicted that the movie—eventually renamed *Modern Times*—would be completed in four months. For one thing Chaplin could not make up his mind whether the film would be a talkie or not. In October he ordered the studio's open-air stage enclosed—a necessary step for sound photography. He and Paulette made sound tests and actually shot some scenes with dialogue. Then, for no obvious reason, the footage was scrapped, and the movie proceeded as a silent film. The human voice would be used on the separately recorded sound track, but very sparingly—in the beginning only the bosses speak, though the Tramp does find his voice in the end.

Two years of virtually round-the-clock coaching had undermined Paulette's natural self-confidence, and she was far from happy about Charlie's decision that she should play her role without makeup. The "gamin [*sic*]" was a barefoot urchin, first seen stealing bananas from the deck of a boat in San Pedro Harbor. Nevertheless, Hollywood leading ladies in the 1930s were expected to look glamorous regardless of the circumstances. When Paulette showed up for the first day's filming with her hair beautifully coiffed, he dumped a bucket of water over her head to get the look he wanted.

Seventeen-year-old Charlie Chaplin (*second row, fourth from left*)
with the company of Casey's Court Circus.
(*Wisconsin Center for Film and Theater Research*)

Tillie's Punctured Romance teamed Chaplin with two great comediennes, the
formidable Marie Dressler and lovely Mabel Normand. (*Wide World Photos*)

Chaplin in 1914. Mack Sennett was aghast to see how young he looked without his stage makeup. (*Wide World Photos*)

A fetching Charlie in the title role of *A Woman*, 1916. (*Wide World Photos*)

Charlie and Edna Purviance relax on the beach with comedian Eddie Foy (*left*) and friends. Roscoe "Fatty" Arbuckle is seated behind Foy. (*Wisconsin Center for Film and Theater Research*)

After a freak snowstorm in 1921, Chaplin's studio looked more like a Tudor village than ever. (*Wide World Photos*)

The proud studio owner in his new office. (*Wisconsin Center for Film and Theater Research*)

Chaplin's cameraman,
Rollie Totheroh.
(*National Archives and
Records Administration*)

Studio manager Alf Reeves.
(*National Archives and
Records Administration*)

Mildred Harris
became the first Mrs. Chaplin
at the age of seventeen.
(*Wisconsin Center for Film and Theater Research*)

Max Eastman.
(*Wide World Photos*)

Florence Deshon.
(*Lilly Library*)

Charlie shaves a nervous Albert Austin. This rare photo is from a sequence shot for *Sunnyside* but cut from the final print. (*National Archives and Records Administration*)

The Tramp and "the Kid,"
Jackie Coogan. (*Wide World Photos*)

Pola Negri and her "Jazz boy, Sharlie," in Berlin, 1921. (*Wide World Photos*)

In *The Pilgrim* Chaplin played an escaped convict who poses as a minister. (*Wide World Photos*)

Charlie clowns with Mary Pickford and Doug Fairbanks on the set of one of Mary's movies. (*Wisconsin Center for Film and Theater Research*)

In 1923 Charlie, Doug, and friends take time out from a doubles match on the court at the Pickford-Fairbanks Studio to show off their gymnastics skills. Spanish star Manuel Alonzo is at center. At the base of the pyramid (*right*) is the American tennis champion "Big Bill" Tilden, who became a lifelong friend of Charlie's. (*Wisconsin Center for Film and Theater Research*)

Charlie and Mack Swain, in training for the rigors of filming *The Gold Rush*. (*Wisconsin Center for Film and Theater Research*)

When Lita Grey was chosen as the leading lady of *The Gold Rush,* the press was invited to witness the signing of her contract. Lita was fifteen, though the studio claimed she was four years older. In November 1924 she and Charlie were married, and her role was taken over by Georgia Hale. (*Wide World Photos*)

The Chaplin brothers in costume, 1925. Syd was a hit in *Charley's Aunt.* (*Wide World Photos*)

Hannah Chaplin and son Charlie in 1928, shortly
before Hannah's death. (*Wide World Photos*)

Lita Chaplin in 1932 with Charles Jr., seven, and Sydney Earle, six.
(*Wide World Photos*)

The individual caught in the gears in this scene from *Modern Times* is Chester Conklin, who first worked with Chaplin at the Keystone Studio in 1915. (*Wide World Photos*)

Chaplin and Paulette Goddard on board the SS *Coolidge* on June 3, 1936, the last day of their Pacific cruise. (*Wide World Photos*)

Catalina, 1937. Charlie and
Paulette on Joe Schenck's yacht,
Invader, with Norma Talmadge
and friend, Franklin Ardell.
(*Wisconsin Center for Film and
Theater Research*)

Brother Syd in 1937.
(*Wide World Photos*)

Jack Oakie had a grand time
playing Benzino Napaloni to
Charlie's Adenoid Hynkel.
At right is Henry Daniell as
Hynkel's aide, Garbitsch.
(*Wide World Photos*)

Oona O'Neill with Stork Club press
agent Murray Lewis, who promoted her
as 1942's "Deb of the Year." Her father
was furious. (*Wide World Photos*)

Joan Barry in her hotel
room, hours after she
learned that Charlie and
Oona had eloped to
Carpinteria, California.
(*Wide World Photos*)

Chaplin and Martha Raye
in *Monsieur Verdoux*.
(*Wide World Photos*)

Three days after *Verdoux*'s premiere,
Chaplin faced hostile questions at a press
conference in the ballroom of New York
City's Hotel Gotham. (*Wide World Photos*)

Charles Jr. and Charlie in a scene
from *Limelight*. (*Wide World Photos*)

On vacation at Saint Jean on the French Riviera, 1957. LEFT TO RIGHT:
Oona, Geraldine, Charlie, Eugene, Michael, Victoria, and Josephine.

Chaplin's family turns out for the premiere of *A Countess from Hong Kong*,
his last film. In the back row are Josephine, seventeen; son Syd; Victoria,
fourteen; Syd's wife, Noelle Adam; Michael's wife, Patrice; Oona (*partially
hidden*); Michael; Eugene; and Geraldine. Jane, nine, and Annette, seven,
are in the foreground with their father. Christopher, five, did not attend.
(*Both photos courtesy Wide World Photos*)

Much later Paulette would acknowledge that Charlie had seen a quality in her that he was able to use very effectively. But the waif was not the role she wanted to play, on the screen or in life. Even as their interaction developed nicely before the cameras—becoming less whimsical and more adult than the Tramp's previous love interests—the off-screen relationship was faltering.

By late spring 1935 Chaplin was putting in sixteen- and eighteen-hour workdays, sleeping on a cot at the studio. Although moviemaking elsewhere had become highly specialized, he still resisted delegating tasks to others. He even produced the sound effects, blowing bubbles to simulate a grumbling stomach, and so on. The final scenes weren't completed until the end of August, and there remained the task of composing and recording the sound track.

Eddie Powell, who was the chief assistant to Alfred Newman, the musical director of UA's corporate studio, recommended twenty-three-year-old David Raksin, already a veteran composer who had worked for Harms and Chappell, arrangers of the scores of most Broadway musicals of the period, and collaborated successfully with Oscar Levant—the noted pianist, composer, and wit—and others. Raksin was thrilled to be working with the great Charlie Chaplin but also "arrogant" enough to give his frank opinion about Chaplin's musical ideas:

I thought that what he was doing was not good enough for the picture, because I wanted it to be more advanced, more modern. . . . .But I really figured, this man is the greatest movie person alive, and his music should be the greatest. And we should do something elaborate and it should be of symphonic dimension. It would have great thematic material. And to work with a tune that went da da da da da da da dum, that's making almost a reel of music out of that little five or six notes.[17]

Unused to such candor, Chaplin fired Raksin at the end of his first week, then hired him back after Newman prevailed on Alf Reeves to arrange a meeting at which Raksin could state his case. Face to face with Chaplin, Raksin swallowed hard and tried to explain that he just wanted the film to have the score it deserved: "If you're looking for an amanuensis, you can buy one for nothing. If you're looking for another hanger on or an acolyte, you already have them by the dozens."[18]

Chaplin listened thoughtfully and agreed to try again, and from that time on the collaboration became fun. Chaplin would arrive at the studio every morning at about ten, usually with ideas for melodies, which he would pick out on the piano for Raksin to develop. Though not a professional musician, Chaplin was a "magpie," Raksin recalled. He knew musical styles and the tonal qualities of individual instruments, and he understood when it was time to move the melody into another register. Instead of using timing sheets, the usual method of scoring a movie, he and Raksin worked with a Goldberg Moviola (a projector that runs film backward as well as forward), coordinating their ideas directly with the action, Chaplin calling for "a bit of Gershwin" here and a "bit of Puccini" there.

Their work was punctuated by spats but also by playfulness. Chaplin did snatches of comedy and talked excitedly about making a picture about Napoleon, recalled Raksin, who had no idea that he was listening to variations on an idea Chaplin had been kicking around for almost two decades: "It was going to be one of those crazy serio-comedies. And I was going to be Henri Marie Beyle, who is Stendhal, the writer." Also, he remembered, Chaplin "was going to make a picture about the Haymarket riots in Chicago, and about all those guys who were victimized, accused, many people believe unjustly. And I was going to play one of the guys who were in jail.[19]

By the end of their work together, Chaplin was treating Raksin almost like a son, inviting him to spend weekends on his yacht and even lending him his chauffeur-driven Cadillac (the Locomobile's replacement) so he could impress a certain actress whom he happened to be dating.

The recollections of David Raksin and Alistair Cooke contradict the impressions of so many others who saw Chaplin's long hours at the studio, his schedule overruns, and his inability to delegate as signs that he was depressed and bogged down in a project he could not bring himself to finish. No doubt there was an element of truth in this view, but on any given day Chaplin often appeared to be having a grand time. In an industry in which the brightest talents—from major stars like Garbo and Cagney to underappreciated screenwriters—felt stifled by the lockstep studio system, Chaplin had beaten the odds. He was the master of his own operation, with complete artistic freedom to work on whatever he pleased, and at his own pace. It would be a mistake to think that he never enjoyed himself.

Unfortunately the freedom was his alone. It wasn't always possible to find talented assistants like Cooke and Raksin, who were willing to accommodate themselves to his eccentricities for the sake of the experience of working with the great Charlie Chaplin, and of course, these fortunate finds had no intention of remaining with the studio for long. In an era when the Writers' Guild and other unions increasingly frowned on producers arrogating creative credits to themselves, Chaplin still routinely did so. Doubtless David Raksin should have been credited as a co-composer of the musical score of *Modern Times,* but he was billed only as the music's co-arranger, with Eddie Powell. As for the script, Carter de Haven's input was nowhere mentioned; he would receive credit only as an assistant director.

Nor was everyone so charmed by Chaplin's leisurely working methods as Raksin. The completed score of *Modern Times* was to be recorded by the UA studio orchestra under the direction of Alfred Newman, a consummate professional and probably the most respected—and the busiest—musical director in Hollywood.

Chaplin had been dissatisfied with the orchestral work on *City Lights.* This time he was bent on perfection and by no means willing to let Newman do his job as he saw fit. He sat in on all the recording sessions, interrupting often, ordering retakes, and overruling Newman's instructions to the orchestra. Chaplin always liked being around musicians, listening to their shoptalk and gossip, and one suspects that he was in no hurry to see the recording sessions end. One day he even showed up with his current house guest, H. G. Wells. As the days rolled on, however, Newman's patience was exhausted, and Chaplin became testy. He kept the musicians working until the small hours of the morning, expressing his disapproval of everything he heard. During one especially tense all-night session, he accused Newman of being lazy, and the conductor stomped out, never to work with Chaplin again. Eddie Powell took over the baton for the final sessions.

✤   ✤   ✤

In March 1935, while Chaplin was engrossed in his work on *Modern Times*, Egon Kisch's Comintern superior Otto Katz arrived in Hollywood, posing as an antifascist resistance fighter named Rudolph Breda. Katz's mission was to help American Communist Party activists set up front groups which would broaden the Communists' influence in the film industry. As Stephen Koch points out in his book *Double Lives*, the Comintern's motives had almost nothing to do with inserting subversive messages into American movies. Katz's goals were to raise funds, find work for Communist émigrés arriving from Germany, and, as Koch puts it, "Stalinize the American glamour culture."[20] With the assistance of Donald Ogden Stewart and Dorothy Parker, Katz established the Hollywood Anti-Fascist League, among whose earliest active members were Charlie Chaplin and Paulette Goddard.

The Anti-Fascist League and other Popular Front groups had tremendous appeal, drawing support from many who were by no means Communists, and in some cases not even left-wingers. Hitler was evil. What could be wrong with joining with Communists to oppose him?

But there *was* something wrong with it. The Communists saw fascism as the end stage of capitalism. In their view of things, the United States and Britain were just a few steps behind Germany on the road to perdition. The antidote to fascism was not democracy but communism. To an amazing degree they succeeded in promoting this outlook within the Popular Front. Anti-American rhetoric, much of it casual and thoughtless, some not so casual, became pervasive. At the same time the Soviet Union was glorified. An unpublished manuscript from Rob Wagner's files, circa 1937, gives his romanticized view of the history of the USSR since 1917: "Almost overnight, 150 million farmers found themselves in control of the biggest country in the world. For the past ten years, Russia has disclaimed world revolution asking only to be left along to work out her problems." Wagner extolled the Soviets' success in building libraries, elementary schools, and hospitals but said not a word about the purges, whose victims had numbered in the millions.[21]

Chaplin, of course, had been enthusiastically pro-Communist during the early twenties, lecturing friends—including, once, a bemused Buster Keaton—about the virtues of communism. By the end of the decade, however, he had found Sovkino boss L. I. Monosson too "conservative" for his tastes, an indication that he may have been influenced by the Trotskyist views of Max Eastman, who returned to the United States in 1927 convinced that Stalin had betrayed the goal of world revolution. Around the time of the mysterious Herr Breda's visit to Los Angeles, there was another shift: Chaplin's disaffection with the Soviet Union—and theirs with him—evaporated. Viscerally and personally offended by the Nazis' racial theories, Chaplin had bought Breda's argument that the Communists were the only true anti-Nazi force in Europe, and the only hope of defeating Hitler.

Also around the time of Breda's visit, someone connected with Chaplin's studio leaked word to the press that the working title of "Production No. 5" was *The Masses*, provoking intense speculation in the trade. Chaplin issued a statement denying the rumor, though of course it happened to be true.

Fear—or, in some quarters, hope—that Chaplin was making a Communist propaganda film intensified in July, when it became known that he had screened his work in progress for members of a visiting Russian trade delegation, the Soviet Cinema Commission, including Boris Shumiatski, the head of the Soviet film industry. Following his return to Moscow, Shumiatski wrote an article in *Pravda*, relating how he had persuaded Chaplin to change the ending of the movie.

The original conclusion of "Production No. 5," as summarized by Shumiatski, called for Charlie and the "gamin" to be separated, only to meet again some time in the future in the aftermath of a world war. The "gamin" has become a Red Cross nurse, finding fulfillment in helping others, and "can no longer return to Charlie and the once 'romantic' world of the hobo and the slum. . . . He, an eternal failure, accepts this betrayal with resignation and withdraws to his old joyless life, a shrunken, bent and solitary man."

According to Shumiataski, the Soviet visitors protested that this was too "fatalistic. . . . We argued with Chaplin, and for a long time he would not yield. But at our departure, he shook hands firmly, and said: 'I am very pleased we met. But this meeting will cost me many weeks of labor on my film.'"

Shumiatski went on to take credit for talking Chaplin into a new ending, in which, as he put it, Charlie and the gamin "decided to work and fight together against the 'machine of time,' a euphemism for capitalist society." This change, he added in a burst of Marxist pride, "must be understood, not as a mere substitution of one scene for another. It must be taken as a stage in the ideological growth of a remarkable artist."²²

A translation of Shumiatski's article appeared in the September edition of the Communist organ, *The New Masses*. In November, three months before "Production No. 5," now called *Modern Times*, was scheduled to open, the story was picked up by the *New York Times*, spreading apprehension among theater owners across the country.

Terry Ramsaye, who had worked with Chaplin during his years with Mutual, had since become a successful journalist as well as an authority on the early history of American motion pictures. After the *Times* story appeared, Ramsaye decided to refute Shumiatski's claims in the pages of the journal he edited, *Motion Picture Herald,* a trade organ read mainly by distributors and theater managers, and he sought out Chaplin at the UA recording studio, hoping for a comment. Chaplin's quarrel with Alfred Newman was well advanced at this point, and he was nursing a broken thumb, which he had caught in a car door, a painful injury that left him more irritable than ever.

Although Chaplin had earlier agreed to be interviewed, he now refused to comment on the record, and Ramsaye was forced to make do with a statement from Alf Reeves, who said: "The Russian story reads deep, terrible social meaning into sequences that Mr. Chaplin considers funny. I can assure you that this picture is intended as entertainment."²³

Reeves was right. *Modern Times* was not a Communist propaganda film, and the final title card, "Buck up—never say die. We'll get along," was a long way from a Marxist battle cry. Nevertheless Ramsaye's article was hardly reassuring. Although his piece was published under the headline CHAPLIN RIDICULES REDS' CLAIM, the fact was that Chaplin personally had not ridiculed, or even denied, Shumiatski's claims. Ramsaye did his best to explain away Chaplin's silence by saying that he was bound by his own self-imposed policy of secrecy, a lame excuse indeed.

Chaplin was well known for his refusal to screen rushes of his work for UA executives, much less representatives of the producers' association or government officials. That he had solicited advance criticism from a delegation of Communist bureaucrats said volumes. And in fact the gist of Shumiatski's article was true. Chaplin had planned an ending similar to the one he described, against the advice of his aides. He changed his mind abruptly in July 1935, at the time of the Soviet delegation's visit.

Its opening delayed by the long postproduction process, *Modern Times* premiered in New York on February 5 at the Rivoli Theater to mixed reviews. To a degree the critics' reservations were justified. Sloppiness had crept into Chaplin's work over the years—there was even a title card announcing DAWN, a cliché the Chaplin of old would have sneered at. Many reviewers found that the plot lacked direction—one critic called it a succession of two-reelers strung together—and they essentially agreed with Upton Sinclair, who reported to Rob Wagner: "Went to see Charlie's picture last night. The part about the factory was very interesting and charming, but the rest just repeats Charlie's old material."

Less understandably, the reviewers seemed to be buffaloed by the blend of slapstick and social satire. They expected at once too much and too little, and perhaps were nervous about praising a film billed by the *New Masses* and the *Daily Worker* as having been vetted by the head of the Soviet film industry. *Life* magazine's Don Herold assured readers that the movie was "simply a succession of swell gags with balletic overtones." On the other hand he complained about the opening montage, an Eisenstein parody that cross-cut images of workers pouring out of the subway and a herd of sheep. "The observation that people are sheep is not new or deep," wrote Herold.[24] (One might point out that the observation that some people are pigs wasn't new either, but that didn't make *Animal Farm* a superficial book.)

Communist critics, meanwhile, had their own dilemma. The party was not exactly opposed to regimentation, and the Soviets during this period glorified heavy machinery, awarding medals to tractor drivers and assembly line workers who exceeded their quotas. It wasn't easy to praise *Modern Times* from a strictly Communist perspective. Fortunately, none other than the head of the Soviet film industry had shown the way, explaining that the movie was to be seen as a stage in Chaplin's "ideological growth." Known and loved around the world as the personification of the Little Fellow, the forgotten man, Chaplin was of such potential value to the party that he would be allowed unusual latitude when it came to deviations from ideological correctness. Following this lead, Rob Wagner's friend Kyle Crichton waxed enthusiastic about *Modern Times* in the *New Masses*, calling it a "historical event" that such a film could emerge from Hollywood. Crichton and others noted that, after all, it was a capitalist factory that had driven the Little Fellow mad.

Privately the Communists and their allies still found the message disturbing. Louis Goldblatt, a CIO organizer who met Charlie over lunch a few years after the picture's release, tried patiently to explain to him why *Modern Times* was misguided and essentially "Luddite." Machines were not the enemy, Goldblatt argued. In fact they were necessary to raise the living standards of the working class. "Why," he added, clinching the argument, "if it weren't for the machine age, the movie camera would never have been invented."

"Good," Chaplin said, interrupting him. "I wish it hadn't."[25]

Goldblatt was too stunned to reply.

Perhaps because they were intent on seeing it as social satire, the critics failed to notice that *Modern Times* was the most autobiographical of all Chaplin's films:

> *In the opening sequence Charlie is employed as a "nut tightener" on an assembly line. Unable to keep up the pace of work, he develops a few loose nuts himself and suffers a nervous breakdown.*

In life Chaplin complained of the assembly-line approach to film production and, indeed, suffered nervous breakdowns trying to keep up.

> *Charlie is chosen at random as a guinea pig to test the Bellows Feeding Machine, whose robot arm stuffs food into his mouth.*

Chaplin became immensely famous through luck and the vagaries of audience taste, and was fed more money and adulation than he could swallow.

After a stint in a mental hospital, Charlie is released to find the depression in full swing. Walking down the street, he picks up a red flag that has fallen off the back of a flatbed truck. Suddenly a parade of demonstrators comes around the corner and falls into step behind him. The police mistake Charlie for the leader of the Communists.

Chaplin recovered from his mental breakdown of 1927 only to find his career threatened by the advent of the talkies and the depression. Through the circumstances of his birth, he identified with the proletariat, only to find himself mistaken for a leader.

Thrown into jail, Charlie is comfortable and content. After his release he is unable to hold a job and tries to get back into jail by strolling into a cafeteria and treating himself to an enormous meal he has no money to pay for.

Chaplin was fascinated by prisons, and very likely it had occurred to him, or perhaps been pointed out to him by Doctor Reynolds, that he felt an unconscious desire to return to the secure, structured routine of the Hanwell orphanage. Nevertheless, even when he defrauded the IRS, he literally couldn't get himself arrested.

Charlie meets a barefoot street urchin (Paulette). Running from the police, they find themselves in front of a cozy tract house. CAN YOU IMAGINE US IN A LITTLE HOME LIKE THAT? he asks. The look on Paulette's face tells us that she can, and Charlie declares: I'LL DO IT. WE'LL GET A HOME EVEN IF I HAVE TO WORK FOR IT.

Lacking confidence in his masculine appeal, Chaplin believed that the only way he could hold on to the love of a woman was through his ability to make her a movie star. Though he had no desire to keep on working, he felt that he must continue to make movies as vehicles for her.

Charlie gets a job as night watchman in a department store. He sneaks Paulette into the store for the night and entertains her by strapping on roller skates in the toy department. On the main sales floor, burglars are looting the store of merchandise. Charlie discovers them in the liquor department, where they shoot up a cask of rum; he accidentally gets drunk.

This sequence, filled with allusions to films of the Essanay and Mutual periods, offers a condensed resume of his career in slapstick.

Charlie and Paulette find jobs in a café To his horror, Charlie learns that besides waiting tables he is expected to entertain the customers by singing. Paulette writes the lyrics of a naughty song on his shirt cuff but the cuff flies off his wrist while the orchestra is playing his intro. Encouraged by Paulette, who mouths the advice NEVER MIND THE WORDS, he mimes an encounter between a fat old banker and a young lady of easy virtue, while improvising lyrics in a nonexistent language:

> *Se bella piu satore, je notre so catore,*
> *Je notre qui cavore, je la qu', la qui, le quai!*
> *Le spinash or le busho, cigaretto toto bello,*
> *Ce rakish spagoletto, se la tu, la tu, la tua. . . .*

The patrons applaud Charlie's song, but soon the police arrive in search of Paulette, who is underage. She and Charlie flee.

Chaplin, "hired" as a pantomime artist, suddenly discovers that with the advent of the talkies he is expected to sing for his supper. The only song he knows is "naughty"—Communist—so he sings it in a private language of his own.

For that matter the story of Charlie and the "gamin" could also be seen as an allegory of the fate of the Gypsies, who find it ever harder to survive in a world dominated by big factories, big government, and disappearing open spaces. If the Tramp is a Gypsy, this explains, for example, why the police always suspect him first. In the café he is applauded by patrons who enjoy his music even though they don't speak his language.

It would be hard to say how much of this was consciously in Chaplin's mind, though he was certainly aware of drawing on his life history in his movies—"Everything is autobiographical," he once said. Pantomime, however, allowed him to create simple situations open to multiple interpretations. One can appreciate Chaplin's satirical view of the regimentation of modern life without necessarily sharing his hatred and suspicion of all machines. For that matter the Communists could see the movie as anticapitalist, and the mainstream reviewers like Don Herold as a laugh fest with no particular social bias.

But the Little Fellow's decision to abandon his silence had marked a turning point. Words were much less ambiguous than gestures and expressions. In the future Chaplin's character would be forced to speak up, and in so doing to define himself and his message at the risk of alienating one segment of his audience or another.

Chaplin saw the trouble coming. Discussing the subject of talking pictures with Rob Wagner, who had been urging him to make the switch since 1928, he once protested: "But what would I say?" Chaplin's fear was not that he would say too little, as Wagner assumed, but that he might say too much.

15

The Great Dictator

Five days after *Modern Times* opened in Los Angeles, Charlie and Paulette departed on the SS *Coolidge* for a vacation in Hawaii. They were accompanied by Paulette's mother, Alta Hatch Goddard, and Frank Yonamori, Chaplin's new valet. After eighteen years, Toraichi Kono had left Chaplin's service, unable to adjust to taking orders from Paulette. Chaplin found Kono a job with United Artists' branch office in Japan; even so he departed under a cloud of bitterness. Chaplin, it developed, had not named Kono and his wife as heirs to one third of his property after all. Kono had served for almost two decades in the expectation of an inheritance that his family would never—and was never slated to—receive.

When their ship docked in Honolulu, Charlie pointed out some shipping crates on the pier labeled for Hong Kong and suggested to Paulette that they change their plans and sail on to China—it would be a great adventure. Paulette protested. She hadn't packed for such a long voyage! What would she wear? What would her mother wear? But Charlie was insistent. Paulette and her mother made a quick foray into downtown Honolulu to shop for travel wardrobes, while he drafted a cable to Alf Reeves, ordering him to close up the studio.

The Asian journey lasted four months, taking in Shanghai, Canton, Hong Kong, Saigon, and the Philippines. This time, Charlie refused official invitations and avoided the press. On shipboard he stayed cooped up in his cabin, emerging occasionally to take walks on deck, looking disheveled and unshaven. Jean Cocteau happened to be a passenger on the same ship, and he noticed that Charlie had a habit of ducking into passageways to avoid chance encounters. When they did meet, Paulette, by now quite fluent in French, did most of the translating. But once, when she had stepped away for a second, Charlie nodded toward her, and Cocteau caught the words, "and then I feel such pity." Cocteau was puzzled. The beautifully coifed and manicured Paulette was like a "little lioness with her mane and superb claws." It was difficult to imagine that there was anything pitiable about her.

Charlie, however, knew what he was talking about. To begin with, Paulette had been tricked into taking their long vacation. As the files of the U.S. Immigration and Naturalization Service (INS) make clear, Chaplin's sudden impulse in Honolulu was a ruse. On February 5, before leaving LA, he had applied to the San Francisco office of the INS for a reentry permit stating that he intended to visit China. He had good cause not to discuss the plan in advance with Paulette, who, after four years in professional limbo, was receiving excellent notices for her performance in *Modern Times*. This was hardly the moment for an ambitious actress who was not getting any younger to depart on an extended sea voyage.

Soon after their return to Beverly Hills in early June 1936, Charlie and Paulette took his sons aside and confided that they had been secretly married in China by the captain of their ship. Charles junior remembered being told the ceremony was held in Hong Kong. Paulette's attorney later said it took place in Canton in June. But she and Chaplin weren't in Canton in June, having reached Los Angeles by the third of the month. Undoubtedly this wedding was another fairy tale. Paulette had made up her mind that she was going to seek roles at other studios, and she needed a story to pacify nervous producers.

Paulette had done her best to make Charlie happy. As Syd senior said of his brother, "He's a rather morose character, and her cheerfulness has helped him out a lot."[1] After four years, however, Paulette's good cheer was wearing thin. Being tricked into the Far East tour was the final insult, and by late 1936, if not before, she had begun seeing other men. Some of her sexual exploits were so indiscreet, and so unlikely, that they can only have been undertaken in an attempt to provoke Charlie's jealousy. The legendary story that Paulette was seen giving Ernst Lubitsch a blowjob in a fashionable Hollywood restaurant is apparently true.[2]

Paulette's most serious affair began in early 1937 at a party at the home of actor Edward G. Robinson, when she was introduced to George Gershwin. Unfortunately the thirty-seven-year-old composer had begun to suffer from debilitating headaches and episodes of poor coordination, symptoms his brother and sister-in-law dismissed as neurotic. Gershwin consulted a psychiatrist, who blamed his complaints on guilt over his cuckolding of Chaplin, whom he knew socially. Gershwin's family detested Paulette, and as his condition deteriorated they kept her from seeing him. When he died on July 11, days after surgeons diagnosed a malignant brain tumor, she was not invited to the funeral. Charlie was, however, and he traveled to New York to attend.

Although he appeared resigned to Paulette having lovers, Chaplin was far from ready to give her her freedom, and he countered the temptations of other men by holding out the promise that he was writing another movie as a starring vehicle for her. On the return voyage from China he had begun working on a script he called *White Russians of Shanghai* or at times *The Countess from Shanghai,* a romantic comedy about a White Russian nightclub singer stranded in China without a passport. The heroine somewhat resembled Skaya, the singer he had met in Paris in 1921, and owed a bit to May Reeves as well. Chaplin also purchased the rights to a Regency period romance and hired a writer named Major Bodley to do a treatment. Either of these stories would have been tailor-made for Paulette, who longed for a chance to wear feminine clothes and display her flair for light comedy. Whether they suited Chaplin's abilities as a director was another matter.

On Christmas Eve 1936, Chaplin's old friend Konrad Bercovici arrived in Los Angeles with his wife and teenage daughter Mirel. Bercovici had spent much of the past eight years traveling in Europe as a writer for *Collier's, Harper's Monthly,* and other magazines, during which time he had interviewed Hitler, Goebbels, and other high-ranking Nazis. More recently, he had been crisscrossing the United States, living in a motor home while lecturing to colleges and clubs about the evils of fascism. As a result, he had been beaten up on a New York street by sympathizers of the Romanian Iron Guards, suffering injuries that kept him hospitalized for months.

From the Communist point of view, however, Bercovici was the wrong kind of antifascist. In his lectures, he said that the Third Reich and the Soviet Union were two sides of the coin of totalitarianism, and he denounced the Stalinist purges along with the Nazi persecution of Jews and Gypsies. So hated was Bercovici by the Communists that on at least one occasion they, too, set up him up for a beating. Booked for a lecture in a remote town in the mountains of northern California, Bercovici found the hall packed with hostile local toughs. Luckily he sensed trouble quickly and managed to escape without injury.

During his lecture tour Bercovici had also been writing a magazine series on the nomadic lives of trailer park residents. His agent, Zeppo Marx, thought he could sell the movie rights, and Bercovici had come to LA to pitch the idea to the studios. After running into Henry Bergman on the street, he got a phone call from Charlie, who took him to lunch and then up to his house to show off his newly resurfaced tennis court. When evening came Charlie took the whole family to dinner at the Old Sweden restaurant.

Later in the week Bercovici returned to Summit Drive to have dinner with Charlie, Paulette, and Charlie's good friend, director King Vidor. After Vidor left, Charlie took Bercovici into his study and asked how long he planned to say in town. That all depended on whether he got some magazine assignments he was hoping for, Bercovici replied.

"Well, that is picking up a few thousand dollars here and a few thousand dollars there," Charlie told him. "Let's do something together that will be really worthwhile. I am sick and tired of pictures about the little man. I want to do something big."[3]

Chaplin explained that he was resigned to making his next film as a talkie and realized that he needed help with script development. He asked what kind of royalties Bercovici got on his books, and when Bercovici said normally it was 15 percent, he proposed that they collaborate on a screenplay. If it was produced and made money, Bercovici would get 15 percent of the profits.

Scanning his library shelves, Chaplin located a book about the

Haymarket riots. This cause célèbre of the Left began during a rally of workers locked out of their jobs at the Chicago plant of the McCormick Harvester Company, when a young anarchist named Louis Lingg threw a bomb into the midst of a group of policemen. Lingg was eventually convicted of murder, as were six other anarchists, indicted on the grounds that their rhetoric had incited Lingg to terrorism.

Chaplin had been thinking about Lingg ever since he learned that he had lived in a rented room above a toy shop. The story he had in mind—"not too propagandistic"—would contrast the mind of the anarchist bomb maker in his garret with that of the toy maker who devotes his life to creating totally useless but entertaining toys. The idea was filled with possibilities—most of them, one suspects, unlikely to be realized in a movie made with the imprimatur of the MPPDA production code.

Although the book Bercovici was given was nonfiction, he realized that the subject had already been tackled by Frank Harris in his novel *The Bomb*. During the course of the year to come, Bercovici drew on *The Bomb* as well as his own research to write four drafts of a screenplay called *In Old Chicago*. After the fourth and final version was delivered, Bercovici recalled, Charlie told him, "We licked it. We are going to do it, but not now because I am still upset about my affairs with United Artists."

The latest round of warfare among the UA partners centered on a bid by Sam Goldwyn to take over the management by having his candidate, Maurice Silverstone, appointed chief executive officer. Goldwyn now owned one-fifth of the company, and his pictures had become its financial mainstay. Dealing with partners who were semiretired and indifferent to modern business practices so frustrated Goldwyn that at one board meeting he denounced Mary Pickford, Doug Fairbanks, and his old friend Charlie as "parasites." Subsequent meetings also degenerated into screaming matches, and Joe Schenck wrote to Mary Pickford, urging her and Douglas to find some grounds for compromise with Goldwyn. "The reason I don't mention Charlie," Schenck added,

is not because I disregard him but simply because I know Charlie and I know how little interest he takes in the company. Furthermore, I know how bitter Charlie can get to be and he wouldn't hesitate to destroy the company rather than do something constructive that may be of some benefit to Sam, whom at the present time he despises.[4]

Though supposedly uninterested in company affairs, Chaplin managed to get his own candidate for CEO elected in Silverstone's place. The final blow to Goldwyn's takevoer hopes was dealt by Mary Pickford, who appealed over his head to Mrs. Goldwyn.

Meanwhile Bercovici had spent the better part of ten months on the *In Old Chicago* project, and his wife, Naomi, was losing patience. Chaplin liked to summon Bercovici to his house for marathon work sessions, and the conversation inevitably got sidetracked into other areas. He would ply his old friend with questions about the European situation until Bercovici came home drained, "more than from any woman," as his daughter put it.

Paulette, meanwhile, was working off her excess energy by supervising the redecoration of Summit Drive. According to Mirel Bercovici, the job was long overdue. She recalls a card table whose green baize surface had been repaired with thumbtacks as typical of the general state of affairs.

With *Old Chicago* on the shelf, Chaplin suggested that Bercovici do an adaptation of "Tinka," one of the "Gypsy tales" from his book *Murdo*, which he felt would be an ideal vehicle for Paulette. "Tinka" was based on a folk tale Bercovici claimed to have heard during his childhood in Romania. Over their parents' objections, a boy and girl from feuding Gypsy clans fall in love. They meet secretly in the forest at night, the boy summoning his sweetheart to their special meeting place by imitating the call of a wolf. Unknown to the boy, his parents have arranged for him to marry another girl. He does his duty and submits to the ceremony. But at the height of the wedding festivities he hears a real wolf howling in the forest, and his heart fills with dread at the knowledge that his sweetheart will mistake the beast's summons for their secret signal.

In the script, which Bercovici called *Cry of the Wolf*, Chaplin insisted that he transform the Gypsy boy into a prince who lives in a castle at he edge of the forest. Bercovici protested that this made the plot ridiculous, since it was out of the question that a prince would ever propose marriage to a Gypsy. "This castle business was

Charlie's idea," he later said, "because in my story, I did not have any castles." It occurred to him that the collaboration was a waste of time, and he was thinking of cutting his losses.

In November 1937, however, Bercovici and his wife attended the ballet at Philharmonic Hall with Charlie and Paulette. During intermission Chaplin recognized a certain Romany singer he knew in the audience, and he approached the man and asked him to stop by the studio the following week, telling him, "I am going to make a Gypsy story and I want you in it." Later he told Bercovici that the real reason he wanted to make *Cry of the Wolf* was because it would give work to various Romany musicians he knew and promote their careers. This idea was irresistible to Bercovici, who soldiered on with a second draft. About ten weeks later he called Summit Drive to set up a meeting to discuss revisions, only to find that the unlisted number had been changed. Calling the studio, he was told that Charlie and Paulette had separated and Charlie had left town.

Unknown to Bercovici Chaplin had also proposed a collaboration with Max Eastman. Since his return to the United States in 1927, Eastman had been in touch with Charlie only sporadically, and as an anti-Stalinist he was regarded as a turncoat by many old friends on the Left. Chaplin, however, continued to think of Eastman as his closest friend, and in the fall of 1937 Paulette called him in New York, saying she was worried about Charlie's state of mind. Paulette begged Eastman to come out to LA, and a few weeks later he arrived with his Russian wife, Eliena.

Eastman found his old friend working at a desk piled high with scripts. "What I'm interested in now is writing," he said, "I don't know how you do it." He then suggested that they write a screenplay together. Eastman was tempted but declined.[5]

Eastman soon learned that had been called to mediate a quarrel over Charlie's promise to produce a film vehicle for Paulette. Two years after the release of *Modern Times*, Charlie still did not have a script. Paulette, meanwhile, had talked their Summit Drive neighbor David Selznick into letting her do a screen test for the role of Scarlett O'Hara in *Gone With the Wind*. Some fourteen hundred actresses were eventually auditioned for the role, and Selznick had probably agreed to the test simply because it was never easy to say no to Paulette. Much to his surprise, however, Paulette's screen test had been impressive, and she continued to improve every time she was called back.

By the autumn of 1937 it seemed that Paulette might be playing Scarlett after all, and that November she informed Charlie that she had hired Myron Selznick, David's brother, as her agent. Charlie was furious. She in turn issued an ultimatum: Either he get serious about making a picture for her, or she would let her contract with the studio lapse and take control of her own career.

Paulette saw Charlie's procrastination as a symptom of a deeper psychological malaise. Max Eastman wasn't sure he agreed. As Charlie reminded him, he had worked hard from the time he was eight years old and felt inclined to take it easy now. Eastman decided that if Charlie wanted to take years to come up with a script, he was entitled to do so. It was Paulette who had the problem, not him. Soon after Eastman reached his conclusion, Charlie abruptly decamped. Paulette also left home for a few days, leaving the guests, Max and Eliena, alone in the house.

Chaplin had departed for Pebble Beach, where he shared a house with his new personal assistant Tim Durant. Born in Waterbury, Connecticut, Thomas Wells Durant enjoyed an independent income from the family businesses, the National Cash Register and Totalizator companies. Once married to a daughter of Charlie's broker, E. F. Hutton, he held a seat on the New York Stock Exchange, but moved to California after the market crashed. Like Harry Crocker, Durant was a Yale graduate, tall and ascetically lean. He talked of becoming a writer or producer, but for the most part he was content to be a satellite. Most recently he had been an unpaid aide to King Vidor before assuming the same role in Chaplin's life.

Durant talked Charlie into renting a house in the posh section of Pebble Beach. At first Charlie was a little nervous about trying to mix with socialites like sugar heiress Geraldine Spreckels, but he was a hit with the area's neglected wives and lonely heiresses, most of whom wanted a soulmate more than a bedmate. "There was a girl who got terribly attracted to Charlie," Durant would recall, "and she used to come over and Charlie used to read poetry to her, and they used to get quite emotional and weep and, you know, *discuss things*, which is very phony to an outsider, but people like that—I mean, they believe in it. So one day they were in the living room talking, and she was reading poetry to him and she started to cry, and he said, 'I can't stand it.' He couldn't cry—he couldn't give—he'd had too much of it. So he rushes into the kitchen, puts some water on his eyes and comes back. Now, that's typical of Chaplin. You'd think he was a prig, if he didn't tell you about it, but I mean, he laughed at it himself."[6]

Chaplin's stay at Pebble Beach lasted through the month of August. Louella Parsons called it "Hollywood's first husband-wife strike," but as usual with Chaplin his motives were far from obvious. In reality, he was hiding out from process servers, who were trying to subpoena him in connection with two plagiarism suits.

The first of these suits was filed in early 1937 by one Michael Kustoff, who claimed that the plot of *Modern Times* was stolen from his self-published autobiography, *Against Gray Walls: Lawyer's Dramatic Escapes* [*sic*]. Kustoff was a colorful character. As a young captain in the Imperial Russian Army, he converted to Bolshevism and fled his homeland to escape a sentence of death by firing squad. Settling in California, he wore his bemedaled dress uniform as an extra in a number of movies and became a fixture in Pasadena's Tournament of Roses parade. While working as a butler for the chairman of the Sun-Maid raisin company, he was accused of writing threatening letters to his employer's son and committed to a state hospital. Released, he became a straight-A law student at the University of California at Berkeley, only to be declared insane a second time—in retaliation for his radical political activities, at least so he claimed.

During this second hospitalization, according to Kustoff, the staff tortured him by pumping poison gas into his room through a duct used for administering oxygen and nitrous oxide. Committed to Napa State, a prison hospital for the mentally ill, Kustoff escaped and made his way to New York, where he passed the bar and became an attorney with the International Labor Defense, working on the Scottsboro case. By 1934 he had returned to Los Angeles and was battling the California Bar Association for the restoration of his license.

It was true that mental institutions in California had been used to incarcerate radicals during the twenties. Whether Kustoff was a victim of political persecution, as he claimed, or a genuine paranoiac, is debatable. At any rate Kustoff saw his autobiography as potential propaganda for the Communist movement. In April 1934 he sent a copy to Earl Browder, the chairman of the Communist Party of the United States, and gave another to Michael Shantzek, a Communist organizer in Hollywood. According to Kustoff, Shantzek had a contact at Chaplin's studio and often passed along material of potential interest.

Kustoff's suit listed more than one hundred specific points of correspondence between his book and *Modern Times*, most of them indiscernible to an objective reader.[7] But there were certain parallels. Like Kustoff, Charlie's character in *Modern Times* is not fundamentally insane but is diagnosed as mad as the result of his conflicts with capitalism—indeed, this was exactly the interpretation of the movie's plot advanced by Boris Shumiatski. And certain incidents in the two works are strangely similar. For example, in the prison ward of the Oakland hospital where Kustoff was supposedly exposed to poison gas, he was visited by a Methodist minister and a middle-aged do-gooder matron. Charlie, in the jail scene of *Modern Times*, is also visited by a minister and a middle-aged woman—in the film, however, it is the woman's digestive difficulties that cause Charlie to "smell gas." (Interestingly, Chaplin, like Kustoff, had something of a phobia about gas. Charles junior wrote that his father refused to sleep in a room heated by gas, and when he traveled he would order Kono to shut off all the radiators in his hotel suite.)

Kustoff soon learned that it was one thing to sue Charles Spencer Chaplin and quite another to locate him and serve the papers. Even the waiters at Chaplin's favorite restaurants were on the alert for process servers and hustled him out through the kitchen if one appeared. If all else failed, Chaplin resorted to hiding out with friends and donning disguises.

Since Chaplin was not a citizen, Kustoff's suit had been filed in federal court, and the responsibility for serving the subpoena ultimately fell to the U.S. marshal's office in Los Angeles. On one occasion federal marshals waited in Chaplin's private office at the studio for most of the day while he hid in a closet just a few feet away.

Almost two years went by before Federal Judge Robert McCormick ended the marshals' misery by ruling that Chaplin could be served in absentia, and the Kustoff suit came to trial in November 1939. The Communist Party organizer, Shantzek, changed his story on the witness stand and admitted that he probably had given Kustoff's book to a Chaplin employee, but he said he could no longer recall just who. Chaplin, too, shifted ground. No longer insisting that similarities between his movie and Kustoff's book were purely coincidental, he suggested that Carter de Haven, the coauthor of the script, might have been familiar with *Against Gray Walls*.

After just a few hours of testimony Judge McCormick called a halt to the proceedings. In his decision, issued some weeks later, McCormick ruled that the two works in question were not "substantially similar." Therefore there was no plagiarism. McCormick did agree, however, that there was circumstantial evidence that someone connected with the film had read Kustoff's book. Fortunately for Chaplin, Angelenos were too preoccupied with war news that winter to pay much attention to a failed lawsuit. Had Kustoff's suit come to trial earlier, the implication that *Modern Times* was based on a Communist's life story—not to mention his charge that the party had a representative on Chaplin's staff—could have been explosive.

Doubtless, however, the trend of Chaplin's testimony was not lost on Carter de Haven. Although de Haven had not received a writing credit on *Modern Times*, now, suddenly, when there was a question of plagiarism and Communist influence, he had been promoted to coauthor. A few years later de Haven would be filing his own plagiarism suit against Chaplin.

The second suit against Chaplin was filed by Films Sonores Tobis, the major European producer of sound films. Tobis contended that the assembly line scenes in *Modern Times* were plagiarized from René Clair's *À Nous la Liberté*. It was not terribly unusual that Chaplin would be sued for plagiarism, and even sued twice over the same screenplay. Although litigation was less common than it is today, few producers escaped the occasional court case. What was amazing was that Chaplin, considering how often he took others to court, should respond to the threat of a lawsuit with unadulterated panic. The Tobis suit scared him more than Kustoff's, perhaps because Tobis had greater resources, and it was the immediate cause of his flight to Pebble Beach.

In November 1937 the Tobis subpoena was entrusted to a professional process server named Oscar Meyerhoff, who proved to be unusually persistent, following Chaplin to the theater, dinner, and even a football game in Pasadena, without quite catching up with him. By January, Meyerhoff had enlisted the help of U.S. Marshal James P. Lavelle. The two men didn't know where Chaplin was living in Pebble Beach, but they learned that he was actually spending several days a week in Los Angeles, sleeping over at an unknown address. Chaplin was in the habit of stopping by Schwab's drugstore when he was in town, and Lavelle asked Bernie Schwab, the proprietor, to notify him the minute Chaplin showed up. Schwab lost his nerve, however, and tipped off Chaplin, who fled minutes ahead of Lavelle's arrival.

As it happens the assembly-line scenes in *Modern Times*—not to mention the look and design of the factory set—do appear to have been influenced by *À Nous la Liberté*. Clair's factory, moreover, manufactures phonograph machines, establishing a symbolic connection between the soulless regimentation of modern life and the coming of the talkies. On the other hand, the Clair movie owes a good deal to Chaplin, so much so that at times it almost seems to be a tribute to *City Lights*. The line between inspiration and plagiarism isn't always easy to draw. But if what Chaplin did was wrong, then Clair was wrong too, and all directors would have to avoid watching one another's films. It is difficult to imagine that an American judge and jury would have convicted Chaplin of plagiarism. This was especially true since René Clair, who no longer owned the rights to *À Nous la Liberté*, had no intention of testifying against him.[8]

Louis Frohlich, a partner of Chaplin's attorney Loyd Wright, informed United Artists that the Tobis suit was "the bunk." Though registered in France, Tobis was "really a German Nazi company" out to harass Chaplin, an outspoken antifascist, he claimed.[9] But there was more involved than politics. Tobis had hoped to sell the script of Clair's much-admired film for a Hollywood remake. There were no takers, but when *Modern Times* was released, several reviewers noted its similarity to Clair's picture. Tobis then hired a private investigator in Los Angeles, who concluded that Chaplin had obtained an unauthorized duplicate print of the Clair film while it was playing at the FilmArte Theater on Vine Street in July 1932. He also secured an affidavit from John D. Palmer, a former technician at the Chaplin studio, who said that as the studio's part-time projectionist he had run the assembly-line sequence from *À Nous la Liberté* for Chaplin at least a dozen times. Palmer's story, if true, was embarrassing at the very least, and it put Chaplin on the defensive.

As in the Kustoff suit, a federal judge finally lost patience with Chaplin's subpoena dodging, and in August 1938 he ordered Chaplin served in absentia. Around this time Chaplin ended his sojourn in Pebble Beach and returned home. Depositions didn't get under way until December, however. Questioned by Tobis's attorneys, Chaplin reasonably argued that an assembly-line speed-up was a generic situation and no one could claim to own the idea. He pointed to Paul Sifton's play *The Belt*, as well as a Disney cartoon about Santa Claus's toy factory, which he had screened at home for his sons, as sources of inspiration.

But Chaplin then went further. Not only didn't he have a pirated copy of Clair's movie, he swore he had never even seen it. He did recall that Alistair Cooke had mentioned the film to him, even warning him that he might run into legal problems, but he took no notice and never bothered to check the movie out.[10]

Alf Reeves backed up his boss. "This is a small, intimate studio," he told the Tobis attorneys. "I knew pretty much everything that was going on. It isn't a big place. . . . We are all here on top of one another. We all knew what was going on, and I don't mind telling you that." To prove his point Reeves produced a plan of the studio and began to talk about traffic patterns and lines of sight.

Not only had no one ever seen Charlie screening Clair's movie in the studio screening room, but no one on Chaplin's payroll, it seems, knew anything at all about *À Nous la Liberté*. Henry Bergman, who declined to state his age but admitted to being "over 68," said that after being hired by Chaplin he had more or less given up going to see other people's movies. Rollie Totheroh swore that he had never even heard of René Clair until a few weeks earlier, when

he was informed that he would have to give a deposition. The head
of the studio carpentry and lighting crews testified that Palmer had
never run the screening-room projector.

It is impossible to say with any certainty whether John Palmer
was telling the truth. But Chaplin and his employees were surely
lying: Their denials were simply too pat to be believed. Alf Reeves
in particular protested too much, in the manner of a man who was a
novice at deception. Had the Tobis suit come to court, these sweep-
ing—and quite unnecessary—denials would surely have hurt
Chaplin's case. But once again his delaying tactics paid off. His
attorneys stretched out the deposition process through the summer
of 1939, and the outbreak of war in Europe did the rest. After a long
series of postponements, the Tobis suit was finally called for trial on
December 2, 1949, thirteen years after it was filed, and the succes-
sors to the Tobis name failed to appear.

Chaplin's tactics had worked. But the humor of his quick exits
and disguises was completely lost on the U.S. marshals. Among
Justice Department and federal court employees he was developing
a reputation as a millionaire radical who scoffed at the law.

While in Pebble Beach during the early part of 1938, Chaplin spent
his time working fitfully on the *White Russians of Shanghai* story.
Around April 1 he and Tim Durant were guests at a cocktail party
given by a Mrs. Reynall, where they ran into Konrad Bercovici and
actor Melvyn Douglas, a popular leading man and spokesman for
liberal causes, who were on their way to San Francisco, where they
had speaking engagements. Chaplin talked about his "White
Russians" project with such an obvious lack of enthusiasm that
Bercovici wondered aloud why he was wasting his time on it. "Why
don't you do something for *yourself?*" he asked.

He'd been intellectually fallow ever since *Modern Times*,
Chaplin said, and he couldn't seem to work up enough enthusiasm
to commit himself to any particular project.

"Well, have I got a story for you, Charlie," Bercovici told him.

"At this point," Melvyn Douglas would recall, "Mr. Bercovici
told a story which, in effect, as well as I can remember it, was
extremely similar to the story which I saw later on the screen in *The*

Great Dictator."[11] Ever the contrarian, Chaplin began to defend
Hitler and Mussolini. Bercovici, Douglas, and other guests, including the president of Occidental College, all took the bait, excitedly
trying to persuade Chaplin that fascism was a bad thing.

This was by no means the first time that someone had urged
Chaplin to make a film about Hitler. The Führer, after all, sported a
version of the "Charlie Chaplin mustache," and the remarkable
physical resemblance between the world's funniest man and the
world's scariest had already been noted by political cartoonists and
pundits. (Among other coincidental similarities, their birthdates
were only four days apart, and both of them had been reported
engaged to Pola Negri, who briefly made a play for Hitler in an
attempt to get the Nazis to stop blacklisting her as a non-Aryan.)
Chaplin later said that the idea of doing a musical-comedy spoof on
Hitler occurred to him as early as 1932. He even wrote the lyrics for
a patter song—"I am Adolph [*sic*], the Great Dictator, once I was a
waiter"—but he did nothing with it because he could see no way to
expand the material into a feature-length movie.[12]

Bercovici and Douglas stayed over at Chaplin's house that night.
Before they left for San Francisco, Chaplin invited them to return in
a week to attend a party for sixty or so guests that he and Durant
were throwing at the Pebble Beach Lodge to repay their social
obligations. The party, held on the evening of April 6, was a gala
affair, with lavish supplies of first-rate caviar and vintage champagne. Once again Douglas and Bercovici spent the night at
Chaplin's house, and this time Bercovici had come prepared with a
synopsis for a movie he suggested calling *The Dictators*, or *Heil
Hitler*, or possibly *The Man with the Chaplinesque Mustache.*
Although the treatment—which filled six closely spaced typed
pages—was hastily written and rife with misspellings, abbreviations,
and repetitions, it outlined a fairly detailed story, including gag
ideas. It read in part:

Charlie, barber or paperhanger, or maybe a peddler, has a fight with
some SS men and is thrown into C.C. [concentration camp]. Escapes from
there wearing a military coat. Taken for Hitler whom he resembles; he runs
away they run after him and Heil Him. They have recognized the Fuehrer
even incognito. They follow him and their numbers grow. . . . He leads the

now grown to an army [*sic*] towards the Austrian border. . . . The real Hitler is on his way to Austria with an army. Charlie could play both parts. . . .

Gross satire done in a Rabelaisian style. No subtlety. . . . The cannon to protect the beloved Fuehrer. . . . It cant be crazy enough. . . . Keep in mind the fact that H isn't imitation Napoleon but Ludwig of Bavaria. . . . Charlei could ballet dance with the globe. Alla Pavlova. Keep to ridicule more than satire. Show him with Benito. Who makes the trains run on time. the bastard rose to power by castor oil.

The thing to do is to introduce Ch first as a nebach [nebbish], a little tramp who doesn't know what has happened in the world. Maybe he has been sick and maybe he doesn't realize what has happened and the people to whom he comes back don't want to tell him yet—so that when the SS men come upon him for the first time he stands up to them. Not afraid. What? They beat him up. The girl takes his part. Maybe she is Jewish and maybe not. . . .

While Ch is in the c.c. . . . This is the time to bring in Benito and the quartering of the melon. . . . Have America one part of the globe. Let them quarrel as to who will take America. they have a fight on that. Benito wants half of America. Hitlers [*sic*] says no. Someone whispers something in Benito's ears. Someone whispers something in Hitler's ears. They are both satisfied. Shake hands. They'll doublcross [*sic*] each other later. . . .

One of the big scenes in the play could be Hitler's speech. Ch could do that in gibberish, the same as the song in *Modern Times* or the opening of City Lights.

Bercovici also suggested a scene of Hitler stripping Göring of his medals and another in which the inventor of an improved parachute tries to test it by jumping out a window—something of the kind had actually happened during his last stay in Germany, he said. He called for a spoof of the Nuremberg rallies, with so many flags and banners that the excess would become laughable, and he suggested that the picture as a whole should make use of a deliberately unrealistic "picture post card decor," inspired by Hitler's own amateurish watercolors.

Chaplin read the treatment overnight. The following morning over a late breakfast he said he was intrigued by Bercovici's ideas, but he wasn't sure such a movie could be made. The United States, after all, still maintained diplomatic relations with Germany and Italy, and a film mocking those countries' leaders could damage U.S. foreign policy. The government might even try to suppress it.

Bercovici pointed out that naturally the names would be changed—the characters in the picture wouldn't be called Benito and Hitler. The government couldn't ban satire, surely.

Nevertheless, Chaplin said, he wanted to consult with a "contact" of his who "knows the attitude of the State Department." He left the room to make a phone call and returned, shaking his head. His contact thought the movie shouldn't be made.

Bercovici was astounded. He'd never known Chaplin to care the slightest about pleasing anyone in the U.S. government. He and Douglas wondered who this influential "contact" might be. To cover the awkward moment, Douglas began to describe another screenplay Bercovici had recently written, in collaboration with William Thiele, about the life of composer Hector Berlioz. Knowing Charlie's interest in music, he suggested that he might want to play Berlioz himself. Instantly Chaplin was reinvigorated. This was exactly the kind of thing he had been looking for—"I will buy this one!" The next day Chaplin called Bercovici's home and talked to Naomi Bercovici, reaffirming his desire to buy the Berlioz story. Konrad then asked Zeppo Marx to withdraw the script from MGM, which had offered $24,000 for it, and send it to Chaplin. Some weeks later, after the Bercovicis had returned to their home in Connecticut, Konrad received a letter from Alf Reeves, proposing to pay him $4,000 for the rights. The figure was so low that Bercovici interpreted it as a brush-off, and he sent Reeves a curt telegram of rejection. The incident was embarrassing since he was responsible for persuading his coauthor, Thiele, to pass up the deal with MGM.

On April 25, 1938, eighteen days after Chaplin last saw Konrad Bercovici, *Variety* announced that his studio, at long last, was being fully renovated for the production of talkies:

Chaplin, who has been at Carmel [*sic*] for the past few months supposedly resting and recreating has been working on several stories. Some time ago Chaplin bought a story in London [the Regency novel] and more recently became interested in an original yarn. The author of his story has been in Carmel recently and it is expected that Chaplin will return here within the next week or so to get started on preparations for his first talking picture. New sound channels have been installed at the Chaplin Studio by RCA, which began the work there last January.

In October the trade papers reported that Chaplin intended to film a spoof on Hitler, entitled *The Dictator*. On reading this, Bercovici sent Chaplin a registered letter asking him what was going on, but he never received an answer. Nor were his calls to the studio returned. In 1939, while he was in Los Angeles on business, he twice ran into Chaplin, once at the Brown Derby and again at the Dome restaurant. The first time Chaplin fled; the second he made a date to meet Bercovici but failed to show up.

In retrospect it is fairly obvious what had gone wrong. No doubt Chaplin brought up the idea of a partnership with an 85 to 15 percent split in a moment of enthusiasm, and then came to regret it. Rather than face the unpleasant task of telling Bercovici that he had changed his mind he kept procrastinating. And the longer he put off the inevitable, wasting Bercovici's time with story conferences and rewrites, the guiltier he felt—and the more resentful.

None of this quite explains why Chaplin did not simply buy the *Dictator* synopsis, avoiding the problems that were sure to crop up once Bercovici realized that his story line was being used without compensation. Perhaps Chaplin became aware that Bercovici would expect a 15 percent share of the picture, per their oral agreement, and couldn't bring himself to pay that much. However, the mysterious phone call to Chaplin's "contact" close to the State Department suggests another explanation. While Chaplin had never been especially worried about Washington's opinion of him, he did care what his friends in the Communist Party thought, and Konrad Bercovici was anathema to the party. The State Department's views on the diplomatic implications of a Chaplin satire on Hitler aren't likely to have changed between April 7 and April 25, but once Bercovici was no longer connected with the project, the party's attitude might indeed be quite different.

Shortly after his return to Los Angeles, Chaplin hired a new assistant to help with him work on the *Dictator* script. Dan James was the son of a well-to-do member of the bohemian set in Carmel, California, whom Chaplin had visited while living nearby in Pebble Beach. After graduating from Yale with the class of 1933, he studied at writing under George Sklar at the New Theater League School in New York and appeared as an extra in *Marching Song* by John Howard Lawson, the screenwriter who was also the leading Communist Party *apparatchik* in Hollywood. James was affable, talented, and a Communist Party member.

One can't help suspecting that James was hired in part to function as a naive witness. Young and impressionable, he would vividly recall those moments sitting around Chaplin's pool or dining at Musso & Frank's or the Cock and Bull, when the process of "chewing the furniture" suddenly gave rise to creative inspiration. Moreover, he kept careful notes of all working sessions, documenting the day in January 1939, for example, when Chaplin first came up with the idea that the Little Fellow was suffering from amnesia, knew nothing of the rise of Nazism, and therefore fearlessly confronted the Storm Troopers when they showed up at his barbershop to harass him. Next came the inspiration of having Charlie march into Osterlich (Austria) at the head of the German army, and a scene mocking "Field Marshal Herring's" passion for medals. James had no way of knowing that all these ideas had been outlined by Bercovici the previous April.[13]

In other instances Chaplin tried to invent new twists that didn't quite work out. At one point he wanted to include a scene in which the Hitler character is induced to test a new invention, a one-man inflatable blimp from which his head "stuck out like a bee." Hitler would fly around a room in his palace, getting his head stuck in a chandelier.[14] But the stunt proved too difficult to set up, and so Chaplin "came up" with a "new" alternative: Hitler is approached by an inventor whose hat doubles as a compact parachute.

One day not long after Dan James was hired, Alf Reeves took him aside and warned him not to let his hopes for the movie ride too high. "Mr. Reeves personally questioned whether it would get before the camera," James later said.[15] Reeves knew that there were many pitfalls, including the possibility that Paulette Goddard would not be available to play Hannah, the girl who helps Charlie battle the Storm Troopers.

❊   ❊   ❊

In his search for the perfect Scarlett O'Hara, David Selznick had eventually narrowed the field from 1,400 to 3—Jean Arthur, Joan Bennett, and Paulette Goddard. Of these Paulette was the candidate he felt enthusiastic about. Unfortunately there was a problem. According to Irene Mayer Selznick, Paulette had told too many contradictory and implausible stories about the circumstances of her marriage. At one point she said she and Charlie had been married years earlier by the mayor of Catalina. But there was no mayor of Catalina.[16]

David Selznick's published memos suggest that he was more worried about Paulette's continuing contractual obligations to the Chaplin studio, which stretched into March 1939. Chaplin was so notoriously litigious that Selznick worried he would find some excuse to sue, tying up his production.[17]

Either way, too much money was being invested in *Gone With the Wind* to risk the baggage that Chaplin's wife—if that's what she was—brought with her, and at the last minute, Selznick decided to give the part to British actress Vivien Leigh. But even though Paulette had lost the chance of a lifetime, Selznick's enthusiasm made her a hot property, and by the summer of 1939 she had as much work as she could handle. Paulette was still willing to play Hannah, fitting the assignment in between roles in the screen version of Clare Boothe Luce's *The Women* and *Second Chorus* with Fred Astaire. Myron Selznick, however, demanded that she be paid $2,500 a week, and then outraged Chaplin by showing up at the studio to talk about improving her billing.

Such negotiations were standard in Hollywood, but not at the Chaplin studio. Interestingly, though most people considered Paulette Goddard highly intelligent and shrewd, Chaplin preferred to see her as a "creature of whims," who was being manipulated by her unscrupulous agent. Myron Selznick happened to be the husband of Marjorie Daw, who had been Mildred Harris's confidante during his first marital breakup, so perhaps Chaplin was prejudiced against him. Still, one wonders if he ever really understood Paulette, or appreciated her strengths.

When filming of *The Great Dictator,* as it was now called, got under way in September 1939, Paulette's presence on the set was the cause of tension. One clue as to how the balance of power between her and Charlie had changed can be seen in Paulette's hairdo. Once again Chaplin had envisioned his leading lady as a fatherless *gamine*. Hannah (as Paulette's character was called) first appears looking a mess, with flyaway hair and smudges of dirt on her cheeks. Soon, however, an excuse is found for Charlie the Barber to do her hair, and she sails through the picture with fluffy curls tied back with a pert hair ribbon, looking ready to tap-dance her way through an MGM musical.

While Paulette was not enjoying herself on the set, Jack Oakie, the actor chosen to play Mussolini—or rather, Benzino Napaloni—would look back on the filming of *The Great Dictator* as "one of the happiest periods of my life." Oakie was returning from Europe on the *Ile de France* in January 1939, when he struck up an acquaintance with a fellow passenger, Syd Chaplin. Syd's wife, Minnie, had died in 1935, and he was now married to a woman named Gypsy, a native of Nice. Nervous about the political situation in Europe, Syd and Gypsy had decided to settle temporarily in LA. Syd talked enthusiastically about Charlie's plans to make a movie in which he would portray Hitler. "Sounds good to me, Syd," Oakie remarked. "After all, Hitler's been trying to imitate Charlie, wearing his mustache."

A veteran campaigner in vaudeville and a popular radio performer, Jack Oakie had enjoyed a brief vogue during the early days of talking films, but his career had been on the skids for some time. Oakie was a prodigious drinker, and his reputation for extended binges had scared off many producers. Fortunate to have advance word of Chaplin's plans, he schemed to win an audition through the influence of his friends Sid Grauman and A. C. Blumenthal. Much to his delight, the studio called.

Chaplin's treatment of Oakie demonstrated the side of his character that could inspire passionate loyalty. Although Oakie was desperate for the role and Chaplin knew it, he never let on. Oakie was a man who enjoyed good food, Chaplin scheduled their meetings for the best restaurants in town, saving the business discussion until they had dined well and expensively. He repeatedly assured Oakie that he wanted an actor, not a Mussolini impersonator. No, he wouldn't think of asking him to shave his head, nor should Oakie make any effort to lose weight. He was *perfect* just as he was.

When Oakie reluctantly broached the subject of his drinking problem, Chaplin was unfazed. "Oakie," he said. "Listen, if you want to drink, go ahead and drink. I don't want you to change your ways. If you get drunk, just don't come in. We're shooting this picture leisurely. We're not in any hurry."

Oakie was so impressed by this "gracious" attitude that he didn't take another drink until the picture was finished. "I didn't want to miss a day."[18]

Unfortunately for Chaplin the days of "leisurely" filmmaking were over. Not only was *The Great Dictator* Chaplin's first talking film, it was the first produced under the new union work rules enforced by the National Labor Relations Board (NLRB). FDR enthusiast that he was, Chaplin detested the new regulations, an attitude shared by many old-timers. The price of job security was the elimination of the spirit of teamwork and spontaneity that had made picture-making fun in the old days. Chaplin, who had been doing his own makeup since childhood, was required to have a makeup specialist, who stood by all day with nothing to do. A potentially more useful addition to the staff was the script girl, whose job it was to ensure continuity from scene to scene. Although her services were sorely needed, Chaplin could never get past his annoyance at having an employee who did nothing but take notes. Day after day he looked around in amazement at the redundant employees on the set. "Who are these people?" he kept asking Jack Oakie.

Along with work rules had come bureaucratic thinking. Asked at the last minute to add an apron to Paulette Goddard's costume, wardrobe master Ted Tetrick called Western Costume, a specialty rental company, and asked them to send one over by express messenger. The bill for the apron, including delivery and pick-up charges, eventually reached four hundred dollars, all for an item that could have been purchased within a block of the studio for fifteen cents.

Still, the Charles Chaplin Studio hardly resembled the glamour factories like MGM and Warner Bros. In addition to Jack Oakie, the cast of *The Great Dictator* included such old timers as Chester Conklin and Hank Mann, a one-time Keystone Kop now cast as a Storm Trooper. Another surprising addition to the studio payroll was Charlie's half-brother Wheeler Dryden, the son of Hannah Chaplin and Leo Dryden. During the early 1920s, while performing in the Far East, Dryden had written to Charlie reintroducing himself. Now he was in the United States, and Charlie had taken him on as an assistant director. A small, nervous man with an impish sense of humor, Dryden was given the job of managing a staff that had more than its share of aging eccentrics. "This schedule is subject to revision at any time due to C.C.'s possible dissatisfaction with what has been shot. Or, as a matter of fact, for any other reason," he scrawled at the bottom of one week's work order. Another note pleaded: "Will the person who took the quart jar of alcohol from the prop room please return it. Clem Widrig has no place to put his teeth."[19]

But the most significant change in the crew was the replacement of Rollie Totheroh, Chaplin's chief cameraman and cinematographer since 1916. It was hardly surprising that Totheroh's work was outdated, considering that he had devoted his entire career to a studio that was timorously venturing into sound production in the era of *Gone With the Wind* and *The Wizard of Oz*. In the early days of the Mutual comedies Totheroh had been fairly inventive, but he got little encouragement from Chaplin, who was so unmechanical, Totheroh once said, that he couldn't use the studio bathroom without locking himself in. Chaplin's belated dissatisfaction with the quality of his cinematography owed a good deal to Syd, who had returned from a decade abroad and could hardly believe how far behind the times the studio was. To Chaplin's credit, Totheroh was demoted, not fired, and Karl Struss was brought in to work over him as director of cinematography.

Karl Struss was no youngster either, having started his Hollywood career in 1918 when he was already twenty-six years old. Struss had filmed the chariot race in Cecil B. De Mille's 1926 epic, *Ben Hur*, and some of Douglas Fairbanks's action pictures, but he was best known for his inventive traveling shots and dramatic use of light in pictures like Murnau's *Sunrise* and Mary Pickford's *Sparrows*. Karl Struss filming a Chaplin picture was like today's Three Tenors singing "My Way"—the technique was utterly disproportionate to the material. Chaplin cared a great deal about quality in acting but regarded fancy camera work as a distraction that took attention away from his performance. With some difficulty Struss did manage to persuade him to use two cameras set at different angles for every shot: "I thought I'd help him, give him something to cut, because he had no knowledge of camera direction, his films were completely 'theater.' It was very routine work with him; you'd just set up the camera and let it go and he and the other actors would play in front of it."[20]

With a script that called for the invasion of Austria, among other episodes, *The Great Dictator* could easily have become a very expensive movie. Chaplin did try staging a "Nuremberg rally" in the San Bernardino Valley, but used little of the footage. For the rest he relied on illusion. The film made heavy use of process shots—filmed backgrounds projected through a screen behind the actors, and the Austrian invasion was shot in the studio with a few dozen extras and two prop tanks.

Even so the picture eventually cost about $1,500,000, still considered a goodly sum, especially for a black-and-white production made in the studio. But the total was somewhat misleading. The largest single item in the budget was Chaplin's own salary of $341,500. Another $37,480 would be listed as the cost of "salaries and expenses" for the development of the screenplay (although Dan James was paid only $75 to $80 a week). Studio rental was on the books at $86,000 and an outlay of $23,324 was somewhat mysteriously attributed to "automobile expense." Only $46,371 was spent for props, wardrobe, and makeup combined; "paint and stores" costed out at $5,383; and "location expenses" totaled a mere $16,890. As a result the picture looked tacky, in a way that Chaplin's 1916 Mutuals, much more cheaply made, almost never did. Oddly enough, however, the tackiness worked in the film's favor—contributing to the concept of Hitler and Mussolini as a pair of second-rate vaudevillians constantly trying to upstage each other.

And upstage each other they did. Jack Oakie's Benzino Napaloni, otherwise known as "Il Digaditch," was the kind of bully who masquerades as a genial uncle. "You a nice-a *leetle* man, Hynkie," he tells his squirming rival. Oakie made a game of trying to one-up Chaplin and would "hop on his lines," coming in with his own dialogue just a little too soon. Much to his amazement, Chaplin had to ask him what he was doing. It had been a long time since he played a speaking role, and his own timing was often uncertain. Chaplin and Oakie enjoyed themselves so much that they sometimes stayed in character even after they left the studio, once show-ing up in costume as Hynkel and Napaloni at a party given by Mary Pickford in honor of Lord Louis Mountbatten.

Chaplin's portrayal of Adenoid Hynkel, "the Phooey," was, of course, the centerpiece of the film. He prepared by watching news-reels of Hitler's interminable harangues and deftly mocked them in the rally scene, in which the Phooey exhorts the Sons and Daughters of the Double Cross: "Der wienerschnitzel und der lagerbieren und der sauerkraut . . . wir muss tighten our belten. . . . Democratie shtunk! Libertie shtunk!" During one especially unin-telligible passage, the microphones literally wilt, and an unctuous interpreter explains that the Phooey has just made reference to the Jews.

Chaplin hadn't been nicknamed "the King" by his own mother for nothing. He understood that every megalomaniac is a big baby at heart, and he dared to imagine the whimsical, childlike side of Hitler. His "Hynkel" is a role player who uses tantrums, intimidation and smarmy, ingratiating rhetoric to manipulate others. Momentarily alone, he dances with a helium-filled globe, lost in his fantasies of world domination until the balloon bursts and he makes a face like a toddler with a broken toy. At fifty Chaplin could still make a standing leap from the floor to his desktop look effortless, and his balletic skills raised the scene from parody to character study.

"Production No. 6" moved along expeditiously by Chaplin's stan-dards—one year of work on the script and another thirteen months from the time the cameras rolled until the premiere. But Hitler moved more quickly. On August 24, 1939, a week before rehearsals were scheduled to begin, Germany and the Soviet Union signed a nonaggression pact. The treaty would allow Stalin to scoop up the Baltic nations while the Wehrmacht invaded Poland, triggering dec-larations of war by England and France. Literally overnight the U.S. Communist Party shifted ground from a war policy to a "peace" pol-icy. The Anti-Fascist League vanished, replaced by the American Peace Mobilization, and Communists who had been screaming for war against Germany were transformed into peace demonstrators who denounced FDR for wanting to use American boys as cannon fodder. The genuine antifascists, who had seen nothing wrong with cooperating with Communists in the Popular Front, were left gaping at this demonstration of hypocrisy.

Chaplin, of course, was far from being a doctrinaire Marxist. His attraction to the Communists was twofold: They presented themselves as the representatives of the oppressed classes, with whom he identified, and they also purported to have the one correct answer to every question. As Harry Crocker put it, "His desire to please the Marxists, whom he erroneously considered to be the great intellectuals they claimed to be, led him into adopting false philosophies."[21] In practice Chaplin was heavily influenced by whomever he had talked to last. During the early stages of making *The Great Dictator* the memory of Bercovici's lectures was still fresh, and he was given to denouncing Stalin as just another power-mad bully. He even threatened to mock him in the film, much to the alarm of Dan James.

Having invested a million dollars in his movie already, Chaplin was not about to abandon it on account of the new Communist "peace" line, but the about-face did influence the script. What most moviegoers are likely to remember about *The Great Dictator* is an early scene in which Paulette Goddard as Hannah brains a Nazi thug with a frying pan. But another episode, a late addition, undercuts that message: Charlie the Barber is part of a group of men from the Pretzelburg ghetto who have made up their minds to assassinate Hynkel. Hannah is asked to serve them a dessert pudding, inserting a coin into one portion. Whoever gets the coin will undertake the suicide mission. Charlie is none too eager to win this contest. He carefully tests the weight of each serving and picks the one that seems the lightest. But luck is not with him. He finds a coin in his pudding . . . and then so do all the others. Hannah has baked a coin into *every* portion to teach them a lesson—not, as one might think, that all must be prepared to sacrifice, but that none of them should. "Our place is at home looking after our own affairs," she tells the men, who are hugely relieved to hear it.

But it was in writing the ending of the film that the question of ideology became hard to finesse. The script called for Charlie the Barber—who has been mistaken for Hynkel—to deliver a speech at the victory rally celebrating the conquest of Osterlich. The speech was a grand opportunity for an actor. But—recalling the question Chaplin once asked Rob Wagner—what would he say?

Chaplin's early notes for the speech show that he still viewed Hitler primarily as a symbol of the increasing regimentation of everyday life—his personal peeve: "It seems our laws are always telling us what not to do—are always keeping us from enjoying ourselves. Human beings are made just as much for having fun as for goose-stepping and sweating in factories."

Furthermore, the way to resist the dictators was through appeasing them: "Yes, let us have appeasement. Let us right the wrongs due to nations. But as the price let us all disarm—totally— till every weapon of death is destroyed." [22]

As the shooting date approached, Chaplin's plans for this final segment, designated "Sequence X" in the shooting script, became ever more grandiose: Charlie's heartfelt appeal, broadcast around the world, would work miracles. A Japanese pilot is about to bomb a Chinese village when, suddenly, his face is suffused with "wonder." He releases his bombs but, magically, instead of instruments of death, parachutes carrying toys rain down on the village. A Spanish firing squad lays down its guns. At the climax a projection of Abraham Lincoln looms up behind Hannah.

This was all very well, but by the spring of 1940 the sentiment "let us have appeasement" was a bit too direct for the mass audience to swallow. And the complaint that Hitler was an enemy of "fun" was no longer relevant. In May, during a working lunch at the Cock and Bull restaurant, Chaplin read another draft of the Barber's speech to Dan James, who was appalled. This version, or one very close to it, included a joke—the Barber *qua* Hynkel tells the Osterlichans: "If I had my way I'd give you back your country. I can't pay taxes on it." Chaplin kept writing. He eventually sought help from others, and the final text of the speech shows the influence of Rob Wagner, always a master of political double entendre.

By the time the filming of Sequence X began on June 26, the Japanese aviator, the Spanish firing squad, and Abraham Lincoln were out. But the speech scene still ran almost six minutes. This was an eternity in cinematic time, and for much of it Charlie stared directly into the camera, addressing his words to the motion picture audience. There were exhortations to "Fight for Liberty!" and bring into being a new world "in the name of democracy." But the politically attuned could still recognize slogans from the current Communist grab bag. At one point Charlie warns, "Soldiers! Don't give yourselves to these brutes. . . . Who drill you—diet you—treat you like cattle and use you as cannon fodder." Theoretically he is addressing *German* soldiers, but in dramatic terms his words are aimed at the movie audience, echoing the Communist charge that Roosevelt was planning to sacrifice American boys to defend British imperialism.

The Great Dictator had its world premiere in New York City on October 15, opening simultaneously at the Capitol and Astor theaters. As might have been predicted, critics loved the lampoon of Hitler but were cool, or worse, to the final speech. In a fairly typical reaction the reviewer for the *New York Post* complained that the speech "makes you squirm" but was willing to give Chaplin credit for "noble" intentions. Syndicated columnist Ed Sullivan, an outspoken anti-Stalinist, was far harsher. Referring to Chaplin's incorporation of the Communist Party line about cannon fodder, Sullivan accused him of "pointing the finger of Communism" directly at his audience.

Nor was Sullivan just being paranoid. David Platt, the film critic of the *Daily Worker*, interpreted the speech in much the same way though, of course, he heartily approved. Platt called the final six minutes of *The Great Dictator* an "eloquent plea for peace" as well as an attack on "the Roosevelts and Churchills and all the little Hitlers" in the arms industry who were trying to lead the world into war. [23]

The ticket-buying public, by and large, was content to take the speech at face value. Laughter and hope were in short supply that autumn, and *The Great Dictator* played to packed houses in New York for fifteen weeks. In England, where it opened at the Prince of Wales theater on December 15, Londoners braved air raids to see it. *The Great Dictator* would go on to earn more than five million dollars in domestic and foreign rentals during its initial release, an amazing total considering that it could not even be shown in occupied countries like France, where Chaplin's movies normally did excellent business.

All in all, though Chaplin had reason to be delighted, he wasn't.

The remarkable feature of Chaplin's character, in retrospect, is not that he allowed himself to be taken in by the Communist line. The times were difficult and distressing, and plenty of people better educated than he was had made the same mistake. Far stranger was Chaplin's inordinate pride in the speech as a piece of writing. His words were duplicitous in that the politically naive thought they meant one thing, while those in the know recognized that they were advocating something else entirely. Yet, as Chaplin saw it, the speech was great writing.

Moreover, even though what many critics disliked about the speech was its suggestion that the United States *shouldn't* go to war against Hitler, Chaplin conveniently chose to believe that anyone who had qualms about his message was a fascist sympathizer. Ever since the subject of *The Great Dictator* was announced, he had been receiving a certain amount of hate mail from pro-Nazi extremists. Fearful that protesters would create a disturbance at the premiere he asked Harry Bridges, the Communist head of the longshoreman's union, to station some of his burly dock workers inside the theater to quell any disturbance that might occur. Bridges wisely refused.

In reality one of the bizarre aftereffects of the Hitler-Stalin pact was that Communists had temporarily found themselves in agreement with isolationist conservatives. As a result Chaplin was asked to read the controversial speech at a meeting sponsored by the Daughters of the American Revolution (DAR) at Constitution Hall in Washington, D.C., where it was to be broadcast over a nationwide radio hookup.

Just hours before the rally he was also invited to meet with President Roosevelt, who received him in his private study. According to Chaplin's account, FDR chided him because the opening of *The Great Dictator* in Argentina had led to pro-German demonstrations in front of the U.S. embassy. But this could hardly have been FDR's main objection. Surely he was more upset by Chaplin's "cannon fodder" remark, and his plans to repeat it at a pro-isolationist rally. Still, Roosevelt gave Chaplin forty-five minutes, their conversation lubricated by a pitcher of dry martinis.

Whatever was said over cocktails, Chaplin left the White House in an agitated mood. Later, while he was reading his speech at Constitution Hall, some in the audience interrupted him with loud coughing and Chaplin suddenly found his mouth so dry that "my tongue began sticking to the roof of my palate and I could not articulate." He was unable to continue until someone from backstage brought him a drink of water. Amazingly, when he came to relate this in his autobiography, Chaplin implied that he was the victim of a plot by the rally organizers, who set him up by failing to leave a glass of water on the podium. It doesn't take a degree in psychology to suspect that he was literally choking on his own words.[24]

At the end of the year, the New York Film Critics Circle voted Chaplin the best actor of 1940, an unusual honor for a comedian. Chaplin, however, wanted to be honored for his writing and directing—which he hardly deserved—and he refused to accept the award. This prompted gossip columnist Sheilah Graham to float the rumor that he also expected an Academy Award and was already writing his rejection speech. In any event, the Oscars passed him by.

Looming over the reception of *The Great Dictator* was the shadow of Konrad Bercovici. On June 24, 1940, after many attempts to arrange a meeting failed, Bercovici had sent Chaplin a letter saying that he wanted no money but did feel that he deserved a screen credit. Chaplin referred the letter to his attorneys, who did not reply. In October, however, when he was in New York for the picture's premiere, Chaplin gave a press conference at the Pierre Hotel, and a reporter who had heard Bercovici's side of the story asked, "Mr. Chaplin, do you know a man named Konrad Bercovici?" Chaplin replied that he did. As a matter of fact, he volunteered, Bercovici had given him the entire plot of the picture "and he didn't get a dime for it."

"But, Mr. Chaplin," another reporter asked, "I thought you stated on the screen that you were the author?"

At this point Chaplin began to rearrange the glasses on the table in front of him and did not answer. He said later that he made the remark "because I wanted to help Bercovici, thinking he was my friend."[25]

And, indeed, he had helped him. Armed with press clippings

quoting Chaplin's admission, Bercovici—who can hardly have been pleased with the twist Chaplin had added to his story—filed a lawsuit charging plagiarism and demanding five million in damages.

By June 1942, when he was deposed in the Bercovici case, Chaplin had come to feel that Bercovici had betrayed him, not the other way around—and, indeed, that it was Bercovici who had been trying to exploit Paulette Goddard. "I didn't want his wares," he said. "He came up to my house as a friend. Twenty years I'd known Bercovici and he never asked me to do a thing and suddenly because I was making a picture for Paulette, he had something to sell."

The extent of Bercovici's contribution to *The Great Dictator* might have been a legitimate subject for litigation, but Chaplin, under oath, chose to rewrite the entire history of their relationship. He swore that there had been just one draft of the *In Old Chicago* script, representing no more than two or three days' work on Bercovici's part. *Cry of the Wolf* had been completely unsolicited. He never made a verbal collaboration agreement with Bercovici; indeed, he didn't recall seeing him at all during the early part of 1937. He had never seen *The Dictator* synopsis either, and he certainly never had a conversation with Bercovici and Melvyn Douglas about calling a contact who knew the attitude of the State Department.

Vacillating between Olympian disdain and petty meanness, Chaplin shrugged off questions about chronology, saying, "Dates mean nothing to me." Asked who had done the research for certain episodes in the film, he denied that anyone had done *any* research, telling the attorneys, "I can put up a good bluff and I can quote all the Latin that you want and I can quote all the medieval characters if I want to. . . . That's an easy thing, to become highbrow."[26]

At this juncture the interrogation took a bizarre turn. Bercovici had mentioned that it was he who, many years earlier, had told Chaplin about Robert Louis Stevenson's story "The Suicide Club," which indirectly inspired the scene in which a coin is cooked into a pudding as a method of drawing lots. When Bercovici's attorney asked Chaplin how he came to write this episode, Chaplin suddenly brightened: "It was a story I've had, called 'The Suicide Club,' for a long time, in which a club is formed by a lot of derelicts for the purpose of living in a state of luxury and at the same time committing a fraudulent act on the insurance companies, by which lots are cast, are drawn, and the one who gets the unlucky number must commit suicide."

"Is that an original idea on your part, Mr. Chaplin?" Bercovici's attorney asked.

"Yes, that's completely original with me."

Bercovici's attorney tried again. "Aren't you aware of the fact that this story was written over fifty years ago by Robert Louis Stevenson?"

"No, it wasn't," said Chaplin.[27]

In fact the plot Chaplin described was not identical with Stevenson's, but he refused to acknowledge, despite prodding, any awareness of the existence of Stevenson's story. At this point Chaplin's attorney, Louis Frohlich, abruptly called for a recess. Frohlich and United Artists had taken Alf Reeves's word for it that Bercovici's claim was baseless.[28] Now they began looking for a technicality that would enable them to get the suit dismissed.

16

Shadow and Substance

Over the years the feisty side of Chaplin's personality had served him well. Without it he could never have pulled himself up from nothing, become a dominant figure in Hollywood, and remained one long after so many of his talented contemporaries were burned out and all but forgotten. As he aged, however, Chaplin seemed unable to let go of the anger that drove him. Feuds, lawsuits, and provocative political speeches became outlets for his rancor.

During the making of *The Great Dictator* it had seemed a safe bet that Chaplin's next all-out battle would be with Paulette Goddard over the terms of their parting. Instead he startled the celebrity-studded audience at the movie's New York premiere by introducing Paulette as "my wife," the first time he had publicly acknowledged her as his spouse. But the concession came too late. Paulette was already involved in an affair with the Mexican muralist Diego Rivera and barely speaking to Charlie. She had traveled to New York separately, and soon returned alone to Summit Drive, where she quietly packed up her belongings for removal to a house in Malibu.

Paulette was either brilliantly calculating or a much nicer person than most people gave her credit for being—or perhaps in this instance the two amounted to the same thing. While her lawyers negotiated quietly, she remained the voice of sweet reason. "If Mr. Chaplin wants a divorce, let him ask for it," she told one reporter. "But I'm too grateful to him for everything, and love him too much, to cause him a moment's anguish."[1]

At last, in the fall of 1942, Chaplin agreed to an out-of-court settlement in the vicinity of a quarter of a million dollars, followed by an uncontested divorce in Juarez, Mexico. When the FBI later looked into Chaplin's marital status, it found that Paulette's attorney had told the Mexican judge that the divorce was being sought "to clear up a possible common law situation."

Not only was Paulette gone from Chaplin's life, but so was his loyal, good-natured friend Douglas Fairbanks, who died in his sleep from heart failure in December 1939. Although Mary Pickford had been divorced from Douglas for several years and was remarried to Charles "Buddy" Rogers, few doubted that she continued to have deep feelings for him. Once he was gone there was nothing left to keep her and Charlie from indulging their mutual antagonism. This time the point of conflict was David Selznick.

After Sam Goldwyn finally gave up his bid to control United Artists, the board of directors had turned to Selznick, granting him generous terms to take over as managing partner. In 1941 UA advanced his company, David Selznick Productions, three hundred thousand dollars to develop three movies—*Jane Eyre*, *Claudia*, and *The Keys of the Kingdom*. A year later, finding himself overextended financially, Selznick transferred the rights to the three properties to another company, Vanguard, which promptly sold them to Twentieth Century–Fox.

United Artists had been left with nothing to show for its three-hundred-thousand-dollar investment. There was no question that what Selznick had done was unfair and even unethical, but as it turned out it wasn't in violation of his contract, which was couched in such vague terms that he wasn't obligated to deliver those three pictures in particular. This technicality made no impression on Chaplin, who may well have blamed Selznick for his troubles with Paulette. In any case by May 1943 he was threatening to sue United Artists and Mary Pickford because they refused to join him in suing Selznick.

In a long, emotional letter, Pickford reminded Chaplin that while other companies formed long after United Artists (no doubt she was thinking of MGM) were now industry giants, "United limps along with barely enough to meet its heavy obligations. Why? Because there has been nothing but dissension for the past fifteen years and because dissension spreads through the management and down to the salesmen in the field." Although she agreed that Chaplin was right in principle, Pickford could not resist reminding him that she and Douglas had waited six years for *The Gold Rush*, so she was prepared to give Selznick time to straighten out his problems as well. And she added:

> You are the last person in the motion picture industry who should ever question my good faith and loyalty to you. But if after twenty-five years of such close partnership, you still don't know me, Charlie, it is useless for me to set forth the innumerable times I have stood loyally by you and have closed by eyes to many hurts, rebuffs and humiliations I have endured at your hand.[2]

Chaplin did not bother to answer this heartfelt letter, and after a chilly encounter at the next stockholders' meeting, Pickford wrote her attorney, Charlie Schwartz, on November 9, informing him that from now on she would deal with Chaplin as a "total stranger."[3]

Chaplin, meanwhile, had no new film project on the horizon but continued his tradition of hosting weekly tennis parties at which such stars as Garbo, Gary Cooper, and John Garfield played tennis with the pros and lunched on English tea fare—cakes, crumpets, and simple sandwiches of chicken on white bread. He dated the lovely Carole Landis, then sultry Hedy Lamarr, but as always he was searching for another "unknown"—the woman who could inspire his flagging ambition to make another movie.

Within three months he had found her.

The woman Chaplin would come to know as Joan Berry, or Barry, began life as Mary Louise Gribble in Detroit, Michigan, in 1920, the daughter of a World War I veteran who committed suicide before she was born. Her mother, Gertrude, then married a man named John E. Berry, and the family moved to New York. Mary Louise, who at some point began to be called Joan Berry, attended a Catholic school in the Washington Heights section of Manhattan and later a public high school in Queens. After graduation she moved to Los Angeles, hoping for a career in the movies.

Berry's red hair, pale complexion, and excellent figure were striking, but with no acting experience and a nasal New York accent her chances of getting a break in Hollywood were almost nil. The landlady of a boardinghouse where she lived for a time would remember her as a quiet, well-behaved young woman who worked hard but never managed to earn enough to dress decently. Berry apparently tried to remedy this problem by shoplifting dresses from a Los Angeles department store. She was twice caught with unpaid-for merchandise, and after her second arrest a judge put her on probation and advised her to go home to New York. She did, briefly working as a legal secretary while living with her mother in Brooklyn, but she was soon back in LA.

This time Berry had brought with her the name of a potentially useful contact, MGM producer Sam Marx, whose uncle, dead for almost two decades, had at one time been married to Berry's aunt. Marx was in his office clearing up some paperwork one Saturday morning, when a receptionist sent word that a young woman claiming to be a relative of his was waiting to see him. Marx could see little future for Berry in show business, but he invited her along on a family outing to Laguna Beach.

Not long after, Marx and his wife returned home from an evening at the movies. While he pulled into the garage, his wife made her way along the unlighted path leading to the front door, where she tripped over a body. It was Joan, limp and apparently unconscious. After being revived Berry told the Marxes that she had swallowed sleeping pills in a fit of depression and then, having nowhere else to go, asked a cab driver to bring her to their house. Observing that Berry had revived quickly, Marx was suspicious. He sent her home in a taxi.

A few evenings later another cab pulled up in front of the Marx house. The cabbie reported that Miss Berry had ordered him on an aimless drive around Beverly Hills, running up a substantial fare, and now had no money to pay him. Again, Marx paid the cabbie and told him to return Joan to her apartment.

After these incidents Berry called Marx at the studio and apologized profusely. Worn down by her calls, Marx agreed to arrange for her to do a reading for the MGM talent department. Much to his astonishment, the studio's head scout was impressed. Joan had "fire," she reported. Unfortunately she needed corrective dental work as well as a year's worth of voice coaching, and MGM wasn't interested enough to make the investment. Neither was Sam Marx.

Berry, meanwhile, had been befriended by a young woman who often went out with wealthy out-of-town businessmen. This woman was not a call girl, exactly, though it was tacitly understood that her dates were inclined to be generous and unlikely to invite her home to meet the family. Through this connection Berry was introduced to the oil magnate J. Paul Getty, who took her out to dinner and clubs, "loaning" her several hundred dollars and advancing the down payment on a new Cadillac.

By April 1941 Berry had followed Getty to his home in Acapulco, where his associate A. C. Blumenthal was arranging a house party for a group of Mexican and American businessmen involved in an oil lease deal. Berry now considered Getty her "boyfriend," and her possessiveness had become a problem. Blumenthal talked her into returning to Los Angeles, and gave her some cash as well as letters of introduction to two friends, director Anatole Litvak and Tim Durant. Berry never heard from Litvak, but Durant called her soon after she returned to LA. "Would you like to meet Spencer Tracy or Charlie Chaplin?" he asked her.

"I'd like to meet Spencer Tracy," Joan said.

Durant got Berry an invitation to a party on Errol Flynn's yacht, where Tracy would be a guest. She went but left early when she began to suspect that she had been set up to be Tracy's date on a solitary midnight cruise. A few days later Durant invited her to meet Charlie Chaplin at Perino's, a fashionable Beverly Hills restaurant. Durant and his date departed early, and Joan poured out her hard-luck story. By the end of the evening, she later said, Chaplin had offered her a movie contract. "I can tell that you have a great deal of talent just by looking at you," he told her. "You're so fresh and alive."[4]

Berry dismissed this as just another line, but Chaplin called her at her hotel at 10:00 A.M. the next morning to ask her out again, and a week or so later he invited her to drive to Santa Barbara to attend an auction. In the backseat of his chauffeured car, Berry later said,

Chaplin "was very insistent and impatient and spent most of the trip pawing and mauling me."

As it happens Chaplin mentions this Santa Barbara trip in his autobiography, and while he says nothing about making a pass, he describes Berry as "a big handsome woman of twenty-two [*sic*], well built, with upper regional domes immensely expansive"—an indication of where his interest lay.[5]

At any rate, on June 23, 1941, Joan Berry signed a contract with the Chaplin studio for seventy-five dollars a week, renewable at one hundred a week after six months. At the same time, the studio decided to change her name to Joan Barry.

Soon afterward Joan went to bed with Chaplin for the first time. As she told it her change of heart had nothing to do with the contract. Rather, she finally gave in to his "verbal persuasiveness"—"his violent insistence that he was madly in love with me."

Barry found an apartment on Shirley Place, and Chaplin (or rather, the studio) paid the first two months' rent. She and Charlie then departed on a cruise around Catalina. "On this trip," Barry would say, "he started giving me voice lessons. I remember that every morning for two hours he would have me scream to the seagulls to strengthen my voice." One evening, as they sat on deck under the stars, Chaplin promised to make her the star of his next picture, which, he insisted, would also be his last. As soon as the shooting was finished, they would leave for an extended cruise across the Pacific. "I want to die in the Orient," he said.

A few weeks later Chaplin announced that he had found an ideal vehicle for her film debut. At a luncheon party he recently attended, the conversation had turned to a discussion of Paul Vincent Carroll's play *Shadow and Substance*, about an Irish peasant girl called Bridget who sees the Virgin Mary in a vision. Barry recalled Chaplin saying that the "woman next to him" had described the play as a modern version of the Joan of Arc story, and he immediately thought "That's for my Joanie!" In fact the "woman" who made this comment was Sinclair Lewis. Barry had either never heard of Lewis or misheard the first name.

Though not religious, Chaplin had long toyed with the idea of using the Virgin Mary and the crucifixion as dramatic subjects. As early as the 1920s he had mimed Christ on the cross during a game of charades at San Simeon, and he once proposed to Igor Stravinsky that they collaborate on a film in which the Passion is played out as an act on the stage of a tawdry nightclub while the patrons prattle on, bored and uncomprehending. Chaplin was amazed when Stravinsky suggested that this idea might be considered offensive, and he was similarly oblivious to the unease generated by the news that he had optioned Carroll's somewhat controversial Catholic-oriented drama for twenty thousand dollars. Joan Barry, meanwhile, had been enrolled in acting classes at the Max Reinhardt WorkShop and was making regular visits to a Beverly Hills orthodontist.

Studio manager Alf Reeves had seen many Chaplin "discoveries" come and go, but he noticed that there was something different about this one. Barry, he would recall, was "erratic, emotional, hard to talk to, and could easily effect a vacant stare in her eyes." Amazingly neither Reeves nor Chaplin considered this behavior an indication that it might be risky to plan a major production around her acting debut. Nor did it occur to either of them to get her medical or psychiatric help. As Reeves observed, Barry's disconcerting qualities made her "ideally suited" for the part Chaplin was writing for her.[6]

Moreover, while other studios normally issued publicity releases announcing the signing of new starlets, Barry was told by Reeves to keep her name out of the papers. Barry, on her part, was in no hurry to have Chaplin find out about her feigned suicide in Sam Marx's driveway. She called Marx and told him that she had found a rich boyfriend, and if they should happen to meet, Marx was to pretend not to know her. A few days later Marx was having lunch at the Brown Derby when Joan walked in on the arm of Charlie Chaplin. Marx pretended to look away, but Joan stopped by his table and greeted him as an old friend. Marx said nothing to Chaplin, but Tim Durant soon spoke with Al Blumenthal, who told him about Barry's odd behavior in the past. Durant passed this information along to Charlie, who refused to believe it.

That autumn Barry found that she was pregnant. This puzzled her, since before she and Charlie slept together for the first time he had assured her that he was incapable of fathering children, and on the strength of this assurance she had not bothered about birth control. When she told Charlie about her condition, she expected him to deny that he was responsible. To her surprise he took the news calmly, admitting that he had no actual reason for believing he was sterile.

Barry was about to drive to New York to see her family. Before she left, Chaplin gave her some money and the name of a physician in New York who would "take care of her." Barry stopped in Denver to see her father, and by the time she returned to LA, weeks later than expected, Chaplin was frantic. After telling her that he had considered reporting her missing to the FBI, he nervously asked, "Are you all right?"—meaning, had she terminated the pregnancy.

"No," admitted Joan.

"For God's sake, you've got to do something about it!" he exclaimed.

"We had a big argument about it," Barry later said, "because he wanted to tell Tim Durant about it so that Tim could fix things up and make arrangements for an operation, and he did tell Tim Durant, which upset me. I really wanted to go ahead and have the baby."[7]

Barry became so upset by Chaplin's attempt to "high pressure" her that she fled to San Francisco. After a few days, however, she called Chaplin and agreed to fly back to Los Angeles, where she was met at the airport by a woman who owned a small private sanitarium on the corner of Sunset Boulevard and Alvarado. The next morning the woman took her to the office of Dr. A. N. Tweedie, who was supposed to perform the abortion. In the doctor's office Barry broke down in tears, and Dr. Tweedie refused to proceed. The sanitarium owner then drove Joan back to her apartment, saying she wanted nothing more to do with the situation.

That evening at Summit Drive, Charlie told Joan that if she wanted the child he would support it and even pay for a full-time baby nurse. However, as part of the bargain she would have to sign an agreement saying that she was voluntarily terminating her contract with the studio. Tim Durant showed up with the papers, and after much tearful discussion, Barry changed her mind again. She had the abortion the next day.

Barry's pregnancy must have been well advanced, because Dr. Tweedie had her remain in his office suite under observation for the next five days. When she returned to her apartment she called

Summit Drive and was told by the butler that Mr. Chaplin was in
Catalina. Joan's stepfather, who had recently arrived in LA, drove
her to the harbor. She took the ferry to Catalina but could not find
the *Panacea* at the marina. Later she learned that Charlie was giving
a party that evening and had instructed his servants that if Joan
called they should tell her he was out of town.

Nevertheless, by early December Joan and Charlie were
together again. Joan's voice lessons and orthodontia had improved
her appearance, and Charlie began taking her out socially. At a party
at the home of Jack Warner and his wife he introduced her to
Marlene Dietrich. Afterward Joan complained that she had been
embarrassed to be the only woman there without a fur, and Charlie
sent her to an LA department store where she picked out a silver fox
coat for $1,100. The studio had renewed her contract, and at
Christmastime she received a $1,000 bonus. She was also invited to
Charlie's family Christmas party, where he read excerpts from the
script for *Shadow and Substance* to the guests, including Syd and
Gypsy Chaplin and Alf and Amy Reeves.

There was only one cloud on the horizon: Joan was pregnant
again.

According to Barry, after her abortion she been fitted with a
diaphragm, but Charlie objected that birth control devices were
unaesthetic and didn't want her to use the thing, and so she had
relied on what she called "ordinary precautions [douches]." When
she broke the news that she was pregnant for a second time, he
laughed "as if it were a big joke" and said, "We'll have to send you to
Dr. Tweedie again." This time Joan didn't object, but she was worried about her mother's reaction. Gertrude Berry had been against
the first abortion, and Joan worried that she would make trouble if
she learned about this one.

Chaplin by now was well aware of Joan's family problems. Her
stepfather was wanted for passing bad checks, and her mother,
though Catholic, had decided to divorce him. Joan proposed using
her Christmas bonus to send her mother to Reno, where after six
weeks' residence she could dissolve her marriage with a minimum
of fuss. This would also keep her out of town until after the abor-

tion. Chaplin agreed to the plan and helped talk Gertrude into going.

According to a statement Joan Barry gave in 1943, Chaplin's chauffeur drove her to Dr. Tweedie's office for the second abortion, and Charlie gave her the money, instructing her to tip the nurse and the receptionist twenty dollars each. Later Tweedie's nurse drove her back to Summit Drive. Joan was half asleep in the "Paulette Goddard room," as it was still called, when she was disturbed by a loud argument going on downstairs. Eavesdropping from the landing, she overheard the nurse scolding Chaplin for his carelessness in getting his girlfriend pregnant twice in three months.

"It's my fault. I know it's my fault," Chaplin said. "But if you think about it, it's a 50–50 proposition. The funny thing is, I just have to look at the girl and she gets pregnant." Unimpressed by this explanation, the nurse continued to berate Chaplin until he eased her out the door with the vow: "I will never let her go through it again." Joan spent the next week in bed, and Chaplin waited on her, bringing her breakfast and reading aloud to her when she was bored.

Soon after this second abortion, Joan developed insomnia and visited Minna Wallis's doctor, telling him that Charle was "driving me crazy and if I [don't] get some sleep I [will] go insane." The doctor wrote a prescription for sleeping pills. In January Joan made screen tests at the Chaplin studio for the role of Bridget, but she soon stopped showing up for her acting classes and dentist appointments. Chaplin, meanwhile, had set aside *Shadow and Substance* to work on a reissue of *The Gold Rush*, which he planned to release with a voice-over narration that he would write and record himself. Worried that *Shadow and Substance* would never be made, Joan went to see Sam Marx again. Reminding him that she now had almost a year's worth of acting training, she begged him to arrange a screen test. He agreed, but since MGM wouldn't test an actor who was already under contract to another studio, she would have to ask Chaplin for a release. Joan went to Alf Reeves, who put the paperwork through. She hadn't seen Chaplin in several weeks.

MGM assigned actor Barry Nelson to prepare a scene with Joan for the screen test. As the date of the test approached, Joan became increasingly nervous. She told Nelson that Charlie Chaplin had offered to give her pointers, and he agreed to go with her to Summit Drive for a coaching session. Much to Nelson's chagrin, Chaplin was obviously not expecting them. The atmosphere was so uncomfortable that Nelson made his excuses and left. After this incident Joan failed to keep several appointments at MGM, and the screen test was canceled.

On May 24, Joan Barry's twenty-second birthday, she picked up her morning newspaper to find that gossip columnist Hedda Hopper had taken belated note of Chaplin's plans to film *Shadow and Substance*:

> This is written for just one girl in Hollywood. I don't know who you are. You haven't been discovered yet. But I can tell you that there's a luscious package waiting for you labeled fame. A gentleman named Charlie Chaplin will be sending it over whenever he's ready. I think you should know what's in it. You'll be the lucky girl chosen by Chaplin to play the top feminine role in "Shadow and Substance." It's your chance, the opportunity of a lifetime. You can say farewell to that one-room apartment with a daybed in one corner and a cookstove in the other. You'll be living in a rosy dreamworld of shining limousines, sables and exploding flashbulbs.
>
> Oh, yes, you will. Or maybe you would have if it hadn't been for wartime restrictions.
>
> Anyway, you'll be somebody. All that will be in your tinseled package. Something more, too. Something not quite so good. There've been many Chaplin leading ladies before you. All got the same package with the same trimmings.

Hopper went on to recount the history of previous Chaplin discoveries. "The tradition of the Chaplin leading ladies has taken on a definite pattern. You were nobody when he discovered you. You were sitting on top of the world for a few months. Then you were nobody again."[8]

A conservative anti-Communist, Hedda Hopper had no shortage of motives for disliking Chaplin, several of them personal. Her late husband, DeWolf Hopper—known on the vaudeville circuit for his rendition of "Casey at the Bat"—had been a compulsive seducer, said to be the only man John Barrymore deferred to when it came to chasing women. Cast as Marion Davies's foster mother in *Zander the Great*, Hopper had been a witness to the beginning of her love affair with Chaplin. Hopper had remained close to Marion over the years and undoubtedly heard a great deal from her about the intimate affairs of Charlie Chaplin. Marion—unlike Hopper—was by no means a stickler for traditional moral standards, and she understood that things would never have worked out for her and Charlie. Still, she had come to regard him as a "contrary" personality, one who had a negative effect on other people's lives. This was precisely Hopper's thrust. Despite what she said in her column, Hopper probably knew that Chaplin already had an actress under contract for *Shadow and Substance*. She may even have heard rumors that Chaplin's relationship with his latest protégée was on the rocks and had hopes that her column would lead to a phone call from the unhappy young woman. If so, she was disappointed. Barry clipped the column but did nothing.

In fact Barry had reached the point where she could not organize herself to do a great deal. During the summer she periodically showed up at Summit Drive and at the studio, where Chaplin would listen to her problems and advance her small sums of cash. On at least one occasion there was a violent argument. Chaplin later said that Barry was hysterical and Tim Durant had to restrain her for her own protection. Barry told her landlady's son that Chaplin and Durant had knocked her around. The young man was so indignant that he called Summit Drive and left a message threatening to come up to the house and beat up Chaplin.

Not long after, Barry announced that she had become engaged to David Hecht, an attorney who worked for Paul Getty in New York. Relieved, Chaplin threw her a going-away party, attended by Tim Durant, Charles junior, and several employees of the studio. The party ended on an amiable note, but Barry did not leave town. She later acknowledged that she had made up the story of her engagement, hoping to spur Charlie's jealousy. As she saw it, when she stirred things up, his interest in her invariably revived. "When I behaved myself, he was bored."

Tim Durant, who would later have occasion to speak very candidly to the FBI about the Barry situation, said that by the summer of 1942 Chaplin was "ashamed" of his role in the affair, knew matters were out of control, and had begun to fear for his own safety.

Even so, he couldn't bring himself to follow a consistent course of action. Said Durant:

> Well, I tell you, there's nobody that knows Charlie any better than I do. I don't know whether I can express it but I know him inside and out. I have no illusions about him. He has a great many faults and I know them d[amn] well. He's a great artist. . . . He has been a great boon to me in many ways—his ability to lift me up when I'm depressed. He's given me a different slant on life, a completely different point of view and character. Not all good, but interesting and certainly it has been very broadening to me . . . [but] he's done nothing for me. I haven't wanted it particularly, but he could have done a great deal, but he's not a person you could expect anything from. . . . I really in a way feel very sorry for him. He has very few friends. He's antagonized everybody. . . .
>
> Psychologically, psychopathically Charlie is a very small person. His success with women has been very poor. He attracts women, but he doesn't hold them. He very seldom holds them, because he's selfish; he's very self-centered; he's very egocentric. He's like Hitler—he wants to dominate and possess, and people can't take that—especially women. He's too absorbing. He expects too much, and he always wants to express himself, not particularly sexually, but he always wants to have people like him and, you know, be involved with him to a certain extent. It's his ego. Actors are that way. . . .
>
> I think in the case of Joan Berry [sic] it was a mistake. She wasn't capable of standing and sustaining anything. She really hasn't the emotional discipline. She couldn't handle a thing like that. I think he really overdid it and I think that was his crime.[9]

While Chaplin was becoming entangled with Joan Barry, dramatic events were taking place on the world scene. On June 22, 1941, having subjugated the Low Countries and France, Hitler repudiated his nonaggression pact with Stalin and launched an invasion of the Soviet Union. Once again the Communist USA Party changed direction. Its "peace vigil" outside the White House was disbanded, literally overnight, and the American Peace Mobilization was dissolved. Instead of charging Roosevelt with wanting to see American boys used for cannon fodder, the party now supported Lend-Lease and an early entry into the war. Within a few months of Pearl Harbor, the Communist Party began calling for the United States to divert troops from the Pacific for an immediate invasion of Europe. Allied landings on the European continent would force Hitler to divert troops from the Eastern Front, taking pressure off the Soviet Union.

Circumstances had made the Soviet Union and the United States allies. As far as anti-Communists were concerned, the animosities aroused by the party's calculated shifts in position were suppressed but hardly forgotten. On the other hand, many liberals, who had begun to come to grips with the reality of Stalinism over the past several years, reverted to their earlier romanticized view of the "people's democracy." Columnist Max Lerner, for example, argued that the Red Army's valiant resistance to the Nazis *proved* that Stalin's regime was basically progressive and popular.

In July 1941, a few weeks after the invasion of the Soviet Union, a meeting was held in Los Angeles to organize Russian War Relief, Inc. (later the American Committee for Russian War Relief). P. Kondratiev, a Soviet diplomat attached to the Los Angeles consulate during the war, writes in his memoirs that when he met composer Dmitri Tiomkin, who was the chairman of the organization at the time, Tiomkin told him how Chaplin shamed the others at the meeting by leaping out of his chair to pledge a donation of one thousand dollars. Chaplin also agreed to be listed as one of the group's official sponsors.

Nothing much came of Chaplin's involvement until the spring of 1942. Calls for the opening of a second front were gathering steam, and a delegation of Soviet newsreel cameramen had arrived in the United States, bringing with them documentary footage of the fighting in Russia—later reedited by Albert Maltz and released in the United States as *Moscow Strikes Back*. When the documentary was screened at Chaplin's studio, Nikolai Litkin, one of the cameramen, noticed that Chaplin remained seated for a long time after the film ended, his head bowed, obviously deeply moved.

A little later, Litkin recalled, Chaplin bent over and a sheet of paper slipped out of his coat pocket. He deftly retrieved it, remarking that it was telegram from a judge who happened to be a fan of his. Chaplin added that he was about to make a speech on behalf of the Second Front in San Francisco, and "I might say something at this meeting which will cause me to need this judge's help."[10]

Chaplin tells a very different story about the San Francisco rally in his autobiography. According to his account, the invitation to speak came the night before the event, when he was asked to substitute for Joseph E. Davies, the former American ambassador to the Soviet Union, who had come down with laryngitis. He arrived expecting to talk for about four minutes (approximately the length of the closing speech from *The Great Dictator*), but shortly before the rally began, the organizers told him to stretch his remarks to one hour. Fortified by a few glasses of champagne, he sat on the platform, listening to the remarks of other speakers, whose lukewarm attitude toward the Soviet Union disgusted him. He was especially incensed by the mayor of San Francisco, who told the audience, "We must live with the fact that the Russians are our allies." When it came his turn to take the microphone, he launched his speech by addressing the audience as "Comrades!"

There was nervous laughter.

"And I do mean comrades. I assume there are many Russians here tonight, and the way your countrymen are fighting and dying at this moment, it is an honor and a privilege to call you comrades."

"I am not a Communist, I am a human being," Chaplin continued. Egged on by the response of the audience, he went on to speak for another forty minutes. Among other statements, he charged that two million Allied soldiers were "languishing" in Ireland while the Russians fought and died for "our way of life."[11]

Only later, when actor John Garfield told him, "You have a lot of courage," did he become depressed by the thought that he might have made trouble for himself.

Chaplin's ability (and, indeed, desire) to quote verbatim from the most controversial portions of this speech in his autobiography suggests that his words were hardly the product of a few too many glasses of champagne at lunch. As Litkin's story suggests, he had written the speech well in advance and knew that it would be widely regarded as offensive and inflammatory.

The Second Front campaign attracted many supporters who were by no means Communists. Such people had wanted to intervene in Europe long before and they feared that the United States, in order to concentrate its efforts on fighting Japan, would put off joining the European war as long as possible. Perhaps we would even wait too long, allowing the Germans to consolidate their advances. Few, however, went so far as to publicly suggest that American troops were "languishing" anywhere. The notion that the invasion of Europe was militarily feasible and was being deliberately delayed by a cabal of right-wing generals was pure Communist propaganda—and seldom so bluntly stated before a general audience, even by Communist Party members.

The United States was at war, though Chaplin seemed scarcely to notice this. While Hollywood mobilized to an extent undreamed of during World War I, Chaplin dickered with the government over compensation for the *Panacea,* which was being commandeered for patrol duty, and showed no visible sign of concern for American troops, meanwhile displaying his pro-Soviet sentiments in ways that were at times politically provocative and at other times just fatuous.

On May 25, a week after the San Francisco rally, he made a very similar speech at a Second Front meeting at the Shrine auditorium in Los Angeles. This Los Angeles rally was occasioned by the arrival in Long Beach of a Soviet freighter on a wartime goodwill visit. During a banquet held for the crew, recalled the Soviet official, Kondratiev, Chaplin sat at the head table and a made an "excited" speech that so impressed the captain that a year later, when his ship once again docked in the city, he brought Chaplin a live bear cub from Kamchatka as a present. The cub was presented to Chaplin at a ceremony arranged by the Soviet consul, Yevgeny Tumantsev.

Another rather bizarre incident from this period was Chaplin's meeting with Ludmilla Pavlichenko, a sharpshooter officially credited with killing 309 fascists (German soldiers). Pavlichenko's tour of the United States with a Soviet youth delegation produced wildly varying newspaper coverage. Some hailed her as a Russian Molly Pitcher or Sergeant York, while others sarcastically described her as another Soviet first, a female mass killer. "Undoubtedly Chaplin was familiar with all the materials about me published in the American press," Pavlichenko would remember. "He read everything, the stories written with good will and the malignant and hostile ones." At a War Relief function, Chaplin made a point of being photographed kissing Pavlichenko's hand. In her 1959 memoir, she interpreted his gesture as "a reply to the insinuations of American fascists."[12]

The Second Front movement reached its peak during the summer of 1942 when news of horrendous losses in the Caucasus inspired fear that Soviet resistance might collapse entirely A rally held on July 22 at Madison Square Garden in New York City was advertised as a "Support the President Rally for a Second Front Now"—a reference to a comment by FDR to Soviet Foreign Minister Vyacheslav Molotov that he wanted to see a second front opened in 1942. The Communist press was by now charging that Roosevelt wanted the Second Front but was being held back by Gen. George Marshall and other military men, who were planning to make a separate peace with Germany. The CIO was listed as the official sponsor of the rally and the evening's speakers included Mayor Fiorello La Guardia, Sen. Claude Pepper of Florida, New York's avowedly pro-Soviet Rep. Vito Marcantonio, and labor leaders Joseph Curran and Mike Quill. Chaplin addressed the rally via a telephone hookup from his home in Beverly Hills, reading a prepared text that began with the ringing phrase: "On the battlefields of Russia democracy will live or die. The fate of the Allied Nations is in the hands of the Communists." He continued:

We hear that the Allies haven't sufficient supplies to support a second front. Then again we hear that they have. We also hear that they don't want to risk a second front at this time in case of possible defeat. That they don't want to take a chance until they are sure and ready. . . . But we cannot afford to lose Russia for that is the aggressive front line of democracy. . . . Then watch out, for the appeasers will come out of their holes. They will want to make peace with a victorious Hitler . . . and then before we are aware of it we will have succumbed to the Nazi ideology. Then we shall be enslaved. Human progress will be lost. There will be no minority rights, no workers' right, no citizens' rights. All that will be blasted too. . . .

Let us aim for victory in the spring.[13]

Chaplin's speech was reprinted in a pamphlet describing him as "the great people's artist of America" and illustrated with a still from The Great Dictator that showed Charlie in the custody of a pair of SS men—on one of them the "double cross" armband used in the film had been airbrushed out and a swastika painted in. Like the Great Dictator speech, the full text of Chaplin's Madison Square Garden remarks was ambiguous—his words could be narrowly interpreted to mean that the Caucasus oil fields were essential to the Allied effort, though the phrase "front line of democracy" clearly implied much more.

By the autumn of 1942 furious fighting in the Pacific theater of war and the imminent Allied invasion of North Africa had taken most of the wind out of the Second Front campaign, and when a group called the Artists' Front to Win the War scheduled another rally in New York for October 14, they rented Carnegie Hall instead of the larger Madison Square Garden. Compared to the July meeting, this event had a distinctly fellow-travelerish orientation, and a larger proportion of the audience were party members.

Chaplin was invited to New York as the keynote speaker, and he opened with a variation on the line that had caused such a sensation in San Francisco: "Dear Comrades, and yes, I do mean comrades. When one sees the magnificent fight the Russian people are putting up it is a pleasure and a privilege to use the word 'comrade.'"

He went on to give a rambling thirty-minute talk. According to newspaper accounts, he said at one point that he personally wasn't worried about predictions that Communism would spread worldwide after the war because "I can live on $25,000 a year."

In November, Chaplin appeared in Chicago. Addressing an audience of about 2,500, mainly party stalwarts, he said: "We are no longer shocked by Russian purges. They liquidated the Quislings and the Lavals, and it was too bad that Norway, Hungary, and other countries didn't do the same. The stigma against Russia is being dissolved like mist in the sun."[14]

The Stalinist purges had often been denied or rationalized, but rarely had they received such a ringing endorsement.

A month later, on December 3, Chaplin was once again in New York, this time appearing as the guest of honor at a Russian War Relief banquet at the Pennsylvania Hotel. This fund-raising event took on the nature of a Chaplin testimonial, and leading pro-Stalinist artists including Dmitri Shostakovich and Ilya Ehrenburg sent congratulatory telegrams, which were read aloud to the assembled guests.

It was the Pennsylvania Hotel banquet that prompted columnist Westbrook Pegler to wonder why Attorney General Francis J. Biddle had not taken steps to have Chaplin deported in light of his "decided partiality to Communism." Pegler excerpted a letter he had received from singer/actress Jeanette MacDonald, who said that she had been approached by Chaplin to lend her name to the Carnegie Hall rally in New York. MacDonald's husband, Capt. Gene Raymond, had recently participated in costly air raids on Dieppe and Rouen, undertaken to test the strength of German fortifications. Since thousands of lives were at stake, including her loved one's, MacDonald said, she had told Chaplin that she was quite willing to leave the timing of the Second Front in the hands of General Eisenhower rather than a bunch of performers. As for Chaplin, she concluded, "I have not given up the hope that he will find it in his heart to go to England, or even Russia, where he could bring great joy" to soldiers returning "half crazed and exhausted" from the front.[15] This response from the normally gentle MacDonald showed just how easy it was to strike a nerve with people who had family members in uniform by implying that Allied troops were not dying quite fast enough.

After a lifetime of relative caution when it came to political involvement, Chaplin was now speaking freely—and none too judiciously. What prompted the sudden outpouring?

Chaplin was quite clear about what motivated him—not Communist doctrine per se, or even opposition to Hitlerism, but his feelings about Soviet Russia. In late 1943 he summed them up in a brief statement in *Script*, which had been taken over by Florence Wagner after her husband's death:

Twenty-six years ago a brave new world was born that gave hope and inspiration to the common man. That world was Soviet Russia, imbued with a dream that would give its people, no matter what race or color, their natural rights to equal liberty, equal justice, and equal opportunity in the pursuit of food and shelter and the life beautiful. And in spite of the ravages of wars, that dream has become a reality, and grows more glorious year by year. Now that the agony of birth is at an end, may the beauty of its growth endure forever.[16]

Chaplin had said in the past, and would often say again, that he was basically an apolitical artist, one who wanted no part of nationalism, patriotism, and militarism. Even many who disagreed with him could respect him for upholding these values. Now, with a handful of speeches he had exposed himself as a hypocrite. If his paean to the Soviet Union wasn't a fervent testament of patriotism, what was it? As for the antiwar, pacifist Chaplin, he too had vanished. In the pages of *Script* Chaplin now called for "More Bombs for Berlin," just as in his speeches he harangued American generals for being reluctant to launch a premature invasion that would have led to the wholesale slaughter of their armies.

Emotions run high during wartime, and Chaplin's fault was surely not that he allowed himself to be touched by the sufferings of the Soviet people, or even that he had made a few speeches at rallies that were arguably organized and manipulated by Communists. But his speeches stood out from those of others who appeared on the same platforms, distinguished by their contempt for American and British interests. Meanwhile all his sympathies were directed toward a country he had never visited, and which he clearly knew little about.

Since the late 1930s Chaplin had been associating mainly with American Communists like Donald Ogden Stewart and his wife, Ella Winter, and with left-wing European émigrés who gathered at the home of Bertholt Viertel (the man who introduced Egon Kisch to Upton Sinclair years before) and his wife, screenwriter Salka Viertel. The recent émigrés were variously unhappy or just ill-at-ease and likely to see a fascist coup around every corner. And one, composer Hanns Eisler, may have been assigned by the Comintern to influence Chaplin in a pro-Soviet direction.

Chaplin's admirers would defend him, then and now, by saying that he was not "really" a Communist but, as Richard Attenborough recently put it, a "limousine liberal." But "limousine liberals" are not popular, especially if they are just dabbling in politics as attitude. And this was exactly what many of Chaplin's contemporaries thought in the mid-forties, including some who counted themselves his friends. As Tim Durant put it:

He's very small; he's very bourgeois, he's very narrow about a lot of things, and yet he's got a lot of spirit and it's usually used in the wrong direction. He's a parlor economist. He's a political amateur and a very absurd one. He's no more of a Communist than I am. He has these ideas that are simply a question of trying to express himself. He's a ham at heart—he admits that. He wanted to startle people and interest people.

None of this quite explains why Chaplin felt so alienated that he needed to look to the Soviet Union as a spiritual homeland. One could understand a certain bitterness toward England, perhaps, as the scene of his youthful poverty. But in the United States he had enjoyed unparalleled success, riches, and the love of millions of devoted fans. And yet he couldn't love them back, even a little.

17

"The Public Wants a Victim!"

One day that autumn Rollie Totheroh arrived at the studio to find a young, exceptionally good-looking brunette waiting by the gate. The girl explained that she had met Mr. Chaplin at a nightclub, presumably in New York, and he had told her to look him up. Now she was in Los Angeles, and living a short distance from the studio.

"Not another one!" Totheroh muttered to himself. He tried to steer the girl to Alf Reeves, but she insisted that she would see Chaplin and no one else. If he wasn't available, she would prefer to come back another day.[1]

The girl was Oona O'Neill, at seventeen already a familiar face at New York's Stork Club, where she had recently been feted as "Deb of the Year." Born in Bermuda in 1925, Oona was the daughter of playwright Eugene O'Neill and his second wife, Agnes Boulton, also a writer. Before Oona's third birthday her parents had separated, launching a nasty battle over alimony. Eugene O'Neill, at first guilt-stricken about leaving his wife, had fallen in love with Carlotta Monterey, the chic, supercompetent ex-wife of Chaplin's friend, Ralph Barton. One of his complaints against Agnes, whose mercurial temperament matched his own, was that she had not devoted herself sufficiently to taking care of him—she was preoccupied with her own writing, and with two toddlers to care for, Oona and Shane, she let the house become a shambles. Agnes, on her part, was stunned by her husband's ingratitude. She had stayed with Gene through years of financial uncertainty and heavy drinking.

Now he was (temporarily) sober and rapidly becoming internationally recognized as America's greatest living dramatist, and she was to be left with nothing.

In his pique over the alimony issue, Gene O'Neill went so far as to hire detectives to investigate Agnes's past, and he threatened that if she delayed the divorce he would simply "starve her out." At this his attorney, Harry Weinberger, warned O'Neill that he was risking the same sort of ugly publicity that had recently arisen from Charlie Chaplin's attempts to deny his wife, Lita, an appropriate settlement. O'Neill angrily denied that there was any comparison: "Chaplin's wife had charged him with ruining young girls, with every form of perversion—and he was guilty as everyone knows. There was every form of dirt to it. But in my case what is there to hide?"[2]

After the divorce Agnes and the children moved around a lot. They lived in Connecticut for a time. Oona was sent to a convent school in Key West and later attended public school in Point Pleasant, New Jersey. She was a precocious, book-loving girl who kept to herself, writing stories and compiling scrapbooks filled with pictures of her favorite movie stars. By her early teens she had the body of a woman, wore makeup, and talked about becoming a movie star, but she paid little attention to boys and was withdrawn, even silent, except with her closest friends. As a girlfriend from Point Pleasant put it, "She was not exactly full of excitement at being alive."[3]

Gene O'Neill wrote Oona and her brother Shane courtly, affectionate letters. He encouraged the children's interest in jazz and drama, and discussed his literary work with them as if they were colleagues whose opinions he valued. Rarely, however, did he express any interest in seeing them or taking on the practical responsibilities of fatherhood. By 1936 even the letters had stopped coming. Ravaged by the effects of a lifetime of drinking, as well as the advancing symptoms of Parkinson's disease and the depression that often accompanies them, he was no longer up to the task. Carlotta occasionally wrote for him.

Oona, her mother, and for that matter many of O'Neill's old friends, could not accept his deterioration. When he ignored them, or lashed out irrationally, they blamed Carlotta. No doubt the chilly, exotic-looking Carlotta, born Hazel Thorsing in Oakland, California, was something of a fake and at times overprotective of her husband's declining energies. But she was less a domineering temptress than a mother figure who had devoted herself utterly to the role of the Great Man's wife-secretary, confidante, fan, and, ultimately, nurse. Oona grew up with the image of Carlotta as a villainness—and yet a powerful woman who had managed to hold on to her husband when her own mother could not.

When Oona was fourteen Agnes Boulton took an apartment in Manhattan, enrolled her in the Brearley School, and began to lobby her Social Register friends to ensure that Oona would be invited to make a formal debut. Scraping up the money to support even a pretense of social acceptability was a challenge, but Oona's status as the daughter of a Nobel Prize winner and critically certified American genius counted for a great deal. Oona was blossoming into a beautiful girl with lustrous black hair, wide-set eyes, and a generous mouth. Agnes hoped she would make the most of her looks and marry someone who could give her financial security.

When Oona was fifteen her mother began taking her to movie premieres and nightclubs. Oona looked like a chorus girl and quickly developed wit and poise beyond her years, but in reality she was completely inexperienced. She and her best friend Carol Marcus were starry-eyed about literature and naively amazed to discover that middle-aged male writers could be interested in them.

But unlike Carol and Carol's other close friend, heiress Gloria Vanderbilt, Oona was a poor girl, pretending to be rich. She knew it, and the realization affected her outlook on life, especially as she entered her senior year at Brearley. Her friends were already moving on, leading glamorous, grown-up lives. Seventeen-year-old Gloria had gone to Beverly Hills to live with her mother, and in December 1941 she married Pat DiCicco, an aide to Howard Hughes. Carol, who had finished school a year ahead of Oona, went to California to be a bridesmaid at Gloria's wedding, and while there met and fell in love with the writer William Saroyan.

Oona had planned to attend Vassar, but now that she was "Deb of the Year" and already a favorite of society-page photographers, freshman English and sorority mixers seemed a little beside the point. Communicating with her father through his attorney, she asked him to support her while she studied at the Neighborhood

Playhouse in New York. But O'Neill was heartbroken that his brilliant daughter was turning down a college education. Unable to cope with Oona's rejection of his dreams for her, he turned bitter and refused to pay for her acting lessons. Writing to Weinberger, he complained that "Deb of the Year" was an ersatz title, cooked up by the Stork Club's publicity agent—which it was—and that Oona had been chosen because of her famous name—which was probably true as well. He also expressed his dismay that Oona had been photographed at a benefit for Russian War Relief, an organization he considered objectionable. As for acting classes, they would have been just "another typical Boulton trick to avoid real work or study," and he dismissed his only daughter as a "spoiled, lazy vain little brat who has, so far, by her actions only proven that she can be a much sillier and bad mannered fool than most girls her age."[4]

After a brief stint in summer stock, Oona headed for California, traveling as a token chaperone for her friend Carol, who was visiting her fiancé, the recently drafted Bill Saroyan. In San Francisco, Oona called Tao House, her father and Carlotta's home in Danville, asking permission to come for a visit. Not only didn't O'Neill wish to see her, he was irate that she had let Carol Marcus pay for her train ticket and furious with her for taking up space on a cross-country train during wartime, when unnecessary travel was severely discouraged. Oona, he complained to Weinberger, appeared to have absolutely no idea that there was a war going on.

Unable to see her father, Oona moved on to Los Angeles, where her mother was working on a screenplay with her current boyfriend, producer Morris "Mac" Kaufman. Wartime housing being scarce, Agnes Boulton was living in a trailer park, but she did have a number of good contacts with producers. Oona began making the rounds of the studios, but the men she spoke with were more interested in getting her into bed than into the movies. She had brought few clothes with her from New York, had very little money, and was rapidly becoming discouraged when she finally got her chance to meet Chaplin.

Chaplin later wrote that he was introduced to Oona by Minna Wallis, a powerful Hollywood agent and close friend of Tim Durant. If so Wallis was acting in a personal, not a professional capacity. Agnes Boulton had known Chaplin for years—some mutual friends say they'd had a brief affair—and she had reason to believe Chaplin might help Oona out for friendship's sake. Moreover, as Rollie Totheroh recalled, Oona had already taken the initiative in seeking out Chaplin.

At any rate, by November 1942 Chaplin was talking about reviving *Shadow and Substance*, with Oona taking over Joan Barry's role. He also began escorting Oona, sometimes accompanied by her mother, to fashionable restaurants in Beverly Hills, and she spent her days by his pool, often dressed in only a brassiere and shorts. "She had nothing," one of Chaplin's servants recalled.

Oona's presence at Summit Drive added another element of tension to an already unhappy household. Chaplin's Japanese servants— including the amiable, American-born Frank Yonamori; Kay, the chauffeur; George, the cook; and Frank's wife, Chiyoko, who supervised the maids—had been placed in internment camps for the duration of the war. The Japanese staff got along with one another, and they had always gone far beyond the requirements of their jobs to cater to Chaplin's whims and anticipate his needs. Without them he was lost.

No doubt Chaplin's resentment of the internment policy— whether on his staff's behalf or his own—had a good deal to do with his jaundiced view of the American war effort in the Pacific. His former chauffeur and aide, Toraichi Kono, moreover, had been interned as a enemy alien two years before the war started, under suspicion of passing military intelligence to a Japanese naval officer. Kono was running an import-export business in LA, and espionage allegations against Japanese businessmen were not uncommon at the time. In Kono's case, however, there was substantial evidence. Kono used his enforced leisure to cooperate with Gerith von Ulm, another detainee, in producing a tell-all book about his years with Chaplin.

The servants who replaced Frank, George, Kay, and the others were far less compliant than their predecessors had been. Their positions were temporary, in wartime Los Angeles jobs were plentiful, and almost from the beginning they were unhappy with Chaplin. Chauffeur and "second man" Andrew Dahl, a naturalized

Norwegian and one of the few citizens on the staff, was particularly upset about his employer's flouting of wartime regulations. When rationing was imposed, Dahl later complained, Chaplin immediately purchased eighty pounds of coffee without declaring it, as well as a freezer that was regularly stocked with steaks and roast beef by a man Dahl called a "meat racketeer."[5]

The "racketeer" in question was Robert Eugene Arden, a somewhat mysterious figure. In addition to working with Chaplin on the *Shadow and Substance* script, Arden had a weekly radio program of foreign affairs commentary on Warner Bros.' Los Angeles station, WTFB. Born Rudolph Kligler in Vienna in 1900, he was active in left-wing politics before fleeing Austria in 1934. Now he was trying to become a citizen through a private bill in Congress, and Chaplin had helped him line up support from Jack Warner and others.

Arden claimed that he could not apply for citizenship through the usual channels because he had been forced to leave Austria in a hurry without his passport or identification papers, and as a Jew, he could not obtain copies. In fact he had been repeatedly told by the INS that he could get around this problem by going to Canada and applying for reentry on the basis of an affidavit. He didn't want to do this, no doubt in part because there were things in his record that might prompt the INS and the FBI to challenge his application for reentry.

Arden had come to the United States for the first time in 1929. A year later he was deported, having overstayed his visa, and although he had supposedly returned to Europe, the INS had reason to believe that he went to Cuba instead. In 1934 he entered the United States on a one-week transit visa for Panama, and had presumably been in the States ever since. Though married to a U.S. citizen for some years, he had made no attempt to straighten out his residency status until the war began, when he decided that he wanted to become a citizen so that he could volunteer for war work. Arden claimed to speak sixteen languages, and he was eager to get involved in propaganda broadcasts and intelligence.[6]

It may be that Arden was just a displaced intellectual, set adrift by the war, but certain factors in his history suggested that he might be a Comintern agent. For whatever reasons, he was almost universally mistrusted by Chaplin's friends as well as by the household staff, who viewed his frequent visits with suspicion.

Then, too, Joan Barry was not quite out of the picture. All summer long Joan had been saying that LA was a "dirty town," but despite much talk of returning to New York, she never went. Barry still believed herself to be deeply in love with Chaplin, and by now she was in too much emotional turmoil to make any plan and stick to it. In October, a few weeks before he headed east to speak at the Carnegie Hall rally, Chaplin offered to buy cross-country train tickets for Joan and her mother. As he would recall it, he was just trying to do the two women (and surely himself) a favor. What Joan heard was that he was inordinately proud of the speech he planned to give and wanted her to be in the audience to share his big moment.

In New York, Joan checked into the Pierre Hotel, which happened to be owned by Paul Getty. David Hecht, Getty's attorney, escorted her to the Carnegie Hall rally, and later that evening they showed up at the Stork Club, where Chaplin was dining with friends. A few days later Chaplin ran into Joan again at the "21" Club, and they went back to his hotel suite, where he gave her three hundred dollars. Joan claimed that they also "had an affair" before she left at about 5:00 A.M. Chaplin would deny this, saying they spent the night engaged in "the usual arguments."

Although Joan soon returned to Los Angeles, she left town again in November, during which time Chaplin began seeing Oona. At the beginning of December she called Summit Drive saying she was back in LA. Chaplin invited her to have dinner with him at Romanoff's restaurant, but asked her not to have anything to drink beforehand. Incapable of keeping her promise, Barry showed up at the restaurant bar at 4:00 P.M. with a writer friend, Hans Reusch. By the time Chaplin arrived at eight, she was drunk, and she insisted on bringing Reusch to the table to meet Chaplin.

"Do you have to flaunt your lover before me?" Chaplin asked, according to Barry.

"Quite an argument" ensued, and that night, back at her hotel, Joan swallowed a handful of sleeping pills. A maid discovered her lying unconscious in her room the next morning, and the hotel manager called in a doctor as well as a private nurse. The Chaplin studio refused to pay the bills for these services, which were eventually covered by J. Paul Getty.

Joan's mental state went downhill rapidly after her suicide attempt. She had no income, and Chaplin agreed to pay her an allowance of fifty dollars a week. Though his offer may have been well-intentioned, it did nothing to solve Joan's problems and was just large enough to keep her in town and dependent on him for regular handouts. She interpreted the arrangement as a sign that Chaplin was still interested in her and wanted to remain in control of her life.

On December 23 Joan showed up at Summit Drive a day early asking for her allowance. Although the next day would be Christmas Eve, Chaplin sent word through Edward Chaney, his new butler, that she would have to wait.

That night, around midnight, Joan returned with a gun and a vague plan to commit suicide in Chaplin's presence. She walked into the house unchallenged and confronted him in the upstairs hallway, where he was on the phone with Florence Wagner. Joan pointed the gun at him, angrily accusing him of having another girlfriend. The standoff was still going on when Charles junior and Sydney Earle came home. Chaplin called out to the boys, ordering them to go to their room and lock themselves in.

Eventually Joan calmed down. As she recalled it, she spent the night in the guest bedroom, and that night and again the next morning she and Charlie made love. The first time the weapon was still on the bedside table, and Charlie remarked that he had never before had sex with a loaded gun pointed at his head, saying: "Well, this is a new twist."

The following night, Christmas Eve, Chaplin had guests. Joan stood outside the house and threw mud at the windows.

On December 30, when Joan showed up again for her allowance, Chaplin agreed to see her, and they sat in front of the fire discussing her problems. Although he rarely drove, he then offered to take her home, but in the car they got into an argument and Chaplin drove to the Beverly Hills police station, pointed to the door, and suggested she spend the night in jail. Joan did go into the police station, but only to call Hans Reusch, who let her sleep at his apartment.

The December 23 incident had frightened Chaplin into hiring Max Watt, the husband of studio secretary Lois Runser Watt, as a night watchman. And on New Year's Eve, while Chaplin was having dinner at Chasen's restaurant, Watt found Barry wandering the property, armed with another gun. He confiscated the weapon and notified Chaplin, who said, "Call the police." Before the police arrived, however, Joan asked to use the bathroom, where she squeezed through a small window and dropped sixteen feet into a bed of ivy. Patrolmen searched the grounds but found no trace of her.

From Summit Drive, Joan somehow made her way to the apartment of her friend Elaine Barrie, the ex-wife of John Barrymore. An hour or so later Barrie called the Beverly Hills police and the *Los Angeles Examiner*, saying that Joan Barry, who had just been dumped by Charlie Chaplin, was planning to kill herself. She also called Summit Drive and spoke with Edward Chaney, who advised the police to check with Hans Reusch. At three A.M. a patrol car found Joan, dressed in Reusch's pajamas, stretched out in the front seat of a car parked on the street in front of Reusch's apartment, her lips smeared with iodine. At the hospital a doctor concluded that she was acting out a "simulated suicide attempt," and she was booked on a charge of vagrancy.

The following morning Robert Arden visited the police station and had a talk with Det. William White, who in turn conferred with police court judge Charles Griffin. White then told Barry that it would be in her best interests to plead guilty. On January 2 Griffin sentenced Barry to ninety days, suspended, on the condition that she stay out of town for two years. Arden paid Barry's hotel bills, and on January 4 he purchased a one-way train ticket to New York in her name.

Joan had no luggage at this point, and Arden asked Ed Chaney to borrow one of Chaplin's suitcases so that he could help her pack. Chaney was very unhappy about this request. Even Chaplin's luggage, it seems, was technically studio property—and therefore tax deductible—so Chaney was required to report the loan to Lois Watt. If the suitcase, which happened to be an expensive one, was not returned, he knew that Watt would try to get him to reimburse the studio out of his own pocket, which he felt was hardly his responsibility. Even so, Chaney decided that the headache was worth it. "At this point I felt just like Mr. Chaplin," he would say. "Anything to get rid of her."

On January 5 Detective White and his wife accompanied Joan to the train station to see her off. As people were boarding the train, White pressed a hundred-dollar bill into her hand. He also tipped the porter, asking him to see that she did not leave the train until it reached New York.

For almost four months Joan Barry dropped out of sight.

Young Charles and Sydney, meanwhile, had been eyeing Oona O'Neill, wondering which of them would work up the nerve to ask her out first. Before long they realized that neither of them had a chance. Charles junior had seen many younger women fall under the spell of his dad's charm, but Oona was a special case: "She worshipped him, drinking in every word he spoke."[7]

Oona, however, was not well. She had developed a bad cough and a chronic respiratory infection. Chaplin insisted that Oona move into the house full-time, putting her up in "the Paulette Goddard room." He told the staff that Oona had tuberculosis, which seems unlikely. True or not, it didn't make them any happier about having to take care of her.

Oona gradually recovered, but she never moved out. Unlike earlier protégées, she was not much interested in nightclubbing or shopping, and spent her time reading her way through his library. Chaplin himself no longer read much of anything except mysteries and the *Police Gazette*, but he enjoyed hearing Oona read aloud and talk about literature, which she did in an unaffected, humorous way. Quite soon he brought up the possibility that they would marry after *Shadow and Substance* was finished—which, at the rate he worked, put the date four or five years in the future. In the meantime, since he was not yet ready to begin shooting, he allowed Oona to test for a role in *The Girl From Leningrad*, a picture being planned by his friend, producer Eugene Frenke.

In late April, Joan Barry returned to Los Angeles. She had spent the intervening months mainly in Kansas City and Tulsa, the site of Getty Oil's home office, registering in hotels under various aliases.

In Tulsa she was arrested for writing bad checks. According to Barry, when the police court ordered her out of LA she had protested to Robert Arden that she had no means of support, and he promised her that Chaplin would continue to deposit her allowance in her Beverly Hills bank account—provided she sent back his $125 suitcase. Barry had forgotten about the suitcase, Chaplin's payments stopped, and her account was empty.

Joan checked into the Château Elysée, a slightly rundown residential hotel in the Hollywood Hills. The Elysée, managed by Tom Ince Jr., happened to be the very property said by Hollywood gossip to have been paid for by W. R. Hearst as a settlement to Nell Ince after her husband's death in 1924. Joan was pregnant again, and sure in her own mind that the child had been conceived on the night of December 23–24, when she and Charlie made love with her revolver beside them on the nightstand.

Not long after her arrival, Joan took a taxi to Summit Drive, entered by the back door, and headed straight upstairs. Throwing open the door of "Paulette's room," she saw a naked woman in the bed. Charlie, fully clothed, was seated at the foot of the bed.

Until this moment Joan Barry had been unaware of Oona O'Neill's existence. Hysterical, she ran downstairs. Chaplin ran after her, promising that if she waited down by the pool he would come out and talk things over. Twenty-five minutes later, when he still hadn't shown up, Joan smashed a glass ashtray on the concrete apron of the pool and attempted to slash her wrists with the shards. She also called the Beverly Hills police, daring them to come up to the house and arrest her. The patrol car took a long time to arrive, and before it showed up Edward Chaney drove Joan back to her hotel.

Joan Barry had not forgotten the Hedda Hopper column that appeared, by an uncanny coincidence, on her birthday. The morning after her visit to Summit Drive, she went to Hopper's house and told her that she was the girl originally signed for *Shadow and Substance*. Now she was pregnant, and Chaplin refused to do anything for her. Hopper made an appointment for Barry with her own physician, William L. Branch, who confirmed the pregnancy. She was prepared to print the story but told Joan she needed time to check it out.

Joan, meanwhile, had taken note of Chaplin's unlisted number, and the next time she called the house Ed Chaney warned her that Chaplin had sent someone around to the Château Elysée to check up on her. Afraid she would be arrested if she returned to her hotel, Joan decided to make one more attempt to confront Charlie.

She arrived at Summit Drive while Charlie was eating dinner with Oona and Tim Durant. Durant went to the door and tried to persuade her to leave, but she parked herself on a stone wall opposite the front entrance and refused to budge while Charlie cowered behind the door, whispering: "I'm afraid she'll shoot me." Eventually he did step outside, shouting, "You dirty little blackmailer. Get the hell out of here. I mean it this time. . . . If you don't get off [*sic*], you'll be put in jail."

Edward Chaney witnessed the scene and decided that Joan was more pathetic than dangerous. "She looked like a little girl of sixteen there, you know. She had her hair tied up in a big ribbon and a pair of slacks on and a long coat, and I felt sorry for the kid, you know. I don't like to see people talk like that to anybody, no matter how bad they are."[8]

This time the police arrived promptly. Joan Barry spent the night in the lockup area of the Beverly Hills police station, where she got into a shouting match with the matron and refused to put on her prison-issue pajamas. The next morning, a Saturday, she was sentenced to ninety days, sixty suspended, and transferred to the women's section of the county jail. A prison doctor estimated that she was about five months pregnant.

Chaplin's attorneys would later allege that Hedda Hopper had advised Barry to goad Chaplin into having her thrown into jail. Such advice would not have been totally out of character for the feisty Hopper, though in Barry's case it would seem superfluous. Hopper swore that she knew nothing about the arrest until the next morning when Joan called her secretary from the jail. Hopper then called Mary Pickford, telling her, "We've got to do something about Charlie Chaplin."

"Well," said Mary, "I don't see that anything *can* be done about Charlie."

Pickford offered to pay Joan a hundred dollars a week out of her own pocket. Later that day, however, she discussed the situation with Arthur Kelly, who assured her that Charlie would reimburse her. But when Pickford reported this to Hopper, she snapped: "Tell him it's too late."

On Tuesday morning Joan was taken off suicide watch and allowed visitors for the first time. Minna Wallis had been in the waiting room since it opened, and she sent word to Joan that she had come to see her at the request of Hedda Hopper. According to Barry, Wallis told her: "I hope that isn't really Charlie's baby, because if it is, we'll never get you out of here." Hearing it put that way, she said: "No, no, it's not Charles's child." Wallis then promised to hire an attorney and warned Joan against speaking to the press.

On her way out of the jail, Wallis ran into Florabel Muir, whose Hollywood column was featured in the *New York Daily News*. "I hope you aren't going to write about this because you don't know the whole story," Wallis told Muir. She added that J. Paul Getty was the father of Barry's unborn child, but Charlie Chaplin "ha[d] been very good to her."

"Why wouldn't he be?" replied Muir. "Men are usually nice to their mistresses until they get tired of them."

Muir couldn't help wondering what Wallis's interest in the matter was. "Hedda Hopper asked me to come down," Wallis said.

Muir knew this wasn't so because *she* had been asked by Hedda to visit Joan Barry. As she later recalled, "Hedda was very excited about the whole thing and thought that there should be something done."[9]

When Muir finally got in to see Joan, she found her completely intimidated. "I don't want any publicity about this," she pleaded. "I'm sure that Charles is only doing this to me to make me suffer so that I can be a great actress."

A brassy redhead in her early fifties, Florabel Muir was married to a studio executive and ran an independent syndication service out of her home. Unlike Hedda Hopper, she had spent years as a police-beat reporter and she saw at once that this was more than just another Hollywood sex scandal. For one thing Joan soon broke down and told her that she had already had two abortions, arranged by Chaplin. As Muir well knew, Hollywood studios often insisted that actresses—occasionally even married actresses—terminate inconvenient pregnancies, and some studios kept abortion doctors on retainer. Any actress who complained risked her reputation and her career. By forcing the district attorney to investigate Barry's allegations, Muir hoped that she might eventually be able to expose this pervasive and despicable practice.

Within hours Muir had talked Joan into giving an interview. She called in not only Hedda Hopper but two reporters from the Hearst-owned *Herald Examiner*—an indication that she was not simply interested in getting a scoop for herself—to listen to Joan's story. "This took a long time to tell," Muir would recall, "because she kept breaking down and crying and telling me Charles was a fine man; that he was a genius, and she didn't want to hurt him in any way. I said, 'He's hurt *you* plenty. He's got you in the can. That's a fine thing for a genius to do.'"

Immediately after the interview Muir went to see Sammy Hash, a local attorney, about getting Barry out of jail. But by the time Hash rounded up a bail bondsman, Barry had been released in the custody of another attorney, Cecil Holland. Holland drove his client to a hotel in Westwood, and from there she was admitted to St. John's hospital in Santa Monica. After two days of trying, Hedda Hopper managed to bluff her way past the nurses at St. John's, but Barry was so heavily sedated—"shot up with hop," as Hedda put it—that she didn't recognize her.

Unlike Hopper, who seems to have known almost nothing about local politics, Muir was aware that Cecil Holland was a part-time Beverly Hills police court judge and a minor player in a raging political battle between the Beverly Hills chief of police and the mayor of Los Angeles. Knowing that Holland could ill afford bad publicity, Muir began calling his office, demanding to know who was paying his fee. If the money was coming from Chaplin, she warned, then he was involved in a conflict of interest.

In fact Holland had accepted a five-hundred-dollar retainer from Minna Wallis, who had introduced herself to him as a friend of Barry's. The same day he heard from Muir, however, Holland received a call from Tim Durant, whom he knew to be personally close to Chaplin. Durant suggested that the case was getting "too hot," and Holland had better withdraw. But it was too late for that.

Holland had already been photographed leaving the county jail with Joan Barry. Nervous about what Muir might write, Holland got Barry discharged from St. John's, returned Wallis's money, and offered to represent Barry for free.

Quite irrationally Joan Barry still believed that Charlie loved her and might even be willing to marry her if it weren't for the interference of Tim Durant and Minna Wallis. As soon as she got out of jail, she called Summit Drive and spoke to Chaplin, who—amazingly enough—said, "I can't tell you not to come up."

Barry took a taxi to Summit Drive, and there followed an emotional four-hour meeting on the patio beside the swimming pool. Chaplin began by assuring Joan that he would support her child, even if it wasn't his. He offered to get her a cottage in Santa Barbara and pay a monthly stipend, if only she would stop talking to reporters. But he drew the line at marriage: "Nobody's forcing me to marry anyone."

Barry's account of the meeting continues:

I was crying and so I went up to the house and went up to Paulette's room and I saw Oona's clothes up there. I ran down by the pool and I said, "Whose clothes are up there? Oona O'Neill's? Is she living here?" and he said, "No." I said, "She is living here." And he said, "It's your unsubstantiated word against mine." He said, "After all, Joan, the most important thing in the world is not you and it isn't me—but it's art. A lot of people have children without getting married. You don't have to get married just because you're going to have a baby." Then he said, "You've got to protect me, Joan. I've got to have peace. Joan, if you bring this into court, you know what it will be. The newspapers will be after you, your picture will be taken—oh, it will be grand for a couple of months. "Then people will forget it. . . . I'll spend my whole fortune if necessary." He said that even if it was proven that he was the father, that he would blacken my name so that won't be the issue involved at all.[10]

The butler, Edward Chaney, arrived at poolside with a plate of sandwiches in time to overhear parts of this monologue. Chaney later said that he had no doubt that Joan's demands were "a bit of a con." Nevertheless, he and his wife, Frances, who was Chaplin's cook, rather liked Joan and felt sorry for her. "The majority of these wealthy guys," Chaney later told a federal investigator, "they've got these girls, but they look after them, you know that—they pay them off—$1,000 or $5,000 is nothing to them. They give them an automobile, they give them a fur coat, but he expected it for nothing. You see, he says because 'I'M CHARLIE CHAPLIN' and that isn't right."

Actually, Chaplin *had* given Joan Barry a fur coat, which Chaney didn't know about. The problem was that Barry had never thought of herself as just another Hollywood mistress. Chaplin had led her to expect so much more—stardom, marriage, true love. Still, at this juncture Chaplin had an opportunity to resolve all his difficulties through a financial settlement. Gertrude Berry had arrived in LA, and she was eager to get Joan out of town and obtain medical treatment for her. If Chaplin settled, Joan would be out of reach of the DA's investigators. Mrs. Berry was asking for $150,000 plus a $100,000 trust fund for the baby, but Cecil Holland, who was representing both Joan and her mother, had no doubt that they would have settled for a few thousand and been glad to get it.

But Loyd Wright, representing Chaplin, seemed determined to make the negotiations as unpleasant as possible. Although Joan's pregnancy had been confirmed by at least three doctors, Wright insisted that she submit to having her uterus x-rayed, telling Holland that for all he knew Miss Barry just "had a tumor." Joan worried that an X ray would damage the fetus, but—astonishingly—Holland's associate told her that she had no choice. When the doctor brought the film in for the lawyers to examine, the associate nudged Joan and joked, "Well, that better be a little Chaplin in there and not a tumor."

This indignity over with, the attorneys began to talk about the money. Wright kept drumming out the refrain that Chaplin owed Joan nothing. His only responsibility, if any, was to the child. At one point Joan actually had the pen in her hand, ready to sign the settlement papers, when Wright began to lecture her, reminding her that she was signing away her child's rights to any claim on the Chaplin estate forever. He implied that by signing Joan would also be admitting that she lied about having intimate relations with Chaplin the previous December. Joan said if that were so, she wouldn't sign.

Wright, it seems, felt he could afford to take a hard line, since he had been assured by Chaplin that there was no possibility of his being the baby's father. In late June, however, Chaney happened to be driving Wright and Chaplin to a meeting when he overheard Chaplin acknowledge that he'd "been with" Joan in October 1942 and again in December. Later he mentioned the conversation to Chaplin's secretary, Catherine Hunter, wondering aloud why, in that case, Chaplin hadn't pushed Wright to make a settlement. Otherwise, said Chaney, "he'll never get rid of this girl." Hunter shrugged. "I don't know why not. He's gotten rid of plenty of others. He'll get rid of this one, too."[11]

By mid-May the *Hollywood Citizen News* had begun a series of editorials, questioning the conduct of Cecil Holland, police court judge Charles Griffin, Detective White, and others. How was it that Joan Barry, who had a hotel room, a weekly allowance from Chaplin, and was often seen around town in a valuable fur coat, had been convicted of vagrancy? Why had White and his wife taken her to her train and paid the conductor to see that she didn't get off at the next station? When Barry refused to put on pajamas and spent the night in her cell half naked, why hadn't she been sent for psychiatric observation? It appeared that the Beverly Hills police and courts had gone out of their way to accommodate Chaplin—who wanted Joan Barry shipped out of town before she could tell her story to the newspapers.

Just as the press appeared to be running out of new angles on the Barry situation, Robert Arden began talking to reporters, telling them that Barry had slept with "a hundred men," himself included, any one of whom could be the baby's father. Hedda Hopper later claimed that Arden admitted over the phone that Chaplin had offered him ten thousand dollars to say the baby was his. Arden denied it.

Florabel Muir, meanwhile, was making it her business to call Los Angeles County DA Fred Howser every morning, demanding to know when he was going to indict Chaplin for conspiracy in arranging two illegal abortions. "I also thought there was a law violation in having these women, her and Oona O'Neill who was then living at the house too, up there at the same time as his two sons were and who were juveniles," Muir said. Neither Muir nor the DA realized that Oona, who turned eighteen a few days earlier, had been a minor when she moved in with Charlie.

Herb Grossman and Philip Tower, investigators from the DA's office, went up to Summit Drive and interviewed young Charlie and Syd, who were indignant at being asked to snitch on their own father. The investigators even managed to get a brief statement from Oona, who cheerfully assured them: "Mr. Chaplin is a wonderful teacher, a wonderful man. But our relationship is strictly esoteric."

The servants also swore that Oona had never spent a night at the house. Chaplin had ordered them to lie, and in varying degrees they were upset and angry about it. Most of the staff were resident aliens and stood to lose their work permits if they got into trouble with the law.

On Memorial Day, Grossman and Tower went to the Château Elysée to interview Joan Barry, but she was too distraught to answer their questions. Cecil Holland had unexpectedly resigned as her attorney that morning, and Barry was so out of control that during the interview she tried to throw herself from the window.

Gertrude Berry told the DA's investigators that her daughter was in no condition to testify in a court case. Gertrude, recalled Muir, "thought the best thing was to take the girl and go back to New York and let the whole thing drop because she didn't want any of Chaplin's dirty money, as she called it, and that it was a terrible disgrace."

Muir, however, found another attorney, John I. Irwin, who told Joan she owed it to her baby to file a paternity suit. Irwin quickly negotiated a temporary support agreement, giving Barry a hundred dollars a week and medical expenses in exchange for agreeing to allow blood tests for herself and the baby. Blood type evidence was not legally binding in California courts at the time, but Joan agreed to drop all claims if the results ruled out Chaplin as the father.

Hedda Hopper had expected that her columns attacking Chaplin would generate a storm of protest. Rather to her surprise, she received only two phone calls, one from David Selznick and the other from Sam Goldwyn, who gently chided her, "Hedda, if we start looking into this sort of thing, where will it lead?"

The rest of Hollywood was waiting nervously to see just that, and when DA Howser failed to file charges promptly, cynics blamed his inaction on pressure from Hal Wallis, Minna's brother, who was head of production at Warner Bros. and widely reputed to be one of the most ruthless executives in the business. Howser had reason to be cautious, however. Joan Barry was an undependable witness at best, and if Chaplin settled the paternity case quickly, there was little chance that she would ever testify. As for Chaplin's household staff, Grossman and Tower knew they were lying and assumed that Chaplin had bribed them to keep quiet.

Up at Summit Drive the appearance of Howser's investigators had created a panic. Chaplin was afraid to come home and was hiding at the Cañon Drive house of Gene Frenke and his wife, actress Anna Sten. Oona, meanwhile, had been temporarily installed in an apartment on Olympic Boulevard. Anna Frenke was not very happy about Chaplin's presence. Gene had recently been investigated by the LA police, though never charged, in connection with a sex ring involved in the procurement of underage girls, and he was not the best person to be shielding a man who, it was assumed, was about to be arrested for contributing to the delinquency of a minor. Moreover, feeding a houseguest during wartime wasn't easy. Chaplin expected meat for dinner and sugar for his tea, items that could be purchased only with precious ration coupons, but he had left home so quickly that he forgot to bring his ration book with him. He promised Anna that he would replace the coupons she used up in shopping for his meals, but never did.

Agnes Boulton had abruptly departed for New York before the DA's investigators could talk with her, and Loyd Wright pleaded with Chaplin to send Oona back East as well. In fact Chaplin wanted her to go, but Oona wouldn't hear of it. She loved Charlie and had no intention of being shunted out of town. As she saw it, the simple solution to the problem was for her and Charlie to move up their wedding date.

Chaplin didn't know where to turn for advice. He was upset with Robert Arden, whose efforts to present himself as the real father of Barry's child had been clumsy in the extreme. And Tim Durant was in a state of agitation over seeing himself portrayed in Joan Barry's statements to the press as "Charlie Chaplin's pimp."

Durant was in love with the African-American dancer and choreo-
grapher Katherine Dunham, and he worried that her name would
be dragged into the scandal. In fact Florabel Muir did write a column about the interracial relationship but changed her mind
about publishing it after a colleague pointed out that the story
might exacerbate racial tensions. Desperate, Chaplin called up
Harry Crocker.

In the years since he was fired from the set of *City Lights*,
Crocker, as a personal aide to William Randolph Hearst, had gained
experience in managing the delicate private entanglements of public
men. Charlie, however, had worked himself into quite a pickle. As
Crocker later told an acquaintance in the Los Angeles office of the
FBI, Charlie was as reluctant to take a wife as ever, but Oona
refused to go away, and one of the Summit Drive maids was threatening to go to the DA unless he paid her several thousand dollars.
Under the circumstances Charlie decided it was time for another
trip to the altar. "Although his attorney advised him not to marry her
[Oona]," Crocker told his FBI contact, "because of the blackmail situation and because of his predicament with Barry he decided to get
out from under one of the situations by marrying O'Neill."[12]

On the evening of June 15, Catherine Hunter drove Oona up
the coast to Santa Barbara, followed by Charlie and Harry Crocker
in a second car. At eight o'clock the following morning, Oona walked
into the county courthouse in Santa Barbara and began the process
of applying for a marriage license. As a former Hearst reporter,
Crocker knew that license bureau clerks in the LA area often had a
button under the counter that they could use to alert courthouse
reporters, so he kept Charlie waiting in his car. Only when the clerk
wondered aloud, "Now, where is the young man?" did Catherine
Hunter race outside and escort him in.

Even so, by the time the license was issued, a knot of reporters
was waiting on the courthouse steps. The wedding party piled into
their cars and sped away, leading the press on an eighty-mile-per-
hour chase out of town. When they had shaken their pursuers they
drove via back roads to the home of Justice of the Peace Linton P.
Moore, a retired Methodist minister, in quiet Carpinteria. Rev.
Moore was seventy-eight and apparently did not read newspapers.
Following a three-minute ceremony, "without fuss, feathers or fol-

de-rol," as he put it, Moore filled out the wedding certificate, giving the groom's name as Charles Chapman.

Crocker had arranged to give an exclusive on the wedding to his old friend Louella Parsons, now the chief rival of Hedda Hopper and Florabel Muir. Parsons released her story within hours of the ceremony, complete with a statement from Chaplin, who said that he and Oona had been drawn together by "our mutual interest in literature."

The wedding caught Hollywood by surprise. That morning, when Hedda Hopper received a tip that Chaplin was about to elope, her first thought was that he had decided to short-circuit the paternity suit by marrying Joan Barry. Calling the Château Elysée for confirmation, Hopper found herself breaking the news to Joan, who realized immediately that the bride must be Oona. Joan called Summit Drive, where Andrew Dahl blurted out, "If he's getting married it's only because you drove him to it." At this Joan collapsed and after what her mother described as "several violent episodes," she voluntarily entered the Garden Grove sanitarium for treatment.

In normal times all this would have been just more grist for the tabloids. But these were not normal times. A whole generation of American young men were in uniform, wondering if they would ever see their wives and sweethearts again, and the news that Charlie Chaplin, fifty-four and a millionaire many times over, had just married a beautiful eighteen-year-old was not a morale booster—especially when the wedding took place just thirteen days after another young woman had announced plans to file a paternity suit against him.

It didn't help that the elopement had involved taking two cars on a one-hundred-mile journey, in defiance of wartime restrictions on inessential travel. The Office of Price Administration (OPA), the agency responsible for enforcing gas and food rationing regulations, received so many complaints that Samuel Leask Jr., the chief of the Southern California district office, sent an investigator to Santa Barbara to question Chaplin and his bride, who were honeymooning in a secluded cottage. Leask was surprised to learn that Chaplin did not have a valid driver's license or own an automobile—his four cars and two trucks were all registered at his studio. After a lengthy investigation, the OPA concluded that no regulations had been broken.

Robert Arden had also assured the DA's investigators that Charlie was not romantically involved with Oona O'Neill. He expressed his reaction to the wedding news by taking an ad in *Variety*: "For sale. Would like to dispose, cheaply, of a slightly used empty bag which I am still loyally holding."

After so much ado the honeymoon was a gloomy affair. For Charlie, marriage and depression went together. Oona tried to cheer him up by reading aloud from George du Maurier's novel *Trilby*. Chaplin had often been called a Svengali, and the old-fashioned melodrama of the original Svengali story provided a degree of comic relief.

So far the FBI's only involvement in Chaplin's problems was Harry Crocker's unsolicited call a week after the wedding, undoubtedly an attempt to fish for information about DA Howser's intentions. Crocker assured his friend at the bureau that Chaplin was just a political naïf who "went overboard" on the Second Front issue and that Joan Barry was a "screwball."

During the course of the phone call, Crocker outlined his plan to rehabilitate Chaplin's image. One idea was for Lou Costello, a great admirer of Chaplin, to take a booth at the Hollywood Canteen, where the stars entertained servicemen and -women and raised money for other canteens overseas. Charlie would appear at Costello's side to sign autographs and, if all went well, he could move up to a booth in his own name. Crocker also thought Chaplin should release some of his old pictures for exhibition to the armed services and publicize his recent purchase of war bonds.

As an example of Chaplin's naïveté, Crocker described a conversation between Chaplin and Waldo Frank, who had been a guest at Summit Drive during the 1942 holiday season. Frank had remarked, in passing, that capitalism was finished, and Chaplin began to speculate enthusiastically on who would run the country under a Communist regime, guessing which figures in the Roosevelt administration would still be around and which ones would go. One can only wonder if the agent's superiors saw this as evidence of Chaplin's ignorance—or, possibly, as an indication that he had inside information.

At any rate, contrary to the contention of the Richard Attenborough film biography, J. Edgar Hoover had no long-standing personal vendetta against Charlie, and the FBI was hardly in a "get Chaplin" mood. The pressure for a federal prosecution was coming from U.S. Attorney Charles H. Carr, who was relatively new in office and highly ambitious. Carr wanted to gain a reputation as the man who cleaned up the Beverly Hills police department, ending a long history of the police serving as a quasi-official security force for the stars. Famous as well as widely disliked, Chaplin was merely a convenient peg on which to hang his corruption investigation.

Chaplin may have thought he was doing the kind thing in getting Joan Barry banished from Beverly Hills the previous January. After all, he could have had her prosecuted for invading his house with a gun. Nevertheless, it was (and is) a violation of federal civil rights statutes for a private citizen to have an inconvenient person railroaded out of town. Carr assumed that Detective White, Judge Griffin, and others had been bribed by Chaplin to get rid of Barry, and in early June he personally told Capt. Robert Bolling of the LAPD to drop his investigaton of the abortion charges. He didn't want Joan Barry embarrassed, because he hoped to use her as a witness in a federal case.[13]

Carr's superiors in Washington were never enthusiastic about this plan. What looked like a pattern of corruption to Carr was likely to strike a jury as penny-ante stuff; in fact, they might even sympathize with Chaplin. In mid-August, however, Robert Hood, the head of the FBI's Los Angeles office, received a tip from a newspaperman, who said that Chaplin had brought Barry to New York at the time of his Carnegie Hall Second Front speech in order to pass her around to his friends. If this allegation proved true, Chaplin might have been in violation of the Mann Act, an antiracketeering statute that made it illegal to transport women across state lines for immoral purposes.

Hood was undoubtedly aware that a similar prosecution had been suggested in another case he supervised. In Ontario in 1942 writer Theodore Dreiser had made a Second Front speech so virulently anti-British that it threatened to disrupt U.S.-Canadian relations. At the time, Thomas B. Thornton, an assistant U.S. attorney in Michigan, wrote a memo pointing out that Dreiser, seventy-one, had shared a hotel room in Port Huron with his much younger mistress and might be a candidate for prosecution under the Mann Act.[14] Nothing came of Thornton's memo, but it probably did inspire Hood to consider throwing a Mann Act charge into the case against Chaplin.

Hood discussed the report in a phone conversation with J. Edgar Hoover who authorized him to investigate—"If [this is] a White Slave violation, we ought to go after it vigorously."[15]

But despite Hoover's authorization nothing much happened for two months. Jack Irwin said that Joan was too ill to cooperate, and another key witness, Ed Chaney, who had served as Chaplin's valet during the trip to New York, was hospitalized with complications from kidney stones. The bureau didn't get around to calling Chaney until late October, and then he was warned not to tell Chaplin that he was coming in for an interview. But of course Chaney did tell. Chaney had lied to the DA's investigators about Oona O'Neill, and he was afraid he might be deported, so he asked Chaplin to get him a lawyer.

Chaplin ignored the request but suddenly became very solicitous about Chaney's health. "You don't have to go in there," he said. "You're a sick man."

Oona happened to be in the room and she interrupted, saying, "Of course he has to go." She talked Chaplin into calling Loyd Wright, but Wright objected that it would be a conflict of interest for him to advise Chaney. Chaplin then refused to pay for Chaney to visit another attorney.

On October 30, when Chaney showed up at the Los Angeles office of the FBI, he was steaming: "You know in domestic work the family says, 'Well, look after him and see that he gets everything,'" he told the interviewing agents. "Well, that son of a gun never sent me an orange down [to the hospital], yet he expects all this of me. . . . But he's scared, you see, because he doesn't know what he's done, and I know what he's done."[16]

Chaney had plenty of unflattering things to say about his boss, but he knew nothing about any orgies in New York. He wasn't even sure that Chaplin had personally bribed anyone to get Joan Barry sentenced to leave town. He recalled that some policemen had come to the house, no doubt expecting a few dollars, but "they didn't know Mr. Chaplin."

In December, Carr traveled to the East Coast in connection with another case and took the opportunity to confer with Attorney General Francis Biddle and Tom Clark, head of the Justice Department's Criminal Division, about the Chaplin situation. Carr expressed his distaste for the Mann Act charge, observing that it lacked the necessary "commercial angle." Clark, on the other hand, thought the civil rights charge was too "complicated" to be worth pursuing, and he advised Carr to drop either all the charges or none of them. The Mann Act count, he reasoned, at least provided a "context" for what happened at the time of Barry's arrest two months later. This was a lawyerly way of saying that while the charge itself was garbage, it would give Carr a chance to introduce unflattering testimony, portraying Chaplin as a man who spent his evenings nightclubbing and scoffed at calls for sacrifice during wartime, bringing his mistress (not to mention his valet!) all the way to New York to hear him give a speech attacking the armed forces for not doing enough.

Carr would have been well advised to drop the case at this point, but he had worked himself into a bind. DA Howser had let himself be called off the abortion investigation and taken a lot of criticism for it. Now someone in Howser's office was leaking rumors of possible Mann Act charges to the press, hoping to embarrass Carr if the case collapsed. More important, perhaps, Carr had become obsessed by the idea that Tim Durant and Robert Arden were bribing witnesses and otherwise doing their best to interfere with his investigation. Chaplin had written to Supreme Court Justice Frank Murphy, a longtime fan, asking him to sound out his contacts in Washington, and it is quite possible that Carr had been subjected to political pressure to drop the investigation. If so, it only made him more stubbornly determined to bring the charges before a grand jury.

If one believed the newspapers, J. Edgar Hoover was running the Chaplin investigation personally, and was on the point of coming to Los Angeles to witness Chaplin's arrest. In fact, these stories were planted by Carr, who wanted to be able to blame Washington if the case fizzled. The truth was that the LA Bureau of the FBI realized that Carr had overreached, and Hoover was trying to stay as far from the mess as possible.

❊   ❊   ❊

On February 10, 1944, a federal grand jury indicted Chaplin on two counts of violating the Mann Act, as well as on a conspiracy count related to the violation of Joan Barry's civil rights. Also indicted on the civil rights charge were Tim Durant, Robert Arden, Det. William W. White and Officer Claude Marple of the Beverly Hills police, Magistrate Charles Griffin, and Jessie Reno, a matron at the Beverly Hills jail. If convicted Chaplin faced up to fifteen years in prison.

Chaplin had hired Jerry Giesler, a colorful criminal defense specialist who had recently defended Errol Flynn against a charge of statutory rape.

Giesler routinely arranged for celebrity clients to be arraigned without attracting undue attention in the newspapers, but the U.S. marshal's office, so often humiliated in its attempts to serve subpoenas on Chaplin, was in no mood to grant him any special consideration. Hundreds of court employees, many visibly overjoyed, lined the corridors, waiting to catch a glimpse of Chaplin when he appeared at the courthouse accompanied by Giesler. Contrary to custom, press photographers were even allowed into the area where Chaplin was about to be fingerprinted. Chaplin objected, and the chief of the marshal's office ordered the photographers out of the room. Before they could go, however, Chaplin suddenly changed his mind, saying, "Who am I to interfere with the operations of the American courts?" One suspects that he realized that the scene, however humiliating, was a great dramatic moment and would gain sympathy for him in the long run.[17]

The virulence of the anti-Chaplin feeling in Los Angeles was almost beyond belief. *Variety* had called for him to be drummed out of the industry, and reporters covering the arraignment abandoned all pretense of objectivity, filling their stories with scathing comments about his bad haircut and choice of clothing—an expensively cut cream-colored sports jacket and mustard-toned sweater that Florabel Muir referred to as his "rainbow garb."[18]

An article by Les Wagner, Florence's son, in the February 4 issue of *Script* reflected Chaplin's own conviction that he was being persecuted for making a laughingstock of Hitler in *The Great Dictator*. That film, Wagner explained, had made Charlie a "shining target for the fascist clique in America." Chaplin himself suggested to Jerry Giesler that Joan Barry was an agent for a proto-Nazi cult. He was annoyed when Giesler refused to take the idea seriously.

David Platt of the *Daily Worker*, meanwhile, wrote that Chaplin had been framed by the "appeasers"—advocates of a negotiated peace with Germany—including William Randolph Hearst and the *Chicago Tribune* publisher, Colonel Robert McCormick. (Platt conveniently forgot that he himself had praised *The Great Dictator* as an anti-interventionist film.)[19]

Blaming "fascists" obscured the obvious: It was the FDR Justice Department that was responsible for the charges against Chaplin. Meanwhile conservatives, including some who had been Chaplin's harshest critics in the past, were generally appalled. Florabel Muir's own paper, the *New York Daily News*, owned by a branch of the McCormick-Patterson family, editorialized that aging men had always been attracted to younger women and punishing Chaplin for doing what came naturally was just another example of a dangerous trend toward "horning in on the private lives of Americans." Westbrook Pegler, who detested Chaplin but disliked FDR even more, called the indictment typical of the "sly tricks" of the Roosevelt Justice Department. Pegler compared the use of the Mann Act against Chaplin with the prosecution of Jack Johnson, the black heavyweight champion who had married a white woman, and the conviction of Al Capone for income tax evasion. The *Washington Times-Herald* said simply, "In our opinion, this is persecution of Chaplin by the federal government."[20]

In any event the trial was an anticlimax. On the morning after his arraignment Chaplin, along with Joan Barry and her daughter Carol Ann, born the previous October 3, presented themselves for blood tests. The tests showed that Chaplin, who was type O, could not have fathered Carol Ann, type AB. In theory the test results had no bearing on the federal prosecution—if anything, they supported the charge that Chaplin had shared his mistress with his friends. But they did nothing for Barry's credibility. As the *New York Daily News* said, the blood test evidence was "a wet towel in the face of the prosecution's case."

Joan Barry had never wanted to testify in the federal case to begin with, and after the blood tests, whose results had clearly been a surprise to her, she began drinking again. When the trial got under way, Jerry Giesler used her history of writing bad checks to portray her as a con artist, pure and simple. Among his witnesses was Rollie Totheroh, who described how he happened to be standing in line at the bank when Barry cashed a check from Chaplin and exulted, "Look, Rollie! Money, money, money!"[21]

But Giesler also introduced a letter written by Barry to Chaplin on November 22, 1942, which made her seem more pathetic than scheming: "I thought loving you and knowing you never wanted or would never allow me to become a part of your life was torture, but now that I know that I am not to be Bridget, 'my cup is full.' I admit though, that after the way I've acted, it's the only thing you could do."

Though no one seemed to notice at the time, this contradicted Chaplin's account that Barry had known she would not be playing Bridget since early in the spring. The letter suggests that for whatever reasons Chaplin had continued to string Barry along with talk of "rehabilitating" her and using her in the movie. In light of this, one wonders if he fully understood his own motives for paying for Barry's trip to New York in October 1942. Had he simply wanted to get rid of her, he could have bought her the ticket months earlier.

In a sense Giesler's defense was almost irrelevant. The case had essentially been won during the pretrial motions, when Federal Judge J. F. T. O'Connor ruled that the Mann Act and civil rights charges must be tried separately. Carr—who for technical reasons had to try the Mann Act case first—knew that he had virtually no chance to win.

Oddly enough, when Judge O'Connor was assigned to the case, Joan Barry had immediately told Carr that she knew him. O'Connor happened to be a good friend of J. Paul Getty and A. C. Blumenthal. In fact Joan and Getty had dined with the judge in a restaurant in August 1942, and a few days later she visited him at his home, where he gave her an autographed copy of his book, *The Banks Under Roosevelt*. The book, retrieved from Barry's stored belongings, was inscribed: "To Joan Barry with kindest regards from her friend, the author, J. F. T. O'Connor, Los Angeles, September 2, 1942." In a memo to Washington, Carr expressed "wonderment" that O'Connor had failed to recuse himself.

During the trial O'Connor allowed J. Paul Getty, a defense witness, to testify to a highly sanitized version of his relationship with Barry—giving evidence that he personally must have known to be untrue. The judge's rulings consistently favored Chaplin, and six days after the verdict was rendered Tim Durant took O'Connor to dinner to thank him for his efforts. Although Chaplin never should have been indicted on the Mann Act charge in the first place, he was not exactly without friends in the courtroom.

Meanwhile Chaplin's behavior throughout the trial was slightly bizarre. One day he clowned for reporters by draping a handkerchief over his head. On the day final arguments began he gave a corridor interview, demonstrating that he had read Westbrook Pegler's column on the case and paraphrasing Pegler's argument in terms hardly flattering to himself: "I never was aware until recently that people considered me an Englishman," Chaplin said:

I never thought about it. I never wanted to vote. I'm an artist! I have never been interested in politics, but I know now I put my foot in it when I made that speech for the second front. . . . The public wants a victim! They are persecuting me on the Mann Act for the same reason that the government went after the gangsters on the income tax. Gangsters had become unpopular and the government couldn't get them on anything but the income tax. I'm in the same boat. [22]

On April 4 the jury took just three hours to find Chaplin not guilty. It was one of those cases in which jurors reach the right conclusion for dubious reasons. One of Chaplin's strongest supporters on the panel argued that he was an artist, and therefore could not have had sex on his mind when he paid Joan Barry's way to New York. Another showed her fellow jurors a picture of her fourteen-year-old daughter, who she was hoping would be discovered by a movie producer like Chaplin.

A week after the verdict Tom Clark met with J. Edgar Hoover, and the two of them agreed that trying the civil rights section of the indictment would be a mistake as "public opinion would tend towards setting up Chaplin as a martyr."[23] Carr was determined to "rock along" with the case a little longer, but Hoover and Clark's arguments soon prevailed.[24]

✿   ✿   ✿

The FBI had taken little if any recent notice of Chaplin's politics, but during the Mann Act investigation its agents began to suspect that Chaplin was planning to visit the Soviet Union—and possibly even to jump bail and defect. To begin with, several sources had suggested to the bureau that Stalin was eager to have Chaplin, now a director of the National Committee for Soviet-American Friendship, pay a goodwill visit to Moscow. A personal invitation from Stalin had reportedly been floated via newspaper correspondent Frederick Othman, and another through Edward Carter of the Institute of Pacific Relations, to Florence Wagner. An anonymous source (surely one of the Summit Drive servants) reported that Wagner had relayed the invitation over the phone to Oona, telling her that she thought Charlie "must accept" such an invitation if it were formally offered. Oona agreed.[25]

Joan Barry, meanwhile, had said in her statement to the FBI that Chaplin had told her that if he defected he had been promised a post as head of the Soviet film industry. Charlie had joked about it, Barry said, asking her, "Well, Joanie, what would you think if I became a commissar?"

And finally, when FBI agents visited the Chaplin studio in November 1943 to get a copy of Barry's contract, Alf Reeves told them that in his opinion Chaplin should get out of the country now and "not wait for them to kick him out." Shortly thereafter, the FBI heard that Charlie and Oona were taking Russian lessons.

In fact the Chaplins *were* learning Russian, though fitfully, and when a second delegation of Soviet documentary cameramen visited the United States in 1944, Chaplin invited them to a screening of *The Gold Rush*—a movie, he pointed out, that was the same age as his wife. Later he entertained the group by playing his impression of a composition by Shostakovich on the piano, singing snatches of Russian folk songs and reeling off a few handy phrases of the language that he had memorized. One of the latter was, *Tvoi guby shepchut o liubvi*—"Your lips are whispering words of love."[26]

Chaplin, of course, had been threatening to pack up and leave the United States since 1916, and despite his enthusiasm for the Soviet Union he had never shown the slightest inclination to place himself or his fortune under Soviet control. The FBI, however, didn't know this, and given Chaplin's susceptibility to flattery and tendency to run away at the first sign of trouble, it is not surprising that the possibility that he would flee to the Soviet Union if convicted was seriously considered. A defection would have been a serious blow to U.S. prestige, and border patrol guards had been put on warning.

The border watch was canceled after the verdict came in, but the Soviets, though still U.S. allies, did not miss the opportunity to use Chaplin's legal troubles as a vehicle for anti-American propaganda. Three weeks after the trial Soviet "art workers" celebrated a two-day Chaplin festival, held under the auspices of VOKS (the All-Union Society for Cultural Relations with Foreign Countries). Featured speaker Ilya Ehrenburg hammered home the message that America was punishing Charlie Chaplin for making *The Great Dictator* and sent him formal greetings, saluting him as an ally in "our common struggle against Hitlerism." Later the audience at the festival was shown clips from several Chaplin films. Ironically, many of those present had never seen the *The Great Dictator*, which had yet to be released in the Soviet Union.[27]

18

Ladykiller

During Chaplin's Mann Act trial, there were sporadic reports that he had abandoned *Shadow and Substance* and was working on a movie called *The Ladykiller* in which he would play a modern-day Bluebeard. This sounded like a case of art imitating life. As it happened Chaplin had acquired the *Ladykiller* property from Orson Welles in July 1941, when his affair with Barry was just getting started.

Welles conceived *The Ladykiller* as a black comedy based on the life of Henri Désiré Landru, a Frenchman who was convicted of murdering eight women and went to his death protesting his innocence. He originally approached Chaplin about playing the lead in a picture which he would direct. Chaplin considered the possibility for a time, then changed his mind, telling Welles, "No, I can't. I've never had anybody else direct me." Since the part had been written with Chaplin in mind, Welles agreed to sell the rights to the title and concept for five thousand dollars. The contract stipulated that if Chaplin eventually made the movie he would give Welles an appropriate creative credit.

In an interview with Peter Bogdanovich, Orson Welles later said that he got the idea for the Landru movie while riding the New York subway. It was

one of the real "Eureka!" kind of things. I saw an advertisement for an antidandruff remedy which had a picture of a bright-faced little hairdresser type making that gesture of the stage Frenchman which indicates that something or other is simply too exquisite for human speech. "*Avez-vous Scurf?*" he was asking us.[1]

This may have been the "eureka" moment for Welles, but the anecdote doesn't explain why Welles connected the bright-faced Frenchman with Landru. And why with Chaplin?

The true, if never acknowledged, source for *The Ladykiller* can be found in the December 1929 issue of the journal *Living Age*, which carried an English translation of "Napoleon and Landru: An Imaginary Dialogue" by the German Expressionist playwright Walter Hasenclever. In Hasenclever's story a schoolgirl contemplates wax figures of the French emperor and the serial killer, which happened to be displayed side by side in the Musée Grevin in Paris. For her Napoleon is boring, a figure from the dusty annals of history: "When everyone knows so much about a man he has no luck with women," she confidently tells a schoolmate. But she stands transfixed before the figure of Landru: "I don't know whether you are a great criminal or a great lover," she says.

After the girl leaves the museum, the wax figures come to life and engage in a dialogue. Landru chides Napoleon, "What is the essential difference between us? You ruined men and I ruined women. We won't inquire into the motives."[2]

Living Age was a periodical followed by Americans interested in European politics and theater, and it happened that two issues preceding December 1929 carried items on Chaplin—one of them was Egon Kisch's article "I Work with Chaplin." Anyone skimming through back issues of the magazine might easily make the connection between Hasenclever's story and Chaplin's well-known obsession with Napoleon. No doubt something like this happened to Welles, whose concept for *The Ladykiller* bore almost no relation to the actual facts of Henri Landru's life and had everything to do with Hasenclever's speculations.

Welles also insisted in later years that he had written a complete script for *The Ladykiller*, which he turned over to Chaplin along with the sale of the rights. Although Welles was unable to produce a copy of his script, which he said was destroyed in a fire, his claim is supported by David Robinson's observation that early notes and drafts for the project, eventually known as *Monsieur Verdoux*, are not to be found in Chaplin's private archive.

According to Welles, Chaplin retained many incidents from his script, including the opening scene in which the fussy, petit-bourgeois *Monsieur Verdoux* (as Chaplin called him) lovingly tends his rose garden while little puffs of smoke issue from the chimney of the backyard incinerator where he is disposing of the remains of his latest wife. Chaplin, however, updated the story from the original World War I–era setting to make Verdoux a victim of the depression. A once hardworking and loyal bank clerk, laid off after more than thirty years' service, Verdoux turns to serial bigamy and murder as a means to support his invalid wife and young son. The Bluebeard Landru was probably originally meant to be the domestic equivalent of Hitler and Mussolini. Chaplin gave the story a Marxist twist, suggesting that murder for profit is just another form of capitalism.

According to Welles his script also had an episode in which the Landru character narrowly avoids becoming the victim of a woman who makes her living by killing rich men. In Chaplin's story the wife-killer's nemesis is an intended victim who, perversely, proves to be unkillable. His Annabella Bonheur is a force of nature. Rasputin-like, she slugs down glass after glass of (apparently) poisoned wine with no ill effects. When Verdoux takes her out in a rowboat intending to drown her, she has a grand time while he succeeds in chloroforming himself. Lusty, busty, and motivated by a vulgar faith in the essential goodness of human nature, Annabella is a misogynist's nightmare, a caricature of the female life force. She is the only one of Verdoux's intended victims who truly loves him, and like the distressingly fertile Joan Barry, she can't be gotten rid of.

"I like women, but I don't admire them," Henri Verdoux says at one point. No doubt Chaplin would have said the same, though the script suggests a deep hostility. Verdoux's true wife—the woman he turns murderer to support—is paralyzed from the waist down, symbolically desexed. The only other female who wins the serial murderer's sympathy is a streetwalker, and Verdoux refrains from killing her because she reminds him of himself. Otherwise the film finds every woman past the first bloom of youth aesthetically and humanly offensive. Having lost their ability to attract men with their looks, such females resort to foolish vanity, nagging, and the lure of their accumulated wealth to snare men. Killing them is a regrettable but necessary task, like plucking the overripe roses that spoil the appearance of Verdoux's garden.

Even if some of the satire was inadvertent, the misogyny of *Monsieur Verdoux* would turn out to be the best thing about the movie. By taking certain social attitudes toward middle-aged women to their logical extreme, the film does suggest, often very humorously, that men who make a fetish of worshipping female beauty are a bit like Nazis celebrating health and fresh air.

The years Chaplin devoted to working on the Bluebeard story were filled with conflict and public humiliation. And yet, ironically, he was also enjoying a relatively happy home life. A few days before he and Oona were married, she informed him that she had no interest in appearing in Eugene Frenke's *The Girl from Leningrad*. In fact she did not want to be in the movies at all, but would prefer to be a full-time wife. No man was ever more intent on having a wife who gave him all of her attention, but Chaplin's habit of using the lure of a movie contract to meet women had made it equally unlikely he would ever find one. Oona's decision both amazed and gratified him.

Florence Wagner, a guest of Oona and Charlie at their family Christmas party in 1943, painted an idyllic picture of domesticity at Summit Drive. Both of Charlie's sons were at home, the last time they would share a family Christmas for several years. Charles junior was in uniform and soon to be shipped overseas; Sydney, still in school, already knew that he would be drafted when he turned eighteen. After dinner, five-year-old Spencer Dryden, the son of Charlie's half-brother Wheeler, read "The Night Before Christmas." Charlie played the accordion and read aloud from a draft of his script. Oona's Christmas present to her husband was a rare two-volume first edition of Edward Sterling's *Old Drury Lane*, a gift that demonstrated taste and an appreciation of his sentimental attachment to the scenes of his childhood. As Wagner observed, Charlie had already become extremely dependent on his much younger wife. Not only had Oona typed his script for him, she sat at his elbow all evening, unobtrusively supplying the odd name or date that happened to slip his mind. "There's a smart little gal, and one who is really interested in and enjoys Charlie's work," wrote Florence Wagner approvingly. "Her dressing table mirror is lined with snapshots of him, and apparently, at last, there is happiness in that house."[3]

Harry Crocker took a less rosy view of the situation. Over the years Charlie's desire to be the center of attention at parties had become less charming. He pontificated and repeated himself, and Crocker wondered how long any intelligent young woman would put up with it. Paulette Goddard, he observed, had also been content to worship at Charlie's knee for a few years, but soon outgrew him. Oona's attitude was already less than worshipful. She had her husband's monologues timed, and could slip out in the car for a milkshake and a hamburger and be back home before he delivered the punch line.[4]

Oona, moreover, missed the East Coast and her friends there. After the Mann Act trial, she and Charlie headed for Manhattan, where they rented an apartment on the East Side, and later spent time in a country house near Palisades, across the Hudson in Rockland County. The idea was for Charlie to find peace and quiet so that he could write, but rural life made him nervous. In the city, on the other hand, they were constantly running into people who remembered Oona from her "Deb of the Year" days.

One evening the Chaplins showed up at the Copacabana nightclub to see the dancing Di Gitanos and a young comedian named Jackie Gleason. Aware of their presence, the management had warned Gleason to cut from his routine several jokes about Errol Flynn's pursuit of underage girls. A friendly columnist who happened to be in the club that evening, observing that Oona, who was seven months pregnant, looked "cute, but tired and worn," approached and tried to cheer her up, reminding her that a few years earlier at her Stork Club press conference he was the fellow who had naively asked: "What does your father do for a living?" Oona warned him off the subject with a stage-whispered "Ssssh!"[5]

For some reason Charlie did not like to be reminded of Oona's days as a deb. More understandably the subject of Eugene O'Neill was also anathema. The king of tragedy had refused to acknowledge his daughter's marriage to the king of comedy. That Oona was looking for a father substitute is almost too obvious to bear mentioning.

It also happened that the substitute she chose was a man her father loathed.

The Chaplins returned to Beverly Hills in time for Oona to give birth to a daughter, Geraldine Leigh, during the early morning hours of August 1. For the first time in his life, Chaplin was proud and happy to be a father.

As usual, however, litigation was on the horizon. As the result of the Mann Act case, Robert Arden had lost his radio show and his bid to become a citizen. Blaming Chaplin for his troubles, he sued for five thousand dollars, money he claimed was owed him for his work on the Bluebeard script and for negotiating the rights to *Shadow and Substance*. He won, and soon departed for Argentina.

Chaplin's animosity toward David Selznick was also keeping United Artists in a state of turmoil. His lawsuit against Selznick was resolved in late 1944, only to be reopened in 1946 when Selznick sold away another set of scripts that UA had financed, this time including the Ingrid Bergman hit *Notorious*. Selznick's second betrayal confirmed Chaplin in his belief that UA should never have gotten involved with financing its producers' pictures. Few others drew the same moral. It was UA's weakness that left producers— even Selznick, who was a partner—with no incentive to give the company their best films. The Selznick era ended with UA agreeing to buy back his stock for two million dollars, saddling it with a debt it could ill afford. As a result UA was counting on Chaplin's next movie for an infusion of cash to stave off bankruptcy.

Compared to the legal sniping over United Artists, Joan Barry's still unresolved paternity suit promised to be a minor annoyance. Barry had reneged on her promise to drop her claim if the blood-test evidence went against her. As a result Jack Irwin, the attorney who negotiated the agreement, had resigned. Barry's new attorney, seventy-seven-year-old Joe Scott, had pinned his hopes for victory on getting the blood test evidence excluded from the civil trial. When Los Angeles superior court judge Harry M. Willis ruled against him, Scott had no case left and he was ready to settle, even for a modest sum.

Joan Barry had caused Chaplin a great deal of trouble, not to mention fear, anxiety and public humiliation. As Chaplin saw it, he owed her nothing. So confident was he of victory that he dismissed Jerry Giesler, who was still trying to collect his fee for the Mann Act defense, and turned the case over to Loyd Wright's partner, Charles "Pat" Millikan, whose experience was primarily in corporate litigation.

The paternity trial began in December 1944, and soon proved to be far rougher than anything Chaplin had experienced in federal court. The white-haired Joe Scott, not just a family man but the father of thirteen children, played the role of the angry patriarch and defender of traditional values. He made sure Carol Ann, by now a chubby toddler, was conspicuously present in the courtroom, and he relentlessly attacked Chaplin as a "Piccadilly pimp," and a "cockney cad." Joan Barry had been a reluctant witness at the federal trial, and her testimony there had left out many of the unflattering details she had earlier told the FBI. Now, in desperation, she filled in the portrait, describing Charlie as a vain man who needed constant reassurance of his virility and was perversely attracted by threats of violence and possessive behavior. Describing the night of December 30, when she brought a gun to Summit Drive to threaten suicide, Barry said, "Charles came over and sat on the edge of the bed. I was kneeling in front of him. He said he was glad I had given him the gun and asked if I had any more. Then he picked up my purse and found a bullet in it and laughed about the whole incident."

She then took off her clothes, Barry said, and Chaplin, also naked, paused to study himself in a mirror, asking, "Joan, do you think I look like Peter Pan?"

"A little," she answered.

"So we went to bed," Barry continued. And afterward, "before I left, he told me he was willing to help me because he wanted to rehabilitate me. He said I was never, never, to break into his house again, and he would phone me when he wanted to see me."[6]

Barry also testified that in May 1943 when she and Charlie discussed her third pregnancy, he assured her that the baby was just a "biological mistake," adding, "I may have lots of babies around here." He then promised her that he didn't love Oona, saying, "Don't be silly. I just felt sorry for her. I know her mother very well. She had been living in an auto court for $18 a month and I just felt sorry for her."

Finally Scott introduced additional excerpts from Barry's letters, including one in which she chided him for his political harangues: "Right you are, Charles, we should destroy soulless, unimaginative money-mad hypocrites who boast of breeding but are more ill-mannered than the lowest serf."

Despite Barry's admissions of past lies and her history of mental instability, her testimony was all too plausible. (With hindsight, moreover, it is also consistent with accounts of Chaplin's other relationships. For example, Chaplin had told other women, including Lita Grey, that he was incapable of fathering children and therefore didn't need to use a contraceptive—something Barry could hardly have known.) On the other hand Chaplin's insistence that his relationship with Barry was over in early 1942 did not fit the evidence, and Joe Scott was far more effective than Carr had been at exposing the inconsistencies in his story. The jury, after hearing two weeks' testimony, including the results of the blood test, deadlocked seven to five for acquittal, ensuring that the emotionally draining ordeal would have to be repeated.

Joe Scott's cross-examination upset Chaplin deeply, and Charles junior believed that his father was never really the same afterward. Scott's attacks, he said, struck at his father's "Achilles' heel"—a deep sense of himself as a victim of some terrible injustice that the younger Chaplin connected with the story his father often told about the time at the Hanwell orphanage when a teacher announced to the assembled orphans that he was unworthy of a Christmas treat because of some "insignificant misdemeanor. . . . The feeling of being unjustly punished that day must have welled up inside him during the paternity trial," Charles junior speculated.[7]

Of course Chaplin had told others, though perhaps not his son, the nature of the "insignificant misdemeanor" that caused him to be held up to ridicule in front of his peers on Christmas Eve—he had soiled his bed. On that occasion he was "guilty" of exercising a bodily function that he was supposed to be able to control but could not. In his summation Scott had unwittingly echoed the teacher's condemnation, warning the jury that Chaplin couldn't control his "lecherous" conduct, therefore they would have to hold him to account. Once again, as Chaplin saw it, he was being singled out and vilified in front of all the world for doing what "everybody" did. The difference, of course, was that at fifty-six he had been in a position to avoid public humiliation. Chaplin seemed to want to be treated like a child, reassured that he wasn't responsible after all.

On New Year's Eve, shortly after the trial ended, Chaplin accidentally locked himself out of the house and vented his frustration by aiming a swift kick at the glass door. A shard of flying glass struck his left leg, cutting a deep gash. Ironically the glass splinter narrowly missed cutting his Achilles' tendon. As it was the glass lodged in his leg within an eighth of an inch of a major artery. At Cedars of Lebanon Hospital, a doctor told Chaplin that he was lucky that he hadn't bled to death. He started the New Year on crutches, unable to work for four weeks.

Meanwhile a new judge, Clarence L. Kincaid, had been assigned to the retrial of the paternity suit. Kincaid wanted to avoid a replay of the theatrics of the first trial, and he offered to arbitrate a settlement. Joan Barry accepted his offer, but Chaplin balked. When the proceedings began in April, however, Chaplin avoided the courtroom. It seems that he could not bring himself to go through the ordeal of being cross-examined by Joe Scott again. It may be, however, that Pat Millikan had advised him not to testify, since he had made a bad impression the last time around. Once again the jury ignored the blood-test evidence, and this time they came to a decision in Barry's favor.

The verdict was attacked in the press as illogical, and later it was even singled out for criticism in a few law review articles. Supposedly the jurors had been too ignorant to grasp the meaning of the blood-test evidence. Perhaps they had heard some of the rumors circulating in Los Angeles that Chaplin had somehow rigged the test. Although it is hard to imagine how the test could have been invalid, even U.S. Attorney Carr had publicly suggested that the results were not to be trusted. Most likely, however, the jury had simply decided the case on the basis of moral responsibility rather than biological responsibility. Even if Chaplin was not Carol Ann's father, he might have been. In the first trial the male jurors had been more inclined to vote against Chaplin, no doubt on the theory that in his place they would have had to pay. At the second trial Chaplin's absence from the courtroom must have made it easier for the jury to find against him.

Financially the loss cost Chaplin little. Judge Kincaid awarded minimal child support of seventy-five dollars a week, later raised to one hundred. Joan Barry expressed shock at the outcome, saying, "Carol Ann will grow up like any other little girl instead of a rich man's daughter."[8] Afterward Barry moved to Pittsburgh, where she married a businessman. By 1953 she was back in California; she soon entered a California state mental hospital, diagnosed as schizophrenic. Her daughter was raised by relatives.

As far as the war was concerned, not much had come of Harry Crocker's plan to rehabilitate Chaplin's image. Chaplin did supply copies of several of his old films, including a specially restored print of *Shoulder Arms,* for exhibition to American troops in North Africa. But his first appearance at a Hollywood benefit—other than for the Soviets—did not come until after V-E day, when he and Oona attended a charity tennis match on behalf of the War Fund. Chaplin's friend tennis pro Bill Tilden was among the competitors, and after the match, when Tilden's racquet was sold in a blind auction, Chaplin offered three hundred dollars, half the winning bid of Barbara Hutton.

Doubtless what drew Charlie and Oona to this event was their desire to support Tilden, the once gallant champion who had fallen on hard times and now used Chaplin's court almost daily for practice and his private lessons. The lanky, impossibly long-legged Tilden had been a friend of Chaplin's since the early twenties, when he often played on the court at Doug Fairbanks's studio. The competitive Fairbanks even invented a game called "dougledyas" which was played with a shuttlecock and governed by rules unpredictable enough to allow him occasionally to win. Tilden was the greatest player of his generation—hailed as a tennis "genius" just as Chaplin was a slapstick "genius"—but ruled the game during an era when it was a true amateur sport. In midlife, having failed as an actor and a writer, Tilden could not reconcile himself to the end of his glory days. He became depressed and increasingly unable to control his sexual attraction to young boys.

By 1941, following a series of hushed-up scandals, Tilden had been quietly banned from major tennis clubs across the country, and he was reduced to giving lessons on the poorly maintained court of the Château Elysée—where financially strapped acquaintances of Chaplin had a way of turning up sooner or later. By 1946 even the Elysée no longer wanted Tilden around. The once dapper champion seldom bathed or changed his clothes. He lost his temper and wept inappropriately in public, and his penchant for young boys was so out of control that he was seen cruising for pickups on Sunset Boulevard in his Packard Clipper and even loitering near school playgrounds.

If anything, attitudes toward pedophiles were somehwat more relaxed in Hollywood during the forties than they are today. At any rate victims of molestation rarely pressed charges—and if they were adolescents, they were often not perceived as victims at all. Tilden got into trouble only when his appearance and strange behavior began to attract attention in public places. In November 1946 he was pulled over on Sunset Boulevard for erratic driving. His passenger, a fourteen-year-old boy, was disheveled, his trousers unzipped. After being indicted on a misdemeanor charge, Tilden blithely told his court-appointed lawyer, Richard Maddox, that there was nothing to worry about. His friend, Charlie Chaplin, would take care of everything. Perhaps Chaplin had pacified upset parents before. This time, however, he advised Tilden to jump bail and flee to the South of France, where Chaplin owned real estate. Maddox, meanwhile, had learned that the boy's parents did not want him to testify in open court, and if Tilden simply pleaded not guilty and demanded a jury trial, the DA would have to drop the charge.

Ignoring both of them, Tilden decided that the gentlemanly thing to do was to plead guilty, express contrition, and throw himself on the mercy of the court. In his statement he insisted that the incident was an aberration, the first homosexual experience he had been involved in since his teenage years. The judge, who happened to be A. A. Scott, the son of Joe Scott, Chaplin's nemesis during his paternity suits, was hardly naive enough to believe that this was Tilden's first offense. Somewhat regretfully he sentenced Tilden to a year at a state prison farm.

Reviewing the episode in the mid-seventies, Tilden's biographer Frank Deford concluded that Tilden was ashamed of his conduct, feared that he was out of control, and, perhaps unconsciously, set a course that led to his incarceration. Indeed he later wrote that he was "eternally grateful" to Judge Scott. Chaplin, however, saw Tilden's problem as caused by American small-mindedness. In January 1949, after Tilden was arrested a second time, Chaplin sent Loyd Wright to Judge Scott, asking him to release Tilden into his custody. He, Chaplin, would then see that Tilden left the country for France.[9]

No doubt Chaplin's loyalty to Tilden was admirable in its way, though it didn't win him any friends among the parents of Beverly Hills and West Hollywood. Tilden used tennis lessons to get close to adolescent boys, and unlimited access to Chaplin's court had doubtless proved convenient over the years. No one knew what to do about Tilden's problem, but Chaplin's proposal to Judge Scott was completely unrealistic, paroling prisoners to the Riviera not being a judicial option. Nor did Tilden want to go to France, or see flight as a solution.

Charlie and Oona did not go out a great deal socially, and the people they saw most regularly were the left-wing émigré writers who gathered at the Sunday salons of Salka Viertel, whose husband Bertholt was responsible for introducing Egon Kisch to Upton Sinclair in the late twenties. The émigrés ranged from Lion Feuchtwanger, considered an important novelist at the time, who lived in a beautiful house crammed with antiques and first editions, to the surly Bertolt Brecht, ensconced in semipoverty in Santa Monica. Few of the émigrés were as well known in California as they had been in Europe, and to varying degrees they were bitter. The Chaplins also saw the Clifford Odetses and Theodore Dreiser and his wife, Helen, as well as high-ranking Communists John Howard Lawson and Donald Ogden Stewart and his wife, Ella Winter, formerly married to Lincoln Steffens. In the country as a whole, anti-Soviet feeling was on the rise, even before the war ended—fueled by continuing revelations about Stalinist purges, the massacre of thousands of Polish officers in the Katyn Forest in 1939, the Amerasia case—the first of many domestic spy scandals—and increasing evidence that the Soviet Union intended to establish hegemony over Eastern Europe. Among Chaplin's friends such negative information was either dismissed or rationalized away. Lion Feuchtwanger quipped that every time he bought a house, the Nazis took over—first Berlin, then Paris, and now Santa Monica.

On May 28, 1946, the Soviet ship *Batumi* sailed through the rapidly changing political winds and docked at Long Beach Harbor. On board were a delegation of Soviet bureaucrats and representatives of Amtorg, the Soviet-American trading corporation, who were hoping to find an American market for crabmeat packed in canneries captured from Japan. Two hundred American guests, including such NCASF stalwarts as Chaplin, actor John Garfield, and director Lewis Milestone, were invited to a shipboard banquet, a lavish spread featuring crab, caviar, and champagne, followed by a showing of a Soviet film, *The Bear*. The Chaplins, along with John Garfield and his wife, were among the last to leave the party, shortly before 4:00 A.M. On disembarking they found customs agents waiting to make a routine check for dutiable items. There were also a few reporters and photographers on hand. Chaplin surveyed the customs agents and remarked to his companions, "Oh, I see we are under the power of the American Gestapo." The story played on the front page of Hearst papers across the country, accompanied by a photograph of a giggling Chaplin, captioned, for some reason, AND ONE SAW RED. Comments overheard by tabloid reporters are always a little suspect. However, Chaplin did talk this way in private. The only unlikely aspect of the story is the implication that he was drunk. Chaplin enjoyed wine and cocktails at this stage of his life, but rarely drank heavily.

Preliminary work on *Monsieur Verdoux* got under way in 1945, but the production did not kick into high gear until March 1946. Most of the characters in the story were middle aged, and Chaplin chose mature, thoroughly experienced character actors, among them William Frawley, soon to become famous as Fred in the *I Love Lucy* TV series. Fred Karno Jr., also had a small part. Edna Purviance tested for Madame Grosnay, a charming lady of a certain age, but she was as camera shy as ever and rather relieved when the role went to stage actress Isobel Elsom. Purviance appears briefly as an extra.

The part of the young streetwalker—eventually changed to a refugee to please the Production Code censors—went to Chaplin's latest "discovery," a University of Arizona premed student named Marilyn Nash who had shown up at one of his Sunday afternoon "tea and tennis" parties. A tall honey blond with a husky voice, Nash had no acting experience apart from drama club productions at her all-girl private school, and when Chaplin asked her to audition for him she read the part of King Lear, a choice that demonstrates the confidence that is so often wasted on the young. Oona, taking no chances, quickly stepped in and organized the grooming of Nash for her role, taking her to her own daily exercise class and signing her up for acting lessons with Max Reinhardt. She also introduced Nash to screenwriter Philip Yordan, another "tea and tennis" regular. By the time the film was released, they were married.

Nash's voice was sexy, but her all-American looks and manner made her unlikely as a desperate Belgian refugee. She played her scenes with Chaplin with an air of bemusement, a good sport gamely cooperating in a venture she knew to be slightly embarrassing. However, she did have the best line in the film. You've "lost your zest for bitterness," she tells Verdoux at one point—a "zest for bitterness" being a salient characteristic of Chaplin's, too.

A far better casting choice was Martha Raye for the role of the cheerfully unkillable Annabella Bonheur. Raye is best known to younger TV viewers as Mel's hash-slinging mother in reruns of *Alice* and the "bigmouth" of the Poli-Grip commercials. In 1946 she was a thirty-year-old with creamy skin and a svelte figure. Born Maggie Yvonne Reed, she had spent her early years living in a Pierce-Arrow automobile, touring the vaudeville and burlesque circuit with her parents, the song-and-dance team of Reed and Hooper. She had a formidable comic technique and had come to stardom on Broadway belting out the song "Mr. Paganini" in *Rhythm on the Range*.

Chaplin told Raye that he'd conceived the part of Annabella especially for her. This was probably not true, considering that he'd been thinking about the story since 1941, and he told others that the role was conceived for Fanny Brice. But Raye did have Annabella's hunger to give and receive affection. She longed to play romantic comedy, but was invariably cast as the comic sidekick. In her private life her need to be needed was so great that she volunteered as a nurse in the maternity and obstetrics ward at Cedars of Lebanon Hospital in Beverly Hills. In 1944, sent to do camp shows in North Africa with the cast of *Four Jills in a Jeep*, she extended her tour to five months. Ironically Raye's commitment to entertaining the troops would eventually make her almost as unpopular within the industry as Chaplin was during the war for *not* entertaining them. She did many shows for soldiers during the Vietnam War and, as a result, found herself scorned within the industry. "They didn't exactly blacklist me in Hollywood," she later said, "but they didn't bother with me."[10]

When Chaplin called Raye to ask her to play a part in his new movie, she took him for a practical joker and hung up on him. On her first day on the set she was "sick with fear." Knowing that in order to act with him she had to overcome her awe of Chaplin's reputation, she called him "Chuck," gave him a hearty slap on the back, and announced in midtake that she was ready for a bite of lunch. Chaplin understood Raye's need for attention and made sure she got it. He personally supervised the design of her clothes and hats and taught her how to smoke for the part, and how to walk. But there was no question who was boss. Though Raye was vain about her figure, he even persuaded her to gain nineteen pounds for the role. "I learned so much from Charlie," Raye would recall. "We became friendly, but if he said jump . . . I jumped."[11]

Monsieur Verdoux illustrates a paradox: A society condemns murder but glorifies war. Unfortunately Chaplin wasn't content to make his point lightly with the character of the elfin sociopath Henri Verdoux. He felt compelled to lecture the movie audience, many of whom, in 1947, had a lot more experience with war and killing than he did and were in no mood to hear his amateur analysis of the subject. In the last segment of the film, Henri Verdoux has been tried for his crimes, and he stands up in the dock to deliver a speech accusing the judge, jury, and spectators of hypocrisy. Why have they condemned Verdoux, a mere cottage-industry killer, while their war machine goes about its business as usual?

As for being a mass murderer, does not the world encourage it? Is it not building weapons of destruction for the sole purpose of mass killing?

Has it not blown unsuspecting women and children to pieces, and done it very scientifically? As a mass murderer, I am an amateur by comparison.

However, I have no desire to lose my temper, because very shortly, I will lose my head. Nevertheless, upon leaving this spark of earthly existence, I have this to say: I shall see you all very soon.

The writer/director/actor who gives himself a "see you all in hell" speech in his climactic scene had better be sure of his ground. Nor should he be surprised if people assume he is speaking for himself as well as his character. But what did Verdoux's speech mean?

The movie's script implies that war is caused by capitalism. Lest anyone miss the point, Verdoux drives it home in his conversation with a reporter in his death cell, minutes before he's led away to be beheaded. "It's all business," he says. "One murder makes a villain, millions a hero. Numbers sanctify."

No doubt Chaplin was horrified by the atomic bomb—a weapon of mass destruction whose devastating power had so recently been demonstrated. Nevertheless, this was the same man who, a few years earlier, had called for "more bombs over Berlin" in his Second Front speeches. When it was a question of coming to the aid of the Soviet Union, he had been quite happy to have the products of the capitalist war machine. Why the change of heart? Significantly, in February 1946, one month before Chaplin started filming, Josef Stalin had made a major speech predicting another war, this time between the Soviet Union and the West. Stalin justified his own attempt to grab territory in Eastern Europe as a response to the supposed aggressive attentions of the United States. *Monsieur Verdoux* embraced the Soviet line that the United States was responsible for the Cold War.

Eerily enough, even Verdoux's quip, "numbers sanctify," was a paraphrase of a remark widely attributed to Stalin: "One murder is a tragedy; a million deaths a statistic." That an actor could use this line as an accusation against capitalists, without even hinting at a criticism of Stalin, the greatest mass murderer of them all, was shocking.

What's more, one could hardly watch *Monsieur Verdoux* without realizing Chaplin was also drawing a parallel to his own experience. While he was being tried by the government on morals charges— not as a "ladykiller," exactly, though Hedda Hopper and Florabel

Muir certainly considered him a baby killer—that same government was deploying a million men in battle and perfecting the atomic bomb for use against Japan. Chaplin made the comparison explicit by including a scene of Verdoux being denounced in court, much as he had been by Joe Scott. Chaplin later insisted that he did not mean to excuse Verdoux's crimes, but even more than Verdoux's words, the arch of his back as he marches off to the guillotine leaves no doubt that he considers himself morally superior to his executioners.

Maybe the government *had* been wrong to prosecute Chaplin under the Mann Act, but his wartime troubles hardly bore comparison with the sufferings of millions who fought and died in World War II. The egotism of this scene would prove embarrassing even to people who agreed with the film's politics.

Chaplin got a foretaste of the reaction to Verdoux's final speech when he submitted the shooting script to the office of Joseph Breen, who administered the Motion Picture Production Code. On first reading Breen's office found the entire script "anti-social" and objectionable.

Chaplin shot back a reply, pointing out in a letter that it wasn't the code enforcer's job to censor his philosophy. In condemning the very premise of the screenplay, Breen was coming "dangerously near encroaching upon Constitutional rights of free speech." He flatly denied Breen's imputation that the script was meant to "indite [*sic*] the system and impugn the present day social structure"— though if not, what was the point?[12]

Chaplin followed up his letter with a personal visit to Breen's office, where he found himself engaging in a "Shavian dialogue" with a Catholic assistant of Breen's who objected in particular to some dialogue in a death-cell conversation between Verdoux and a priest. Pressed into a theological debate, the aide threw up his hands, dismissing Verdoux's verbal fencing about the nature of sin as just "a lot of pseudo-philosophizing."

Chaplin took great pride in his battle with the Breen office, devoting twelve pages of his autobiography to the episode. In fact it was little more than a skirmish. Joe Breen was a simple man of relatively middle-of-the-road views whose mandate from the Motion Picture Association of America was to keep "smut" out of the movies. In 1947 his main preoccupation was cleavage—just how much, if any, could be shown on the motion picture screen. Breen had loved *The Great Dictator* and was well aware of Chaplin's reputation as one of the few—if not the only—serious film artists in Hollywood. He wanted to protect his job and had no desire to lock horns in a battle over political censorship.

In the end the Breen office demanded that Marilyn Nash's character be changed from a streetwalker to a refugee who did time in jail for stealing a typewriter. A few other minor changes were laughable. Instead of telling Verdoux to "come to bed," one of his middle-aged and by no means appealing wives was to order him to "go to bed." The words "indecent moon" were ordered cut from a speech.

Actually Chaplin would have done well to give serious thought to the critiques of Breen and his assistant, since they were a foretaste of the public's response. In March 1947, as Chaplin was wrapping up the postproduction work, word of the film's theme began filtering out. Newspaper columnist Dorothy Kilgallen summarized the industry's view of the picture, reporting that Verdoux, before going off to be guillotined, says that "the makers of the atom bomb are the real murderers, and so are the heroes of the last war."[13]

Panic had descended on UA's corporate headquarters. The company had been counting on Chaplin's film to erase the red ink from its books. Now all thoughts of profit vanished as the company braced itself for a public relations disaster.

Verdoux would have been problematic enough in normal times, but it was being released just as the House Committee on Un-American Activities was investigating links between Popular Front organizations and Moscow.

In February 1947 former German Communist Party organizer Ruth Fischer testified that her brother Gerhart Eisler was "a most dangerous terrorist" and a Comintern hit man who had organized a purge of Communist Party leaders in China and plotted the death of Nikolai Bukharin, a former member of the Soviet Politburo executed on trumped-up charges in 1938. Fischer also said that since 1935 Gerhart Eisler had been the chief Comintern agent in the United States.

Gerhart Eisler had first come to the United States in 1935, using a forged passport in the name of Samuel Liptzin. During the war, he kept a secret radio transmitter in his apartment and served as a conduit, replaying messages from the Communist hierarchy to leaders of the U.S. Communist Party and prominent fellow travelers. There were hints, never fully documented, that Eisler was also involved in an effort to glean classified information from J. Robert Oppenheimer, the chief physicist of the Manhattan Project. For a time Eisler had received a salary of $150 a month from the Joint Anti-Fascist Refugee Committee—evidence suggesting that contributions to this supposedly independent organization were used to support Soviet espionage.

Ruth Fischer also said that another brother, Johannes "Hanns" Eisler, had been in touch with Gerhart during these years and supported his work. A well-regarded composer of film scores, Hanns Eisler had been a pupil of Arnold Schoenberg. At the time of his sister's HUAC appearance he was working with Bertolt Brecht on a theatrical production of Brecht's *Galileo*, starring Charles Laughton. When Laughton heard about Fischer's charge, he was indignant. "Eisler a Communist?" protested Laughton. "Nonsense. His music is just like Mozart!"[14]

Not all of Hanns Eisler's music was like Mozart, however. He had composed the music for dozens of agitprop revolutionary songs, most of them with lyrics by his frequent collaborator, Bertolt Brecht. The "Comintern March" was fairly typical:

The Comintern calls you,
Raise high the Soviet banner,
In steeled ranks to battle.
Raise sickle and hammer;
Our answer: Red Legions,
We raise in our might;
Our answer: Red Storm Troops.
We lunge to the fight. . . . [15]

Eisler's "revolutionary" work was no secret. Indeed, it was far better known than his serious orchestral compositions. He was described as a Communist in the *Great Soviet Encyclopedia* of

1933, and during the mid-1930s he was hailed in many articles published in the Soviet Union, and in the United States in the *Daily
Worker*, as a "great revolutionary composer." He was also the chairman of the International Music Bureau, an organization formed in
Moscow for the purpose of spreading revolutionary consciousness
among composers and professional musicians.

When Eisler tried to emigrate to the United States, the State
Department wanted to exclude him, and he was listed on the INS's
"watch list." Eisler managed to gain a residence visa anyway, thanks
in part to letters of support written by prominent individuals like
Clifford Odets, Malcolm Cowley, film director Joseph Losey, and,
not least of all, Eleanor Roosevelt. On entering the United States
Eisler swore under oath that he had never been a Communist Party
member, and under questioning by an immigration official he said,
"I hate Stalin as much as I hate Hitler."

Soon after his arrival in California in 1940, Eisler met Chaplin,
and in an interview in East Germany a few years later, he would
proudly take credit for persuading Chaplin to make his films more
explicitly political.[16] It is quite possible that Eisler was also responsible for influencing Chaplin to get involved with Russian War Relief,
since it seems that Chaplin first came into the organization through
a meeting organized for composers and musicians.

Eisler's left-wing friends in Hollywood knew about his "proletar-
ian" songs. What they couldn't accept was the suggestion that the
International Music Bureau was ultimately controlled by Stalin's
secret police. They wanted to believe that the inspiration for Eisler's
"revolutionary" music was pure. Chaplin, as it turned out, had a suspicion that there might be something to the charges, but he dismissed the idea. When it was a case of the U.S. government versus a
personal friend, there was no question which side he was on.

Early hints that Chaplin might soon be called to testify before
HUAC added more political baggage to a movie that already carried
quite enough. And even on nonpolitical grounds, *Monsieur Verdoux*
would not be an easy film to market. For the first time in his career
Chaplin was appearing in a feature film in a role that bore no relationship to the beloved Little Fellow. Film historian Charles Silver
has observed that Henri Verdoux was "the Tramp grown old."[17] But
he was also the Tramp grown rich—and arrogant. Americans were

used to films that gave them a protagonist they could identify with; a movie in which the "hero" is not likable is always a hard sell.

The good news was that Charlie Chaplin's transition to a new character was highly promotable. Yet, as early as March 1946, the UA publicity department had begun to receive complaints about the uncooperative attitude of Chaplin's studio: An entertainment writer for the *New York Times* wanted to do a feature story about the production but couldn't get permission to visit the set. The United Press had requested stills for a photo spread on "Chaplin Through the Years," but a studio representative refused to supply any, informing UP that the very subject of the story was "anathemic [*sic*] to Mr. Chaplin" who wanted to put the Tramp behind him.

With *Verdoux's* April 11 New York premiere only a few weeks away, only a select group of UA executives had been permitted to see the film at a special screening, and one of them on his return summed up *Verdoux* in an interoffice memo as Chaplin's "most pretentious film to date." Tom Waller, head of UA's publicity office in New York, complained that he had yet to see a synopsis of the story. Chaplin's studio had always supplied the copy and artwork for the pressbooks distributed to critics and the trade. By March 25, however, the only word Waller had from the studio was a memo warning that on no account was the publicity for *Verdoux* to use "any of the following words or similar words: Wives, Lover, Passionate, Bigamy, Sex."[18]

Laboring under this asinine directive, Waller's department put together a PR campaign that was easily funnier than the film itself. In a faint echo of children's box office promotions of the past, the press book announced that "inexpensive replicas" of Verdoux's unappealing mustache would be made available to exhibitors as giveaways. It also suggested that theater owners arrange co-op ad campaigns with their local banks: Widows would be urged to keep their money safely on deposit with the slogan, Don't Let a Verdoux Do You! (Presumably the bankers would not be sharp enough to notice that the film indicted them as agents of mass murder.)

As if Waller didn't have trouble enough, rumblings of discontent were issuing forth from Orson Welles, who had learned that the creative credit guaranteed him in his 1941 contract was nowhere in the final print. Indeed, one of the items of press-book copy eventually supplied by the studio was a story that identified "Oscar Wilde's portrait of Thomas Wainwright" as the inspiration for the script. Robert Arden had told Chaplin about Wainwright, the storied English forger and poisoner described by Wilde in "Pen, Pencil and Poison." Reproached for killing a woman, he is said to have remarked, "Yes, it was a dreadful thing to do, but she had very thick ankles." No doubt there was a bit of Wainwright in Henri Verdoux, but this didn't change the fact that the plot was based on Welles's Landru, who was nowhere mentioned in the film's publicity.

When Welles inquired about his credit, Chaplin sent word that he couldn't afford to include it just yet because Konrad Bercovici's long-postponed plagiarism suit was scheduled for trial two weeks after the premiere. Chaplin didn't want to acknowledge that *Verdoux* was based on an idea by Orson Welles because in his deposition for the Bercovici case he had insisted that he *never* used other people's story ideas. Thus cheating Bercovici in 1940 became the rationale for cheating Welles in 1947. Since Welles was a notorious credit hog in his own right, there was a certain poetic justice in this.

Some of the confusion over *Verdoux*'s advance publicity might be attributed to disarray at the studio. Alf Reeves, on whom Chaplin had depended for many years, had recently died, and his temporary successor, John McFadden, was neither popular nor effective. Oona's influence was a more serious problem. She often sat in on business discussions, and it was difficult to argue with Charlie while she was at his side, ready to take offense on his behalf at any hint of criticism.

In the past Chaplin had always been his own best PR representative, carefully nurturing his personal relationships with the most influential New York critics. This time Arthur Kelly sent advance word from California that Chaplin would go to only "the most important" interviews. Waller duly set up lunches and one-on-one meetings with a handful of important newspaper and magazine writers known to be Chaplin admirers. When he arrived in town, however, Chaplin refused to keep the appointments. Marilyn Nash and Martha Raye hadn't come East to promote the film either, so Waller, grousing that he'd had the "whole Book of Obstacles" thrown at him, had no one to send to these meetings but Robert Lewis, who played a tiny part as Verdoux's friend. Meanwhile Chaplin found time to talk to representatives of obscure foreign publications like *FilmIndia,* and at night he and Oona partied at "21," El Morocco and the Stork Club with friends like Carol and Bill Saroyan, at times sitting tables away from some of the very critics who had been spurned.

The day before the picture opened, Chaplin did give a press conference, but it was for foreign reporters only—no Americans allowed. He told this group that he had no idea why he was being criticized by Westbrook Pegler and others for failing to become a U.S. citizen. After all, many American businessmen lived in England for years and the British press didn't attack *them.* What's more, under American tax laws he paid taxes on all his income from motion pictures even though 70 percent of it was earned from foreign distribution. So, he concluded, "I am a well paying guest."

It was true that the citizenship issue was a red herring. Many foreign-born movie stars had never applied for U.S. citizenship—starting with "America's sweetheart" Mary Pickford, who was Canadian and proud of it. But Chaplin's statement would have been better received by Americans who learned of it indirectly had he left out the words "well paying," which implied that the United States was a sort of luxury hotel where guests were entitled to muss up their rooms a bit. Moreover, one can safely assume that an American living in England who mixed in radical politics, got involved in tabloid sex scandals, and held himself aloof from the war effort might well find himself unwelcome.

One might almost surmise that Chaplin had decided to write off the domestic release of *Monsieur Verdoux* in favor of the 70 percent of his income earned abroad. However, the New York press was not to be ignored entirely. On April 3 Chaplin ordered Waller to arrange a "mass meeting" of the press for Monday, April 14. Everything about this plan foretold disaster. The date was three days *after* the premiere, when the critics' reviews would already have been written, and an open press conference was bound to attract journalists who cared nothing about the film—or any film—and were interested solely in Chaplin's politics. Waller tried "strenuously" to dissuade Chaplin by listing some of the tough questions he was sure to be asked, but to no avail. "Chaplin expects that this will be controversial," he reported to the West Coast, "and understands that we can do nothing to protect him or [the] picture once he submits to mass questioning."[19]

Unable to talk Chaplin out of the press conference, the UA publicity department apparently decided that it might as well generate as much controversy as possible. One employee even called the fiercely anti-Communist Ed Sullivan and tried to talk him into attending. Sullivan declined, suspecting a setup, but did publish a column listing the questions he hoped others at the press conference would think to ask. Also, though Chaplin had asked that the group be limited to people with "recognized press credentials" (whatever that meant), Waller's office approved a pass for James W. Fay, who wrote for the newsletter of the Empire State Catholic War Veterans. Fay had read Ed Sullivan's list of questions and intended to pose as many of them as he could.

On Friday, April 11, Chaplin arrived at the Broadway Theater with Oona on one arm and, on the other, Mary Pickford, who had set aside her personal feelings to make a show of support for her longtime partner. The house had been papered with friendly celebrities like sculptor Jo Davidson, chairman of the Independent Citizens' Committee of the Arts, Sciences and Professions (ICCASP), who had recently refused to ban Communists from his organization. But even this overwhelmingly liberal, politically sophisticated audience took offense at the film's ending. Seated between his young wife and his longtime antagonist, Chaplin, for the first time in his life, heard an opening-night audience boo and hiss his work.

At the after-show party, guests avoided Chaplin's table, a sure sign of a disaster. The reviews confirmed it. The *Times*'s Bosley Crowther loved the film, but Howard Barnes of the *Herald Tribune* called it "something of an affront to the intelligence." *The New Yorker*'s review was titled "Chaplin and His Murky Message."[20]

No sooner were the first reviews in than an acknowledgment of Orson Welles was added to the movie's credits. "The next day—after they'd all said, you know, 'Who gave him this *awful* idea?'—up on the screen went my billing," Welles groused.[21]

On Monday morning an overflow crowd jammed the ballroom of the Hotel Gotham for Chaplin's "mass meeting." While nervous UA executives paced at the back of the room and a sound crew recorded the proceedings for broadcast that evening over radio station WNEW, Chaplin stood alone behind a bare conference table and announced that he would be not be making an opening statement. "Proceed with the butchery," he invited the assembled reporters.

After an opening question about Orson Welles, the subject quickly turned to politics. Asked to define his political beliefs, Chaplin said:

"Well I think that is very difficult to do these days, to define anything politically. There are many generalities, and life is becoming so technical that if you step off the curb—I think you need a guidebook—if you step off the curb with your left foot, they accuse you of being a Communist. But, I have no political persuasions whatsoever. I've never belonged to any political party in my life, and I have never voted in my life! Does that answer your question?"

This didn't satisfy James W. Fay, who wondered why Chaplin took pride in saying he never voted. "Don't you think that as a citizen [sic] you should be interested in getting qualified people in government?"

Chaplin replied: "I don't believe in making any divisions of people. I think that any division—I mean is very dangerous. I think that leads to fascism. Citizens are citizens of the world over."

The suggestion that voting leads to fascism was certainly an interesting perspective, but Fay was not quick-witted enough to follow it up. Instead he brought up Chaplin's failure to return to Britain during World War II, and the two of them got into a rambling colloquy about patriotism.

Another journalist then asked if it was true, as reported, that *Monsieur Verdoux* expressed Chaplin's conviction "that contemporary civilization was making mass murderers of us all."

"Well," said Chaplin, "all my life I have always loved peace and abhorred violence. Now I think these weapons of destruction—I don't think I'm alone in saying this; its a cliché by now—that the atomic bomb is the most horrible invention of mankind, and I think it is being proven so at every moment. I think it is creating so much horror and fear that we are going to grow up as neurotics."[22]

By no means was everyone in the room hostile. One reporter defended Chaplin's right to "think as you please," and a few others lobbed easy questions, such as, "Are you going to make any more films for children?" (Had he ever made any?) Chaplin, however, seemed dazed. Asked to comment on changing audience tastes, Chaplin drifted back to politics: "We're going into another war."

From his seat in the balcony, James Agee, then a movie reviewer for *Time* magazine, had been listening to the proceedings with mounting outrage. Suddenly he spoke up, his voice trembling with emotion:

> What are people who care a damn about freedom—who really care for it—[to] think of a country and the people in it, who congratulate themselves upon this country as the finest on earth and as a "free country," when so many of the people in this country pry into what a man's citizenship is, try to tell him his business from day to day and exert a public moral blackmail against him for not becoming an American citizen—for his political views and for not entertaining troops in the manner—in the way they think he should.

Agee's words were inaudible in the front of the room, so he found a microphone and repeated them. Chaplin thanked him, and the press conference soon drew to a close.

In 1969 *Film Comment* printed a transcript of the Hotel Gotham proceedings with remarks by George Wallach, who covered the event for WNEW, calling it "more like an inquisition than a press conference." If so, it was an inquisition staged by Chaplin, who cast himself in the role of the heretic—much like the protagonist of Brecht's *Galileo*, which Brecht and Eisler were even then preparing for its opening the following July. Chaplin, after all, had set the ground rules and been warned well in advance of the questions he would be asked. And James Fay, while obviously hostile, was also an amateur interviewer, who flitted from one loosely phrased query to the next without any follow-up.

Chaplin had been glibly parrying the questions of the press for thirty years. No doubt he had reason to think that he would come off better under "mass" questioning than in one-on-one interviews with the press. And he was right. In the aftermath of the conference, few paid much attention to Chaplin's statements. What would be vividly remembered was Chaplin as, in George Wallach's words, "the personification of the universal underdog."[23]

Or course it is wrong to expect artists to pass a political litmus test. If Chaplin wanted to make a movie that pointed the finger of blame at capitalism (and by extension, the United States), he had a perfect right to do so. But surely James Fay and others had an equal right to ask him what he meant by it. Chaplin's views on Communism and World War II were hardly irrelevant to the message of his movie, and his insistence that he had "no political persuasions" was disingenuous. Indeed, Chaplin's performance at this press conference goes far to explain why people of James Fay's political stripe thought all liberals were two-faced and elitist. Chaplin may have been an artist, but he was also a multimillionaire producer. Fay, the Catholic war veteran, was far closer to representing the voice of "the people," yet as soon as he posed a few hard questions, he was cast as a bully and an "inquisitor" and Chaplin as his victim.

The debate over *Monsieur Verdoux*'s political message necessarily obscured its other qualities. Although a talky, old-fashioned looking movie—ironically, much like the early sound films Chaplin criticized in the late 1920s—it was nevertheless a drama of ideas, quirky and unpredictable, which made it startlingly different from the typical American movie of the 1950s—and, unfortunately, today. James Agee, who had never met Chaplin before the Hotel Gotham press conference, loved *Monsieur Verdoux* for precisely this reason. In retrospect he, too, found Verdoux's final speech distasteful. What he saw in the film was a fable of sexual politics—the story of "Responsible Man" whose efforts to support his family in the "modern world" cause him to become alienated from them: "The wife and child are shut away in a home which is at once a shrine and a jail; and there, immobilized, and cut off from the truth, they virtually cease to exist as living objects of love; they become an ever more rigid dream."[24]

Agee's lengthy three-part review of *Verdoux* in the *Nation* never explained why this dilemma is unique to "modern" man. Surely men in centuries past were forced to make moral compromises to earn their livings, and had duties that separated them from their wives and children for long periods of time. The contemporary viewer can't help thinking that Henri Verdoux's motives for becoming a bigamist and then a murderer have little or nothing to do with the need to support his invalid wife and child. Verdoux dashes from one "wife" to another, reinventing himself every time he takes a new mate. With Annabella he pretends to be a sea captain; with another "wife," he poses as a globe-trotting engineer, and so on. Henri Verdoux demonstrates why the modern world is so fascinated by serial killers—they practice the ultimate form of self-expression, leaving no inconvenient witnesses to hinder their quest.

While *Monsieur Verdoux* appealed to a certain kind of movie fan, it did not have the ingredients that make a commercial hit. With hindsight, one suspects that Chaplin realized that the best way to generate box office was to provoke as much controversy as possible. Indeed, the strategy might even have worked to some extent if he had followed up the New York press conference with a national publicity tour. Chaplin had never found this necessary in the past, and this time he couldn't consider a tour even if he wanted to because he was preoccupied with the Konrad Bercovici plagiarism suit, which was scheduled to come to trial in New York State Supreme Court at the end of April. Chaplin had never expected Bercovici's complaint to get as far as it had, since Loyd Wright had assured him that the suit would be thrown out on a technicality. But Wright had miscalculated, and after six years of delays, the judge brushed aside Chaplin's request for yet another postponement.[25]

In court a few unpleasant surprises awaited. Bercovici had a new attorney, the celebrated Louis Nizer, a master of the art of cross-examination. Moreover Melyvn Douglas, whose wife, Helen Gahagan Douglas, was a popular liberal Democratic member of the House of Representatives, had come from California to support Bercovici's version of the events in Pebble Beach.

Douglas was uncomfortable about testifying against Chaplin at a time when he was under attack for his pro-Communist beliefs, but his unease only made his testimony more credible.

On a Friday afternoon, the eighth day of the trial, Chaplin was called to the stand. Since he had already told reporters in 1941 that Bercovici gave him the idea for *The Great Dictator*, he was hard pressed to deny it now. In the process he managed to add a few more improbable denials to the story he had given in his depositions. He said, for example, that he had never had any special interest in Gypsies or Gypsy culture, a statement even an attorney less resourceful than Nizer could easily have challenged.

Over the weekend Chaplin's attorneys contacted Nizer and offered to settle the case out of court for ninety thousand dollars. Nizer told his client: "You can win, but it might take you five years to get paid." Bercovici was sixty-five and suffered from bleeding ulcers, a condition aggravated by the stress of hearing Charlie publicly disavow their twenty-five-year friendship. He decided to settle. Afterward Chaplin told friends that he would have won the case but had come under heavy pressure from the judge, who was eager to wind up the trial so he could visit his dying brother. The notion that Chaplin had spent six years and thousands in legal fees only to settle to accommodate the schedule of the judge was, of course, ridiculous.[26]

During the course of the trial Chaplin found time to have dinner with Max Eastman. Having lived in Moscow during the twenties, Eastman had no illusions about Soviet methods. He had no doubt that Hanns Eisler was a "cultural emissary of the Communists" who had taken advantage of Chaplin's trust. His attempt to persuade Chaplin of this made no impression, however. "Why, the idea of his being subversive is perfectly fantastic!" Charlie exclaimed when Eisler's name came up. "He is a charming fellow, a gifted musician and a very good friend of mine."[27]

Verdoux played in New York for four weeks, to steadily shrinking audiences, and by the time he returned to Los Angeles, Chaplin had decided to withdraw it until the autumn. Russell Birdwell, a top public relations specialist who had designed the marketing campaign for *Gone With the Wind,* was hired by the studio to prepare for the reissue. Birdwell recognized that audience resistance to Chaplin's new character could not be ignored. The ad campaign he designed put the onus on movie fans, challenging them with the slogan: Chaplin Changes! Can You?

Birdwell also sent Marilyn Nash and her husband, Philip

Yordan, to New York on a publicity junket. New York was sweltering in an August heat wave, and Marilyn Nash, eight months pregnant, looked exhausted. Yordan was the author of *Anna Lucasta*, a play with a plot that reminded many of *Anna Christie*, and an all-black cast. As Patrick McGilligan reported in his book *Backstory 2: Interviews with Screenwriters of the 1940's and 1950's*, it was whispered at the time that Yordan had hired an unemployed black writer to "Negro-up" the dialogue.[28] *Anna Lucasta* had been a success, but it made Yordan a somewhat controversial figure in theatrical circles, and, for whatever reasons, the press appeared to have it in for the couple. By the time they returned to California, Nash was so exhausted that she checked into a hospital to recuperate.

Chaplin scheduled the re-release of *Verdoux* for Washington, D.C., on September 26—the same week Hanns Eisler was scheduled to testify before HUAC. The Communist Party, meanwhile, was holding "Free Gerhart Eisler" rallies, where speakers protested the notion that Moscow exercised control over the Communist movement in the United States or had espionage agents in the country. In June, Chaplin signed a petition calling on the federal courts to delay the contempt of Congress trials of Gerhart Eisler and two officials of the Communist Party USA, Leon Josephson and Eugene Dennis, who were accused of helping him obtain a false passport, on the grounds that "anti-Communist hysteria" would make it impossible for them to get a fair trial.

In July it was reported that Chaplin himself would be among the first witnesses summoned by HUAC when Congress resumed in the fall, and he fired off an open telegram to committee chairman J. Parnell Thomas:

> From your publicity I note that I am to be quizzed by the House un-American Activities Committee in Washington in September. . . . Forgive me for this premature acceptance of your invitation. . . . While you are preparing your engraved subpoena I will give you a hint where I stand. I am not a Communist. I am a peacemonger.[29]

For years afterward Chaplin would entertain his friends by enacting the performance he would have given had he actually been summoned to testify before HUAC. He planned to appear, he said, in his Tramp makeup and costume, to expose the hearings for the farce they were. In the event he was not so brave. At Chaplin's request Russell Birdwell sent telegrams to the members of the committee inviting them to attend the premiere of *Verdoux* on September 26. The invitations served as advance notice that Chaplin was planning something dramatic, and Parnell Thomas canceled his appearance, announcing that he had no intention of helping Chaplin publicize his latest film.

Hanns Eisler did testify, however. Echoing Chaplin's own statements at the Hotel Gotham press conference, Eisler insisted that he was a nonpolitical artist. Committee counsel Robert Stripling countered by reading from Eisler's own articles, including one in which he described his music as "a particular kind of political seminar on problems of party strategy and politics." Reminded that he had told an INS investigator that he hated Stalin as much as Hitler, Eisler, who faced likely deportation to the Communist bloc, became flustered, saying, "If I really made such a stupid remark I was an idiot. . . . There must be a misunderstanding, or it is a completely idiotic, hysteric remark."[30]

HUAC's investigation had started out with a strong, well-informed witness, Ruth Fischer. But a congressional hearing room was never the place to conduct a serious investigation of espionage and political infiltration. Members like John Rankin of Mississippi were intent on using the hearings to embarrass Roosevelt Democrats and flog the liberals, introducing an element of partisan backbiting into the proceedings that made the Committee's work all too easy to discredit. Matters deteriorated further when the committee turned its attention to Communist activity in Hollywood, launching a bootless attempt to demonstrate that Communist screenwriters had slipped subversive political messages into the films they made for the major studios. *Monsieur Verdoux,* one movie that did have such a message, was roundly scored by critics and booed by audiences, suggesting that the citizenry could look out for itself.

The committee had subpoenaed nineteen "unfriendly" witnesses, mainly screenwriters who were Communist Party members with a long history of political activism. "The Nineteen," as they were called, arrived in Washington with the support of the most dazzling political lobby ever assembled, the ad hoc Committee on the First Amendment, whose members included John Huston, Humphrey Bogart, Lauren Bacall, Gene Kelly, Danny Kaye, Jane Wyatt, Frank Sinatra, Judy Garland, and Paulette Goddard, among many others. The stars were prepared to risk their careers to support their colleagues on free-speech grounds. But the "unfriendlies"—except for Bertolt Brecht, a noncitizen—had their own strategy and were intent on turning the hearings into political theater. In the process of refusing to answer the committee's questions, the first ten witnesses who were called lectured the representatives on "the principles of Americanism"; accused them of waging a "cold war" on Jews and on blacks; compared them to Hitler, Goebbels, and Göring, and addressed staff attorney Robert Stripling as "Mr. Quisling." The eleventh witness, Brecht, denied being a Communist—"No. No. No. No. No!"—and fled the country the next day.

Perhaps Chaplin in his Tramp costume would have been more effective, but the Hollywood Ten did not make a good impression. With a few exceptions, they came off as belligerent ideologues who publicly proclaimed their belief that the U.S. Congress was a hotbed of fascists. One by one the stars bailed out, and on November 26, 1947, Eric Johnston of the producer's association announced that the Unfriendly Ten would be banned from the industry. It was the beginning of the Hollywood blacklist.

Chaplin's strategy of tying *Monsieur Verdoux* to the HUAC hearings had backfired. The picture did fairly good business in Washington but soon sank from sight, its failure helped along by negative public reaction to the performance of the Hollywood Ten. As it happened the Communist Party was not especially eager to have its followers see *Monsieur Verdoux* either. The party's limited sense of irony did not extend to a film that put Marxist sentiments in the mouth of a serial wife murderer. Arnaud d'Usseau, in a lengthy and tortured analysis in the Communist journal *Mainstream,* took comfort in the fact that Henri Verdoux ultimately submitted to the authority of the state—going willingly to the guillotine.[31]

No doubt there was something in Chaplin's personality that drove him to get into situations in which he identified with the alienated and despised of society and, indeed, cast himself as one of society's victims. Unlike Rob Wagner, who regardless of politics had always tried to protect Chaplin's reputation, his Communist friends during the 1940s were all too ready to take advantage of him. The most egregious example of manipulation occurred later on during the Eisler affair. Hanns Eisler had been detained at Ellis Island pending deportation proceedings, and on November 21, Chaplin wired Pablo Picasso in Paris, urging him to organize a protest on Eisler's behalf at the American embassy. The telegram also asked Picasso to keep Chaplin informed of his plans, so that protests in France could be coordinated with actions in Los Angeles.

Chaplin did not know Picasso personally, and organizing political demonstrations anywhere was out of character for him. Very likely the telegram was sent on the instigation of Ella Winter, who was in Paris in early November with her husband, Donald Ogden Stewart, and Joel Forster of the *New Masses* and apparently in contact with Picasso.[32] Communist demonstrations on Eisler's behalf in Paris were hardly likely to convince the U.S. government that Eisler was not a Communist, or to make his deportation less likely.

Though Picasso declined to get involved, copies of Chaplin's telegram mysteriously found their way to left-wing journals in Paris. When the story broke in the United States there was an uproar. Previously all Chaplin had done was express his opinions, but for a noncitizen to be organizing an anti-American protest abroad did cross a line between free speech and meddling. The Picasso telegram reenergized the veterans' organizations, whose opposition to *Monsieur Verdoux* had run out of steam. It also antagonized the film industry, which was collectively hoping that the HUAC fiasco would soon be forgotten. On December 11 the *Hollywood Reporter* weighed in, wondering why Chaplin was still permitted to live in the United States when "it has become quite obvious that he is not satisfied with the conduct of our government and continually criticizes its actions."[33]

As so often happened, Chaplin had put his reputation on the line for nothing. Hanns Eisler and his wife Lou had no intention of remaining in the United States permanently. At most, they wished to delay their return to Germany until they could be sure that their enemies within the German Communist Party had been neutral-ized. In the meantime, like a number of other Comintern operatives, they planned to take refuge in Czechoslovakia. According to the FBI, Chaplin himself approached Bohun Beneš, a Czech diplomat in Los Angeles and a nephew of Edvard Beneš, who headed the coalition of democrats and Communists in power in Prague, asking him to arrange visas for Hanns and Lou Eisler.

On February 13, 1948, even as his supporters were organizing a concert on his behalf at Town Hall, Hanns Eisler signed an agreement to forgo hearings and accept voluntary deportation. His and Lou's departures were delayed for a month when France balked at granting him a transit visa. By the time they left the United States on March 24, the Beneš government had been overthrown by a Communist coup, and the Czech patriot, Jan Masaryk, forced to commit "suicide." As a composer of atonal music who had lived many years abroad, Eisler had reason to fear that Stalin would try to eliminate him, and he and his wife found refuge in Vienna for a time. In 1949, however, Gerhart Eisler jumped bail and fled the United States as a stowaway on the Polish ship *Batory*. He was soon appointed chief of the East German propaganda ministry, and Hanns and Lou returned home.

19

Limelight

In December 1947 Hollywood learned from a report in the British press that Charlie Chaplin had written its obituary. He told a British reporter of his plans to leave the United States "before long" because he had "lost confidence" in the American film industry:

Hollywood is now fighting its last battle, and it will lose that battle unless it decides once and for all to give up standardizing its films—unless it realizes that masterpieces cannot be mass-produced in the cinema, like tractors in a factory. I think, objectively, that it is time to take a new road—so that money shall no longer be the all-powerful god of a decaying community.

And, he added in conclusion: "I, Charlie Chaplin, declare that Hollywood is dying."[1]

Even if one agrees to some extent with Chaplin's complaints about formulaic movies, this display of ego was ill-timed. The year 1947 had been a hard one for the industry. Television had hurt movie revenues, jeopardizing the jobs of workers at all levels, and anti-Communist sentiment was still on the rise in the country as a whole. Within a few years publications like *Red Channels* and *Counterattack* would be outing alleged Reds, at times on the basis of ludicrous misinformation.

What Hollywood did not need at this point was another slam from Chaplin, who had announced his departure more times than anyone could count. This time, however, he really did intend to go—and not just for political reasons. New tax laws designed to protect the struggling British film industry would make it financially advantageous for Chaplin to shoot his next picture in London.

Chaplin's status as a resident alien had become the pet peeve of a handful of conservative representatives and veterans' groups, and when he applied for a permit assuring his right to reenter the United States, he was told that he would have to submit to an interview first. On the afternoon of April 17, 1948, INS Deputy Commissioner John P. Boyd showed up at Summit Drive accompanied by an FBI special agent, prepared with a list of questions that covered everything from Chaplin's morals ("Have you ever committed adultery?") to his association with various Communist front groups.

Chaplin's name had been used at one time or another by a long list of questionable groups like the People's Radio Foundation, formed during the war to secure broadcasting licenses for pro-Communist stations. Chaplin insisted that he had never heard of the People's Radio Foundation. Given his close association with left-wing broadcaster Robert Arden, one wonders if this could have been true. Nonetheless Chaplin had a point when he complained that he was inundated by "hundreds of requests from all sorts of organizations" and often cooperated without knowing exactly what they were about: "As a matter of fact, I don't know these people, and so forth, and they say in the cause of justice will you lend your name to such and such a thing and so forth."[2]

Chaplin gave the impression of being slightly fed up with his political friends. He was bitter that *Monsieur Verdoux* had "strangely enough" not been approved for showing in the Soviet Union, and at one point in the interview, he cut short his answer to a question to exclaim, "I have $30,000,000 worth of business—what am I talking about Communism for?"

Overall Chaplin came off rather well on this occasion. However, when the transcript was returned to him, his attorney, Pat Millikan, advised him not to sign it. The INS waived its demand for a signature and issued him a reentry permit on April 28.

Chaplin's immediate problem was not with the INS but the IRS, which wanted him to post a bond of a million and a half dollars to cover his potential liability on a disputed tax bill. Rather than put up the money, he canceled his and Oona's ship and hotel reservations and stayed home.

In time Pat Millikan was able to negotiate a compromise with the IRS. Still, it wasn't easy for a man with a young American wife, a growing family, and recurring tax problems to leave the country in a huff. He and Oona now had two children, Geraldine and two-year-old Michael, born in 1946. Over the summer Oona became pregnant for the third time, and she and Charlie decided not to go to Europe that year after all. The baby, Josephine Hannah, was born the following March 28. Meanwhile Geraldine was ready to start school, and Oona was planning a major renovation of the Summit Drive house, removing the two-story atrium and adding five new bedrooms.

Monsieur Verdoux had won Chaplin at least one new and devoted admirer. James Agee had moved to Los Angeles in 1948 and was now a frequent guest at Summit Drive. Undeterred by the experiences of Konrad Bercovici and Orson Welles, Agee was eager to write a script for Chaplin, who led him to believe that he might consider resurrecting the Tramp if the right material presented itself. Agee proposed a story set in a New York City devastated by atomic war. Here the Tramp would encounter a utopian sect of survivors who had banished sexual jealousy along with the traditional family, raising all their children in common. The villains of the piece were a group of scientists, intent on controlling what remained of society with their technological expertise.

Agee's equation of the threat of nuclear destruction with sexual repression now seems almost quaint. He labored over the concept, but by the time he had completed a sixty-six-page scenario, called *Scientists and Tramp*, he could see that it wasn't working. For one thing, in an antimaterialist utopia the Tramp was no longer distinctive. Nor, one suspects, was Chaplin serious about reviving his character—as he realized, he was now so changed physically that this would have been quite difficult. When the idea came to nothing there were no hard feelings on either side.

Chaplin was already busy working on his own idea, the semi-autobiographical story of a "washed up clown," the alcoholic music hall comedian Calvero. (The very name suggests Calvary—and Calvero was another incarnation of the universal victim.) Whatever Chaplin's shortcomings in his private life, he could not be accused of avoiding difficult issues in his work. The Calvero story, eventually the basis of his film *Limelight,* tackled a great and important theme—it is often easier to love others than to accept their love for us.

Certainly this was the root of much of Chaplin's chronic loneliness. He could never trust the love and admiration that came his way. Fearing rejection, he managed to spurn others before they had a chance to hurt him. This was true not only of Chaplin's romantic relationships. It was also the governing principle of his career, and he knew it. The first page of the manuscript version of the story said of Calvero: "Necessity made him turn to comedy, which he loathed, because it demanded of him an intimacy with his audience which he did not feel and which never came natural [*sic*] to him."[3]

While Chaplin labored over his story, his and Oona's lives went on as before. Despite the banning of the Ten from the industry, Hollywood remained a bastion of leftish sentiment. In 1948 it was a center of support for the Progressive Party candidacy of Henry Wallace, who favored a policy of friendship with the Soviet Union. The Chaplins were among Wallace's prominent supporters and at one rally at the Hollywood Bowl it was announced that Charlie—the nonpolitical nonvoter—pledged a thousand dollars. Whether the Progressives got the money was another matter. Chaplin had a habit of making pledges in a moment of enthusiasm, then leaving the checks unsigned on his desk for months.

The Progressive Party was not overtly Communist, but Party members and sympathizers played a prominent role. As long as the campaign lasted, Wallace's followers could sustain the illusion that they were still at the center of the political debate. On election day, however, the Wallace ticket drew only a million votes nationwide. Before long, the Chaplins' activist friends were reduced to supporting local causes like raising funds for the progressive Westland School, where Geraldine and Michael were enrolled. Charlie made several films available for school benefits, but Westland was Oona's enthusiasm, not his. Privately he thought progressive education silly.

Despite the changing political climate, Charlie continued to support the Party's pet causes. That April he became a sponsor of the World Peace Congress in Paris, an event organized by the French Communist Party to spread anti-American propaganda and foment opposition to NATO. Although the congress had been condemned in advance by the State Department, Chaplin dispatched a congratulatory telegram to the delegates, which was released to the press by the convocation's president, Dr. Frédéric Joliot-Curie. Asked by a reporter for the *Los Angeles Times* if he wasn't a bit suspicious of the organizers' motives, he said, "I am never suspicious of anybody who is working for world peace."[4]

The Joliot-Curie telegram was the final straw for Louella Parsons, who had held herself aloof from the anti-Chaplin chorus during the Joan Barry scandal, the HUAC hearings, and the clamor over *Monsieur Verdoux*. "I can hardly believe that Charlie Chaplin has the nerve to plan another movie in America," fumed Parsons. "I think his conduct has reached the point where even his old friends can no longer continue to apologize for him."[5]

In fact Chaplin was far from sure he would make another picture in the United States. As late as the spring of 1950 he still hoped to film the Calvero story in England, but when he applied for another reentry permit, he was informed through Pat Millikan that the permit, even if issued, would not guarantee him the right to return to the United States. Under a recent reorganization of the federal bureaucracy, reentry permits were issued routinely by the local office of the INS, whose decisions could be overruled at any time by the Justice Department.[6]

Chaplin was caught in a web of inertia. Old enough to remember the Red Scare of 1919–20, he kept thinking that the political winds blowing from the right would die down within a few months, a complete misreading of the situation. In the meantime, Oona, who had never been to Europe, was eager to go abroad and kept pressing him to firm up his plans for filming in London. Oona was an intelligent, well-read woman, but when it came to politics and practical affairs, she inhabited a world of gossamer illusion—partly because Charlie chose to keep her there. Although the implications of the INS warning had to be quite clear to Charlie and Pat Millikan, she managed to remain oblivious.

At times Chaplin seemed to be reaching out to his old audience, preparing the ground for his next film. In 1950, for example, he rereleased *City Lights*, his last nonpolitical movie. Unfortunately, disdaining television and the small fees involved, he had passed up offers to make live appearances and/or permit the showing of some of his First National–era films on television. When WPIX in New York announced plans to air a selection of his earlier two-reelers, the Empire State War Veterans threatened to picket the station.

Probably nothing Chaplin could have done at this point would have defused the animosity of the veterans' organizations. At times, however, he seemed to enjoy provoking them. In March 1950, after an Australian journalist floated a rumor that he was about to apply for U.S. citizenship, the Hollywood post of the American Legion passed a resolution urging the government to deny his application. Instead of ignoring this development, Chaplin felt obliged to issue a rebuttal: "As a believer in 'one world' I wish to respectfully state that my position is unaltered and that I have not made any request officially or unofficially for citizenship. *These rumors and lies are part of a conspiracy instigated by my enemies to try and embarrass me* [italics added]."[7]

Just who Chaplin thought was conspiring to make it appear that he wanted to be a U.S. citizen was unclear. But the statement guaranteed that the Hollywood post's anti-Chaplin resolutions would be placed on the agenda of the legion's next national convention, which duly voted to boycott his next picture.

Unsure of his future plans, Chaplin had also been unable make up his mind what to do about United Artists, which was on the brink of bankruptcy. In 1949 he and Mary Pickford, the only remaining partners, were offered $12.5 million by a group of investors organized by Si Fabian, president of the Fabian theater chain. Chaplin's $5 million share of the selling price was to be paid in cash, but the deal collapsed hours before the signing of the papers. Chaplin and Pickford blamed each other, though *Variety* reported that it was Chaplin who had balked.[8]

By 1950 Chaplin appeared to have mentally written off his interest in the struggling company. A new management team had taken over, headed by Paul McNutt, a former governor of Indiana, and Max Kravetz, a promoter and old friend of Pickford's. The McNutt

management team failed to win the confidence of independent producers, releasing just two B pictures during its tenure. With foreclo-
sure just days away, a pair of prominent entertainment industry
attorneys, Arthur Krim and Robert Benjamin, offered to step in.
Although two years earlier Si Fabian had been prepared to pay
$12.5 million, in February 1951 Krim and Benjamin were able to
acquire half the company for nothing, in exchange for saving it from
total collapse.

The Krim takeover marked the turning point in UA's fortunes
and assured that Chaplin would have a U.S. distributor for his next
picture, if he wanted one. But Chaplin's paranoid mood had
infected his business associates as well. Max Kravetz believed that
Chaplin had schemed to undermine the McNutt management, in
part by inducing Sam Spiegel (aka S. P. Eagle) and other producers
to withhold their pictures. Kravetz had no hard evidence to back up
his suspicions, and most industry observers blamed McNutt's failure
on his lack of financial clout and industry experience. Still, it was
true that McNutt was a former commander of the American Legion,
which Chaplin believed was engaged in a fascist conspiracy to
destroy him.

Max Kravetz filed a suit against Chaplin and United Artists, and
he was also involved in litigation with Mary Pickford, who had lent
him some of the money that evaporated with the Krim takeover. UA
dismissed Kravetz's complaint as a nuisance suit, but nothing could
be resolved until Chaplin gave a deposition, which he kept avoiding.
Mary Pickford became so incensed that she tried to get a federal
judge in New York to indict the manager of the Sherry Netherland
Hotel for repeatedly helping Charlie to evade subpoenas.

Charlie and Oona were not exactly pariahs in Beverly Hills.
Geraldine and Michael were on the kiddie birthday party circuit,
and as late as 1951 the Chaplins threw an elegant A-list party to celebrate Carol and Bill Saroyan's second try at marriage. Carol's first
marriage to the overbearing Saroyan had left her self-esteem in tat-
ters. Charlie urged her to try again on the grounds that the love of a
great writer like Bill Saroyan was worth suffering for. By the evening
of the ceremony, Carol knew she was making a terrible mistake, but

it was too late to cancel Charlie and Oona's perfect party. Two hundred guests appeared for the wedding dinner, and the lighting, flowers, and music were exquisite.

Compared to the old days, however, Summit Drive had become a social black hole. In a town where chance encounters at parties could make or break careers, Charlie's famous "tea and tennis" gatherings had long enveloped him in an aura of power. Invitations were so sought after that Tim Durant had become a minor celebrity in his own right, courted by people who knew he controlled the guest lists. Since Chaplin's get-togethers filled a need, even the Joan Barry affair had not dimmed their cachet. In the post-HUAC era, however, it was no longer smart to be seen there.[9]

Ironically Chaplin was not really accepted by Hollywood's rank-and-file Communists either. For one thing party members tended to be straitlaced, almost puritanical about sex. For another, Chaplin, with his own studio and an international audience, was in a unique position to help out blacklisted screenwriters, yet their plight failed to move him to action.

Alvah Bessie, a member of the Hollywood Ten who had met Chaplin only in passing, came to Summit Drive one day to pitch his idea for a modern-dress version of *Don Quixote*, starring Walter Huston as the Don and Chaplin as Sancho Panza. He arrived to find Chaplin playing his pipe organ while Oona was on the tennis court with Bill Tilden, who had recently been released from the prison farm. A very young and petulant friend of Tilden's was watching the game from the terrace, increasingly impatient because it was taking so long. Chaplin listened to Bessie's pitch, then shook his head. "If I were to tamper with a great classic like that, they'd crucify me. For another, I like the things I do to be my own."

The subject was closed, but Chaplin insisted on ordering tea for both of them, produced a copy of his Calvero manuscript, and began to read portions of it aloud. He then launched into a long discourse on his efforts to save Tilden from the prison farm. When Bessie got up to leave, Chaplin pressed a hundred-dollar bill into his hand. The gesture was kindly meant, no doubt, but so much less than Bessie had hoped for that he was humiliated. He was left with an overwhelming impression of "a man who was far more interested in himself than he was in anybody else."[10]

Chaplin filled in his time during these years by taking an interest in the Circle Theater, a repertory company that Sydney junior organized with his partner, Jerry Epstein, after the war. The army had transformed Syd from an overweight kid into a devastatingly handsome young man with a taste for fast cars, smooth whiskey, and beautiful women. Syd gave the impression that he took nothing seriously, but his accomplishments with the Circle Theater were impressive. The group had started with nothing. A Los Angeles woman let them stage their first production in her living room, and the opening performance was interrupted when her husband came home unexpectedly. Within a few years, however, the Circle had three theaters and a long list of impressive credits.

In time Charlie began to attend rehearsals and even quietly directed a few productions, including *Rain* with June Havoc, and a misbegotten staging of Camus' *Caligula*, a play he almost certainly never actually read. Syd professed to be delighted by his father's involvement though, with hindsight, the more the theater became Charlie's hobby, the less in control Syd seemed to be. The experiment ended with Lillian Ross of *The New Yorker* using the theater's last production as the basis of a long article that was later published as a book called *Moments with Chaplin*—and she didn't mean Syd. Charlie then hired Jerry Epstein, Syd's friend and partner, to be an associate producer on his forthcoming film, *Limelight*.

By 1951 the Calvero story had grown to more than a thousand pages of prose, only to be reduced once more to screenplay length with the help of James Agee. The character of Terry, the young dancer who loves Calvero, was obviously a composite—based partly on Hannah Chaplin and Oona, among others. Terry also bore a definite resemblance to Florence Deshon. In fact the screenplay opened with a reenactment of Deshon's suicide. After rescuing Terry—as Charlie had failed to rescue Florence—Calvero then frees her to love a tall, handsome young composer, played by Sydney junior.

Limelight had the potential to be a brilliantly original film about a May-December love affair, seen from the perspective of the insecure older man. Unfortunately Chaplin's approach to filmmaking had become shamelessly self-indulgent. The script was marred by his need to idealize Terry and at the same time turn the movie into a sentimental farewell turn for himself. The casting became a family affair, with roles for Syd junior, brother Syd, and Wheeler Dryden, as well as brief appearances by Charles junior, Geraldine, Michael, and Josephine.

Chaplin's score for the movie would include a ballet sequence, danced by André Eglevsky and Melissa Hayden, based on a musical idea Chaplin had been mulling over since 1920. A young pianist named Ray Rasch, who had never done any transcribing before, became the picture's musical director. Rasch got five dollars an hour, plus an extra ten dollars per sheet for doing the orchestral arrangements.

The production got under way with the usual search for an "unknown." The studio placed an ad in the Los Angeles papers:

"Wanted. Young girl to play leading lady to a comedian generally recognized as world's greatest. Must be between 20 and 24 years of age. Stage, ballet experience preferable but not necessary. Apply Charles Chaplin Studios, Hollywood. Send photo."

Young Syd helped screen the hundreds of women who responded but—fortunately, one feels—none of the applicants struck Chaplin as suitable. Even so he could not let go of the fantasy that the next young woman he passed on the street might turn out to be his great discovery. Visiting New York with Oona, he was struck by the appearance of a Rockette pictured on a three-year-old poster outside Radio City Music Hall. Although the Rockette hadn't danced in some time and was a recent mother, she was tracked down at her home in a New Jersey suburb and brought to New York to audition for Mr. Chaplin. No sooner did she open her mouth to say hello than Chaplin realized her accent would never do for Terry. The young woman was philosophical, Chaplin wistful. In the silent film days, he recalled, "all I had to do . . . was to stamp on an applicant's foot to see if she could register emotion."[11]

After six months of searching the only plausible candidate was Claire Bloom, a young English actress recommended to Chaplin by playwright Arthur Laurents. Chaplin was lucky to find an actress whose purity of intention enabled her to speak the hoary line, "I can walk!" without a hint of self-parody. Bloom's work would earn her excellent reviews, but Chaplin himself was never quite satisfied that she was right for the part. As he complained to Clifford Odets, Bloom had the problem common to all English actresses—"no clitoris." (He hastened to add that he didn't mean this personally.)[12]

The high spots of *Limelight* were Calvero's onstage performances. Chaplin had long been fascinated by the problem of how to go about playing a bad comedian without actually being one. Here, at last, he found the solution in Calvero's impersonation of Professor Bosco, the ringmaster of a flea circus whose invisible performers happen to be having a very bad night.[13]

At the climax of the story Calvero's friends hold a benefit concert in his honor—as the friends of Charlie's father once held a benefit for him. This time, Calvero is a hit in a double act with another comic, played by Buster Keaton. Chaplin/Calvero is a violinist bothered by a problem with a mysteriously receding leg; Keaton is his deadpan accompanist.

Keaton in his prime had never been a star of Chaplin's magnitude, and during the 1930s he fell prey to the twin demons Chaplin had managed to dodge—alcoholism and bankruptcy. Hiring him may well have been the inspiration of Jim Agee, who had recently done a major article on Chaplin, Keaton, and Harold Lloyd for *Life* magazine. Chaplin had known Keaton during the early twenties but hadn't seen him for years and thought of him as a sad case. He was surprised when Keaton showed up looking limber and ready to work.

"How do you manage to stay in such good shape?" he asked.

"Television," said Keaton.[14]

Still a major star in Europe, Keaton had recently been a headliner at the Cirque Medrano in Paris, and, as Chaplin might have known had he owned a TV, a highly successful guest appearance on Ed Wynn's television show in December 1947 had revived Keaton's career at home. During the spring of 1948 he had his own show on Los Angeles station KTTV, and while the show never went national it led to guest appearances on network television as well as star bookings in major European houses. Keaton never became rich and no one ever called him a genius—"No man can be a genius in slap shoes and a flat hat," he once said—but by the time he shot his scene in *Limelight* in 1951, he was known and loved by a younger audience who had never seen Chaplin's best comedies on a movie screen. In spite of all his troubles, Keaton considered himself a much happier man than Chaplin, which was surely true.

The shooting of *Limelight* must have been a pleasant experience for Chaplin in many ways. He was essentially filming a tribute to himself, surrounded by his family, first-rank talents like Claire Bloom and the dancers Eglevsky and Hayden, and old friends from the glory days of silent screen comedy like Loyal Underwood and one-time Essanay comedian Snub Pollard, who appeared in small parts. But all this effort was going into a movie that might never be shown in the United States, a prospect that left him angry and bitter.

In a letter to Clifford Odets written in June 1951, when *Limelight* was still being cast, Chaplin vented his frustrations. The country, he complained, had been taken over by the "American fascists," and he was filled with contempt—not for his political enemies but for his friends, who had allowed it to happen. "Oh for the halcyon days of Pearl Harbor!" he exclaimed. Oona had recently given birth to her fourth child, a girl who had been named Victoria, and the family would be spending the summer in a rented house while builders pulled out his beloved pipe organ and renovated Summit Drive. The inconvenience was pointless, he told Odets, since "I know I shall never see the day when I shall live in it."[15]

Harry Crocker had returned to handle publicity for *Limelight*, and he broke with long-established tradition by opening the set to the press. He even coaxed Louella Parsons to stop by to watch the filming of Chaplin and Keaton doing their musical duet. Parsons, who had known Chaplin since 1915, was eager to make peace for old times' sake. But "I felt the chill in the air as soon as I walked onto the sound stage," she wrote. Chaplin "eyed me coldly with no trace of the charm and graciousness I had known for so many years. . . . As was always the case with Chaplin, he didn't feel he had deserved one word of criticism. I was the one at fault. I could hardly wait to get out of the studio."[16]

By the spring of 1952 *Limelight* was in the editing stage, and Chaplin began telling friends that when the film was finished he was thinking of moving abroad, perhaps to Jamaica. On April 2 he quietly transferred his stock in United Artists to Oona, an indication that he was reorganizing his finances in preparation for exile. He had scheduled the world premiere of *Limelight* for October 23 in London, three months before its official opening in the United States. Applying for yet another reentry permit, he said he planned to make a "world tour" with his family, returning via the Orient and San Francisco some time in the spring of 1955. By the end of the summer Charlie had added Oona's name to his bank accounts and drawn up a power of attorney for her. She went on a shopping spree, buying a full-length mink coat, an ermine stole, and other luxury items that happened to be much more heavily taxed in Europe than in the United States.

As the law stood, an alien who chose to fight deportation could keep his case tied up in the courts for years, and if he happened to be a public figure with good legal advice, he had an excellent chance of winning. In retrospect Chaplin's frequent statements like, "I am not a Communist! I am a peacemonger!" may even have been deliberately intended to create a pattern of denials that would come in handy in court. At the end of the year, however, a new law would take effect, making it easier for the government to exclude aliens considered undesirable. Undoubtedly Chaplin had been advised by Millikan to go abroad while the old law was still operative.

The Chaplins were to depart from New York on the liner *Queen Elizabeth* on September 17, 1952. At 5:00 A.M. Harry Crocker smuggled Chaplin onto the ship, where they were joined a few hours later by Oona and the children. At sailing time, while his family stood on deck waving good-bye to well-wishers, Chaplin remained below, locked in his cabin. Jim Agee, a dear friend, arrived on the dock hoping to say good-bye. Oona sent word to Charlie, but he dared not come out, so he pressed his face to the porthole in his cabin, hoping Agee would see him. He didn't.

Chaplin would recall this distressing moment in his autobiography. It hurt to be leaving the United States so "ignominiously" after forty years' residence, he wrote.[17] But his humiliation had nothing to do with his immigration problems, at least not directly. Process servers hired by Max Kravetz's widow, Rina, and Mary Pickford had learned of his sailing plans, and hoped to hand him subpoenas before the ship left New York waters. At this point a subpoena would have been highly inconvenient and might have forced him to miss Limelight's London premiere, but this was a situation that need never have developed if he had cooperated at any time during the past year.

On his second full day at sea, September 19, Chaplin learned via the ship's radio that Attorney General James P. McGranery had revoked his reentry permit. McGranery was quoted as saying that he thought the INS had a "pretty good case" for excluding Chaplin under the law banning political and moral undesirables.

The attorney general's statement led to much speculation about the nature of the "case" against Chaplin. In fact there was no case. An FBI security index investigation conducted between 1946 and 1949 had failed to come up with hard evidence that Chaplin was formally a member of the Communist Party. One former regional party organizer from Florida recalled hearing that Chaplin inquired about membership in 1935, but was told that he would be more useful if he remained a member at large. But however plausible, this was hearsay. At any rate even the Justice Department did not think that Chaplin had done anything that made him legally excludable on political grounds.

With questions about Chaplin's immigration status being raised in Congress, McGranery had discussed strategies that might be used to bar him. The government's only secret evidence had to do with the Joan Barry abortions, which had been merely hinted at in the press at the time. McGranery's idea was to ask Chaplin under oath if he had conspired to obtain two illegal abortions. If he admitted it, he could be excluded from the United States as morally unfit. If he denied it, he could be charged with perjury. But this was theoretical. No one had actually done any research to see if the strategy was feasible.

The speculation among Chaplin's friends was that President Truman had ordered his permit rescinded in a fit of temper, after learning that—at a party during a visit he and Oona made to New York that summer—Charlie had done a wicked imitation of his daughter, Margaret, singing. Truman, however, wrote journalist James O'Donnell in 1958 that Chaplin's parody was "news to me."[18]

The real reason for McGranery's action, it seems, was that the Justice Department had learned that Chaplin was reorganizing his financial affairs so that his wife could manage his assets if he failed to return to the United States. The English, French, and Italian premieres of *Limelight* had been scheduled for the two weeks preceding the U.S. presidential election. No doubt the Justice Department feared that Chaplin was planning some sort of dramatic announcement. Whatever he had in mind, it was hardly likely to be in the interests of the United States, and Congress would blame McGranery for allowing it to happen.

Whether Chaplin had any such plans is debatable, though the European Communist parties doubtless intended to make the most of his visit. As wiser heads might have predicted, the cancellation of Chaplin's reentry permit only generated more sympathy for him in Europe, turning him into a martyr figure. While Chaplin had been warned that revocation was possible at any time, the attorney general's move came as a surprise to the public, and certainly struck many people as a sneaky trick. The *New Republic*, the *Nation*, and the *New York Times* all protested the action. And once again, Chaplin also had his defenders on the right. Writing in the *American Mercury*, William Bradford Huie called him a "twenty-four carat, ring-tailed stinker," but added that Chaplin, even if a noncitizen, had lived under the Constitution for four decades and was entitled to "the sovereign right to make himself obnoxious."[19] Huie's defense might not have pleased Chaplin's admirers, but surely he had zeroed in on the real issue when he said that the law existed for the unpopular as well as the popular.

McGranery's action wasn't winning raves within the government either. At a September 29 meeting, Assistant Commissioner Raymond F. Farrell of the INS told FBI liaison John E. Foley that if Chaplin tried to reenter the United States before December 24, when the new law took effect, there was no doubt he would be readmitted. Farrell also pointed out that if the INS had to enforce McGranery's order "it would involve a question of detention which might well rock INS and the Department of Justice to its foundations."[20] After this meeting the FBI reopened its files on Chaplin, and quickly learned that proving his connection to the ten-year-old abortion case would not be easy. No one doubted that the operations had occurred—two ex-nurses of Dr. Tweedie admitted it, but the doctor himself was dead and Barry, apparently, unavailable to testify.

✿   ✿   ✿

Arriving in Cherbourg, Chaplin met the press and announced, with his usual humility, "This is not the day of great artists. This is the day of politics." He then told reporters about a dream he'd had (not for the first time) about an immigrant who arrives in the New World speaking an ancient language that the customs officials are incapable of understanding. The dream would give him the germ of a script idea—he was already thinking about how to translate his latest defeat into his next movie.

London had taken the U.S. expulsion of its native son to heart, and the city rallied to his support. A crowd had gathered at Waterloo Station, and many followed the limousine carrying Chaplin and his family to the Savoy Hotel. Chaplin was feted at a Variety Club luncheon attended by 450 guests and by the city's most fashionable hostesses. Princess Margaret was in the audience the night *Limelight* opened; later in the week he was presented to Queen Elizabeth.

In France the crowds were even larger, and certainly more unruly. *Limelight* opened in four Paris theaters simultaneously, playing to packed houses, and Chaplin was invited to lunch by President Vincent Auriol and his wife and made an officer of the Legion of Honor, a higher order of the award he first received in 1931. He dined with Louis Aragon and Jean-Paul Sartre, and the owner of the famous Tour d'Argent restaurant opened a bottle of 1803 vintage port in his honor. The French Communist newspaper *L'Humanité* hailed *Limelight* as a film by a man who had survived "unimaginable persecutions," and Radio Moscow asserted that Chaplin was being punished for refusing to spy on his colleagues for the FBI.[21]

As during his 1931 tour, Chaplin's progress was never quite as smooth as his press coverage suggested. At the Variety Club luncheon he was invited to say a few words at the end of the program and launched into a partisan and rambling defense of the British National Health Service, a controversial political issue at the time. He later stunned the show business elite who had welcomed him by ducking an invitation to appear at the annual Royal Variety Show Concert. According to Harry Crocker, who had accompanied the Chaplins as their press agent and personal assistant, a man named Mr. Swaffer had called Chaplin's suite wanting him to make a charity appearance, and someone in his entourage turned him down without knowing whom he represented.

Despite much talk, public and private, about turning his back on "fascist" America, Chaplin was emotionally unprepared for exile. Suddenly homesick for Summit Drive, he talked about returning to fight McGranery's decision. Harry Crocker wanted to keep the tour from becoming too politicized, though it wasn't easy. The French Communist Party had called for demonstrations at the Paris openings of *Limelight*, but the police, fearing riots, quietly arrested the demonstration leaders. In fact the only picketer at the theater Chaplin attended was a self-described Surrealist, who carried a placard reading, "Chaplin is finished." In Italy, however, a reception organized by director Vittorio de Sica drew a hundred right-wing demonstrators who pelted Charlie and Oona with ripe tomatoes and broccoli.

On November 17 Oona quietly flew back to the States, accompanied by Arthur Kelly. She attended a United Artists board meeting, gave notice to the servants at Summit Drive, and arranged to have the house closed up and the furniture shipped to Europe. She also emptied Chaplin's safe deposit boxes and quietly transferred more than four million dollars to accounts abroad.

While she was gone Charlie came close to having another nervous breakdown. He couldn't sleep and was near hysterics, tortured by fears that her plane would crash, leaving him alone in the world. His inability to stand the stress of even this brief separation dispelled any lingering notions he might have had about fighting for his reentry permit.

Limelight received only limited distribution in the United States. In addition to pressure from the American Legion against local theater owners, the picture was boycotted by the Fox West Coast and RKO theater chains. The RKO ban was by personal order of Howard Hughes, whose uncle Rupert Hughes, the writer, had never forgiven his onetime best friend, Rob Wagner, and Wagner's protégé, Chaplin, for their stance during World War I.

During the decade that followed, few traces of Charlie Chaplin remained in Hollywood. His Summit Drive property was broken up into parcels. The house itself sold for $150,000. Some years later it passed into the hands of actor George Hamilton and became the subject of a lawsuit by the Philippine government, which claimed that Hamilton was acting as agent for Ferdinand and Imelda Marcos.

Closing Chaplin's studio proved to be a slow process. Worried that his papers and film archives would be seized by the FBI or the IRS, which still had unsatisfied claims, Wheeler Dryden painstakingly packed everything into small brown-paper packages and forwarded them to Europe by parcel post. Like Summit Drive, the studio was eventually sold for far less than the asking price, fetching under a million dollars. Since 1966 it has been owned by A&M Records, and in 1985 it was the scene of the all-star recording, "We Are the World."

In 1958, when the Hollywood Walk of Fame was planned, Chaplin was not included among the stars to be honored. Ironically one of the very few to protest was Mary Pickford, who denounced this rewriting of motion picture history as "ridiculous."

Sydney junior signed a contact with Universal Pictures, but his career in Hollywood movies never amounted to much. Producers, he said later, "had no idea what to do with me, . . . so they slapped a coat of dark greasepaint on me and cast me as an Indian or an Egyptian." Among Syd's greasepaint roles was a part in the epic *Land of the Pharaohs*, during which he met Joan Collins, one of the many female stars he loved and left. But on Broadway, if not in Hollywood, Syd's career flourished, highlighted by his starring role opposite Judy Holliday in *Bells Are Ringing* and his later appearance as Nick Arnstein (to Barbra Streisand's Fanny Brice) in the musical *Funny Girl*.

While Sydney honed his reputation as a bon vivant, Charles Chaplin, Jr., became a casualty of his father's exile. It was well known in Hollywood that Charles had never approved of his father's political views, and for several years West Coast gossip writers, seeking to do him a favor, missed few opportunities to mention these father-son differences in ther columns. The publicity became an embarrassment to Charles, who still loved his father, and in 1960, after his father's name was once again omitted from plans for the Walk of Fame, he filed suit against the Hollywood Chamber of Commerce in a vain attempt to force a change in policy. Many career disappointments, two failed marriages, and an off-and-on struggle with alcoholism all took their toll. In 1968 he died from a massive pulmonary embolism suffered after a bad fall at home.

If a single word could be used to summarize the tangle of scandals, lawsuits, and political tiffs in which Chaplin was enmeshed during his final fifteen years in the United States, it would be "unnecessary." His legal troubles could have been settled out of court, his political and immigration problems largely avoided if he had chosen his battles, and his words, a bit more carefully. No one saw this more clearly than his longtime cameraman Rollie Totheroh. When the La Brea Avenue studio was being vacated, it was Totheroh who was asked to hand-carry Chaplin's favorite cane and bowler hat to Europe. Totheroh was honored by the errand, and delighted by the stir he caused passing through customs. Still, when it came to the theory that his boss was an innocent victim, Totheroh could be blunt. "He figures he's been treated terrible," he told film historian Timothy Lyons in 1967. "But I think a lot of it was his own fault."[22]

20

"A King in Switzerland"

A year after leaving the United States, Chaplin wrote his good friend Clifford Odets saying that he felt as if he had been released from the penitentiary after serving a forty-year sentence. He looked back on America as a nightmare, a "large ugly boil" on the body of the world, and an "old fashioned" country where the people want to "castrate" dissenters.[1]

Writing to Lion Feuchtwanger the same day, Chaplin developed his theme, describing the United States as a "torrid, dried-up, prune-souled desert." In retrospect the very landscape now struck him as disgusting—the deserts were endless, the Pacific Ocean "bleak," the horizon spoiled by hideous oil derricks.[2]

Chaplin had a right to feel aggrieved and even a valid point about the intolerance of American public opinion. Still, for an Englishman who sat out two world wars in Beverly Hills to wax enthusiastic about how much more "civilized" Europe was demonstrated a certain lack of perspective.

The welcome the Chaplins received from the British public could not have been warmer. Charlie was even approached by a group of Labourite politicians who were eager to have him stand for Parliament. For the next twenty years Chaplin would make his native city the center of his business and social life. His doctors, dentist, and tailor were there. The Savoy Hotel became his and Oona's home away from home. The only thing he didn't do there was pay taxes.

Charlie's official home was to be Switzerland—ironically, the one nation he had singled out during his 1931 world tour as not especially appealing to him. Brother Sydney, however, had long ago discovered the charms of the Swiss banking system, and there was never any question of where Charlie and Oona would settle. There are many fates worse than tax exile, but it was a strange choice for a man who had endured so much criticism for the sake of his pro-Communist views. In order to avoid paying for the social services he strongly advocated, he would be forced to ration carefully the number of nights he slept at the Savoy, lest he inadvertently become a legal resident of Britain.

Immediately after Oona's return from the States, she and Charlie began househunting in the vicinity of Lake Geneva, bidding for likely homes under the pseudonym Crocker. Within a few months they settled on Manoir de Ban, an eighteen-room house in Corsier-sur-Vevey. Purchased from a wealthy American, the house had been remodeled just six years earlier. The grounds covered thiry-seven acres, including fruit trees and a garden that yielded prize strawberries, asparagus, peas, and currants. The Chaplins had their gardener plant corn and added a barbecue grill to the patio, California customs that mildly shocked their European guests.

Family life at the Manoir de Ban was organized along Edwardian lines. The children, with Edith "Kay-Kay" MacKenzie and Mabel Rose "Pinnie" Pinnegar, occupied the third floor of the house, seeing their parents at mealtimes. Both nannies were beloved figures, strict but affectionate. Still, as son Michael later noted, it was a bit like growing up in an orphanage.

When he chose, Charlie could be a charismatic father. He would entertain the children by reading them fairy tales and improvising "Nice Old Man" stories, about an old man who dreamed up grotesque and fantastic ways to torment babies and small dogs. At other times, however, the children got on his nerves. Charlie always overreacted to any threat of violence, in one direction or another. Where the children were concerned he was likely to read dark motives into normal roughhousing. In June 1951, when the family was still living in Beverly Hills, Michael accidentally pushed his three-year-old sister Josephine into the pool. Josephine came up dog-paddling and was rescued by the swimming teacher. None the worse for wear, she proudly told her father, "I swummed." Charlie, however, brooded over the incident, which became in family lore that time "that Michael tried to drown his little sister," leaving the boy feeling like a "failed murderer."[3]

Young Aram Saroyan had an eerily similar experience when he spent a few days at Vevey while his mother was in London. Playing outdoors with the girls, he dropped Josephine, who ran to the house in tears. Later Chaplin took the ten-year-old Aram for a walk in the woods and asked such probing questions about his motives that he, too, was frightened into wondering if he was a "possible murderer."[4]

Chaplin worried about his children growing up spoiled, and made it a point to send them to the strictest schools he could find. Geraldine was enrolled in a convent school, where the nuns taught that it was sinful to look at one's own naked body and made the girls wear plastic shifts to bathe in. An adaptable girl, she fit in and even became fervently Catholic for a time. Michael was sent to the École Nouvelle de Paudex, where he was the youngest boarding student. Unlike Geraldine, he was quick to get upset and slow to make friends, and he had tough time of it.

During his first six months abroad, Chaplin seemed not to have made up his mind about attempting to return to the United States. He declared he was through with Hollywood forever, but at other times he hinted that he might take his chances on returning. In April 1953, however, the Internal Revenue Service sent a bill for $516,167, and he responded by paying a visit to the American consulate in Zurich and tossing his now invalid reentry permit on the consul's desk. Unfortunately this gesture did not resolve the tax problem, since he was still liable for taxes on income earned in the United States. The process of dissolving his U.S. interests took months, involving complicated legal and accounting advice. His new personal corporation, Roy Enterprises (named for his English pronunciation of the French word for king), was based in Tangiers, a locale known for easy and confidential currency transfers.

During the summer of 1953 Rollie Totheroh and Lois Watt spent time in Vevey, helping Chaplin reorganize studio files and archival films shipped from Los Angeles. Another visitor was Lou Eisler, who had recently resettled with her husband in East

Germany, where brother-in-law Gerhart was the chief of propaganda. In California the Eislers had been perpetually short of cash. Now Lou was better dressed and groomed than the Chaplins had ever seen her. East Germany was dull and stodgy, she said, but luckily she and Hanns were able to get away periodically to enjoy living "under corruption" in Vienna. Oona confided in a letter to Lion Feuchtwanger that she and Charlie had suspected all along that some of the allegations against the Eislers "must be slightly true." Now she was relieved to know they weren't—Lou had assured her of it.[5]

In June, Chaplin also spent several days in Zurich with Jarwaharlal Nehru, who was in Switzerland as a UN mediator, trying to resolve the problem of prisoner repatriation, which had stalled negotiations to end the Korean conflict. North Korea and China were insisting that POWs in South Korea be returned to them, even against their will. By chance he was in Nehru's office on June 19, when he learned that South Korean President Syngman Rhee had ordered the gates of the POW camps opened, allowing some twenty-five thousand to flee. Chaplin had no doubt that the United States was the aggressor in Korea, and could work himself into a rage over the *International Herald Tribune*'s coverage of the fighting. The desperation of the prisoners, who preferred flight to repatriation, did nothing to change his mind. Writing to Feuchtwanger, he described Nehru's shock and dismay over Rhee's action. At the same time, he commented on his mixed feelings, as an Englishman, about Indian independence.

Although he had been invited to visit India, and the Soviets were eager as ever for him to come to Moscow, Chaplin was far more interested in making movies. For all his talk about retirement, he never felt so much zest for living as when he was working on a new project. By the spring of 1954 Chaplin was once again talking about filming *Shadow and Substance*. He had discovered an English girl whom he planned to cast in the role of Bridget, and he wrote Clifford Odets, predicting that she would become the next Eleanora Duse. The girl was fifteen years old.

After finishing *Shadow and Substance*, he added, he was planning a film about a deposed king who flees to the United States incognito to escape an assassination attempt. The story, he promised

Odets, would be a "satire on Americano and the *modus operendi* of the day [*sic*]."[6]

Oona was not one to pour out her heart, even to close friends. But it was no secret that she was having a harder time adjusting to life in exile than Charlie. Oona, one suspects, had never believed that the family would be forced to flee Los Angeles; otherwise she would hardly have invested so much energy in planning the remodeling of Summit Drive. Now that it had happened, however, she was prepared to make the best of it. But she still hoped, in the beginning, that she would be able to return to the United States to visit friends and family.

By 1951 Eugene O'Neill was in the final stages of his agonizing physical decline, and his relationship with his wife, Carlotta, had devolved into a psychodrama, marked by stormy arguments and tearful reconciliations. O'Neill was falling a good deal, sustaining serious injuries on several occasions, and his longtime agent Saxe Commins and Saxe's wife, Dorothy, suspected Carlotta of abusing him mentally and even physically. The Comminses and Eugene O'Neill's other friends in New York were still unwilling to recognize the nature of his illness and too eager to blame Carlotta, whom they had never liked. Nevertheless it was a distressing situation; the great American playwright was pathetic and increasingly helpless in his last days, cut off from his children and many old colleagues.

When Oona and Charlie passed through New York in September 1952, O'Neill was in Doctors Hospital, and Oona sent him a letter through Saxe Commins, begging him to let her visit. O'Neill read the letter, told Commins that he would love to see his daughter again, and put it under his pillow for safekeeping. Before Oona could get to the hospital, however, Carlotta arrived. The letter disappeared, and there was no visit.

During her first year abroad, Oona lived with the knowledge that her father had (apparently) wanted to see her, and that a reconciliation might have been possible had she been nearby. She named her second son, born in April 1953, Eugene, in her father's honor. Still there was no word from New York, and O'Neill died the following November, cut off from both Oona and her brother, Shane.

Meanwhile Shane's problems with drugs were becoming more apparent. Oona kept in touch with Shane's wife by letter and, it seems, helped the family out financially.

But Oona's plans to visit them were frustrated by the tax situation. Charlie might be beyond the reach of the U.S. government, but Oona was not. The UA stock was still in her name, and she would eventually inherit a share of her father's literary estate. Moreover, she had helped her husband remove from the country assets on which he owed back taxes, and the IRS was surely interested in details of the transfer. Potentially it might even make a case that she was criminally liable. On February 10, a month before the 1954 income tax filing date, Oona visited the American embassy in London and announced that she wished to renounce her citizenship. The Chaplins called a press conference at the Savoy, and Charlie announced that Oona had acted without telling him, as a gesture of loyalty—an unlikely story. Giving up her passport did not free Oona from her obligation to pay taxes on any American income she might have, but an attempt by the IRS to get at Chaplin through her would now qualify as an international incident.

That August, Oona made plans to visit New York while the children vacationed on the Riviera with their nannies, Kay-Kay and Pinney. But now, in addition to lingering unertainty about the tax situation, there was another problem. Rina Kravetz's lawyers had discovered that Oona was the legal owner of her husband's former shares in United Artists, and a New York State Supreme Court judge had issued a subpoena in her name. The other defendants in the case continued to dismiss it as a nuisance suit, but Kravetz's attorneys would surely have been eager to question Oona about her and Charlie's finances. Indirectly they could be doing spadework for the IRS. Thus the New York trip was canceled.

That June the World Peace Congress awarded Chaplin its highest honor, the Stockholm Peace Prize, otherwise known as the Lenin Peace Prize. To the distress of the Chaplins' conservative neighbors, the award ceremony was held on the patio at Manoir de Ban. Oona failed to emerge from the house to witness the presentation, touching off rumors that she and Charlie were at odds over his politics. There was a crisis in the marriage, but it had less to do with politics per se than with the mounting obstacles to either of them returning to the States, even as visitors. Oona did not speak French, and the Chaplins' acquaintances in Vevey included concert pianist Clara Haskil, painter Theodore Bosshard, and Ena (Victora Eugenia), who reigned as queen of Spain until her husband, Alfonso XIII, was forced to abdicate in 1931. She was twenty-eight, and living among people in their fifties, sixties, and seventies, for whom everything of interest had happened before World War II.

In February 1955 Chaplin's American attorneys learned that the IRS planned to place a lien against Oona's United Artists stock. Within twenty-four hours he had negotiated the sale of the shares to Arthur Krim for $1.1 million dollars. Mary Pickford by now had come to believe that there was something to the Kravetzes' theory of a conspiracy by Chaplin against the McNutt group. Unable to get to Charlie, Pickford turned her suspicions on Arthur Krim, hiring attorney William Shea (for whom New York's Shea Stadium was to be named), and press agent Richard Condon, later a bestselling novelist, to press her claims. Shea found no evidence of a conspiracy, much less of Krim's involvement, but Pickford never gave up her conviction that Charlie was somehow behind the crash of the company's stock.

Chaplin's tax problems went unresolved until 1959, when he agreed to pay $425,000 to settle a bill that had mounted to more than $700,000 in penalties and interest. As a result of the voluntary payment Oona, and later her children, could travel to the United States and even own property there if they wished. By this time, however, any plans Oona may have had to lead an independent life, see American friends, and shop for the classic jazz recordings she enjoyed were moot. Charlie claimed that he couldn't sleep without Oona in the house, and couldn't bear the thought of her taking a vacation away from him.

Oona enjoyed shopping in London and Paris, and if a dress by Dior caught her fancy, she might order three or four in different colors. But she seldom had anywhere to wear such clothes, and they hung in her closet. To occupy her time she concentrated on becoming the perfect housekeeper. She kept meticulous household accounts, planned the rose garden, and prepared gourmet feasts on the cook's day off. She was said to be an excellent cook, though there were often last-minute kitchen disasters of the sort experienced by overambitious and possibly tipsy chefs. She loved cats and dogs and schemed to introduce them into the house over the objections of Charlie, who had liked animals when he was younger but now found barking dogs and shedding cats bothersome.

And the children kept coming: Eugene, the fifth child, was a tall, mischievous boy, known at home as "Tadpole." He was followed by Jane Cecil, born in May 1957; Annette Emily, born in December 1959; and Christopher, born in July 1962, when his father was seventy-three years old.

Chaplin's relations with the Swiss began well. Shortly after he purchased his home, the cantonal authorities honored him with a banquet in Lausanne, presenting him with a gold watch, and he responded in kind, arranging a special showing of his films in Vevey. But before the year was over, a chill had set in. Neither Chaplin's contractor nor his preservation-minded Swiss neighbors agreed with his plans to remodel his distinguished old home—removing hand-carved paneling and lowering the ceilings. Vevey looked askance at his taste in furnishings, a mixture of valuable antiques from different periods and aging curiosities, including a white couch that had been used as set decoration in *City Lights*. Understandably Chaplin felt he had a right to suit himself in these matters, but his disagreements with the contractor degenerated into petty squabbles over the noise made by the workmen and the cost of materials.

Since Chaplin did not speak French, the task of communicating his complaints to the workmen fell to his secretary, Isobel Deluz. A former script editor for Alexander Korda, Deluz was working for a minimal forty dollars a week, in part because she admired Chaplin's films and considered him a victim of political persecution. And at first she found Chaplin a delightful employer. "Well, Isobel, old girl, let's get to work," he would say every morning. "Life is short." For three or four hours, pausing only for a quick yogurt at lunchtime, Chaplin gave stream-of-consciousness dictation, skipping back and forth between ideas for *Shadow and Substance* and his anti-American satire. When he was in a good humor, he was magnetic. One day Deluz was amused and touched to find him on the terrace, improvising a declaration of love to a large, ungainly insect. The end of the workday, moreover, was usually signaled by Oona playing a recording of one of Charlie's own compositions, the ballet music from *Limelight*, on an antique hand-cranked Victrola.

As the weeks went by, however, the secretary's patience began to fray. She was expected to get rid of strangers who showed up at the gate, including one rather pathetic young woman who arrived carrying a package wrapped in yellowed paper, which she claimed contained documentary proof that she was Chaplin's daughter.

And the squabbles with the construction crew were becoming more irrational. The final insult came when Deluz accepted delivery of a load of granite slabs, to be used to line the new swimming pool. The stones arrived on a rainy day, and as they were wet they looked darker than they had when Chaplin selected them. He saw them and threw a fit. "Tombstones!" he fumed. "I won't have my children swimming in a graveyard!" He then accused Deluz of conspiring with the workmen to cheat him and informed her that the cost of the stones would come out of her salary. Indignant, she put on her coat and walked out. Chaplin later refused to accept her apologies. She was discharged.

Deluz was so upset that her doctor prescribed two weeks of bed rest. Deluz then sued Chaplin for severance pay as well as two weeks' vacation pay, to which she was entitled under Swiss law. The claim came to a total of 2,899 francs, or $680. Rather than pay, Chaplin fought the claim. The domestic staff of the Manoir, and even Oona, were trotted into court to back up his version of the quarrel. Technically Chaplin emerged a winner, ordered to pay only 222 francs, less than he had already offered in settlement; but the moral victory went to Madame Deluz, and the locals were not charmed to learn that Chaplin had accused Swiss workers of being lazy and dishonest.

The Deluz case proved to be just a warm-up for Chaplin's battle with the commune of Vevey over the municipal firing range, where all men up to forty years of age were required to take target practice as part of their military service requirement. Real estate in Vevey was not cheap even in the 1950s, and Chaplin had purchased the Manoir de Ban at a bargain price, reportedly about two hundred thousand dollars. Chaplin had boasted to friends that the previous owner had died after a fall down the staircase, and the house came cheap because it was thought to be haunted. But Vevey was filled with two- and three-hundred-year-old houses that many people had died in, and the class of buyers who could afford them was unlikely to be deterred by superstition. The real reason for the moderate price of the property was its proximity to the firing range. Interestingly the noise did not bother Chaplin during the six months he lived in the house before exercising his option to buy. It was only after his relations with his neighbors began to go sour that the sound of rifle fire began to prey on his nerves, upsetting him so much that he couldn't work. The commune tried to accommodate him, cutting back on the range's hours.

Around this time Ella Winter wrote Chaplin asking him to spearhead a campaign to force the U.S. government to restore the passport of "our old friend Paul" (Robeson). Winter's plan was to arrange for British and European celebrities to invite Robeson to sing a concert in England. The invitations, she emphasized, must be made to look "non-political," and she suggested that Chaplin "start the ball rolling," perhaps lining up Picasso and Sartre for a joint appeal. Winter reminded Chaplin that there weren't "so damned many" great artists left—meaning, pro-Communist great artists— "you are in the company of five or six maybe." If this transparent sycophancy was an example of how Chaplin's closest friends approached him, it is little wonder that he had become both arrogant and cynical.[7]

Cedric Belfrage, the British left-wing journalist and editor who had spent many years in the United States, was dispatched by Winter to Vevey to discuss the details of the campaign. During the course of Belfrage's visit, Chaplin gave him an interview, complaining that the noise of the "artillery" banging away had made him a prisoner in his own home. He also managed to imply that the commune of Vevey was making a profit by opening the range to men from other towns, and that greed was the real issue. This undiplomatic accusation, which happened to be untrue, reopened his battle with the Vevey authorities. They adopted a plan to erect sound dampers and a concrete wall to contain the noise. Chaplin complained that the plan was inadequate, and in October 1956 he filed suit, asking $125 a day in compensation for his pain and suffering.

Chaplin had managed the considerable feat of reducing the tolerant "civilized" Swiss to sputtering outrage; indeed they had begun to sound a lot like his critics in the United States, England, and France. Referring to the Hungarian uprising, which was much in the news at the time, the Zurich paper *Die Weltwoche* steamed: "Why does the noise of Swiss militia soldiers in Vevey disturb Charlot so much more than the noise coming from Budapest? Why are the rifle shots from a Swiss army service weapon so much worse than the cannon of Russian panzers?"[8]

Chaplin eventually reached a compromise, agreeing to pay part of the cost of renovating the firing range. No sooner was this issue settled than he began complaining that his house was pervaded by the smell of sewer gas. When plumbers failed to discover the cause of the problem on his property, he began badgering the local authorities to dig up the pipes under the public road.

In truth he was also out of sorts with his Communist friends during these years. The refusal of the Soviets to pay market prices for distribution rights to his films had always been a sore point, and Chaplin regretted deals he had made for individual pictures in the past. A friendly meeting with Chou En-lai in Zurich in the summer of 1954 turned acrimonious when the Chinese premier proposed acquiring the rights to his work for an insultingly low figure. A meeting with Khrushchev in London in 1956 was private and apparently cordial, but it was no secret that the Russians were disappointed by Chaplin's continuing refusal to visit Moscow or to become more active politically. A song recorded in the mid-fifties by Arkady Raikin expressed the Soviet concept of Chaplin as a "brooding" semirecluse who must be encouraged to speak out:

We love and respect you,
But still we all expect
That someday we shall hear your voice.

Privately Chaplin was annoyed by these expectations. When the wife of Grisha Alexandrov, the Soviet director who had been Eisenstein's assistant, showed up in Vevey with a friend asking for pages from his scripts and musical scores for a Moscow museum, Chaplin complained: "Get rid of these damned Communists.

They're all the same. They take everything that's not nailed to the floor."[9]

In his old age Chaplin seemed to identify more and more with his royalist neighbors, like Queen Ena of Spain. Still, in his public statements Chaplin excoriated the West and upheld the Soviets. In February 1955 the Dickens Fellowship Society of London invited him to be its guest of honor at their annual Jubilee Dinner, and instead of confining his remarks to Dickens, Chaplin launched into a call for unilateral disarmament. As usual he argued the subject from a purely emotional position, and put 100 percent of the blame for the Cold War on British and American "hypocrisy" and "double-talk." The mainly elderly and conservative Dickensians were not ripe for such sentiments. One leaped to his feat and began to argue back, while others cheered him on.

Why Charlie persisted in defending the Soviets, even after the Hungarian uprising, perplexed many of his friends. Perhaps the best explanation was a statement he made in a 1971 conversation with reporter Sven Kisslin: "My daughters, of course, are mad about Castro and what he calls 'the Cuban miracle.' How else do you expect them to imagine their father's struggle to achieve all the luxury they were born in?"[10] One suspects that this leap of imagination mattered less to Chaplin's daughters than to him. Leftist politics had become an exercise in nostalgia, a sentimental link with the struggles of his childhood.

Perhaps the true cause of Chaplin's irritability in 1954–55 was his inability to adjust to the quiet routine of retirement. He was impatient to be back in the studio again, but his fifteen-year-old "Duse" had not worked out, and a request for a six-month visa to make a film in Mexico fell through, possibly because of reports that the subject matter would be political. Chaplin therefore decided to film his "Americano" satire—the story of the deposed King Shahdov (Shadow?) who loses the throne of Estrovia during a popular uprising and flees to the United States, where he has a run-in with HUAC.

Jerry Epstein had settled in London with his wife, Bernice, and was to serve as Chaplin's producer. He rented space at the

Shepperton Studios outside London, and Oona and the younger children settled into a nearby hotel for the duration of the filming, which began in May 1956. Dawn Addams, a chic British actress who happened to be married to an Italian prince, was cast as the female lead, backed up by a cast of experienced British character actors. None of these people looked or sounded especially American—nor did the black-and-white film's cut-rate sets and backgrounds evoke New York, but the disparity was no greater than in the Hollywood back-lot recreations of Paris familiar from Chaplin's earlier films.

McCarthyism was certainly a ripe subject for satire, but to deal with it effectively would have required political sophistication, not to mention a sense of perspective that Chaplin sorely lacked. His script attacked American culture with the verbal equivalent of the Fatal Mallet—taking wild swings at targets big and small, worthy and unworthy. Judging by *A King in New York*, the trouble with America was the pervasiveness of rock and roll, Cinemascope, TV commercials for deodorants, progressive education, drivers who honk their horns for no reason, and loud jazz in nightclubs. Many of King Shahdov's complaints sounded like the grouchiness of an aging man, used to being deferred to, in a country where "the people" are free and prosperous enough to enjoy themselves as they see fit.

A scene in which King Shahdov goes to the movies and sees previews for three awful new releases typifies the lack of focus. One of the three movies lampooned is obviously *Glen or Glenda?: I Changed My Sex*, a low-budget pseudodocumentary by Edward D. Wood Jr., a director whose sincere awfulness earned him a cult following. However bad, *Glen or Glenda?* was the antithesis of the slick, mass-produced Hollywood movies Chaplin had been criticizing for two decades. The reference was also outdated; *Glen or Glenda?* had been released in 1952.

A King in New York gave Chaplin a chance to visualize how he might have deflated the pretensions of HUAC with slapstick and—more strangely—to revisit his most humiliating moment, when he was publicly fingerprinted during his arraignment on Mann Act charges. Perhaps he realized that a deposed king did not make the most sympathetic of victims, so the HUAC thread of the plot involves a boy, Rupert Macabee, whose parents have been accused of being Communists. The part was inspired by a false report in the

Italian press some years earlier, which had claimed that Chaplin was interested in adopting the sons of Julius and Ethel Rosenberg. After searching for a child actor for the role of Rupert, Chaplin ultimately decided to cast his own son, ten-year-old Michael, who had shown a remarkable facility for imitating his dad's performance in *The Great Dictator*.

But here again Chaplin's script missed the mark. HUAC had its faults, but one thing it didn't do was pressure children to bear witness against their own parents. And while the FBI may have visited the schools of the children of suspected Communists, it didn't grill twelve-year-olds for hours on end. Moreover, the speeches Chaplin wrote for the precocious schoolboy were a mélange of Marxist slogans and callow cynicism. Far from being shamed by the young boy's words, one begins to feel that the parents who pumped their son so full of angry rhetoric probably are monsters who deserve what is happening to them.

Chaplin made no attempt to open *A King in New York* in the United States, but even the British critics, eager to see a director take on McCarthyism, were dismayed. "Is it right to spit through the mouth of a child?" asked Donald Gomery of the London *Daily Express*. Kenneth Tynan, a Chaplin admirer, also disliked the film, but made the point that for all its faults, *A King in New York* bristled with the quality of abrasive individuality so lacking in British and American movies—and even more lacking today, one might add. "Nobody has subjected the script to 'a polishing job,' which is the film industry's euphemism for the process whereby rough edges are planed away and sharp teeth blunted," wrote Tynan. "The result, in the fullest sense of the phrase, is 'free cinema,' in which anything, within the limits of censorship, can happen."[11]

Because the political satire received so much attention, few critics bothered to notice another and rather more interesting theme of *A King in New York*—voyeurism. Like any normal man—at least so the movie implies—Shahdov cannot resist the temptation to spy on the beautiful woman (Dawn Addams) who is occupying the hotel suite adjoining his own. Indeed Addams's character, a scheming PR woman named Ann Kay, *knows* that she will be spied on and entraps the king by lolling seductively in her bubble bath. The notion of the Peeping Tom as victim appears in one of Robert Louis Stevenson's stories about the Suicide Club, but it also recalls that Chaplin was paddled at the Hanwell orphanage for peeking through a keyhole at a female student.

But the voyeurism doesn't stop there. Ann Kay has a motive for capturing Shahdov's interest. The ex-king is famous for his impromptu after-dinner performances, and she lures him to a banquet where his antics are captured by a hidden camera and broadcast live on television, during a show sponsored by her company. Improbable as this may be in context, Chaplin in real life was indeed famous for his party turns—including blue material like "The Geisha Girl" and "The Woman with a French Lover" (in which he played all three parts, the woman, the lover and the cuckolded husband) as well as impersonations of Margaret Truman, Noel Coward, Pola Negri (emoting at the funeral of Rudolph Valentino), and Aly Khan (who boasted of his ability to prolong the sexual act for many hours). Unfortunately, the sample performance Chaplin gave in this film hardly lived up to the promise of his fabled repertory. Shadhov does a few seconds of a dentist's-chair routine reminiscent of *Laughing Gas*, then recites Hamlet's "To Be or Not to Be" soliloquy—and does it badly, spraying spittle at the camera, misquoting Shakespeare, and generally demonstrating why the universal comedian's dream of playing tragedy is better left unindulged.

What Chaplin seems to be saying here is that the camera (or perhaps the mass audience) is a voyeur that has "stolen" his art. Considering how much money he made in films, he had no cause for personal complaint on this score, but he did have a point. The movies, TV, and the other mass media do impose a form of dictatorship by default. The performer who must please everyone ends up pleasing no one, including himself. In the end there is no room for art, only celebrity.

A King in New York may have been inspired by bitterness, but making it was hardly a bitter experience. Jerry Epstein would recall that Charlie had great fun with the production and was eager to get to the set every morning. Moreover, despite slams from influential British critics, the film received its share of respectful notices and did fairly good business in London and Paris.

Rejuvenated by the experience, Chaplin even hinted that he was thinking of reviving the Tramp by moving him into the atomic age—

perhaps he was thinking of James Agee's "Scientists and Tramp" concept. Though nothing more was heard of this idea, he did put together a reissue of three First National comedies, *A Dog's Life*, *Shoulder Arms*, and *The Pilgrim*, introduced with home-movie footage from the early days of the La Brea Avenue studio and an original score.

Michael Chaplin had fallen in love with Kenya on an earlier trip, and in 1958 Charlie, Oona, and the older children went on a photographic safari in East Africa. Oona, not he, was the photographer, enthusiastically shooting a charging rhino through the sun roof of the guide's vehicle, while Chaplin forgot his panic long enough to direct her efforts. Two years later the family made a VIP around-the-world tour, cheered by crowds everywhere, from Japan and Hong Kong to India. Seeing so much poverty from inside the cocoon of first-class hotels, limousines and official guides had a depressing effect on fifteen-year-old Michael, who soon after their return developed a crush on a working-class Polish woman of twenty-one. The relationship was part puppy love and partly an attempt to shock his parents, who carefully vetted the children's friends. Chaplin responded by hiring a detective, who scared the young woman off by warning her that she could be arrested for corrupting the morals of a minor—an interesting move considering his own history as well as his many attempts to shield the notorious Bill Tilden.[12]

Chaplin's major project during these years was writing his autobiography. Rejecting suggestions that he work with a collaborator, he insisted on writing the book himself. In an age of ghostwritten celebrity bios, his desire to be the author of his own life story was praiseworthy, but the project may have been more than he bargained for. Chaplin wrote by dictating to a secretary, Eileen Burnier. Given Chaplin's short attention span and a tendency to leap from one subject to another, Madame Burnier had her work cut out for her. Chaplin had told stories about his early struggles for years, and despite an understandable desire to protect his mother and a tendency to borrow from *Oliver Twist*, his favorite novel, the results were satisfactory. Nonetheless, Chaplin had promised Max Reinhardt the book in 1958. The first third of the manuscript wasn't ready to hand in until 1962, and by then his patience and composure had begun to fail him.

When he came to his experience with First National—ironically, the period during which he achieved creative "freedom"—the quality of Chaplin's recollections changes, becoming an exercise in the famous-people-who-knew-and-admired-me school of autobiography. As he began delving into the more troubled years of his adulthood, Chaplin began to brood, finding some topics too difficult to confront. The pages of anecdotes about meetings with George Bernard Shaw, Cocteau, Churchill, and myriad others mounted. He sought editorial help and advice from Truman Capote and, reportedly, other well-known visitors to Vevey, but took little of it. As late as 1963 Chaplin was thinking about stretching the work to two volumes.

A year later, with the book already in proofs and ready to go to press, he had yet to sign the contracts, and Oona wrote Ella Winter confiding that he was depressed and "horribly nervous."[13] Among the things that bothered him were cigarette smoke (now that he had given up his own tobacco habit), houseflies, the insecticide that Oona and the servants sprayed to get rid of houseflies, the noise made by the children's pets, sewer gas (imaginary), cut flowers (which ate up oxygen, he believed), taxes (Swiss), the varicose veins of a longtime member of the household staff, and the fear that he hadn't asked a high enough advance for his life story.

And, as always, the lawsuits rolled on. In 1963, when Orson Welles mentioned in an interview with the London *Times* that he had written the first version of *Monsieur Verdoux*, Chaplin was "furious," Oona wrote Ella Winter. He fired off a letter to the editor, so virulent that the *Times* refused to print it. Chaplin, who was worth at least forty million dollars, then threatened to sue Welles and the *Times* for libel. Welles was having financial problems, and the *Times*, to protect him, paid a settlement of five hundred pounds.[14]

A year later, in September 1963, Chaplin successfully sued the owner of a clinic in Nice, France, for claiming him as a patient, along with Konrad Adenauer and King Ibn Saud of Saudi Arabia. The clinic claimed that its version of Prof. Paul Niehans's "rejuvenation" therapy, consisting of injections containing cells from sheep and calf embryos, had contributed to Chaplin's ability to father four children after the age of sixty-four.[15]

Except on rare occasions when the children were involved, Oona invariably took Charlie's side. Since very few people could be counted on to share this loyalty, the number of people she could rely on as friends was limited. Ella Winter, who seems to have been one of the few she confided in, was not much help since she, too, suffered from recurring bouts of depression.

Director Harold Clurman, one of the founders of the Group Theater, had directed a production of Eugene O'Neill's *Desire Under the Elms*, and his acquaintance with the Chaplins dated back two decades. A guest at Vevey at the end of June 1962, he found Charlie in an "ebullient" mood. Oona was eight months pregnant, and eight days away from giving birth to Christopher James, her eighth and last child. Like many longtime acquaintances, Clurman admired Oona's beauty, her "flesh like soft marble" and jet-black hair, now showing a few strands of gray. But Oona was also more than a little mysterious. She had a way of remaining on the sidelines of every conversation, revealing little or nothing of herself. Clurman speculated that this was "an acquired gift . . . developed by having lived in the wake of two overpowering personalities: her father and her husband. Whatever the cause of Oona's effortless ease—her capacity to sit back, listen and absorb—it is a quality so rare in American women nowadays as to seem miraculous."

One may wonder if "miraculous" was the right word. However pleasant Oona's company may have been for others, her attention focused more and more on trivialities. She doted on pets and one of her letters to Ella Winter shows her scheming in a rather childish way to smuggle a puppy into the household over Charlie's objections, a plan he foiled in the end.

Harold Clurman, moreover, noticed with mild amazement that the younger children were not really fluent in English. Since Charlie had never learned French, and Oona was not especially comfortable in the language, this observation said a great deal about the closeness of family life in the Chaplins' Swiss retreat.[16]

Chaplin gave Clurman a portion of his book to read, and confided that he thought the United States "came off rather well."

When the book appeared in the fall of 1964—titled *My Autobiography* (who else's would it have been?)—it sold briskly, but the reaction of reviewers and his American admirers was disappointment. There was something at once sad and annoying about Chaplin's need to validate his fame by chronicling the famous people like Gandhi and Einstein who had paid court to him. His account of his troubles in the 1940s, blaming everything on the machinations of underground "Nazi sympathizers," reopened issues that many of his former opponents might have been willing to let pass. More shockingly, he failed to mention, even in passing, important collaborators like Rollie Totheroh, Eddie Sutherland, Georgia Hale, and his half-brother Wheeler Dryden. Rob Wagner was acknowledged only in passing; Henry Bergman and Albert Austin were reduced to names in a list; Stan Laurel and Buster Keaton were also among the missing. His omission of Florence Deshon, Konrad Bercovici, and Carter de Haven was more understandable; not so his dismissal of Lita Grey Chaplin, the mother of two of his sons, in three brief sentences. Mary Pickford, who stood by him in public on so many occasions regardless of their private differences, was portrayed as a miser.

This was the sort of autobiography that called for rebuttal—and got it. Pola Negri, astounded at Chaplin's "phenomenal" lack of perspective, paid him back in her autobiography. Far more damaging, Lita Grey Chaplin published her own recollections, *Life with Chaplin*. Although criticized at the time for its intimate revelations, the book was extraordinarily generous by today's standards.

Mary Pickford, still living at Pickfair as a semirecluse, was one who did not strike back. Her decades-long feud with Charlie could not disguise the fact that they were similar personalities—two strong, determined people who had fought hard to overcome early hardships, and who suffered greatly when the characters they created were rendered obsolete by age, changing audience tastes and the coming of the talkies. A few years later Douglas Fairbanks Jr. decided to try to bring about an end to the hostilities. Visiting Pickford in Beverly Hills, he mentioned his recent meetings with Charlie in London and suggested—without any real evidence—that perhaps his feelings toward her had mellowed. Pickford, by now bedridden but still recognizable as the sweet-faced blond whose sunny disposition had charmed a generation of movie fans, managed to raise herself up in bed to deliver her reply. "I don't care," she said. "He's still a son of a bitch."

The attitude of Chaplin's children toward their famous father was very much that of people who chance to live in the shadow of an active volcano. They tried to stay out of the way of his periodic eruptions, but if they cursed their fate at times, they were also proud of their old man, an indomitable if at times remote personality. Chaplin wanted his children to have the solid academic education that had been denied to him, and to become professionals—doctors, lawyers, or professors. They disappointed him by turning out to be very much like their father and interested in the same things—writing, acting, and the circus.

Since Geraldine and Michael happened to come of age during the sixties, their differences with their parents seemed to epitomize the rebellion of the younger generation, making both of them celebrities in their own right. Geraldine, who became a full-time ballet student in London at age sixteen, had her father's high-strung personality and dramatic looks, a combination of her parents' most striking features. Almost immediately rumors were floated that she was being considered for important movie roles. Charlie had let his eldest daughter go to London on condition that she live with a companion and take a chaperone along on dates, rules that became more unrealistic as she reached her eighteenth birthday and became romantically involved with Georges Govriloff, a dancer in his early thirties.

In January 1965 Geraldine was cast as a featured dancer in a Paris production of Prokofiev's *Cinderella*, and the French press went wild over the gamine daughter of Charlot. Charlie made no secret of his displeasure at this development, refusing to attend her opening night and accusing her of trading on "his" name. The charge so angered her that she announced her intention to drop her surname entirely and be known, henceforth, simply as Geraldine. A year later David Lean cast her in *Doctor Zhivago*, evidence that her acting ambitions were serious, and the dispute with her parents was resolved.

Michael, meanwhile, had entered the Royal Academy of Dramatic Arts in London. He grew his hair long, skipped classes, and smoked marijuana—all without severing relations with the family friends who were looking out for him, or skipping regular sessions with his analyst, who reported to Oona in Vevey. During a jaunt to Spain over the 1964 Christmas season Michael and his girlfriend, actress Patrice Johns—another "older" woman at twenty-five—stayed with a friend who happened to be the great-granddaughter of the actor Sir Herbert Beerbohm Tree. Deciding on impulse to get married, Michael and Patrice went to see the British consul. Too late they learned—as Charlie's agents had learned in Mexico four decades earlier—that the law required a public notice of marriage license applications. While the press swarmed around the hapless couple, another complication developed: Michael was just eighteen and not could wed in Spain without parental consent. A free-lance photographer offered to pay for an elopement to Scotland, where the laws are more tolerant.

Three months later Michael and Patrice were back in London and he had signed up for welfare at twenty-nine dollars a week. When his parents passed through town on their way to an Easter season fishing vacation in Ireland, Oona told a reporter: "The young man is a problem and I am sorry he was given national assistance. . . . If I do not wish to indulge him as a beatnik that is my privilege."

Michael signed a recording contract and accepted a surprisingly meager advance for a ghostwritten tell-all book about life in Vevey. Six months later he, too, had reconciled with his parents, joining them in an effort to suppress his own book. The British courts were not sympathetic, and the book appeared anyway, minus a few of its more unflattering anecdotes.

Charlie had now reached the age when most of his contemporaries were long retired. The elder Sydney Chaplin, who for many years had divided his time between Nice and Montreux, writing unpublished waltzes and enjoying life, died on April 16, 1965, Charlie's seventy-sixth birthday. Even young Syd, pushing forty, had given up a flourishing career on the stage and was in the restaurant business in Paris. Charlie, who still had three children under ten, had every intention of going on forever. He talked of filming a spoof on Hollywood epics and writing an opera based on Hardy's *Tess of the D'Urbervilles*. For several years he had worked sporadically on a script about a condemned convict in a Kansas jail, a part he hoped would reestablish his son Syd as a movie actor. Few were surprised in the fall of 1965, when Chaplin announced that he was about to begin production on his eighty-first movie.

The project Chaplin had chosen was not the convict script or the Hollywood parody, but *A Countess from Hong Kong*, a revised version of the story of a stateless nightclub singer turned stowaway and the stuffy diplomat who falls in love with her, originally envisioned as a vehicle for Paulette Goddard and Gary Cooper. Although Chaplin had not had a critically successful movie in many years, his reputation as Hollywood's persecuted genius had grown brighter during the sixties with the political shift leftward and the rise of the *auteur* school of film criticism. Casting his first color wide-screen film, Chaplin had his pick of the hottest actors in the business, and he settled on Sophia Loren to play the singer and Marlon Brando the diplomat.

Astoundingly Brando, Loren, and the supporting players signed their contracts without reading the script. Chaplin, secretive as ever about his plot, had refused to send copies to the stars or their agents.

Tippi Hedren, the cool, blond star of Alfred Hitchcock's *The Birds*, had been cast as Brando's wife. The part, she was promised, would be a major supporting role, with scenes throughout the picture. She arrived in England with her husband and young daughter (the future star Melanie Griffith), to find that her character did not even make an appearance until the final third of the picture. That evening, over dinner with Chaplin, she chided him for lying to her. "If you had said, 'Tippi, come over and do a cameo,' I would have said, 'I'd love to.'"

"I didn't think you would come," Chaplin admitted.[17]

Meanwhile Marlon Brando, seeing what he was in for, retired to his hotel room and began issuing bulletins on his medical condition through his physician.

Chaplin had updated his story to sometime after World War II. But yet he hadn't. Sophia Loren's character, Countess Natascha, was still supposed to be a White Russian aristocrat, who had fled the

Bolsheviks to become a dance hall girl in Hong Kong, a type common in the twenties, perhaps even the thirties, but hardly still decorating Asian dance halls in the late forties. The situation of a beautiful female stowaway in a man's cabin was treated as an occasion for much scrambling around, as in a pre–World War I Keystone comedy. There was a surfeit of seasickness jokes, long an unfortunate predilection of Chaplin's. All of Chaplin's successful pictures, and some unsuccessful ones, too, had been about loners. He had no idea of how to make two worldly, sophisticated adults interact on the screen. It was if the entire history of romantic comedy, from *It Happened One Night* to Cary Grant and Katharine Hepburn, not to mention Grant and Audrey Hepburn, had never existed.

Chaplin suffered a serious bout of flu just before shooting on *Countess* began and never regained his full strength. Still, when it came to establishing his authority he was more than a match for Brando, who had a way of arriving on the set of a new film like an alpha wolf taking over a pack. When he decided to come to work, Brando showed up late and did his best to intimidate Loren, remarking on her black nose hairs during the shooting of a love scene and, once, reaching out to give her a possessive pat on the backside as she walked past him. Chaplin put a stop to such antics, telling Brando that if they couldn't get along they could take their grievances public. "You call a press conference, and I'll call one, and we'll see who gets the biggest audience."

Brando had been a guest at Chaplin's Summit Drive tennis parties when he was starting out in Hollywood. Though he respected Chaplin's genius, he hadn't liked him much then, and he liked him even less as a director. He was appalled by the way Chaplin would tear into his son, Syd, who was playing a supporting role, and indignant that Jerry Epstein, who was acting as a producer, was not getting a percentage of the picture.

Chaplin's approach to directing belonged to another era. He had worked out everyone's performance for them, down to the last gesture. "I wish someone would have been allowed to do a documentary," Tippi Hedren said later. "The way he directed was unlike anyone I ever saw. He acted out all the parts himself. He did Sophia's part, then Marlon's part, then Sydney's part, then mine, and then he'd say, 'Okay, now you can do it.' Which would be impossible, to mimic the master. It was incredible. None of us believed it. Marlon hated it."[18]

Chaplin had high hopes for *Countess*, and celebrated its London opening at a dinner party for thirty-two thrown for him by the American jet-setter Slim Keith and her British banker husband, Kenneth. The guest list demonstrates how far the Little Tramp had come. Among those present were Princess Alexandra (who "must be seen to be believed," gushed columnist Suzy Knickerbocker) and her husband, Angus Ogilvy. Also present were the Marqués and Marquesa de Santa Cruz, the earl of Hardwicke, the earl of Carnarvon, the duke of Marlborough, Lady Ashcombe, and the American songwriter Jule Styne and his wife. Paul Getty, Liza Minnelli, Lord Louis Mountbatten and reigning supermodel Jean Shrimpton were among the B-list crowd present at a post-screening party at the Savoy.

By the time the partying began, Chaplin had already attended the press preview and knew he was in trouble. The negative reaction to *Countess* should hardly have come as a surprise. Film buffs loved Chaplin because he was the antithesis of Hollywood. To an audience sated by a diet of porterhouse steak he served up a dish of bouilla-baisse, a spicy change of pace even if the individual ingredients were sometimes questionable. With *A Countess from Hong Kong* he was no longer challenging Hollywood but competing with it, and in the genre of romantic comedy it did very well indeed. He was doing it, moreover—had gone mainstream—at the very moment when the movies were more challenging than they had been in years. Chaplin loathed the trend toward explicit sex, drugs, and violence in the cin-ema—and one feels in retrospect that his objections were valid. But wasting the talents of Loren and Brando on a creaky farce was not the alternative.

Stung by the critics, Chaplin's circle was in a state of denial. Jerry Epstein blamed the projectionist at the press screening for using the wrong lens and suggested in his memoir, *Remembering Charlie*, that *New York Times* critic Bosley Crowther panned the film out of spite because Chaplin had refused a request for an inter-view on grounds of exhaustion. Chaplin himself called the press "idiots," and took the opportunity to mention that he had found *Dr. Zhivago*, his own daughter's breakthrough film, "banal."

"My old man told off the British critics, the ones that murdered it," Sydney explained to Broadway columnist Earl Wilson. "He doesn't want crazy camera angles, with cameras up people's nostrils. They say he's old fashioned. My old man says THEY'RE old fashioned. . . . My old man says London has never liked one of his pictures when they opened. Twenty years later they're works of art."

Syd added that he didn't believe that *Countess* would be his father's last picture, as everyone assumed. "My old man is loaded and he's almost eighty. He's probably going to make another one."[19]

Chaplin was indeed writing another script, *The Freak*, about a young girl with wings who is discovered by scientists in Argentina. This tale of a fragile nonconformist, a sort of angel cruelly thrust into the spotlight—promised to be more original and interesting than the material in which he had invested his effort in recent years.

But time was running out. In October 1966, while finishing postproduction work on *Countess* at the Pinewood Studios, Chaplin fell in the street, breaking his ankle. Immobilized by his injury, he was forced to give up tennis, which he had continued playing, casually, with Oona.

Almost as ominous as the accident was Oona's hysterical reaction. She had often accompanied Charlie to the studio, but on this particular day he had gone to work without her. For some years Charlie had resented any interest that took Oona away from him for more than a few minutes. He wanted 100 percent of her attention. Now she had denied him, and look what had happened! On their return to Vevey, Oona devoted herself more completely than ever to her husband's needs.

In the beginning Chaplin had envisioned roles in *The Freak* for two of his daughters, Josephine and Victoria, both large-eyed, ethereal-looking girls who had been giving impromptu shows at home since they started school, dressing up as film stars like Marlene Dietrich, or, after a visit to the Peking Opera, restaging a scene complete with their version of the high-pitched, incomprehensible singing.

Josie, however, was not especially interested in acting at this point in her life. An aspiring singer, she idolized Maria Callas and studied with her for a while but eventually decided against trying for a career in opera. In 1969 she married Nick Sistovaris, scion of a family of Greek furriers. Charlie, who firmly believed that a beautiful woman was nothing without a rich husband, was delighted by the match, and gave the couple a gala wedding at Vevey. Truman Capote, Graham Greene, and an assortment of titled and demi-titled Europeans attended. Josie and her husband settled in nearby Geneva, skied in Gstaad, and had a son, Charles Alexander. She took up acting, appearing as Patient Griselda in Pier Pasolini's film version of *The Canterbury Tales*.

Victoria, who studied ballet as a child, had finished her convent school education and was putting off plans to enter the Royal Academy of Dramatic Arts in London on account of *The Freak*. Charlie had a pair of angel wings made and began coaching his daughter for the role, as he had coached so many other protégées in the past. Even when he was in good health, Charlie often took years to get a movie into production and the delays became a strain on Vicki. Charlie, who had become plump in old age, worried constantly about weight, and Vicki began to show signs of anorexia. Oona finally stepped in, telling Jerry Epstein to suspend plans to put the movie into production. Charlie at times appeared to be unaware of her decision. As late as 1972 he told a reporter who ran into him while he was vacationing at the Hotel du Cap in Antibes that he planned to direct Josie and Vicki in the film.

But Victoria had eloped in 1969 with an impoverished French actor, Jean-Baptiste Thiérrée, who traveled around the countryside in a van performing as a street busker. Charlie liked to tell friends that Vicki had fallen in love with Thierrée at first sight and run off with him the first day they met. It was a romantic story, but not true. In fact the couple had been in love for some time, evading Charlie's ban on unchaperoned dates for his daughters with the connivance of sympathetic family friends. After the elopement Vicki joined her husband in his nomadic life, performing with him in an act called "Vicki et Baptiste" and giving birth to her first child, Aurelia, five months later in a municipal hospital.

Vicki and Baptiste made a brief appearance in Fellini's *The Clowns* (1970). In 1971 they opened their family circus at the Avignon Festival. More than two decades later they and their acrobat son, a near double for Charlie, would still be touring with their minimalist show, Le Cirque Imaginaire.

Charlie and Oona did not quite know what to make of Vicki's husband, surprisingly, since he was the modern equivalent of the street musician Charlie had portrayed so touchingly in *The Vagabond*. Jean-Baptiste had studied psychology and was interested in the therapeutic uses of performance art. The young couple's first visit to Manoir de Ban was awkward. Geraldine, visiting them in Paris a few years later, was taken aback at first to find them living in an apartment filled with dirty laundry and unwashed dishes. Baptiste, however, won her over by commenting that he, personally, wouldn't mind having a maid but Vicki didn't want one. "I guess all this is a reaction against her upbringing," he commented wryly.

If Charlie and Oona's children had one characteristic in common, apart from their interest in the arts, it was a determination to avoid having their lives ruled by servants. Geraldine brought up her son Shane, by Spanish director Carlos Saura, without benefit of a nanny, even though it meant staying up with him at night and reporting to the set the next morning on a few hours' sleep. Michael, who was divorced from Patrice, by whom he had two sons, in 1969, was a playwright and scriptwriter, who lived simply with his second wife, the former Patricia Beauduvier, a British subject of West Indian extraction.

Although *The Freak* had been canceled, Chaplin continued to work when he could, composing a new score for the reissue of his 1928 film, *The Circus*. More often now he was content to take pleasure in small things. "I know I'm rich when I can take *two* clean handkerchiefs out of my drawer every morning," he told Oona.

He had been looking for a distributor to reissue his older films for some time, since breaking his contract with Lopert Films in the early sixties. In 1971 at Cannes he struck a deal with Mo Rothman. Representing himself and several investors, including Bert Schneider, the producer of *Easy Rider*, and at the time a major financial supporter of Huey Newton and the Black Panther Party, Rothman paid some six million dollars plus 50 percent royalties for the distribution rights to seventeen classic UA and First National films. The sale came as a blow to Sydney, who had earlier been told by his father that he would be allowed to broker the sale. Syd, who was in need of cash for his restaurant business, had lined up a bidder only to be embarrassed when they got a chilly welcome at Vevey from Charlie, who had begun dealing with Rothman in the meantime. Syd shrugged off the disappointment. A few years later he opened another restaurant, this time in Palm Springs, California.

Legally Chaplin had been free to return to the United States since he settled with the IRS in 1959. Dean Rusk, whom he met in 1962 when they both received honorary degrees from Oxford University, had assured him that he would have no trouble getting a visa, and Chaplin briefly considered a U.S. tour to promote *A Countess from Hong Kong*, a plan that fizzled along with the movie. By 1972 anti-Communism was viewed as an embarrassment by the reigning generation in Hollywood, and the Academy of Motion Picture Arts and Sciences was eager to make up for past slights by honoring Chaplin, who had never won a competitive Oscar. Although he was persuaded by Rothman that a visit to the United States would help promote his films, Chaplin was extremely nervous. "I like America. And I'm prepared to be shot," he told *Cue* magazine's film critic, William Wolf, who saw him in Switzerland in March 1972.

The following month he and Oona flew to New York, where he was feted by the Film Society of Lincoln Center and awarded the Handel Medallion by Mayor Lindsay. A week later, on April 10, he received a special Academy Award. These events were an emotional high for loyal Chaplin defenders and old leftists like Zero Mostel, who led the cheers at the Lincoln Center gala. Chaplin, for better or worse, remained his crusty self, far from swept away by the sentiment of the moment. "My God, the affection of the people," Chaplin said the day after the Lincoln Center gala, "So sweet. Like little children after they've been slapped down and they're sorry they've done something." In a more reflective mood, he added, "It's very hard to respond to affection. I can respond to antagonism. But love and affection . . ."[20]

Syd Chaplin later said that if pickets had appeared in front of Lincoln Center, his father was prepared to return to Switzerland immediately, skipping the Academy Awards altogether. "Like anyone else, if you go to a cocktail party and it stinks, you leave."[21]

In fact there were no demonstrations of any kind in New York.

In Hollywood, an unknown person did attempt to deface Chaplin's star on the Hollywood Walk of Fame, which had only recently been added, and the exhibition of a Chaplin statue in the atrium of the American Airlines office at the corner of Hollywood and Vine ended after reported bomb threats.

The one honor Chaplin did dearly want, his friends agreed, was a knighthood. The elevation to Sir Charles, rumored since the early sixties, finally came in March 1975. Chaplin, eighty-five and wheel-chair-bound, was ushered in to the ballroom at Buckingham Palace to the strains of the theme from *Limelight*, the best known of his half-dozen compositions that had become popular standards. Too weak to kneel, he was knighted sitting down, and appeared, to some observers, slightly bewildered. Outside the palace, Oona prompted him to smile for the photographers. "I'll make another picture," Chaplin managed to say before his limousine whisked him away.

Chaplin had suffered a broken back during a fall in his bed-room, an injury that was not recognized and properly diagnosed until some time later. Frail and easily tired, he now spent most of his time watching his old pictures or French-language television. He still did not understand the language but amused himself by mimick-ing the acting. Occasionally he reread his battered copy of *Oliver Twist* and on good days, tried to work on a new musical score for *The Kid*. He had little interest in seeing friends or family. Oona had become his entire world.

In 1976 Chaplin suffered a stroke that left him partially para-lyzed. When he appeared for the last time at his favorite restaurant, L'Auberge de l'Onde, he did not recognize the proprietor and Oona had to feed him and wipe his mouth. Even so he had been a domi-nant force for so long that his children found it hard to imagine that the end was near. Geraldine, though she acknowledged being told that recovery was all but impossible, said: "My father is eternal. He'll outlive us all." Oona, recognized by a British reporter as she wheeled Charlie on the promenade that runs along the shore of Lake Geneva, said: "I wouldn't have changed a thing. All of the trauma and difficulties and heartbreak I have been through with Charlie—it was worth every minute of it."[22]

Chaplin died a month after this interview, on Christmas Day, 1977. After a private ceremony, he was buried in the small cemetery in Corsier-sur-Vevey. Two months later his grave was found to have been dug up, the coffin missing.

In a way it seemed fitting that even Chaplin's passing, at the advanced age of eighty-eight, was marked by mayhem, mystery, and controversy. Rumors flew that the grave-napping was the work of anti-Semites, who objected to the burial of a (supposed) Jew in a Christian cemetery. In fact money was at the root of the bizarre crime. The coffin thieves were demanding a huge ransom, and when their calls to the house and the family's attorney in Geneva produced no response they became abusive and threatening. After seventy-six days the macabre incident ended when the intact coffin was discovered buried in a farmer's field near Villeneuve at the eastern end of Lake Geneva. Roman Wardas, a Polish auto mechanic, and his Bulgarian accomplice were arrested and convicted in the attempted extortion plot.

Chaplin was survived by nine children. (Charles junior died in 1968.) Except for Sydney, who had retired from the stage and was settled in Rancho Mirage, California, and Eugene, who ran a shop in Vevey, all the children were involved in the arts. Christopher, the youngest, made his acting debut in the 1984 film, *Where is Parsifal?* A decade later it was already the grandchildren's turn, with Aurelia Thiérrée beginning to make her mark as an actress.

After a lifetime haunted by the fear of slipping back into poverty, Chaplin died a wealthy man. His estate, protected by the secrecy afforded Swiss bank accounts and privately held corporations, was estimated at about ninety million dollars. What Chaplin had missed out on was a sense of what wealth can accomplish, beyond an ample supply of clean socks and a very comfortable home. He had avoided the major follies that drain the bank accounts of many of the newly rich; but neither was his name associated with any important charitable endeavors.

Oona, just fifty-two years old, withdrew into herself. Her childhood friend Carol Grace Marcus, now Mrs. Walter Matthau, persuaded her to come to the United States for a time. In 1979 Gloria Vanderbilt Cooper threw a party in Southampton to reintroduce her to New York society. Oona bought a co-op in New York City, appeared at the fashionable Studio 54, and was seen around town escorted by screenwriter Walter Bernstein. Still a beautiful woman but shy and unhappy, she had trouble coping with the details of everyday life; her habit of us-them snobbery, born of years of private jokes shared with Charlie, was not attractive. Her sense of futility and loss grew worse with time. Then her health began to fail. She suffered a stroke, and died in 1991 back home in Vevey, after being bedridden for several years.

In 1993 it developed that Dr. Christ Zois, who had been Gloria Vanderbilt's psychiatrist and sometime business partner (an arrangement that ended in a court fight and bitter recriminations), had borrowed half a million dollars to buy a house in New Jersey on the strength of a promissory note bearing Oona's signature. Her estate claimed that the signature was a forgery and successfully sued in U.S. District Court in Manhattan, disclaiming the debt.

That same year a huge auction of Chaplin memorabilia, including a violin said to have been the one he played in *The Vagabond*, was held in Geneva, Switzerland, despite the vocal protests of eight of his children. The sale included hundreds of items, from pajamas, cast-off clothes, and toiletry items to fan letters and handwritten notes for *The Freak*, collected over the years by Mirella Canese, who had been the housekeeper at Manoir de Ban for more than two decades.

Of course the true legacy of Charlie Chaplin is not the memorabilia, his considerable fortune, or even in his genius for bitterness. It lies in the films—which, ironically, were shrouded in the mists of memory for much of his life and only just becoming widely available through the medium of home video at the time of his death. Today, thanks to Chaplin's voluminous archives they are available in meticulously restored laser disc editions.

Looking back on Chaplin's work, one is struck by what a fragile mix comedy and the film medium have turned out to be. Comedy may be a craft, even a business, but laughter depends on surprise and the illusion of spontaneous connection between performer and audience. Movies make everything and everyone familiar. They seemed to call for more—feature-length stories, romance, character development, special effects, a message. The golden era of the Mutual comedies lasted little more than a year. The rest was struggle.

Author's Note

Charles Spencer Chaplin was fond of the argument that artists should not be judged by the same standards as other people. Therefore his life, more than most, raises the question of the public's relationship to those creative people who give so much pleasure through their work yet turn out to be less than admirable in their private lives. Carol Matthau, in her recent memoir, *Among the Porcupines*, expresses the outrage felt by many of Chaplin's friends and admirers over the events that led to his being excluded from the United States, arguing that his fate was a horrible example of "the way we treat our artists." This, indeed, is a problem, given the celebrity machine's habit of raising stars up only to grind them down at the first opportunity. On the other hand, for many Americans at the time, the issue was quite different: a matter of how our artists treat us.

Since Chaplin was a complex personality, it is not surprising that the many books written about him fall into two distinct camps—admiring tributes to his film art on the one hand, and the bitter reminiscences of individuals who were close to him on the other.

In the first category are biographies by Theodore Huff, Roger Manvell, and John McCabe (who incorporated the reminiscences of Chaplin's onetime roommate, Stan Laurel). These books were written at a time when the general public, and in many cases even serious students of film, had no ready access to Chaplin's movies, and the authors devote considerable space to narrating their story lines. Today, thanks to videotapes and laser disc technology, nearly all of Chaplin's eighty-one films are easily obtainable. Of special interest is the CBS/Fox Video laser disc series of digital remasters from the Chaplin archives, *Chaplin: A Legacy of Laughter*. Those who know Chaplin's movies only from old, grainy prints will find the remastered versions a revelation. These discs also include restored footage and archival material, and one, *A First National Collection*, gives us a complete eleven-minute "home movie": *Nice and Friendly*, starring Lord and Lady Mountbatten and Jackie Coogan.

David Robinson's 791-page *Chaplin: His Life and Art* was the first biography to give a documented account of Chaplin's childhood and also provided detailed production histories of his films. But Robinson, the film critic of the *Times* of London, was writing with the cooperation of Lady Chaplin, and he passed very lightly over the more controversial areas of his subject's private life.

Another interesting book, Charles J. Maland's *Chaplin and American Culture: The Evolution of a Star Image*, filled in some of the gaps left by Robinson but was limited by its focus on Chaplin's "star image" as reflected in the press.

Reading Robinson and, indeed, many reminiscences by Chaplin's devoted admirers, it is hard to comprehend how the American public could have turned against such a charming and versatile genius. Indeed, many of Chaplin's admirers tend to echo, if more discreetly, his own explanation for this train of events—blaming scheming women, McCarthyite persecutions, and the philistinism of the American press and public.

The other school of Chaplin biography is the personal reminiscence.

Gerith von Ulm's *Charlie Chaplin: King of Tragedy* was a gossipy insider's story, based on information provided by Toraichi Kono, Chaplin's longtime chauffeur, valet, and bodyguard. Jim Tully's magazine articles and Carlyle Robinson's memoir, which I found only in the French version, *La Vérité sur Charlie Chaplin: Sa vie, ses amours, ses déboirs* (The truth about Chaplin: His life, his loves, his heartbreaks), are works by ex-employees. *My Life with Chaplin* is the autobiography of Lita Grey Chaplin, the complainant in the most scandalous divorce case Hollywood had seen up to that time.

Lita Chaplin stood by everything in her 1966 book: "It's all there," she said.

Two of Chaplin's sons also wrote books. *My Father, Charlie Chaplin* is a remarkably graceful book by an eldest son who was estranged from his father but still idolized him. Michael Chaplin's *I Couldn't Smoke the Grass on My Father's Lawn* was produced in the throes of youthful rebellion, and its bleak picture of family life at Chaplin's retirement home in Vevey presents an interesting contrast to *Remembering Charlie*, by Jerry Epstein, Chaplin's producer and an intimate friend of the family.

The objectivity of such highly personal narratives is always suspect. But, despite some errors in chronology, doubtless attributable to the process of collaboration with ghostwriters, these books proved to be generally accurate and, in most cases, remarkably generous in comparison to the revenge memoirs so common today. My research into the papers of such close Chaplin associates as Max Eastman, Rob Wagner, and Harry Crocker—as well as the records of his many bitterly contested lawsuits and confrontations with government officials—quickly showed me that Chaplin was capable of bizarre behavior, with unfortunate consequences for those close to him.

Chaplin suffered a form of what today would be called manic-depressive, or bipolar, illness. Paradoxically, when his personal life was spinning out of control, he was often intensely creative in his work. Such contradictions present problems for the biographer, especially in an age when one risks being accused of "pathography," but certainly in Chaplin's case one cannot begin to understand the artist without knowing the man, and the same qualities of sensitivity and self-absorption that made him so very successful also led to his downfall as an American idol.

Endnotes

Abbreviations used in the notes:

BR   Billy Rose Theater Collection of the New York Public Library for the Performing Arts at Lincoln Center, Astor, Lenox and Tilden Foundations

CHLA   David Robinson, *Chaplin: His Life and Art* (New York: McGraw-Hill, 1985)

CCMM   Harry Crocker, "Charlie Chaplin: Man and Mime" typescript in the Harry Crocker Collection of the Margaret Herrick Library.

COH   Oral History Research Office, Columbia University, New York

CU   Special Collections, Butler Library, Columbia University

FBI   Federal Bureau of Investigation

LILLY   Lilly Library, University of Indiana, Bloomington, Indiana

MA   Charles Spencer Chaplin, *My Autobiography* (New York: Simon & Schuster, 1964)

MHL   Margaret Herrick Library of the Academy of Motion Picture Arts and Sciences

MoMA   Museum of Modern Art, Film Study Center

NARA   National Archives and Records Administration, including the center for the Northeast Region in New York City (NY) and the center for the Pacific Southwest Region in Laguna Niguel, California

RLC   Robinson Locke Collection of Dramatic Scrapbooks, a division of the Billy Rose Theater Collection

SMU Oral History Collection on the Performing Arts, DeGolyer Library, Southern Methodist University

UCLA Department of Special Collections, University Library, University of California at Los Angeles

USC University Library, University of Southern California

WHS Wisconsin Historical Society, including the United Artists Collection, Wisconsin Center for Film and Theater Research

Chapter 1 "They Were Nothing . . . *Nothing* . . . NOTHING!"

1. *MA*, p. 19.

2. Peter Steffens, "The Victorian Tramp," *Ramparts* (Mar. 1965): 17–24.

3. *MA*, p. 23.

4. The article tracing Chaplin's descent from a family named Thonstein appeared in volume 3 of *Who's Who in American Jewry*. See Harold Manning, "Charlie Chaplin's Early Life: Fact and Fiction," *Historical Journal of Film, Radio and Television* 3, no. 1 (Mar. 1983): 35–43.

5. Reginald R. Chaplin, "Charlie Chaplin's Ancestors," *Historical Journal of Film, Radio and Television* 5, no. 2 (1985): pp. 209–32.

6. CCMM, chap. 1.

7. Steffens, "The Victorian Tramp." The article was based on a visit with Chaplin in September 1964.

8. CCMM, sec. 1, p. 4.

9. "Gipsy Life Around London," *Illustrated London News*, Nov. 29, 1879, p. 503.

10. *CHLA*, p 10.

11. Ibid., pp. 11–12.

12. Harry Geduld, ed., *Charlie Chaplin's Own Story* (Indianapolis: Indiana University Press, 1985), pp. 1–2. An annotated reprint of the suppressed "as told to" biography based on interviews Chaplin gave in 1915. Feverishly melodramatic, full of errors, yet revealing of what the young Chaplin believed, or chose to believe, about his childhood.

13. Ibid., pp. 4–5.

14. Interview with Albert Edward Sutherland, Feb. 1959, COH.

15. CCMM, sec. 1, pp. 15, 31.

16. John Burnett, *Plenty and Want: A Social History of Diet in England from 1815 to the Present Day* (London: Nelson, 1966), pp. 159–63.

17. Geduld, *Charlie Chaplin's Own Story*, p. 28.

18. CCMM, sec. 1, p. 6.

19. The program is reproduced in Charles Chaplin, *My Life in Pictures* (New York: Grosset & Dunlap, 1975), p. 43.

20. Harry C. Carr, "Charlie Chaplin's Story: As Narrated by Mr. Chaplin Himself to Photo Play Magazine's Special Representative," *Photoplay*, June 20, July 4, July 18, 1915, RLC.

21. Letter to an unidentified English newspaper, clipping, Chaplin file, 1950–59, MoMA.

22. Thomas Burke, "Orphanage," in *The Wind and the Rain* (London: Thornton Butterworth Ltd., 1924), pp. 94–95.

23. *MA*, p. 33.

24. Ibid.; see also CCMM, sec. 1, p. 17.

25. *CHLA*, p. 19.

26. CCMM, sec. 2, p. 8.

27. Carr, "Charlie Chaplin's Story," June 20, 1915.

28. Ibid.

29. *MA*, p. 51.

30. Ibid., p. 19.

31. CCMM, sec. 2, p. 12.

32. Ibid., pp. 37–38.

33. Dana Burnet, "Garbo and Chaplin Talked for Me," *Photoplay*, June 1936, pp. 26–27 ff.

34. *CHLA*, p. 40.

Chapter 2 . . . *A Romance of Cockayne*

1. "When Little Charlie Chaplin Played in a Traveling English Road-Show," *New York Journal-American*, May 31, 1931. This interview with Edith Green, later Edith Scales, appeared originally in the English press; see a partial photocopy in Chaplin, *My Life in Pictures*, pp. 50–51.

2. *CHLA*, pp. 55–58.

3. *MA*, p. 93.

4. John McCabe, *Mr. Laurel and Mr. Hardy* (1961; reprint, New York: New American Library, 1985), p. 25.

5. J. P. Gallagher, *Fred Karno: Master of Mirth and Tears* (London: Robert Hale, 1971), p. 78.

6. *MA*, p. 107.

7. CCMM, sec. 4, p. 16.

8. Alf Reeves, in the *Philadelphia Record*, Apr. 2, 1912, RLC, vol. 110.

9. McCabe, *Mr. Laurel and Mr. Hardy*, p. 39.

10. Ibid., 41.

11. "List or Manifest of Alien Passengers . . . ," NARA (NY). Chaplin gave his next of kin as "Sid Chaplin, Camberwell, SE, London."

12. *Vancouver News*, April 12, 1912; *Los Angeles Examiner*, May 21, 1912; RLC, vol. 110.

Chapter 3 *A Film Johnnie*

1. Gene Morgan, "Where Are Chicago's Big Shoes?" *Chicago Herald*, Jan. 10, 1915, RLC, vol. 110.

2. Linda Arvidson (Mrs. D. W. Griffith), *When the Movies Were Young* (1925; reprint, New York: Benjamin Blom, 1968), pp. 77–78.

3. Harold Lloyd interview, 1964, COH.

4. In a contemporary interview Chaplin said he arrived at Edendale in a cab; this became a trolley in his autobiography. Edendale *was* on the trolley line, but Chaplin is unlikely to have been familiar with the route after one day in town.

5. Carr, "Charlie Chaplin's Story," July 18, 1915.

6. Mack Sennett and Cameron Shipp, *King of Comedy* (New York: Doubleday, 1954), p. 156.

7. Andy Edmonds, *Frame-Up!: The Untold Story of Roscoe "Fatty" Arbuckle* (New York: William Morrow, 1991), p. 73.

8. *MA*, p. xx.

9. Harry M. Geduld, *Chapliniana: A Commentary on Charlie Chaplin's 81 Films*, vol. 1 (Bloomington, Ind.: University of Indiana Press, 1987), pp. 10–11.

10. Sennett and Shipp, *King of Comedy*, pp. 156–57.

11. Ibid., pp. 158–59.

12. "Charlie Chaplin's Million Dollar Walk," *McClure's Magazine*, July 1916.

13. Geduld, *Chapliniana*, p. 26.

14. Kalton C. Lahue, *Mack Sennett's Keystone: The Man, the Myth and the Comedies* (South Brunswick, N.J.: A.S. Barnes & Co., 1971), p. 157.

15. *MA*, p. 142.

16. Charles Chaplin, "Does the Public Know What It Wants?" *The Adelphi* 1, no. 8 (Jan. 1924), Chaplin file, 1930–39, MoMA.

17. No one knows the actual shooting dates of either film, and the question of which came first has been the subject of considerable debate. Conklin's account in *King of Comedy* clearly states that *Mabel's Strange Predicament* had been delayed on account of rain. In court documents defending his proprietary rights to his character Chaplin named *Mabel's Strange Predicament* as the Tramp's debut.

18. *CHLA*, p. 119.

19. Harry Geduld and a few other Chaplin scholars argue, largely on the basis of internal evidence, that two of Chaplin's comedies, *Cruel, Cruel Love* and *The Star Boarder,* were directed by Sennett, not Nichols. Chaplin's reminiscence on this

point is somewhat vaguely worded but seems to indicate that Nichols was the director of a series of four films, made around the same time as *A Film Johnnie*.

20. *MA*, pp. 147–48.

21. Betty Harper Fussell, *Mabel* (New York: Ticknor & Fields, 1982), p. 72.

22. Chaplin, "Does the Public Know What It Wants?"

23. Sennett and Shipp, *King of Comedy*, p. 164.

24. Geduld, *Chapliniana*, p. 154.

25. Quoted in Gerald D. McDonald, Michael Conway, and Mark Ricci, *The Films of Charlie Chaplin* (New York: Bonanza Books, 1965), p. 59.

26. *What Do These Old Films Mean?*, vol. 1, *Great Britain, 1900–1912*, prod. Hubert Niogret, dir. Noël Burch, 26 mins., Facets Video, 1985, videocassette.

27. *MA*, p. 152.

28. Fussell, *Mabel*, p. 108; *MA*, 156.

29. Frances Marion, *Off with Their Heads* (New York: Macmillan, 1972), pas-sim; also, "Marie Dressler Estate, Complete Statement, Feb. 20, 1936, Box 17, Robert Leicester Wagner Papers, UCLA.

30. Sennett and Shipp, *King of Comedy*, p. 187.

31. *CHLA*, p. 132.

Chapter 4   *Work*

1. Interview with Gilbert Anderson, 1958, COH.

2. Interview with Buster Keaton (popular arts, series 1, vol 60, COH.

3. May Tinee, "Charlie Chaplin, a Modest Violet," *Buffalo Courier*, Jan. 10, 1915, RLC, vol. 110.

4. Mary E. Porter, "Charlie Chaplin, Cheerful Comedian," *Picture-Play Weekly*, Apr. 24, 1915; Morgan, "Where Are Chicago's Big Shoes?"; both RLC, vol. 110.

5. Charles J. McGuirk, "Chaplinitis," part 1, *Motion Picture Magazine*, July 1915, pp. 85–85; see also part 2, Aug. 1915, pp. 121–24.

6. Gloria Swanson, *Swanson on Swanson* (New York: Random House, 1980), p. 40.

7. Timothy J. Lyons, "Roland H. Totheroh Interviewed," *Film Culture* 62, no. 2 (Spring 1972): 285.

8. Terry Ramsaye, "Chaplin—and How He Does It," *Photoplay*, Sept. 1917, pp. 19–23 ff.

9. Fred Goodwins, "The Little Lady of Laughter," *Pictures and Picturegoer*, May 6, 1916, Purviance file, MoMA.

10. Ibid.

11. McGuirk, *Chaplinitis*, part 2.

12. Various advertisements and clippings, vol. 110, RLC; see also Charles J. Maland, *Chaplin and American Culture*, pp. 10–11.

13. "How Much Does Charlie Chaplin Own?" *Literary Digest*, Feb. 2, 1934. p. 44 and ff.

14. *Chicago Herald*, July 15, 1915, vol. 110, RLC.

15. *Variety*, Mar. 26, 1915; *New Jersey Mail*, Apr. 10, 1915; *Picture Play Weekly*, Apr. 4, 1915; *Chicago Tribune*, Apr. 25, 1915, vol. 110, RLC.

16. *CHLA*, p.144; Roger Manvell, *Chaplin* (Boston: Little, Brown, 1974), p. 89.

17. Carr, "Charlie Chaplin's Story," Oct. 1915.

18. Goodwins, "The Little Lady of Laughter."

19. *Charles Chaplin v. Vitagraph-Lubin-Selig-Essanay, Inc. and the Essanay Film Manufacturing Co.*, Equity Case Files 684, Box 1574-57A300, RG 21, National Archives, Great Lakes Region; see also *Moving Picture World*, July 10, 1915, clipping, vol. 110, RLC.

20. *MA*, p. 172.

21. McDonald, Conway, and Ricci, p. 99.

22. "Is Charlie Killing the Golden Goose?" *Chicago Tribune*, July 16, 1915, RLC, vol. 110.

23. Terry Ramsaye, *A Million and One Nights* (1926; reprint, New York: Simon & Schuster, 1964), p. 733.

Chapter 5 *The Vagabond*

1. Ramsaye, "Chaplin—And How He Does It."

2. Ramsaye, *A Million and One Nights*, p. 735.

3. *New York World*, Feb. 22, 1916; see also *New York Herald Tribune*, Feb. 22, 1916, and Robert Grau, "The More People Laughed at the Idea of Chaplin's Salary, the More They Had to Pay," *Motion Pictures Magazine*, May 1916, vol. 110, RLC.

4. "Charlie Chaplin Should Be Barred, Says Citizen," *New Orleans American*, Sept. 7, 1915; *Minneapolis Tribune*, Mar. 14, 1917.

5. J. B. Hirsch, "The New Charlie Chaplin," *Motion Pictures Magazine*, Jan. 1916.

6. *Toledo Blade*, Mar. 10, 1916. vol. 110, RLC.

7. *Harper's Weekly*, May 6, 1916.

8. Lyons, "Roland H. Totheroh Interviewed," p. 285.

9. Buster Keaton, *My Wonderful World of Slapstick* (New York: Doubleday, 1960), p. 126.

10. Syndicated newspaper interview, excerpted in *CHLA*, p. 164; "Chaplin—And How He Does It."

11. "A Day in 'The Pawn Shop'," *Motion Picture Classic*, Nov. 1916.

12. Harry Crocker, "Henry Bergman," *Academy Leader*, April 1972, p. 17.

13. CCMM, sec. 11, p. 4.

14. CCMM, sec. 6, p. 33.

15. Mutual publicity release, excerpted in *CHLA*, pp. 205–8.

16. Interview with Archie Bell in the *Cleveland Plain Dealer*, June 23, 1918, vol. 111, RLC.

17. Mutual publicity release, Edna Purviance file, MoMA. Answering *Photoplay*'s annual questionnaires in 1916, Edna continued to do her best to correct the mistaken impression given by Ramsaye's story. Though she fudged slightly on her age, claiming to have been born in 1895 rather than 1894, she left the question about higher education blank and replied to the query about previous experience in the negative, saying, "never have been on stage." She went on to list her hobbies as "lawn tennis, horseback riding, motoring, lingist [*sic*], and music."

18. Goodwins, "The Little Lady of Laughter"; *Photoplay* questionnaire (Lone Star period), ibid.

19. Ivan Gaddis, "Secret Griefs and Cankers in the Bosom," *Motion Pictures Magazine*, Apr. 1916, vol. 110, RLC.

20. Sven Kisslin, "The Bittersweet Memories of Charlie Chaplin," *Daily News Sunday Magazine*, Apr. 18, 1971, p. 12.

21. *New York Telegraph*, Mar. 18, 1916.

22. Sutherland interview, COH.

23. Chaplin later made a promotional film with Scottish comedian Harry Lauder, during which Lauder drew a cartoon profile of him with "Semitic" features. Chaplin responded by indicating that he was not Jewish but Syd was. See Kevin Brownlow and David Gill's documentary *Unknown Chaplin*, part 2, 55 mins., Thames Television/HBO Video, 1983, videocassette.

24. One descendant of J. G. Chaplin refused to be interviewed, and another failed to respond to a written request; however, a member of the immediate family confirmed in a telephone interview that casual contacts between the two Chaplin families continued as late as the early 1970s, when two members of the family visited with Oona Chaplin at her and Charlie's home in Switzerland. For more on J. G. Chaplin, see James A Porter, "Versatile Interests of the Early Negro Artist: A Neglected Chapter of American Art History," *Art in America* (Jan. 1936), pp. 16–27.

25. Theodore Huff, *Charlie Chaplin* (New York: Arno Press, 1972), p. 71.

26. David Robinson quotes extensively from correspondence on this subject in the Chaplin archives, *CHLA*.

27. *Brooklyn Eagle*, Apr. 9, 1916; *New York Variety*, Apr. 14, 1916; *Moving Picture World*, Apr. 22, 1916; *New York Morning Telegraph*, Apr. 9, 1916.

28. Equity Case Files, Box 484, NARA (NY).

29. *Keystone Film Co.* v. *Herman S. Waldman, Trading Under the Name of "Chaplin Film Company,"* E12-375, NARA (NY).

30. *New York Star,* June 28, 1916, RLC, vol. 110.

31. Ramsaye, *A Million and One Nights*, p. 37.

32. CCMM, sec. 7, p. 11.

33. Rob Wagner to Upton Sinclair, Feb. 8, 1918, Upton Sinclair Papers, LILLY.

34. Mabel Condon, "In Chaplin's House of Glass," *Picture-Play* Magazine, Dec. 1916, RLC, vol. 110.

35. Alistair Cooke, *Six Men* (New York: Berkley, 1978), p. 30.

36. Ramsaye, "Chaplin—and How He Does It."

37. CCMM, sec. 6, p. 30. Danny Hall, speaking to Crocker, says this occurred during the filming of "Shanghaied—I think it was." But the "fish gag" occurs at the beginning of *The Immigrant*, not *Shanghaied*.

38. *Variety,* Apr. 6, 1917, p. 1.

39. Ibid. June 29, 1917, p. 1.

40. Julian Johnson, "Charles, Not Charlie, *Photoplay*, n.d., MHS.

41. Theodore Huff, *Charlie Chaplin*, p 86.

42. *Variety*, June 22, 1917, p. 20; as noted in a page one article the same day, actors of draft age were required to obtain a permit from the War Department before leaving the country. As a British subject, Chaplin could refuse the U.S. draft, but at the price of exile.

43. James E. Hilbert, "A Day on Location With Charlie Chaplin," *Motion Picture News*, Nov. 1917 (but describes interview of July 13), RLC, vol. 110.

44. Maland, *Chaplin and American Culture*, p. 37. Chaplin's statement is cited by Maland from the Feb. 23, 1918, issue of *Pictures and Picturegoer.*

Chapter 6 "Camouflage"

1. *MA*, p. 189.

2. Rob Wagner, "Mr. Charles Spencer Chaplin: The Man You Don't Know," *Ladies Home Journal*, Aug. 1918, vol. 111, RLC.

3. *MA*, p. 204

4. Arvidson, *When the Movies Were Young*, pp. 237–38.

5. Marion, *Off with Their Heads!*, p. 52.

6. *MA*, pp. 206–7.

7. *New York Tribune*, Dec. 30, 1917, vol. 111, RLC.

8. *MA*, p. 210.

9. *New York Tribune*, Apr. 9, 1918, clipping, WHS.

10. *New York American Magazine,* May 1, 1918, vol. 111, RLC.

11. *MA*, pp. 220–221.

12. Sutherland interview, COH.

13. *Boston Post*, Mar. 21, 1920, vol. 111, RLC.

14. *MA*, p. 226. Chaplin, whose memory for first meetings is invariably unreliable, says he met Mildred at a party given by Samuel Goldwyn—Sutherland and

Mildred are quite specific about the Owen Moore party, however. Chaplin also gives Mildred's age as "almost nineteen."

15. *Boston Post*, Mar. 21, 1920.

16. *New York Times*, Nov. 10, 1919.

17. *CHLA*, p. 247

18. *Toledo Blade*, Aug. 4, 1920, RLC, vol. 111.

19. *MA*, pp. 221–22.

20. *Moving Picture World*, Feb. 1, 1919. For a more complete account of UA's founding see Tino Balio, *United Artists: The Company Built by the Stars* (Madison: University of Wisconsin Press, 1976).

21. O'Brien Legal File, Box 209, Tax Assessment File, United Artists Collection, WHS.

22. Max Eastman, *Great Companions: Critical Memoirs of Some Famous Friends* (London: Museum Press, 1959), pp. 213–14.

23. William L. O'Neill, *The Last Romantic: A Life of Max Eastman* (New York: Oxford University Press, 1978), p. 66.

24. Eastman, *Great Companions*, p. 210.

25. Lita Grey Chaplin, *My Life with Chaplin* (New York: Bernard Geis, 1966), p. 298.

26. Raymond Lee, "I was a Chaplin Kid," *Classic Film Collector* 17 (Winter-Spring, 1967), Chaplin file, 1960–69, MoMA.

27. Ibid.

Chapter 7 "The Black Panther"

1. ME to FD, May 26, 1919, Florence Deshon Collection, Max Eastman Papers, LILLY.

2. Eastman, *Great Companions*, p. 219.

3. FD to ME, 24, 1919, Deshon Collection, Max Eastman Papers, LILLY.

4. ME to FD, Dec. 26, 1919, ibid.

5. Interview with Nixola Greeley-Smith, *New York World*, Feb. 19, 1916, vol. 110, RLC.

6. FD to ME, Jan. 7, 1920, Deshon Collection, Max Eastman Papers, LILLY.

7. FD to ME, Feb. 12, 1920, ibid.

8. FD to ME, Feb. 12, 1920, ibid.

9. Robinson details the vagaries of the production schedule; see *CHLA*, pp. 255–59.

10. FD to ME, Feb. 19, 1920, ibid.

11. FD to ME, Mar. 29, 1920, ibid.

12. Gerith von Ulm, *Charlie Chaplin, King of Tragedy* (Boise, Idaho: Caxton, 1940), p. 108.

13. Irene Mayer Selznick, *A Private View* (New York: Alfred A. Knopf, 1983),

p. 32; Marjorie Daw, "A Little Journey to the Home of Mr. and Mrs. Charles Chaplin," *Detroit Journal* (and syndicated), June 31, 1920.

14. Sutherland interview, pp. 44–45, COH.

15. *Toledo Blade*, Aug. 4, 1920, RLC, vol. 111.

16. FD to ME, July 8, 1920, Deshon Collection, Max Eastman Papers, LILLY.

17. *CHLA*, p. 339.

18. *New York Times*, Aug. 11, 1920, p. 18.

18. Frank Harris, *Contemporary Portraits: Fourth Series* (New York: Brentano's, 1923), pp. 60–63.

20. John McCabe, *Charlie Chaplin* (New York: Doubleday, 1978; reprint, London: Robson, 1992), p. 108.

Chapter 8 "A Total Stranger to Life"

1. Eastman, *Love and Revolution*, p. 206.

2. Ibid., p. 207.

3. Ibid. Eastman says that Florence remained with him for two months after Chaplin's return to Los Angeles. Actually, as their correspondence makes clear, it was Florence who left New York first, on October 6, 1920, and Chaplin who remained in New York for about three more months.

4. FD to ME, Oct. 10, 1920, Deshon Collection, Max Eastman Papers, LILLY.

5. Gorham Munson, *The Awakening Twenties* (Baton Rouge: Louisiana State University Press, 1985), p. 233.

6. Benjamin de Casseres, "The Hamlet-Like Nature of Charlie Chaplin," *New York Times*, Dec. 12, 1920, sec. 3, p. 5.

7. Eastman, *Love and Revolution*, p. 231.

8. Theodore Huff, *Charlie Chaplin* (New York: Henry Schuman, 1951), pp. 148–49.

9. FD to ME, June 17, 1921, Deshon Collection, Max Eastman Papers, LILLY.

10. ME to FD, undated letter from the first half of July 1921, ibid.

11. Visa Name Files, 1914–40, 811.111 Chaplin, Mrs. H[annah], 1921. Record Group: 059 State. NARA-Pacific Southwest.

12. Eastman, *Great Companions*, pp. 220–21.

13. Frederick James Smith, "Shadowland," undated clipping (but published shortly after release of *The Kid*), WHS.

14. *Toledo Blade*, Jan. 22, 1922, vol. 111, RLC.

15. *MA*, p. 267; see also Charles Chaplin, "A Comedian Sees the World," *Woman's Home Companion*, part 1, Sept. 1933, p. 9.

16. It seems almost cruel to point out that Frank's admiration for Chaplin's

work flowered only after he learned that Chaplin was a friend of people he knew, and a man who shared his tastes and politics. In 1917 Frank wrote, "Chaplin is a brilliant clown, but he is also an unhealthy one." In 1919, even as word spread of Chaplin's left-wing sympathies, he opined, "His art is indeed a symbol of health in a complexly moral world." His discovery that Chaplin admired Schopenhauer opened yet another door of appreciation.

17. A year earlier Max Eastman had suggested to Florence that she take Charlie to see the clown Grock, who was appearing in Los Angeles. Assuming she did so, this would not have been Chaplin's first exposure to his friends' enthusiasm for clowns.

18. Alexander Trachtenberg, ed. *The Memoirs of Waldo Frank* (Amherst: University of Massachusetts, 1973).

19. Charles Chaplin, *My Trip Abroad* (New York: Harper & Row, 1922). Citations in the following pages are from the British edition, published as *My Wonderful Visit* (London: Hurst & Blackett, 1922).

20. Cami, "Charlot jouera-t-il Napoléon???" *Les Chroniques du Jour: numero double consacré a Charlot* 7, nos. 7–8 (Dec. 31, 1926).

21. Interview with Mirel Bercovici, Feb. 3, 1995.

22. *My Wonderful Visit*, p. 36 and passim. Chaplin entered the United States in 1910 and 1912 as a nonimmigrant alien, and thus did not pass through Ellis Island. The entries on the ship's manifest from 1912 are all in Alf Reeves's handwriting, and one would assume that he handled the formalities for his entire troupe.

23. Anita Leslie, *Clare Sheridan* (New York: Doubleday, 1977), p.175.

24. Ibid., pp. 180–81.

25. Munson, *The Awakening Twenties*, p. 233.

26. *CHLA*, p. 296.

27. Sidney D. Kirkpatrick points out several connections between Chaplin and Taylor: both had dated Claire Windsor; they shared the same accountant, and so on. Perhaps most important was the connection with Edward Knoblock, Charlie's "great friend"—as he put it. A number of factors in the Taylor murder suggested that his death was related to his homosexuality. His butler had recently been arrested for soliciting in a public park, perhaps on Taylor's behalf. The suspect seen leaving Taylor's house on the night he died was described as a man who had an "effeminate" walk and wore heavy stage makeup. Kirkpatrick, however, concludes that the killer was a woman in man's clothing—specfically, the mother of Paramount star Mary Miles Minter. See Sidney D. Kirkpatrick, *A Cast of Killers* (New York: E.P. Dutton, 1986).

28. Report by A. A. Hopkins to Mr. Hood, Aug. 15, 1922. Originally LA Bureau File 180/10; 100–127090, Section 1, FBI.

29. Hays to Wm. J. Burns, Director, Sept. 6, 1922, 100–127090, Section 1, FBI.

30. 100–127090, Section 1, FBI. Both a photostat of the original Jan. 12, 1932, *Pravda* review and a translation credited to C. L. McMahon are included.

31. Statement of Max Eastman to INS, Oct. 22, 1952, INS file 0030-27798, Max Eastman Papers, LILLY.

Chapter 9 *A Woman of Paris*

1. "Eastman Denies Rift with Miss Deshon," *New York Times*, Feb. 6, 1922; see also "Actress Dies of Gas Poison," Feb. 5, 1922.

2. Marie Howe to Max Eastman, Feb. 6, 1922; Marie Alamo Thomas to Eastman, Feb. 6, 1922, Deshon Collection, Max Eastman Papers, LILLY.

3. Eastman, *Great Companions*, pp. 236–37.

4. *MA*, p. 297.

5. According to Jerry Epstein's memoir of Chaplin, he was familiar with the original Willie Howard routine, and often quoted the line, "Comes the revolution, you'll eat strawberries and cream. . . ." See Jerry Epstein, *Remembering Charlie: A Pictorial Biography* (New York: Doubleday, 1989).

6. *MA*, p. 298.

7. Ibid., p. 277.

8. Pola Negri, *Memoirs of a Star* (New York: Doubleday, 1970), Quotations in the following section are from pp. 209 ff.

9. Ibid. p. 215.

10. Ibid. p. 219.

11. Ibid.

12. CCMM, sec. 9, p. 7.

13. Normand Zierold, *Sex Goddesses of the Silent Screen* (Chicago: Regnery, 1973), p. 8.

14. *MA*, p. 301.

15. CCMM, sec. 9, p. 8.

16. Adolphe Menjou and M. M. Musselman, *It Took Nine Tailors* (New York: Whittlesy House/McGraw-Hill, 1948), pp. 106–15.

17. Konrad Bercovici, "Charlie Chaplin—An Authorized Interview," *Collier's*, Aug. 15, 1925, p. 5.

18. Jean-Pierre Liégeois, *Gypsies: An Illustrated History* (London: Al Saqi Books, 1986), pp. 82–83.

19. Interview with Mirel Bercovici.

20. Jim Tully, "The Real-Life Story of Charlie Chaplin," *Pictorial Review*, Jan. 1927, p. 34.

21. Ibid., April, 1927, p. 22.

22. Brom Weber, ed. *The Letters of Hart Crane*, 1916–1932 (New York: Hermitage House, 1951), p. 157.

23. Ibid., pp. 51–22.

24. For the trial see *New York Times*, Jan. 19, p. 10; Jan 22, p. 21; and Jan. 23, p. 21. Other stories on the case appeared on Jan. 2, p. 1; Jan. 3, p. 1; Jan. 4, p. 17; Jan. 5, p. 3; Jan. 6, sec. 1, part 2, p. 5; Jan. 8, p. 25; Jan. 10, p. 18; and Feb. 7, p. 19.

Chapter 10 *The Gold Rush*

1. *Variety*, Mar. 8, 1950.

2. Eddie Manson, typescript, "Charlie Chaplin's Secrets," p. 3. MHL.

3. Sutherland interview, COH.

4. CCMM, sec. 9, p. 21.

5. Sutherland interview, COH.

6. Jim Tully, "The Real Life Story of Charlie Chaplin," *Pictorial Review*, Mar. 1927, p. 54.

7. Jim Tully, *A Dozen and One*, (Hollywood: Murrary & Gee, 1943), p. 28.

8. Lita Grey Chaplin, *My Life with Chaplin*, pp. 102–3.

9. Lyons, "Roland H. Totheroh Interviewed," p. 285.

10. Sutherland interview, COH.

11. Pickford to O'Brien, June 18, 1923, O'Brien Legal File, UA.

12. Ibid., July 5, 1922.

13. O'Brien memo, Oct. 17, 1923, Box 209, Folder 14, ibid.

14. Adela Rogers St. Johns, *The Honeycomb* (Garden City, N.Y.: Doubleday, 1969), p. 192.

15. Statement released by Chaplin's studio to the press in January 1926.

16. Fred Lawrence Guiles, *Marion Davies* (New York: McGraw Hill, 1972), pp. 184–96. Guiles interviewed Vera Burnett and Eleanor Boardman d'Arrast, as well as numerous Davies relatives and friends. Unfortunately his account has the yacht party beginning on Tuesday, Nov. 18. See also W. A. Swanberg, *Citizen Hearst* (New York: Scribner's, 1961), pp. 374–75.

17. Guiles, pp. 191–92,

18. St. Johns, p. 191.

19. Ibid., 189–90.

20. *New York Times*, Dec. 11, 1924.

21. Von Ulm, *King of Tragedy,* p. 207.

22. Lita Grey Chaplin, *My Life with Chaplin,* p. 4.

23. *CHLA*, 353–54.

24. Raoul Sobel and David Francis, *Chaplin: Genesis of a Clown* (New York: Horizon Press, 1978), p. 179.

25. *CHLA,* p. 354.

26. *Variety*, July 1, 1925.

27. *New York Daily Mirror*, July 22, 1925, p. 25; for rumors of Swain's disappearance, see July 13, p. 17.

28. CCMM, sec. 9, p. 27. Crocker heard the story from d'Arrast; Chaplin gives his version of the "nervous breakdown" in *MA*, p. 305. The diagnostic criteria for hypomania are summarized in Kay Redfield Jamison's *Touched with Fire: Manic Depressive Illness and the Artistic Temperament* (New York: Free Press, 1993), pp. 13–14, 265.

29. With his usual disregard for chronology, Chaplin says in his autobiography that this incident happened two days before he returned to Los Angeles. This would put the visit to Coney Island in October, by which time New York was in the grip of an early snowstorm; there were no swimmers and certainly no lifeguards on the beach at this time. A body *was* recovered off Rockaway Point (not Coney Island) on August 18, 1925, but the victim was a boater, not a swimmer. In short, Chaplin may have seen swimmers pulled out of the water, but he did not see anyone die.

30. Louise Brooks, "Charlie Chaplin Remembered," *Film Culture* 40 (Spring 1966): 5–6. See also Barry Paris, *Louise Brooks* (New York: Alfred A. Knopf, 1989), pp. 107–9, which draws on later comments by Brooks in conversation with Kenneth Tynan and her correspondence with film historian Kevin Brownlow. Also of interest is "Marion Davies' Niece," in Brooks's *Lulu in Hollywood* (New York: Alfred A. Knopf, 1982).

31. Paris, *Louise Brooks*, p. 110.

32. *New York Mirror*, Sept, 25, 1925, p. 29.

33. *New York Mirror*, Sept, 2, 1925, p. 2.

34. Manson, "Charlie Chaplin's Secrets," p. 104.

Chapter 11   *The Circus*

1. Balio, *United Artists*, p. 61.

2. Ibid., p. 62.

3. *New York Times*, Nov. 29, 1925, p. 29.

4. Maurice Willson Disher, *Clowns & Pantomimes* (1925; reprint, New York: Benjamin Blom, 1968), p. 91 passim.

5. CCMM, sec. 10.

6. *Daily Mirror*, Aug. 25, p. 27.

7. Production schedules for *The Circus* are excerpted on the CBS/Fox laser disc reissue, prod. David H. Shepard, 72 mins., CBS/FOX Video, 1993.

8. Lita Grey Chaplin, *My Life with Chaplin*, pp. 213–15.

9. Ibid., pp. 227, 225.

10. CCMM, sec. 10, p. 17.

11. Rob Wagner, "Hollywood," Manuscript draft, Box 21, Robert Leicester Wagner Papers, UCLA.

12. Lyons, "Roland H. Totheroh Interviewed," p. 273.

13. Ibid.

14. Tax assessor's report and memoranda, O'Brien Legal File, Box 209, UA.

15. Memo, 1/29/27, Box 207–4, ibid.

16. Manson, "Charlie Chaplin's Secrets," pp. 110–11.

17. *New York Herald Tribune*, Dec. 11, 1926, clipping, DeMott Collection, BR.

18. Ed Sullivan, ed., *Chaplin vs. Chaplin* (Los Angeles: Marvin Miller Enterprises, May 1965). A reprint of the original divorce complaint and Chaplin's reply appear on p. 9.

19. Lyons, "Roland H. Totheroh Interviewed, p. 273.

20. *CHLA*, p. 376.

21. Lyons, "Roland H. Totheroh Interviewed, pp. 273–74.

22. "Picking on Charlie Chaplin," *The New Yorker*, July 23, 1927, p. 18, DeMott Collection, BR. This "Talk of the Town" item was written by Chaplin's close friend, New Yorker cartoonist Ralph Barton. See Bruce Kellner, *The Last Dandy, Ralph Barton: American Artist, 1891–1931* (Columbia: University of Missouri Press, 1991).

23. *CHLA*, p. 383.

Chapter 12 *City Lights*

1. Wagner to Sinclair, July 30, 1928, Box 17, Robert Leicester Wagner Papers, UCLA.

2. The manuscript is not among his papers at UCLA, and its whereabouts are unknown.

3. Harry Crocker, typescript, "I Read You Every Morning . . . Small Talk by Great People," Folder Six, Harry Crocker Collection, MHL. See especially pp. 7–8, 63, 154–55, 182, 248.

4. CCMM, sec. 9, p. 9.

5. Arthur Gelb and Barbara Gelb, *O'Neill* (New York: Harper & Brothers, 1962), pp. 617–18.

6. Charles Chaplin Jr., with N. and M. Raw, *My Father, Charlie Chaplin* (New York: Random House, 1960), p. 72.

7. Von Ulm, *King of Tragedy*, p. 98; also, Rob Wagner, "Mr. Charles Spencer Chaplin: The Man You Don't Know," *Ladies' Home Journal*, Aug. 1918, RLC, vol. 111.

8. Konrad Bercovici, "A Day with Charlie Chaplin," *Harper's Monthly Magazine*, Dec. 1928, pp. 42–49.

9. Ibid.

10. Stevenson also wrote a story, "David and Goliath"—perhaps the inspiration for the David v. Goliath sermon in *The Pilgrim*.

11. Harold Lloyd interview, COH.

12. Kevin Brownlow, *The Parade's Gone By* (New York: Alfred A. Knopf, 1968; reprint, Berkeley: University of California, 1975), p. 570.

13. Ibid., p. 573.

14. See E. V. Durling, *New York Journal,* June 24, 1957; *Variety,* Jan. 2, 1931, clippings, Sydney Chaplin file, BR.

15. *MA,* p. 325.

16. *New York Times,* Mar, 19, 1928, p. 23; also *Variety,* Apr. 4, 1928, as discussed in Maland, *Chaplin and American Culture,* pp. 111–12.

17. Gladys Hall, "Charlie Chaplin Attacks the Talkies," *Motion Picture Magazine,* May 1929; see also for Jolson's reply, August 1929.

18. Fairbanks interview, New York City, Apr. 7, 1993.

19. Gerard Molyneaux, *Charles Chaplin's City Lights* (New York: Garland, 1983), p. 50.

20. Upton Sinclair's correspondence with Kisch is found in the Sinclair Collection, LILLY. For background on Kisch and the Comintern's focus on the film industry, see Stephen Koch, *Double Lives* (New York: Free Press, 1994). The ditty was recalled by Joel Agee, to the author.

21. Ivor Montagu, *With Eisenstein in Hollywood* (New York: International Publishers, 1967), p. 28; also G. V. Aleksandrov, *Epokha i Kino* [The epoch and cinema] (Moscow: Politicheskaya Literatura Pub., 1976), 0. 116.

22. Quotations are from the English translation of the article, which appeared as: Egon Erwin Kisch, "I Work with Chaplin," *Living Age,* Oct. 15, 1929, pp. 230–35.

23. Montagu, *With Eisenstein,* p. 66.

24. Harry Geduld and Ronald Gottesman, *The Making and Unmaking of* Que Viva Mexico! (Bloomington: Indiana University Press, 1970), p. 11.

25. Sergei Eisenstein, "Charlie the Kid," in *Film Essays and a Lecture,* Jay Leyda, ed. (Princeton, N.J.: Princeton University Press, 1982), pp. 108–39.

26. Léon Moussinac. *Sergei Eisenstein* (New York: Crown, 1970). p. 50.

27. Montagu, *With Eisenstein,* pp. 96–97.

28. Ibid.

29. Wagner to Sinclair, Mar. 24, 1931, Upton Sinclair Papers, LILLY.

30. Eisenstein, "Charlie the Kid," p. 29.

31. Molyneaux, *Charles Chaplin's City Lights,* p. 2.

32. Carlyle Robinson, *La Vérité sur Charlie Chaplin: Sa vie, ses amours, ses déboirs* (Paris: Société Parisienne, 1933), p. 39; *CHLA,* pp. 406–7. The screen test of Georgia Hale and an interview with Virginia Cherrill can be seen in Brownlow and Gill's *Unknown Chaplin.*

33. *Rob Wagner's Beverly Hills Script,* Feb. 7, 1931, vol. 4, Robert Leicester Wagner Collection, UCLA.

34. Alexander Bakshy, "Charlie Chaplin Falters," *Nation,* Mar. 4, 1931, Chaplin file, MoMA; *Variety,* Feb. 11, 1931, p. 14.

Chapter 13 "Disillusion of Love, Fame and Fortune

1. Charles Chaplin, "A Comedian Sees the World," *Woman's Home Companion*, Sept. 1933, p. 7. This serialized article continued monthly through Jan. 1934.

2. Carlyle Robinson, *La Vérité,* p. 180.

3. "A Comedian Sees the World," p. 88.

4. *New York Times*, May 21, 1931, p. 1.

5. Charles Chaplin, "A Comedian Sees the World," part 2, Oct. 1933, p. 16.

6. *New York Times*, Mar. 15, 1931, p. 12.

7. *Les Plus Beaux Yeux du Monde,* in Solomon A. Rhodes, ed., *Contemporary French Theater* (New York: Crofts, 1942).

8. *New York Times,* Mar. 27, p. 29.

9. Carlyle Robinson, *La Vérité,* p. 226.

10. *CHLA,* p. 434, quoting an unsourced interview by Reeves with Kathryn Hayden, a journalist who was a favorite of Chaplin and his aides.

11. May Reeves, *Charlie Chaplin Intime* (Paris: Gallimard, 1935).

12. Alf Reeves to Wagner, July 27, 1931, Box 17, Robert Leicester Wagner Papers, UCLA. Reeves was writing to congratulate Wagner on an article putting down antismoking activists—those "gasper glarers," he called them. Gasper was Cockney slang for a cigarette.

13. CCMM, sec. 14, p. 10.

14. The interview was excerpted in "John Bull Hit by a Chaplin Pie," *Literary Digest*, May 23, 1931, p. 10.

15. *Comoedia*, May 23, 1931, translated excerpt in Box 208, File 10, O'Brien Legal File, UA.

16. "John Bull Hit,"*Literary Digest,*

17. Guedalla to Silverstone, Oct. 30, 1931; May Shepherd v. Chaplin, Box 208, File 10, O'Brien Legal File.

18. *A Comedian Sees the World*, part 4 (Dec. 1933), p. 23.

19. *New York Times*, June 14, 1932, p. 26.

20. Von Ulm, *King of Tragedy,* p. 370; *New York Times,* Jun. 14, 1932, p. 26.

Chapter 14 *Modern Times*

1. Lyons, "Roland H. Totheroh Interviewed." Chaplin says in his autobiography that he met Paulette at a party aboard Joe Schenck's 138-foot yacht, *Invader*. Apparently such a party did take place, but he already knew Paulette and the two of them, along with Schenck's girlfriend of the moment, were the only guests.

2. "Lucky Star," *Picture News* (Sunday Magazine supplement of *PM*) June 30, 1946, Goddard file, MoMA.

3. Fairbanks interview, New York City, Apr. 7, 1993.

4. Joe Morella and Edward Z. Epstein, *Paulette* (New York: St. Martin's Press, 1985), p. 13.

5. "Lucky Star."

6. Charles Chaplin Jr., *My Father*, p. 60.

7. Ibid., p. 57.

8. Anthony Slide, ed., *The Best of Rob Wagner's Script* (Metuchen, N.J.: Scarecrow Press, 1985), p. 27.

9. Ibid., pp. 82–87. See also vol. 20, no. 476, Sept. 1938, Wagner Collection, UCLA.

10. Cooke, *Six Men*, pp. 23–33.

11. David H. Shepard, producer, archival materials for *Modern Times*, prod. David H. Shepard, 103 mins., CBS/FOX Video, 1992, laser disc.

12. Chaplin to Sinclair, Dec. 4, 1933, Upton Sinclair Papers, LILLY.

13. Wagner to Sinclair, Dec. 8, 1933, ibid.

14. Wagner to Browne, Sept. 25, 1934, Box 17, Robert Leicester Wagner Papers, UCLA.

15. Upton Sinclair, typescript review of Chaplin's *My Autobiography*, written for the *Los Angeles Times*, Sinclair Papers, LILLY. Sinclair says the rally was at Grauman's Theater, though other accounts place it at the Shrine Auditorium, the usual venue for left-wing fund-raisers.

16. Cooke, *Six Men*, pp. 41–42.

17. Ronald L. Davis, interview with David Raksin, SMU, p. 36.

18. David Raksin interview, Shepard archival materials, *Modern Times*.

19. Davis interview, SMU.

20. Koch, *Double Lives*, p. 79.

21. Untitled typescript, Box 21, Wagner Papers, UCLA.

22. Leon Dennett, trans., "Charlie Chaplin's New Picture," *New Masses*, Sept. 24, 1936, pp. 29–30.

23. Terry Ramsaye, "Chaplin Ridicules Reds' Claim," *Motion Picture Herald*, Dec. 7, 1935, pp. 13–14. Ramsaye was editor of the *Herald*.

24. Don Herold, *Life*, Apr. 1939, p. 20; reprinted in Slide, *The Best of Rob Wagner's Script*.

25. Louis Goldblatt interview, COH.

Chapter 15 *The Great Dictator*

1. Unidentified clipping from the Hearst press, Dec. 16, 1937, Goddard file, MoMA.

2. Mirel Bercovici recalled that her father was in the restaurant and came home and told her mother, "You wouldn't believe what they were doing!" He added that a waiter quickly set up a folding screen around Goddard and Lubitsch's table.

3. Testimony of Konrad Bercovici, trial transcript, p. 109. *Bercovici* v. *Chaplin*, Civil Case 14–190, NARA (NY).

4. Ibid., p. 257.

5. Eastman, *Great Companions*, pp. 226–28.

6. Tim Durant interview, 31–68496, Section 4, p. 57, FBI.

7. Eastman, *Great Companions*, pp. 226–28.

8. George Charensol, "To Fight the Machine," Introduction to *À Nous la Liberté and Entr'Acte: Films by René Clair*, translated by Richard Jacques and Nicola Hayden (New York: Simon & Schuster, 1970).

9. Frohlich to Alf Reeves, Mar. 30, 1939, O'Brien Legal Files, Box 208-12, United Artists Collection, WHS.

10. *Films Sonores Tobis, Société Anonyme* v. *Charles Chaplin, et al.*, E. 85–125, NARA (NY).

11. Testimony of Melvyn Douglas, trial transcript, p. 478, *Bercovici* v. *Chaplin*.

12. Deposition of Charles Chaplin, ibid., p. 136.

13. Deposition of Daniel James, ibid., p. 267. See also James's deposition in *Carter de Haven* v. *Charles Chaplin & United Artists Corporation*, Civ. 13–366, U.S. Dist. Court, Southern Dist. of N.Y., NARA (NY).

14. James Deposition, *De Haven* v. *Chaplin*, p. 16.

15. Ibid., p. 178.

16. Selznick, *A Private View*, p. 214.

17. Rudy Behlmer, ed., *Memo from David O. Selznick* (New York: Viking Press, 1972), p. 181–82.

18. Jack Oakie, *Jack Oakie's Double Takes* (San Francisco: Strawberry Hill Press, 1980), pp. 72–73.

19. Shepard archival materials supplement, chap. 25, CBS/FOX Video laser disc edition of *The Great Dictator*, 1993.

20. Charles Higham, *Hollywood Cameramen: Sources of Light* (Bloomington: Indiana University Press, 1970), p. 131. Struss is referring to two cameras placed at different angles. Chaplin had long used a second camera to produce a duplicate negative.

21. CCMM, sec. 11, p. 27.

22. Notes from the speech are among the archival materials included on the laser disc edition of *The Great Dictator*.

23. *Daily Worker*, Oct. 16, 1940.

24. *MA*, p. 405.

25. Chaplin deposition, *Bercovici* v. Chaplin, pp. 25–33. The press conference was reported in the *New York Daily Mirror*, Nov. 1, 1941.

26. Chaplin deposition, Bercovici vs. Chaplin, p. 258.

27. Ibid., pp. 255-56.

28. Alf Reeves to Paul O'Brien, June 28, 1941, O'Brien Legal File, Box 207, United Artists Collection, WHS.

Chapter 16 *Shadow and Substance*

1. Morella and Epstein, *Paulette*, p. 66.

2. Pickford to Chaplin, Oct. 18, 1943, O'Brien Legal Files, Folder 209-6. United Artists Collection, WHS.

3. Pickford to Charles Schwartz, Nov. 9, 1943, ibid.

4. 31–68496, Section 6, p. 10, FBI. Quotations in this section are taken from Barry's statements of Jan. 7, 10, & 11, FBI.

5. *MA*, p. 413–14.

6. 31–68496, Section 4, p. 30, FBI.

7. Statement of Joan Berry [*sic*], 31–68496, sec. 6, p. 13, FBI.

8. Hedda Hopper, June 2, 1943, clipping (1940-49), MoMA. Hopper here reprints her earlier column with "I told you so" commentary.

9. 31–68496, Section 4, pp. 50–59.

10. N. Litkin, "Kak v kino. Zapiski kinoooperatora" (Like in the movies. Notes of a camerman), *Molodaya Gvarkiia (Young Guards) Journal* (1985), no. 3.

11. *MA*, pp. 408–9.

12. V. Pavlichenko, "V trudnye gody" (Over difficult years), *Iskisstvo Kino* (1959), no. 5, p. 156.

13. Reprint issued by the Greater New York Industrial Council, Chaplin file, 1940–49, MoMA.

14. 100–127090–25, p. 10, FBI.

15. *New York World-Telegram*, Dec. 21, 1942.

16. *Rob Wagner's Script* 29, no. 667, Nov. 20, 1943, Robert Leicester Wagner Papers, UCLA.

Chapter 17 "The Public Wants a Victim!"

1. Lyons, "Roland H. Totheroh Interviewed," pp. 274–75.

2. O'Neill to Weinberger, April 23, 1928. In Travis Bogard and Jackson R. Breyer, eds., *Selected Letters of Eugene O'Neill* (New Haven: Yale University Press, 1988). p. 296.

3. Thomas B. Morgan, "The May-December Marriage of Charlie Chaplin," 1958 clipping, Chaplin file, 1950–59, MoMA.

4. Bogard and Breyer, *Selected Letters of Eugene O'Neill*, p. 533.

5. 100–127090, Section 3, p. 36, FBI.

6. Att. Gen. Biddle to Hon. Samuel Dickstein, Nov. 13, 1943; Arden's testimony and supporting letters are from the Bill Files of the 77th and 78th Congresses, 77-A-D14 and 78-A-D12, NARA Legislative Archives Division.

7. Charles Chaplin Jr., *My Father*, p. 272.

8. 31–68496, Section 8, p. 265, FBI.

9. Interview with Florabel Muir, 31–68496, sec. 8, p. 273, FBI.

10. Ibid.,sec. 6, pp. 43–44.

11. Summary report of Nov. 9, 1943. pp. 32–34, 31–68496. Section 1.

12. "Memorandum for the Director: Re Charles Chaplin," from R. B. Hood, Special Agent in Charge (SAC), June 24, 1943, 31–68496. Section 1. This memo reflects a lengthy telephone conversation between a longtime friend of Chaplin and an unidentified government employee, presumably an FBI agent in Los Angeles. The source's name and the name of the person he spoke with have been blacked out, but the source identifies himself as the one who arranged the Chaplin-O'Neill wedding and is clearly, from this and other statements, identifiable as Harry Crocker.

13. Hood to Director, May 11, 1944, 31–68496, sec. 5, FBI.

14. The annotation and excerpt are dated April 7, 1932. See also "Memo for the Director, Re: Theodore Dreiser" from the Detroit office, dated Jan. 7, 1943," and following documents in Dreiser's FBI files, 100–54750-X.

15. "Memorandum for Mr. Tamm, Re: Charles Chaplin," Aug. 26, 1943, 31–68496, sec. 1, FBI.

16. Interview with Edward Chaney, 31–684–96, sec. 8, p. 270, FBI.

17. *New York Daily Mirror*, Feb. 15, 1944; also *Los Angeles Times-Herald, Washington Times-Herald, Washington Post*, same date. Unpaged clippings, 31–68496, sub. A, sec. 1, FBI.

18. *Washington-Times Herald,* Ibid.

19. *Daily Worker*, Apr. 3, 1944, p. 5.

20. *New York Daily News*, Feb. 19, 1944, and Westbrook Pegler's syndicated column, Feb. 21, 1944, unpaged clippings, 31–68496, Section 3, FBI.

21. "Joan Berry Recalled to Witness Stand in Chaplin Trial," *Washington Star,* Mar. 24, 1944, p. 2; "Chaplin Court Bars Quiz on Other Man," *Washington Post,* Mar. 23, 1944, p. 5; also, Lyons, "Roland H. Totheroh Interviewed."

22. *Washington Times-Herald*, Apr. 4, 1944. 31–68496, Sub A, Section 2.

23. "Memorandum for Mr. Tolson, Mr. Tamm & Mr. Rosen," Apr. 11, 1944, 31–68496, Section 6, FBI.

24. R. B. Hood to Hoover, May 11, 1944, ibid.

25. Hood to Director, Dec. 22, 1943, 31–68496, Section 2.

26. V. Mikosha, *Gody I strany. Zapiski kinooperatora* [Years and countries: Notes of a cameraman] (Moscow: Iskusstvo Publishers, 1967).

27. *Moscow News*, Apr. 29, 1944. Chaplin file, 1940–49, MoMA.

Chapter 18 *Ladykiller*

1. Orson Welles and Peter Bogdanovich, *This Is Orson Welles* (New York: HarperCollins, 1992), p. 135.

2. Walter Hasenclever, "Napoleon and Landru: An Imaginary Dialogue," *Living Age*, Dec. 1929, pp. 433–40.

3. *Script*, Jan. 8, 1944, sub. A, sec. 1, 31–68496, FBI.

4. Memorandum for the Director, June 24, 1943, R. B. Hood, SAC; see also Carol Matthau, *Among the Porcupines* (New York: Turtle Bay/Random House, 1992), p. 86.

5. *New York Post*, June 7, 1944, unbylined clipping, Chaplin file, 1940-49, MoMA.

6. Virginia MacPherson, "Joan's Version of Chaplin Romance," *New York Daily Mirror*, Dec. 21, 1944, p. 2; for additional reports of the paternity suit see 31–68496, sub. A, sec. 2, FBI.

7. Charles Chaplin Jr., *My Father*, p. 298.

8. *Washington News*, Apr. 19, 1945.

9. Frank Deford, *Big Bill Tilden: The Triumphs and the Tragedy* (New York: Simon & Schuster, 1976), p. 258 and chaps. 17 and 18, passim.

10. Viola Hegyi Swisher, "Getting Serious," *After Dark*, Mar. 1980. Martha Raye file, MoMA.

11. Ibid.

12. Chaplin to Breen, Mar. 5, 1946, MPPA Collection, MHL.

13. Dorothy Kilgallen's column, Mar. 22, 1947, Chaplin file, 1941–49, MoMA.

14. John Fuegi, *Brecht & Company: Sex, Politics and the Making of Modern Drama* (New York: Grove Press, 1994) p. 474.

15. The testimony of Ruth Fischer is excerpted in Eric Bentley, ed., *Thirty Years of Treason* (New York: Viking, 1973), pp. 61–73. For a summary of the Eisler affair, see Walter Goodman, *The Committee* (New York: Farrar, Straus & Giroux, 1968), chap. 7.

16. Hans Bunge, *Fragen sie mich über Brecht: Hanns Eisler im Gespräch* (Ask me about Brecht: Hanns Eisler in conversation) (Munich: Rogner & Bernard, 1970), pp. 58–59.

17. Charles Silver, *Charles Chaplin: An Appreciation* (New York: Museum of Modern Art, 1989), p. 53.

18. Memo to Advertising, Mar. 25, 1947, Section 6D, Box 6–6, United Artists Collection, WHS.

19. Ibid.

20. *New York Herald Tribune*, Apr. 12, 1947, p. 8; *The New Yorker*, Apr. 19, 1947, p. 42.

21. Welles and Bogdanovich, *This Is Orson Welles*, p. 136.

22. "Charlie Chaplin's Monsieur Verdoux Press Conference," Introduction by George Wallach, *Film Comment* (Winter 1969), pp. 34–42. Transcript of tape recorded by Wallach for radio broadcast. The article mistakenly gives the date of the press conference as April 12.

23. Ibid.

24. Agee's three-part review originally appeared in *The Nation* on May 31, June 14, and June 21, 1947. It is reprinted in *Agee on Film* (New York: Grosset & Dunlap, 1967), vol. 1, pp. 252–62.

25. Bercovici had filed suit as a resident of Connecticut. Chaplin's attorneys visited Bercovici's home to take a deposition, noticed that it appeared to be in New York State, and decided that they could get the suit dismissed on a technicality. What they didn't realize was that Bercovici's property straddled the state line. His claim to be a Connecticut resident was upheld by the court.

26. Chaplin repeated this story in his autobiography, much to the distress of Bercovici's daughters, who solicited a letter from Nizer confirming their memory of the circumstances. During the trial even the leftish newspaper *PM*, sympathetic to Chaplin, took note of his poor performance on the witness stand. The idea that he would spend six years and thousands in legal fees only to settle in order to accommodate the judge's schedule is ridiculous.

27. Statement of Max Eastman to INS, Oct. 22, 1952, NS file 0030–27798, Max Eastman Papers, LILLY.

28. Patrick McGilligan, *Backstory Two: Interviews with Screenwriters of the 1940s and 1950s* (Berkeley: University of California Press, 1991).

29. *New York Times*, July 21, 1947, p. 12.

30. For Eisler's testimony, see Bentley, *Thirty Years of Treason*, pp. 73–105.

31. Arnaud d'Usseau, "Chaplin's Monsieur Verdoux," *Mainstream* 1 (Summer 1947), pp. 307–17.

32. Fuegi, *Brecht & Company*, p. 487.

33. *New York Times*, May 14, 1949, p. 19. For a comprehensive review of Chaplin's forays into politics and the furor they provoked, see Terry Hickey, "Accusations Against Charles Chaplin for Political and Moral Offenses," *Film Comment* (Winter 1969), pp. 44–56.

Chapter 19 *Limelight*

1. "I Have Had Enough of Hollywood," *Reynolds News*, Dec. 7, 1947; quoted in "Chaplin's Swan Song . . . ," *New York Times*, Dec. 14, 1947, clipping, MHL.

2. 100–127090–46, Section I, Part II, p. 15, FBI.

3. *CHLA*, p.

4. *Los Angeles Times*, Apr. 5, 1949, clipping, MHL.

5. Quoted by Parsons from her April 1949 column, in "Star's Red Leanings Draw Public Fire," *Los Angeles Examiner*, Sept. 25, 1952, sec. 1, p. 15.

6. *Variety*, Sept. 27, 1950, clipping, MHL.

7. *Variety*, Mar. 9, 1950, clipping, MHL.

8. Balio, *United Artists*, p. 315.

9. Matthau, *Among the Porcupines*, pp. 80–81.

10. Alvah Bessie, *Inquisition in Eden* (New York: Macmillan, 1965), pp. 239–42. Bessie placed this incident in the summer of 1949, surely the wrong date since Tilden was in prison from February through mid-December of that year. Mostly likely Bessie's visit occurred after Tilden's release from this, his second incarceration.

11. Leonard Lyons's column, *Los Angeles Times*, Oct. 13, 1950, clipping, MHL.

12. Chaplin to Odets, undated but June 1951, Clifford Odets Collection, LILLY.

13. The flea circus routine can be seen in primitive form as early as the Essanay film *By the Sea*. Chaplin also played Professor Bosco in *The Professor*, a never-released film that dates from the First National period.

14. Keaton, *My Wonderful World of Slapstick*, p. 271.

15. Chaplin to Odets, undated but June 1951.

16. Parsons, *Los Angeles Examiner*, Sept. 25. 1952, p. 15.

17. *MA*, p. 464.

18. Jes O'Donnell, "Charlie Chaplin's Stormy Exile," *Saturday Evening Post*, part 1, Mar. 8, 1958.

19. William Bradford Huie, "Mr. Chaplin and the Fifth Freedom: The Sovereign Right to Be a Fool," *American Mercury*, Nov. 1952, pp. 122-28; see also Irving Kristol, "McGranery and Charlie Chaplin," *Commentary*, Nov. 1952, p. 9.

20. A. H. Belmont to D. H. Ladd, FBI memo, Sept. 30, 1952, 100–12790, sec. 2, FBI.

21. *L'Humanité*, Nov. 1, 1952, p. 7; the Radio Moscow claim is according to United Press International, see *Hollywood Citizen News*, Nov. 13, 1952, clipping, MHL.

22. Lyons, "Roland H. Totheroh Interviewed," p. 282.

Chapter 20 "A King in Switzerland"

1. Chaplin to Odets, Sept. 2, 1953, Clifford Odets Collection, LILLY.

2. Chaplin to Feuchtwanger, Sept. 2, 1953, Lion Feuchtwanger Collection, USC.

3. Michael Chaplin, *I Couldn't Smoke the Grass on My Father's Lawn* (New York: G. P. Putnam's Sons, 1966), p. 6; Charles Chaplin's account of the accident is found in his letter to Clifford Odets, June 1951, Clifford Odets Collection, LILLY.

4. Aram Saroyan, *Trio* (New York: Simon & Schuster, 1985), pp. 210–11.

5. Oona Chaplin to Feuchtwanger, undated but summer/early fall 1953, Feuchtwanger Collection, USC.

6. Chaplin to Odets, Mar. 11, 1954, Clifford Odets Collection, LILLY.

7. Ella Winter to Chaplin, Oct. 5, 1955, Ella Winter Papers, Box 1, CU.

8. James O'Donnell, "Charlie Chaplin's Stormy Exile," *Saturday Evening Post*, part 2, p. 110.

9. Epstein, *Remembering Charlie,* p. 160.

10. Sven Kisslin, "The Bittersweet Memories of Charlie Chaplin," *New York Daily News,* Sunday Magazine section, Apr. 18, 1971, clipping, Chaplin file, 1970s, MoMA.

11. Kenneth Tynan, "Looking Back in Anger," *Observer*, Sept. 1957, clipping, Chaplin file, 1950–59, MoMA.

12. Michael Chaplin, *I Couldn't Smoke,* p. 98.

13. Oona Chaplin to Ella Winter, June 25, 1964, Box 1, Ella Winter Papers, CU.

14. Oona Chaplin to Ella Winter, n.d., Ella Winter Papers, Box 1, CU; see also Welles and Bogdanovich, *This Is Orson Welles*, p. 136.

15. *New York Herald Tribune*, Sept. 17, 1963, clipping, Chaplin file, 1960–69, MoMA.

16. Harold Clurman, "Oona, Oxford, America and the Book," *Esquire*, Nov. 1962, p. 86 ff.

17. Ronald L. Davis, interview with Tippi Hedren, July 24, 1982, SMU.

18. Ibid.

19. Earl Wilson's column, Mar. 16, 1967, clipping, Lester Sweyd Collection, BR.

20. Quoted from remarks Chaplin made to critic Richard Meryman, Pete Hamill's column, *New York Daily News,* Dec. 26, 1977, clipping, Chaplin file, 1970s, MoMA.

21. Will Tusher, "Any Sign of Hostility Would Have Sent Chaplin Packing," *Hollywood Reporter*, Apr. 17, 1972, clipping, ibid.

22. Natalie Gittelson, "My Father, Charlie Chaplin," *McCall's*, Mar. 1978; Tom Smith and John South, *National Enquirer,* Nov. 29, 1977, clipping, Chaplin file, 1970s, MoMA.

Acknowledgments

It is impossible to produce a book like this without the assistance of Many people. Terry Karten, my editor, has been unstinting in her support, and Sue Llewellyn has been not just a copy editor but my most discerning and critical reader.

Special thanks also to Charles Silver of the Film Study Center of the Museum of Modern Art. The center's extensive clipping files made it possible to gain an overview of the vast number of newspaper and magazine articles on Chaplin. Mr. Silver also kindly made it possible for me to view the museum's collection of Chaplin Keystones.

The Margaret Herrick Library of the Academy of Motion Picture Arts and Sciences is home to the Harry Crocker Collection, including Crocker's unpublished manuscripts, as well as Eddie Manson's *Secrets of Charlie Chaplin*, files of the Breen Office (MPAA), and many clippings from *Variety*, the *Hollywood Reporter*, and other West Coast sources underrepresented in other locations. Many thanks to Sam Gill and Fay Thompson for directing me to this material.

The Wisconsin Center for Film and Theater Research, at the Wisconsin State Historical Society in Madison, houses the corporate archives of the pre–1951 United Artists, including correspondence of the founders, minutes of board of directors' meetings, legal files, press books, stills, and other materials.

Also invaluable were the resources of the Billy Rose Theater Collection, especially the Robinson Locke scrapbooks, a treasure trove of information about the early Hollywood careers of both Charlie and Syd Chaplin.

The story of Chaplin's friendship with Max Eastman and his love affair with Florence Deshon was reconstructed mainly through correspondence between Deshon and Eastman. Many thanks to curator Saundra Taylor for making available these letters, which have previously been restricted, and to the Lilly Library's staff for their assistance in tracking down relevant materials in the vast Upton Sinclair

Collection, including information on Sinclair's meeting with Egon Kisch and his friendship with Robert Leicester "Rob" Wagner.

Anthony Slide's anthology, *The Best of* Script, led me eventually to Wagner's papers at UCLA, which provided invaluable insights into Chaplin's political views and activities. In addition to correspondence and manuscripts, Wagner's papers include a back file of his "little magazine," *Script* (also called *Beverly Hills Script*). Produced by "ye ed," Wagner, with the help of his wife, Florence, *Script* published occasional pieces by many of the biggest names in the film industry.

Greg Plunges, of the National Archives and Records Administration (NARA) New York center, unearthed many legal documents that I could never have located on my own. The story of Chaplin and Konrad Bercovici unfolded in the depositions and trial record of the latter's lawsuit—C. 14–190, Box 754 and 755 (273351–52A) and (167586). Also in New York are the depositions from *Tobis* v. *Chaplin* (E.–85–125); as well as records from *Keystone Film Co.* v. *Herbert S. Waldman, trading as the "Chaplin Film Co."* (12–375); *Charles Chaplin* v. *the Film Exchange et al.* (14–352); *Charles Chaplin* v. *the New Apollo Feature Film Co. and Hugo Maienthau* (14–299); *Chaplin* v. *Potash and Peskov* (15–296); *Chaplin* v. *Otis Lithograph Co.* (14–344); *Chaplin* v. *Jim Tully* (E. 40–13); and *Chaplin et al.* v. *Mary Pickford* (C. 66–294).

Bill Doty of NARA's Pacific Southwest records center in Laguna Niguel, California, tracked down material on the Michael Kustoff lawsuit (RG21, E–1300-M, Box 1239), including a complete copy of Kustoff's self-published book, *Against Gray Walls*, as well the case files of the Mann Act trial and Robert Eugene Arden's attempt to become a citizen. Thanks also to Martha Wagner Murphy of the Archival Programs Branch of the Center for Legislative Archives.

George Spoor's long-standing dispute with Chaplin began in New York (E. 13–244, Box 484) and continued in the Northern District of Illinois, Eastern Division. The latter file is located in NARA's Great Lakes Region records center—*Chaplin* v. *Vitagraph-Lubin-Selig-Essanay, Inc. etc., et al.* (E. 648, Box 1574, 57A300).

FBI files released under the Freedom of Information Act made it possible to trace the chain of events that led up to Chaplin's indictment on charges of violating the Mann Act in 1944. The records of the investigators (FBI 31–68496) include first-person statements given by Tim Durant, Joan Barry, Edward Chaney, Florabel Muir and others, offering a far more candid and detailed account than was presented in the courtroom or the press.

Chaplin's radical connections are covered in a separate file (100–127090). While this file comprises four sections, it is not lengthy by FBI standards and suggests that the federal government was not actively investigating Chaplin's political activities until his immigration status became an issue after the Mann Act trial.

The Popular Arts program of Columbia University's Oral History Project performed a great service during the late 1950s and early 1960s by conducting interviews with pioneers of the silent era. Broncho Billy Anderson, Gloria Swanson, Buster Keaton, and Harold Lloyd were among those who reminisced about Chaplin. Thanks also to Dr. Ronald L. Davis and the staff of DeGolyer Library for making available interviews from SMU's Oral History Collection on the Performing Arts.

Marje Schuetze-Coburn of USC's University Library located Lion Feuchtwanger's correspondence with Charlie and Oona Chaplin. I found additional correspondence in the Ella Winter Papers at Columbia University.

Todd Weinberg and his staff at NewEurope International provided research on Russian-language sources, including materials from the Goskino Library, the Library of the Research Institute of Cinematography, and the Russian State Library, all in Moscow. Additional research was provided by genealogist Carmen DiCiccio.

Dr. Ian F. Hancock, president of the International Roma Federation, enlightened me as to some of the reasons why Chaplin, like some current stars, would have been ambivalent about acknowledging his Romany heritage.

The Manuscript of this book was almost completed when I discovered Kay Redfield Jamison's *Touched with Fire: Manic Depressive Illness and the Artistic Temperament*. The parallels between Chaplin's chameleonlike moods and those of the poets, novelists, and composers discussed by Jamison are striking.

Finally, special thanks to Douglas Fairbanks Jr. and Mirel Bercovici, who were generous with their time. Also, Pamela Paumier, executor of the Chaplin estate; Dr. David H. Shepard; Brian Andersson; Herbert J. Brownell; the late Lita Grey Chaplin; Alistair Cooke; Richard Lingemann; Yvette Eastman; Jan-Chris Horak, Curator of Eastman House in Rochester, New York; Gillian Anderson of the Music Division of the Library of Congress; Randall Roffe, who lives in the bungalow where Chaplin and his "brain trust" held story conferences and suspects the place is haunted; Marion Davies's biographer Fred Lawrence Guiles; Robert Board; Ken Cobb, director of the New York City Municipal Archives; Chuck Lee of the Historical Society of Western Pennsylvania; Joel Agee; Stephen Koch; Erik Wensburg; Patrick McGilligan; Anthony Slide; Philip Yordan; Joel Agee; Charles and Gail Lynch, and Ermine Allen.

Index